THE AUTO REPAIR BOOK

JOHN DOYLE

J. G. FERGUSON PUBLISHING COMPANY/CHICAGO

1983

Library of Congress Cataloging in Publication Data

Doyle, John.
The auto repair Book.

Includes index.
1. Automobiles—Maintenance and repair.   I. Title
TL152.D64 1982   629.28'722
ISBN: 0-89434-031-X
Library of Congress Catalog Card Number 82-15530

FOREWORD

This book was planned, written and produced by the author and publisher to meet the needs of the serious amateur who wants to maintain and repair his own car. The first consideration in developing the book was that the reader knew relatively little about the mechanics of his car. It was also assumed that the reader had only the standard tools available, rather than the expensive and complicated tool sets and electronic equipment available to the professional mechanic. And finally, it was assumed that the reader could do all his own work up to the point when he should call on the experienced mechanic, rather than attempting repairs that only the factory-trained technician should handle.

The text examines your car by its various systems and explains how each one works and relates to the other systems. The writer makes even the most technical and complicated mechanical procedures thoroughly understandable. The book is superior in coverage, clarity, organization and thoroughness in each topic discussed. The material is presented in step-by-step method with illustrations to clarify and supplement text. It offers information and instruction that can be understood and followed by the amateur and appreciated by the professional.

CONTENTS

1

ELECTRICITY AND MAGNETISM FOR AUTOMOTIVE MECHANICS

Contents

ELECTRICITY

Purpose of the Chapter

Although an auto mechanic is not expected to be an electrician, some basic understanding of electricity and magnetism is very helpful in trying to locate and correct faults in the electrical systems of modern automobiles.

The purpose of this chapter is to provide a basic understanding of electricity and magnetism. The discussion is thoroughly practical, involves no mathematics, is easy to read and understand, and requires little time to read.

Introduction to Electricity

In many ways an electrical system in an automobile resembles the water-supply system found in a home. In the electrical system, however, *wires* replace pipes and *electrical current* replaces water.

In the water-supply system, pumps are used to maintain the hydraulic pressure needed to force water through pipes. Similarly, *electrical pressure* is needed to force current through an electric circuit. In an automobile, the basic source of electrical pressure is a *battery*. In order for the battery to maintain a steady electrical pressure it must be kept *charged*, and this is the job of the *alternator*.

Finally, in the same way that the friction of pipes and fixtures opposes the flow of water, the wires and all parts connected in an electric circuit oppose the flow of current. This opposition to current is called *resistance*.

The *amount* of current passing through an electric circuit is measured in *amperes* (often shortened to amps); electrical pressure, commonly called *voltage*, is measured in *volts;* and resistance is measured in *ohms*.

When the resistance of a circuit is some definite value (as it is in any circuit which is operating properly), an *increase* in voltage causes an *increase* in current, and a *decrease* in voltage causes a *decrease* in current.

When the voltage applied to a circuit is some fixed value, a *decrease* in resistance causes an *increase* in current, and an *increase* in resistance causes a *decrease* in current.

Finally, it should be noted that current, in passing through any resistance (either the resistance of the wire or any part connected in the circuit), creates *heat*. If the amount of heat is excessive, the wire, or part, or both, will *burn out*.

Conductors and Insulators

In electric circuits it often is necessary either to confine the current to a given path, or to prevent contact *between* or *with* conductors. *Insulators* are used for this purpose.

The *plastic coating* on most conductors (another name for wires) is an insulator which confines the flow of current to the conductor in the same way that piping confines the flow of water. The insulation also keeps a person from coming into contact with a bare wire. Since your body is a very good conductor of electricity, the passage of current through your body to ground results in an electric *shock*.

Air is another good insulator, and is used in switches. An open switch prevents the flow of current through a circuit simply by breaking the current path at a selected point.

Other insulators that find wide application in automobiles include *rubber* and *porcelain*.

When too much pressure is applied to a water system, the pipe breaks down and water escapes. The same thing can happen in an electric circuit. Too much voltage applied across an insulator causes the insulator to break down.

Electric Circuits

Electric circuit *diagrams* show the arrangement and interconnection of parts. To keep the diagrams from being cluttered, so-called *schematic symbols* are used in place of pictorial sketches. Letter symbols which often appear on schematic diagrams include I for current, E (or V) for voltage, and R for resistance. If there is more than one current, voltage, or resistance, numerical subscripts are used with the letter symbols in order to distinguish one from another. The resistances represented by the filaments of three light bulbs, for example, may be designated R_1, R_2, and R_3.

Incidentally, you may also encounter components marked *resistor*. This is simply a part into which some particular value of resistance has been *lumped*. Resistors have leads at each end to permit easy connection into a circuit.

All practical electric circuits, regardless of how simple or how complex they may be, require *four* basic parts. These four parts are (1) a *source of voltage* (electrical pressure) to force current through the circuit; (2) *conductors* (wires) for carrying current around the circuit; (3) a *load*—that is, a device to which the source supplies electricity; and (4) a *control device* to turn the circuit on or off.

The schematic diagram of a simple electric circuit is shown in Fig. 1-1. Here, the voltage source is a battery. The conductors usually are copper, but aluminum or some other material may be used in place of copper. The control device is a switch. When the switch is open, as shown, current cannot flow through the circuit. A complete path, which permits the flow of current, is formed when the

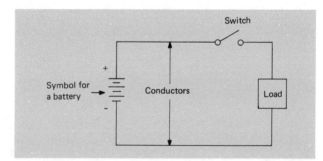

Fig. 1-1   Schematic diagram of a simple electric circuit.

switch is closed. The load may be any one of a wide variety of devices, such as a light bulb or a motor.

Notice that one terminal of the battery in Fig. 1-1 is marked with a minus (−) sign. This terminal is called the *negative* terminal. The other terminal is marked with a *plus* (+) sign and is called the *positive* terminal. During circuit operation, current always flows in the *same* direction—from the negative terminal of the battery, through the external circuit, and back to the positive terminal. Current whose direction never changes is called *direct current*, abbreviated dc, and the sources which provide dc are called *dc sources*. Thus, a battery is a dc source of electricity.

The *condition* of being positive or negative is called *polarity*. *Positive polarity* is indicated by a *plus* (+) sign and *negative polarity* by a *minus* (−) sign.

Measuring Current, Voltage, and Resistance

The basic instrument used to measure current is called an *ammeter*. The symbol for an ammeter is a circle enclosing the letter A. The scale of a typical ammeter is marked as shown in Fig. 1-2. The *maximum* current-carrying capability of this particular meter is 1 amp, the highest value indicated on the scale. Each major calibration mark represents one-tenth of an amp. For flexibility, many ammeters can cover several different ranges (current-carrying capabilities). The choice of range is made either by rotating a *range switch*, located on the front of the instrument, or by inserting the instrument test leads into appropriately labeled *jacks* mounted on the front panel.

Because an ammeter measures the *current through* a circuit, it is connected end-to-end with other parts, as shown in Fig. 1-3. Thus, the circuit must be broken to permit the insertion of an ammeter at the point where current is to be measured.

Also notice in Fig. 1-3 that, in the case of a dc source, such as a battery, it is necessary to observe polarity; that is, connect + to + and − to −. If the meter is connected with the wrong polarity, it may be ruined quickly.

Always make sure you use a range large enough to measure the circuit current. If the value of current is unknown, use the highest range available for the first measurement. Then, if the current is small enough, switch to a lower range.

A voltmeter is used to measure either the source voltage or the voltage across the terminals of any device external to the source (usually called a *voltage drop* and designated V). Thus, a voltmeter is always connected *across* a device,

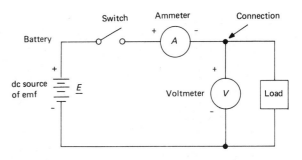

Fig. 1-3 An ammeter is connected end-to-end with other parts and a voltmeter is connected across the part whose voltage drop is to be measured.

as shown in Fig. 1-3. In the case shown, the voltmeter is being used to measure the voltage drop across the load.

Again, in a dc circuit, polarity must be observed. If the voltmeter is connected with the wrong polarity, the meter pointer will move off scale and the meter may be damaged. It is also necessary, of course, to use a range large enough for the voltage rise or drop being measured. The schematic symbol for a voltmeter is a circle enclosing the letter symbol V.

The instrument used to measure resistance is called an *ohmmeter*. Usually, the ohmmeter is part of a *multimeter*; that is, a meter that may be used to measure either voltage, current, or resistance. On a multimeter, the quantity to be measured is selected by means of a *function switch* or by inserting the instrument test leads into appropriate jacks located on the front panel of the instrument. The correct range is then selected by means of a range switch.

The following precautions must be taken when using an ohmmeter:

1. In the circuit under test, turn all power *off* before making resistance measurements. An ohmmeter contains its own battery power supply and will be destroyed if connected into a *hot* circuit (one with power applied).

2. Always connect the ohmmeter leads *across* the part or circuit whose resistance is to be measured.

3. Before using the meter, touch the two test leads together and turn the *zero adjust control*, located on the front panel, until the pointer rests directly over the zero position on the meter scale. If a zero reading cannot be obtained, change the internal battery.

4. For most accurate readings, use the range that keeps the pointer near the *low end* of the scale.

5. Multiply the scale reading by the setting of the range selector switch.

6. When the ohmmeter is not in use, turn the function switch to some position other than *ohms*. If the switch is left on ohms and the test probes come into contact with one another, the internal battery will be discharged and will have to be replaced.

All instrument manufacturers supply literature with

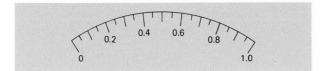

Fig. 1-2 The scale of an ammeter with a range from 0 to 1A. Each major calibration mark represents 0.1A.

Table 1-1

Prefix	Meaning	Abbreviation
Mega	One million	M
Kilo	One thousand	k
Milli	One thousandth	m

their instruments that give detailed operating instructions. *Never use an unfamiliar instrument until you have read those instructions.*

Prefixes

Currents smaller than 1 amp, voltages as high as several thousand volts, and resistances in the millions of ohms are not uncommon. To indicate such values, certain *prefixes* are added to the basic units. The most common prefixes are shown in Table 1-1. Referring to the table, 1 million ohms is read as one *megohm*, abbreviated 1 MΩ (where Ω means ohms), one one-thousandth of an amp is read as 1 *milliampere*, abbreviated 1 mA, 1000 volts is read as 1 *kilovolt*, abbreviated 1 kV, and so forth.

Types of Electric Circuits

An electric circuit, in which all the parts are connected end-to-end is shown in Fig. 1-4. When the switch S is closed to complete the circuit, the current has but *one* path to follow: from the negative terminal of the source, through each load device in turn, and back to the positive terminal of the source. Circuits of this type are called *series* circuits. From what has been said, it is quite obvious that, when an ammeter is connected at *any* point in a series circuit, the same current reading is obtained.

As far as current is concerned, the situation existing in a series circuit is identical to that existing in a simple water system where one tank is located at a point of greater elevation than a second tank and the two are joined by a single pipe. The water is confined to a single path in moving from

the higher tank to the lower tank. In the series-type electric circuit, current is also confined to a single path.

Since the current must pass through every resistance in a series circuit, it is apparent that *the total resistance of a series circuit is equal to the sum of the individual resistances.* Another characteristic of a series circuit is that *the sum of the voltage drops is always equal to the source voltage.*

In a so-called *parallel* circuit, the parts are connected in a side-by-side manner and more than one path exists for the passage of current. See Fig. 1-5. Each current pathway is called a *branch.*

Notice in Fig. 1-5 that each of the three load resistances, R_1, R_2, and R_3 is connected directly across the terminals of the voltage source. This means that *the same voltage exists across all branches of a parallel circuit.*

Finally, notice that the total circuit current must pass from the negative terminal of the voltage source to point A. At point A, the current divides, and part passes through resistance R_1 and the remainder goes to point B. At point B, the current again divides; part passes through resistance R_2 and the rest through resistance R_3. At point C the currents through all three branches recombine and return to the positive terminal of the source. Thus, *the total current in a parallel circuit is equal to the sum of the individual branch currents.*

In practice, electric circuits often are a combination of the series and parallel arrangements. A typical *series-parallel* circuit is shown in Fig. 1-6. Since resistance R_1 is in series with the voltage source, the total circuit current passes through R_1. At point A, resistances R_2 and R_3 are connected in parallel. Thus, the total circuit current divides at point A, with a portion passing through R_2 and the remainder through R_3. At point B, the currents through R_2 and R_3 recombine and pass through resistance R_4 in returning to the positive terminal of the source.

Opens and Shorts

An *open circuit*, usually referred to as an *open*, is simply a break in the conducting path. The resistance of an open cir-

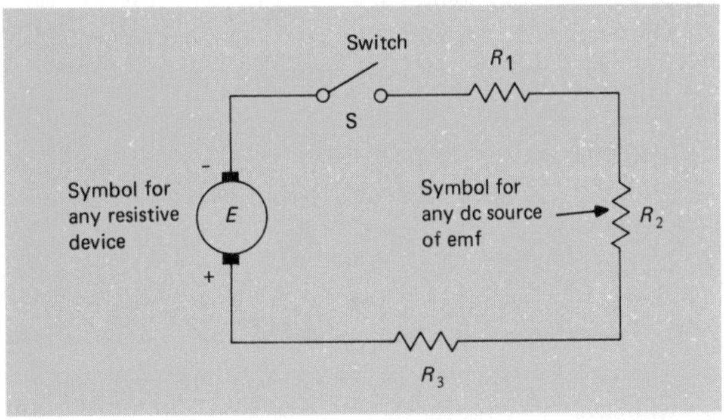

Fig. 1-4 A series circuit; all parts connected end to end.

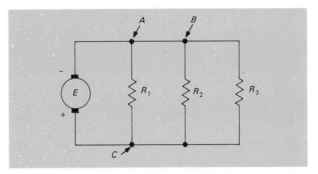

Fig. 1-5 A parallel circuit; all parts connected in a side-by-side manner.

cuit is so high that it cannot be measured with most instruments since air (an excellent insulator) replaces the conductor.

When an open occurs in a series circuit, there is no complete path through which current can pass. The current at all points in the circuit, therefore, is zero. If the circuit contained, for example, a string of series-connected lights, as shown in Fig. 1-7, and the filament of one light, L_5, burned out, all the lights would be extinguished since the circuit current would be zero.

In a parallel circuit, the location of the open determines what effect it has on circuit operation. In Fig. 1-8, where ten lamps are connected in five parallel branches, an open in the main line at point A has the same effect as in a series circuit because the total current passes through point A. On the other hand, if the filament of any one lamp burned out and created an open in one of the branches, both of the lamps located in that branch would go out because the branch current would be zero. All the remaining lights would continue to operate, however, because each of the branches in which they are located is still connected across the voltage source and still forms a complete path for current. The current in each complete branch remains unchanged since the voltage across, and the resistance of, the branch is unchanged. The total circuit current decreases, however, by an amount equal to the current that normally passes through the branch in which the open occurs.

A *short circuit*, usually referred to as a *short*, occurs when a portion of the resistance normally found in an electric circuit is bypassed (short-circuited). Let us see, first of all, how a short affects a series circuit.

Suppose, in Fig. 1-9, two bare conductors come into contact with one another at points A and B, thereby forming a short. The only resistance between points A and B, under these conditions, is the very small resistance of the wire. Since current follows the path of least resistance, essentially the total line current passes from point A to point B; the current through resistances R_2, R_3, and R_4, for all practical purposes, drops to zero. The effective removal of R_2, R_3, and R_4 from the circuit causes a sharp increase in the total circuit current. Due to the excessive amount of current which R_1 and R_5 must then handle, these devices, whatever they may be, will be destroyed by heat. Once these devices burn out, an open circuit exists.

To summarize, in a series circuit, a short usually results in the destruction of those devices connected between the

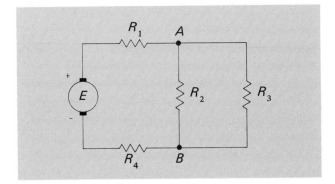

Fig. 1-6 A series-parallel circuit.

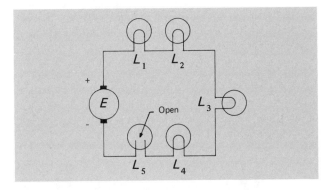

Fig. 1-7 The open filament of lamp L_5 causes the circuit current to be zero and all the lights are extinguished.

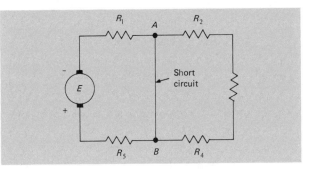

Fig. 1-9 A short-circuited series circuit. The current through R_1 and R_5 increases while the current through the remaining components is essentially zero.

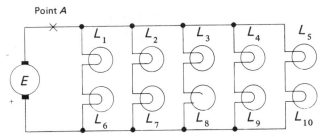

Fig. 1-8 In a parallel circuit, the effect of an open depends upon the location of the open. Note that each branch is a series circuit containing two lamps connected end to end. Thus this is an example of a series-parallel circuit.

voltage source and the point at which the short occurs. It should be understood, of course, that the source itself may also be damaged or destroyed. Those components bypassed by the short are not affected, since the current through those components is essentially zero.

In the parallel circuit of Fig. 1-10, a short is assumed to exist between points A and B. Because the resistance of the short-circuit path is practically zero, the current reaches a very high value of, perhaps, several hundred amps, and produces so much heat that the source, the conductors, or both, may ignite and burn.

The devices represented by resistances R_1 and R_2 in Fig. 1-10 are made inoperative as a result of the short circuit because the current through these branches drops to essentially zero; however, the devices are not damaged and may be reused when the circuit fault is repaired.

To sum up, a short in a parallel circuit causes a dangerously high current that may either damage or destroy the source. In any event, rapid and severe overheating of the source and the conductors between the source and the short will occur, and a fire is very possible. The devices connected in the normal branches are not affected by the short but are made inoperative until the circuit fault is fixed.

Ground-Return Circuits

A *ground-return circuit* is not to be confused with a short circuit. A ground-return circuit is formed when any part of

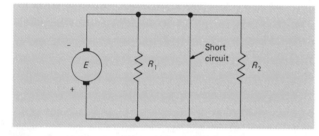

Fig. 1-10   A short-circuited parallel circuit. Practically the entire circuit current passes through the short circuit and the conductors attached to the source of emf. Essentially zero current passes through R_1 and R_2.

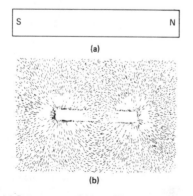

Fig. 1-11   (a) Bar magnet. (b) Iron filings arrange themselves in a line when placed on cardboard above bar magnet.

the automotive electrical system is intentionally connected to the *frame* of the automobile. The parts of the metallic frame, as a whole, are excellent conductors. Grounding a circuit intentionally for reasons of safety is common practice. For example, one terminal of the battery is connected to the chassis (ground) and the other terminal is connected to the wiring. General practice in the automobile industry is to connect the *negative* terminal of the battery to the chassis, but there are some exceptions. The chassis forms one conductor of the electric circuit and the current passes through the chassis on its way to and from the load. This is a ground-return circuit. Very frequently, either vibration or rust or dirt result in imperfect connections to the ground-return circuit. Such faults are easy to locate by using an ohmmeter to check for very high (or infinite) resistance.

MAGNETISM

Some Basic Ideas About Magnetism

A compass needle is a small *magnet*. As you know, one end is called the *North pole* and the other end is called the *South pole*. If two compasses needles are brought close to each other, two North poles or two South poles *repel* each other, but a North pole and a South pole *attract* each other. Thus, *like poles repel, and unlike poles attract*.

The region about a magnet in which the force of attraction or repulsion is present is called a *magnetic field*. This field is made up of *magnetic lines of force*, often called *flux*, as shown in Fig. 1-11. The *direction* of the flux is from the North pole to the South pole in the region *outside* the magnet, and just the opposite *inside* the magnet. The *intensity* of the field is indicated by the density of the lines, and its *direction* by the arrows.

When current passes through a conductor, a magnetic field is built up around the conductor. If the conductor is bent in the form of a loop, a much stronger field is produced inside the loop. If the conductor is coiled into a number of turns, as in Fig. 1-12, the lines of force due to each loop combine to produce a still larger field. Such a coil (or helix),

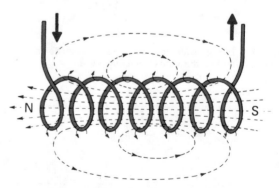

Fig. 1-12   Magnetic field around a current-carrying conductor bent into the form of a loop.

with its length long compared to its diameter, is called a *solenoid*. The diagram of Fig. 1-12 shows that the field about a solenoid is like the field about a bar magnet.

When a coil is wound on a bar of *magnetic material* (iron, steel, or their alloys), the combination is known as an *electromagnet*. The bar of magnetic material is called the *core* and the wire winding is called the *magnetizing coil*.

To prevent a short circuit between turns of the magnetizing coil, it is wound with insulated wire.

Because of its magnetic core, an electromagnet produces a very strong magnetic field.

Although we have distinguished between the terms solenoid and electromagnet, manufacturers of electrical equipment use the term *solenoid* to mean an electromagnet having a *movable* iron core which is free to move in and out of the coil and, by so doing, to perform mechanical work.

Some Applications of Electromagnets

The electromagnet lends itself to many practical applications, such as *relays*, *motors*, and *alternators*.

Relay. A relay is a special type of switch actuated by an electromagnet. See Fig. 1-13. When switch *S* in the auxiliary circuit is closed, current passes through the solenoid and magnetizes the core. The electromagnet attracts a soft-iron piece called the *armature*, which presses upward and closes the relay contacts in the main circuit. When the switch is opened, the solenoid core is demagnetized and the spring action of the relay contacts causes them to open so that the main circuit is broken.

The motor principle. If a current-carrying conductor is placed in a magnetic field at right angles to the magnetic lines of force, it experiences a sideways thrust directed at right angles to the field. This is known as the *motor principle*.

To understand this principle, it is necessary to consider the interaction of two magnetic fields: (1) the external field produced by *field magnets*; and (2) the field produced by the current in the conductor.

A current-carrying conductor situated in a magnetic field produced by two permanent (field) magnets is shown in Fig. 1-14(a). Current is directed *out* from the page and the magnetic field around the conductor is in a *clockwise* direction. Above the conductor the two fields are in the *same* direction; the resultant field is therefore *stronger* than either field. See Fig. 1-14(b). Below the conductor the two fields are in *opposite* directions and the resultant field is *weaker* than either field. The lines of force tend to repel each other when they are in the same direction and also tend to contract in length. A downward force is exerted on the conductor. This thrust is in a direction at right angles to both the current and the magnetic field. If either the direction of current in the conductor or the direction of the magnetic field is reversed, the direction of the force is reversed. See Figs. 1-14(c) and (d).

The simple dc motor. The electric motor is a practical application of the motor principle. The dc motor in its simplest form is shown in Fig. 1-15(a). A current-carrying conductor, in the form of a rectangular loop, is supported in a magnetic field so that it can rotate about the axis *XY*.

Current from a battery is supplied to the loop through a rotating switch called a *commutator*. The commutator consists of an insulating cylinder of ebonite attached to the shaft and two cylindrical copper sections called *Commutator bars* fixed to its surface. The commutator bars are insulated from each other by gaps in the copper. The loop ends are connected one to each section as shown. Current is supplied to the loop through a pair of *fixed carbon brushes* which make continuous contact with the copper sections as the commutator rotates. The brushes are placed opposite each other so that when one brush makes contact with section *A*, the other contacts section *D*.

Current flows from the battery through commutator bar *A*, along side *B* of the loop, around side *C*, and leaves by commutator bar *D*. An upward force is exerted on side *B* and a downward force on side *C*. The resulting turning ef-

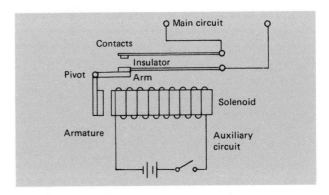

Fig. 1-13 A simple relay.

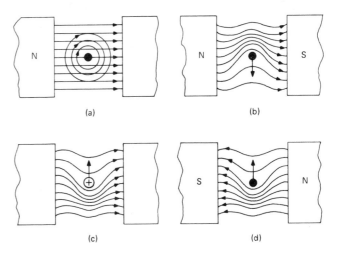

Fig. 1-14 Effect of a magnetic field on a current-carrying conductor which is free to move.

fort, called *torque,* causes the loop to rotate in a clockwise direction to the position shown in Fig. 1-15(b). In this position the forces act outward from the center of rotation and exert no torque. The momentum of the loop carries it past this neutral position. If the current were to continue in the same direction the torque would reverse and oppose rotation. At this point, however, each commutator bar breaks connection with one brush while still making connection with the other. The brush that was in contact with segment *A* now contacts segment *D,* and the current in the loop flows in the reverse direction. See Fig. 1-15(c). Thus, rotation in the clockwise direction is maintained by the action of the commutator which *reverses* the current in the loop every half revolution.

In a practical motor the loop is replaced by a number of coils wound in longitudinal slots on a cylindrical soft-iron core. A commutator of many bars is mounted on the same shaft as the coils and core. This assembly is known as the *armature.* The armature rotates in a strong magnetic field provided by powerful electromagnets.

Notice that the motor is a device that changes electrical energy into mechanical energy. Alternators, on the other hand, are devices that convert mechanical energy into electrical energy. Alternators are discussed in Chapter 2.

How a Transformer Works

If so-called *primary* and *secondary* coils are placed as shown on Fig. 1-16 and a *changing* current is applied to the primary coil, the magnetic lines of force around the primary will alternately *expand* and *collapse.* In doing so, they will *cut across* the turns of the secondary winding. The voltmeter will show that a voltage is *induced* (generated) in the secondary winding. This is the basic principle on which a transformer operates.

A special type of transformer, called an *autotransformer,* Fig. 1-17, contains only one coil which is *tapped.* The portion of the coil between the tap and one end forms the primary while the entire coil forms the secondary. The secondary contains many more turns of wire than the primary. As a result, the voltage induced in the secondary is many times greater than that of the primary.

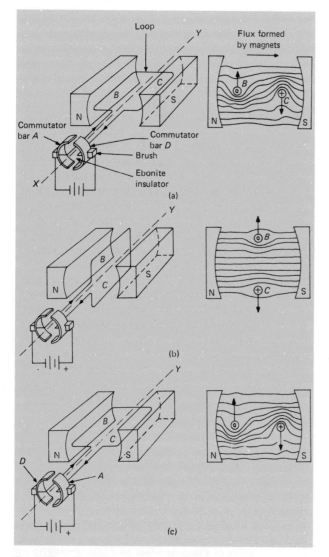

Fig. 1-15   The operation of a simple dc motor.

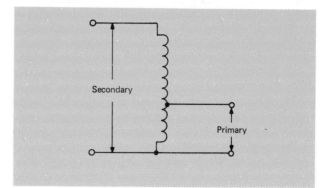

Fig. 1-16

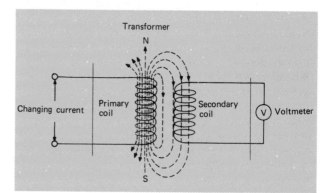

Fig. 1-17

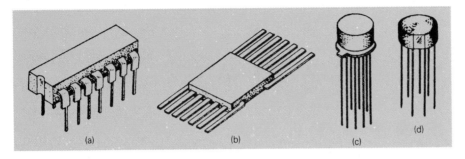

Fig. 1-18. Typical IC packaging. (a) Plastic DIP (Dual Inline Pack); (b) Ceramic flat pack; (c) Metal can T pack; (d) Plastic T pack.

THE PACKAGING OF ELECTRONICS SYSTEMS

Electronics and the Automotive Mechanic

Electronics devices and systems are playing an increasingly important role as each new model year comes around. Fortunately, however, this does not mean than an automotive mechanic will also have to become an electronics technician. The majority of electronics modules used in autos are of the plug-in, "go no-go" variety whose operating condition can be verified quickly by using simple testers. Either the modules work (go) or they do not work (no-go) and need replacement.

In some instances, however, special test equipment is needed to check the performance of an electronics system and it appears likely that some adjustments and individual parts replacement (as opposed to module replacement) will become standard practice. It is advisable, therefore, to at least know a little about the packaging arrangements you are very likely to encounter.

Printed Circuit Boards

The operating power levels of modules encountered in automotive work are generally low enough to permit the use of small components which are mounted on insulating board that plugs into a connector. The board is usually copper-clad and the parts interconnection pattern is etched (by a chemical process) into the copper. The board is then called a *printed-circuit board*, abbreviated PCB.

Integrated Circuits

Integrated circuits, or ICs, are commonly mounted on PCBs to form dules or subsystems.

By definition, an IC is a circuit that combines the previously separate disciplines of materials, devices, and circuits into a single discipline. The use of the word *integrated*

as the modifier for this form of electronics does not, as is sometimes erroneously assumed, signify just the combination of previously discrete (individually distinct) components into a single functional entity.

ICs represent a complete departure from older equipment design and manufacturing techniques. Conventional building blocks disappear as separate entities. Their functions are accomplished by microscopically small depositions or growths of material layers, or films, which are generally unrecognizable and inseparable from a complete circuit. In fact, entire complex electronics circuits have become so thoroughly united that the complete circuit function, rather than individual parts, is the basic component of electronics equipment. Because they are so very small, ICs are frequently called *microcircuits* and many computers of the type being used in automobiles and trucks are called *microprocessors*.

Typical IC packages are shown in Figure 1-18. They may plug into sockets (for quick and easy replacement) or they may be soldered into a circuit to prevent problems as a result of vibration or careless handling. A PCB containing multiple ICs of the so-called DIP (Dual Inline Pack) variety is shown in Figure 1-19.

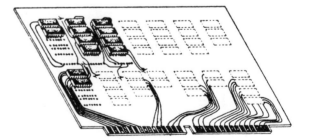

Fig. 1-19. Multiple ICs mounted on a PCB and interconnected to form a module or subsystem.

2

ALTERNATORS

Contents

INTRODUCTION

Alternator vs dc Generator

It was common, at one time, for a *dc generator* to be used to keep the battery charged in an automobile. On newer vehicles, however, *alternators* have replaced dc generators.

Alternators (sometimes referred to either as *ac generators* or simply generators) have the distinct advantage of greater current output at low speed. While the low-speed output varies with different alternators, some will deliver as much as 40 amps at an idle speed of approximately 1000 rpm (revolutions per minute). This output may be compared to the 28 amps for an extra-output dc generator. Most dc generators, however, will not approach this figure. The high output at idling speed is important. In city traffic, an engine may idle half the time, and with a conventional dc generator an automobile must travel in excess of 20 mph before the battery receives a charge. An alternator, on the other hand, charges the battery while the engine is idling.

Another advantage of the alternator is that it requires less input current. In addition, it is designed so that it cannot be damaged when operating at high speeds—a distinct possibility with dc generators.

Basic Operation of an Alternator

If a conductor cuts across a magnetic field, a voltage is induced (generated) between the ends of the conductor. This is the operating principle of the alternator.

The induced voltage, and the induced current resulting from it, will be greater if: (1) the magnetic field is made stronger; (2) the number of conductors cutting across the magnetic field is increased; or (3) the speed of relative motion between the magnetic field and conductors is increased.

In a practical alternator the magnetic field is made very strong by the use of electromagnets. The field of the electromagnet is controlled by varying the strength of the current flowing through it, and this permits variation of the output voltage.

Since a *steady* magnetic field is required, direct current must be sent through the electromagnet. *Starting* field current is provided by the battery. Once the alternator is started, direct current is provided by the output of devices called *rectifiers* (discussed later).

To increase the number of conductors cutting across the magnetic field, many turns (loops) of insulated copper wire are wound on an iron core. The complete assembly is called the *armature*, and the coil, which is inserted into slots in the core, is called the *armature coil*. The core not only supports the coil, but also furnishes an easy path for magnetic flux from the North field pole to the South.

Finally, the speed of relative motion between the magnetic field and conductors is increased by belt coupling between a pully on the alternator shaft and a pully on the shaft of the radiator fan.

A simple alternator is shown in Fig. 2-1. Notice that the ends of the armature coil are connected to metal *slip rings*, which are mounted on the armature shaft but insulated from it. Carbon *brushes* make a wiping contact with the slip rings and connect the output voltage to the external circuit.

Figure 2-1 shows that the output of an alternator is so-called *alternating current*, abbreviated ac. Alternating current, instead of flowing in the same direction (− to +) at all times, reverses *direction* periodically. Thus the output voltage appearing between the brushes also reverses *polarity* periodically.

Figure 2-2 shows how the alternator produces ac. When a single loop of the armature coil is perpendicular to the magnetic field, the sides of the loop are passing between the flux lines. Since no lines are being cut, the induced voltage is zero. This happens twice during each full revolution of the loop. When the loop is parallel to the magnetic field, its sides are cutting straight across the flux lines. Since the rate at which the flux lines are being cut is maximum, the induced voltage is maximum. This also happens twice during each revolution; however, in one position of the loop the polarity of the induced voltage is positive (+), while a half-revolution (180°) later, it is negative (−).

At all other positions of the loop, its sides are cutting the magnetic flux at an angle. Because it then takes the sides of the loop longer to go from one flux line to the next, the induced voltage is somewhere between the maximum value and zero, becoming less as the angle of the loop increases from parallel to perpendicular.

The *waveform* (graph) of the induced voltage is called a *sine wave* and each complete revolution of the loop produces *one cycle* of sine-wave voltage. The *number* of cycles completed each second is called the *frequency* of the ac voltage and is expressed in *cycles per second*, abbreviated cps. (A newer term, *hertz*, is sometimes used in place of cps. Since most mechanics still use the older expression, however, we shall use it here.)

Practical Automotive Alternators

Although the voltage produced by a single loop on the armature coil is very small, the output voltage of the alterna-

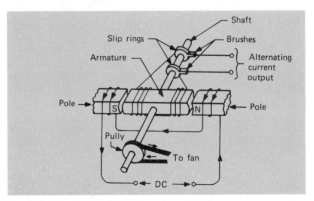

Fig. 2-1 Simplified illustration of an alternator.

tor is the *sum* of the voltages induced in all loops of the armature coil.

When an alternator delivers relatively low power, slip rings operate satisfactorily. When large amounts of power are involved, however, it becomes difficult to insulate slip rings satisfactorily, and they are, therefore, a frequent source of trouble. Because of this, automotive alternators have a *stationary* armature and a *rotating* field. (It makes no difference whether the magnetic field is stationary and the conductor cuts through it, or the conductor is stationary and the magnetic field moves across it.) In such alternators the armature coils are permanently mounted around the inner circumference of the housing, while the field coils and their pole pieces are mounted on the shaft and rotate within the stationary armature. Because the field rotates, it is called the *rotor*. Similarly, because the armature is stationary, it is called the *stator*.

With a stationary armature, the alternator output can be connected directly to an external circuit without the need for slip rings and brushes. This eliminates the insulation difficulties that would otherwise exist if large currents and voltages were delivered to the load through slip rings. Of course, since the field winding rotates, slip rings must be used to connect the winding to its dc source. However, the voltages and currents are small compared to those of the armature and there is no difficulty in providing sufficient insulation.

Another advantage of a stationary armature is that it makes possible much higher speeds of rotation and, therefore, higher voltages than can be obtained with rotating armatures. At very high speeds of rotation the large centrifugal force that results makes it difficult to properly insulate the armature winding. No such problem exists when the field winding rotates at high speeds.

Instead of using a single armature coil, automotive alternators use *three*, each coil being wound 120° from its neighbor, as shown in Fig. 2-3(a). As the field rotates, a voltage is induced in each armature coil, but these voltages are not *in step* with each other; that is, they start and end at *different* times. See Fig. 2-3(b). The voltage of coil *B* is 120° behind that of coil *A*, and the voltage of coil *C* is 120° behind that of coil *B*. When voltages are not in step, they are said to be *out of phase*. In this case we have three out-of-phase voltages, so the alternator is called a *three-phase alternator*.

Although the alternator of Fig. 2-3 produces three-

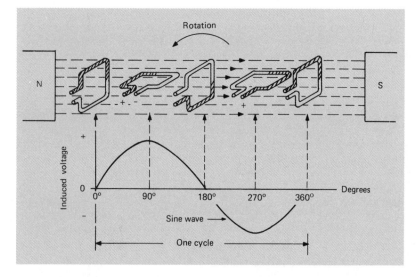

Fig. 2-2 How an alternator produces ac.

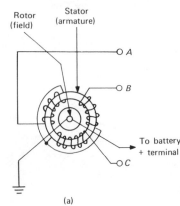

(a)

Fig. 2-3 A three-phase generator. (a) Coil arrangement. (b) Three-phase output voltage.

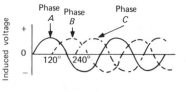

(b)

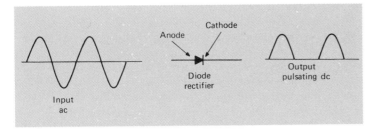

Fig. 2-4 Operation of a diode rectifier.

phase ac, charging current for the battery must be dc. To change ac to dc we use electronic devices called *silicon diodes*.

Figure 2-4 shows how a silicon diode works. Notice the symbol for the diode. The straight line portion of the symbol is called the *cathode* and the arrow head is called the *anode*. When the *positive* half-cycle of the input ac waveform is applied to the diode, its anode becomes positive *with respect to* its cathode. Under these conditions the diode acts like a *very low resistance* and permits the passage of current. The direction of current is from the cathode toward the anode. When the *negative* half-cycle of the input ac waveform is applied to the diode, however, its anode becomes negative with respect to its cathode. When this happens, the diode acts like a *very high resistance* and blocks the passage of current. Thus the negative half-cycle of the input waveform is no longer present in the output. Because the output is always positive, it is dc. The strength of the output voltage is not constant, however, as in pure dc, but varies in value. For this reason it is called *pulsating* dc.

Now, if we connect a device called a *capacitor* (formerly called a *condenser*) between the output of the rectifier and ground, as shown in Fig. 2-5, the shape of the output waveform is changed. The capacitor is simply a storage device. As the rectifier output voltage rises the capacitor *charges*, and as the rectifier output voltage drops the capacitor *discharges*. Before the capacitor discharges completely, however, it is recharged by another positive pulse. As a result, the space between the positive output pulses is partially filled in. The fluctuations in the level of the output voltage are called *ripples*.

In a three-phase alternator, two silicon diodes are connected to the output of each armature coil, as shown in Fig. 2-6(a). The diodes marked *A* conduct (pass current) when the output voltage of their respective windings is negative. (When the cathode is negative, the anode is relatively positive; hence the conduction.) Since the diodes then represent a very low resistance, the armature windings are effectively grounded, and their output is zero.

The diodes marked *B* conduct when the output voltage of their respective windings is positive. Thus, the positive portion of each cycle is passed to the output.

The input to the capacitor is shown in Fig. 2-6(b). Notice that the ripple in the output is much smaller than in Fig. 2-5 since the positive pulses are spaced much closer together and the capacitor has much less time to discharge. For this reason, the output from the capacitor is very nearly

equal to the maximum voltage induced in the armature coils. The decreased ripple plus a higher output explains why a three-phase alternator is used in preference to a single-phase alternator (one with a single armature winding).

One additional modification of the simple alternator is incorporated in automotive alternators. Instead of using one set of pole pieces to produce the magnetic field, we use *two sets*. With this arrangement, two cycles of ac are produced in each armature winding during each revolution of the rotor (field). Thus, the frequency of the output pulses is dou-

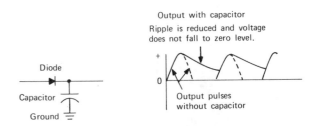

Fig. 2-5 Using a capacitor with a rectifier.

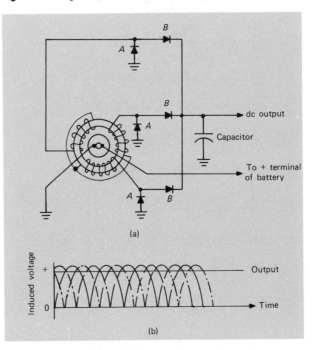

Fig. 2-6 (a) Three-phase alternator with diodes and capacitor. (b) Output voltage at capacitor.

bled and the ripple is reduced even more. The output of the capacitor is then a very close approximation to dc and is entirely suitable for charging the battery. This dc is also used, as noted earlier, to supply current to the field electromagnets once rotation of the alternator begins. Recall that the initial starting current is supplied by the battery.

Regulating the Alternator

The load current of an alternator flows through the armature windings which have resistance. Since a voltage drop is produced across this internal resistance, the available output voltage changes with changes in load current. The voltage drop across the armature winding also depends on the frequency of the output voltage. (This is due to a characteristic of the windings called *reactance*.) Since speed is one factor that determines frequency, the internal resistance of an alternator changes with speed.

To keep the output voltage steady despite changes in load current, use is made of a *voltage regulator*. Typical regulators are discussed in Chapter 3.

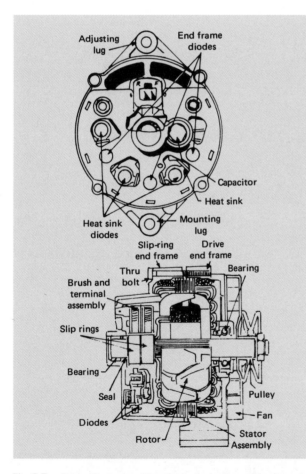

Fig. 2-7 Internal construction of a typical automotive alternator. *Courtesy of Delco-Remy Division, General Motors Corporation.*

A Typical Automotive Alternator

The main components of the alternator, shown in Fig. 2-7, are the rotor, stator, diodes, and enclosing case. Other mechanical features, such as the brush and terminal assembly, slip rings, bearings, fan, drive pulley, oil seals, and frame are also shown. As explained previously, the rotor carries the field current and revolves inside the stator. Three diodes are mounted in the slip ring end frame and three in the heat sink which is attached to, but insulated from, the slip ring end frame. The heat sink absorbs heat and thereby protects the diodes, which are susceptible to heat damage. The battery terminal of the alternator is also attached to the insulated heat sink. The heat sink is cooled by the flow of air blown across its surface by the fan, which is mounted on the main shaft of the alternator and is belt-driven from the automobile engine.

The case acts as one lead of a diode and is marked either $(+)$ or $(-)$ to indicate its polarity. In a negative-ground system (the usual case), the negative-case diodes are mounted in the slip ring end frame, and the positive-case diodes are mounted in the insulated heat sink. A diode with a negative case has a single positive-polarity lead, and a positive-case diode has a single negative-polarity lead.

SERVICING

Alternator Disassembly

The typical alternator of Fig. 2-7 has four assemblies: two end frames, a stator, and a rotor. To disassemble the unit, first remove the four through-bolts and separate the drive end frame and rotor assembly from the stator assembly. This is done using a screwdriver at the stator slot to pry apart both assemblies. Scribe marks will aid in reassembling the parts correctly.

After disassembly, place a piece of *pressure-sensitive tape* over the slip ring end-frame bearing and over the shaft on the slip ring end to keep dirt from the bearing and shaft. *Never use friction tape;* it will leave a gummy deposit on the shaft.

To remove the drive end frame from the rotor, place the rotor in a vise and tighten the vise only enough to permit removal of the shaft nut. *Excessive tightening of the vise may cause distortion of the rotor.* Remove the shaft nut, washer, pulley, fan, and collar, and then separate the drive end frame from the rotor shaft.

Diode Replacement

To replace a diode, a support tool, a press tool, and a shouldered installing tool are needed. These tools are available from most automotive parts manufacturers.

As shown in Fig. 2-8, the end frame is held by the support tool and the diode is forced out of the end frame by pressure exerted on a diode-removing tool (not shown) by an arbor press. *Never strike a diode with a hammer;* the shock may damage other diodes.

Select a replacement diode having the proper marking or identification. (For Delco-Remy alternators, the negative diodes in the end frame have black markings and the positive diodes in the heat sink are red.) Support the outside end of the frame around the diode hole on a flat, smooth surface, and press the diode into place with the shouldered installing tool and an arbor press. Make sure the diode is square with the end frame and started straight into the hole. Avoid bending or moving the diode stem; excessive flexing may cause internal damage and result in diode failure.

Bearing Replacement and Lubrication

The bearing in the drive end frame is removed by first removing the retainer plate screws and then pressing the bearing from the end frame. If the bearing is in satisfactory condition, it may be reused and should be one-quarter filled with a lubricant specified by the manufacturer. Add the lubricant before reassembly, and avoid overfilling, which may cause the bearing to overheat.

Press in a new bearing with a tube or collar that just fits over the outer race of the bearing. Install a new retainer plate if its felt seal is hardened or worn excessively.

Replace the bearing on the slip ring end frame if its grease supply is exhausted. *Never reuse an old bearing.* To remove the bearing, press it out with a tube or collar that just fits inside the end-frame housing. Press from the outside of the housing toward the inside.

To install a new bearing, place a flat plate over the bearing and press from the outside toward the inside of the frame until the bearing is flush with the outside of the end frame. Support the inside of the frame with a hollow cylinder to prevent breakage and avoid misalignment or undue stress on the bearing. Saturate the felt seal with SAE (Society of Automotive Engineers) 20 oil, and reassemble the seal and steel retainer.

Brush Replacement

When the slip ring end-frame assembly is removed, the brushes will fall down onto the shaft and pick up shaft lubricant. Before the brushes are reused, they must be cleaned thoroughly with a soft, dry cloth. The shaft is also cleaned before reassembly.

Inspect the brush springs for damage or corrosion. If their condition is doubtful, replace them.

To install new brushes, remove the brush-holder assembly from the end frame by detaching the two brush-holder assembly screws. An exploded view of the brush-holder assembly is shown in Fig. 2-9. Install the springs and brushes in the brush holder and insert a straight wire or pin into the holes at the bottom of the holder to retain the brushes. Then attach the brush-holder assembly onto the end frame, noting carefully the proper arrangement of parts.

Allow the straight wire to protrude through the hole in the end frame.

Heat Sink Replacement

The heat sink is replaced by removing the battery and ground terminals from the end frame and the screw attaching the capacitor lead to the heat sink. During reassembly note very carefully the proper arrangement of parts. An exploded view of the heat-sink assembly is shown in Fig. 2-10.

Reassembly of Alternator

To reassemble the alternator, reverse the disassembly procedure. When assembling the pulley, secure the rotor in a vise only tight enough to permit tightening of the shaft nut to 50 to 60 foot-pounds of torque, as indicated by a torque wrench. Excessive pressure applied against the rotor can cause distortion of the assembly. To join the slip ring end-frame assembly to the rotor and drive end-frame assembly, remove the tape over the bearing and shaft. Make sure the shaft is perfectly clean. Insert a straight wire through the holes in the brush holder and end frame to retain the brushes in the holder. After the alternator is assembled, withdraw the wire and let the brushes drop onto the slip rings.

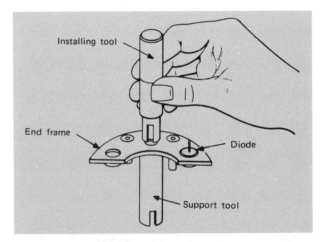

Fig. 2-8   Replacing a diode.

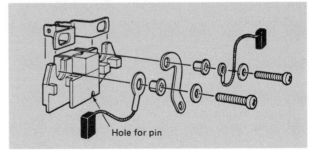

Fig. 2-9   Exploded view of brush holder. *Courtesy of Delco-Remy Division, General Motors Corporation.*

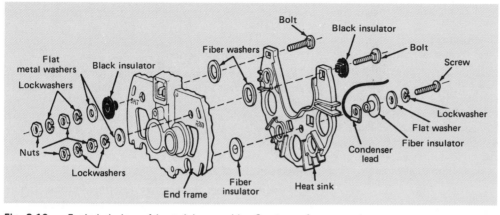

Fig. 2-10   Exploded view of heat-sink assembly. *Courtesy of Delco-Remy Division, General Motors Corporation.*

Tests and Maintenance

Even though the alternator is constructed to give long periods of trouble-free service, regular inspection procedures should be followed to obtain maximum life. Also, certain tests should be made and maintenance procedures carried out, such as cleaning slip rings, checking the rotor electrically, checking stator windings, and making sure all diodes are functioning properly. The checks to be made on an alternator are summarized in Table 2-1. A more detailed listing of troubleshooting steps is given in Table 2-2.

Alternator Inspection

The frequency of inspection is determined largely by operating conditions. High-speed operation, high temperatures, and dust and dirt increase the wear on brushes, slip rings, and bearings. At regular intervals, inspect the terminals for corrosion and loose connections and the wiring for frayed insulation. Check the mounting holes for tightness, and the belt for alignment, proper tension, and wear. Belt tension should be adjusted according to the recommendations of the engine or vehicle manufacturer. When increasing belt tension, apply pressure against the stator laminations between the end frames, *not* against either end frame.

Noise from the alternator may be caused by worn or dirty bearings, loose mounting bolts, a loose drive pulley, a defective diode, or a defective stator.

Slip-Ring Servicing

Dirty slip rings may be cleaned and finished with 400-grain or finer polishing cloth. Do not attempt this job, however, unless you have access to a lathe or some other means of spinning the rotor as the polishing cloth is held against the slip rings. Attempting to clean slip rings by hand, without spinning the rotor, may result in flat spots on the rings. Flat spots cause brush noise.

Table 2-1.   Summary of Alternator Checks

Component	Connection	Reading	Result
Rotor	Ohmmeter from slip ring to shaft	Very low	Grounded
	110-V test lamp from slip ring to shaft	Lamp lights	Grounded
	Ohmmeter across slip rings	Very high	Open
	110-V lamp across slip rings	No light	Open
Stator	Ohmmeter from lead to frame	Very low	Grounded
	110-V test lamp from lead to frame	Lamp lights	Grounded
	Ohmmeter across each pair of leads	Any reading very high	Open
	110-V test lamp across each pair of leads	No light	Open
Diode	Ohmmeter across diode; then reverse connections	Both readings very low	Shorted
		Both readings very high	Open
	12-V test lamp across diode; then reverse connections	No light in both checks	Open
		Lamp lights in both checks	Shorted

Table 2-2 Alternator Troubles and Remedies

Condition	Possible Cause	Correction	Condition	Possible Cause	Correction
Alternator fails to charge battery (no output)	Blown fuse wire in regulator	Locate and correct cause of fuse blowing. Install new fuse wire. Solder ends securely.		Low regulator setting	Adjust voltage regulator.
	Drive belt loose	Adjust drive belt according to specs.		Shorted or open rectifier	Perform current output test. Remove and dismantle alternator. Test rectifiers. Replace as needed.
	Worn brushes and/or slip rings	Install new brushes and/or rotor.		Grounded stator windings	Remove and dismantle alternator. Test stator windings. Install new stator if necessary.
	Sticking brushes	Install new brushes.			
	Open field circuit	Test all field circuit connections and correct as necessary.	Excessive charging rate to a fully charged battery	Regulator set too high	Reset regulator according to specs.
	Open charging circuit	Inspect all connections in charging circuit and correct as necessary.		Regulator contacts stuck	Install new voltage regulator.
				Regulator voltage winding open	Install new voltage regulator.
	Open circuit in stator windings	Remove alternator and disassemble. Test stator windings. If necessary, install new stator.		Regulator base improperly grounded.	Correct regulator base to ground connection.
			Regulator contacts oxidized	High regulator setting	Reset regulator according to specs.
	Open rectifiers	Remove alternator and disassemble. Test rectifiers. Install new ones if needed.		Regulator air gap set improperly	Reset air gap and lower contact gap.
				Shorted rotor field-coil windings	Test current draw of rotor field coil. If excessive, install new rotor.
	Loose drive belt	Adjust belt according to specifications.	Regulator contacts burned	High regulator setting	Reset regulator according to specs.
	High resistance at battery terminals	Clean and tighten terminals.		Shorted rotor field-coil windings	Test current draw of rotor field coil. If excessive, install new rotor.
	High resistance in charging circuit	Check charging circuit resistance. Correct as required.	Regulator voltage coil winding burned	High regulator setting	Install new regulator. Test setting and adjust if necessary.
	High resistance in body to engine ground lead	Tighten ground lead connection. Install new lead if needed.	Regulator contact points stuck.	Poor ground connection between alternator and regulator	Correct ground connection. Install new regulator. Adjust.
	Open stator winding	Remove and disassemble alternator. Test stator windings. Install new stator if necessary.	Noisy alternator.	Alternator mounting loose	Properly install and tighten mounting.
				Worn or frayed drive belt	Install new drive belt and adjust.
Low generator output and low battery	High resistance in the charging circuit	Test charging circuit resistance. Correct as needed.		Worn bearings	Remove and dismantle alternator. Replace bearings.

(Continued)

Table 2-2 (continued)

Condition	Possible Cause	Correction
	Interference between rotor fan and stator leads or rectifiers	Remove and dismantle alternator. Correct interference as needed.
	Rotor or rotor fan damaged	Remove and dismantle alternator. Install new rotor.
	Open or shorted rectifier	Remove and dismantle alternator. Test rectifiers. Install new ones as needed.
	Open or shorted windings in stator	Remove and dismantle alternator. Test stator windings. Install new stator if necessary.

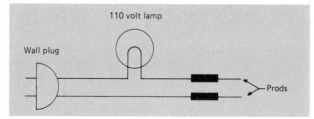

Fig. 2-11 Typical test lamp.

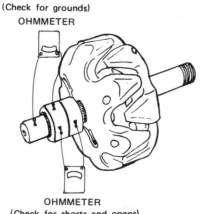

Fig. 2-12 Checking stator for grounds, shorts, and opens. *Courtesy of Delco-Remy Division, General Motors Corporation.*

Rotor Checks

The rotor may be checked electrically for grounded, open, or short-circuited field coils by use of an ohmmeter or a 110-volt test lamp, such as that shown in Fig. 2-11.

To check for grounds, connect the test lamp or ohmmeter, as shown in Fig. 2-12, from either slip ring to the rotor shaft. If the ohmmeter reading is low, or if the lamp lights, the field winding is grounded.

To check for opens, connect the ohmmeter or test lamp across the slip rings. This, too, is shown in Fig. 2-12. If the ohmmeter reading is very high (infinite), or if the lamp does not light, the winding is open. If an open condition does not exist, the winding is tested for short circuits by again connecting an ohmmeter across the slip rings. If the resistance reading is below the value specified by the manufacturer, the winding is shorted. If the manufacturer does not state the resistance directly in ohms, divide the specified voltage by the specified current to obtain your answer. If the rotor is not defective and the alternator fails to supply the rated output, the trouble is either in the stator or in the diodes.

Stator Checks

The stator leads are connected to the slip ring end frame by three nuts, as shown in Fig. 2-13. Remove the nuts, disconnect the stator leads, and then separate the stator assembly from the end frame. See Fig. 2-14. If the lamp lights, or if the meter reading is low when the meter is connected between any stator lead and the frame, the windings are grounded. If the lamp does not light, or if the meter reading is high when the meter is successively connected between each pair of stator leads, the windings are open.

A short circuit in the stator winding is difficult to locate unless you have access to a laboratory-type ohmmeter, because the resistance of the windings is very low. However, if all other electrical checks are normal and the alternator

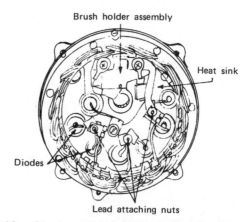

Fig. 2-13 Slip-ring end frame, showing location of stator lead nuts. *Courtesy of Delco-Remy Division, General Motors Corporation.*

fails to supply its rated output voltage, shorted stator windings are indicated as the trouble.

Diode Checks

Each diode may be checked electrically for a shorted or open condition. Any of the following three methods may be used.

Ohmmeter method.   The ohmmeter should have a 1.5-volt internal cell, and the lowest available test range should be used.

With the stator disconnected, a diode in the heat sink may be checked, as shown at the left of Fig. 2-15, by connecting one ohmmeter lead to the heat sink and the other ohmmeter lead to the diode lead. Note the reading. Then reverse the ohmmeter lead connections and again note the reading. If both readings are either very low or very high, the diode is defective. A good diode gives one low reading and one high reading.

To check a diode mounted in the end frame, connect one of the ohmmeter leads to the end frame and the other ohmmeter lead to the diode lead, as shown to the right in Fig. 2-15. Note the reading. Then reverse the ohmmeter lead connections and again note the reading. Again, if both readings are either very high or very low, the diode is defective.

Test-lamp method.   An alternate method of checking the diodes is to use a test lamp of not more than 12 volts. With the stator disconnected, connect the test-lamp leads across each diode as described above, first in one direction and then in the other. If the lamp either lights or fails to light on both checks, the diode is defective. If the diode is good, the lamp will light on only one of the checks.

Special-meter method.   Special meters are available for checking the diodes without disconnecting the stator. Before

you use any such tester, read the manufacturer's instructions carefully.

Alternator Polarity

Since the alternator is designed for use on systems having a particular polarity, certain precautions must be observed when working on the charging system. Failure to observe any of the following precautions will result in serious damage to the electrical equipment.

1. When installing a battery, make sure the ground polarity of both the battery and alternator are the same.

2. When connecting a booster battery, connect the negative terminals together and the positive terminals together; that is, connect the two batteries in parallel.

3. When connecting a charger to the battery, connect the charger positive lead to the battery positive terminal and the charger negative lead to the battery negative lead (in parallel).

4. Never operate an alternator on an open circuit. Make sure all connections in the circuit are secure.

5. Do not short-circuit or ground any terminal on either the alternator or the regulator.

6. Never ground the field circuit between the alternator and the regulator. Damage to the regulator will result if either field terminal is grounded.

7. When adjustments are needed on the voltage regulator, circuit breaker, or relay, always use an insulated tool. Grounding of an uninsulated tool will damage the alternator.

8. To resolder a diode lead, grasp the lead between the sol-

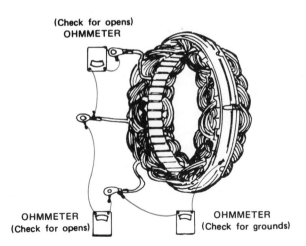

Fig. 2-14   Checking stator windings. *Courtesy of Delco-Remy Division, General Motors Corporation.*

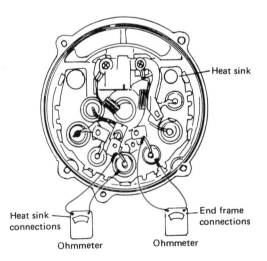

Fig. 2-15   Checking diodes with an ohmmeter. *Courtesy of Delco-Remy Division, General Motors Corporation.*

der joint and diode with a pair of pliers. The pliers act as a heat sink. Use a 25- or 35-watt iron and resin-core solder. Never use acid-core solder or any additional soldering flux.

9. Most cars have a negative ground system, but always check to make sure. Reversed polarity may damage the diodes, wiring system, or other parts of the charging circuit.

In conclusion, it should be realized that mechanical assembly and disassembly procedures vary somewhat for different makes of alternators. Refer to the manufacturer's literature whenever possible, and work slowly and carefully. Arrange all parts in correct order. Incorrect arrangements can cause damage that is difficult to locate or can result in inoperation.

3

VOLTAGE REGULATORS

Contents

ELECTROMECHANICAL REGULATORS

Basic Regulator Operation

A typical circuit used to regulate the alternator output voltage is shown in Fig. 3-1. One side of the alternator field winding is connected directly to the negative side of the rectifier diodes (ground). The other side of the field winding is connected to the positive side (terminal BAT) of the alternator output either through resistor R or through the lower contacts (known as the *series* contacts) of the voltage regulator relay. Thus the field winding is either directly across the alternator output (series contacts of relay closed) or it has the resistor connected in series with it (series contacts of relay open).

The series contacts of the relay are held closed by a spring so that when the alternator first starts to operate the contacts are closed and the field winding is connected directly across (in parallel with) the alternator output. Notice that the winding on the relay is also connected in parallel with the alternator output.

As the speed of the generator increases, its output voltage (and current) increases. Thus, a greater current passes through the relay winding and creates a stronger magnetic field around the coil. This strong field attracts the relay armature. When the magnetic attraction is greater than the pull of the spring, the series contacts open. Since the field current must then flow through the resistor, it decreases in

value. This reduced field current weakens the magnetic field of the alternator, causing its output voltage to decrease. The decreased output voltage, in turn, weakens the magnetic field of the regulator coil and the spring causes the series relay contacts to reclose. The cycle described is repeated many times per second to limit the alternator output voltage to a preset value at *average* alternator speeds.

At high alternator speeds, the magnetic field surrounding the relay coil is strong enough to pull the upper (shorting) contacts closed. When this happens, the alternator field is grounded. With both of its ends grounded, the field is effectively removed from the circuit; hence, no current passes through the field. With no current through the field winding, the alternator voltage decreases. The decrease in alternator voltage causes a decrease in the magnetic pull of the relay coil and permits the shorting contacts to open. With the shorting contacts open, field current passes through the resistor. As the voltage increases, the shorting contacts again close. This cycle is repeated many times per second to limit the voltage to a preset value at high alternator speeds. The voltage regulator unit thus operates to limit the value of voltage throughout the alternator speed range.

A regulator of the type shown in Fig. 3-1 is called a *single-unit* regulator. *Two-unit* regulators also include a *field relay*. See Fig. 3-2.

When the ignition switch is closed, before the engine

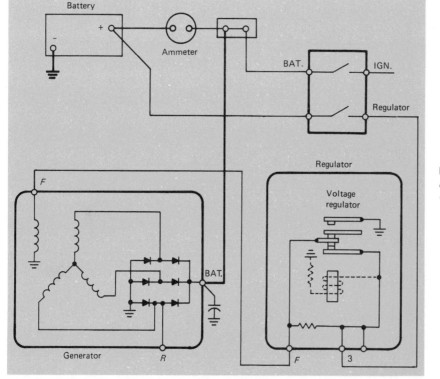

Fig. 3-1 A single-unit regulator. *Courtesy of Delco-Remy Division, General Motors Corporation.*

is started, the indicator lamp lights to indicate that the alternator is not charging the battery. Current then flows from the grounded terminal of the battery (and field winding) through the field winding to terminal *F* on the regulator. From terminal *F* it passes through the series contacts of the regulator to terminal 4, through the indicator lamp and resistor in parallel, and back to the positive terminal of the battery. This current energizes the field winding sufficiently to ensure voltage buildup in the stator windings when the engine starts.

When the alternator starts to operate, voltage from the *R* (relay) terminal on the alternator housing is impressed, through the regulator No. 2 terminal, across the field-relay winding, causing the relay to close. This connects the regulator No. 4 terminal directly to the battery through the field-relay contacts, causing the indicator lamp to go out. Alternator field current then flows from the negative terminal of the battery, through the alternator field winding to the F terminal on the regulator, through the series contacts of the regulator, then the contacts of the field relay, and back to the positive terminal of the battery. The indicator is then turned off.

Operation from this point on is identical to that described for the single-unit regulator.

Some units also contain an indicator-lamp relay, and are called *three-unit* regulators.

Troubles in Charging System

Trouble in the charging system generally shows up as one or more of the following conditions: faulty indicator-lamp operation, an undercharged battery, or an overcharged battery.

Before making any electrical checks, inspect all connections, including the slip-on connectors at the regulator and alternator, to make sure they are clean and tight. Since the regulator terminals are of the slip-on type, a special cable assembly (adapter) must be used during testing so that the meter connections can be made to the terminals. Such an adapter is available from the various test-equipment manufacturers and tool companies that supply the automotive field. Always proceed carefully and follow the instructions for use of the adapter.

Indicator-lamp relay. If the lamp fails to light when the switch is closed, check for a burned-out bulb. If the lamp fails to go out when the switch is open, check for a shorted diode in the alternator. If the lamp fails to go out with the

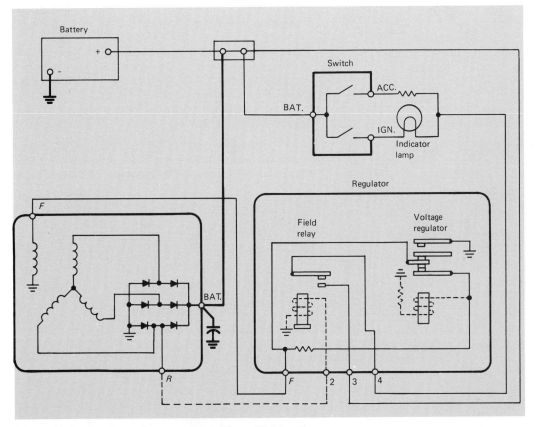

3-2 A two-unit regulator. *Courtesy of Delco-Remy Division, General Motors Corporation.*

alternator operating, the fault may be either in the relay or in the alternator. To determine which device is at fault, connect a voltmeter to the adapter, as shown in Fig. 3-3. Then operate the alternator at moderate speed and note the reading of the voltmeter. If the voltmeter reading is 5 volts or above and the indicator lamp does not go out, the indicator relay is defective and must be replaced. If the voltmeter reading is below 5 volts, the trouble is in the alternator and the battery may be undercharged.

Undercharged battery. An undercharged battery, as evidenced by slow cranking, may be caused by a loose drive belt, a defective battery, excessive circuit resistance, defective field relay, defective alternator, or a low voltage-regulator setting. In some cases, the indicator lamp may operate properly.

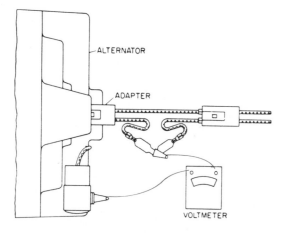

Fig. 3-3   Checking indicator lamp circuit.

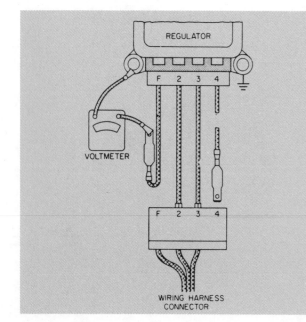

Fig. 3-4   Checking field relay.

If the drive belt is loose, it should be tightened in accordance with the manufacturer's specifications.

A sulfated battery, or one with an intermittent open at a terminal post or in one of the cell connectors, will remain undercharged under normal operating conditions.

For high circuit resistance, inspect all connections and make sure they are clean and tight.

To check the relay, make the connections to the adapter shown in Fig. 3-4, turn the switch to the IGN position, and observe the voltmeter. If the reading is zero, either the line between the switch and terminal 2 of the regulator is open, or the field relay is defective and must be checked.

To determine if the alternator is operating properly, connect an ammeter in the circuit of the BAT terminal of the alternator and a voltmeter from the BAT terminal to ground. Then load the battery, by turning on the headlights, to prevent high voltages. Do not let the voltage exceed the recommended voltage setting of the regulator. If necessary, turn on other accessories for additional loading. Finally, make the adapter connections shown in Fig. 3-5 and check the operation of the alternator against the manufacturer's specs.

If no circuit defects are found but the battery remains undercharged, the most likely cause is a low-voltage setting of the regulator. This is corrected by adjusting the regulator in the manner described shortly.

Overcharged battery. An overcharged battery, as indicated by an excessive use of water, can be caused by a shorted cell, excessive circuit resistance, or a high-voltage setting of the regulator.

Adjusting Voltage Setting

It is important to remember that the voltage setting for one type of operating condition may not be satisfactory for a different type of condition. Temperature under the engine

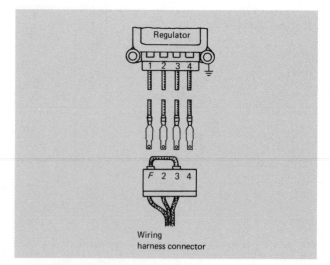

Fig. 3-5   Checking alternator output.

hood, operating speeds, and nighttime service are all factors that help determine the proper voltage setting. The proper setting is attained when the battery remains fully charged with a minimum use of water.

If no defects are found in the circuit but the battery remains undercharged, raise the setting by 0.3 volt, and then recheck the battery after a reasonable period of time. If the battery remains overcharged, lower the setting by 0.3 volt and recheck the battery again.

Three checks and adjustments are required on the voltage-regulator unit: point opening, air gap, and voltage setting. If the voltage can be adjusted properly, the point opening and the air gap need not be checked.

Point opening. With the lower contacts touching, measure the point opening between the upper contacts. Adjust by bending the upper contact arm as shown in Fig. 3-6. Use care not to bend the hinge.

Air gap. Measure the air gap with a feeler gauge between the armature and core when the lower contacts are touching. To adjust the air gap, turn the nylon nut on the contact support. Only an approximate air-gap setting should be made by the feeler-gauge method. The final adjustment must be whatever is required to obtain the specific difference in voltage between the upper and lower sets of contacts.

Voltage setting. The voltage at which the regulator operates varies with changes in the ambient temperature, which is the temperature of the air ¼-inch away from the regulator cover.

Procedure for Setting Voltage

Check and adjust the voltage setting as follows:

1. Connect an ammeter and a one-quarter ohm resistor with a rating of 25 watts or more in series with the alternator BAT terminal, as shown in Fig. 3-7. If the battery is discharged, the resistor will limit the output to 10 amps or less, which is required to make the regulator voltage setting.

2. Make the connections to the adapter shown in Fig. 3-7. Use a 25-ohm, 25-watt variable resistor in series with the alternator field winding and the *F* terminal of the regulator, and connect a jumper between lead 3 of the regulator and the BAT terminal of the alternator. Also connect a voltmeter between regulator terminal 3 and the regulator ground terminal. Do not let lead 4 of the regulator touch ground. Turn the variable resistor to its closed (zero resistance) position.

3. Run the engine at 1500 rpm for 15 minutes. At this engine speed, the alternator will turn at about 6000 rpm. Leave the cover on the regulator so that its operating temperature can be determined. Make sure all accessories and lights are turned off.

4. After 15 minutes, cycle the regulator. To do so, first turn the variable resistor to its full-resistance (off) position. Then disconnect and immediately reconnect the jumper lead at the alternator BAT terminal. Now return the variable resistor to its zero-resistance position. Finally, bring the engine speed up to 2500 rpm and note the reading of the voltmeter. With the equipment operating, the voltage should be as indicated in Table 3-1. The reg-

Table 3-1

Temperature	Voltage Range		
0	14.0	to	14.6
20	13.9	to	14.5
40	13.8	to	14.4
60	13.7	to	14.3
80	13.7	to	14.3
100	13.6	to	14.2
120	13.5	to	14.1
140	13.4	to	14.0

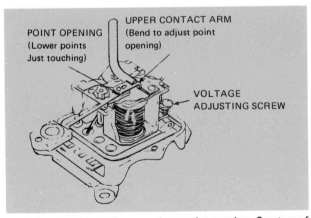

Fig. 3-6 Checking voltage regulator point opening. *Courtesy of Delco-Remy Division, General Motors Corporation.*

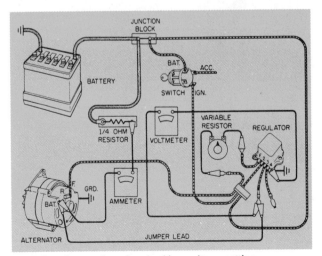

Fig. 3-7 Connections for checking voltage setting.

ulator should be operating on the upper (shorting) contacts. If not, the battery needs recharging before proceeding.

5. To adjust the regulator voltage setting, turn the regulator adjusting screw shown in Fig. 3-6. When removing or installing the regulator cover, always disconnect the jumper at the alternator BAT terminal to avoid accidental grounds. Always make the *final* setting by turning the regulator adjusting screw clockwise. This assures that the spring holder will be against the head of the screw. If it is ever necessary to turn the screw counterclockwise, do so until its head is approximately ⅛-inch above the adjusting bracket, pry the holder up against the screw head, and then turn the screw clockwise to make the final adjustment.

6. After making the setting, cycle the regulator again by repeating step 4.

7. Run the engine at 2500 rpm and make the regulator setting. Readjust if necessary. Always take the final reading with the cover in place.

8. After making the voltage setting with the regulator operating on the shorting contacts, check the setting during operation on the series contacts. This is done by slowly increasing the resistance of the variable resistor, with the engine operating at 2500 rpm, until the regulator begins to operate on the series contacts. Note the voltage reading and compare it with the manufacturer's specs. If operation on the series contacts cannot be obtained, return the resistor to its initial position, turn the headlights on, and rotate the variable resistor until operation on the series contacts is obtained.

   The best method to determine if the regulator is operating on the series contacts is to connect a set of earphones in series with the regulator *F* terminal and ground. As the variable resistor is turned, and operation

switches from the shorting to the series contacts, sound will first fade completely and then return when the series contacts operate.

9. The difference in voltage between the operation of the shorting and series contacts can be increased by slightly increasing the air gap between the armature and the center of the core. The difference can be decreased, of course, by slightly decreasing the air gap. If the air gap is adjusted either way, the voltage setting for both sets of contacts must be rechecked. In any case, the final voltage setting must be made with the regulator cover in place.

Checking the Field Relay

Three checks are required on the field relay: air gap, point opening, and closing voltage.

Air gap.   With the regulator removed from the vehicle, check the air gap with the points just touching. If adjustment is necessary, carefully bend the flat contact support spring.

Point opening.   Measure the opening between the points. If necessary, adjust by bending the armature stop. If the unit does not have an armature stop, this check is not required.

Closing voltage.   The closing voltage of the field relay may be checked by connecting a 50- to 70-ohms variable resistor and a voltmeter to the adapter, as shown in Fig. 3-8. Turn the resistor to its full-resistance position, leaving the ignition switch in the off position. Then slowly decrease the resistance and note the closing voltage of the relay. If necessary, adjust by bending the heel iron, as shown in Fig. 3-9.

Regulator Maintenance

The contacts of the voltage regulator should not be cleaned unless the electrical performance indicates that this is necessary. A sooty or discolored condition after a relatively

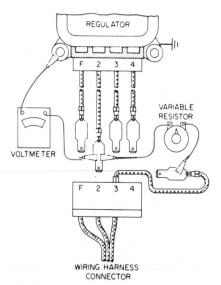

Fig. 3-8   Checking closing voltage of field relay.

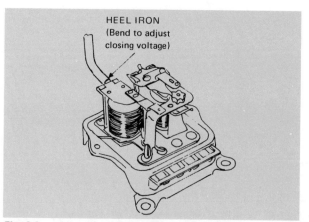

Fig. 3-9   Adjusting closing voltage of field relay.

short period of operation is normal. If the voltage fluctuates, however, as evidenced by an unsteady voltmeter reading, the contacts may have excessive resistance or be sticking. Cleaning is then necessary. First, however, make sure the unsteady voltage is not caused by loose connections or high resistance elsewhere in the system.

Never clean the regulator contacts with a metal file. A strip of No. 400 silicon carbide paper should be folded over and pulled back and forth between the contacts. After cleaning, wash the contacts with alcohol to remove any residue. Repeat if necessary.

To clean the field-relay contacts, use a thin, fine-cut, flat file. Remove only enough material to clean the points. Never use emery cloth or sandpaper to clean contact points.

TRANSISTORS

The transistor is an electronic device that can be used as a switch to turn a circuit either on or off. Thus, a transistor may be used to replace the contacts of a regulator completely, or to work in conjunction with contacts. When transistors are used by themselves in a regulator, the assembly is called a *transistor* regulator. When the transistors and contact points are used together, the assembly is called a *transistorized* regulator.

Compared to contact points, transistors offer the advantages of virtually unlimited life, no periodic maintenance, high current-carrying capability, insensitivity to vibration, and the elimination of periodic adjustments. Transistors are, however, temperature sensitive. To dissipate heat, and thereby minimize the possibility of damage due to heat, the transistors used in automotive regulators are made from silicon and are mounted on relatively large heat sinks.

All transistors have three terminals called the emitter (*E*), base (*B*), and collector (*C*). Leads are attached to these terminals to permit connection into a circuit. Quite often, however, the lower portion of the transistor housing is used as the collector lead. An arrangement of this type is shown in Fig. 3-10. The large area of the collector acts as a heat sink.

You may encounter either one of *two* types of transistors in a given system—the so-called *NPN* type or the *PNP* type. Never use an *NPN* type in place of a *PNP* type, or vice versa. If you do, the new transistor will be destroyed immediately. Schematically, the two types are designated by the symbols shown in Fig. 3-11. Note the direction of the arrowhead on the emitter lead for each type.

TRANSISTORIZED REGULATORS

Basic Circuit Operation

The basic operation of transistorized regulators can be seen in Fig. 3-12. When switches S_1 and S_2 are open, current

through the circuit is zero. With S_1 closed, current flows from the emitter to the base. Let's assume this current is 5 amps and that the collector current is zero because S_2 is still open.

When both switches are closed, the total current remains at 5 amps, but the base current drops to 0.1 amp while the remainder, 4.9 amps, passes through the collector circuit.

With S_1 open and S_2 closed, both the base and emitter currents are essentially zero. Effectively, then, the emitter-to-base resistance is *very high*. This is just the opposite of the condition existing with both switches closed. Under the latter conditions, the emitter-to-collector resistance is *very low*, as indicated by the high collector current. The effective change in resistance from low to high, and vice versa, is the characteristic of a transistor which makes it suitable for regulator applications.

Actual regulators are quite similar to the circuit of Fig. 3-12. The generator field is connected in series with the emitter, the regulator contact points are located in the base circuit in place of switch S_1, and switch S_2 is eliminated since the collector circuit is always grounded.

The current values used in the preceding discussion merely illustrate transistor operation. The values actually

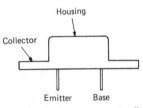

Fig. 3-10   Lower portion of case acts as collector.

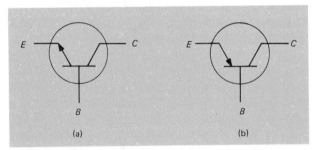

Fig. 3-11   Symbols for (a) NPN and (b) PNP transistors.

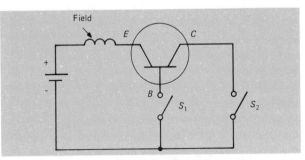

Fig. 3-12   Basic operation of transistor regulators.

encountered in automotive transistorized regulators may vary considerably from these values.

A Four-Terminal Transistorized Regulator

A *four-terminal* transistorized regulator has a field relay, one transistor, and a voltage regulator. When the field relay is energized, its contact points close. This connects the alternator field windings and regulator *shunt* (parallel) windings to the battery. When the relay is not energized, a spring holds the contacts open.

The transistor is mounted under the base of the regulator on a flat aluminum plate which acts as a heat sink.

When the solenoid in the voltage regulator is not energized, its contact points are held closed by a spring attached to the armature. When the solenoid is energized, the contacts open, the emitter-base current of the transistor drops to zero, and the alternator field current drops to zero.

A four-terminal charging circuit contains the alternator regulator, battery, ignition switch, and ammeter. The alternator output appears between its BAT terminal and ground. An increase in alternator speed or in alternator field current causes the output to increase. Similarly, a decrease in either speed or field current causes the output to decrease. To pro-

vide a constant output the regulator decreases field current as speed increases.

Refer to Fig. 3-13. When the ignition switch is closed, the field-relay winding is connected across the battery, and the field-relay contacts close. This connects the alternator field windings to the battery. The field circuit is completed to ground through the emitter-collector circuit of the transistor. It is also completed through the emitter-base circuit of the transistor and the contact points of the voltage regulator which are normally held closed by a spring.

When the field-relay contacts close, the two windings on the voltage regulator are also connected across the battery. The resulting magnetism, however, is not strong enough to overcome the tension of the spring, so the contacts remain closed. Thus the alternator field is completed to ground as soon as the ignition switch is closed and the alternator field windings carry the full field current. For the sake of illustration, let's assume the full field current is 4.5 amps.

With the alternator in operation, a dc voltage appears at its BAT terminal and is applied across the two parallel windings of the voltage regulator. When this voltage is high enough, the magnetism created by the regulator windings is strong enough to overcome the spring tension and the regulator contact points open. With the regulator contacts open, the emitter-base current and emitter-collector current of the transistor both drop to zero. Thus the alternator field current is cut off when the voltage-regulator contacts open.

Without field current, the alternator output voltage drops. The reduced voltage drives less current through the regulator winding and the magnetic field around the winding is reduced in intensity. This lets the spring pull the armature away from the core and the contacts again close. This cycle is repeated many times per second, resulting in a constant voltage from the alternator.

Since the voltage-regulator contacts are in series with the emitter-base circuit of the transistor, the current through these contacts is small—perhaps, for the sake of illustration, 0.3 amps when the generator field current is at the assumed value of 4.5 amps. In regulators without a transistor, the full generator field current passes through the regulator contact points—about 1.5 amps. Since contact points cannot handle higher currents safely, the generator field currents are limited to approximately 1.5 amps.

The voltage-regulator winding, connected to regulator terminal *F2* and then to ground through a resistor and the regulator points, carries no current when the voltage contacts are open. Thus, after the contacts open, the magnetic pull created by this winding disappears. This loss of magnetic attraction, combined with the reduced magnetic pull of the winding connected directly to ground, allows the armature spring to reclose the contacts within a very short time interval. Once the contacts are closed, the magnetic pull is restored and added to the magnetic field of the normally grounded winding. The contacts then reopen immediately. Because the voltage-regulator winding which is

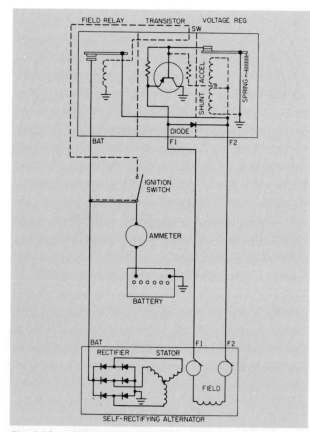

Fig. 3-13 Charging circuit of a four-terminal regulator.

grounded only through the contact points speeds up the frequency of vibration, it is called an *accelerator* (ACCEL) winding.

When the voltage-regulator contacts are open under high-temperature conditions, the resistor connected between the emitter and base of the transistor prevents emitter-to-collector current leakage. At high temperatures, however, there is still some tendency for current leakage even though the contact points are open. The resistor in series with the ACCEL winding and contact points is a compensating resistor that permits the use of the required wire size for the winding.

The diode connected directly across the generator field acts as a safety valve. If the voltage contacts were to open without a diode in the circuit, the sudden interruption of field current would induce a high voltage in the field coils and cause transistor failure. The diode provides an alternate current path to avoid inducing a high voltage in the field windings.

When the ignition switch is opened, the field-relay winding is disconnected from the battery. The flexible spring then pulls the armature away from the core and opens the contacts, disconnecting the generator field windings from the battery. When the generator is not operating, the battery does not discharge into the stator windings because the diodes prevent this *reverse* current flow.

Three-Terminal Transistorized Regulator

A *three-terminal* transistorized regulator usually contains an indicator-light relay, a single transistor, and a voltage regulator. The transistor and regulator circuits are similar to those used in four-terminal regulators. The indicator-light relay is similar to the regulator relay, but has only one winding which is connected between the BAT terminal of the regulator and ground.

Troubleshooting Transistorized Regulators

Although some minor details of a given transistorized regulator may differ from those discussed here, you should experience no difficulty in understanding how they operate and in carrying out any particular instructions a manufacturer might provide.

Several precautions merit repeating. (1) The alternator and regulator must be operated on the same polarity. (2) When installing a battery, make sure the ground polarity of the battery and alternator are the same. (3) When connecting a booster battery or charger across a battery, make parallel connections. (4) Never operate the alternator on an open circuit. (5) Never short-circuit or ground any terminals on the alternator or regulator.

Now let's run through some procedures for determining the most likely sources of trouble in a transistorized-regulator charging system.

Indicator-lamp relay. If the indicator lamp does not go out when the alternator is operating, connect a voltmeter be-

tween the R terminal of the lamp relay and ground and note the reading. If the voltage is above the opening voltage specified by the manufacturer and the lamp stays on, the relay is defective and should be replaced.

An undercharged battery. An undercharged battery may be caused by a loose drive belt, defective battery, defective alternator, excessive circuit resistance, low setting of the voltage regulator, defective field relay, open transistor, or a defective regulator diode. Correction of the first two faults should require no additional comment.

To check the operation of the alternator, connect an ammeter between the battery terminal of the junction block and the BAT terminal of the alternator. Connect a voltmeter from the BAT terminal of the alternator to ground. Connect a so-called *carbon-pile rheostat* (available from auto-supply houses) across the terminals of the battery. This places a load on the battery and prevents high voltage. Remove the lead from the regulator F terminal and connect it to the regulator V terminal. Then, slowly increase the alternator speed and check its rated output at each given speed. If the alternator does not provide the rated output, it should be checked for defects. Do not allow the alternator output voltage to exceed the manufacturer's recommended voltage setting of the regulator.

If, in the test for a defective alternator, the alternator provides the rated output, check for excessive circuit resistance. To do so, first reconnect the lead to the F terminal of the regulator. Then connect a voltmeter between the ungrounded lead of the battery and the V terminal of the regulator. Turn on the switch, but do not run the alternator. Note the reading of the voltmeter. If an oil-pressure switch is used, put a jumper across its terminals temporarily. If the voltage reading is greater than 0.3 volt, excessive line resistance is indicated. Correct by replacing the wiring, then clean and tighten all wiring connections. If this does not correct the excessive voltage drop, check the alternator for shorted or grounded fields.

To check for a low voltage-regulator setting, connect a voltmeter from the regulator F terminal to ground. Turn on the ignition switch, but do not run the alternator. If an oil-pressure switch is used, put a jumper across its terminals temporarily. If the voltmeter reads 9 volts or more, the regulator is probably in good condition. The cause of the undercharged battery is probably a low voltage setting.

If a reading of less than 9 volts is obtained, either the field relay contacts are not closed or the transistor is burned out. To replace a defective transistor, unsolder the connections and remove the two attaching screws. When resoldering, keep the soldering time to a minimum, hold the lead between the iron and the transistor body with a pair of pliers which will act as a heat sink, and use a small wattage iron. After replacing the transistor, clean the voltage contacts.

To check diodes in the regulator, disconnect the regulator V and F leads, remove the cover, and unsolder the two diode leads. Do not move the diode leads more than necessary, and use the same precautions noted for resoldering the transistor. Next, connect an ohmmeter across the diode and note the reading. Then reverse the ohmmeter connections and note the reading. If both readings are either very low or very high the diode is defective.

To check any diode, use an ohmmeter powered by a 1.5-volt cell and use the lowest range available.

Adjusting Voltage Setting

Two adjustments may be made on the voltage regulator: the air-gap adjustment and the voltage setting. The air gap seldom requires adjustment. When adjustment is needed, however, push the armature down against a suitable gauge and then adjust the upper contact supports so that the contacts are aligned squarely and just touch when the contact support screws are tightened.

The voltage at which the regulator operates varies with changes in the ambient temperature. Most regulators should operate at 13.3 to 13.9 volts when the ambient temperature is 125°F. If the ambient temperature is not 125°F and a new setting is desired, the data in Table 3-2, if applicable, may be used to make the desired setting. For example, setting

Table 3-2

Regulator Ambient Temperature °F	Voltage			
165	13.0	13.2	13.4	13.6
145	13.2	13.4	13.6	13.8
125	13.3	13.5	13.7	14.1
105	13.5	13.7	13.9	14.1
85	13.7	13.9	14.1	14.3
65	13.8	14.0	14.2	14.4
45	13.9	14.1	14.3	14.5

the voltage at 14.1 volts at an ambient temperature of 85°F will give an operating voltage of 13.7 volts when the ambient temperature is 125°F.

Other procedures for setting the voltage regulator and the field relay were covered earlier in this chapter. If necessary, review these procedures.

Maintenance

Operating the regulator with an open transistor can cause the voltage contacts to oxidize and this condition requires

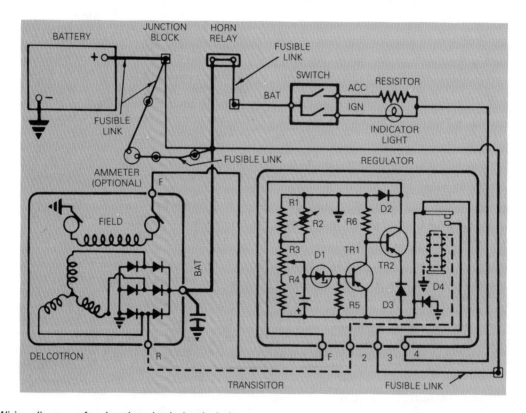

Fig. 3-14. Wiring diagram of a charging circuit that includes a transistor regulator with an integral field relay. *Courtesy of Delco-Remy Division, General Motors Corporation.*

cleaning of the points. Normally, however, the points require cleaning only after extremely long periods of operation.

TRANSISTOR REGULATORS

A transistor regulator, as noted earlier, depends entirely upon the action of transistors to control the alternator voltage. A transistor regulator may or may not include an integral field relay.

Transistor Regulator with Integral Field Relay

The wiring diagram of a charging circuit that includes a transistor regulator having an integral field relay is shown in Figure 3-14. The operation of the field relay is similar to that of the field relay in the two-unit electromechanical regulator discussed earlier.

Regulator voltage is adjusted by turning a screw located in the base of the regulator. To avoid the possibility of short-circuiting a transistor, a fiber rod is used to adjust the screw. Rotation of the screw varies the resistance of resistor R_2. Transistor TR_1 is the driver stage and TR_2 is the output stage. Diode D_1 is a special type of diode called a *Zener* or *breakdown* diode and plays a special role in the operation of the regulator.

When the ignition switch is turned ON, transistor TR_1 is also turned ON. Then TR_1, in turn, switches output transistor TR_2 ON. With both transistors conducting, current passes through the field winding of the alternator. Then, when the car engine is started, the alternator voltage builds up and the alternator charges the battery.

When the alternator output voltage reaches a specified value, Zener diode D_1 conducts and the resulting voltage drop across resistor T_5 turns TR_1 and, consequently, TR^2, OFF. The resulting cessation of current through the alternator field winding causes the alternator output voltage to drop. Once the voltage drops below a specified value, Zener diode D_1 is cut OFF and this causes TR_1 to conduct. The sequence of events just described is then repeated.

Integral (Built-In) Regulators

The alternators on most new cars have integral (built-in) transistor regulators. The regulator is an integrated circuit and is encapsulated in plastic to make it impervious to dust and moisture. The complete regulator package is about the size of a silver dollar with most of the bulk attributable to the plastic encapsulation. Operation of the charging system is basically the same as that described in the preceding topic with the two transistors turning the alternator field current on and off as needed to maintain a specified alternator output voltage.

Servicing Transistor Regulators

Except under conditions of extreme heat, transistor regulators are seldom the cause of trouble in the charging system. If other checks indicate regulator trouble, however, refer to the manufacturer's literature before making any tests or replacements. The in-circuit testing of transistors and diodes requires a special tester available from many electronic test-equipment manufacturers.

4

STARTING MOTORS

Contents

BASIC PRINCIPLES

The Starting System

Modern automobiles use a built-in electric motor powered by the battery to start the engine. This motor is called the *starting* or *cranking* motor and is controlled by the ignition switch.

Figure 4-1 shows the starting system of an automobile in greatly simplified form. When the ignition switch is turned *on*, current flows from the battery to the starter. The solenoid completes the circuit and is needed because the motor draws a starting current higher than the ignition switch can handle. The starting motor engages and turns the flywheel ring gear, and this turns over the engine. As soon as the engine begins to run under its own power, the starting motor disengages automatically and is turned off by the solenoid switch.

The starting-motor armature must rotate at high speed in order to produce sufficient power to crank the engine. Because the motor itself starts at a low speed, its drive pinion is very small compared to the flywheel ring gear, the ratio being typically 20 to 1. Thus the starting motor can develop a relatively high armature speed and develop considerable power while turning the engine at low speed.

When the engine starts, its speed may increase rapidly to 1,000 or more rpm. At this speed the starting motor would spin at 20,000 rpm (assuming a 20:1 gear ratio) and would be ruined. To prevent such damage, the drive pinion must be disengaged from the flywheel ring gear as soon as the engine starts.

Several different *drive mechanisms* have been designed to solve this problem. The drive mechanism is the mechanical linkage that engages the drive pinion with the flywheel ring gear when the engine is cranked, and disengages the two gears when the engine starts. The drive mechanisms discussed here are made by the Delco-Remy Division of General Motors Corporation. They include the *Bendix drive,* the *overrunning clutch drive,* the *Dyer drive,* and the *Delco-Remy inertia drive.* Although other manufacturers make drive mechanisms and starting motors, all operate on the same principle. If you understand the types described here, you should have little difficulty with any type or make of starting motor.

General Description of Starting Motors

A starting motor consists, in general, of a drive mechanism, a frame, field windings, an armature, and brushes. In most starting motors, the total battery current passes through both the field and armature windings; i.e., the motors are *series wound.* Such motors can develop very high torque.

In high-voltage starting motors, *shunt*-connected coils are added to the circuit to reduce the maximum free-running speed of the motor. In a series motor, operated with no load, the speed increases without restriction and may cause destruction of the motor.

Some starting motors contain a magnetically operated switch which controls the circuit between the battery and the motor. Others, with an overrunning clutch or a Dyer drive, have a solenoid-type magnetic switch that closes the battery-motor circuit and also shifts the starting motor drive pinion into mesh with the flywheel ring gear.

A relay may also be used in conjunction with the solenoid. The relay-type solenoid requires less current to operate the control circuit, thus allowing the use of lighter switches and smaller wire. When the ignition switch is turned *on*, the relay contact points close and connect the solenoid to the battery. This makes the solenoid operate, shifting the drive pinion into mesh and closing the starting-motor circuit.

Starting motors are designed to operate with very heavy current, and this creates considerable heat in the wires. Thus, operation of the starting motor at any one time should be limited to 30 seconds. If the engine does not start within 30 seconds, the starter motor should be allowed to cool off for a few seconds before it is reused.

Most starting motors are now located under the engine and are exposed to road splash, slush, and mud. To keep moisture and other foreign particles out, the motor is completely enclosed. Low-temperature lubricants are used to prevent icing and freezing.

Starting motors operate in essentially the same manner described in Chapter 1 for the simple electric motor. If necessary, review this section before proceeding.

As noted earlier, the field windings and armature of most starting motors are series connected. All of the windings are made of low-resistance, heavy-gauge copper wire to permit the flow of the heavy currents needed to develop large amounts of torque.

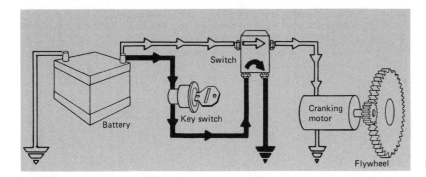

Fig. 4–1 Simplified version of starting system.

Types of Starting Motors

Figure 4-2 shows the coil and pole circuits and brush arrangements commonly used in starting motors.

Two-coil four-pole circuit. A so-called two-coil four-pole starting motor is shown in Fig. 4-2(a). To keep resistance to a minimum, only two field coils are used to create a magnetic field in all four poles. This is possible because a magnetic pole cannot exist by itself; an opposite pole is always created to balance it. In this motor, the two coils are wound in such a way as to make north poles at their physical location. The shape of the field frame then causes south poles to develop at the two remaining pole pieces.

In all starting motors, adjacent shoes must be of opposite polarity. A compass may be used at the faces of the poles to check this condition.

Four-coil four-pole circuits. The starting motor of Fig. 4-2(b) has four poles, four field windings, and four brushes. Two of the brushes are insulated and two are grounded. Half of the total current flows through one set of field windings to one insulated brush; the other half flows through the

second set of field windings to the other insulated brush. From the insulated brushes the current flows through the armature and then returns to the battery through the grounded brushes.

With four field-coil windings of low resistance, it is possible to create stronger magnetic fields, greater torque, and more cranking ability than with the two-coil four-pole circuit.

In the starting motor shown in Fig. 4-2(c) all four brushes are insulated. Two of the brushes are connected to the motor terminal, and the other two are connected to one end of the field coils. The opposite ends of the field coils are connected to ground.

When a completely insulated starting motor is needed, the two field leads are connected to a second insulated terminal on the field frame.

Six-coil six-pole circuits. The starting motor shown in Fig. 4-2(d) is designed for heavy-duty operation and uses six coils and six brushes. The current is split three ways; one-third flows through each pair of field windings to an insulated brush, and the three remaining brushes are grounded.

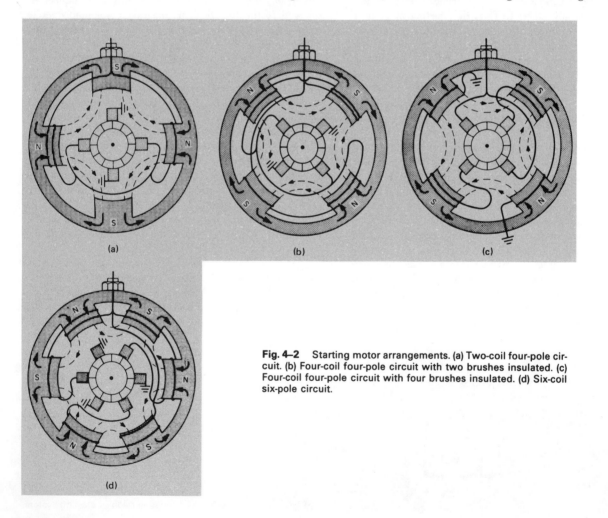

Fig. 4–2 Starting motor arrangements. (a) Two-coil four-pole circuit. (b) Four-coil four-pole circuit with two brushes insulated. (c) Four-coil four-pole circuit with four brushes insulated. (d) Six-coil six-pole circuit.

As a rule, insulated brushes are connected to each other by means of a jumper. This is done to equalize the voltage across the brushes. Without equalization, too much current may flow in one brush. This would cause arcing and burning of the commutator bars, damage to the contact surface, and, eventually, an open circuit between the brushes and commutator that would stop operation.

It is also interesting to note that the pole shoes of most starting motors have a longer tip on one side than on the other. When a shoe is installed, the longer tip should point in the direction of armature rotation. This design creates an improved magnetic field that provides greater torque.

Shunt-coil motors.   All of the motors described so far have been series wound. This type of motor can develop great torque, but if it is permitted to run free, that is, with no external load, it will destroy itself.

To limit the maximum free speed, a shunt coil may be connected in parallel with the armature. The magnetic field of the shunt coil remains constant and does not vary with speed. The magnetic field of the armature, in cutting through the field of the shunt coil, creates a counter voltage which increases with increasing speed. This counter voltage opposes, and thereby limits, any further increase in speed.

DRIVE MECHANISMS

Standard Bendix Drive

The standard Bendix drive depends on inertia to provide meshing of the drive pinion with the flywheel ring gear. A starting motor equipped with a standard Bendix drive is shown in Fig. 4-3. The drive assembly consists of the drive pinion, sleeve, spring, two screws used to fasten the spring to the assembly, a counterbalance, and a drive head. The drive pinion, is normally unbalanced by the counterbalance on one side, has screw threads on its inner bore. The sleeve, which is hollow, has screw threads cut on its outer diameter, and these threads engage those of the pinion.

When the ignition switch is turned on, current flows in the starting motor and its armature starts to rotate. The rotating motion is transmitted through the drive head and spring to the sleeve, so that all of these parts start to rotate and increase in speed directly with the armature.

Because the pinion is fit loosely on the sleeve screw thread, however, its speed does not increase at the same rate as the sleeve. In other words, the inertia of the drive pinion keeps the pinion from beginning to rotate immediately. Thus the sleeve rotates within the pinion. Since the pinion is actually threaded onto the sleeve, this rotation causes the pinion to ride out along the threads until it meshes with the flywheel ring gear.

When the pinion reaches the pinion stop, it begins to rotate together with the sleeve and armature, meshing with the flywheel ring gear. This rotation is thus transmitted to the ring gear (the Bendix spring takes up the shock of meshing), and the flywheel starts to turn. The engine is now being cranked.

When the engine begins to operate, the flywheel begins to drive the pinion. This makes the pinion spin faster than the starting-motor armature, causing the pinion to ride back down the threads until it is out of mesh with the flywheel ring gear. Thus the Bendix drive pinion and flywheel ring gear crank the engine and then disengage automatically when the engine starts operating.

During the operation of a starting motor equipped with a Bendix drive, certain precautions must be observed. Intentional backfiring of the engine should be avoided at all times. Any condition that causes the engine to backfire while it is being cranked should be corrected immediately. When an engine backfires with the pinion gear in mesh and the starting motor in operation, enormous stress is placed on the starting motor, which is attempting to spin the drive pinion in one direction while the engine is turning the drive pinion in the opposite direction. Such opposing forces on the Bendix drive may ruin the Bendix spring.

Damage may also occur when the engine starts momentarily and then stops. The tendency of the driver is to engage the starter immediately. But at this moment the engine is coming to rest, and in so doing, often rocks back (rotates in the reverse direction) for part of a revolution. When the starting motor is engaged during this rock-back period, serious damage will result. The drive housing on the cranking motor will probably break, or the Bendix spring will be damaged.

Burred teeth on the flywheel ring gear are an indication of an attempted re-engagement of the starting motor during engine rotation. Any burred condition should be corrected to make full engagement of the drive piston possible. If the pinion does not fully engage, it cannot travel all the way to the pinion stop. This situation applies a screw-jack force to the commutator end frame, which may cause a fracture in the end frame.

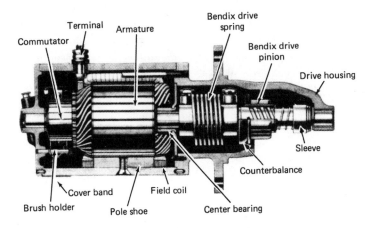

Fig. 4-3 Sectional view of a standard Bendix Drive. *Courtesy of Delco-Remy Division, General Motors Corporation.*

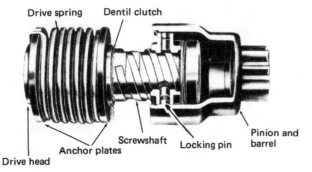

Fig. 4-4   Folo-Thru Bendix Drive. *Courtesy of Delco-Remy Division, General Motors Corporation.*

Variations of the Bendix Drive

A Bendix drive, known as the *Folo-Thru,* is shown in Fig. 4-4. This is a barrel-type drive mechanism with a pin used to lock the drive in the cranking position. The locking pin prevents disengagement on false starts. The pin is thrown out by centrifugal force when the engine is running, and the pinion then disengages. The screw shaft is in two pieces, connected by a dentil clutch (similar to a ratchet), which acts as a safety factor to prevent overspeeding of the starting-motor armature. If the engine drives the piston at a rate faster than the free speed of the armature, the clutch will slip and allow the pinion-and-barrel assembly to overrun the armature shaft.

The Overrunning Clutch

The overrunning clutch is a distinctly different type of drive mechanism than the Bendix drive. The clutch assembly, shown encircled in Fig. 4-5(a), transmits cranking torque from the armature to the engine flywheel. As soon as the engine starts, however, it disengages the drive pinion from the rest of the clutch assembly and the armature. This feature prevents the armature from being driven at excessive speed by the engine.

The overrunning clutch provides positive meshing and demeshing of the drive pinion with the flywheel ring gear. The clutch mechanism uses a shift lever to actuate the drive pinion. The pinion, together with the clutch mechanism, is moved endwise along the armature shaft, and either into, or out of, mesh with the flywheel ring gear. The shift lever may be either manually or solenoid operated.

A cross-section of the overrunning clutch is shown in Fig. 4-5(b). The clutch consists of a shell-and-sleeve assembly, the sleeve being a hollow shaft that fits over the armature shaft. The inside of the clutch shaft is splined to mesh with the splines on the armature shaft (some units have straight splines while others have spiral splines). The shell contains the pinion-and-collar assembly, and a gripping mechanism consisting of rollers, plungers, and springs, as shown in Fig. 4-5(c). Notches are cut into the shell, and a hardened-steel roller is assembled into each notch. The notches taper inward slightly, allowing adequate space for

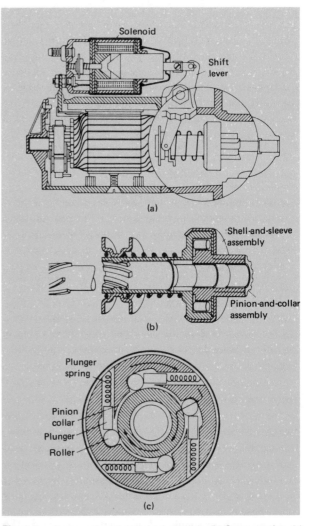

Fig. 4-5   Overrunning clutch. (a) Assembly. (b) Cross section. (c) Operation. *Courtesy of Delco-Remy Division, General Motors Corporation.*

the rollers. The pinion collar can rotate freely in a clockwise direction, that is, in the direction that tends to move the rollers against the plungers and plunger springs.

When the pinion meshes with the flywheel gear and the armature begins to rotate, the shell rotates in the direction of cranking, as shown in Fig. 4-5(c). The rollers rotate between the shell and collar until they are forced tightly into the smaller part of the notches. When the rollers jam between the collar and shell, they force the pinion to rotate with the shell. The resulting transmitted torque causes the engine to be cranked.

When the engine begins to operate, it drives the pinion faster than the armature. This action returns the rollers to the larger portion of the notches, allowing the pinion to rotate freely in the shell.

Clutch with accordion springs.   A clutch shell of small diameter was introduced with starting motors having enclosed

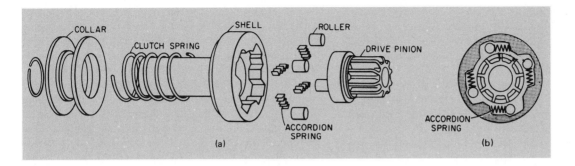

Fig. 4-6 Clutch with accordion spring. (a) Assembly. (b) End view. *Courtesy of Delco-Remy Division, General Motors Corporation.*

shift levers. The mechanical strength of the smaller clutch is maintained by accordion springs, which are used in place of the plungers and plunger springs. An exploded view of the clutch with accordion springs is shown in Fig. 4-6(a), and an end view of the assembly, showing the position of the springs, in (b).

Operating precautions. As soon as the engine starts, the circuit to the cranking motor should be *off*. If the circuit is not *off*, the drive pinion will remain in mesh and will continue to overrun the armature. The overrunning clutch cannot be operated in this condition for any more than very brief periods of time. After too long a time, overheating occurs and the clutch lubricant melts and escapes. The clutch is then likely to seize and spin the armature at high speed. A similar effect will result if the operator opens the throttle too wide during initial starting. Either condition puts an excessive load on the overrunning clutch and may ultimately cause it to seize.

Both the armature and the clutch may be ruined by excessive heat and too much overrunning. Such abuse is evident if the clutch bearings are galled under the drive pinion, resulting in a blue discoloration or a deposit of bearing metal on the armature shaft. This type of clutch should be protected from all extremes of heat, which might melt the lubricant.

The overrunning clutch must never be cleaned by using high temperatures or grease-removing methods, as such procedures remove the special lubricant originally packed in the clutch. If the lubricant is removed, rapid clutch failure can be expected. The clutch should always be cleaned with a brush dipped in oleum or other neutral spirits.

Pinion clearance. On many solenoid switch-operated starting motors, the linkage between the shift lever and the solenoid plunger must be adjusted so that a clearance exists between the pinion and the housing when the clutch is in the operating position. This clearance, shown in Fig. 4-7(a), should be checked in accordance with the manufacturer's instructions, with battery current being used to hold the plunger in the bottomed position. To check this clearance, disconnect the lead from the solenoid to the starting motor

so that the motor will not operate. Close the solenoid circuit and push the plunger in by hand. The battery current will hold the plunger in while the pinion clearance is checked.

Extruded-frame starting motors do not permit disconnection of the solenoid and motor terminals. To check these units for pinion clearance, a heavy jumper lead must be connected between the grounded motor terminal and the positive side of the 6-volt cell strap of a 12-volt battery, as shown in Fig. 4-7(b). This supplies only half the operating voltage, which is not enough to turn the armature.

SOLENOID CIRCUITS

Solenoid Circuit Function and Description

The solenoid is energized, either directly or through a relay, by closing the starter switch, which is usually part of the

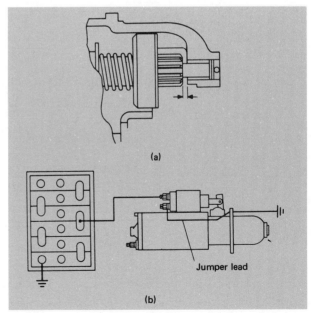

Fig. 4-7 Pinion-to-housing clearance. (a) Operating clearance. (b) Jumper connection for extruded frame motor.

ignition switch (see Fig. 4-8(a)). The solenoid, through the shift lever and its linkage, shifts the drive pinion into mesh with the flywheel ring gear. At the same time, the solenoid closes the circuit between the battery and the starting motor through an internal switch.

Figure 4-8(b) is an internal view of the solenoid. When the starter switch is closed, current flows through the pull and hold windings and creates a magnetic field which pulls the plunger to the right. Since the plunger is connected to the shift lever, this action meshes the pinion with the flywheel ring gear. In some designs, notably the Dyer drive, the plunger cannot complete its travel until the gears are fully meshed. In any case, however, when the plunger does move all the way to the right, the contact disk touches the battery and motor terminals. This completes the circuit from the battery to the starting motor, causing the armature to rotate and crank the engine.

The pull and hold windings are made of different size wire, but contain about the same number of turns. The pull winding is needed to start plunger movement. The plunger completes its movement when the contact disk closes the main switch contacts and the battery is connected directly to the starting motor. This action also shorts out the pull winding, which is connected across the main contacts. Sufficient current continues to flow through the hold winding, however, to hold the plunger in its inward position. The heavy current in the pull winding occurs only during plunger movement and is too brief to register on an ammeter.

When the control circuit is broken by releasing the starter switch, current no longer reaches the hold winding from this source. However, current flows from the battery, through the contact disk, through the pull winding in a reverse direction, and through the hold winding to ground. With the same number of turns on each of the two windings, and with the same current through each, the windings generate magnetic fields which effectively cancel each other. The tension of the return spring is then sufficient to cause the plunger to return to its at-rest position, which breaks the starting-motor circuit.

Solenoid Relay

In some starting-motor applications, a solenoid relay is used to prevent the starting motor from operating when the engine is running. The solenoid relay also allows the starting switch to handle only the relay-coil current instead of the much heavier solenoid current. Thus, a small starting switch can be used.

A circuit using a solenoid relay is shown in Fig. 4-9. When the ignition switch is turned on, current flows from the battery, through the ammeter, ignition switch, neutral safety switch, vacuum switch, solenoid-relay winding, regulator and ground circuit, back to the battery. The vacuum switch and neutral safety switch may not be found in some circuits. This current energizes the solenoid relay, closing

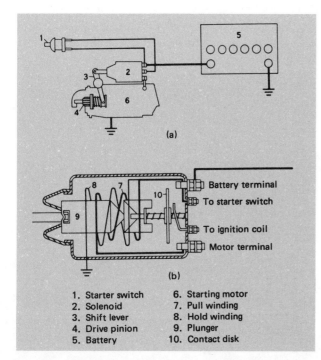

Fig. 4-8   (a) Functions and connections, and (b) internal view of solenoid.

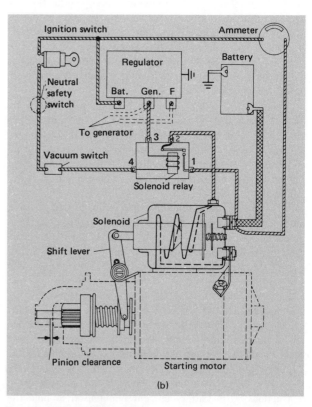

Fig. 4-9   Circuit using relay.

the circuit from the battery through the solenoid windings to ground and thereby cranking the engine.

When the engine starts to run, the generator begins to rotate; the buildup of generator voltage opposes the battery voltage across the solenoid-relay coil, which stops the flow of current through the coil. The relay contacts then open, disconnecting the starting-motor solenoid from the battery. This breaks the circuit to the starting motor, and the circuit ceases to operate, even if the ignition switch is still on. Thus the starting motor cannot be made to operate while the engine is running. This is a valuable safety feature.

Solenoid relay checks. To check the operation of a solenoid relay, first connect a battery across terminals 3 and 4 of the relay. Then connect a jumper from terminal 4 to terminal 1. Finally, connect a voltmeter between terminals 2 and 3. The voltmeter lead connected to terminal 3 must be of the same polarity as the battery lead connected to that terminal. The voltmeter should read battery voltage. If the voltmeter reading is zero, the relay is defective and should be replaced.

Solenoid failure. As noted earlier, the solenoid is released by cancellation of the magnetic fields in the pull and hold windings. If just a few of the turns on the pull winding become shorted together, the coil cannot generate enough magnetic force to oppose the force on the hold winding. Thus the main switch contacts in the solenoid remain closed and the starting motor continues to operate. Continued cranking after the control circuit is off usually indicates the existence of shorted turns in the pull windings. However, this condition may also result from binding of the solenoid plunger. The binding is caused by the solenoid mounting being out of line.

Either low system voltage or an open circuit in the hold winding will cause the plunger to oscillate instead of pulling in firmly. The pull winding has sufficient magnetic strength to close the main contacts, but when the contacts are closed, the pull winding is shorted out. If the hold coil is open, there is no magnetic force to keep the contacts closed. Whenever chattering of the switch occurs, check for a complete circuit in the hold winding. If the chattering continues and the windings are good, check the condition of the battery. Also check any other wiring systems that may be causing a heavy battery drain and consequent low system voltage.

If the solenoid plunger does not move at all when the start switch is closed, there is probably an open circuit between the battery and the solenoid. Check for loose connections, broken wires, or a defective start switch.

Disk replacement in solenoid. Some solenoids used with the Dyer drive have a replaceable contact disk which is adjustable. When assembled, the disk should be 1-1/32 inches below the edge of the housing when the plunger is in a retracted position. This setting is important during the cranking cycle because it provides the correct pressure between the contact disk and the terminal contacts. Adjustment of the setting is made in the same way as the pinion-travel adjustment described earlier.

Adjusting solenoid pinion clearance. The clutch-type cranking motor must have the piston clearance checked without the pinion spring being compressed. Some units have a stud adjustment in the plunger of the solenoid. Other units have slotted holes in the mounting bracket which make it possible to shift the position of the entire unit on the motor frame. A third type of unit has a serrated linkage adjustment that should be made in accordance with manufacturer's instructions. Always check the alignment of the linkage on these units to prevent binding.

The correct pinion clearance must be maintained because the pulling power of a solenoid increases as the air gap of the plunger is reduced. Locating the pinion adjustment at the high limit on either the clutch or Dyer-type motors reduces the air gap, and this gives a more powerful magnetic field. Whenever the solenoid on a motor is replaced or adjusted, always check the pinion clearance. Satisfactory performance depends upon this adjustment.

MAINTENANCE AND TROUBLESHOOTING

Lubrication

Some starting motors need lubrication only during overhaul. However, others require lubrication every 5,000 miles or 300 hours of operation, and have lubrication fittings. To lubricate, proceed as follows: (1) Use hinge-cap oilers or oil tubes sealed with a pipe plug and apply 8 to 10 drops of medium-grade (SAE 20) engine oil. (2) For grease cups, turn down one turn and refill with bearing grease if necessary.

When the motor is disassembled for any reason, it should be lubricated as follows: (1) Oil wicks, if present, should be resaturated. (2) Coat bushings with a lubricant specified by motor manufacturer. (3) Coat armature shaft lightly with lubricant specified by manufacturer. (4) Wipe drive assembly clean and coat with light oil. Do not wash the drive assembly in solvent, and avoid excessive lubrication.

Troubleshooting

To avoid a lot of unnecessary work, several visual and electrical checks should always be made before a starting motor is removed from a vehicle.

Check the battery voltage and the specific gravity of the battery electrolyte.

Inspect the wiring for frayed insulation or other damage and replace as needed. Inspect all connections to the starting motor, solenoid or magnetic switch, ignition switch or any control switch, and battery. Make sure all ground connections are clean and tight. Refer to the manufacturer's literature and check the allowable voltage drop in the cranking circuit.

If any switch is suspected of being defective, connect a jumper across the switch to remove it from the circuit. If the circuit operates properly with the switch jumpered, replace the switch.

If the specified battery voltage is measured at the motor terminal of the solenoid (allowing for a voltage drop in the circuit) and the engine is functioning properly but the cranking system does not work, it is time to remove the motor from the vehicle for more extensive tests.

Mechanical Test

When a starting motor is defective and is removed from the engine for repair, several tests may be applied to locate the difficulty. Mechanical checks should always be performed before electrical tests. If there is any mechanical trouble, the high-speed running required for electrical tests might worsen the trouble.

Check the pinion for freedom of operation by turning it on the shaft. Check the armature for freedom by turning the pinion together with the armature. If any stiffness, binding, or scraping is detected, dismantle the motor and correct the fault. Typical causes of these conditions are tight, dirty, or worn bearings, a bent armature shaft, and loose pole shoes or screws. Too much play in the armature shaft is usually caused by worn bearings.

After any obvious mechanical defects are corrected, the motor is ready for electrical testing. Since a mechanical defect may have been overlooked, however, check for unusual noises and/or excessive vibration while the electrical tests are in progress.

No-Load Test

With the motor clamped in a vise, or otherwise mounted in a fixed position that permits free rotation of the armature, make the connections shown in Fig. 4-10. To start the mo-

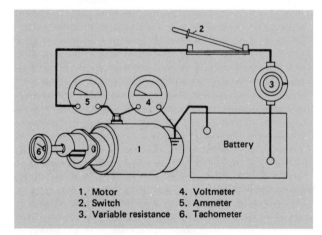

1. Motor	4. Voltmeter
2. Switch	5. Ammeter
3. Variable resistance	6. Tachometer

Fig. 4-10 Connections for no-load test.

tor, close the switch. With the motor running, adjust the variable resistance to make the voltmeter read the voltage specified by the motor manufacturer for this test. When the correct voltage is set, read and record the motor current as indicated by the ammeter, and the motor speed as indicated by the tachometer attached to the armature shaft. Then turn the motor off.

No-load test results. If the motor current and speed are correct, the motor is probably in good electrical condition.

If there is high current at low speed, either there is mechanical trouble—the armature cannot turn freely—or an electrical short or ground in the motor windings.

A grounded armature can be detected by raising the grounded brushes off the commutator and insulating them with cardboard. Then a test lamp and test prods can be used to check between the insulated terminal of the starting motor and the motor frame. When this check is being made, the ground connection of the shunt coils, if such coils are used, must be removed. If the lamp lights, there is a ground. To locate the ground, raise the other brushes from the armature and check the armature and fields separately. On some motors, the current passes through the armature windings first and then goes to ground through the field windings. On such units it is necessary to disconnect the ground leads before making any checks for abnormal grounds.

If these checks fail to locate the cause of a low no-load speed and a high current draw, the armature should be removed and tested on a growler. The procedure for testing the armature is the same as that used in testing the armature of a dc generator.

If there is high current, but no rotation, a direct ground exists at the switch, at the terminal, or at the brushes or field connections. Frozen or binding shaft bearings also produce an overloaded condition.

If there is no current draw, an open circuit exists in the fields, the armature, at the terminal connections or brushes, or between the brushes and commutator. Broken or weak brush springs, worn brushes, or high mica on the commutator all prevent good contact and cause an open-circuited or high-resistance condition.

If there is low current at low speed, there is too much resistance in the motor circuit. On units where the current takes two or three parallel paths, one of the field windings may be open-circuited. This would reduce the current drain and, consequently, the torque.

If there is high current at high speed, there is a shorted field. Since the fields have a low resistance, a short may be difficult to detect. If a shorted field is suspected, the one sure test is to install a new field and check for improved performance. Because of the high current drain of starting motors under load, all interconnecting cables must be sufficiently heavy to carry the current. Clean connections, firmly made, are also essential to maintaining the required low resistance.

Stall, or Resistance, Test

For a stall, or resistance, test, the motor is clamped in a vise and is hooked up as shown in Fig. 4-11. A variable resistance that can handle the high current, an ammeter, a battery, and a switch are connected in series with the motor. The battery must be large enough to supply the required test voltage with the variable resistance in the circuit. The test voltage is much lower than the normal operating voltage of the motor. A voltmeter is connected across the motor. When the switch is closed, the variable resistance is adjusted to produce the specified voltage at the motor. The current drain is then noted and compared with the value specified by the manufacturer. If the current drain is below the minimum specified value, a high resistance exists as a result of poor connections or improper brush seating. An excessive current reading indicates grounded or shortened conductors.

Lock-Torque Test

The lock-torque test requires the equipment and connections shown in Fig. 4-12. Again, the variable resistance must have a high current-handling capacity. The motor should be securely mounted, and a brake arm should be hooked to the drive pinion. Use extreme caution during this test. Make sure the end of the brake arm does not slip off the pinion when current is applied. When the specified current is applied, the torque is computed from the scale reading. A 12-inch brake arm will indicate pound-feet directly. Compare the indicated pound-feet of torque with the manufacturer's specifications. If the torque is low, the motor must be disassembled for further tests and repair.

Disassembling Starting Motors

Never attempt the disassembly of a starting motor unless you have access to the manufacturer's maintenance handbook for that particular motor. Because there is such a wide variety of starting motors on the market, no general disas-

sembly procedure can be given. If you attempt the job, do exactly as the manufacturer instructs, and disassemble the motor only as far as necessary.

As a precaution, wear safety glasses when attempting this job.

Inspection and Repair

In general, there are three main points of inspection for a starting motor: the brushes and brush holders, the armature, and the field coils.

Brushes and brush holders. Inspect the brushes for wear by comparing them with a new brush. If the brushes are worn to one-half their original length, they should be replaced. Make sure the brush holders are clean and that the brushes do not bind in the holders. The full brush surface should ride on the commutator, with proper spring tension. The brush leads and screws should be tight and clean.

Armature. The armature should be checked for short circuits, opens, and grounds. Short circuits may be located by rotating the armature in a growler while holding a hacksaw blade on the armature. If the blade vibrates, there is a short in that area. Shorts between commutator bars are sometimes produced by brush dust or copper particles between the bars. Undercutting the mica will eliminate these shorts.

To find an open circuit, look for loose or broken solder joints at the points where the conductors are joined to the commutator. Poor connections cause arcing and burning of the commutator. If the bars are not badly burned, resolder the leads in the riser bars and have the commutator turned down in a lathe. Then undercut the mica between the commutator bars by 1/32 inch.

Grounds in the armature can be detected by using a test lamp. If the lamp lights when one test prod is placed on the commutator and the other prod on the armature core or shaft, the armature is grounded.

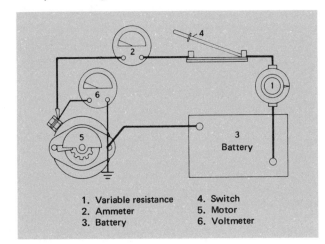

1. Variable resistance
2. Ammeter
3. Battery
4. Switch
5. Motor
6. Voltmeter

Fig. 4-11 Connections for stall test.

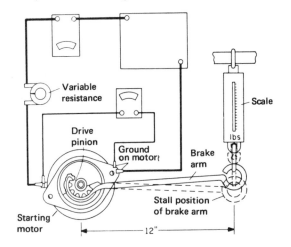

Fig. 4-12 Connections for lock-torque test.

Use a test lamp to check the field coils for grounds or opens. For ground checks, disconnect the ground connection of the field coil. Connect one test prod to the field frame and the other to the field connector. If the lamp lights, the field coils are grounded. To check for opens, connect the test prods to the ends of the coil winding. If the lamp does not light, the winding is open.

If the field coils must be removed for repair or replacement, a pole-shoe spreader and a pole-shoe screwdriver should be used. Take care when tightening the coils in place to prevent grounds or shorts. Where the pole shoe has a long lip on one side, it should be assembled in the direction of armature rotation, as noted earlier.

Assembling Cranking Motor

Again, follow the instructions given by the manufacturer. Do not attempt to force parts into place. If they do not fit readily, check your work to determine why.

5

IGNITION AND LIGHTING SYSTEMS AND INDICATING DEVICES

Contents

ELECTRICAL SYSTEMS

The Five Main Systems

The five main electrical systems in an automobile, shown in Fig. 5-1 are: (a) *electrical generating;* (b) *starting (cranking);* (c) *ignition;* (d) *lighting;* and (e) *signaling.*

The *heart* of the electrical generating system is the storage battery, which performs three primary functions: (1) supplies power to the cranking motor and ignition system for starting and operating the engine, (2) supplies power to lights, radio, heater, and so on, when the requirement for these accessories is greater than the output of the alternator (or generator), (3) serves as a voltage stabilizer for all electrical systems. Satisfactory operation of an automobile without a properly functioning battery is impossible.

The alternator (or generator) provides a regulated flow of electricity to keep the battery charged and to operate other electrical systems, except the starting system, upon demand. The generating circuit proper contains the alternator (or generator), regulator, ammeter, junction block, battery, and car frame. Of course, the ammeter, junction block, battery, and car frame are common to all systems. Thus, when the alternator (or generator) is inoperative or defective, the other electrical systems will operate only so long as the battery remains charged.

Operation of the cranking motor is controlled by the ignition-starter switch. Each of the other systems has some

form of switch control. In the generating system, for example, the cutout relay in the regulator does the switching automatically. For interior lighting, a separate switch is generally used for each light.

The ignition system contains two circuits: the *low-voltage* (6 or 12 volt) *primary* circuit, and the *high-voltage* (20,000 to 30,000 volts) *secondary* circuit. The primary circuit includes the battery and associated items (ammeter, etc.), ignition-starter switch, ignition resistor, distributor points and capacitor (formerly called condenser), special connecting wires, and the primary winding of the ignition coil. The secondary circuit includes the secondary winding of the ignition coil, distributor cap and rotor, spark plugs, and cables.

In some shop manuals, the generating system is considered to be part of the ignition system because it supplies power to the primary circuit during operation at high engine speed. During idle or low engine speed, the battery becomes part of the ignition system. An alternator, when used, will charge even at idling speeds.

The lighting system, Fig. 5-1(d), includes both exterior and interior lighting. Each circuit operates independently.

In addition to the horns shown in Fig. 5-1(e), the signalling system also includes turn-signal lights, switch, and flashing unit.

The electrical generating and starting systems were covered in Chapters 3 and 4, respectively.

Because none of the systems described in this chapter

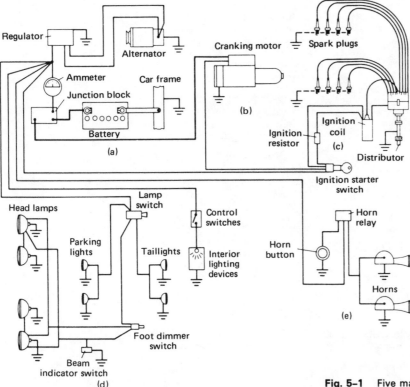

Fig. 5-1 Five main electrical systems.

can operate when the storage battery of an automobile is defective, it seems appropriate to begin the chapter with a discussion of this extremely important component.

THE STORAGE BATTERY

General

The modern automobile battery is a 12-volt lead-acid unit having a specified *ampere-hour capacity;* that is, the capacity to supply a certain amount of current in amperes for a given length of time in hours.

Six 2-volt cells are enclosed in compartments in the battery case, which is made of hard rubber or an acid-and-shock resistant plastic.

When purchased, most automobile batteries are dry and *electrolyte* (a mixture of water and sulfuric acid) must be added. If you must fill the cells with electrolyte, be extremely careful since the mixture is highly corrosive and will cause severe burns if it comes into contact with your skin or eyes. Follow each step of the manufacturer's directions carefully. Make sure that the funnel you use to fill the cells with electrolyte is either glass or acidproof plastic. A metal funnel will contaminate the electrolyte and seriously shorten battery life.

Terminals for connecting the battery into the various electric circuits are located either on the top of the battery or on the side of the case. On top-terminal batteries, the positive (+) terminal is larger in diameter than the negative (−) terminal. Side-terminal batteries must be installed so that the terminals are exposed. Two cable connectors are then in position for attachment to the proper terminal. Both arrangements prevent connection of the battery with reverse polarity since any such connection can destroy the alternator and regulator.

Vent and filler plugs are installed in the cell covers. When it is necessary to add water the plugs are removed. Each plug has a vent hole that permits the escape of gas that is generated during the charging process. If the gas is not permitted to escape freely, a battery may explode while being charged. When a battery is connected to a charger located within a closed space, make sure that the space is well ventilated for the removal of gas and that no one enters the space while smoking or attempts to light a cigarette while inside the space.

Sealed Batteries

Some batteries have a sealed top and do not require the usual maintenance. There is no filler cap, but a small vent is provided at one edge of the battery top.

There are two types of sealed batteries in current use: one has a charge indicator eye and the other does not. The testing procedure for either type is as follows:

1. Check the condition of the case. If the loss of electrolyte is possible, replace the battery.

2. Check the condition of the charge indicator eye. On batteries that have no charge indicator eye, charge the battery using a rate and time selected from Table 5-1. Do not charge the battery for more than 50 ampere-hours. If the green dot appears or electrolyte squirts out of the vent, stop the charge and go on with Step 3.

3. Either disconnect the high-voltage coil wire or the engine harness (electronic ignition) and crank the starter motor for 15 seconds.

4. Connect a voltmeter and a 230-ampere load across the battery terminals.

5. Take a voltmeter reading after the load has been connected for 15 seconds, then disconnect the load.

6. Consult Table 5-2. If the battery voltage is that specified (or more) for the given ambient temperature, the battery is good. If the voltage falls below that specified, the battery is in poor condition and must be replaced.

Overfill Prevention

When an excessive amount of water is added to battery cells, gas created during the charging process forces droplets of electrolyte out of the vent plugs. This loss of electrolyte shortens the lifetime of the battery. Moreover, the electrolyte is highly corrosive to any material on which it is deposited.

To prevent the loss of electrolyte as a result of overfilling, many batteries now have devices in their cell covers that permit visual observation of the electrolyte level.

Table 5-1. Charging rates and times for sealed batteries. Notice that all combinations equal 50 ampere-hours.

Charging Rate in Amperes	Charging Time in Hours
75	⅔
50	1
25	2
10	5

Table 5-2. Acceptable terminal voltages at different ambient (surrounding) temperatures. Notice that the acceptable terminal voltage drops with lower temperatures.

Ambient Temperature in °F	Voltage in volts
70 or above	9.6
60	9.5
50	9.4
40	9.3
30	9.1
20	8.9
10	8.7
0	8.5

Periodic Servicing Notes

Water usage. Excessive usage of battery water indicates that the battery is being overcharged. Most common causes of overcharge are high battery temperatures or a too high voltage regulator setting.

No appreciable usage of water, over two or three months of average vehicle use, indicates an undercharged battery condition. Poor cable connections or a too low voltage regulator setting could be the cause.

Cleaning. The external condition of the battery should be checked periodically for damage or dirt and corrosion. The top of the battery should be kept clean. Acid film and dirt may permit current to flow between the battery terminals, resulting in current leakage. This will slowly discharge the battery. For best results when cleaning the top of the battery, wash it first with a diluted ammonia or a soda solution to neutralize any acid present, and then flush off with clean water. Care must be taken to keep vent plugs tight so that the neutralizing solution does not enter the cells.

Cables. To ensure good electrical contact, the battery cables should be clean and tight on the battery posts. If the battery posts or cable terminals are corroded, the cables should be disconnected and the terminals and clamps cleaned separately with a soda solution and a wire brush. After cleaning, apply a thin coating of petroleum jelly on the posts and cable clamps to help retard corrosion.

Carrier and hold-down. The battery carrier and hold-down should be clean and free from corrosion before installing a battery. The carrier should be in sound mechanical condition so that it will support the battery securely and keep it level.

To keep the battery from shaking in the carrier, the hold-down bolts should be tight. However, they should not be tightened to the point where the battery base will be placed under severe strain.

Testing Procedures

Light load test. The light load test is simple, quick, and accurate and should be used on all batteries having *individual* cell covers. This test is *not suitable* for batteries having one-piece covers. A typical voltmeter intended for this purpose is shown in Figure 5-2. Each scale division represents 0.01 volt. Since each cell contains two groups of plates, positive and negative, and plate straps for each group are located on opposite sides of the vent cap (near the outer edge of the battery), the test prods of the voltmeter must come into contact with the straps. The light load test should be made before batteries are charged. Otherwise, defective cells may pass the test and give a false diagnosis.

If the battery is in the vehicle, place a load on the battery by holding the starter switch on for three seconds or until the engine starts. If the engine starts, turn off the ignition. When the battery is out of the vehicle, place a 150-ampere load on it for three seconds.

Next, turn on the headlights (low beam), or if the battery is out of the vehicle, place a 10-ampere load on the battery. After one minute, with the lights still on or with the 10-ampere load still connected, read the voltage of each battery cell with the tester. Note the exact voltage. It is necessary either to remember or record for later reference the highest and lowest cell voltages.

If the cells read 1.95 volts or more and the difference between the highest and lowest readings is less than 0.05 volt, the battery is good and sufficiently charged.

If cells read both above and below 1.95 volts, and the difference between the highest and lowest readings is less than 0.05 volt, the battery is good but needs charging.

If any cell reads 1.95 volts or more and there is a difference of 0.05 volt or more between the highest and lowest cell, the battery is defective, damaged, or worn out and should be replaced.

If all the cells read less than 1.95 volts, the battery should be charged before the light load test is repeated. Charge all 6-volt batteries for 30 minutes at 60 amperes. Charge 12-volt batteries rated at 100 ampere-hours or less for 20 minutes at 50 amperes. Charge 12-volt batteries rated over 100 ampere-hours for 30 minutes at 60 amperes. If the charger being used will not give the rate specified, charge for an equal length of time at the next lower rate available.

If, after charging, the battery is found to be good, it should be fully recharged before being placed back in service. If none of the cells comes up to 1.95 volts after the first boost charge, repeat the charge. Batteries that do not come up to the required voltage readings after the second boost charge should be replaced.

Full charge hydrometer test. This test should be used on batteries that have tested well using the light load test, but which subsequently fail in service.

First, remove the battery from the vehicle and add wa-

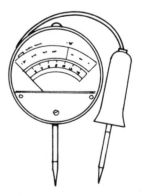

Fig. 5-2. Typical voltmeter for light-load test. *Courtesy of Delco-Remy Division, General Motors Corporation.*

ter, if necessary. Then charge the battery fully and note the specific gravity of the electrolyte in each cell.

A full charge hydrometer reading of less than 1.230 on any cell indicates that the cell is defective and the battery must be replaced.

Full charge hydrometer readings above 1.310 on any cell indicates that the cell was either improperly filled at time of activation or improperly serviced. Short life will result.

If all cells read between 1.230 and 1.310, and the difference between the lowest and highest cells is 0.050 or more, the battery is defective. Otherwise the battery is good.

Other battery tests.   Although they require the use of special testers which are seldom available to the "do-it-yourself" mechanic, two additional tests are worthy of brief mention here.

The so-called 421 test was originally designed to test batteries having a one-piece cover, but is actually suitable for use on any battery. The test requires a special tester which applies a discharge load and then a charge, each for a specified number of seconds. The open-circuit (no load) voltage readings of the battery are taken immediately after the discharge and charge cycles, and the difference in readings shows the condition of the battery.

The cadmium-tip test requires a special tester with cadmium tips that are inserted into the electrolyte of adjacent cells after the filler plugs are removed. Electrolyte must be up to the proper level. If the car has been operated or the battery charged within eight hours, turn on the headlights for one minute and then turn them off. The test is started by putting a red probe into the cell that has the positive terminal post. A black probe is then inserted into the adjacent probe. Note the meter readings. Next, move the red probe to cell 2 and the black probe to cell 3, and so forth. Battery replacement is recommended when any cell readings vary by five or more scale divisions.

Removing and Installing Batteries

Although there is nothing difficult about removing or installing batteries, a lot of people use the wrong tools and/or a wrong procedure and end up having to buy a new battery. Today, a new battery can be very expensive.

In removing a battery, *always* detach the ground cable first. If you attempt to remove the "hot" (ungrounded) cable first, any tool you are using may come into contact with a grounded object. If it does, a very heavy current is drawn from the battery and may cause irreparable damage.

To remove a nut-and-bolt type cable clamp, use either special battery-cable pliers or a box wrench to loosen the clamp nut about 3/8-inch. *Do not use* ordinary pliers or an open-end wrench. The jaws of the pliers or wrench may swing around and break the cell cover. If the clamp sticks to the battery terminal post, use a clamp puller to remove

the clamp. If you use a pry bar or a screwdriver to loosen the clamp, you will place a strain on the terminal post and its attached plates. The plates may break loose or other internal damage that ruins the battery may occur.

To loosen a spring-type cable clamp, squeeze the ends of the prongs together with a wide jaw, vice grip, or channel-lock pliers. The expanded clamp can then be lifted off the post.

To install a battery having nut-and-bolt type cable clamps, place the clamps over the terminal posts and tighten the nuts with battery-cable pliers or a box wrench. If necessary, use a clamp spreader to spread the cable clamps far enough to ensure full seating of the clamp on the terminal post. *Never* hammer or force the clamp down on the post since this may break the cell cover or cause internal damage that ruins the battery. And do not overtighten the nuts since this could damage the clamps. When the tightening is completed, there should be some space between the jaws of a clamp. If there is no gap between the jaws, the clamp is probably loose on the terminal post.

Make the battery hold-down clamp "snug" but do not overtighten since this may damage the battery case.

Using a Booster Battery to Start a Car Engine

If the battery is too low to start an engine, a *booster* battery, connected in *parallel* with the battery in your car, can supply the necessary current to the starting motor. Once again, this is not a difficult task, but it is usually performed in such a manner as to create an unnecessarily hazardous condition. Here is how the job should be done.

1. Remove the vent caps from both batteries and place a clean cloth over the openings to prevent contamination of the electrolyte should an explosion occur.

2. Shield your eyes.

3. If the booster battery is being used in the electrical system of another vehicle (the most common situation), do not permit the two vehicles to come into contact with each other.

4. Turn off all electrical equipment in both vehicles other than the ignition of the car to be started.

5. Connect one end of a jumper cable to the positive (+) terminal of the booster battery. Then connect the other end of the jumper cable to the positive terminal of the dead battery.

6. Connect one end of a second jumper cable to the negative (−) terminal of the booster battery. Then connect the other end of the jumper cable *to the engine block* of the car being started. Do not make the second connection to the negative terminal of the dead battery (a very common practice). If you do, you may damage electrical equipment or cause a battery to explode! And keep your face away from the battery while making this connection.

7. *Now* start the car containing the booster battery. Only

then should you start the second car containing the dead battery.

8. When the disabled car is running, first remove the engine-block connection of the negative cable. Then remove the other end of the negative cable.

9. Finally, disconnect the positive cable, being careful not to ground the end of the cable removed first.

One final caution about supplying a battery boost to another vehicle. *Never* operate your starting motor for more than 30 seconds at a time. Wait a few minutes before operating the starting motor again. This motor draws a heavy current and heats up quickly.

NON-ELECTRONIC IGNITION SYSTEMS

More About Electric Circuits

Before we can describe the operation of the ignition system in a technically correct (and easy to understand) manner, we must take a quick look at a second *property* of all electric circuits called *inductance*. (Resistance is also a property of all electric circuits.)

In Chapter 1, you learned that when a *changing* current passes through the primary winding of a transformer, the magnetic lines of force (magnetic flux) produced around the primary alternately expand and collapse. In doing so, they cut across the turns of the secondary winding and induce an electromotive force (emf) or voltage in the secondary. *But this is not the only emf induced in the transformer windings.*

Look at the circuit of Figure 5-3 that consists of a battery, switch, and two-turn coil connected in series. When the switch is first closed, the increasing magnetic flux produced by the rising current in turn A induces an emf into turn B. In like manner, the rising current in turn B induces an emf into turn A. These emf's are in series and both have a direction that *opposes* the increasing flux. Since the increasing flux is due to the rising current, the induced emf opposes the applied emf so that current *cannot rise instantly.*

The generation of an emf in an electric circuit by a changing current in the *same* circuit is called *self-induction.* And since the induced emf opposes any change in current, it is called a *counter emf* or *cemf.*

When the switch is opened in the circuit of Figure 5-3, the magnetic field collapses and again induces an emf in both turns. But the polarity of the self-induced emf is reversed as the coil tries to maintain current flow by having the polarity of its cemf such that it adds to the battery emf, thus raising the total emf in an attempt to sustain current flow in the circuit.

The *property* of an electric circuit that opposes any change in current in that circuit is called *self-inductance.* But because it is quite apparent in circuit diagrams whether the induction action in question is self-induction or *mutual* induction (as in a transformer), we usually omit the word *self* and simply speak of the inductance of an electric circuit.

The magnitude of the cemf caused by inductance is directly proportional to the *rate of change of current* which is always greatest at the instant when current flow through a circuit either commences or is interrupted.

Finally, note that the opposition to current caused by inductance ends once the current reaches its maximum value since the rate of change is then zero. Resistance, on the other hand, opposes the flow of current at all times.

Basic Operation of the Ignition System Primary Circuit

The wiring diagram of a non-electronic ignition system is shown in Figure 5-4. The so-called *primary* circuit is shown in black and the *secondary* circuit in white. For improved clarity, the distributor cap is removed from, and shown above, the *distributor.*

When the ignition switch is turned to START, the distributor contact points close and current passes through the series connected primary circuit consisting of the battery, distributor points, ignition coil primary, and ignition switch.

In passing through the primary winding of the ignition coil, the increasing current produces an expanding magnetic field around the coil. Due to the presence of inductance, however, the field does not reach its maximum immediately, but does so only after an elapsed period of time referred to as the *build-up time.*

Although it is quite brief, build-up time nevertheless

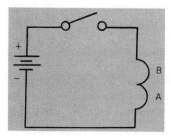

Fig. 5-3. Self-induction

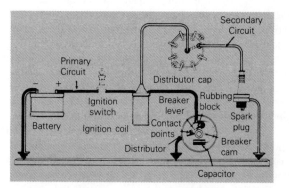

Fig. 5-4. Wiring diagram of a non-electronic ignition system.

has an adverse effect on the performance of the ignition system, particularly at high engine speeds, because the contact points are then closed for such short periods of time that current (and, therefore, the magnetic field around the coil) never reaches its maximum value. In a properly designed and operating ignition system, however, the overall effect of the build-up time is not serious.

Unlike resistance, inductance does not convert the energy supplied by the source of emf (battery) into heat or light. Instead, the energy from the source is stored in the magnetic field since the rising current forces the magnetic lines of force to expand against their natural characteristic of trying to become as short as possible. Once the current reaches a steady, maximum value, a constant amount of energy is stored in the magnetic field.

The breaker cam is rotated by a distributor shaft which is driven, in turn, by gearing from the camshaft of the engine. The distributor shaft and breaker cam rotate at one-half engine speed and the cam *usually* has the same number of lobes as there are engine cylinders. When a lobe passes under the breaker-lever rubbing block, the breaker points open.

When the points open, the energy stored in the magnetic field of the coil is returned to the circuit. But, again, as a result of inductance, a brief time must elapse before the current can change. Thus, at the instant the contact points open, the circuit current is the same as it was just before the points opened.

To help us understand the effect of interrupting current flow in a dc circuit containing a coil, we shall give a specific value of 500 kilohms to the *leakage resistance* of the open contacts. Figure 5-5 shows this resistance connected across the contact points and the resistance of the coil primary, 2 ohms, is shown in series with the primary winding. Just before the contact points open the current is

$$I = \frac{E}{R} = \frac{12}{2} = 6 \text{ amperes}$$

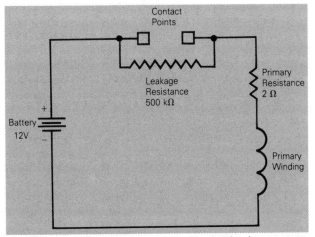

Fig. 5-5. Schematic diagram of primary circuit when contact points open.

At the instant the contact points open, the current through the coil is still 6 amps. Since this is a simple series circuit, this 6-ampere current must flow through the leakage resistance of the contact points, creating a voltage drop across the contact points of

$$E = IR = 6 \times 500,000 = 3,000,000 \text{ volts}$$

This extremely high voltage drop is matched by the cemf generated in the turns of the coil by the rapidly collapsing magnetic field. If we permit such a high voltage to be induced in practice, not only will there be arcing between the contact points, but the insulation of the coil will break down.

To prevent sparking of the breaker contacts, a capacitor is connected across the contact points (in place of the leakage resistance of Figure 5-5). While the points are closed, the voltage across the capacitor is zero volts. Since the voltage cannot rise instantaneously when the contact points open, there is sufficient time to move the contact points far enough apart that they do not spark. Some of the energy released by the collapsing magnetic field of the coil is transferred to the capacitor as it charges. The capacitor then partially discharges, building up a smaller magnetic field around the coil in the opposite direction. Several cycles of diminishing energy transfer take place until the energy stored is all dissipated in the resistance of the coil.

Although it is not shown in Figure 5-4, the non-electronic type of ignition system includes a resistance wire (also called a *ballast* resistance) which is in series with the ignition-coil primary when the car engine is running. This protects the distributor points from excessive current. During cranking, however, the ignition switch shorts out this resistance so that full battery voltage is applied to the primary circuit to aid proper circuit performance. On some cars the ballast resistance is a separately mounted part, but on most cars it is included in the wiring harness.

Operation of the Secondary Circuit

The secondary circuit of the ignition system consists of the secondary winding of the ignition coil connected in series with the spark plugs. A *rotor* (revolving contact) located in the distributor cap connects each spark plug (in turn) to the coil at an appropriate time.

When the breaker points open and primary current is interrupted, the rate-of-change of current and, therefore, the cemf generated across both windings of the coil, reach maximum values. Typically, the voltage across the primary winding reaches about 250 volts while that across the secondary winding is approximately 25,000 volts. When the high voltage across the secondary winding appears across the small air gap of the spark plug, the air gap "breaks down" and a spark "jumps" across the gap. This spark ignites an air-fuel mixture in the combustion chamber of an engine cylinder. As the burning gases expand, they drive a piston (inside the cylinder) downward and this action provides the power that propels the car.

To understand why the secondary voltage is so much higher than the primary voltage and why the ignition coil is constructed in a certain manner, let us "detour" briefly to take a look at certain features of transformers.

More About Transformers

A typical ignition coil, Figure 5-6, is a special type of transformer and contains three essential parts: (a) a primary winding of a few *hundred* turns of fairly heavy wire, (b) a secondary winding consisting of several *thousand* turns of fine wire, and (c) a laminated soft-iron construction which concentrates the magnetic field and ensures that essentially all lines of force about the primary also cut the secondary. Thus the magnetic *coupling*, for practical purposes, is assumed to be perfect. The primary winding is assembled around the outside of the secondary winding and the laminated iron is distributed so that one portion serves as a core for the winding and the remainder serves as a shell around the entire subassembly. This subassembly is placed in a seamless, one-piece case, and the case is filled with oil to provide waterproofing. A cap is then assembled to the case, and sealing gaskets are used between the cap and case on all terminals.

In our example of circuit operation, we assumed primary and secondary voltages of 250 volts and 25,000 volts, respectively. Thus, the ratio of the two voltages is 250 to 25,000 or, dividing each number by 250, 1 to 100. In other words, the secondary voltage is 100 times greater than the primary voltage.

Now, here are two very interesting things about transformers. (1) The ratio of primary voltage to secondary voltage is the same as the ratio of primary turns to secondary turns (or vice versa). (2) The ratio of primary current to secondary current is the inverse or opposite of the ratio of primary turns to secondary turns.

In our example, we arrived at a primary to secondary voltage ratio of 1 to 100. Now, if the primary of the coil shown in Fig. 5-6 contains, say, 200 turns, and the ratio of primary to secondary turns is the same as the voltage ratio, the secondary winding must contain

$$200 \times 100 = 20,000 \text{ turns}$$

also, the secondary current must be equal to just $\frac{1}{100}$ th of the primary current. If, for example, the primary current is 6 amperes, the secondary current will be 60 milliamperes. The required current-handling capabilities of the two windings account for the difference in wire sizes.

The Distributor

Figure 5-7 is a partially exploded view of a typical ignition distributor. This device has three jobs. First, to open and close the ignition primary circuit and thereby produce the changes in current needed to cause alternate expansions and contractions of the magnetic field surrounding the ignition coil. Second, to distribute the high-voltage surges through the distributor rotor, cap, and high-voltage wiring to the spark plug that is ready to "fire." Both of these jobs have been discussed in detail and it is the third job with which we are concerned here; namely, the timing of each spark across a spark-plug gap so that it occurs just as the piston in the engine cylinder reaches its TDC (top-dead center) position, *regardless of engine speed*. This is accomplished by means of *centrifugal advance* and *vacuum advance* mechanisms, callouts 1 and 2 in Figure 5-7.

Spark Advance

To obtain good engine performance, the timing of the spark with respect to the piston position in the cylinder must vary. Thus, at high speed, the spark must occur at the plug earlier in the compression stroke in order to give the fuel-air mixture ample time to ignite, burn, and give up its power to the piston as it starts down on the power stroke. Also, under part-throttle engine operation, a small amount of fuel-air mixture (by weight) enters the cylinder so that the mixture is less highly compressed. Under this condition, advancing the spark (causing it to appear earlier in the compression stroke) will permit fuller utilization of the fuel-air charge.

Centrifugal advance mechanism. Delco-Remy distributors use a centrifugal advance mechanism which advances (moves) the breaker cam ahead of the distributor shaft (and thus the camshaft, crankshaft, and pistons). This mechanism consists of an advance cam that is integral with the breaker cam, a pair of advance weights, springs, and a weight base that is integral with the distributor shaft.

Figure 5-8 illustrates the two extreme positions of a typical centrifugal advance mechanism. At the left is the idle

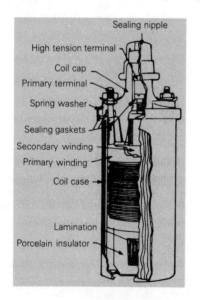

Fig. 5-6. Cutaway view of hermetically sealed and oil-filled ignition coil with one-piece case. *Courtesy of Delco-Remy Division, General Motors Corporation.*

Sealing nipple
High tension terminal
Coil cap
Primary terminal
Spring washer
Sealing gaskets
Secondary winding
Primary winding
Coil case
Lamination
Porcelain insulator

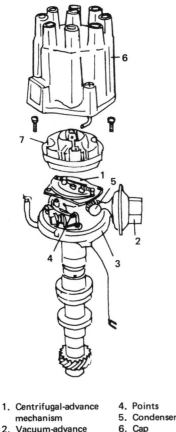

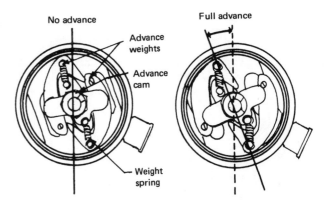

Fig. 5-8   Two positions of centrifugal advance mechanism. *Courtesy of Delco-Remy Division, General Motors Corporation.*

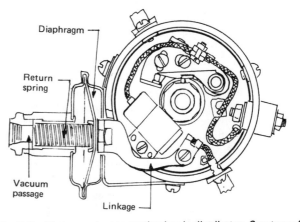

Fig. 5-9   Vacuum advance mechanism in distributor. *Courtesy of Delco-Remy Division, General Motors Corporation.*

1. Centrifugal-advance mechanism	4. Points
2. Vacuum-advance assembly	5. Condenser
3. Breaker cam	6. Cap
	7. Rotor

Fig. 5-7   Partially exploded view of a typical ignition distributor. *Courtesy of Delco-Remy Division, General Motors Corporation.*

(no-advance) position, while at the right is the high-speed (full-advance) position.

Different spark advance is required on different engines throughout their speed ranges. The centrifugal advance for any particular engine is determined by operating the engine at wide-open throttle on a dynamometer and varying the spark advance at each engine speed until the advance is found that gives maximum power at that speed. Centrifugal advance weights, advance cam contours, and weight springs are designed to supply this advance through the engine speed range. Maximum advance designed for some engines is only a few degrees. Other engines can use as much as 42° advance (spark occurs 42° engine-crankshaft rotation before piston reaches top dead center) at high speed.

Vacuum advance mechanism.   Under part-throttle operation there is a partial vacuum in the intake manifold so that the fuel-air charge taken into the cylinder is not as highly compressed. This means that the speed of burning of the compressed mixture is somewhat reduced. In order to utilize maximum power from this mixture, the spark must oc-

cur somewhat earlier in the stroke. The vacuum advance mechanism used to achieve this advance contains an airtight, springloaded diaphragm, which is linked to the distributor breaker plate or the distributor housing (see Fig. 5-9). The spring-loaded (airtight) side of the diaphragm is connected by a tube to an opening in the carburetor. This opening is on the atmospheric side of the throttle valve when the throttle is in the idle position so that there will be no vacuum advance. However, when the throttle is opened, it swings past the vacuum-passage opening, as shown in Fig. 5-10. The intake manifold vacuum can then function through this passage on the vacuum-advance diaphragm, causing the spring to be compressed and the distributor housing or breaker plate to be rotated. This moves the contact points ahead of the breaker cam so that the points close and open earlier in the compression stroke. This provides the desired vacuum spark advance. The amount of throttle opening determines, in part, the amount of intake manifold vacuum and thus the amount of spark advance obtained.

Combined centrifugal and spark advance.   At any particular engine speed, there will be a certain definite centrifugal advance due to speed in addition to a possible advance re-

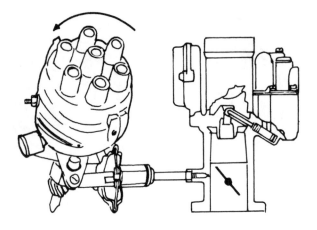

Fig. 5-10 Vacuum passage between vacuum advance mechanism and carburetor. *Courtesy of Delco-Remy Division, General Motors Corporation.*

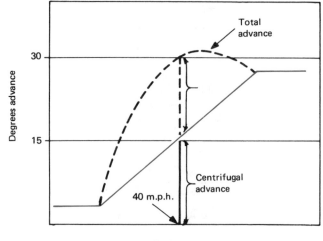

Fig. 5-11 Centrifugal and vacuum curves on a typical application. Vacuum advance is in addition to centrifugal advance. *Courtesy of Delco-Remy Division, General Motors Corporation.*

sulting from vacuum conditions in the intake manifold. One typical centrifugal vacuum advance curve is shown in Fig. 5-11. On this application, the centrifugal advance will supply 15° advance at 40 mph while the vacuum advance mechanism will provide up to 15° additional advance under part-throttle operation. However, with wide-open throttle, there will be little vacuum in the intake manifold and consequently little vacuum advance will be obtained. In actual operation the total advance achieved will be somewhere between the centrifugal advance curve and the total possible advance. Thus, with wide-open throttle, economy will be reduced. Part-throttle operation permits the vacuum advance mechanism to operate so that greater economy will be achieved.

Spark Plugs

In addition to the regular spark plug used in most passenger automobiles, there are many specialized types. A special plug is used, for example, in high-compression overhead-valve engines and for correcting fouled-plug conditions at low engine speeds. Other plugs offer greater resistance to the high-voltage surges from the ignition coil and, as a result, produce a hotter-than-normal spark at the spark-plug gap. These plugs are used to prevent misfiring caused by heavy carbon and oil deposits on and around the spark gap. Still other plugs are made to withstand high mechanical stresses that may be encountered in severe operating conditions. The plug is sealed from external exposure by an integrally made outer shell. The shell keeps oil, dirt, and water from collecting on the plug.

The heat range of plugs governs, to a large extent, the performance of the engine under different conditions and speeds. The heat range classifies plugs according to their ability to transfer heat from the spark-gap end of the plug to the engine cooling system. The rate of heat transfer, that is, the heat range, is controlled by the distance between the inside gasket and seat and the insulator tip.

A cold spark plug has a short insulator nose and transfers heat to the cooling system rapidly. This plug is used in heavy-duty or continuous high-speed operation to avoid overheating. A hot plug has a much longer insulator nose and transfers heat at a relatively slow rate. This makes the plug operate hotter. In doing so, the plug burns off deposits that tend to foul it during prolonged periods of low-speed operation. Both regular and special plugs are made in several heat ranges to suit different engines and operating conditions.

Ignition System Troubleshooting

A great deal more is said about the ignition system in Chapter 6, which is concerned with engine tune-up. For the time being, our comments will be brief. However, the maintenance of a typical ignition distributor will be discussed in detail.

If one has a basic knowledge of the manner in which the ignition circuit operates, and how testing instruments are used to check whether a circuit is being completed normally, electrical diagnosis is simply a matter of logical application.

If the ignition system fails to deliver a hot-enough spark to ignite the air-fuel mixture, the fuel mixture itself may be too rich or too lean or the fuel lines may be restricted. In the latter case, the fuel system is unable to supply the combustion chamber the right kind of combustible vapor.

A quick way to determine if the trouble is in the ignition system (and not the fuel system) is to remove the high-voltage lead from either the center terminal of the distributor cap or from a spark plug and hold it about a quarter-inch from the engine block while the engine is being cranked. If there is no spark, the ignition system needs attention.

Ignition Distributor Maintenance

The best assurance of obtaining maximum service with minimum trouble from ignition systems is to follow a regular inspection and maintenance procedure.

Lubrication. Always follow the precise recommendations of the distributor manufacturer. Avoid excessive lubrication. If too much oil is used, the excess may get on the contact points and cause them to burn.

Vacuum advance mechanism. Make sure the vacuum advance mechanism operates freely. On the type that rotates the complete distributor, turn the distributor in its mounting by hand and then release it. The vacuum advance spring should return it to its original position without sticking. On the type which rotates the breaker plate only, turn the plate by hand. The breaker plate should return to its original position when released.

Centrifugal advance mechanism. Check for freeness by turning the breaker cam in the direction of rotation and then releasing it. The advance springs should return the cam to its original position without sticking.

Cap. Wipe out the distributor cap with a clean cloth and inspect it and the rotor for chips, cracks, and carbonized paths which would allow high-voltage leakage to ground. Such defects require replacement of the parts.

Contact points. The point opening of new points can be checked with a feeler gauge, but the use of a feeler gauge on older, rougher points is not recommended since accurate gaugings cannot be done on such points. See Fig. 5-12. The gauge measures between high spots on the points instead of the true point opening. The opening of used points is best checked with a dial indicator, as shown in Fig. 5-13. To adjust the point opening, loosen the lock screw and turn the

eccentric screw (see Fig. 5-14). Tighten the lock screw well after the adjustment is complete.

A cam angle meter can be used to check the cam or contact angle. This angle is the number of degrees a break cam rotates from the time the points open until they close again. Refer to Fig. 5-15. The cam angle increases as the point opening is decreased and it is reduced as the point opening is increased.

The contact point pressure should be checked with a spring gauge to see if it meets the manufacturer's specifications. Typical readings are from 17 to 21 ounces, or from 19 to 23 ounces. The scale should be hooked to the breaker lever and the pull exerted at an angle of 90° with the point surface. Readings should be taken just as the points separate. The pressure can be adjusted by bending the breaker-lever spring. If the pressure is excessive, it can be decreased

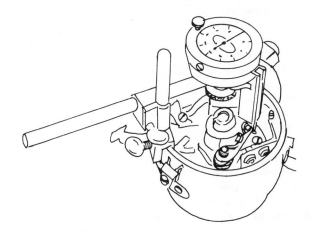

Fig. 5-13 Using dial indicator to check contact-point opening. *Courtesy of Delco-Remy Division, General Motors Corporation.*

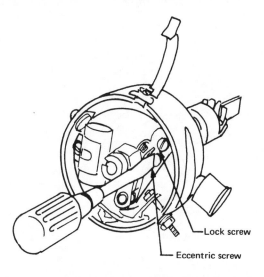

Fig. 5-14 Adjust point opening by loosening lock screw and turning eccentric screw. *Courtesy of Delco-Remy Division, General Motors Corporation.*

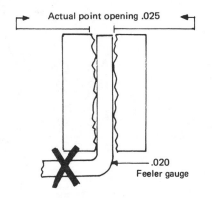

Fig. 5-12 The use of a feeler gauge is not recommended on rough contact points, since it measures the distance from high spot to high spot and not the actual opening. *Courtesy of Delco-Remy Division, General Motors Corporation.*

by pinching the spring carefully. To increase pressure, the lever must be removed from the distributor so that the spring can be bent away from the lever. Avoid excessive spring distortion. New breaker-lever springs may be stronger than required in service; be sure to check the spring tension of all new levers when installed. Remember that excessive pressure causes rapid wear in rubbing block, cam, and contact point, while insufficient pressure will permit high-speed point bounce, which will, in turn, cause arcing and burning of the points and missing of the engine.

Clean the contact points, if necessary, with a few strokes of a clean, fine-cut contact file. Do not attempt to remove all roughness or dress the contact points down smooth—remove only the scale or dirt. Never use emery cloth or sandpaper to clean points since particles will embed and cause arcing and rapid burning of the points.

Under most normal operating conditions, distributor contact points will provide many thousands of miles of service. Points which have undergone several thousand miles of operation will have a rough surface or slight transfer of material, but this does not mean that they are worn out.

Rough contacts which are grayish in color have a greater area of contact than new contacts, and will provide satisfactory service until most of the tungsten is worn off.

Pitted or transferred contacts are normal and should not necessarily be replaced until the transfer has exceeded 1/20 inch.

Contact point burning will result from high voltage, the presence of oil or other foreign material, defective capacitor, and improper point adjustment.

High voltage causes an excessively high current flow through the contact points, burning them rapidly. High voltage can result from an improperly adjusted or inoperative voltage regulator. Oil or crankcase vapors that work up into the distributor and deposit on the point surfaces will also cause them to burn rapidly. This condition is easy to detect, since the oil is a smudgy line under the contact points, as shown in Fig. 5-16. Clogged engine breather pipes permit crankcase pressure which will force oil or vapors up into the distributor. Overloading the distributor will also produce the condition.

If the contact point opening is too small (cam angle too large), the points will be closed for too much of the total operating time. Current flow through the points will be excessive, the points will burn rapidly, and arcing between the points will cause low secondary voltage and engine miss.

High series resistance in the capacitor circuit is another condition that will cause rapid deterioration of the contact points. The high resistance may be caused by a loose capacitor mounting, a loose lead connection, or by poor connections inside the capacitor.

Cables.   The low- and high-voltage cables should be examined carefully for brittle or cracked insulation and broken strands. Defective insulation will permit missing or cross-firing of the engine. All connections should be clean and bright.

Spark plugs.   Spark plugs should be inspected and serviced every 3,000 to 4,000 miles per 150 hours of operation. Cracked, broken, or worn plug insulators require plug replacement. Oily plugs should be degreased, dried thoroughly, and sand-blasted clean to prevent gumming and packing of the cleaning compound. Always refer to the manufacturer's literature for details of spark-plug service.

The center electrode should be filed to a flat surface with a sharp edge. When readjusting the spark gap, bend the outer electrode only. Bending the center electrode may cause the porcelain to crack.

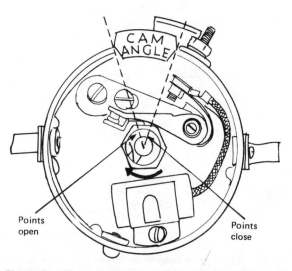

Fig. 5-15   Cam angle is the number of degrees of breaker cam rotation from time points open until they close again.

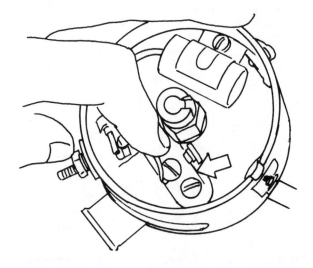

Fig. 5-16   A smudgy line under the contact points indicates oil or crankcase vapor is getting between the points, causing rapid burning of the points.

Timing and synchronization.   Set advance adjustment arm or selector to zero and tighten arm holddown bolt before attempting to time the distributor to the engine. Motor vehicles have fly-wheel markings to facilitate timing. Refer to the engine manufacturer's instructions for timing. All ignition distributors with manually controlled sparks should be timed in the full manual advanced position to eliminate variations in the manual control linkage. Some distributors with vacuum-controlled sparks have a ⅛-inch hole in the advance arm and clamp arm. On these units it is necessary to align the holes with a ⅛-inch pin before timing. To correct timing, loosen the distributor clamp bolt(s) and rotate the distributor in its mounting. Tighten the bolt(s) after timing is completed.

On some engines it is not possible to synchronize double breaker-lever distributors on the engine without special synchronizing tools. This is particularly true on engines having more than eight cylinders.

Disassembly and reassembly.   Because the disassembly and reassembly procedures vary according to the type of distributor, never attempt this job unless you have access to the manufacturer's instructions.

Installation.   When installing a distributor, always observe the following precautions: (1) Be sure the distributor mounting is clean so there will be a good ground connection. (2) Check engine breather pipes, since clogged pipes cause crankcase pressure which will force oil up into the distributor. (3) If the advance mechanism of the old distributor was found to be worn, check the engine for worn timing gears on oil pump, since these cause backlash which produces torsional vibration. This type of vibration, in turn, causes rapid wear of the advance mechanism. (4) Be sure to install the new distributor all the way down in its mounting well. If the distributor is not pushed all the way down, the distributor shaft may freeze in the housing and ruin the distributor completely. (5) Be sure that the vacuum line to the distributor, where used, is open.

ELECTRONIC IGNITION SYSTEMS

Electronic ignition systems have been around for nearly a decade, having become standard equipment on U.S. built cars in the mid 1970's. Four representative systems, covering the period from 1973 forward, are examined here. With this background, little difficulty should be experienced in understanding the operation of any electronic ignition system that may be encountered.

Except for the physical appearance and placement of a few parts, especially the ignition coil, and the use of different names to identify components that perform essentially the same functions, there is surprisingly little change in going from one system to the other. Also, as mentioned in

Chapter 1, the replacement of electronic control units (or modules) is a simple matter based on a few go no-go tests using such common test instruments as a voltmeter and ohmmeter.

TRANSISTOR-CONTROLLED IGNITION SYSTEM

Comparison of Transistor-Controlled and Conventional Systems

The simplified wiring diagram of Fig 5-17 (a) shows the circuit of a conventional ignition system. As you know, when the ignition switch is in the *run* position, current flows from the battery through the ignition coil primary, the contact points, and back to ground. This causes a magnetic field to build up in the ignition coil. When the contact points open, current through the primary circuit ceases, the magnetic field collapses, and a high voltage is induced in the secondary winding. This high voltage creates a spark at the plug gap, and the spark ignites the air-fuel mixture in the engine cylinder. Thus the contact points in the conventional system act as a trigger to open and close the primary circuit in order that the high secondary voltage can be produced.

The simplified wiring diagram of a transistor-controlled ignition system is shown in Fig. 5-17(b). Ignition systems of this type are often referred to as *solid-state* ignitions, since the transistor belongs to the solid-state family of electronic devices. The battery, resistor, switch, secondary wiring, and spark plugs are similar to those used in the conventional system. This ignition coil is similar in appearance to the conventional coil, but quite different electrically. It has a different number of turns of wire in both the primary and secondary windings to permit increased current. The conventional coil and that used in the transistor system are not interchangeable. (For the sake of illustration, the transistor system discussed shortly is the Delco-Remy Delcotronic Transistor-controlled Magnetic-pulse Type Ignition System.)

The *magnetic-pulse distributor* is similar in external appearance to the conventional distributor, and has some features that are the same. For instance, both the centrifugal and vacuum advance mechanisms are the same in both units. However, the breaker cam, contact points, and capacitor used in the conventional distributor are not found in the magnetic-pulse distributor. In their places are a permanent magnet, a timer core, and a pick-up coil. These units, which can be likened to the breaker cam, produce an alternating voltage when the distributor is in operation. This voltage is transferred to the control section of the *ignition pulse amplifier*.

The ignition pulse amplifier is an entirely new unit not used in conventional systems. It functions as a set of contact points to turn the primary current on and off. The ac voltage developed by the distributor either decreases or increases the voltage applied to the base of the transistor, and thereby controls the on-off action of the transistor.

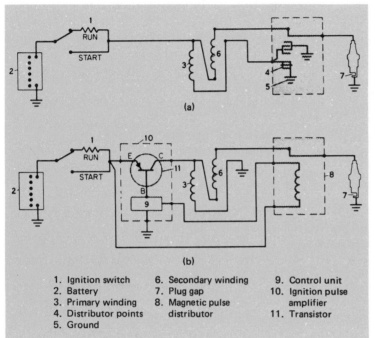

Fig. 5-17 Simplified diagrams of (a) conventional and (b) transistor-controlled ignition systems.

1. Ignition switch
2. Battery
3. Primary winding
4. Distributor points
5. Ground
6. Secondary winding
7. Plug gap
8. Magnetic pulse distributor
9. Control unit
10. Ignition pulse amplifier
11. Transistor

With the ignition switch in the *run* position, current flows from the battery through the emitter-collector circuit of the transistor, the primary winding of the ignition coil to ground, and back to the battery. The primary circuit current builds up a magnetic field in the ignition coil just as it does in a conventional system.

Voltage produced by the magnetic-pulse distributor is then applied to the base-emitter circuit of the transistor. When the base voltage is higher than the emitter voltage, the transistor is back-biased and is turned off. Under these conditions, current flow through the primary circuit is interrupted, the magnetic field surrounding the ignition coil collapses, and the now familiar series of events occurs. It is apparent, therefore, that the transistor simply replaces the contact points in a conventional system. However, since a transistor can pass more current than contact points, more secondary output voltage is available at all engine speeds.

The Delcotronic System

The Delcotronic transistor-controlled magnetic-pulse type ignition system features a specially designed pulse distributor, an ignition pulse amplifier, and a special ignition coil. The other units in the system—the resistors or resistance wires, switch, and battery—are of standard design. A typical magnetic-pulse distributor is shown in Fig. 5-18.

As shown in the partially exploded view of Fig. 5-19, an iron timer core replaces the conventional breaker cam. The timer core has the same number of equally spaced projections, called vanes, as engine cylinders.

The timer core rotates inside a magnetic pick-up assembly, which replaces the conventional breaker plate, contact point set, and capacitor assembly.

The magnetic pick-up assembly consists of a ceramic permanent magnet, a pole piece and a pick-up coil. The pole piece is a metal plate having equally spaced internal teeth, one tooth for each cylinder of the engine.

The magnetic pick-up assembly is mounted over the main bearing on the distributor housing, and is made to rotate by the vacuum control unit, thus providing vacuum advance. The timer core is made to rotate about the shaft by conventional advance weights, thus providing centrifugal advance.

The ignition-pulse amplifier, Fig. 5-20, consists primarily of transistors, resistors, diodes and capacitors mounted on a printed-circuit panelboard. Since there are no moving parts, the control unit is a completely static assembly. Some models have a wiring harness as a permanent part of the assembly, instead of a plug-in connector as shown in Fig. 5-20. The information that follows is applicable to either type.

Since the ignition-pulse amplifier is a completely static unit, and the distributor shaft and bushings have permanent-type lubrication, no periodic maintenance is required. The distributor lower bushing is lubricated by engine oil through a splash hole in the distributor housing, and a housing cavity next to the upper bushing contains a supply of lubricant which will last between engine-overhaul periods. At time of engine overhaul, the upper bushing may be lubricated by removing the plastic seal and adding SAE 20 oil to the packing in the cavity. A new plastic seal will then be required since the old one will be damaged during removal.

A wiring diagram showing the complete circuit for a typical transistor ignition system is given in Fig. 5-21. The two current-limiting resistors, R_5 and R_6, may be separate devices or they may be in the form of resistance wire in a

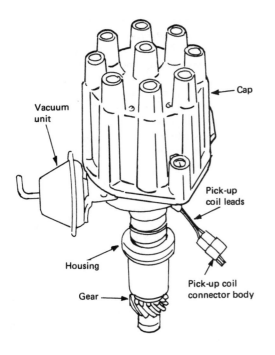

Fig. 5-18 Typical magnetic pulse distributor. *Courtesy of Delco-Remy Division, General Motors Corporation.*

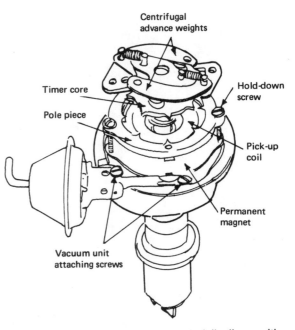

Fig. 5-19 Partially exploded view of typical distributor with cap removed. *Courtesy of Delco-Remy Division, General Motors Corporation.*

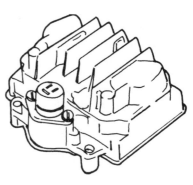

Fig. 5-20 Typical ignition pulse amplifier. *Courtesy of Delco-Remy Division, General Motors Corporation.*

harness. Resistor R_5, connected directly to the switch, is bypassed during cranking, but R_6 is always in the circuit. On some applications, the bypass lead may be connected to the cranking-motor solenoid.

To produce a spark at the plug, a high voltage is induced in the ignition-coil secondary by disrupting current through the primary circuit. When the switch is closed and the engine is not running, current flows through that part of the circuit indicated by light lines. The current can be traced from the battery through the switch and resistor R_5 to the amplifier. Current then flows through inductor (coil) L, transistors TR_1 and TR_2, resistors R_1 and R_2, the ignition coil primary, and resistor R_6 to ground. This completes the circuit back to the battery. With full current flowing through the ignition-coil primary, capacitor C_1 is charged with the polarity indicated.

When the engine is running, the vanes on the rotating iron core in the distributor are in line with the internal teeth on the pole piece. This establishes a magnetic path through the center of the pick-up coil, causing a voltage to be induced in the pick-up coil. This voltage makes transistor TR_3 conduct. The resulting current flow is shown by the lighter lines in Fig. 5-22.

The charge on capacitor C_1 causes transistor TR_2 to turn off, which, in turn, causes transistor TR_1 to turn off. This switching sequence interrupts the circuit to the ignition-coil primary winding, and the high voltage needed to fire the spark plug is induced in the secondary winding of the coil.

The current-flow conditions shown in Fig. 5-22 exist until

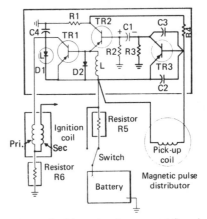

Fig. 5-21 Internal wiring, showing current flow in light lines, with switch on and engine not running.

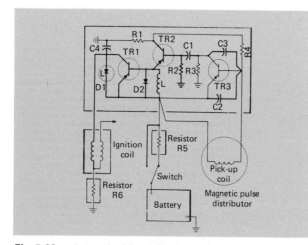

Fig. 5-22 Internal wiring, showing current flow in light lines, when spark plug fires.

the charge on capacitor C_1 is dissipated through resistor R_2. When this happens, the system reverts to the current-flow conditions shown in Fig. 5-21. The system is then ready to fire the next spark plug.

Resistor R_4 is called a *feedback resistor*. Its purpose is to turn TR_3 off when TR_2 is turned back on. Diode D_1 is a special type of diode, called a *Zener diode*, and is used to protect transistor TR_1 from high voltages that may be induced in the primary winding of the coil. Capacitors C_2 and C_3 protect transistor TR_2 from high voltages that appear in the system. Inductor L and diode D_2 help turn off transistor TR_1. Capacitor C_4 reduces the amount of power transistor TR_1 must dissipate. Although the physical arrangement of some of the components used in this, and other, solid-state ignition systems may change from time to time, basic operation of the circuit will remain essentially unchanged. *Always* refer to manufacturers' service literature before attempting to do *any* work on *any* solid-state system.

Troubleshooting Procedures

Faulty engine performance is usually indicated by engine miss, engine surge, or a dead engine.

Engine miss. If the trouble is not due to carburetion, check the ignition system in the following order making sure the switch is *off* whenever connecting or disconnecting leads: (1) timing, as specified by engine manufacturer, (2) spark plugs, (3) wiring, (4) distributor. The distributor pick-up coil may be checked by separating the wiring harness connector and connecting an ohmmeter across the coil. The resistance of the coil should be from 550 to 650 ohms. If the reading is infinite, the coil is open; and if the reading is low, the coil is shorted. The pick-up coil may be checked for grounds by connecting the ohmmeter from either coil lead to the distributor housing. The reading should be infinite. If it is not, the coil is grounded. (5) Ignition coil. The ignition-

coil primary winding can be checked for an open condition by connecting an ohmmeter across the two primary terminals. An infinite reading indicates an open. If the engine runs but misses occasionally, the primary winding may have an intermittent open. The secondary winding of the coil can be checked for an open by connecting an ohmmeter from the high-voltage center tower to either of the primary terminals. (6) Ignition-pulse amplifier. If all of the previous checks are satisfactory and the amplifier is properly grounded, the engine miss is probably caused by a defective ignition-pulse amplifier. Use a substitute unit to determine the condition of the amplifier. If a substitute unit is not available, have the amplifier checked by a competent factory-trained technician, or return the unit to the manufacturer for repair. If complete manufacturer's literature is available, you may be able to check out the amplifier on your own, but follow all instructions carefully. Transistor circuits can be damaged quickly when subjected to improper testing and/or repair procedures.

Engine surge. Engine surge may be caused by reversal of the two distributor leads in the connector body, or by an intermittent open condition in the distributor pick-up coil. When the distributor leads are properly assembled, those bearing the white and green stripes are positioned in the connector body as shown in Fig. 5-23. If the leads are reversed, a severe surging condition will result. A surge may also result from the action of the vacuum advance unit that causes a broken lead in the distributor pick-up coil wiring to open and close intermittently. This may be checked by disconnecting the vacuum line and observing the engine behavior at idle speed.

To complete the checks on the primary coil, connect an ohmmeter to the two distributor-coil terminals in the connector body. The resistance should be 550 to 650 ohms. If the resistance is infinite, the coil is open, and if the resistance is low, the coil is shorted. Also connect the ohmmeter from either terminal to the distributor housing. The reading here should be infinite. If it is not, the winding is grounded.

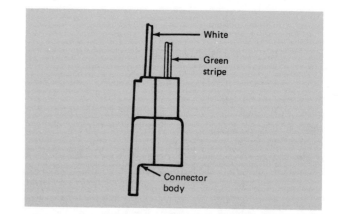

Fig. 5-23 Location of distributor leads in connector body.

Dead engine. If the engine will not run, remove the lead from one of the spark plugs to check for the presence of a spark to the engine block when the engine is cranked. If a spark occurs, the ignition system is not at fault. If a spark does not occur, check the ignition system as follows: (1) wiring, (2) ignition-coil primary for an open condition as described earlier, (3) check for continuity by connecting a voltmeter from the ignition-coil positive terminal to ground, as shown in step 1, Fig. 5-24. Turn the ignition switch on and note the reading. If the reading is 6 to 7 volts, go on to the next check. If the reading is battery voltage, there is an open in the circuit between the positive terminal and ground. If the reading is zero, there is an open between the positive terminal and the battery. To check further, connect the voltmeter as shown in step 2 of Fig. 5-24. Note the reading with the switch on. If the reading is zero, there is an open between the resistor terminal and the battery. If the reading is battery voltage, there is an open circuit between the amplifier and the ignition coil. (4) Distributor. Check the distributor as described earlier.

Chrysler Electronic Ignition System

This system consists of a pulse-sending distributor, an electronic control unit, a two element ballast resistor, and a special ignition coil. A rotor, called the *reluctor,* replaces the breaker points and capacitor of a conventional ignition system.

The ignition primary circuit includes the battery, ignition switch, primary side of the ignition coil, and the electronic control unit. The negative terminal of the battery and the control unit are grounded to complete the circuit. The secondary circuit is the same as that found in non-electronic systems.

The magnetic pulse distributor is also connected to the control unit. As the distributor shaft rotates, the reluctor passes in front of the pick-up coil assembly. Notice that the reluctor contains eight teeth (one for each engine cylinder). For a six-cylinder engine there are six teeth on the reluctor. In either case, as each reluctor tooth passes a facing tooth on the pick-up coil it induces a voltage pulse in the magnetic pick-up unit. This pulse is transmitted to the control unit where it causes a switching action in the transistor circuit that cuts off current in the ignition primary circuit. The resulting collapse of the magnetic field around the ignition coil initiates the series of events with which you are now familiar.

Testing. Use a voltmeter having a sensitivity of not less than 20,000 ohms per volt and an ohmmeter with a 1.5 volt internal battery. The emf of the auto storage battery should be at least 12 volts.

NOTE: In the procedures that follow, *always* turn the ignition *OFF* before removing or replacing the control unit connector. See Figure 5-25.

1. Remove the wiring plug from the control unit.

2. Turn the ignition switch to its ON position and make sure that all accessories are turned off.

3. Connect the negative (black) lead of the voltmeter to ground.

4. Insert the positive (red) test lead of the voltmeter into cavity 1 of the wiring harness connector. The voltage reading should be within 1 volt of the battery emf (that is, at least 11 volts when the storage battery is a 12-volt unit). If it does not, check the continuity of the circuit leading back to the positive (+) terminal of the battery.

5. Repeat the process of Step 4 with the positive lead of

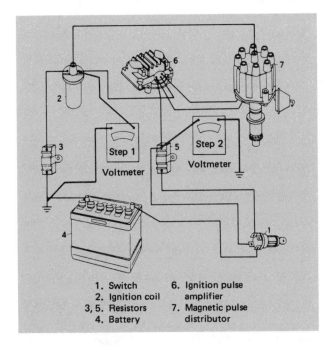

1. Switch
2. Ignition coil
3, 5. Resistors
4. Battery
6. Ignition pulse amplifier
7. Magnetic pulse distributor

Fig. 5-24 Voltmeter connections for circuit checks.

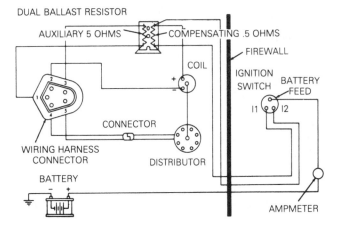

Fig. 5-25. Wiring diagram of the Chrysler electronic ignition system. *Courtesy of Chrysler Corporation.*

the voltmeter inserted in cavity 2 of the wiring harness connector.

6. On 1979 models *only,* repeat the procedures of Step 4 with the positive lead of the voltmeter inserted into cavity 3 of the wiring harness connector. On 1980-1981 models there is no No. 3 connection.

7. Turn the ignition OFF and disconnect the voltmeter.

8. Connect the ohmmeter leads to cavities 4 and 5 of the wiring harness connector. The indicated resistance should be within the 150-900 ohm range. If it is not, detach the dual-lead connector from the distributor and check the resistance of the connector. If it is not within the 150-900 ohm range, replace the distributor pick-up coil.

9. Connect one ohmmeter lead to ground and the other lead to either lead of the distributor connector. If the ohmmeter pointer deflects from its normal (infinite resistance) position, replace the distributor pick-up coil.

10. Connect one ohmmeter lead to ground and the other to pin 5 on the control unit. (The control unit is not shown in Figure 5-26, but plugs into the wiring harness connector.) There should be continuity (i.e., the ohmmeter pointer should swing to zero ohms). If not, remove and reconnect the control unit and check again. If there is still no continuity, replace the control unit.

11. Replace the control unit and distributor connector plugs.

12. Check the air-gap adjustment of the magnetic pick-up coil (procedure described shortly).

13. Remove the center wire from the distributor cap. Very carefully, using insulated pliers and a heavy glove to prevent shock, hold the cable end about 3⁄16 inch from the engine block and have the starter operated. If there is no spark, replace the control unit and try the test again. If there is still no spark, replace the coil. If a spark is now obtained, return the original control unit to the circuit and repeat the test. This will avoid the unnecessary replacement of a satisfactorily operating control unit.

Air-gap adjustment. Through 1977 all Chrysler distributors had two pick-up coils. The *start* pick-up has a larger connector than the *run* pick-up. The two pick-ups have different air gaps, but are adjusted in the same manner. Some 1980-1981 models also have two pick-up coils. The start pick-up has a dual-prong male connector while the run pick-up has a male to female connector.

1. Align one reluctor tooth with the tooth on the case of the pick-up coil. On dual pick-up models, align the reluctor tooth with the tooth on the start pick-up coil.

2. Loosen the pick-up coil hold-down screw.

3. Insert a non-magnetic feeler gauge between the reluctor

tooth and the tooth of the pick-up coil. The gauge should be 0.008-inch-thick through 1976 and 0.006-inch-thick for later models.

4. Adjust the air gap so that simultaneous contact is made between the feeler gauge and the two teeth.

5. Tighten the hold-down screw and (without force) remove the gauge.

6. Check the setting of the air gap by trying to insert a thicker feeler gauge (0.010 inch through 1976 and 0.008 inch for 1977 and later) into the gap. Without using force, the thicker gauge should not fit.

7. On dual pick-up models, align one reluctor tooth with the tooth on the run pick-up coil.

8. Loosen the coil hold-down screw.

9. Using a 0.012-inch-thick feeler gauge, set the air gap (as described in Step 4).

10. Check the setting of the air gap (as described in Step 6) by using a 0.014-inch-thick feeler gauge.

Replacing a pick-up coil (1974 only).

1. Remove the distributor from the engine.

2. Remove the pick-up coil mounting screw.

3. Remove the wires from the retainers on the upper plate and distributor housing.

4. Remove the pick-up coil from the upper plate.

5. Position the new pick-up coil on the pivot of the upper plate and install (but do not tighten) the mounting screw.

6. Insert the wires in the correct retainers.

7. Install the distributor.

8. Set the air gap.

Replacing a pick-up coil (1975) and later).

1. Remove the distributor from the engine.

2. Using two small pry bars or screwdrivers (maximum 7⁄16 inch-wide), pry the reluctor off the shaft from the bottom (being careful not to damage the reluctor teeth).

3. Unfasten the screws that attach the vacuum control to the distributor housing and remove the vacuum unit after disconnecting the arm from the upper plate. NOTE: Some 1980-1981 model distributors do not have a vacuum-advance diaphragm.

4. Unfasten the pick-up coil wires from the distributor housing.

5. Unfasten the two screws that hold the lower plate to the distributor housing. Lift out the lower plate, upper plate, and pick-up coil.

6. Separate the upper and lower plates by depressing the retainer clip on the underside of the plate and slide it away from the stud. The pick-up coil and upper plate cannot be separated and must be serviced as an assembly.

Installation is the reverse of removal. Place a small amount of distributor grease on the support pins on the lower plate.

Troubleshooting the Chrysler Ignition System

Engine will not start (fuel and carburetion satisfactory).

1. Check the resistance of the dual ballast resistors and replace if faulty. With an ambient temperature in the 70 to 80°F range, the resistance of the compensating resistor should lie between 0.5 and 0.6 ohm and that of the auxiliary resistor between 4.75 and 5.75 ohms. If replacement is necessary, make sure the wires are correctly inserted in the keyed molded connector.

2. Use a coil tester to check the ignition coil for a carbonized tower. With an ambient temperature of 70 to 80°F, the resistance of the primary should lie somewhere between 1.41 and 1.79 ohms while that of the secondary should lie between 9200 and 11,700 ohms. Replace the coil if the readings lie outside of the specified ranges.

3. Check the resistance of the pick-up coil. It should be somewhere between 400 and 600 ohms.

4. Using the procedures described earlier, check the air-gap setting of the pick-up coil.

5. Once the air-gap setting of the pick-up coil is known to be correct, run the distributor on a test stand and apply vacuum advance. Make sure the core of the pick-up does not strike the reluctor teeth. REMEMBER, some 1980-1981 model distributors do not have a vacuum-advance diaphragm.

6. Visually inspect all wiring and connectors and verify their continuity by using an ohmmeter.

7. After going through the above procedures, if the engine still will not start, replace the control unit making sure that the wires are correctly inserted in the keyed molded connector.

Severe engine surges (carburetion satisfactory)

1. Check for loose connections and/or broken conductors in the wiring harness.

2. Disconnect the vacuum advance. If the surging stops, replace the pick-up unit.

3. Check the ignition coil for an intermittent open in the primary winding.

Engine misses (carburetion satisfactory).

1. Check the spark plugs. Clean and regap or replace, as necessary.

2. With an ohmmeter, check the continuity of the wiring in the high-voltage secondary of the ignition system.

3. Use an oscilloscope (procedure described in Chapter 6) to observe the operation of the ignition system.

4. Use a coil tester to check the ignition coil for a carbonized tower.

5. Tighten and clean all loose and/or dirty connections.

6. Disconnect the vacuum advance. If the missing stops, replace the pick-up unit.

7. If all of the above checks are negative, replace the control unit.

Chrysler Corporation Omni/Horizon Hall Effect Electronic Ignition

General. If a current-carrying metal conductor is inserted into a magnetic field that lies across the conductor, a voltage is produced between the two edges of the conductor. This is the so-called Hall Effect.

The Omni/Horizon Hall Effect Electronic Ignition System is used in conjunction with the Chrysler Lean Burn/ Electronic Spark Control System (covered in Chapter 7). The 1979-1981 models consist of a sealed Spark Control Computer, ignition coil, spark plugs, ballast resistor, and four engine sensors (vacuum transducer, coolant switch, carburetor switch, and Hall Effect pickup assembly). Earlier models included a fifth engine sensor, a throttle position transducer.

The Hall-Effect pickup assembly is contained in the distributor, Figure 5-26, and supplies the computer with information on engine speed and crankshaft position. The pickup produces an output signal in the form of a pulse when one of the rotor blades passes between the two arms of the sensor. Keep in mind, however, that this is only one of several signals the computer uses as input to determine ignition timing.

Operation. The Spark Control Computer operates in two modes: *start* and *run*. The start mode is used during engine cranking when the only input signal to the computer is derived from the Hall Effect pickup. This input is interpreted to provide a fixed number of degrees of spark advance. The computer shuts off coil primary current in accordance with this input. As in conventional systems, primary current shutoff causes a collapse of the coil magnetic field and the production of a high voltage that is used to fire a spark plug.

Once the engine starts (and during normal operation), the computer functions in the run mode. The Hall Effect pickup signals then constitute just one of several inputs to the computer and serve as reference signals indicating maximum possible spark advance. Using information provided by other sensors, the computer then determines how much of this advance is necessary, and shuts down the primary current accordingly to fire the spark plug at the exact moment when this advance (crankshaft position) is reached.

Should the computer fail, the ignition system operates in the so-called "limp-in" mode that results in poor engine performance but does allow the operator to get the car to a

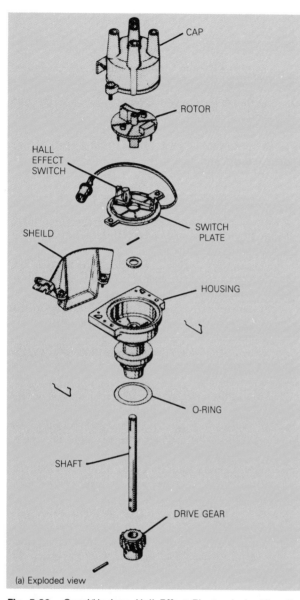

(a) Exploded view

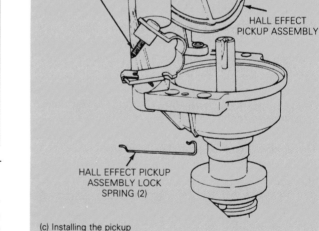

(b) Removing the rotor

(c) Installing the pickup

Fig. 5-26. Omni/Horizon Hall Effect Electronic Ignition System. *Courtesy of Chrysler Corporation.*

repair facility. During the limp-in mode, the Hall Effect device provides the only input to the ignition system. If the Hall-Effect device also fails, the engine will neither start nor run.

Tests.   Test procedures are covered in Chapter 7. The ignition coil can be checked, however, on a conventional coil tester. Include the ballast resistor in all such tests. For a Chrysler Prestolite coil the primary resistance (at 70°F) should be within the range of 1.60 to 1.79 ohms. For a Chrysler Essex Coil the reading should be somewhat lower—1.41 to 1.62 ohms.

Secondary resistance for the Prestolite coil should be

9400 to 11,700 ohms and, for the Essex coil, 8900 to 11,200 ohms.

Through 1979, the ballast resistor should measure 0.5 to 0.6 ohm at 70°F. On 1980-1981 models the resistor should measure 1.2 ohms at 70°F.

Hall-Effect pickup replacement.

1. Loosen the distributor cap retaining screws and remove the cap.

2. Pull straight up on the rotor and remove it from the shaft.

3. Disconnect the pickup assembly lead.

4. Remove the pickup lead hold-down screw.

5. Remove the pickup assembly lock springs and lift off the pickup.

6. Install the new pickup assembly and fasten it into place with the lock springs.

7. Fasten the pickup lead in place with its hold-down screw.

8. Reconnect the lead to the harness.

9. Press the rotor back into place on the shaft. Do not wipe off the silicone grease on the metal portion of the rotor.

10. Replace the distributor cap and tighten the retaining screws.

AMC Solid State Ignition System

The SSI system is standard equipment on all 1978 and later six-cylinder and eight-cylinder AMC cars. The new four-cylinder engines, 1980-1981, use an improved version of the Delco Remy system described earlier.

The SSI system consists of a sensor and toothed trigger wheel inside the distributor, coil, spark plugs, ignition wires, and a sealed electronic control unit that determines dwell (the number of degrees of distributor rotation while the ignition primary circuit is supplied current).

The trigger wheel rotates on the distributor shaft. As one of its teeth nears the sensor magnet, the magnetic field shifts toward the tooth. When the tooth and sensor are aligned, the magnetic field is shifted to its maximum, signalling the electronic control unit to switch off the primary-circuit current. This starts an electronic timer inside the control unit, which allows the primary current to remain off only long enough for the spark plug to fire. The timer adjusts the amount of time the primary current is off according to conditions, thus automatically adjusting dwell. Another special circuit within the control unit detects and ignores spurious signals. Spark timing is adjusted by both centrifugal and vacuum advance.

Testing the secondary circuit.

1. Disconnect the coil wire from the center of the distributor cap by first twisting the rubber boot slightly in either direction, then grasping the boot and pulling straight up. Do not pull on the wire and do not use pliers.

2. Hold the wire ½ inch from a ground and watch for a spark as the engine is cranked. (To prevent shock, hold the wire with insulated pliers and wear a heavy glove.)

3. If a spark appears, reconnect the coil wire.

4. Remove the wire from one spark plug and test for a spark (as above). If a spark occurs, the fault is in the fuel sys-

tem or ignition timing. If no spark occurs, check for a defective rotor, cap, or spark plug wires. NOTE: On auto models 1977 through 1979, do not remove the spark plug wires from cylinders 3 or 5 of a 6-cylinder engine. On 1980 and later models, do not remove spark plug wires from cylinders 1 or 5 of a 6-cylinder engine or 3 or 4 of a V8 engine. Removal of the spark plug wires indicated may cause sensor damage.

5. If no spark occurs from the coil wire in Step 2, check the resistance of the coil wire. It should not exceed 10,000 ohms.

Primary circuit test.

1. Turn the ignition ON and connect a voltmeter between the positive (+) terminal of the coil and ground. If the voltage is between 5.5 and 6.5 volts, go to Step 2. If the voltage is above 7 volts, go to Step 4. If the voltage is below 5.5 volts, disconnect the capacitor lead and measure the voltage again. If the voltage is then 5.5 to 6.5 volts, replace the capacitor. If the voltage is still lower than 5.5 volts, go to Step 6.

2. With the voltmeter still connected as in Step 1, read the voltage while cranking the engine. If battery voltage is indicated, the circuit is satisfactory. If not, go to Step 6.

3. Check for a short-circuit or an open-circuit in the wire connecting the (+) terminal of the coil and terminal 1 on the starter solenoid and make sure the solenoid is operating properly.

4. Disconnect the red resistance wire from terminal 1 of the starter solenoid. Turn the ignition ON and have the voltmeter connected as in Step 1. If the voltage drops to 5.5 to 6.5 volts, replace the solenoid. If not, connect a jumper between the negative (−) terminal of the ignition coil and ground. If the voltage drops to 5.5 to 6.5 volts, go to Step 5. If not, the resistance wire is defective.

5. Check for continuity between the negative terminal of the coil and D4, and D1 to ground. If there is continuity, replace the control unit. If not, check for an open wire and go back to Step 2.

6. Turn the ignition OFF. Connect an ohmmeter between the positive terminal of the coil and dash connector AV. If the resistance is higher than 1.4 ohms, the resistance wire is defective.

7. With the ignition still OFF, connect the ohmmeter between connector AV and terminal 11 of the ignition switch. If the resistance is less than 0.1 ohm, replace the wire and/or the switch. If the resistance is higher than 0.1 ohm, check for defective wiring and/or connections.

Coil test.

1. Check the coil for cracks, carbonated tower, etc., and replace as necessary.

2. Remove the coil connector and measure the resistance of the coil primary by connecting an ohmmeter between

the (+) and (−) terminals. If the resistance is between 1.13 and 1.23 ohms (at 75°F) go to Step 3. If not, replace the coil.

3. Measure the coil resistance between the center tower and either the (+) or the (−) terminal. If the resistance is between 7700 and 9300 ohms the coil is good. If not, replace.

Control unit and sensor test.

1. With the ignition ON, remove the coil high-voltage wire from the distributor cap and, with insulated pliers, hold it about ½ inch from ground. Disconnect the 4-wire connector at the control unit. If a spark occurs (normal), go to Step 2. If not, go to Step 5.

2. Connect an ohmmeter between D2 and D3. The resistance should read between 400 and 800 ohms. If it does not, go to step 3. If it does, go to Step 6.

3. Disconnect and then reconnect the 3-wire connector at the distributor. If the ohmmeter reading is then 400-800 ohms, go to Step 6. If not, disconnect the 3-wire connector and go to Step 4.

4. Connect an ohmmeter across B2 and B3 of the distributor connector. If the reading is between 400 and 800 ohms, the wiring between the A and D terminals is defective. If not, replace the distributor sensor.

5. Connect the ohmmeter between D1 and the negative terminal of the battery. If the reading is 0.002 ohm or less, go to Step 2. If the resistance is higher than 0.002 ohm, there is a poor ground in the cable or at the distributor. Repair and retest.

6. Connect a voltmeter across terminals D2 and D3. Crank the engine. The voltmeter pointer should fluctuate. If it does not, either the trigger wheel is defective or the distributor is not turning. Repair as necessary.

Ignition feed to control unit test. (Do not perform until *after* the coil primary circuit is tested.)

1. Turn the ignition ON and then unplug the 2-wire connector (E to F) at the control unit. Connect a voltmeter between F2 and ground. If the reading is battery voltage, replace the control unit and go to Step 3. If not, go to Step 2.

2. The voltage reduction is caused either by a defective ignition switch or a corroded dash connector. Repair as necessary. Then check for a spark at the coil wire. If a spark is obtained, the system is performing correctly. If not, replace the control unit and recheck for proper operation.

3. Reconnect the 2-wire connector at the control unit and unplug the 4-wire connector (D to C). Measure the resistance between terminal C1 and ground. It should be between 0.9 and 1.1 ohms. If it is not, replace the control unit.

LIGHTING SYSTEMS AND EQUIPMENT

Automotive Lamps

The lights used on automobiles are classified as miniature lamps, with the largest rated at about 60 watts. (The watt is the unit of power and is equal to the product of voltage and amperage. With a 12-volt battery, a 60 watt lamp draws a current of 5 amperes; that is, 12 volts times 5 amps equals 60 watts.)

Motor vehicle lighting requirements for safety and convenience in night driving are specified by the Society of Automotive Engineers (SAE).

Internally, one lead-in wire is soldered to the rim of the lamp base and another to the center contact. The lead-ins are insulated from one another by a glass insulator, which appears as a black ring around the center contact.

The general shape of miniature lamps is indicated by a letter or combination of letters, such as G (globe shape), S (straight side), RP (reflector, pear shaped), and PAR (parabolic).

Group Classifications

Motor vehicle lamps may be grouped, according to their functions, into four general classifications: (1) roadway lamps, (2) instrument and indicator lamps, (3) interior and utility lights, and (4) marker and signal lights.

Roadway lamps use a precision combination of filament, lens, and reflector to give a controlled beam pattern. Included in this group are headlamps, driving and passing lamps, fog lamps, spot lamps, and back-up lamps.

Instrument and indicator lamps are usually smaller than headlamps, and are fitted with miniature bayonet bases to permit installation in a very limited space. The lamps in this group include dial lights or instrument lights, such as those used for the speedometer; fuel, oil, and water gauges; generator; clock; radio; and so on. Also included in this group are lights that show when the headlamps are on high beam and when the turn-signals are in use.

Interior and utility lamps include those used for dome lighting, front compartment, map, trunk, etc.

Marker and signal lamps mark the car from the front, side, and rear, illuminate the license plate, and signal intention to stop or change direction.

Headlamps

An automobile headlamp must throw a strong beam of light in one direction. Since the lamp is usually in the 60-watt range, the light rays issued from the filament in all directions must be reflected in the direction in which illumination is desired. This reflection is obtained by means of a parabolic reflector, which is made of a borosilicate, heat-resistant glass with an aluminum inner surface.

The sealed-beam headlamp, which appeared initially in 1940 model cars, offers the advantages of standardization, simplicity, and little loss of efficiency throughout the life of the lamp. The standard sizes (diameters) are 4½, 5¾, 7, and 8 inches.

The sealed-beam lamp cannot be opened, and each element is adjusted at the factory in correct unchangeable relationship to the others. Since the lamp is sealed, dirt and moisture cannot reach the interior and deposit on the mirrorlike surface of the reflector. Because of this, the reflecting power remains practically constant throughout the life of the lamp filament.

While seal-beam lamps vary in some design details, comparable units, interchangeable on a particular make and model of car, are made by all headlamp manufacturers.

Four-Headlamp Arrangements

In a four-headlamp system, there are three possible arrangements of the lamps; horizontal, diagonal, or vertical. Regardless of the arrangement, however, all systems operate in the same manner. The outer lamp in a horizontal or diagonal arrangement, and the upper lamp in a vertical arrangement are called the outboard lamps. The other lamps are called inboard lamps.

The inboard lamps have a single filament and are used only for high-beam operation. Outboard lamps have two filaments and are used for both low- and high-beam operation.

With the headlamps on and the dimmer switch in the position for low-beam operation, only the outboard lamps are lit. Depressing the dimmer switch for high-beam operation switches on both inboard and outboard lamps. The inboard lamps are wired to the high-beam terminal of the outboard lamps, and as a result the inboard lamps will light only for high-beam operation.

Replacing Sealed-Beam Headlamps

To remove a sealed-beam lamp from an automobile, proceed as follows:

1. Remove the screws from the headlamp trim, and lay the trim aside. In a typical installation, two to four screws hold the trim in place.

2. Back out the three retaining-ring screws, Fig. 5-27. In some installations it may be necessary to rotate the retaining ring in a counterclockwise direction until the screw heads will pass through the enlarged end of the keyhole slot of the ring lug to remove the ring and sealed-beam lamp. In some installations the retaining ring can be lifted off as soon as the screws are loosened merely by giving the ring a slight turn to the left.

3. Pull off the plastic plug at the back of the lamp, and snap the lamp out of the retaining ring.

To replace the lamp, reverse the instructions given above.

Four-Headlamp Adjustments

All headlamps must be aimed properly to obtain maximum road illumination. With the four-lamp system, proper aiming is extremely important because the increased range and power of these lamps make even slight variations from recommended aiming hazardous to approaching motorists. The light from the lamps must be checked for proper aim whenever a new seal-beam lamp is installed and after any adjustment or repair to the structural members or front panels.

Regardless of the method used to check the aim of the lamps, the car must be at curb weight, including gas, oil, water, and spare tire, but no passengers. The tires must be uniformly inflated to the pressure specified by the manufacturer. If the car normally carries a heavy load in the trunk or pulls a trailer, these loads should be on the car when the check is made. Some state governments have special requirements for headlamp aim, and these requirements should be known and observed.

In a typical installation, there are two adjusting screws on each headlamp for aiming purposes. As shown in Fig. 5-27, the vertical adjusting screw is at the top of each lamp, and the horizontal adjusting screw is at the side of each lamp. Each screw is first turned counterclockwise to make the adjustment. Different procedures can be used for aiming the lamps. Since this is a job that requires special equipment and a particular type of physical layout, a discussion of aiming techniques is not useful in a book of this type and will not be attempted.

DIRECTIONAL SIGNAL SYSTEMS

Signal Lamps and Indicators

Usually the front directional signal light is produced by a 32-candlepower filament in the dual-purpose bulb mounted in the front parking lamp. The rear directional signal lamp is usually also a 32-candlepower filament in the bulb of the rear-lamp assembly. This filament also serves as a stop light.

When the ignition switch is turned on and the directional signal switch is manually operated to indicate a turn,

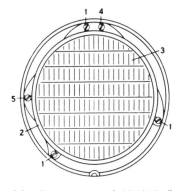

1. Retaining-ring screws
2. Retaining ring
3. Sealed-beam lamp
4. Vertical adjusting screw
5. Horizontal adjusting screw

Fig. 5-27 Sealed-beam lamp and retaining ring.

the front and rear signal lights flash on and off on the right or left side of the car, depending on the direction of the intended turn. The flashing of the signal lights is caused by a flasher that is connected into the proper signal circuit by contacts made in the directional switch when the switch is set for a turn.

When a directional signal light is flashing, a corresponding signal-indicator bulb on the instrument panel also flashes. The signal indicator is a flashing green light, which shows the direction of the turn.

Switching Operation

The directional signal switch is mounted on the steering-mast jacket, and its control device is housed within the jacket, just below the steering wheel. Movement of the control device is transmitted to the signal switch through the operating lever, Fig. 5-28, which runs into the jacket and then is connected inside through a lever plate and a rod crank.

The lower end of the two-piece operating lever is crank-shaped and fits in a slot in the lever plate. The lower end of the rod crank is attached to the signal switch by a spring pin, which is not shown. The exposed operating lever is threaded into the lever plate, connecting it to the rod crank. When the operating lever is moved up or down, it causes the lever plate to rotate around a pivot screw, and rotates the rod crank in turn. A detent spring mounted in the housing holds in place a nylon roller mounted in the lever plate whenever the turn position is set. Bosses in the housing provide stops for the plate when it is set for either turning direction.

The trip (cancellation mechanism) for returning the switch to the OFF position after a turn has been completed, consists of a trigger spring on the lever plate and a switch-cancelling pin on the steering-wheel hub. The pin extends through the level plate, but when the switch is in the OFF position, the lever plate is centered so that the pin cannot contact the trigger spring as the steering wheel is turned.

When the operating lever is moved clockwise to set the switch for a right-hand turn, the lever plate is moved down, bringing the upper loop of the trigger spring into the path of the cancelling pin. As the steering wheel is turned left at the completion of the right turn, the cancelling pin pushes the loop of the trigger spring against a stop on the lever plate; this forces the lever plate and switch back to the OFF position.

A similar action, but in the opposite direction, takes place when the switch is set for a left-hand turn. If the switch is erroneously set to indicate a turn in one direction and the turn is made in the opposite direction, the cancelling pin will contact the trigger spring and return the switch to the OFF position as the turn is started.

Signal-Lamp Circuit

In a typical installation, the directional signal lamps are independent of the headlamp lighting switch and circuit breaker. The wiring circuits are protected by a fuse on the fuse block under the cowl. The flasher is also mounted on the fuse block, which serves as a terminal block for the signal switch and the chassis wiring.

The directional signal circuit, with no turn indicated, is shown in Fig. 5-29. For a left-hand turn, all three contacts of the directional-signal switch move to the right. For a right-hand turn, the contacts move to the left. For either turn, the flasher is connected into the circuit and the stop-light switch is opened.

Fiber Optics

With little space available, the location of many indicator lamps in the dash becomes a real problem. One solution to this problem that has been used in some cars is fiber-optic conductors. These conductors are fine fibers (threads) of glass. They are highly flexible and are bound together in bundles (cords). Each thread is hollow and can conduct light, even around sharp corners. Thus, only one light source is needed to feed light to all of the many points where it is needed. Because the fiber bundles are very

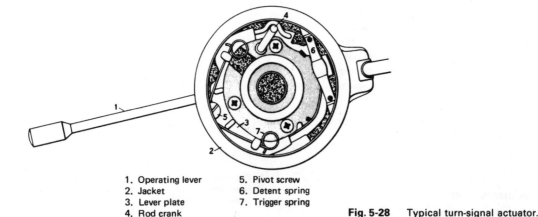

1. Operating lever
2. Jacket
3. Lever plate
4. Rod crank
5. Pivot screw
6. Detent spring
7. Trigger spring

Fig. 5-28 Typical turn-signal actuator.

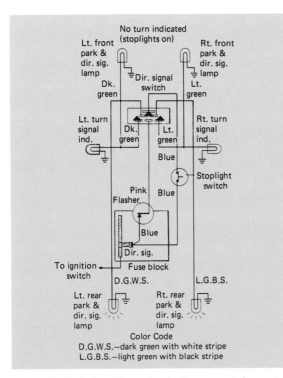

Fig. 5-29 Typical signal-lamp circuit. *Courtesy of General Motors Corporation.*

sturdy and durable, about the only servicing required is the replacement of the single bulb when it burns out.

INDICATING DEVICES

General

Most automobiles have four indicating devices mounted on the instrument panel; a fuel gauge, an oil-pressure indicator, an engine-temperature indicator and a battery charge indicator. These four gauges may be categorized as *magnetic*, *bimetal* or *thermal*, *Bourdon tube*, or *vacuum*, depending on their manner of operation.

Fuel Gauges

Magnetic. A magnetically operated fuel-gauge system, commonly referred to as a "balancing-coil" system, Figure 5-30, contains a tank unit and dashboard (dash) unit. Operating power is derived from the electrical system storage battery when the ignition key is turned ON. The battery and ground coils of the dash unit are connected in series with the battery through a set of contacts on the ignition switch. A rheostat (variable resistor) in the tank unit is connected in parallel with the ground coil of the dash unit. The sliding contact on the rheostat is positioned by a lever which, in turn, is connected to a float.

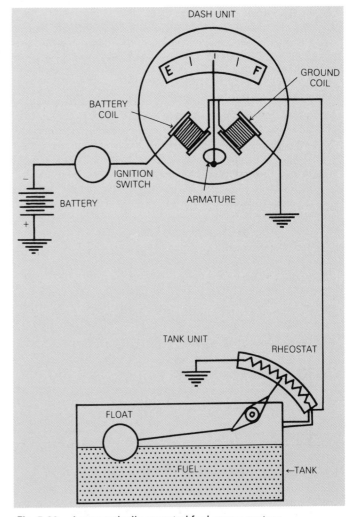

Fig. 5-30. A magnetically operated fuel-gauge system.

When the fuel tank is full, the maximum resistance of the rheostat is included in the circuit. As a result, essentially the total circuit current flows through the two series-connected coils of the dash unit. These coils are wound in such a way that the magnetic field of the ground coil is then stronger than that of the battery coil. Consequently, the gauge armature (with its attached pointer) pivots to the extreme right and the pointer shows that the fuel tank is full.

As the level of fuel in the tank drops, the float lever moves the sliding contact on the rheostat so that progressively less resistance is contained in that branch of the circuit. As the resistance of the rheostat decreases, more and more current passes through the rheostat and current through the ground coil of the dash unit decreases in a corresponding manner. This causes the relative intensities of the magnetic fields surrounding the battery and ground coils to change. The field around the ground coil becomes steadily weaker while that around the battery coil becomes steadily stronger. When the tank is nearly empty, essentially all of the circuit current passes through the battery coil and rheostat. Since the magnetic field surrounding the battery coil then approaches its maximum intensity while that surrounding the ground coil virtually disappears, the gauge armature is pivoted to the left and its attached pointer indicates a nearly empty tank.

To check the accuracy of the fuel gauge first substitute a tank unit of known accuracy in place of the in-use unit. To do so, look on the back of the dash unit and disconnect the wire leading to the tank unit. Attach one end of the wire jumper in its place. Connect the opposite end of the jumper to the rheostat connector on the test unit. Then attach a second wire jumper between the frame of the test unit and ground. Turn the ignition key to its ON position and move the float arm of the test unit through its entire range. The dash gauge should respond proportionately. If it does not, and the wiring to the gauge is in good condition, the dash

unit is defective and should be replaced. But if the gauge response is satisfactory, the tank unit is at fault.

Remove the tank unit and check the float, linkages, and lever arm for mechanical soundness. If no problem is detected, check the continuity of the rheostat over its entire range and the condition of the conductor running from the rheostat to the connector on the dash unit.

One operating characteristic of the magnetically operated fuel-gauge system is that the pointer on the dash unit may stop at any position when the ignition is turned OFF. This does not indicate a malfunction. When the ignition is again turned ON the gauge pointer will snap to its correct position.

Bimetal.   A bimetallic element consists of two dissimilar metal strips welded or riveted together along their lengths. When heated, one metal expands more than the other, causing the element to bend.

In a bimetal fuel-gauge system, Figure 5–31, the tank unit again includes a rheostat whose resistance is varied as the float moves up and down. When the tank is full and the float is up, the resistance of the rheostat is at a minimum so the circuit current is maximum. Under these conditions, a heating coil that surrounds (but is electrically insulated from) the bimetal arm in the dash unit reaches its highest temperature and this causes maximum warpage of the bimetal arm. The movement of the bimetal arm is carried by linkage to the gauge pointer which then indicates a full tank.

As the float in the tank unit drops, proportionately more resistance of the rheostat is included in the circuit. Consequently, circuit current decreases, the heating coil on the dash unit cools and there is less warpage of the bimetallic element. When the tank is near empty the bimetal arm is straight and the gauge pointer is at the left end of the gauge scale.

The voltage regulator contains a bimetallic arm and heating coil and two contacts. When the bimetallic arm bends the contacts open and the heating coil is disconnected from the battery. The coil then cools, the arm straightens, and the contacts again close. This process is repeated over and over and keeps the voltage applied to a gauge system from increasing beyond the designed value.

To test gauge operation, turn the ignition switch to its OFF position. Then place four series-connected D-type flashlight cells across the gauge terminals.

If the gauge reads half-full and was not operating properly before, a fault in the tank unit is likely to exist.

If both the fuel gauge and temperature gauge show similar errors, the voltage regulator is probably defective.

During testing, be very careful not to ground *any* gauge supplied by the regulator since a full current through the regulator will probably burn out its heating coil.

If the dash unit operates properly, connect a wire jumper between the gauge and tank unit. If the gauge operates, the existing wire is defective and needs replacement.

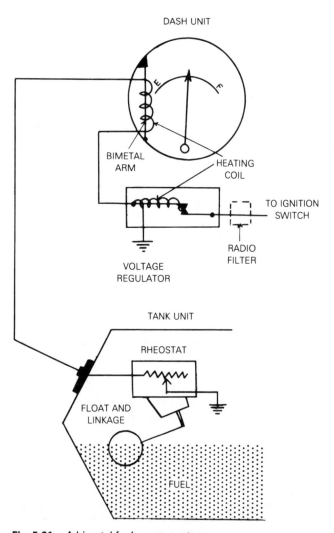

Fig. 5-31.   A bimetal fuel-gauge system.

But if the gauge still operates improperly, replace the tank unit.

Unlike the pointer of a magnetically operated gauge, that on a bimetallic-type gauge moves slowly to its gauging position and drops to zero when the ignition switch is turned to its OFF position.

Incidentally, the presence of a voltage regulator will cause radio interference. But it is easy to eliminate the interference by placing a filter in the position shown by dashed lines. The filter consists of nothing more complicated than a resistor connected in series with a special type of coil called a *choke* coil.

Engine-Temperature Gauges

Temperature indicators generally use either a magnetic or a bimetallic dash unit in combination with a water-temperature sensor that is screwed into the water jacket of the cylinder head or the engine block.

A temperature indicator that uses a magnetic dash unit is shown in Figure 5–32. The water-temperature sensor is simply a flat disk, called a *thermistor*, protected by a metal housing. The term thermistor is used to indicate that the device is a thermally sensitive resistance. But its behavior is just the opposite of what you might expect. As its temperature increases the resistance of a thermistor decreases. Thus, as the temperature of the engine coolant increases the resistance of the thermistor decreases and more current passes through the right-hand coil of the dash unit. As a result, the gauge armature and pointer swing to the right and the pointer indicates the higher temperature. The opposite action occurs, of course, when the temperature of the engine coolant declines.

The bimetal-type engine-temperature indicator is very similar to the bimetal-type fuel-level gauge. Except for scale calibration, the dash units are essentially the same. The thermistor engine unit is identical to that just described.

Oil-Pressure Gauges

Oil-pressure gauges may be of the magnetic or bimetallic types or they may employ a device called a Bourdon tube.

A Bourdon-tube gauge, Figure 5–33, contains a flattened tube that is bent to form a curve. The curve tends to straighten under internal pressure caused by engine oil pressure. The curved tube is geared or lined to a pointer that moves across a scale that is calibrated in pounds per square inch (psi).

The gauge is connected by means of a small copper or nylon tube that runs from the gauge to the main oil passage in the engine oiling system. The pressure developed by the oil pump is then applied directly to the gauge mechanism.

Bourdon-tube gauges are most often encountered on expensive and *sporty* automobiles, such as some Corvettes.

When the gauge pointer flutters, chances are that oil has entered the gauge tube as a result of a gauge or tube leak or improper installation. If the leak cannot be corrected it is necessary to replace the gauge. When the system is put back together, free the gauge-to-engine line at both ends and blow it clear. Then connect the gauge end first.

If a gauge reads zero pressure or abnormally low pressure, the gauge-to-engine line may be obstructed. Disconnect the line from the gauge and hold the loose end over an empty container. Then start the engine. After a few bubbles, oil should flow steadily.

If the oil does not flow steadily, check the oil level and the operation of the oil pump. If both are satisfactory, the fault is in the gauge or in the line. First make sure the line

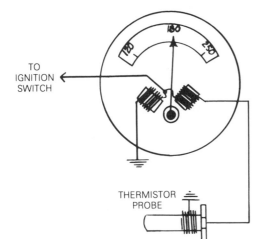

Fig. 5-32. A magnetic dash unit used in combination with a thermistor engine unit.

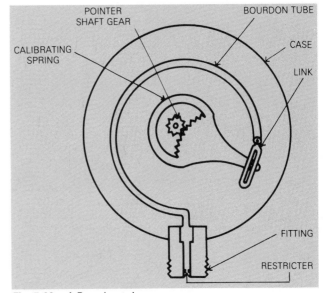

Fig. 5-33. A Bourdon-tube gauge.

is unobstructed. Then remove the gauge from the instrument panel. The hole leading to the Bourdon tube must be clear and the lever linkage and pointer gears must operate freely. If the trouble still persists, the Bourdon tube is defective and a new gauge is needed.

In a balancing-coil oil-pressure gauge, Figure 5–34, there is a variable resistance in the engine unit. Increasing oil pressure pushes the oil-pressure diaphragm upward and this causes the sliding contact on the rheostat to place more resistance in the circuit. Consequently, the field of the right-hand coil in the dash unit becomes stronger than that of the left-hand coil and this causes the pointer to swing to the right and indicate a higher pressure.

In the bimetallic-type oil-pressure gauge, movement of the oil pressure diaphragm acts on a bimetallic arm contained in the engine unit. Operation is basically the same as that of a bimetallic-type fuel-level gauge.

When either a magnetic-type or a bimetallic-type oil

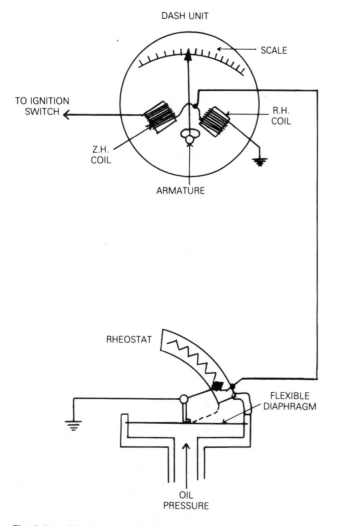

Fig. 5-34.   A balancing-coil oil-pressure indicating system.

pressure gauge registers zero with the engine running, turn the ignition switch to its OFF position and remove the engine unit from the engine block. When the engine is restarted and allowed to idle for a while, oil should flow from the hole into which the engine unit is normally inserted. If no oil flows from the hole, the engine lubricating system is at fault. If oil does flow from the hole, either the engine unit, dash unit, or the connecting wiring is defective.

If the dash unit is a bimetallic type, check the gauge by grounding the connecting wire for a *brief* (repeat, *brief*) instant with the ignition switch ON. The pointer of a good gauge will jump to its maximum reading. If it does, the engine unit is defective.

If the gauge does not move when it is grounded, check the wiring for continuity. If all is well in the wiring, the gauge is defective.

When the dash unit is a magnetic type, the troubleshooting procedures are essentially the same as those described for a fuel-level indicator.

Battery-Charging Gauge

An ammeter, connected in series with the battery and the alternator, indicates that the battery is either charging or discharging and also gives some indication of the intensity of current. To reduce pointer fluctuations as a result of regulator action, the ammeter is usually equipped with a mechanical damping device.

The ammeter scale reads zero at its center position and the pointer rests on zero when the ignition switch is turned OFF. With the engine running, the ammeter pointer moves to the right of zero when the alternator (or generator) is charging the battery and to the left of zero when the battery is discharging.

When the battery approaches a fully discharged condition, its charging rate should become increasingly higher (the ammeter pointer should swing farther to the right of zero). When the battery approaches a fully charged condition, on the other hand, the ammeter pointer will move just a short distance to the right of the center-scale zero.

With the lights and all accessories turned off, the ammeter pointer should move to the right of zero when the engine is first cranked. The extent of this movement depends on the condition of the battery, as indicated above.

When the speed of the vehicle is about 30 mph or greater, and all lights and accessories are turned on, the ammeter should always indicate that the battery is charging. If the battery is discharging, something is wrong with the alternator (or generator) or the regulator. Follow the testing procedures given in Chapters 2 and 3.

To check the operating condition of an ammeter, turn the headlights on but do not start the engine. The ammeter should indicate that the battery is discharging. If it indicates the opposite condition, reverse the connections of the ammeter. If there is no movement of the ammeter pointer check all connections and the continuity of the wiring. If the pointer still rests on zero, replace the ammeter.

Fuel-Economy Gauge

Some cars also have a fuel-economy gauge. The scale of the gauge is divided into three segments marked poor, good, and decelerate. The gauge is actually showing manifold vacuum as a function of throttle position and engine load. At normal cruising speeds or when idling, a consistently "poor" gauge reading is a pretty reliable indicator that the ignition timing is off or that manifold vacuum leakage is occurring.

Most manufacturers insert a vacuum pulsation restrictor in the vacuum line at a point close to the manifold connection. This allows the hose to act as a small vacuum reservoir between the gauge and manifold, thereby reducing manifold vacuum pulsations and damping the gauge movement when sudden acceleration occurs.

A hand-operated vacuum test pump is most often used to test the vacuum system. However, the engine can be used as the vacuum source if you have an attaching tee and a separate vacuum gauge. Here is the procedure to follow when using a hand-operated test unit.

Disconnect the vacuum tube at the manifold, insert the tester (via a connecting hose and adapter) into the vacuum tube and pump to about 20 inches vacuum.

If the reading of the test gauge drops, disconnect the hose from the connector on the back of the test gauge, wrap a short length of teflon tape around the threads of the connector (to act as packing) and reconnect the hose.

Again pump to 20 inches vacuum. If the vacuum reading still drops, replace the tester gauge assembly.

If the vacuum reading is steady, the vacuum tube and the tester gauge are in satisfactory condition. Disconnect the test gauge, make sure the restrictor is in place in the vacuum hose and remake the manifold vacuum connection.

Next, connect the test pump to the fuel-economy gauge and pump to approximately 20 inches vacuum.

If the test gauge shows a loss in vacuum, replace the fuel-economy gauge.

If the vacuum remains steady, replace or repair the hose leading to the engine manifold vacuum port.

Warning Lights

Temperature. This system has a temperature-sensitive switch (bimetallic element) that is enclosed in a metal container. The assembly is screwed into the engine block and senses change in the temperature of the engine coolant.

Most often the temperature-sensitive switch has a single set of contacts which remain open until the temperature of the engine coolant reaches about 250°F. The contacts then close and turn on a red warning light to let the operator know that the engine is overheating.

Sometimes, however, the temperature-sensing switch has two sets of contacts. See Figure 5 – 35. When the engine is cold, one set of contacts is closed and this turns on a blue light. When normal operating temperatures are reached, the bimetal has bent far enough to open the "cold" contacts and turn off the blue light. Again, the red light comes on should overheating occur.

With a dual-light system, the blue lamp should light when the ignition switch is turned to its ON position. If it does not, try a new bulb. If there is still no light, check the wires running from the light to the bimetallic element. To

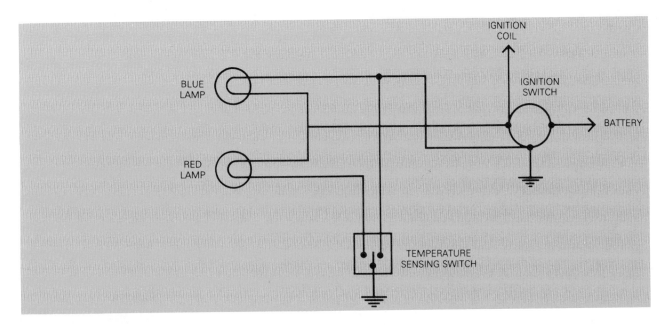

Fig. 5-35. Temperature-sensing switch with two sets of contacts for control of blue and red lamps.

do so, simply connect a test jumper in parallel with the existing wiring. If the light still remains off, remove the test jumper and disconnect the original wiring from the connector on the temperature-sensitive switch and touch it to ground. If the blue light turns on, the bimetallic element is faulty.

Pressure. A red oil-pressure lamp lights when the ignition switch is turned ON. Once the engine is started and the oil pressure builds up, the light should turn off. If not, the oil pressure is about 5 psi or less and the lubrication system should be checked without delay.

The oil-pressure sensor contains a diaphragm, spring, linkage, and electrical contacts and this assembly is tapped into the main oil gallery. The warning light is wired in series with the sensing unit.

When the indicator light does not operate as it should, use the same test procedure given for the temperature-indicator light.

Battery charge. A charge-indicator light is used on many cars in place of the more expensive ammeter. When the battery is discharging, a red light goes on. When the alternator (or generator) is charging the battery, the light goes off.

A simplified diagram of the charging circuit is shown in Figure 5–36. When the ignition switch is turned to its ON position, the field current needed by the alternator passes through the resistor connected in parallel with the indicator lamp in getting back to the positive terminal of the battery. The resulting voltage drop across the resistor is sufficient to activate the light. Once the alternator starts charging the battery, however, the resistor/light combination is bypassed and the light, therefore, is extinguished.

If the light does not glow when the ignition switch is turned ON, replace the bulb. If the light still remains off,

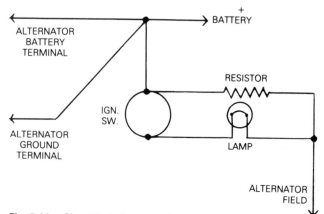

Fig. 5-36. Simplified diagram of charging circuit.

check for continuity in the series circuit formed by the alternator field, resistor, ignition switch, and battery. If the light stays on, the alternator (or generator) is not operating properly and must be tested using the procedures described in Chapter 2.

Coolant level. Some GM automobiles have a warning light that is activated when the level of coolant in the radiator drops below a specified level. The system includes a sealed liquid-level sensor that is threaded into the side tank of the radiator, a module mounted behind the instrument panel, and a warning light. As a bulb test, the light should turn on when the ignition switch is turned to START. If it doesn't, check the light and all wiring. If both are satisfactory, remove the lead from the sensor. If the light then comes on, replace the sensor; if not, replace the module.

Sometimes the light may stay on even though the level of coolant is correct. Check for a short-circuit in the sensor-to-module wiring. If the wiring is good, replace the module.

6

ENGINE SERVICING AND TUNE-UP

Contents

INTRODUCTION

Four-Stroke Power Cycle

The four-stroke power cycle is illustrated in Fig. 6-1. The transfer of power generated by the combustion process is shown in (a). Briefly, the spark ignites a gas-air mixture in the combustion chamber. Power created by the combustion drives the piston downward. The downward motion of the piston is changed into circular motion by the crankshaft, and the circular motion is transmitted to the rear axle to make the wheels turn.

The *intake stroke*, the first of four in the cycle, is shown in Fig. 6-1(b). As the piston moves downward, the carburetor delivers a gas-air mixture through the intake valve of the combustion chamber. The second stroke, called the *compression stroke*, is shown in (c). Here the piston moves up, the intake valve closes the port, and the piston compresses the gas-air mixture in the combustion chamber. Just before the piston reaches top dead center (TDC), the high-voltage spark ignites the mixture, as shown in (d). The mixture burns until just after TDC, and the energy developed by this combustion drives the piston downward in the *power*

stroke, (e), turning the crankshaft and transferring the energy to the wheels. The fourth and last stroke, called the *exhaust stroke*, is shown in (f). The piston moves up, forcing hot gases out through the exhaust port and thereby completing the cycle.

Basic Troubleshooting Equipment

Very often, the only tools needed for troubleshooting are wrenches (open-end, box, and socket), pliers (slip-joint, box-joint, and lap-joint), and screwdrivers with various tips, such as standard, thin-blade, clutch-type, and Phillips. Of course, a tremendous variety of tools is available, but unless you plan to become a professional mechanic, the investment is usually prohibitive.

For tune-up work some special tools, such as a plug scope are needed. This instrument is particularly useful since the engine need not be under load and the plugs need not be removed from the cylinders. The particular scope shown adjusts automatically to either 6- or 12-volt ignition systems, and measures the high voltage delivered to each plug.

A typical set of scope patterns, Fig. 6-2, shows a

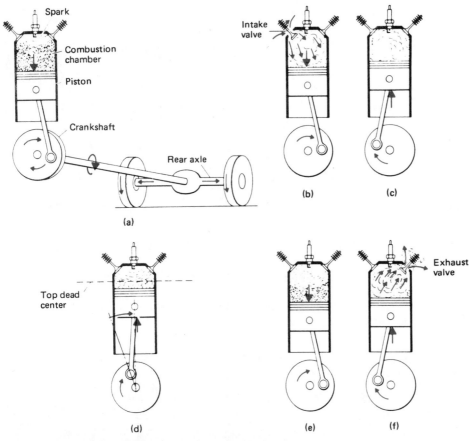

Fig. 6-1   Four-stroke power cycle. (a) Power transfer, (b) intake stroke, (c) compression stroke, (d) point of ignition, (e) power stroke, and (f) exhaust stroke.

Fig. 6-2   Shorted or fouled plug pattern on scope screen. *Courtesy of Champion Spark Plug Company.*

shorted or fouled plug, as indicated by the small circle, which may be caused by plug fouling or leakage to ground within the distributor cap or to the plug cable, or by a narrow spark-plug gap. The actual cause is determined by identifying the defective plug. The plug to which a certain trace pattern belongs is located by clipping a connector from the plug scope to the plug cable leading to the cylinder that fires last in the firing order. The trace patterns then appear on the screen, from left to right, in the firing order of the engine, and the defective plug is easily identified. Once removed from the cylinder, the defective plug is left open-circuited so that it does not spark to ground. The engine is then started. If the plug is faulty, the pattern approaches the top of the screen. If the pattern is still low, either the plug wire or distributor cap is grounded.

Other special tune-up tools include a spark-plug gap gauge, standard compression tester, low-reading voltmeter with 0.01-volt gradations, cam-dwell indicator, timing light, and electric tachometer. Most minor tune-ups can be handled with the equipment discussed thus far, and at a nominal investment. More sophisticated timing lights, incorporating a meter to indicate degrees of advance, are also available.

The oscilloscope, often referred to as an ignition analyzer, is an electronically operated device (resembling a TV set) that provides a series of patterns (pictures) which show the condition of the ignition system. These instruments vary in price, size, ease of operation, and special features.

Types of engine analyzers.   The method of presenting the patterns on the screen of an engine analyzer identifies the analyzer as to type. A so-called paradepattern display is shown in Fig. 6-3(a), and a stacked (raster)-pattern display in (b).

In a parade-pattern analyzer, (a), each cylinder pattern is connected to the preceding cylinder pattern; the number of connected patterns is determined by the number of engine cylinders.

In a stacked-pattern analyzer, (b), the cylinder patterns are stacked one above the other to permit a quick comparison of the character of the spark lines and their lengths. Variations caused by mechanical or electrical defects are exposed immediately.

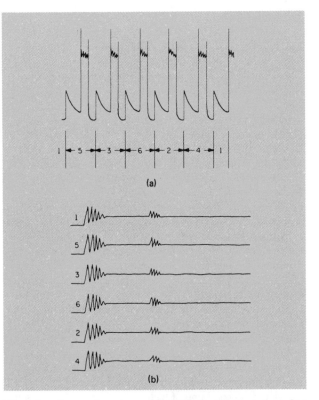

Fig. 6-3   Types of analyzers identified by display patterns. (a) Parade-pattern, and (b) stacked (raster) pattern.

Use of an oscilloscope allows the entire ignition system to be analyzed prior to the start of any tune-up work. This lets you determine if an ignition problem actually exists, and, if so, where it is and whether or not it is serious.

PREVENTIVE MAINTENANCE

Purpose and Frequency

Every part of an automobile requires attention during the life span of the automobile. Very often, the failure of one part causes damage to other parts. Thus preventive maintenance is extremely important.

The preventive maintenance suggestions given here are flexible because of the varying habits of drivers and the actual driving conditions.

The checklist embodies a progressively broader approach to preventive maintenance. During the early mileage on a car, only the quick-wearing parts are checked. As the mileage adds up, however, the longer wearing parts often need to be repaired or replaced.

Check manufacturer's literature for recommended frequency of inspections, but always give due consideration to the two factors noted earlier—driver habits, and driving conditions.

A General Checklist

Lubricate chassis and change crankcase oil.

Check level of battery electrolyte; do not overfill.

Check level of water and condition of antifreeze in radiator.

Check condition and tension of fan belt.

Check for leaks in cooling system, transmission, and differential.

Lubricate door latches.

Check air pressure in each tire, including spare.

Lubricate manifold valve shaft with recommended lubricant.

Change oil filter, as specified by engine manufacturer.

Replace positive crankcase ventilator valve.

Check level of fluid in master brake cylinder. Use fluid specified by manufacturer. Never add mineral oil to the hydraulic brake system.

Check level of oil in transmission and differential, while units are at operating temperature.

Check fluid level in power-steering unit while it is at operating temperature.

Clean and oil carburetor air cleaner and oil filter cap.

Clean and set spark plugs.

Adjust distributor points.

Rotate tires.

Check operation of windshield wiper and all lights.

Flush cooling system and add a rust inhibitor.

Check overall condition of battery.

Check front-end alignment, balance front and rear wheels, and repack front wheel bearings.

Check effectiveness of shock absorbers; refill with fluid or replace shocks.

Inspect break linings, adjust brakes when needed, and lubricate emergency brake cable.

Adjust automatic transmission bands, where used, and replace fluid and filter. Do not flush transmission.

Adjust clutch, where used.

Examine muffler and exhaust system for leaks.

Check universal joint, and refill with oil if necessary.

Give engine a minor tune-up.

Tighten screws and bolts in body and sheetmetal joints.

Clean exhaust emission air-pump filter.

Inspect windshield wiper blades.

Check starter and dc generator brushes.

Inspect and clean alternator slip rings and brushes.

Inspect and repack alternator bearings, when necessary.

Clean fuel pump and then check pump pressure.

Clean and adjust carburetor.

Install new brake linings and inspect wheel drums.

Overhaul starting motor.

Check alternator diodes; replace if necessary.

Replace dc generator brushes and adjust voltage regulator.

Overhaul carburetor and fuel pump.

Overhaul master brake cylinder and wheel cylinders. This may be done when new brake linings are installed.

Check tie rods and wheel suspension; replace all worn parts.

Check shock absorbers and replace if necessary.

Check air conditioner for leaks and operation.

ANALYZING SPARK-PLUG CONDITIONS

Plug Selection

Of all automobile parts, spark plugs are the most frequently replaced. Thus the correct selection of spark plugs is essential to proper engine performance.

The life of a plug depends in part on the automobile, but still more on the driving habits of the operator. For this reason it is necessary to keep a careful check on the plugs to maintain engine efficiency. When new plugs are installed, the ignition points and capacitor should be checked.

In general, the plug type recommended by the automobile manufacturer should be used. However, factory recommendations are based on average driving conditions only, and the driving habits of the operator may make the use of the recommended plug impracticable. If most driving is at high speeds, a cooler plug may be needed. If, on the other hand, the car is used mainly for city driving or for short trips, where the engine does not run at high temperatures, a hotter plug may be better.

A spark plug that is too hot for a given engine causes preignition, rough operation, and loss of power on hard pulls or under conditions of sustained wide-open-throttle operation.

If the insulator of a spark plug has accumulated a gray, fluffy deposit, or is covered by carbon and a wet, oily deposit, the plug is running too cold and should be replaced by a plug one or two steps higher in the heat scale. The effects produced by a plug that is too cold are hard starting, slow warming up, fouling, and missing.

A yellow deposit sometimes found on plugs is caused by the use of ethyl gasolines. The amount of the deposit varies, depending on the amount of such fuel used. This deposit does not affect the operation of the plug if it is in otherwise good condition.

If carbon streaks are found on the top section of the insulator, there is a leakage between the insulator and shell. As a rule, plugs that show this condition are also badly burned. Such trouble is usually caused by improper installation.

Plug Conditions

Normal and excessive plug wear. It is usually possible to determine if the proper plug is being used by noting its physical appearance after a period of operation. If the plug has the proper heat characteristics, the insulator is tan in color, is not sooted, and the electrodes appear grayish at the point where the spark jumps the gap. Such plugs may be cleaned, regapped, and reinstalled. Worn-out electrodes and a pitted insulator are indications of 10,000 miles or more of service. These plugs should be replaced for better gas mileage, quicker starting, and smoother engine performance.

In a plug running too hot, the insulator is free of carbon, and its appearance ranges from a whitish in mild cases to pock-marked, blistered, and burned. The burned or blistered insulator nose and badly eroded electrodes indicate improper spark timing or low-octane fuel detonation and overheating. Lean air-fuel mixtures, cooling-system stoppages, or sticking valves may also result from this condition. As noted earlier, sustained high-speed service may require the use of colder plugs.

Carbon-fouled plug. Has a dry, fluffy black deposit, resulting from an overrich carburetion, overchoking, sticking manifold heat valve, or clogged air cleaner. Faulty breaker points, weak coil or capacitor, or worn ignition cables can reduce voltage and cause misfiring. Also, excessive idling and low speeds under light load can keep the engine temperatures so low that normal combustion deposits are not burned off. Try a hotter plug.

Oil-fouled plug. Wet, oily deposits may be caused by oil leaks between worn piston rings and the cylinder wall. The break-in period of a new or overhauled engine may also produce this condition. A porous diaphragm in the vacuum booster pump, or excessive clearances in the valve-stem guide can also cause oil fouling. Usually, oil-fouled plugs can be degreased, cleaned, and reinstalled. A hotter plug reduces the amount of oil fouling, but an engine overhaul may be necessary to correct the condition.

High-speed glazing. May cause misfiring. The shiny deposit is usually yellow or tan. The existence of a glazed deposit suggests that the engine temperature rose suddenly during a hard acceleration, and the normal deposits did not get a chance to chip off. Instead, they melted and formed a conductive, glazed coating. A colder plug and regular cleaning are recommended.

Turbulence burning. Causes electrodes to wear on one side and is the result of normal turbulent patterns in the combustion chambers of certain engines. Such burning can be ignored if normal plug life is obtained. If the gap growth appears excessive, follow the corrective measures suggested later in the overheating section.

Fuel-scavenger deposits. Deposits are white or yellow. The plug may appear bad, but the deposits shown are normally expected with some branded fuels. In these fuels, certain ingredients are added to change the chemical nature of the deposits on the plugs and lessen the tendency to misfire. The accumulation of the deposit on the ground electrode and shell areas may be very heavy; however, the material is easily flasked off during cleaning. Such plugs are considered good and can be cleaned with standard procedures and techniques.

Preignition damage. Caused by excessive engine temperatures. Preignition produces melting of the center electrode, and eventually, of the ground electrode. The insulators appear relatively clear of deposits. Remember, a spark plug is like an electric fuse; plug melting is a warning that other troubles may exist in the engine. Check for correct plug heat range, overadvanced ignition timing, and other reasons for overheating (covered later).

In its extreme condition, preignition damage usually involves the melting of the ceramic firing tip. Since such melting requires temperatures above 1700°F, other engine components have probably been damaged. Careful overall inspection of the engine and adjustment of all electrical systems is needed.

Splash fouling. Sometimes occurs after a long delayed tune-up. During the delay, deposits have had adequate time to build up after continuous misfirings, and when normal combustion is restored by the tune-up, these deposits are suddenly loosened. During a highspeed run, the loosened materials are thrown against the hot insulator surface. The deposits can be removed with regular cleaning techniques, and the plugs can be reused.

Chipped insulator. Usually results from bending the center electrode during regapping of the spark plug. During engine operation, severe detonation may also split an insulator tip.

The insulator chip is not likely to cause damage to the piston or cylinder bore since, in a four-cycle engine, the fragment of ceramic is easily thrown out through the exhaust. When a plug is chipped, replace it.

Mechanical damage. Caused by a foreign object in the combustion chamber. Small objects travel from one cylinder to another because of the overlap design of the valves. Always check the complete bank of cylinders for the presence of foreign objects when working on an engine, and never leave the carburetor throat and spark-plug holes uncovered during servicing.

Gap-tool pressure defect. An improperly used pressure-type gap tool can place an extremely high pressure on the center electrode of a spark plug and distort the negative electrode. The high pressure is caused by the compression between the end of the center electrode and the top of the shell.

Reversed polarity coil defect. The spark-plug condition caused by reversed-coil polarity is often detected by a depressed-surface (dish) effect on the shell electrode. Although the center electrode does not wear badly, it wears enough to cause inefficient engine operation. Over a period of time, excessive wear can cause both misfiring and rough idle. Install new plugs and reverse the primary leads to the ignition coil.

Gap Setting

The spark-plug gap should be set with a round-gauge wire. The form of the combustion chamber, type of ignition coil, heat characteristics of the engine, and similar factors all affect the plug setting. It is therefore impossible to set any rule on the amount of gap that will apply in all cases. Follow the manufacturer's specifications. In some cases, however, these specifications may have to be altered. For instance, when high-speed performance is the most significant requirement and good idling is a secondary consideration, a closer plug gap should be used. Care must be taken in changing from a recommended gap setting because the change, while satisfying one requirement, may cause operating problems in other parts of the engine.

An inaccurate gap setting eventually causes plug failure. A gap that is too wide causes flashover, in which wet, unburned fuel is deposited on the plug, eventually burns to carbon, and adheres to the plug core. A wide setting can also cause an engine to miss at high speeds. A gap that is set too closely, on the other hand, causes plug fouling and engine missing at low speeds.

A typical gap-setting gauge and gauge-adjusting tool is shown in Fig. 6-4(a). This gauge is used to set gaps ranging from 0.022 to 0.040 inch. Proper positioning of the gauge is shown in (b). Flat gauges provide false settings and should not be used. The proper method of adjusting the plug gap is shown in (c). The adjustment is always made on the outer electrode. Using the center electrode may result in a broken insulator.

Installing Plugs

Cracked insulators are usually due to careless regapping or to installing the plugs too tightly in a cold engine. The only remedy is to install new plugs. A damaged or cracked plug shell may also be caused by overtightening with a conventional box wrench. The safest method of installing plugs is to screw and tighten them into their seats by hand, run the engine until it is warmed up, and then tighten the plugs securely with a torque wrench, applying the torque recommended by the manufacturer (usually 30 foot-pounds).

When a plug is being installed, the gasket should be compressed to prevent combustion gases from leaking and damaging the plug. Applying the proper torque provides the proper gasket compression between the plug shell and cylinder head. New gaskets should always be used with new plugs.

High-Voltage Cables

High-voltage cables should be checked and tested at the same time as the plugs, since they are exposed to heat, cold, moisture, oil, and corona. Corona is the electric field set up around the cables by the passage of current. This electrical field combines with the oxygen of the air to form ozone, which attacks the rubber covering on the cable and tends to destroy its insulation properties. New forms of insulation minimize the corona problem.

The cables are subjected to bending each time the dis-

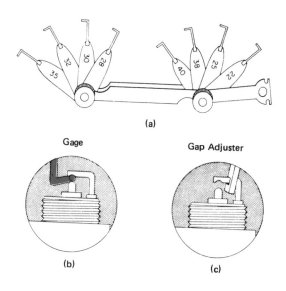

Fig. 6-4   Gap setting and adjusting. (a) Gauge and gap adjuster, (b) gauge in position, and (c) proper use of tool. *Courtesy of Champion Spark Plug Company.*

tributor cap is removed. Both visual and electrical checks are necessary because cracks revealed by visual inspection may be harmless as long as the cable is dry, but if the cracked cable becomes wet, current might leak through the cracks to the outside of the cable and follow along the damp covering to ground.

To attain top engine efficiency, change all high voltage cables after every two years of operation and always handle them with great care. When cables are removed from the plugs, never pull on them like a rope. Instead, grasp the boots over the plugs and rotate the boots while pulling them off the plugs.

When new cables are installed, all connections must be tight and clean, and the cable end terminal must be set properly into the distributor-cap tower. If an air gap is left at this point, it forms a high-resistance path for current going to the plugs. Corrosion may also form at the tower terminal and add resistance to the secondary circuit.

Most engines are now fitted with nonmetallic core (rather than copper) high-voltage cables to reduce interference with radio and TV reception caused by the emission of high-frequency waves by the ignition system. Careless handling of such cables may break the center conductor and cause ignition failure. When removing a lead from a spark plug or distributor cap, grasp the wire as close to the end as possible and apply a steady pull, using the least pull necessary, to remove the wire. Never jerk the wire, as this will surely crack the graphite center. When checking continuity with an ohmmeter, you should get a reading of about 5,000 ohms per foot of wire. An ordinary light bulb continuity tester cannot be used to check the continuity of this type of cable.

CAUSES OF ENGINE OVERHEATING

Detecting Troubles

Excessive-temperature operation can cause serious damage to an engine. The heat thins out cylinder oil, and engine parts wear more rapidly than normal.

Checks for overheating should begin with the more obvious or common causes. First, note the conditions under which the heating takes place—short or long runs, long pulls, steep grades, etc. Then, you are ready to start work.

Coolant level and radiator leaks. Check the coolant level in the radiator; it should be about one inch below the bottom of the filler neck. Examine the radiator from front and back. Check all hose connections, the gasket seal in the radiator cap, and the cylinder jacket. Also, look under the engine for signs of dripping water. The radiator cap in a pressurized system *MUST* be removed cautiously, particularly when the engine is hot, since pressures as high as 35 pounds per square inch may be encountered.

Lubrication. With the engine running, look at the oil gauge or warning light on the dash to see if the oil pump is working. If the gauge shows low oil pressure or if the warning light remains on, stop the engine and check the oil in the crankcase. If the supply of oil is adequate, note its condition; if it is very thin and consists mostly of gasoline or kerosene, drain it out and fill the crankcase with clean oil of the proper viscosity.

If the oil gauge does not register, the gauge itself or the oil pump may be defective.

Fan belt. A fan belt may slip if it is loose or oily, or if the shaft binds in its bearings. Check by attempting to turn the fan by hand. A V-shaped belt in good condition can be turned only with difficulty when one of the fan blades is pushed downward. If the fan turns easily, there is too much slack in the belt, and it should be adjusted. If the belt is oily, or too slack when the limit of the belt adjustment is reached, install a new belt. In an emergency, an oily belt can be made to pull better by wiping it clean and sprinkling powdered chalk on the inner side.

If the fan blade cannot be pushed downward, the belt is too tight or the fan bearing is binding, probably due to the lack of lubrication. Adjust the belt and lubricate the bearing. When time permits, remove, clean, and then replace the fan bearing.

Radiator hoses. A defective radiator hose can usually, but not always, be detected by inspecting its outer surface. A good piece of hose is springy when pinched with the fingers, and returns to its original shape as soon as the pressure is released. In older neoprene or plastic composition hoses, the lining sometimes breaks away from the body and acts as a shutoff valve. The only sure way to determine the condition of the hose is to remove and examine it thoroughly, particularly when persistent overheating occurs.

Frozen radiator. A steaming radiator in freezing weather usually means a frozen radiator or evaporation of the coolant; in other words, insufficient coolant remains in the radiator to cool the engine. Pass your hand along the bottom of the radiator and also along the lower hose connections. If both are cold while the top of the radiator is hot, there is no circulation, and freezing has probably occurred.

Thaw a frozen radiator in a heated garage, and run the engine at idle speed for only one or two minutes at a time. Allow an interval between running times for the cylinder heat to dissipate into the radiator.

Thermostat. Overheating can also be caused by a thermostat stuck in its closed position as a result of rust and sediment. A thermostat installed upside down will also be inoperative. Always make sure that the proper type and range of thermostat is used.

Air circulation. Overheating is often caused by insects, mud, or dirt on the radiator honeycomb, which prevents air circulation. Clean the honeycomb.

Brakes. Another cause of overheating is that brakes are set so tightly they drag on the brake drums. A quick test is to stop the automobile on a smooth, level surface, set the gears in neutral, release the brakes, and then try to push the automobile. If it moves easily, the brakes are not at fault. Run the automobile for a while before making this test, since the brakes may be free enough when cold, but bind when warm.

High engine friction. A new or recently overhauled engine frequently runs at high temperatures because parts are tight. Some of the things most likely to cause high friction include improperly fitted piston rings, rings of excessive tension, either by themselves or in conjunction with inner expansion rings, rough finish on rebored cylinder walls, bearings set up without sufficient clearance, or dirt, even in the form of microscopic grit. For this reason, cleanliness in all engine servicing work cannot be overemphasized. If the engine does not loosen up after a few hundred miles, and the overheating does not cease, the only remedy is to tear down the engine, and locate and remove the cause.

Clogged radiator. A radiator may be blocked internally by dirt, rust, or other foreign matter. Try cleaning with washing soda or one of the many solutions now available for this purpose.

Ignition. When engine overheating is not traceable to the cooling system, check the ignition system. Irregular or weak ignition may be caused by pitted or dirty contact points, weak breaker springs, or dirty or improperly set spark plugs. If the ignition is irregular or weak, a greater demand is made on the engine and overheating results. A late spark may also cause overheating even in an engine that originally was timed properly. Wear of the rubbing block on the breakerpoint cam, sticking of the automatic advance, or a broken vacuum diaphragm in the advance mechanism are possible causes of late ignition timing.

Fuel mixture.   If the cooling and ignition systems are in good condition, check the fuel system next. A fuel mixture that is either too rich or too lean is slow burning and noneffective, making the engine overwork.

Transmission.   A slipping clutch or an automatic transmission that will not shift will cause an engine to overheat. To test for a slipping clutch, slow the automobile down to a speed of about 12 mph with the transmission in high, and then press down quickly on the accelerator. If the engine starts to race, but there is no appreciable increase in the speed of the automobile, the clutch is slipping.

When an automatic transmission fails to shift into high gear, the engine acts as a braking force as soon as the accelerator pedal is released. Thus the engine is running continually at high speed, causing rapid wear of all parts, overheating, and short engine life.

Pump impeller.   Pump-impeller trouble is rare in late-model automobiles, but it may occur if the water pump is allowed to freeze. This causes the impeller pin to shear off. In older cars, wear sometimes occurs between the impeller and pump housing, resulting in little or no water circulation.

The quickest way to check pump action is to remove the upper hose connection at the radiator end, fill the radiator with water until it starts to run out of the open end of the hose, and then start the engine. If the pump is working properly, the water should be forced out of the hose under pressure.

Fan blade.   If fan blades are not set at the correct angle, sufficient air is not drawn through the radiator to cool the engine. Trouble of this kind is usually the result of a front-end collision. To test the fan efficiency, let the engine run and hold a piece of newspaper against the front of the radiator. When the fan is working properly, the paper is held against the radiator by suction.

Water flow.   Restriction of water passages between the cylinder jacket and cylinder head is usually encountered only with older automobiles. The openings that connect the cylinder jackets and the cylinder head may be shut off by the use of the wrong head gasket, or the proper gasket may be installed upside down; this prevents the free passage of water from the cylinder jackets to the head. A baffle plate or an engine-block manifold that is rusted, loose, or damaged will also cause overheating.

TESTING COMPRESSION AND VACUUM

Definitions

Compression ratio is the space between the pistons and the top of the chamber at the top of the piston stroke, as compared to this same space at the bottom of the piston stroke.

Compression pressure is the actual pressure within the cylinder at top dead center at the beginning of the firing stroke. It is measured in pounds per square inch (psi), as indicated on a gauge. When the pistons, piston rings, and valves are in factory condition, compression pressure will average 160 psi for a 9.0 to 1 ratio and 180 psi for a 10.25 to 1 ratio. On older cars with lower compression ratios, such as 6.2 to 1, an average of 130 psi can be expected.

Making a Compression Check

A compression check is a vital part of every tune-up. In a typical compression tester, Figure 6-5, pressure is exerted against a diaphragm in the tester and this causes movement of the pointer across a scale that is calibrated (marked) in pounds per square inch (psi).

Before using the tester, disconnect the wires from all spark plugs and loosen each plug one turn. Connect the yellow lead of a tachometer to the negative ($-$) terminal of the ignition coil and the black lead to ground. (A tachometer shows engine speed in revolutions per minute—rpm—and has a switch that permits use with 4-, 6-, or 8-cylinder engines.) Now reconnect the spark-plug wires. Start the engine and let it run for a few moments at 1000 rpm. The combustion gases generated during this interval will blow out of the plug wells any dirt that could fall into the cylinders when the plugs are removed. The gases also blow out of the combustion chamber and loose carbon that has accumulated around the exposed thread end of the plugs. This keeps carbon particles from getting under a valve and keeping the valve open when a compression test is being run.

Now screw the compression-tester fitting into the spark-plug hole of cylinder 1 and disconnect the distributor lead from the negative terminal of the ignition coil to protect

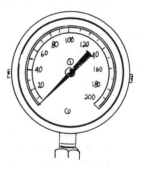

Fig. 6-5   Typical compression tester gauge.

the coil against high voltage. Then hold the throttle wide open and crank the engine.

Modern compression gauges operate on an accumulated pressure principle. This simply means that the engine must be cranked several times until the pressure reading shows no further increase. Typically, 10 to 12 compression impulses produce maximum pressure.

In some high-performance engines, the loss of compression past the valves can lead to an inaccurate diagnosis. Because the camshaft holds the valves open longer at a low cranking speed, a great amount of air in the cylinders is lost past the open valves. To minimize this loss, run the engine at a minimum of 1500 rpm while making the compression test. This speed minimizes errors introduced by air rushing back into the intake manifold. Variations in pressure are more meaningful than maximum gauge readings on these engines.

Specifications are supplied by the automobile manufacturer for the compression cranking speed. While these specifications are not guaranteed to be absolutely accurate, they serve as a guide to what the engine compression should be.

Compression tests are most valuable in indicating variations in compression among cylinders. The compression should not vary more than about 15 psi in any cylinder. If the variation is greater than 15 psi, trouble is indicated.

Interpreting Compression-Gauge Readings

An irregular compression buildup is a sign of sticking valves. Low readings on adjacent cylinders indicate leakage of the gasket between the cylinders. However, before the gasket is condemned and replaced, make sure the cylinder-head bolts are tight. A low reading on one cylinder indicates either improper valve seating or piston and ring blow-by.

When the pressure is not up to maximum, check the rings. Introduce heavy oil, such as SAE 40, onto the tops of the pistons with an adjustable neck oiler. Be sure to keep the oil away from the valves. The pressure is then taken again and the improvement noted. For example, the initial test may show 100 psi, while the specifications show that it should be 160 psi. After the oil is put on the cylinder, the gauge may register 140 psi. This would mean that, of the original 60 psi loss, 40 psi is attributable to ring leakage and 20 psi to valve loss. Follow this procedure with each cylinder.

Low compression may result from leaky piston rings (due to wear of either the rings or the cylinder wall), or from gummed rings. A good gum solvent in the crankcase oil may free the rings and raise compression. In some cases, however, it is necessary to remove the pistons and clean them by hand.

Valve leakage also causes low compression. The only remedy, in most cases, is a valve-grinding job. Poorly adjusted valves may be held open when they get hot. Resetting will usually stop this leakage. Leaky head gaskets will

also cause trouble. Oil leaks around the gaskets usually indicate this condition.

Occasionally, the compression may be higher than it should be by as much as 10 psi, but variations among the cylinders should not exceed 15 psi. Greater fluctuations show that carbon has accumulated in the combustion chamber, making the chamber smaller and raising the compression ratio and pressure. This same type of carbon buildup may occur in the engine manifold of high-compression engines, causing frequent stalling at idle speed. Such a condition is not unusual when an automobile is used exclusively for heavy stop-and-go driving.

Vacuum

A *vacuum* (that is, a space devoid of air) exists in the space between the top of a cylinder piston and the throttle valve so long as no air leaks into the cylinder when the piston moves downward on its intake stroke. A vacuum gauge connected to the top of the cylinder registers this vacuum. A dial-type vacuum gauge is shown in Fig. 6-6.

An *atmospheric pressure* of approximately 14.7 psi is exerted on the area around the cylinder and manifold. If there is a very small hole through which the atmosphere is forced into the cylinder, the cylinder loses its vacuum slowly. If the opening is large, the vacuum is lost much more rapidly. If the engine condition is normal, the only leakage to the space above the throttle is around the throttle, which must be opened to permit the passage of the fuel-air mixture. As the throttle opening is increased, the mixture drawn into the cylinder increases and the vacuum decreases.

The scale of a vacuum gauge is calibrated in inches of mercury, abbreviated in. Hg. When an engine is operating

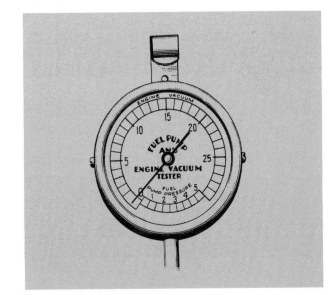

Fig. 6-6 Dial-type vacuum gauge.

satisfactorily, the vacuum reading is typically between 17 and 22 in. Hg.

Engine Effect on Vacuum Gauge

When a vacuum gauge is connected to an engine that has a loose manifold bolt, thus allowing a slight amount of air to enter the cylinder, the loss of vacuum is less than if one valve is held open. If both valves are closed tight, but the piston rings do not form a tight seal to the cylinder wall, vacuum is lost because air leaks past the rings.

If vacuum were lost in a one-cylinder engine, the vac-

uum hand of the gauge would return to zero. However, in a four-stroke eight-cylinder engine there are four intake (displacement) strokes during each revolution of the crankshaft. If no vacuum exists in one cylinder, the gauge does not drop to zero because the intake stroke of another cylinder keeps the indicator at a higher reading.

The extent to which air can enter the manifold and cylinder depends on the throttle opening and the engine rpm. Therefore, a vacuum gauge is a comparative tachometer. Any adjustment that increases the rpm with a set throttle opening also increases the vacuum. The vacuum is also increased if the rpm is maintained but the throttle opening is

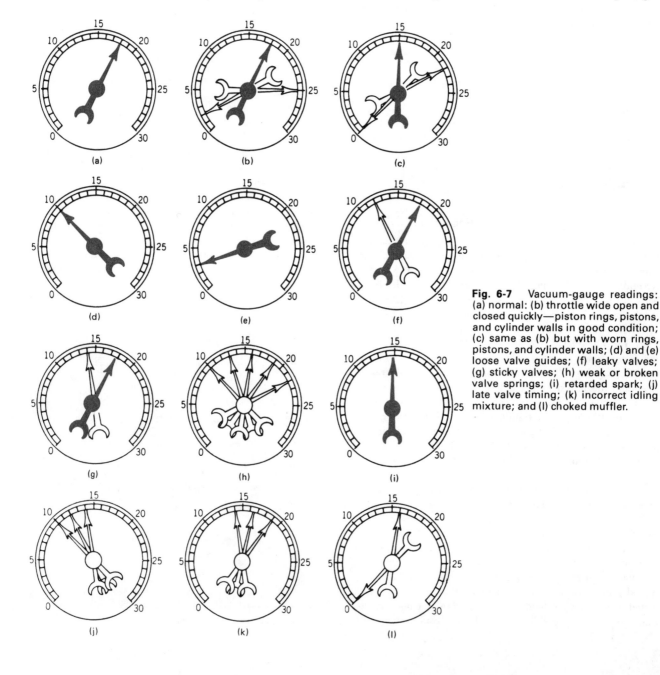

Fig. 6-7 Vacuum-gauge readings: (a) normal: (b) throttle wide open and closed quickly—piston rings, pistons, and cylinder walls in good condition; (c) same as (b) but with worn rings, pistons, and cylinder walls; (d) and (e) loose valve guides; (f) leaky valves; (g) sticky valves; (h) weak or broken valve springs; (i) retarded spark; (j) late valve timing; (k) incorrect idling mixture; and (l) choked muffler.

decreased. No vacuum reading takes place if the air enters the manifold fast enough to keep the space above the piston filled with air as the piston moves downward.

Practical application of the foregoing statements may be understood by recalling that, when the ignition is advanced, there is a slight increase in the rpm of the engine. As this is accomplished without changing the throttle opening, a higher vacuum reading results. Conversely, if the timing is retarded without changing the throttle opening, a lower vacuum reading results. If the ignition is advanced to a point where the spark occurs before the piston reaches the top-dead-center position, a backward pressure is created on the piston head, which reduces the rpm of the engine and causes a vacuum drop.

Interpreting Vacuum-Gauge Readings

The gauge readings shown in Fig. 6-7 are for various conditions that affect the proper operation of the engine. After connecting the vacuum gauge to the intake manifold, check the cylinder head and manifold bolts to make sure they are tight.

Run the engine slightly faster than normal idling. If the ignition, carburetion, and mechanical parts are operating correctly, the vacuum needle remains steady and somewhere between 17 and 21 in. Hg., as shown in Fig. 6-7(a). When the throttle is opened wide and then closed quickly, and the piston rings, pistons, cylinder walls, and oil are in good condition, the needle drops to approximately 2 in. Hg. and then rebounds to about 25 in. Hg. or more, as shown in (b).

If the piston rings, pistons, or cylinder walls are worn or if the oil is too thin, the vacuum is lower than normal. When the throttle valve is opened and closed quickly, the gauge needle drops to zero on opening and does not rebound to 25 psi. See Fig. 6-7(c).

Loose valve guides produce a low reading on the vacuum gauge, with very little movement of the needle, because atmospheric pressure is passing through the guides constantly and partially destroying the vacuum in the intake manifold. Gauge readings of this nature are shown in (d) and (e). Loss of power and greater oil consumption results from this condition.

A bad manifold leak also causes a low gauge reading. If you suspect this condition, seal the intake manifold gaskets with some heavy oil. If the reading becomes higher, the gasket leaks; if not, the valve guides are worn.

A leaky guide does not adequately seal compression in the cylinder, and every time the valve is on its seat, which occurs at equal intervals, the needle drops several inches, as shown in Fig. 6-7(f). The amount of drop depends on the extent to which the valve remains open. A blown cylinder-head gasket produces a similar effect on the vacuum gauge, but if the trouble is located in the valve, a small quantity of oil introduced into the intake manifold temporarily speeds up the engine and holds the vacuum steady; no such effect is noted if the head gasket is blown or defective.

Sticky valves are indicated when the gauge needle drops four or five points at regular intervals. See Fig. 6-7(g). This reading may also indicate a rich or lean mixture, an occasional spark-plug miss, or internal carburetor trouble.

When the gauge needle fluctuates over a wide range, Fig. 6-7(h), and increases with higher engine speeds, the valve springs are weak or broken.

A retarded spark causes a low, steady reading on the gauge, as shown in part (i) of the figure. If, however, the amount of retard is excessive, not only is the vacuum lower than normal but the needle also swings backward and forward.

Late valve timing also causes a low vacuum reading, with possibly a slow back-and-forth movement of the needle, as shown in Fig. 6-7(j). This results from the charge being forced back through the intake valve during the compression stroke.

For an incorrect idling mixture the gauge needle swings slowly back and forth, (k), but at a higher pressure than shown in (j). A fuel-air mixture that is too rich or too lean burns more slowly than a normal mixture, and combustion sometimes continues until the intake valve opens, causing the vacuum to be interrupted. Also, too lean a mixture can cause an irregular drop of the gauge needle.

When the gauge shows a normal reading at the start, but the needle drops gradually, a choked muffler is indicated. See Fig. 6-7(l).

FUEL SERVICING PROBLEMS

Fuel Consumption

Failure to operate economically may be the result of your driving habits or the conditions under which the driving is done. If due consideration is given to both of these factors and still fuel consumption is high, it may be due to trouble in the carburetor. Such troubles include the float level being too high, the needle valve leaking, the accelerator pump out of adjustment, the throttle stop-screw set for too-fast idling, the metering jet being too large, the automatic choke not opening fully, the economizer valve acting too quickly, the economizer piston stuck in its cylinder, or valve stem stuck in its guide.

Hard-to-Start Hot Engine

An engine that is hard to start when hot usually indicates fuel-system problems related to the flow of fuel and the fuel-air mixture to the cylinders. Check all of the conditions mentioned earlier in the section relating to overheating. There may also be mechanical problems, such as burned or leaking valves, a stuck heat valve in the manifold, or carburetor and fuel-pump defects.

Certain electrical troubles may also be causing the difficulty, especially the battery or ignition system. A systematic check of all electrical parts usually leads to the solution of the problem. Quick checks may be made for high resistance in the distributor system, or for a defective ignition switch or starting motor solenoid. Should the starting motor require more than 150 amperes during a cranking cycle, the trouble is likely to be in the starting motor.

Testing the Fuel Pump

Fuel-pump pressure is measured at the fuel-pump level, and should run from about 4½ to 6½ lbs. in most high-compression engines. In lower compression engines, the range is from 2½ to 3½ lbs. Adapters are available to connect the gauge into the gasoline line, making it unnecessary to disconnect the line.

A high pump pressure and a leaky diaphragm are common causes of low gasoline mileage. If the fuel-pump diaphragm is leaking, gasoline escapes through a hole in the pump body. In the upright (vertical) type pump, a leaking diaphragm causes oil to leak into the vacuum chamber and then pass into the intake manifold and engine. In the inverted-type fuel pump, oil that works its way into the pump is expelled through the vent hole in the upper half of the pump body. This vent hole must be kept open. A leaky seal around the diaphragm shaft is indicated by oil passing out of the vent hole.

Some newer pumps have a small, calibrated bypass hole drilled between the inlet and outlet passages of the pump. This passage provides a controlled leakage path back to the fuel tank. Fuel, expanding in the fuel line and fuel pump, must have a place to go. Hotter running engines, confined space under the hood, and in-line filters have made this expansion more of a problem. If there were no return passage, the expanding fuel would be forced into the carburetor, making it difficult to restart a hot engine.

ABNORMAL ENGINE NOISES AND THEIR CAUSES

Tracing Knocks

Unless an engine is first tuned up to fire on all cylinders, it is very difficult to apply the test required to locate noise causes.

Loose main bearing. This noise is always loudest under a load or pull. In tone, it is a dull pounding sound or thud. A loose main bearing is also noticeable when a car is running on a level road at from 15 to 25 mph, but unless the bearing is very loose the noise is not audible when the engine idles except when it is not firing evenly.

If a main bearing is unusually loose, it causes a pronounced dull thud and the engine vibrates when it is steadily accelerated from 35 to 50 mph. This vibration may be felt in the car floor, or it may be detected by placing your hand on the door sill with the car door partially open.

The noise can be reduced by shorting out certain spark plugs. To determine which main bearing is loose, you must know how many main bearings are in the engine. If the crankshaft is carried on three main bearings, the services of two persons are needed. One sits in the driver's seat and starts the engine. After a warm-up period, he applies the emergency brake, moves the selector lever of an automatic transmission into drive position, or engages the high gear in a standard transmission, and then puts a load on the engine by making it pull slightly against the brakes. The second person then shorts out the spark plugs in front cylinders to locate a noisy front bearing, or shorts out the plugs in the rear cylinders to locate a noisy rear bearing. The shorting should be done on two cylinders at a time, one on each side of, and nearest to, the main bearing.

If a main bearing is badly pounded, burned, or worn, the noise is audible at all engine speeds. The center bearing of a three-bearing crankshaft is usually the first to knock.

Loose lower connecting-rod bearings. This noise is usually most audible at an engine speed corresponding to a road speed of 25 mph, but may occur at about 20 mph and again at 35 mph. In tone, the noise is similar to a light pound; in some engines it produces a clatter, or rattling sound, or a series of short raps. The tone is always sharper than the dull thud caused by main bearings, and unless the bearing is burned out the noise never gets louder.

If the bearing is badly worn or burned, the noise will be audible at all engine speeds and even while the engine is being cranked. Ordinary looseness that shows up at 25 mph generally is not detected at idling speed.

The location of a loose lower connecting-rod bearing is detected by shorting out spark plugs. On most engines, shorting out the plugs reduces the intensity of the noise.

A low oil-pressure reading usually indicates loose bearings. If the automobile is not equipped with an oil-pressure gauge, connect one temporarily. A rapid drop in pressure as the oil gets warm, if ignored for too long, may cause parts to be damaged beyond economical repair.

Bent or sprung connecting rods. Abnormal noise due to one or more bent connecting rods, such as the one shown in Fig. 6-8, is sometimes difficult to identify. The illustration greatly exaggerates the tilt of the piston and the bend in the connecting rod with reference to the center line x-x. The sound produced is somewhat like a piston slap; that is, a hollow and tinkling bell-like sound, but a little sharper. Although usually loudest at idling speed or during acceleration, this sound may be constant above 20 mph. Noises caused by bent connecting rods cannot be silenced entirely by shorting out spark plugs. Shorting does, however, reduce the intensity of the noise somewhat. This noise can also be detected by exerting pressure against the front or rear end of the crankshaft with the handle of a hammer or a stout wooden rod or stick. If the top of the connecting rod is bent forward, pressure exerted on the front end of the crankshaft reduces the sound and may even eliminate it. If the top of the connecting rod is bent backward, the sound intensity increases.

Piston slap. This is caused most frequently by a piston that is too loose diametrically in the cylinder bore, and is always most pronounced when the engine is accelerated. It may also be heard as a loud knock at idling speeds when the engine is not under load, but it is always present under load. The noise is a hollow and tinkling bell-like sound. If the automobile is driven on level ground at 11 to 14 mph and then accelerated quickly, the slap shows up in the form of a clicking noise. When the throttle is released for coasting or slowing down, the sound disappears.

To detect which piston is producing the noise, short out the plug of the suspected cylinder. If the piston is loose, the noise is greatly reduced or eliminated.

Another method is to remove a spark plug and pour about one or two ounces of heavy engine oil into the spark-plug hole of the cylinder containing the suspected piston. After a minute or so, start the engine. If the piston is loose, oil fills the clearance, and the noise is either reduced or eliminated. The oil thins out in a few minutes and then the slap should return.

An engine should never be tested for piston slap until it is warm. A cold engine makes many noises that cease when the engine reaches its normal operating temperature. In general, however, the noise caused by a loose piston is most pronounced when the engine is first started. Slight piston noises, which occur when the engine is cold but cannot be heard when the engine is warm usually can be disregarded.

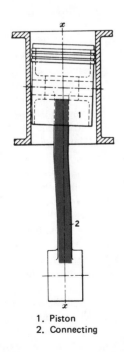

1. Piston
2. Connecting

Fig. 6-8   Bent connecting rod.

Tight piston. The combination of a tight piston and a loose piston pin produces a sound very similar to that caused by piston slap. A *tight* piston is one with insufficient diametrical clearance, but not necessarily so tight as to score the cylinder. This combination may be encountered in a new or recently rebuilt engine. Checking the piston clearances or removing and examining the pistons quickly reveals whether they were too loose or too tight in their respective cylinders. Loose pistons are evenly polished all over; tight pistons will show evidence of binding by localized polished spots and slight scratch marks.

On pistons equipped with two-piece rings, or rings that have a steel, crimped inner ring, a light piston slap may be produced by carbon lodging in the groove and holding the ring compressed, or by the weakening or breaking of the inner ring. Before replacing a piston, check the diametrical clearance. The fouling or loss of wall pressure of the ring may produce the slap, even though the clearance between the piston and cylinder wall is correct.

Other piston or ring noises are covered later.

Timing gear and chain noises. The noise caused by timing gears that are either loose or have an excessive amount of backlash is always loudest at idling speed. This noise may cease at speeds of 15 to 20 mph but becomes pronounced again at speeds of 25 to 35 mph. In tone, the noise differs with the type and make of engine, but sounds either like a sharp clatter or a solid and heavy knock. Timing-chain looseness usually causes a loud rumble at idling speed or when accelerating.

A knock from the timing chain or gear case cannot be shorted out. However, when the water pump is located at the side of the engine, the handle of a hammer may be pried against the exposed part of the pump shaft to act as a brake and take up the backlash. If, in so doing, the knock cannot be heard or is considerably reduced in intensity, it is due to too much backlash or to worn bearings in the gear hub.

If the gears are fitted too tightly, insofar as meshing is concerned, they produce a howl that increases in intensity as the engine speed is increased up to as high as 40 mph.

Foreign matter between the gear teeth shows up as a decided rattling knock; in some cases, it appears as a dull knock, usually accompanied by vibration that can be felt at the engine auxiliary shaft.

When the cover of either the timing gear or chain case is removed, the sprockets and gears should be checked for mesh and alignment of their faces, as well as for tightness on their shafts. A loose key, hub screw, or bolt produces a knock that is hard to find, even though the mesh of the gears is perfect. The same may be said regarding excessive end play and a loose front bearing on the camshaft, crankshaft, auxiliary shaft, or idler gear. All front bearings in either the timing gear or the chain case should be tightened or replaced when the gears are installed.

Loose piston pins. Noises produced by loose piston pins are always loudest when the engine is idling, but in rare cases may occur with the same intensity at 20 to 30 mph. They are usually less audible when the spark is retarded than when it is advanced. The noise from a loose piston pin is usually a sharp, metallic double knock occurring at twice the engine speed, i.e., twice for every revolution of the crankshaft. This knock may be confused with the knock caused by the lower bearing of the connecting rod, especially when the pin is badly worn or very loose. There are two methods of checking for a loose piston pin; both are very simple. In the first method, let the engine idle, then insert the point of a screwdriver between the stem of the exhaust valve and the top of the tappet screw. Hold open the exhaust valve on the suspected cylinder by prying up or down with the screwdriver to raise the valve fully off its seat. Relieving the pressure in this way eliminates the knock unless the pin is exceptionally loose, and even then, it noticeably diminishes the sound.

In the second method, idle the engine and short each plug in turn. When a cylinder is suspected, place the point of a screwdriver against the upper part of the cylinder and the handle end against the ear. Then remove the screwdriver from the cylinder and place it on the crankcase. If a loose piston pin is causing the knock, the noise is much louder and more distinct with the screwdriver held against the cylinder. If the noise is louder when the screwdriver is held against the crankcase, the trouble is a loose lower connecting-rod bearing.

Because it is difficult to distinguish piston-pin noise from noise caused by the piston and connecting rod, it helps to remove the piston and connecting rod and check for piston-pin looseness with your fingers.

Sticking valves. The noise occasioned by sticking valves is usually very noticeable when the engine is accelerated, but can often be heard when the engine is idling. The sound varies from a hollow drumlike noise to a dull thud slightly sharper than the thud caused by a loose main bearing. The dull knock is usually audible at idling speed and speeds up to about 15 mph. The sound varies because the knock may be produced either by uneven compression or by a valve that is delayed in closing and then slaps against its seat.

Valve noises cannot be shorted out. A visual inspection of the valve action with the engine running is a preliminary method of checking for this trouble. The only positive method, however, is to remove the valves and examine the stems for carbon deposits and shiny spots that indicate a sticking condition.

In hydraulic valve mechanisms, air may become entrapped and form bubbles in the oil because the oil level in the crankcase is too high. Air bubbles cause irregular operation and excessive lash clearances in the linkage.

Loose vibration damper, crankshaft gear, or sprocket. Usually indicated by a bump or a thud at the front of the engine during acceleration from idle, or when the engine idles unevenly at low speed. The sound is a sharp clatter at low engine speed with uneven idle. When

checking either condition, short out one or two plugs to obtain uneven idling.

Piston rings. Noise of this type may be caused by interference of the top piston ring with the cylinder-head gasket, variation in the diameter of the cylinder bore, worn piston-ring grooves, or a slightly exposed piston top ring. A light tap, but quite often a click or a sharp rattle, are typical noises. Shorting out one or more plugs usually diminishes the noise slightly but does not eliminate it.

The noise caused by the top ring slapping against the cylinder wall and then back into the groove is often diagnosed as a piston slap. This noise nearly always occurs in engines in which the top ring overruns the top of the cylinder bore.

If the piston does not come to the top of the bore, a shoulder may form near the upper end of the bore at the point reached by the top ring. After continued service with a slight loosening of the connecting-rod and piston-ring bearings, the top ring may strike this and should produce a knock. The characteristic sound of this knock is a light and either regular or irregular rap occurring at moderate engine speed. Removal of the shoulder with a hone or a special chamfering tool eliminates the noise.

A small ridge anywhere along the bore due to defective reaming or grinding of the cylinder causes a similar click at regular intervals. The sound cannot be eliminated by shorting out spark plugs.

Detonation and preignition. Both are usually encountered on high-compression or high-efficiency engines, and occur only under heavy load or when the engine is overheated. The higher the efficiency or compression ratio of the engine, the greater is the susceptibility of the engine to detonation and preignition.

Detonation may cause missing and firing back into the carburetor when the preignition stage is reached, and a noise similar to a sharp connecting-rod knock is audible. In some cases, the noise may be accompanied by vibration of the whole engine. The noise cannot be shorted out unless the test is made with the engine pulling at full load.

If the cooling system is in good condition, the engine is carbon-free, and the combustion chambers have no sharp projections, look for faulty spark plugs. High-compression engines require special plugs. An oil-proof plug is, in general, designed to keep the insulated electrode operating at a temperature high enough to burn off oil. In a spark plug designed for high-compression, high-efficiency engines, the insulator carries away heat fast enough to keep the electrode temperature much lower than that of an oil-proof plug. Closed-end (foulproof) plugs should not be used in high-compression engines. Preignition damage to spark plugs was discussed earlier.

Valve heads that are not properly cooled or are coated by heavy oxide deposits also produce detonation and preignition.

Preignition and detonation may occur in a mild form, with no knocking or missing. Generally, in these cases, the maximum speed of the engine will be reduced by as much as 400 rpm.

Fuel knock. Caused by too lean a fuel mixture or by a fuel not suited to the engine, the knock may be confused with spark knock. It cannot be shorted out. The noise is loudest when accelerating, and can be diminished or eliminated by using a richer fuel mixture. Before deciding that the noise is a fuel knock, check the ignition unit and the automatic advance mechanism, which may be stuck in the advanced position or be advancing too rapidly.

Carbon knock. A carbon knock is usually a sharp, clattering noise, which appears under load or rapid acceleration. If the noise is due entirely to carbon, it will not diminish noticeably when the spark is retarded. Visual inspection of the combustion chambers is the surest way to determine whether carbon deposits are sufficient to cause knocking.

Spark knock. This is a tinkling sound, similar to a slight piston slap, and is very hard to distinguish from a fuel or carbon knock. A slight spark knock at low engine speeds with the engine under full load usually indicates the need for an antiknock fuel. If a spark knock occurs at all speeds, examine the automatic advance. It may have weak springs. The weights then move out and advance the spark both too much and too quickly. Also check the ignition timing.

TROUBLESHOOTING

Starting System

If the starter fails to crank the engine at normal speed, the trouble could be at any point from the battery to the starter.

Battery. Turn the lights on and try to start the engine. If the lights dim as the starter engages, the battery is partially discharged or has a bad cell. If the lights do not go on, use a voltmeter to check the battery voltage. A reading of 12 volts indicates a fully charged battery. A reading of less than 12 volts shows that the battery needs recharging or is defective.

Battery cables. If the battery is good, test the cables. The simplest test is to move the cables back and forth while the starter is engaged. If the starter then cranks the engine intermittently, the cable may be defective or its battery-terminal post may be loose.

If a hissing or bubbling sound comes from the terminal when the starter is engaged, the terminal is loose. If no sound is noted, the cable terminal may still be loose. Insert the blade of a screwdriver between the cable terminal and the battery terminal post. If cranking improves, the terminal is loose. Another indication of a loose terminal on a solenoid-equipped starter is the chattering of the solenoid plunger in the switch when the starter is engaged.

Starter. If the battery and cables are good, check the starter. If the starter just barely turns the engine, there may be a ground or a short in the starter, a burned commutator, or burned and worn brushes. To isolate the trouble to the starter, test across the terminals of the solenoid switch with pliers. If there is a sharp spark, the starter is at fault. If the starter turns freely when the switch is shorted, the switch is at fault.

Occasionally, the starter pinion will not engage with the flywheel ring gear. When this happens, the starter will turn very rapidly without cranking the engine. The piston may be stuck on its shaft by excessive oil or gum, or the starter spring may be broken.

Fuel System

If the engine cranks properly, failure to start may be due to trouble in either the fuel system or the ignition system. Because the lack of gasoline is a common cause of failure to start, it may be best to check the fuel system first.

Fuel gauge. Just keep in mind that the fuel gauge may be defective and give a false reading.

Fuel pump. On older cars look at the glass sediment bowl at the base of the fuel pump. If there is gasoline in the tank, the bowl should be filled with colored liquid. If the liquid in the bowl is clear, water may be in the gasoline. Drain the tank, the sediment bowl, and the carburetor. On newer automobiles, the gas-line filter cartridge should be checked. Replace if it is clogged.

Carburetor. To see if the carburetor is getting gasoline, remove the air cleaner and have someone work the accelerator pedal back and forth several times while the throat of the carburetor is checked. If there is gasoline in the carburetor, a spurt will come out of the accelerating-pump jet every time the accelerator pedal is depressed. If it does not, and if the fuel pump is known to be in good condition, the trouble is in the carburetor.

While the air cleaner is off, check the choke valve. When the engine is cold, the choke valve should be closed; if it is not, the choke unit may be defective. However, the choke can be closed by hand to start a cold engine, or opened by hand to start a warm engine.

Ignition System

The operation of the ignition system can be tested by removing a wire from one plug and holding it about ½ inch from a good ground, such as the cylinder head. A spark should jump from the end of the wire to ground when the engine is cranked.

Primary circuit. To test the primary circuit, turn the engine over until the distributor points close. Then remove the ignition coil secondary wire from the distributor cap. While the distributor points are opened and closed with a screwdriver, hold the end of the secondary wire about ½ inch from a good ground. A sharp spark to ground every time the points open shows that the coil and the primary circuit are in good condition. No spark or a very weak spark indicates a defective coil or capacitor. If the points do not spark, the primary circuit is either grounded or is not getting current.

Now turn the engine over until the points are open. While holding the secondary wire one-half inch from ground, short the movable contact point to the distributor plate by moving the screwdriver up and down to make and break contact with the plate. A sharp spark from the secondary wire to ground, if previously there was a weak spark, indicates bad distributor points. No spark, or a weak spark, means trouble at some point other than the distributor points or the coil.

Every time the screwdriver contacts the distributor plate in the preceding test, a small spark should occur between the screwdriver and the plate. No spark shows a defective capacitor. To test the capacitor, remove it from its mountings but leave the pigtails connected. Again move the screwdriver up and down to make and break contact with the distributor plate. If a spark occurs with the capacitor out of the circuit, the capacitor is bad. If no spark occurs, there is an open in the primary circuit.

Secondary circuit.   Remove both secondary wires from the distributor cap and the distributor cap itself. Turn the engine until the points are closed. Hold the secondary wire about one-half inch from a good ground and open and close the distributor points. If the secondary circuit is good, a sharp spark will jump from the end of the secondary wire to ground. If it does not, the coil or the secondary wire from the coil to the distributor cap is defective.

If a good spark jumps from the secondary wire to ground but none occurs at the spark plugs, the trouble is likely to be in the distributor rotor or the distributor cap. To test the rotor, hold the end of the secondary wire from the coil to the distributor cap one-quarter inch from the contact of the rotor (the center-tower contact) while the engine is cranked. A spark from the end of the wire to the rotor contact shows the rotor is grounded and must be replaced. No spark means that the trouble is in the distributor cap, spark-plug wires, or spark plugs.

All of the plugs or plug wires will rarely be defective at the same time, so trouble at these points can be discounted. The distributor cap can be at fault in several ways. It may have corroded terminals, carbonized leads inside the cap, or grease or dirt on the outside of the cap which cause the secondary current to short to ground.

Ignition Timing

A spark must reach the spark plug in each cylinder a specific number of degrees before the piston reaches TDC (top dead center) on the compression stroke. To make the spark arrive at the right time, it is necessary to adjust the distributor and this process is called *ignition timing.*

First, we shall look at the timing procedure for a conventional ignition system. Then we shall examine the procedure to be followed with three typical electronic ignition systems; namely, the Solid-State Ignition (SSI) system used by AMC, the Breakerless Induction-Discharge (BID) ignition, also used by AMC, and the Delco-Remy High-Energy Ignition (HEI) system.

Conventional system.   The distributor is adjusted by being turned in its mounting. Rotation in the direction opposite to normal cam rotation advances the spark (makes it occur earlier). Rotation in the same direction as normal cam rotation retards the spark.

There is a timing mark on the crankshaft pulley and a timing pointer is mounted adjacent to the pulley. Timing is correct when the pulley mark and the pointer are aligned.

Of course, with the engine running, it is not possible to see the pulley mark. To overcome this difficulty use is made of a stroboscopic light called a *timing light.* This light flashes every time the No. 1 plug fires and during these flashes of light the pulley appears to stand still.

A timing light has two leads for connection to the battery: one red (+) and one black (−). A third lead goes to the plug. To avoid the possibility of a shock *always* make the battery connections first. When the timing is completed, *always* remove the plug lead first.

To set the timing, loosen the clamp that holds the distributor in its mounting and turn the distributor in either direction. The markings on the pulley will then move ahead of the pointer or drop to a position behind the pointer. Move the distributor as necessary to make the mark and pointer align. Retighten the distributor clamp and check the timing once again before disconnecting the timing lamp.

Electronic ignition systems.   A scale located on the timing-chain cover and a notch milled into the vibration damper are used as references to set the ignition timing.

On the BID or SSI systems, first connect a tachometer to the ignition system (that is, to the distributor side of the coil and ground). There is a TACH terminal on HEI distributor caps. Some tachometers may not work with BID, SSI, or HEI ignition systems and there is a possibility that they could be damaged. It is good practice, therefore, to check with the tachometer manufacturer to make sure that it can be used.

Now disconnect the vacuum hose at the distributor vacuum unit. Plug the vacuum line to prevent leakage.

Next, connect a timing light in accordance with the manufacturer's instructions. If the light has an advance control, turn it OFF.

Start the engine and adjust the carburetor curb idle screw so that the engine on models through 1977 idles at 500 rpm. For 1978 models and later, set the screw at the specified idle speed at operating temperature. If there is a throttle-stop solenoid, it must be disconnected electrically.

Loosen the distributor clamp nut and, with the timing light aimed at the pointer marks, rotate the distributor until correct timing is achieved.

NOTE: On some models, a white paint mark is applied to the scale for the specified initial timing setting. Do not mistake this mark for TDC.

After the distributor clamp is retightened, check the timing again.

Finally, remove the plug from the vacuum hose and reconnect the hose at the distributor vacuum unit. Set the idle speed to specifications.

Other Difficulties

Four basic requirements must be met for an engine in good mechanical condition to start when cranked and to continue to run: a proper fuel-air mixture, sufficient compression, adequate ignition, and proper timing relationship of the valves and ignition to the piston stroke.

When an engine stops of its own accord, the cause of stoppage is often indicated by the action of the engine itself. If the fuel supply is cut off for any reason, the engine usually coughs or backfires and then gradually slows down. Electrical trouble is usually indicated by an irregular firing or a sudden stoppage of the firing. In either case, check the ignition system first and then the fuel system. Tests for both of these systems, as well as for timing and compression, have already been discussed.

Engine starts hard. This condition is often noted during the winter. When a condition of hard starting fails to improve after the usual checks and adjustments are made, a change from regular to high-test or to another brand of gasoline may eliminate the trouble.

Oils of lighter viscosity (10-10W or 20-20W), or all-weather oils, are intended for winter use. These oils let the pistons move more easily when the engine is cold, and the oil circulates more freely through the passages of the engine bearings. The use of heavy oil during cold weather imposes an extra load on the storage battery which is already working at reduced efficiency. Multiple viscosity oils, such as 10W-30, are recommended by most engine manufacturers.

Flooding, a common ailment during cold weather, is usually caused by a faulty automatic choke.

The ignition breaker points may be pitted, dirty, or improperly spaced.

Spark plugs may be fouled, improperly spaced, shorted by carbon, or have cracked insulators.

Because of the low battery efficiency during cold weather, the trouble may be due to a dirty starter commutator. High resistance caused by dirt increases the current required to turn the starter, and the ignition does not provide a hot enough spark.

Other causes of hard starting include the choke not closing fully, wrong ignition timing, a stuck valve, or the carburetor float level too low.

Engine misfire. A steady engine miss confined to one or two cylinders is usually easier to locate than an irregular miss. A so-called dead miss occurs when there is no cylinder explosion.

On V-8 engines, except those having a two-plane crankshaft, test each bank of cylinders as a separate four-cylinder engine. Assuming one cylinder has a dead-miss condition, remove the spark plug from that cylinder and insert it in a correctly firing cylinder. If the plug again causes a miss, the plug is at fault. If the miss does not follow the plug, the trouble is elsewhere. The most frequent causes of a dead miss under these conditions include the following: (1) spark-plug cable broken, grounded, or pulled partly out of the distributor socket; (2) wires interchanged at two spark plugs or in the distributor-cap sockets; (3) burned, warped, or sticking valves; (4) broken valve springs; or (5) cylinder-head gasket blown out at one cylinder or between two cylinders. A blown-out gasket between cylinders causes compression loss and missing on two adjacent cylinders. A blow-out into a cylinder water jacket causes water to appear in the cylinder spark plug. Another possible cause for the dead miss is the presence of carbonized paths in the distributor cap that cause a ground.

Idle or light-load misfire. When an engine misfires at idling speeds or under light loads, check the following: (1) spark-plug gap too small. (2) Intermittent high-voltage failure. Check by creating a small gap between the end of each plug wire in rotation and the plug terminals. Watch for skipping. When skipping is noted, check the various ignition units. (3) Incorrect fuel mixture resulting from air leaks in the intake manifold or the gaskets. A broken windshield-wiper hose will cause missing or erratic operation with a fully or partially closed throttle. To check, remove each line from the intake manifold and securely close the opening. The disappearance of the trouble indicates a leak in the line being tested. The fuel mixture may also be affected by air leaks at the valve guides. (4) Insufficient valve clearance may cause irregular operation at idling speeds by changing the opening and closing time of the valve, or by preventing complete closing under certain engine-temperature conditions.

A final cause for idle or light-load misfire is improper carburetion caused by any of the following: (a) float level too high or too low, (b) partially clogged idle-air passage or idle-gasoline jet, (c) improperly balanced idle-adjusting screws of duplex carburetor, (d) throttle valves of duplex carburetors not synchronized, (e) air leak between the upper and lower carburetor bodies around the idling tube, (f) air leak around the carburetor throttle shaft, (g) valves incorrectly timed—usually too early, (h) wrong spark timing—high-speed engines require at least 35° maximum advance, (i) ignition not synchronized, (j) cracked cylinder head or cylinder forming a passage through which compressed gas escapes into the water jacket, and (k) a defective positive crankcase ventilator valve or a leak in some part of the ventilating system.

Heavy-load or high-speed misfire.   Spark-plug gaps set too wide often cause missing under heavy pulling, quick acceleration, or high speeds, particularly when the ignition coil is not designed for a large gap load, short dwell, or short buildup period at high-speed operation.

When a high-speed engine misses and backfires at speeds above 35 mph, especially when warm, the spark plugs may be breaking down.

Plugs may be good but not operate correctly if they are the wrong type; e.g., if the insulators usually look pale white after use for some time, the plug is too hot and a cooler type should be substituted. Also, if the plug insulators crack at the lower end and the plugs are the type specified, the engine is probably running under hotter than normal conditions. Change to a cooler plug. Finally, if the upper part of the insulator is blackened just above the shell but the lower part of the plug is not sooted, use a cooler plug.

Other points to be checked when a miss occurs at high speed include the following: point gap too wide or too close; weak breaker-lever spring; breaker lever sticking; a weak or defective ignition coil or one not designed for high compression, high speeds, or the larger spark-plug gaps now specified for some engines; defective high-voltage wires; worn bearings on the distributor cam; burned contact points; an improperly adjusted carburetor; an obstruction in the fuel line; imperfect fuel-pump operation; improper operation of the hydraulic-valve mechanism; and preignition.

Lack of power at high speed.   This condition may result from several factors:

1. Cylinder compression unequal or insufficient. To check for unequal compression, run the engine at a speed corresponding to a road speed of 20 mph and listen to the exhaust noise. Uneven compression causes an uneven exhaust. Test the cylinders for compression with a pressure gauge. As a further check, pour about a teaspoonful of heavy engine oil into each cylinder through the spark-plug openings, and repeat the gauge test. If the gauge shows increased compression, leakage at the pistons and rings is indicated because the oil forms a temporary seal at these points. With no increase in gauge pressure, the leakage is probably at the valves. Leakage at the cylinder-head gasket between two cylinders is indicated when the gauge reading of the adjacent cylinders is low.

2. Improper carburetion due to poor carburetor adjustment, partial obstruction in the carburetor fuel line, carburetor air inlet obstructed, choke valve not opening fully, carburetor throttle loose on shaft, improper fuel-pump operation, or play in the accelerator linkage that prevents the throttle from opening completely.

3. Back pressure caused by obstructions or restrictions in the exhaust pipe, muffler, or tail pipe.

4. Excessive friction in running parts of engine, which might result from excessive tightness of main or connecting-rod bearings, use of inner rings in pistons, too heavy engine oil, or out-of-alignment connecting rod and piston. Rolling friction may result from dragging brakes, an out-of-line rear axle, or low tire pressure.

5. Carbon in the cylinders, improper ignition, incorrect ignition or valve timing, or a leaking intake manifold.

Backfiring through intake pipe and carburetor.   Backfiring through the carburetor when a cold engine is started is often unavoidable, and results from an improper mixture entering the cylinders at subnormal temperatures. When the engine warms up, the backfiring should stop if the choke is operating properly and the carburetor is adjusted correctly.

If the backfiring continues after warmup, look for one or more of the following causes: stuck or warped valves, especially the intake valve; an excessively lean mixture, caused by partial stoppage in the intake manifold; wrong valve timing; defective cylinder-head gasket between cylinders; incorrect ignition timing; preignition; poor quality fuel; and high-voltage wires improperly connected to spark plugs.

When an automobile engine backfires on a downhill grade with the throttle closed, the exhaust-pipe gasket may be broken or worn out, or the throttle may be closed too tightly. Depressing the accelerator pedal should stop the annoyance. A permanent remedy is a slightly increased idling speed.

Excessive engine vibration.   Some vibration accompanies the running of most engines and is most pronounced at the so-called critical speed.

Abnormal vibration may result from any of the following causes: unequal compression in the cylinders; misfiring; variations in piston and connecting-rod assembly weights in different cylinders; an improperly functioning vibration damper—the result of improper assembly or adjustment, looseness on crankshaft, or sticking in place; unsynchronized ignition-break contact points; unbalanced fan or loose fan blade; engine loose on mountings; unbalanced or sprung crankshaft; unbalanced flywheel; excessive clearance of camshaft or crankshaft front bearing or both; or excessive friction in engine due to a too-small clearance at pistons, connecting rods, or crankshaft and also to scored pistons, or too-heavy engine oil.

Troubleshooting Chart

The chart that follows shows various engine troubles, possible causes, and remedies. Use of this chart will save much time in correcting a given trouble.

Trouble	Cause	Remedy	Trouble	Cause	Remedy
Engine will not turn over.	Run-down battery	Recharge or replace.		Defective valve action	Make compression, leakage, and vacuum tests.
	Open starting circuit	Locate and eliminate.		Defective rings	Make compression, leakage, and vacuum tests.
	Bendix drive jammed.	Eliminate jamming.		Engine overheating	Check cooling system; service as needed.
	Starting motor jammed	Remove motor and repair.		Clogged exhaust	Locate and eliminate clogging.
	Engine jammed	Locate and eliminate source of jamming.		Manifold heat-control valve sticking	Service valve as needed.
Engine turns over slowly, but fails to start.	Run-down battery	Recharge or replace.	Engine lacks power, acceleration, or high-speed performance when hot.	Engine over-heating	Check cooling system; service as needed.
	Starting motor defective	Repair or replace.		Choke not operating properly	Repair or replace.
	Poor connections in starting circuit	Check, clean, and tighten all connections.		Manifold heat-control valve sticking	Service valve as needed.
	Undersized battery cables	Replace cables.		Vapor lock	Shield fuel line. Use different fuel.
Engine turns over normally, but fails to start	Ignition-system defect	Check ignition system and timing. Make spark test.	Engine lacks power, acceleration, or high-speed performance when cold.	Automatic choke sticking	Repair or replace.
	Fuel-system defect	Check fuel pump, choke, carburetor, and fuel line.		Thermostat sticking	Replace.
	Air leakage in carburetor or intake manifold	Check gaskets and replace if needed. Tighten all mountings.		Engine valves or manifold heat-control valve sticking	Service valves as needed.
	Defective engine	Make compression and leakage tests. Check valve action, timing, etc.	Engine lacks power, acceleration, or high-speed performance when hot or cold.	Ignition system	Check entire ignition system. Service as needed.
Engine runs, but cylinder misses.	Defective spark plug	Clean or replace.		Fuel system	Check fuel pump, carburetor, and air cleaner.
	Defective distributor cap or lead	Replace.		Throttle valve not opening fully	Adjust valve linkage.
	Defective rings or piston	Replace rings. Service piston as needed.		Compression loss	Make compression and leakage tests.
	Head gasket defective	Replace. Tighten all mountings.		Defective valves	Make compression, leakage, and vacuum tests.
Engine runs, but different cylinders missing.	Ignition system	Check ignition system and timing.		Clogged exhaust	Locate and eliminate clogging.
	Fuel system	Check fuel pump and carburetor.		Excessive engine carbon	Remove carbon.
	Compression loss	Make compression and leakage tests.		Wrong fuel or coil	Change as as needed.

Trouble	Cause	Remedy	Trouble	Cause	Remedy
Engine over-heating.	Resistance caused by low tire pressure, dragging brakes, etc.	Locate and correct as needed		Engine over-heating	See previous remedy.
	Lack of coolant	Add as needed.		Crankcase venti-lator valve malfunctioning	Service valve as needed.
	Loose or broken fan belt	Adjust or replace.		Defective carburetor dashpot	Replace or adjust as needed.
	Defective thermostat	Replace.	Engine backfires.	Ignition timing	Adjust as needed.
	Late ignition timing	Adjust as needed.		Wrong spark plugs	Change plugs.
	Water jackets clogged	Clean out.		Fuel mixture too lean or too rich	Adjust or repair carburetor or fuel pump.
	Defective hoses in cooling system	Replace.		Engine over-heating	See previous remedy.
	Defective water pump	Repair or replace.		Excessive carbon	Remove carbon
	Lack of engine oil	Add as needed.		Sticking valves	Service valves as needed.
	Late valve timing	Adjust as needed.		Distributor cap cracked	Replace cap.
	Fuel mixture too lean	Adjust carburetor.	Smoky exhaust.	If smoke is blue, cause is excessive oil consumption	See excessive oil consumption.
	Faulty or incorrect head gasket	Replace.		If smoke is black, cause is excessive fuel consumption	See excessive fuel consumption, below.
Engine idles roughly.	Carburetor idle adjustment incorrect	Adjust as needed.	Excessive oil consumption.	External leaks	Replace seals and gaskets as needed. Tighten all mountings.
	Crankcase venti-lator valve mal-functioning	Clean or replace.		High-speed driving	Adjust driving habits.
Engine stalls while warming up.	Choke valve stuck closed	Open valve. Repair automatic choke.		Oil being burned in combustion chamber	Check valve-stem clearance, piston rings, cylinders and cylinder walls, rod bearings, and vacuum pump diaphragm. Service as needed.
	Engine over-heating	See previous remedy.			
	Idling speed too low	Adjust as needed.			
	Sticking manifold heat-control valve	Service valve as needed.			
	Crankcase ventila-tor valve mal-functioning	Service valve as needed.	Excessive fuel consumption.	High-speed driving	Adjust driving habits.
Engine stalls after idling or low-speed driving.	Defective fuel pump	Repair or replace.		Short-run driving	If possible, extend runs.
	Engine over-heating	See previous remedy.		Fuel-pump pressure excessive, or pump leaks	Adjust or repair as needed.
	Carburetor float level high	Adjust as needed.		Choke remains partly closed after warmup	Repair or replace choke.
	Idling speed incorrect	Adjust as needed.		Air cleaner clogged	Clean or replace.
Engine stalls after high-speed driving.	Vapor lock	Shield fuel line. Use different fuel.		Carburetor float level high	Adjust as needed.
	Defective carburetor venting or idle compensa-tor valve	Replace or repair.			

Trouble	Cause	Remedy
	Float needle valve dirty or sticking	Free and clean thoroughly.
	Carburetor jets worn	Replace.
	Metering rod or full-power piston stuck	Service as needed.
	Idle adjustment too rich or too fast	Adjust as needed.
	Leaking carburetor	Service carburetor as needed.
	Accelerator-pump check valve stuck	Free and clean.
	Ignition system	Check plugs, coil, capacitor, points, wiring, and timing. Service as needed.
	Compression loss	Make compression and leakage tests.
	Defective valve action	Make compression, leakage, and vacuum tests.
	Clutch slipping	Adjust or repair as needed.
	Resistance caused by low tire pressure, dragging brakes, etc.	Locate and correct as needed.
Low oil pressure.	Engine bearings worn	Replace.
	Oil diluting or foaming	Replace oil.
	Lubricating system defective	Check oil pump, valve, and liners. Service as needed.
Engine knocks: Steady clicking.	Valves and tappets	Adjust valve clearances.
Ping or chatter on acceleration or load.	Fuel, carbon, or advanced timing (see engine backfires also.)	Change to higher octane fuel. Remove carbon, adjust timing.
Light knock or pounding with engine floating.	Worn connecting-rod bearing or crankpin, bent rod, or lack of oil	Replace bearings. Service crankpin. Realign rod. Add oil as needed.
Light metallic double knock, particularly during idling.	Worn or loose piston pin or bushing. Lack of oil	Service pin or bushing as needed. Add oil as needed.
Rattling or chattering during acceleration.	Worn or broken rings, low ring tension, or worn cylinder walls	Replace rings, and service cylinder walls as needed.

Trouble	Cause	Remedy
Hollow, bell-like sound when engine is cold.	Piston slap or lack of oil	Service pistons, cylinder walls and rods as needed. Add oil as needed.
Heavy and dull metallic sound during acceleration or under load when engine is cold.	If sound is regular, worn main bearings.	Replace bearings.
	If sound is irregular, worn end thrust bearings	Replace bearings.
Other noises or rattles.	Loose generator or alternator, horn, oil pan, or accessories.	Locate and tighten all mountings.
Engine continues to run after ignition turned off.	Idle speed too high	Adjust idle speed.
	Combustion chamber deposits	Remove heads and clean out carbon.
	Spark plug heat range too hot	Replace with correct heat range plugs.
	Engine over-heating	See previous remedy.
	Defective wiring or switch	Check and correct.

7

FUEL AND EMISSION CONTROL SYSTEMS

Contents

FUEL SYSTEMS

Gasoline Additives

Tetraethyl lead. The antiknock additive used in most brands of gasoline is tetraethyl lead (TEL). Refiners use TEL almost universally because, with it, a given octane number is attained more cheaply than by the extra refining steps needed to bring clear (white) gasoline up to an equivalent quality.

With pollution making headlines, unleaded gasoline may help meet the limitations imposed on exhaust emissions. The reasons most often given for the reduction of TEL are: (a) lead may be a potential health hazard; (b) lead particles contribute to impaired visibility; (c) lead deposits increase hydrocarbon emissions; and (d) lead interferes with advanced emission control.

Antioxidant inhibitor. Additives found in all acceptable gasolines are the antioxidant inhibitors which, for periods of six months to a year under normal storage conditions, keep oxygen in the air from joining the unstable hydrocarbons found in gasoline. One antioxidant, known as chelate, guards against the damage gasoline causes to certain metals, particularly copper.

Tricresylphosphate. Tricresylphosphate (TCP) and trimethylphosphate (TMP) are additives that soften the deposits on spark-plug electrodes and within cylinder heads to the point where the electrodes and cylinder heads become self-cleaning. The deposits are simply blown out of the exhaust during normal engine acceleration. Either TCP or TMP can at least double spark-plug life. It is claimed by several marketers that boron does the job equally as well as TCP.

Other cleaning additives, called detergents, are found only in certain premium gasolines. One company thinks highly enough of its detergent to guarantee regular users that it will, over a short period of time, literally give the carburetor a mechanical enema.

Alcohol and platformate. Alcohol has become a popular winter additive to prevent carburetor and fuel-line icing. The alcohol absorbs and neutralizes the water that forms through condensation in the fuel system. Fuel-system icing, surprisingly, is most prevalent in a damp spring or early fall when temperatures average 40°F.

Platformate is an additive that gives higher lbs. and volatility. This increases mileage slightly, but measurably.

Combustion

Fuel ratios. One gallon of gasoline, weighing 6.2 lbs. when combined with 94 lbs. of air and burned in an engine, theoretically produces 19.1 lbs. of carbon dioxide, 8.9 lbs.

of water, and 72.2 lbs. of nitrogen. Thus the air-to-fuel ratio is approximately 15 to 1. In practice, the carburetor varies this ratio from about 12 to 1 at idle to as much as 17 to 1 at cruising speeds. At ratios under 15 to 1, there is not enough oxygen to burn off the hydrogen and carbon in the gasoline mixture, and the partially burned materials leave the engine in the form of carbon monoxide, methane, and other more complex gaseous hydrocarbons.

Since air is less dense at high altitudes than at sea level, the air-to-fuel ratio can vary enough to require some carburetor adjustment in long trips from low-altitude to high-altitude regions.

Mixtures of gasoline and air. A lean mixture is one that contains less vapor than it can absorb. A rich mixture is one that contains more vapor than it can absorb. The ideal air-to-gasoline vapor ratio is 15.17 to 1, but is not achieved in automobile engines. Actual ratios run from 11 through 17 to 1 while a well-tuned engine is operating through its normal speed range.

As a general rule of thumb, if the exhaust pipe of a car is coated with an almost black deposit, an overly rich mixture is being burned. If the deposit is medium to light gray in color, the proper mixture is being received. Finally, if the coating is more white than gray, the mixture is too lean. This rule does not hold true, however, for a properly tuned car that has made only short trips, or for properly tuned but badly worn engines.

A lean mixture will burn, but gives less power and creates more heat. Continued operation on an excessively lean mixture may burn and warp the exhaust valves, or may, at least, create a condition that promotes preignition.

A rich mixture wastes both power potential and fuel. Continued rich operation causes rapid wear within the engine, since the unburned gasoline dilutes the lubricating oil. Under certain conditions, gasoline vapors collecting in the crankcase may explode, and there is also the possibility of secondary, uncontrolled ignition in the cylinder head.

Combustion. Combustion is simply the joining together of two or more elements so rapidly that heat and light are produced. Oxygen seeks out the hydrocarbons that make up gasoline. When gasoline in vaporized form is pressed by the piston against the cylinder head and ignited, the mixture of oxygen and carbon tends to burn explosively. The release of this tremendous force (estimated to range from 2 to 4 tons) against the head of the piston powers the car. Further, only a tiny amount of gasoline is burned on each power stroke.

Combustion must be precisely controlled if its potentially destructive force is to be turned into useful work. In a four-cycle engine, the mixture for the carburetor must be sucked through a valve that opens at a specified time. Then, as the piston nears the top of its compression stroke, the distributor must signal the spark plug to fire. The spark is usually timed so that peak pressures from the resulting combustion occur on the power stroke between 10° and 20° after the piston reaches top dead center. Finally, the piston pushes the exhaust gases out through another valve.

Each of these events occurs approximately 7,100 times per minute in the V-8 engine of a car traveling at 70 mph. The wall of flame spreading out from the plug when it fires travels between 20 and 150 feet per second. Pressures within the cylinder jump from 160 to almost 600 psi each time the charge is fired. If these forces were not properly timed, the engine would be destroyed in a fraction of a second.

Detonation.   Detonation is simply the explosion of the last part of the fuel-air charge. The ping one hears comes from the explosion banging against the metal of the combustion-chamber parts, usually the piston itself. If severe, or prolonged, detonation may be destructive. In any case, a power loss is noticeable during periods of detonation. Except in the most severe cases, the bulk of the charge is burned in a normal, controlled manner. However, the advancing wall of flame compresses the overheats the remaining unburned charge, and the charge explodes. This explains why detonation is sometimes called self-ignition or autoignition.

The two most common causes of detonation are use of a fuel with an octane number lower than that required by the engine, and a spark setting that is too advanced.

Preignition and postignition are advanced forms of detonation that require immediate attention to prevent destruction of the engine. The causes are various. They include carbon deposits and cooling-system blockages, improper spark plugs, rough edges on a reconditioned valve, and exposed gasket edges. In effect, the distributor loses its control over the firing of the charge, and the result is almost immediately cumulative. The additives TCP and TMP are effective in preventing the formation of deposits that contribute to preignition and postignition.

PRINCIPLES OF CARBURETION

A carburetor *atomizes* and *vaporizes* gasoline and mixes the vapor with air in the proper proportions to form a combustible mixture at all engine speeds.

Atomizing means changing the liquid fuel mechanically into a very finely divided spray. *Vaporizing* means to change the spray into a vapor. For all practical purposes, both processes take place simultaneously in a carburetor. Atomizing is accomplished by having the liquid fuel issue from a small orifice or jet at fairly high speed into an air current moving at high speed and low pressure. Vaporizing is accomplished by applying heat to the atomized fuel-air mixture.

Fuel is pumped into a carburetor through an inlet seat and fills the float bowl. See Figure 7-1. The fuel, rising in the bowl, lifts the float, which pushes a needle into the seat.

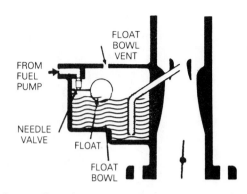

Fig. 7-1.   Carburetor float circuit. *Courtesy of United Delco Division, General Motors Corporation.*

Whenever the float drops enough to let the needle come off its seat, additional fuel flows into the bowl. Too much fuel in the bowl will make the fuel-air mixture too rich, and too little fuel will make the mixture too lean.

Main Metering System

Gasoline from the float bowl is then mixed with air and fed into the carburetor. The base of every carburetor is simply an air valve with throttle plates suspended on a shaft controlled by the accelerator pedal. When you step on the pedal, the throttle valve opens and the amount of air entering the engine increases. To mix air and gasoline in correct proportions, a tube is run from the float bowl to the middle of the air stream. The end of the tube is called the *main nozzle* and is positioned in the center of the *venturi*, which is the narrow section of the air passage. Because the venturi is narrow, it causes reduced pressure at the end of the tube, and this reduced pressure (suction) draws fuel from the float bowl. (Actually, the atmospheric pressure exerted through the float bowl vent pushes fuel out of the nozzle.) When the fuel enters the air stream it atomizes, then goes past the throttle valve on its way to the combustion chamber. The main nozzle is connected by a tube to the *main well*, which is located at the bottom of the float bowl. Fuel enters the main well through a calibrated hole called the *main jet*.

There may be *air bleeds* (small baffles) in the main nozzle and vacuum- or mechanically-operated *metering rods* in the main jet. These refinements ensure the metering of the correct amount of fuel to the engine under all operating conditions. Between idling and wide-open throttle, the metering rods are moved further into the jet stream.

Mechanically-operated rods are lifted by a lever hooked to the throttle. Vacuum-operated rods are pushed out of the jet by a spring and pulled down into the jet by engine vacuum acting on a piston hooked to the top of the rod. A passageway from the intake manifold runs up through the carburetor so that engine vacuum can act on the piston.

A carburetor must have engine vacuum in order to work. At idling speed, the vacuum that exists below the

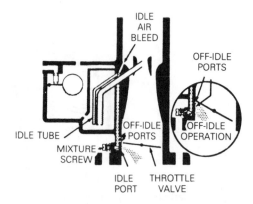

Fig. 7-2. Carburetor idle and low-speed circuit. *Courtesy of United Delco Division, General Motors Corporation.*

throttle valves of a properly operating engine ranges from about 18-in. Hg. to 21-in. Hg. As the throttle is opened, the vacuum drops off until, at wide-open throttle, it is zero.

The Idle System

At idle, the engine draws air through the throttle valve, which is slightly open. However, the air is not mixed with fuel at this point. Instead, the fuel comes through an *idle port* located below the throttle plate. See Figure 7-2. An *idle-mixture screw* (needle valve) screws into the outside of the throttle body and is used to regulate the amount of fuel flowing through the port.

Fuel enters the idle system through a tube mounted in the carburetor; usually between the float bowl and the carburetor throat (air horn). The end of the tube is a calibrated hole called the *idle air bleed* or *idle jet*.

As the throttle opens, vacuum beneath the throttle valve decreases and less fuel flows through the idle port. To keep the engine running, another hole, called the *off-idle port* or the *idle transfer*, is uncovered, and through it more fuel is fed to the engine. In a very short time, enough air is coming through the venturi to let the main metering system resume operation. Surprisingly enough, however, the idle system in most carburetors continues to operate at speeds up to about 70 mph.

Accelerating Pump

If the throttle is suddenly opened wide, a large amount of air passes through the throttle plates, but fuel from the main nozzle is inadequate to prevent lean operation and poor engine performance. An *accelerating pump*, Figure 7-3, is used to solve this problem. This pump is simply a piston which operates in a well or cylinder. The piston is hooked to the throttle linkage. When the accelerator is depressed, a squirt of fuel goes into the carburetor throat. The pump operates only when the throttle is opened suddenly.

The pump system includes intake and discharge check valves to let the piston pull fuel from the bowl into its cyl-

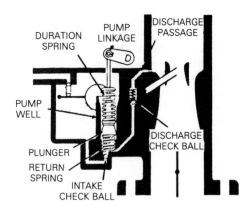

Fig. 7-3. Accelerator pump circuit. *Courtesy of United Delco Division, General Motors Corporation.*

inder on the upstroke and squirt fuel into the carburetor throat on the downstroke.

Some pumps have a so-called duration spring that pushes the pump down and makes it operate for a fixed length of time, regardless of how fast the accelerator is depressed.

The jet that controls the amount of fuel injected by the accelerating pump is usually built into the pump nozzle, which is mounted above the venturi.

Power System

Main metering jets, with or without metering rods, provide adequate fuel for the idling and most cruising speeds. At wide-open throttle, however, more fuel is needed, and is provided by the *power system*. See Figure 7-4.

To admit more fuel, another passage runs from the main well up into the main nozzle. This passage is closed except when the throttle is opened wide enough to let engine vacuum fall below approximately 10-in. Hg. A spring, which opposes the engine vacuum, then opens a power

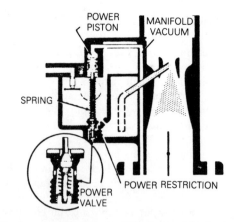

Figure 7-4. Carburetor power circuit. *Courtesy of United Delco Division, General Motors Corporation.*

valve to let additional fuel enter the main well and go through the main nozzle into the venturi.

Both mechanical and vacuum-operated power valves are in use. In some carburetors, the power valve is at the bottom of the accelerating pump well. At wide-open throttle, the accelerating pump bottoms and tips a plunger to open the power valve. The power valve that operates by means of engine vacuum opposed by a spring may be a piston operating in a cylinder or a diaphragm.

High-speed pullover

To cut down on emission, the main jets on late-model cars are lean, and there is not enough fuel supplied when the car operates in a high-rpm, part-throttle condition. At part throttle, the metering rod does not lift to its high-speed position because the engine vacuum is still too high, but the engine needs more fuel because of the high rpm. To provide the additional fuel, some carburetors include a *pullover* system. This sytem consists of a passageway from the float bowl up to the carburetor air horn, which is located above the choke valve. Because the opening is sensitive to air velocity, the pullover hole feeds additional fuel into the airstream when the engine operates at high rpm. Pullover starts at about 50 mph on part throttle. Other names used for pullover include high-speed fuel feed and auxiliary fuel feed.

Choke system

A *choke system*, Figure 7-5, is needed to start the carburetor. If the engine could be heated to operating temperature before starting there would be no need for a choke.

A cold engine makes fuel condense out of the mixture onto the intake manifold passageways and walls of the combustion chamber. Since fuel must be mixed with air to burn, more fuel must be supplied to compensate for that which condenses. The choke is an air valve located above the main nozzle so that it can shut off all air going to the engine. The

high vacuum in the carburetor throat then lets the pressure in the fuel bowl push more fuel through the main nozzle.

A major problem with chokes is getting them to open at the right time. The choke is closed by a thermostatic coil spring and opened by the same spring when heat from the exhaust manifold is adequate. For more positive action, a vacuum piston opposes the spring, and the choke valve itself is offset so that air entering the carburetor tends to push it open. The combination is called an automatic choke.

While the choke is operating, the engine must run at a faster than normal idle to use the extremely rich mixture. To accomplish this, a fast-idle cam and linkage works in conjunction with the choke.

Multiple-Barrel Carburetors

In a two-barrel carburetor, the main metering and idle systems are duplicated for the second barrel (throat). A single fuel bowl has enough capacity to supply the two main jets, and only one accelerating pump is needed. The pump has two nozzles, however, one for each barrel.

The power system is basically the same, but feeds two main metering systems. The choke valve is simply made big enough to cover both carburetor throats.

In a four-barrel carburetor, the engine runs normally on two barrels, called the *primaries;* the other two referred to as the *secondaries*, operate only at high engine speed.

The design of four-barrel carburetors varies widely, and there is no general method of feeding the secondaries. There is, of course, a main metering system, but there may also be a power system and even an idle system.

Secondaries may be controlled mechanically or by vacuum. The mechanically controlled type start to open when the primaries reach about three-quarter throttle. The secondaries open at a faster rate than the primaries so that all are wide open at full throttle.

On mechanically controlled secondaries, the driver may open the throttle excessively at low speed. Compensation for this is provided by an air valve, or velocity valve, located in the secondary barrels above the throttle valve. This valve does not open until the air velocity is great enough to raise a weight or compress a spring.

Vacuum-controlled secondaries are operated either by manifold vacuum or venturi vacuum and open only when the engine needs more air.

Carburetor Heat

At low speeds, the fuel mixture is moving slowly through the intake passages, and there is a tendency for droplets of fuel to fall out of the airstream. A heated manifold helps keep the fuel vaporized. The exhaust gases, which are channeled up under the base of the carburetor, produce heat to the intake passages. To keep the heat from the fuel in the carburetor bowl, some carburetors are installed on the manifold with a large insulating block or extra thick gasket.

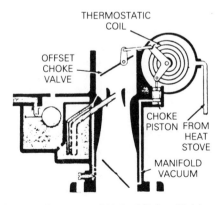

Fig. 7-5. Choke system. *Courtesy of United Delco Division, General Motors Corporation.*

Anti-stall Dashpot

If the accelerator is pressed down hard, then released suddenly, an anti-stall dashpot, also known as a slow-closing throttle dashpot, keeps the engine from stalling. This device keeps the throttle open for a few seconds and allows it to come down to idle slowly. Thus, the engine has enough time to burn off the rich mixture.

CARBURETOR TROUBLESHOOTING

Cleaning

Most problems attributed to the carburetor are actually caused by bad ignition timing, worn spark plugs, loss of compression, poor fuel delivery to the carburetor, or a clogged air cleaner. Before you even touch the carburetor check the heat riser, intake-manifold bolts, compression, ignition, fuel-pump pressure and volume, and the crankcase vent system.

With so few moving parts, carburetors are not usually subject to wear. Probably the biggest offenders in this respect are the throttle shaft and the accelerating pump. Nevertheless, a carburetor does get dirty. Regardless of how well you maintain the air cleaner and fuel-line filter, both admit some dirt into the carburetor. In addition, the heavier fractions of gasoline form a gumlike substance in all parts of the carburetor.

Cleaner added to the gas tank three or four times a year from the time a car is new does a fairly good job in keeping the carburetor clean.

Cleaning solvent can also be introduced directly into the carburetor through a gravity-feed kit, such as that made by the Gumout Division of Pennsylvania Refining Co. To use this cleaner, disconnect the gas line at the carburetor and block off the line with the fitting provided with the kit. Attach the flexible hose supplied with the kit to the gas-inlet port, using the adapter that fits the hole. Start the engine and run it at various speeds. Occasionally, place the palm of your hand over the carburetor to block off air and force the cleaner into all gasoline and air passages.

If the above procedures prove ineffective, it is time to dismantle the carburetor for cleaning. Before starting, make yourself one promise. Do the disassembly, cleaning, and reassembly without making any adjustments, even if you have to replace parts such as accelerating pumps and needle seats. Replace both old and new parts in the same positions in which you found them, and check the manufacturer's specifications carefully.

To take off the carburetor, first remove the base nuts, then the throttle linkage, hot-air tube to the choke housing (if used), and any wires to such things as transmission kickdown switches, or air-conditioning idle speed-up switches. Now place the carburetor on a clean working surface.

Dismantle the carburetor only to the extent needed. As a rule, remove anything with a gasket so that the gasket can be renewed during reassembly. Remove any screw-in jet so that the cleaning fluid can enter the passages behind the jet. If the choke vacuum pistons are built into the carburetor, remove them also. The same applies to screw-in power valves, but if they are pressed or staked in, leave them alone.

Keep all small parts together in a close-screened container, and place the large parts in the basket that comes with the cleaner. Make absolutely sure any rubber or neoprene parts are removed before immersing the remaining parts in the cleaner. If you don't, the cleaner will ruin them. Keep your fingers away from the cleaner—it's a very powerful chemical solution. It is also wise to wear safety glasses to protect eyes against splashing.

Immerse all parts for the length of time recommended by the cleaner manufacturer, then remove the parts from the cleaner and allow them to drain. Then, to wash out the cleaner, submerge all parts in kerosene. Use a brush to remove any remaining deposits.

Remove all parts and blow all passages with compressed air, or with a tire pump, to remove any remaining stubborn dirt.

While reassembling the carburetor you will set the float level, but this is usually the only internal adjustment. After the carburetor is reassembled, refer to the sheet included with the repair kit, or to auto repair manuals or shop manuals, to make the many external adjustments needed for the carburetor to work properly.

Idle-Mixture Adjustment

If possible, always use your fingers to adjust mixture needles. If it is absolutely necessary to use a screwdriver, be careful to avoid screwing the needle in too far. If you force it into the idle porthole, it will either be ridged or break off.

The needle is screwed inward for a leaner mixture and outward for a richer mixture. On older cars, not equipped with smog-control devices, the usual setting is about 1½ to 2 turns out from the completely closed position. Emission-control carburetors may require as many as 3 turns to keep running. When making the adjustments, the engine must be at operating temperature, with the choke not operating, and the fast-idle cam must not be holding the throttle open.

Obtain and carefully follow the specifications for the car on which you are working. On some cars, for example, the headlights must be on when the idle-adjustment is made. Always know for sure what conditions must be met.

The idling point at which the engine starts to falter is called the *lean fall-off point*. The idling point at which the mixture is so rich that the engine starts to run rapidly is called the *rich fall-off point*.

On autos not equipped with smog-control devices, the idle needle usually is set a bit toward the lean fall-off point to obtain better mileage. On late-model cars, the mixture is made progressively leaner until the rpm drops by a specified amount. This is necessary so that the car can pass the idle emission test. If the adjustment is done in strict accordance with factory specifications, the idle will prove satisfactory.

Engines with air pumps must burn up hydrocarbons, thus requiring a somewhat richer mixture. The usual setting is about one-quarter turn (in the richer direction) from the lean fall-off point.

Air-Fuel Mixture

Power, performance, and smoothness are all dependent upon having the correct air-fuel mixture. A good carburetor mechanic uses an exhaust-gas analyzer to measure the air-fuel ratio accurately. The analyzer samples the exhaust, and the ratio of air to fuel (by weight) is indicated on a meter. With emission-control carburetors, mixtures as lean as 20 to 1 are not uncommon. On older cars, the mixtures run from about 11 to 1 through 16 to 1.

Most exhaust-gas analyzers will not handle mixtures as lean as 20 to 1 and the trend is toward the use of hydrocarbon meters, which are very expensive. To avoid a big investment, let a properly equipped shop do the job for you.

If a satisfactory mixture cannot be obtained, and the car idles unsatisfactorily or stalls frequently, the carburetor probably needs a good cleaning. First, however, check for such things as vacuum leaks, continuity in the ignition wiring system, initial ignition timing, the condition of distributor points, the distributor dwell angle, and the spark plugs.

Float Level

A leaking or dented float cannot maintain the proper level. In either case, replace the float. A leak can be detected by removing the float and shaking it; if there is gasoline in the float, it will slosh around. Also keep in mind that the only time a float can be dented is when it has been installed improperly.

Checking and setting the float level requires special gauges that vary from one make or model of carburetor to another. However, a combination straightedge and steel scale may be substituted. The level is usually specified by a measurement from the top of the float to the edge of the bowl flange. Sometimes the float may not be in a perfectly horizontal position when set to the specified level. In any case, the setting varies among carburetors, so consult the manufacturer's specfications. To change the level, remove the float and gently bend the vertical lip only (toward the float to raise the level and away from the float to lower the level). On some carburetors the small float hinge pin drops out easily, so guard against losing it.

Crankcase Ventilation Valves

These valves, often called smog valves, cause mixture problems because they allow crankcase vapors to enter the engine. On an engine in good condition, the vapors are mostly unburned fuel or just air, but if the engine is badly worn, oil smoke is mixed with the vapors.

Make sure the valve is clean and that all connecting hoses have no leaks. If the valve is an orifice type, visual inspection is adequate. On plunger-type valves, shake the valve to make sure the plunger is free inside.

Most car manufacturers recommend replacement rather than cleaning of crankcase ventilator valves. When cleaning is approved, use a carburetor cleaner.

To see if the valve is plugged or restricted, pinch the hose or put your finger over the end of the valve. Since this takes away some air and gasoline from the idle mixture, the engine should idle slower.

Accelerating Pump

Trouble in the accelerating pump can be diagnosed only during a road test. A malfunction is indicated by flat spots when accelerating heavily from a low speed while in high gear or drive. Stop the car, remove the air cleaner and, while accelerating the engine by hand, note the stream from the pump outlet. If the pump is O.K., it produces a healthy squirt of fuel. If the stream is thin, deflected, or just a dribble, inspect the pump jet for clogging or damage. Most often, though, the leather on the piston has shrunk or dried. The most common cause of premature deterioration of the leather packing is water in the fuel system. Also, dirt may get under the ball check valves in the pump system and keep them from seating properly. This symptom is most noticeable at low speeds.

All carburetors provide for alternate settings of the pump stroke. Most car owners don't bother changing the settings, but use the medium stroke (middle hole in the linkage) as it is set at the factory. For optimum pump performance in winter, however, the long hole (farthest away from the throttle shaft) should be used. During extremely hot weather, use the nearest hole. The short stroke should also be used for high-altitude driving, but remember to change the setting back to the middle hole as soon as driving conditions permit. The adjustment is very easily made.

Choke

About all that can go wrong with a manually operated choke is binding, which is caused by wear in the linkage or damage to the carburetor air horn. Neither the choke nor the throttle linkage should be oiled on modern cars, since the bearings are made of self-lubricating nylon. If the bearings wear, they are easy to replace. Some choke linkages are composed mainly of a flexible cable that will not work properly if kinked. Damage to the carburetor air horn invariably stems from overtightening the air cleaner. If, on a carburetor equipped with an automatic choke, the moving parts just described can be actuated freely by hand, the governing (sensing) unit is faulty and should be replaced.

Carburetor Air Cleaners

The two most common types of air cleaner are the throwaway accreted-paper type and the polyurethane type, which

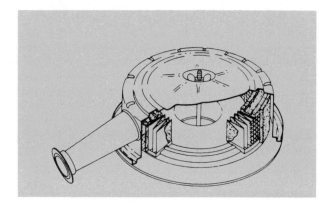

Fig. 7-6   Combination type air cleaner.

can be cleaned and reused. A combination type, shown in Fig. 7-6, features an oil-wetted paper element and an outer covering of oil-wetted polyurethane which is removable for cleaning. Heavy-duty air cleaners provide a well to hold additional engine oil.

An element should be cleaned every 6,000 miles or every six months, whichever comes first. When the car is operated on unpaved roads or in desert country, the frequency of cleaning should be increased considerably. The element is easily removed by simply unscrewing the wing nut holding the cover in place and lifting off the entire cleaner assembly. The assembly itself should be cleaned thoroughly when the element is cleaned or replaced. Be sure to obtain the proper new part number; although one element may look much like another, small differences in dimensions may render it ineffective in the wrong housing. Some elements also act as the carburetor air silencer and must not be installed upside down.

Ram-Air Intake

The ram-air induction system used on some *muscle* cars allows cooler, and thus denser, outside air to be forced through the hood scoops and into the air cleaner during open throttle or heavy load conditions. During normal engine operation, air enters the air cleaner through the conventional duct and valve assembly.

A manually operated ram-air intake consists of a valve mounted behind the hood scoops, which is operated by a cable inside the car. Air enters by way of the hood scoops or from under the hood, depending on the position of the valve. The air is then routed to a plenum, where it is directed to the carburetor by way of the air cleaner.

In a vacuum controlled ram-air intake, when intake manifold vacuum drops, as during periods of open throttle or heavy load conditions, the vacuum motor causes the ram-air door to open. When the engine is running under normal conditions, the intake manifold vacuum is high, and the vacuum motor keeps the ram-air door closed.

Exhaust Manifold Heat Valve (Heat Riser)

A thermostatically controlled heat valve in the outlet passage of the exhaust manifold directs heat from the exhaust manifold to the floor of the intake manifold for better fuel vaporization during engine warm-up.

When the engine is cold, the valve is closed, directing the hot exhaust gases through a passage in the intake manifold. As the engine warms up, the thermostatic heat-control valve opens, and the exhaust gases are no longer passed through the intake manifold.

The valve must operate freely and should be lubricated as recommended by the automobile manufacturer. The valve and components may be replaced with a service kit.

A vacuum operated heat-riser valve is now used on many engines. The valve is controlled by a temperature sensitive vacuum switch. Names used for this type of arrangement include Power Heat Control Valve (Chrysler), Early Fuel Evaporation (General Motors) and Vacuum Operated Exhaust Heat Valve (Ford).

All heat-riser valves are closed by manifold vacuum and exhaust gases are forced through a crossover passage in the intake manifold. In addition, there is a temperature-sensitive device that shuts the vacuum off once the engine is warmed up.

Ford and Chrysler products have a temperature-sensitive vacuum switch on the intake manifold coolant passage. The Ford switch has three hose connections, but one is a vent with a filter that keeps dirt out. The Chrysler switch has only two hose connections. But in addition to shutting off the manifold vacuum, this switch also controls the vacuum supply to an idle enrichment system and an air switching valve.

General Motors uses either a coolant vacuum switch or a vacuum solenoid connected to an oil-temperature switch. The coolant vacuum switch has two hose connections and a vent when it controls the heat valve only. When it is joined to other emission control systems, it has up to five hose connections plus a vent. Some GM products also have a check valve in the hose so that vacuum is trapped in the heat valve actuator when the engine is accelerated. This keeps the heat valve closed and prevents a rattle.

Gasoline Strainers

On any car that does not come with a factory installed gasoline strainer, do yourself a favor and install one. It is placed in the fuel line directly ahead of the carburetor to prevent the passage of lint, dirt, dust, water, and metallic particles.

Most auto manufacturers recommend cleaning or replacing the element, depending upon the type, at least every 12,000 miles. To replace the filter, simply disconnect the fuel line at the filter, insert a new filter, and reconnect the line.

Water and Other Foreign Material in the Gas Tank

A missing gas-tank cap may let water enter the fuel tank. Even a small amount of water, when mixed with gasoline, causes poor engine performance; any substantial amount causes engine stoppage. Of course, the only remedy is to remove the drain plug and empty the tank. Then replace the drain plug, fill the tank with clean fuel, and install a new cap.

Dirt in the fuel tank may clog the filter, which is located inside the tank. If this happens, remove the drain plug to empty the tank and disconnect the supply line to the engine at any convenient point prior to connection with an accessory. Apply a very limited amount of compressed air through the point of disconnection toward the tank. Increase the air pressure gradually as the filter starts to open. When the filter is completely clean, flush the tank with a little clean gasoline. Then reinstall the drain plug and fill the tank with clean gasoline.

FUEL PUMPS

Mechanical Fuel Pump

Figure 7-7 shows a cross section of a modern mechanical fuel pump. Power is applied to the *rocker arm* by an *eccentric* machined into the engine crankshaft. The rocker arm, which is pivoted on the *pin*, pulls the fuel *diaphragm* upward by means of the *connecting pull rod*. The vacuum created by the upward motion of the diaphragm causes atmospheric pressure to push gasoline from the supply tank through the inlet valve and into the fuel chamber of the pump. The need for atmospheric pressure at all times in the supply tank accounts for the fact that air must be allowed to enter the tank. The return stroke, caused by the rotating

eccentric, releases the compressed diaphragm spring, expelling fuel through the outlet valve and sending it to the carburetor bowl. The rocker-arm spring holds the rocker arm in contact with the eccentric on the engine camshaft, so that the rocker arm swings up and down as the shaft rotates.

Fuel pumps are usually designed to pump from two to three times the amount of gas required by the carburetor. Thus, when the immediate needs of the engine have been satisfied, continued operation of the fuel pump starts to fill the carburetor bowl and causes the float to rise. At a point determined by the float adjustment, the float arm seats the needle valve. The seated valve prevents more fuel from entering the carburetor. When the needle valve is closed and held in place by the pressure of the fuel on the float, the pump builds up pressure in the fuel chamber until it overcomes the pressure of the diaphragm spring. This pressure results in almost complete stoppage of diaphragm movement until more fuel is needed.

Air-conditioner equipped cars use a fuel pump with a bypass passage that continually returns part of the fuel to the fuel tank. This bypass also returns fuel vapors that may form in the lines or pump under high operating temperatures.

Electric Fuel Pump

Electric fuel pumps come in a variety of designs in which operation depends on the movement of a plunger, diaphragm, bellows, or impeller. The impeller type, Figure 7-8, is mounted in the fuel tank and has a motor-driven impeller that pushes fuel through the fuel line to the carburetor. Tank mounting is preferred for electric fuel pumps because the entire line to the carburetor is then pressurized. Consequently, vapor bubbles are very unlikely to form even if the line gets hot, and this virtually eliminates the possibility of a vapor lock. Moreover, the pump runs cooler in this location than it would, for example, in the engine compartment.

Electric fuel pumps are very reliable. But in any system where they are on the line and in action whenever the ignition switch is on, they are potentially dangerous should

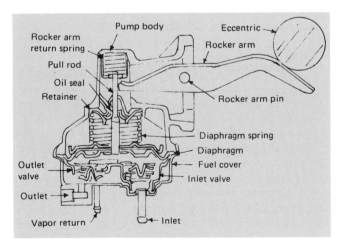

Fig. 7-7 Typical mechanical fuel pump. *Courtesy of AC Spark Plug Division, General Motors Corporation.*

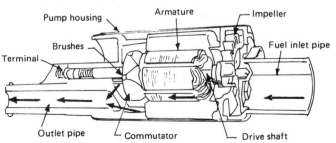

Fig. 7-8 Impeller-type electric fuel pump. *Courtesy of Buick Motor Division, General Motors Corporation.*

the fuel line be accidentally ruptured. One relatively simple way to avoid this hazard is to have a single-pole double-throw switch controlled by the action of a diaphragm located in the engine oil system.

When the engine is cranked, the starter solenoid is energized through the ignition switch. As long as the starter solenoid is energized and the engine oil pressure is less than 3 psi, current is also supplied to the fuel pump through normally closed contacts on the control switch.

When the ignition switch is turned off, the pump circuit is de-energized. The same thing occurs, of course, should the engine stop or stall.

TROUBLESHOOTING FUEL PUMPS

Rate of Fuel Flow

Once a fuel pump is known to be defective, replace it with a new unit. An attempt to repair or rebuild the old pump is frequently unsatisfactory.

A fuel pump may supply either too little, or in some rare cases too much, fuel. To check the rate of flow observe the following procedures:

First, disconnect the pump-to-carburetor line at any convenient point. If you disconnect the line at the carburetor, however, keep in mind that either the line itself, or the fuel filter, may be the cause of difficulty. Leave the pump in place initially.

In a road emergency, cranking the engine with the line disconnected will show if the fuel is flowing from the pump. Holding a finger over the line will give an indication of the degree of pumping action, but this check is very inconclusive unless you are very familiar with how the pump normally acts. It is preferable to use an inexpensive fuel-pump analyzer, which can be obtained at any auto-supply house. The analyzer is placed in the line to measure the pressure delivered by the pump at cranking speed. Acceptable pressure ranges, specified by the pump maker, run from 1 lb. to as much as 12½ lbs. The most common spread in a light six-cylinder car is from 2 to 4 lbs. Higher spreads and maximums are encountered in V-8 engines.

In addition to the analyzer reading you should also obtain a flow reading. Attach a flexible line to the open connection and direct the flow of gasoline into a graduated container. The average car should deliver about three-quarters of a pint at cranking speed, and not more than 1 pt., in exactly one minute. The exact amount for each common make of pump is specified in the literature furnished with the analyzer.

In most analyzer designs, a bypass valve is provided to feed gasoline to the graduated container.

During any of the tests just described, make sure the ignition switch is in the OFF position; operate the starter by jumping the solenoid terminals.

Too Little Flow

If the analyzer shows little or no fuel flow from the pump, first check for a leak in the bowl gasket. A gasket problem is easy to spot. Next look for loose fuel-line connections, checking all the way back to the gas tank. Actually, a serious leak is not always as evident as a minor one, because the heavier flow of gasoline, as compared to the seepage, washes away the telltale dye contained in the gasoline. Thus, it is wise to make a physical check of each fuel-line connection. While following the line to the supply tank, watch for deterioration of, or damage to, flexible hose or for kinks in the metal portion of the line. Near to the tank, check to make sure it is properly vented. If the pump is equipped with an integral strainer or filter, remove the element and clean it with solvent and compressed air. If the element is of the secreted (porous aggregate) throwaway variety, replace it with a new one.

If none of the preceding checks bring fuel flow, disconnect the main supply line at the inlet side of the pump and blow it out with compressed air. Be sure to remove the gasoline cap first. Never inject compressed air into the pump itself, as damage is sure to result. If these minor services fail to restore fuel flow, the fuel pump must be removed for overhaul or replacement.

Excessive Flow

An oversupply of gasoline from the fuel pump is caused usually by damage or maladjustment within the carburetor. Thus, the first step should be to remove the carburetor bowl cover to see if the float is punctured. Gasoline will remain inside if it is. If the float is sound, check for an obviously bent float arm or a defective carburetor needle valve. Evidence of wear or scratching of the valve usually can be detected with the fingers. Accurately determining the level of an apparently undamaged float and arm requires a special gauge, and this gauge and the settings vary from carburetor to carburetor. Another possible cause of excessive flow is the automatic choke sticking in its closed position.

Vapor Return Line

Cars have a fuel pump mounted under the hood and air conditioning should have a *vapor return line* connected between the pump and the fuel tank. Vapor tends to form in the fuel pump as a result of high under-the-hood temperatures caused by inefficiency of the cooling system during idle and operation of the air-conditioner condenser. The resulting vapor lock prevents proper fuel delivery to the carburetor and causes the engine to stall.

The vapor return line is connected to a special outlet in the fuel pump and lets any vapor in the pump flow back to the fuel tank. In addition, any excess fuel being pumped through the line is also routed back to the fuel tank. Because this circulation of excess fuel cools the pump, it acts to prevent the formation of moisture.

Sometimes a vapor separator is connected between the fuel pump and the carburetor. Vapor bubbles produced by the pump enter the separator together with fuel. The bubbles rise to the top of the separator and are forced, by fuel-pump pressure, into the fuel-return line and back to the tank where they condense back into liquid.

Vehicle Vapor Recovery (VVR) System

When a pre-1970 car is parked and its engine is not running, gasoline vapor can escape from the fuel tank and carburetor. To prevent the resulting atmospheric pollution, cars produced since 1970 have a *Vehicle Vapor Recovery* (VVR) system.

In a VVR system, the fuel tank is sealed and any vapors that try to escape must pass through a vapor-recovery line to a cannister that contains charcoal particles. Inside the cannister, the charcoal particles absorb and retain the vapor. When the engine is operated, air flows through the cannister on its way to the carburetor and, in the process, picks up the stored vapor. Upon arriving at the carburetor, the vapor is mixed with the air-fuel mixture and is burned instead of being permitted to enter the atmosphere as a pollutant. As you will see later in this chapter, a VVR system functions as part of the emission-control system.

ELECTRONIC FUEL INJECTION (EFI)

Electronic fuel injection is standard on Cadillac Sevilles through 1976 and later full-size models.

In an EFI system, selected engine operating conditions are monitored and this input is fed to a *microprocessor* (a very compact computer made with integrated circuits). The computer output is used to electronically meter the fuel needed by the engine to meet the monitored conditions.

Four subsystems make up the EFI system: namely, the fuel-delivery system, the air-induction system, a network of sensors, and an electronic control unit (generally referred to as the ECU).

In 1980 a so-called Digital Fuel Injection (DFI) system was introduced on the Sevilles and in 1981 it was made standard on all 368 cubic-inch (6 liter) engines.

The DFI system includes eight subsystems: the same four as in the EFI system plus an Electronic Spark Timing (EST) system, an Idle Speed Control (ISC) system, the Exhaust Gas Recirculation (EGR) system, and an Electronic Control Module (ECM).

As a result of the additional subsystems, the ECM used in the DFI system is considerably more sophisticated than its EFI counterpart, the ECU.

Fuel Delivery System

This system contains two electric fuel pumps (one in-tank and one chassis mounted), a fuel filter, fuel-pressure regu-

lator, feed rails (in EFI), either one injector for each cylinder (in EFI) or two injectors in the throttle body (DFI), and supply and return lines.

The two fuel filters are connected in parallel to the ECU/ECM and are activated by the computer when the ignition is turned on and the engine is either cranking or operating. If the engine stalls, or the starter is not engaged, the pumps stop operating in about one second. Fuel is pumped from the tank, through the supply line, filter, pressure regulator and feed rails (EFI) to the injectors. Any excess fuel is returned to the fuel tank.

The in-tank fuel pump supplies fuel to the chassis-mounted pump or to the throttle body pressure regulator.

The chassis-mounted pump contains a check valve that prevents the return of fuel to the tank. The flow rate of this pump is 33 gallons per hour and the pump maintains a minimum pressure of 39 psi. To protect the system from excessive pressure, an internal relief valve opens at 55 psi.

The fuel pressure regulation used in an EFI system is mounted near the front of the engine and can be serviced separately. But its counterpart on the DFI system is integral with the throttle body and cannot be worked on separately. Both regulators maintain a constant pressure of 39 psi across the fuel injectors and both contain an air chamber and a fuel chamber separated by a spring-loaded diaphragm. (The air chamber on EFI systems is connected to the throttle body by a hose.) Pressure in the air chamber is the same as in the intake manifold. As changes in manifold pressure occur, the spring moves the diaphragm causing it to either open or close an orifice (opening) in the regulator fuel chamber. Excess fuel leaves the regulator and returns to the fuel tank.

The fuel injectors in EFI systems are solenoid-operated pintle valves. They are located on the intake manifold above the intake valve of each cylinder and meter fuel to the cylinders. Electrical pulses from the ECU control the operation of the injectors. When a valve is energized, it opens just long enough to spray an exact amount of fuel droplets into the cylinder. When the valve is de-energized, fuel flow to the cylinder is cut off.

The eight injectors in the EFI system are divided into two groups of four each. Injectors 1, 2, 7 and 8 form group one and 3, 4, 5 and 6 make up group two. All injectors in a group are opened and closed simultaneously and the two groups operate alternately.

A DFI system has only two fuel injectors. They are located on the throttle body and are controlled by the ECM. Each injector, as shown in Figure 7-9, contains a spring-loaded ball valve controlled by a solenoid. When the solenoid plunger lifts the ball valve off its seat, fuel is fed through the atomizer into the throttle bore.

Air-Induction System

The air-induction system includes the throttle body assembly, the idle speed control and the intake manifold.

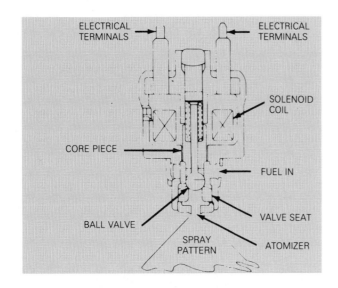

Fig. 7-9. A solenoid-operated fuel injector. *Courtesy of Cadillac Division, General Motors Corporation.*

Throttle body. Upon entering the throttle body, combustion air is controlled by throttle valves which are connected to the accelerator pedal linkage. The throttle body housing has two bores and two shaft-mounted throttle valves. These valves are preset slightly opened when the throttle lever is resting against the idle stop position. DO NOT CHANGE THIS ADJUSTMENT. A set screw, located on the front of the throttle body, is used to set the warm-engine idle speed. It does so by adjusting an idle bypass air passage in the throttle body and this allows a certain amount of air to bypass the throttle valves.

On the 1978 Seville and later models, a solenoid-operated idle air compensator provides additional air to the engine when the air conditioner clutch is engaged at idle.

Fast idle valve. The fast-idle assembly, Figure 7-10, has a plastic body that contains an electric heater and thermal element, a spring, and the valve. The assembly is located in a large port on top of the throttle body.

The valve is connected electrically to the fuel-pump circuit through the ECU. When the engine is started cold the valve is open and allows extra air to bypass the throttle valve.

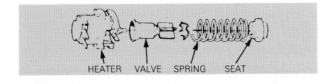

Fig. 7-10. An exploded view of the fast idle valve assembly. *Courtesy of Cadillac Division, General Motors Corporation.*

As the heater element warms it expands and pushes the valve toward the seat against the opposition of the spring. This reduces the amount of bypass air. Eventually, the valve is firmly seated, the bypass air is cut off, and the engine operates at normal idle speed. The warmup process takes about 90 degrees when the ambient temperature is 68°F and about 5 minutes when the temperature is −20°F.

Intake Manifold. Only a few differences distinguish the intake manifold of an EFI system from that used on a carbureted engine. On the EFI system, only air passes through the manifold. There is a hole above each cylinder into which an injector fits and a port is available for the installation of an air-temperature sensor. There is no exhaust-heat crossover and the exhaust passage from the right cylinder head is for exhaust gas recirculation (EGR).

Engine Sensors

All engine sensors are electrically connected to the ECU (in EFI) or the ECM (in DFI). Each sensor monitors a specific operating condition and transmits this information to the ECU/ECM.

Manifold absolute pressure sensor. This sensor monitors pressure changes in the intake manifold which are produced by variations in engine load, engine speed, and barometric pressure. When the manifold pressure increases, more fuel is needed and when the pressure decreases, less fuel is needed. This information is processed by the ECU/ECM and the computer output controls the length of time the fuel injectors are energized.

The manifold absolute pressure sensor is mounted within the ECU and a manifold pressure line runs from the sensor to the front of the throttle body.

Temperature sensors. Variable-resistance-type sensors are used to monitor the air temperature in the intake manifold and the temperature of the engine coolant. They are identical.

The resistance of each sensor varies in step with change in temperature. When the temperature is high the resistance is high and only a small current passes through the sensor. Thus, a small voltage drop appears across the resistive element. The opposite conditions hold true when the temperature is low. The voltage drops across the sensors are monitored by the ECU and appropriate warning signals are displayed when necessary.

Throttle position switch. This switch is mounted on the throttle body and monitors the opening and closing of the throttle valves by sensing the movement and position of the throttle valve shaft. Appropriate signals are then transmitted to the ECU/ECM where they are processed to determine the engine fuel requirement.

Speed sensors. On EFI systems, the speed sensor is encased in plastic and is an integral part of the distributor. The sensor consists of two reed switches and a magnet that rotates with the distributor shaft.

When the magnet passes the two switches, they open and close, thereby producing two pulse-type signals which synchronize, by way of the ECU, activation of the proper injector group with the opening of the intake valves.

The ECU. The ECU/ECM is a pre-programmed computer that is electrically connected to the car's power supply, all elements of the EFI/DFI systems, and to the EGR solenoid. The ECU/ECM is located either in the glove box or under the dash.

When the ignition system is turned to either ON or CRANK, the ECU/ECM is activated and starts receiving and processing information from the various engine sensors in order to determine the exact fuel requirement for the engine. The ECU/ECM then transmits pulses to the fuel-injector solenoids that cause the injectors to open only for a specific length of time. Of course, the fuel requirement (and the duration of the injector sprays) varies as the operating conditions change.

Each model vehicle uses a particular ECU/ECM and these units are not interchangeable. There are also differences between the ECU/ECM's mounted on cars sold in California and those on cars sold in the other states.

EFI TROUBLESHOOTING

Special test equipment is needed to diagnose suspected faults in the ECU. DO NOT ATTEMPT ANY SUCH DIAGNOSIS ON YOUR OWN. Only mechanical and simple electrical problems are considered here.

Before any part of the fuel-delivery system of an EFI-equipped automobile is disconnected, pressure in the fuel lines must be bled off. Unless this precaution is observed, fuel may spray out and ignite.

The correct pressure-bleeding procedure is described in steps 1 through 4 in the section that describes the installation and removal of the chassis-mounted fuel pump.

Engine cranks but will not start. If the rest of the vehicle's electrical system is operating properly, proceed as follows.

1. Turn the ignition key to its ON position. Listen carefully for a whining sound emitted by the chassis-mounted fuel pump when it is operating. If the sound lasts for only one second and then stops, the fuse in the fuel pump electric supply line is open. Depending on the auto model year, this fuse may be rated at 10 amperes or 20 amperes. Of course, if the sound of the fuel pump continues, the fuse is O.K. But if no sound is heard, either the chassis-mounted pump is defective, the supply line is open-cir-

cuited, or there is a poor connection in the fuel pump wiring harness.

2. Check the wiring harness of the ECU for a poor connection.

3. Check for an open circuit in the purple wire between the ECU and the starter solenoid and the green wire between the ECU and the BAT terminal on the alternator.

4. Check the engine cooling sensor. There may be a poor connection or open circuit in the wiring or in the sensor itself when the engine is cold. The resistance of the sensor should not exceed 1600 ohms.

5. Check the speed sensor on the distributor. There may be a poor wiring connection or the trigger of the sensor may be stuck closed.

6. Disconnect the throttle-position switch and try starting the engine. If the engine does start, the wide-open-throttle section of the switch is shorted. Replace the switch.

7. Check for a restriction in the fuel-delivery system.

Hard starting.

1. Same as Step 6 above.

2. Turn the ignition key to its ON position and make sure the chassis-mounted fuel pump continues to operate. Check the pump for other faults.

3. When the engine is cold, check for an open circuit in the engine coolant temperature sensor.

4. The fuel pressure regulator may be malfunctioning. Instructions for the removal and installation of the regulator are given shortly.

Engine stalls.

1. Check for a poor connection or open circuit in the black and yellow wire between the ECU and the fuse block.

2. When the engine is cold, check for an open circuit in the engine coolant temperature sensor.

3. On a 1978 or later Seville, check the operation of the idle air compensator solenoid.

Rough idle.

1. Check the vacuum hose on the manifold absolute air pressure sensor. It may be loose, disconnected, pinched or leaking.

2. When the engine is cold, check for a poor connection or open circuit in the air temperature sensor and its wiring. An ohmmeter connected across the sensor terminals should read no less than 700 ohms.

3. When the engine is cold, check for an open circuit in the engine coolant temperature sensor.

4. Check all connections at the injectors.

Prolonged fast idle.

1. Adjust the throttle position switch.
2. Check the fast-idle valve for poor connections and/or an open heating element.
3. Check for any leaks around the throttle body.

Engine hesitates when accelerating.

1. Check the vacuum hose of the manifold absolute air pressure sensor for leakage, disconnection or restriction.
2. Make sure the throttle position switch is adjusted and working properly.
3. When the engine is cold, check for a poor connection at the EGR valve solenoid and make sure the solenoid is not stuck open.
4. Check the wiring harness of the ECU for poor connections.
5. Check the speed sensor trigger (at the distributor).

Poor fuel economy.

1. Make sure the manifold absolute air pressure sensor is properly connected and is not leaking.
2. Check the connections of the vacuum hose at the fuel pressure regulator and throttle body.
3. Check both temperature sensors as described earlier.

Poor high-speed performance.

1. Check the adjustment and operation of the wide-open throttle section of the throttle position switch.
2. Check the fuel filter for any restriction.
3. Check the operation of the chassis-mounted fuel pump.
4. Check the operation of the speed sensor trigger.
5. Look for an open circuit in the purple wire between the ECU and the starter solenoid.

Component Removal and Installation Procedures

Chassis-mounted fuel pump.

1. Locate the pressure fitting in the fuel line and remove the protective cap.
2. Loosely install the special valve depressor (G.M. Tool No. J-5420) on the pressure fitting.
3. With a towel wrapped around the pressure fitting to block any spray, slowly tighten the valve depressor until the pressure is released.
4. Remove the valve depressor and reinstall the protective cap.
5. Remove the fuel hoses from the pump.
6. Roll back the rubber boot and remove the nut (metric threaded) and lead from each electrical connector.

7. Remove the two screws and flat washers that hold the fuel pump to the bracket. This frees the fuel-pump assembly for removal.
8. Follow the reverse procedures to reinstall the pump. The green wire goes to the positive (+) terminal on the pump and the black wire to the negative (−) terminal. Make sure the pump sits evenly on its two mounts and is not grounded against the bracket or frame.

In-Tank Fuel Pump.

1. Disconnect the battery from the pump.
2. Open the fuel tank filler door and remove the tan wire that is connected to the tank unit.
3. Raise the rear of the car one foot higher than the front and siphon all fuel from the tank.
4. Remove the screw that connects the ground wire to the cross member.
5. Disconnect the fuel line, evaporative emission lines and return lines from the front of the tank.
6. With the tank supported by a jack and wooden block, remove one screw on each side that secures the tank support straps to the body at the front of the tank.
7. By means of the jack, lower the tank enough to be able to disconnect the pump electrical lead.
8. Remove the fuel tank from the car.
9. Remove the locknuts that secure the tank unit and pump feed wires to the tank unit.
10. Using a soft, non-ferrous punch and hammer, turn the cam locking ring counterclockwise. Once the lock ring is removed the tank can be lifted clear.
11. Follow the reverse procedure to install an in-tank pump. Use a torque of 25 foot-pounds to tighten the screws in the tank-retaining straps.

Fuel Filter.   To replace a filter element simply unscrew the bottom cover and remove the element. With the new element in place, retighten the bottom cover. To replace the fuel-filter assembly, proceed as follows.

1. Bleed the pressure from the fuel delivery system (see Steps 1 through 4 for the removal of the chassis-mounted fuel pump).
2. Remove the inlet and outlet hoses from the fuel filter.
3. Remove the two screws that secure the fuel filter in its bracket and take out the filter assembly.
4. Remove the filter assembly inlet and outlet fittings and install them on the replacement unit. Use sealer on the threads.
5. Attach the filter to its retaining bracket. Use a torque of 12 foot-pounds to tighten the retaining screws.
6. Using new clamps, connect the filter inlet and outlet lines.

Throttle-body assembly.

1. Remove the air cleaner.

2. Disconnect the two throttle return springs from the throttle lever.

3. Remove the cruise control, control chain retainer, and chain on cars so equipped.

4. Remove the clip and disconnect the throttle cable from the throttle lever.

5. Remove the left rear throttle body mounting screw.

6. Remove the screw that holds the throttle bracket to the intake manifold.

7. Remove the downshift switch from the throttle lever and position bracket.

8. Disconnect the throttle position and fast idle valve electrical connectors and slide the wiring out of the notch in the throttle body.

9. Disconnect the throttle lines from the valve body.

10. Remove all remaining retaining screws and remove the throttle body.

11. Remove all gasket material from the intake manifold and the throttle body.

12. Use the reverse procedure to install the throttle body. Install the throttle return springs between the throttle lever and pressure regulator bracket with the open end of the spring on the outside of the throttle lever.

Throttle position switch.

1. Remove the throttle body from the engine.

2. Take out the mounting screws and remove the switch from the throttle body.

3. Install the switch on the right side of the throttle body so that the tab on the switch engages the flat on the throttle shaft.

4. Install the two mounting screws and tighten them until the switch is firmly in place but can still move.

5. Adjust the throttle position switch using the procedure described earlier.

6. Reinstall the throttle body.

Fast idle valve.

1. Remove the air cleaner and the electrical connection to the valve heater.

2. Remove the air cleaner mounting stud.

3. Remove the fast idle valve heater by pushing down and twisting it 90° counterclockwise.

4. Remove the valve, spring, and seat from the throttle body.

5. Install the fast idle valve seat, spring, and valve in the throttle body.

6. Position the heater on top of the fast idle valve. Push it down to compress the spring but be very careful not to damage the contact arm of the microswitch located on the bottom of the heater housing.

7. Align the tabs on the fast idle valve heater with the cutout portion of the throttle body, and compress the spring further.

8. To secure the heater in position, rotate it clockwise 90°.

9. Connect the electrical lead.

10. Install the air cleaner stud and the air cleaner.

Fuel Injector. Except Seville. NOTE: When removing the fuel lines, use a back-up wrench to avoid any kinking of the lines.

1. Relieve pressure from the fuel system by following the procedure given in Steps 1 through 4 for the removal of the chassis-mounted fuel pump.

2. Remove the clamp that secures the pressure regulator to front fuel line.

3. Remove the flare nut from each end of the fuel line.

4. Disconnect the front line from the pressure regulator and remove it from the engine compartment.

5. Remove the fuel inlet line from the rear fuel line. (Note: The rear fuel line has three inlet lines: a rear line and two side lines.)

6. Remove the flare nut from each side line and remove the rear fuel line.

7. Remove the electrical conduit from the injector brackets.

8. Remove the screws that hold each injector bracket to the inlet manifold and remove the brackets and grommets.

9. Disconnect the electrical lead from all injectors on the fuel rail being removed.

10. Remove the fuel rail and injectors from the engine as an assembly.

11. Should any injectors stick to the intake manifold or come off with the fuel rail, remove the injectors from the manifold and fuel rail as necessary.

12. Remove and discard all used O-rings that seal the injectors at the fuel rail and intake manifold.

13. Lubricate the new O-rings with a suitable lubricant and install them on the fuel-rail end of each injector.

14. Install the injectors in the fuel rail with their electrical connectors facing inward.

15. Install new O-rings in each injector port in the intake manifold.

16. Install the fuel-rail and injector assembly on the intake manifold. Make sure that each injector is properly positioned in the manifold O-ring.

17. Install the new rubber grommets, flanges down, on the fuel rail and place the injector brackets in position.

18. Using a torque of 5 foot-pounds, tighten the bracket retaining screws.

19. Route and secure the electrical harness along the bracket.

20. Connect the eight injectors as follows: the injectors for the two front and two rear cylinders are connected to the red and black wires; the injectors for the four center cylinders are connected to the white and black wires.

21. Install the front and rear fuel rails.

22. Turn the ignition ON and OFF a few times to build up fuel pressure in the system and check for leaks.

23. Start the engine and check for leaks. Because the fuel lines were drained, you may have to crank the engine for some time before it will start.

Fuel injector. Seville. NOTE: Use a back-up wrench to avoid kinking the fuel lines during removal.

1. Disconnect the electrical lead from all injectors on the fuel line that is being removed.

2. Remove the fuel-system pressure. See Steps 1 through 4 under the removal procedure for the chassis-mounted fuel pump.

3. Remove the fuel inlet line at the fuel rail.

4. Disconnect the return and vacuum hoses at the fuel pressure regulator.

5. Disconnect the fuel line from the pressure regulator.

6. Remove the retaining screws from the injector brackets and remove the brackets.

7. Remove the fuel line and injectors as a unit.

8. With new O-rings, reverse the above procedure during installation.

Fuel pressure regulator.

1. Remove the vacuum hose from the top of the regulator.

2. Bleed the pressure in the fuel delivery system (Steps 1 through 4, removal of the chassis-mounted fuel pump).

3. Disconnect the flexible fuel hose between the fuel rail and the pressure regulator.

4. Disconnect the fuel return line.

5. Remove the metric threaded nut that secures the regulator to the bracket and remove the regulator.

6. Reverse the above procedure to install the regulator.

IDLE SPEED AND THROTTLE POSITION SWITCH ADJUSTMENT

Idle speed adjustment.

1. Adjust the ignition timing to the correct specifications.

2. Disconnect and plug the distributor vacuum line at the distributor, the parking-brake release-cylinder vacuum line at the release cylinder, and the air-leveling compressor hose at the air cleaner.

3. Set the parking brake and block the wheels.

4. Connect a tachometer to the engine, then start the engine and let it reach normal operating temperature.

5. Set the transmission selector at DRIVE and make sure the air conditioner is turned off.

6. Loosen the lock nut on the idle bypass adjusting screw located on the front of the throttle body. (On 1978 and later Sevilles, a conventional spring-loaded adjustment screw is used.)

7. Using an allen wrench, adjust the idle bypass adjusting screws to obtain an idle speed of 600 rpm for 1976, 650 rpm for 1977, 600 rpm for the 1978 Seville, 650 rpm for 1978 and later fuel-size Cadillacs, and 600 rpm for the 1979-1981 Eldorado and Seville.

8. Tighten the lock nut on the adjusting screw, stop the engine, remove the tachometer, and install the air cleaner and vacuum hoses.

Throttle position switch.

1. Loosen the two throttle position switch mounting screws.

2. Hold the throttle valves in the idle position and turn the throttle position switch counterclockwise until the end stop is reached. Be very careful in doing so.

3. Tighten the mounting screws.

4. Make sure the throttle valves close to the throttle stop. If they do not, readjust.

5. Rotate the throttle lever until the first click is heard.

6. Insert a feeler gauge between the throttle lever and the idle stop screw. The clearance should not exceed 0.020-inch. If it does, rotate the switch slightly clockwise and repeat the adjustment described above. Ideally, the clearance should be about 0.019-inch. Replace the throttle position switch if proper adjustment cannot be achieved.

Similar Electronic Fuel Injection Systems

Fuel injection systems similar to that described here have been developed by other manufacturers and are available as either optional or standard equipment. Although the systems are called by different names, as are component parts of the systems, they all operate pretty much the same.

MODULATED DISPLACEMENT

The Modulated Displacement system is used as the base power plant in the 1981 Cadillac DeVille, Brougham, and Eldorado. It is optional on the Seville.

In a conventional spark-ignition engine, the power output is controlled by the throttle. At low power outputs, the throttle is nearly closed in order to limit the amount of fuel-air mixture drawn into the cylinder. However, this small throttle opening introduces a "throttling loss," which is the energy the engine must use in expanding to draw fuel-air through the throttle opening. Because of this, an engine runs most efficiently when unthrottled.

An unthrottled condition can be approached by operating only the number of cylinders needed to give the required power, and operating them at high power cylinder levels. In doing so, the throttle is at a wider opening and there are fewer cylinders drawing air through that opening. This reduces the vacuum in the intake manifold, thereby reducing the throttling loss per cylinder. In addition, there are fewer cylinders experiencing throttle loss and the fuel requirement is reduced. The result is a fuel economy improvement. Reducing the number of operating cylinders is accomplished through use of valve selectors. At low power levels, valve selectors deactivate both intake and exhaust valves on two or four cylinders; for full power output, normal valve operation is restored.

In each of the deactivated cylinders, the piston continues to travel, but the intake and exhaust valves are closed. Since the gases in the cylinders are merely compressed and expanded by the piston, no energy is consumed as pumping losses, although normal frictional losses are still present. Furthermore, by closing both valves, the cylinders are not allowed to cool and, consequently, there is a smooth flow of power once the valves are reactivated and the cylinders return to power operation.

MD System Components

To provide a valve selector system that gives acceptable driveability, several engine operating features must be considered. These features are monitored by the sensors currently used by the DFI system for fuel control. Information used includes engine rpm, coolant temperature, throttle position, and intake manifold absolute pressure.

Information from the sensors is sent to the ECM of the DFI system and the computer processes the data. Based on this input and the programmed logic, the ECM determines the number of operating cylinders required. The ECM then energizes the electrical solenoids in the valve selectors. Each selector controls both the intake and exhaust valves on one cylinder.

Using four valve selectors allows the selective operation of 4, 6, or 8 cylinders to effectively reduce the engine from a 6.0 liter 8 cylinder to either a 4.5 liter 6 cylinder or a 3.0 liter 4 cylinder. Valve selectors are installed on cylinders 1, 4, 6 and 7. In the 6-cylinder mode, cylinders 1 and 4 are deactivated and when the 4-cylinder mode is chosen, cylinders 6 and 7 are also deactivated.

Valve Selector Operation

The operating principle of valve selectors is to control the point of pivot of the rocker-arm assembly, and by doing this

be able to either cause the rocker arm to open the valve or allow the valve to remain closed while the remainder of the valve gear operates through its normal travel.

During active operation, the rocker arm pivots near the center of the rocker arm (the fulcrum point). As the cam reaches its high point the valve is opened, allowing the fuel-air mixture to enter the cylinder.

When the valve selector is activated (4 or 6 cylinder mode) and the cam is again on the high point, the valve will not open because the rocker arm does not pivot at the center of the arm. The selector will shift the rocker arm pivot point and allow the rocker arm to slide up and down its mounting stud. This in effect shifts the fulcrum point to the tip of the now stationary valve. With the valve being held closed by its spring, the cylinder is inactive.

The valve selectors are mounted on the intake and exhaust-valve rocker arms above the rocker-arm fulcrums. When the solenoid is not energized, the selector body is restrained from moving upward by contact between the "body projections" and the "blocking plate" above it. The rocker arm pivots near its center and the valves operate normally.

When the selector is energized (to deactivate the valves), the blocking plate is rotated by the solenoid to align the "windows" in the blocking plate with the body projections. As the rocker arm is lifted by the push rod, the rocker arm and body ride up the stud since the body is no longer restrained by the blocking plate. The rocker arm now pivots at the tip of the valve, and the valve remains closed.

The body is spring-loaded downward by an internal spring. This internal spring provides valve-gear action and normal hydraulic-lifter function when the valve gear is deactivated by providing tension in the valve body and maintaining zero valve lash.

The solenoid force is less than that required to overcome blocking plate/body friction when the valve is lifted. This prevents deactivation of the valve while it is lifted, which would cause the valve to seat abruptly.

The valve selector, if found defective, must be replaced as an assembly. Separate valve selector components are not available.

Other Engine Differences

Engine components changed or modified to accomodate the MD, which are specific to these engines, include the ECM, rocker arm covers, rocker-arm supports for modulated cylinders, and wiring harnesses. In addition, other components or systems have been modified to accomodate the operating characteristics of the MD system.

Vacuum pump. Due to the decreased engine vacuum levels during the 6- and 4-cylinder modes, an auxiliary vacuum pump is used to allow normal operation of the various vacuum operated systems (power brakes, air conditioning, etc.). A belt-driven vacuum pump is used.

Engine lubricating system.   The oil pump is mounted on the right side near the front of the engine. Oil enters the pump through a screened intake pick-up pipe and is pumped through the oil filter and through an angular passage in the cylinder block into the right longitudinal header. It then crosses over to the left longitudinal header through intersecting vertical passages above the No. 2 camshaft bearing. The oil continues up the left longitudinal header to the oil pressure signal switch.

Main bearings Nos. 2, 3, and 4 are lubricated by oil from the right longitudional header through holes drilled in the block. Main bearings Nos. 1 and 5 are lubricated in the same manner by oil from the left longitudinal header. The camshaft bearings are lubricated by oil from the corresponding main bearing through holes drilled in the block. Oil from each main bearing also lubricates adjacent connecting-rod bearings through holes drilled in the crankshaft.

The longitudinal headers feed the hydraulic valve lifters through drilled passages. The oil then flows under pressure into the lifters and up through the hollow push rods to the rocker arms. The amount of oil is controlled by a small metering disc in the valve filter.

The oil comes through a small feed hole in the rocker arm and flows onto the arm, lubricating the rocker arm pivot points as well as the push-rod tip and the valve tip.

Oil drains from the cylinder heads into the valve-lifter compartments and returns to the oil passage through a hole on the bottom of the compartment.

Exhaust manifolds.   The exhaust manifolds are designed to provide space for the upper control arms and reduce weight. All screws are torqued to 35 foot-pounds and use locks to secure the screws.

EMISSION CONTROL SYSTEMS

Closed Positive Crankcase Ventilation System

Since 1968, all automobiles are required to pass emission tests specified by Federal law. This law also requires the use of a closed crankcase ventilation system.

The closed positive crankcase ventilation (P.C.V.) system performs two functions; it helps control air pollution caused by crankcase blow-by gases and it ventilates the crankcase with clean air, scavenging the blow-by and preventing the formation of sludge and other undesirable products.

The closed P.C.V. system consists of an air filter, P.C.V. valve, and hoses. The location of the components varies, but operation is always the same.

At idle or normal road speeds, fresh air is drawn through the air cleaner. The air is then routed through the air filter, a hose, into the rocker-arm cover, and then into the crankcase, where it joins with crankcase vapors.

This mixture is then drawn through a P.C.V. valve to

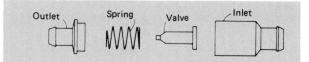

Fig. 7-11   Positive crankcase ventilation (P.C.V.) valve.

the intake manifold, where the vapors are mixed with the normal fuel-air mixture and burned.

During high road speeds or heavy acceleration, intake manifold vacuum is decreased and engine blow-by is increased. The crankcase vapors are routed through the connecting hose from the rocker-arm cover into the air cleaner. This mixture joins the normal air-fuel mixture and passes into the intake manifold for burning.

The P.C.V valve, Fig. 7-11, is kept closed by spring force when the engine is shut off. This prevents any hydrocarbon fumes from gathering in the intake manifold, which could lead to hard starting. When the engine is started, manifold vacuum pulls the valve open against the force of the spring. The valve floats as long as there is engine vacuum, allowing crankcase fumes to enter the intake manifold.

In case there is an engine backfire through the intake manifold, the P.C.V. valve closes and prevents the ignition of crankcase fumes.

P.C.V. Valve Maintenance

Once a year, or every 12,000 miles, whichever comes first, the P.C.V valve should be replaced. The crankcase ventilation filter should be removed and washed in kerosene. The rest of the system should be serviced by washing the parts in kerosene and blowing out the hoses and pipes, or both, with compressed air.

Every time the closed P.C.V. system is serviced, the carburetor should be adjusted to idle specifications.

During normal operation, the P.C.V. valve may become plugged and remain closed. This will cause high crankcase pressure at highway speeds and may cause the engine to blow out oil through the engine seals and gaskets. A rough idle definitely results from a plugged valve. To see if the P.C.V. is the cause of the rough idle, make the following check. (1) Connect a tachometer to the engine. (2) Start the engine and adjust the curb idle. (3) Clamp off the hose that goes from the P.C.V. to the base of the carburetor. (4) If the P.C.V. system is O.K., the engine will change by 50 to 60 rpm. Also, you may hear the valve click shut when clamping and releasing the line several times. If the P.C.V. valve or hoses are plugged, no change in engine rpm occurs.

EVAPORATION EMISSION CONTROL SYSTEMS

An evaporation emission control (EEC) system prevents the escape of fuel vapors into the atmosphere from the fuel tank and carburetor fuel bowl.

There are three variations of the EEC system: the carbon canister (General Motors and Ford), the crankcase air cleaner (Chrysler), and the cylinder head cover design (American Motors). The canister system was mentioned during our discussion of fuel systems. At that time it was called a vehicle vapor recovery (VVR) system.

All systems serve the same purpose and operate in similar manners. Each is a closed system that cuts off the escape routes for volatile gasoline to the atmosphere. Gasoline may escape as vapor discharged from the fuel tank or carburetor bowl, when the engine is not in use, as liquid overflow caused by overfilling the fuel tank, from temperature expansion of gasoline in the tank, or from spillage from the tank during extreme driving maneuvers.

Carbon Canister System

Gasoline vapors are controlled through the use of a charcoal canister that absorbs the fuel vapors and stores them until they can be removed to be burned in the engine. See Fig. 7-12.

Removal of vapors from the canister to the engine is accomplished by air drawn through a line to the engine air cleaner. In addition to the charcoal canister, a nonvented cap is used on the fuel tank. The fuel tank also has extra vents to a liquid-vapor separator.

The liquid-vapor separator prevents liquid gasoline from entering the vapor system to the canister. As vapors are generated in the fuel tank they flow through the liquid-vapor separator to the carbon canister, where they are stored. The vapors from the canister are then routed to the carburetor where they are burned during normal combustion.

Fuel tank. Although Ford and General Motors both use the carbon canister, they use different methods to allow for fuel expansion. Ford uses a fuel tank with an extended filler neck that provides an air space for fuel expansion after the fuel gauge indicates full.

General Motors has a filling control device added to the

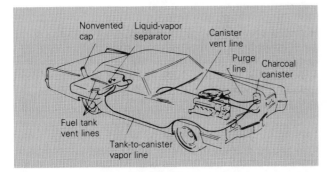

Fig. 7-12. Evaporation emission control system: charcoal canister system. *Courtesy of Cadillac Division, General Motors Corporation.*

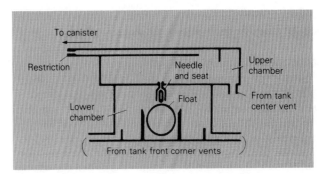

Fig. 7-13. Liquid-vapor separator. *Courtesy of Cadillac Division, General Motors Corporation.*

fuel tank to limit the fill of the tank. This overfill protector provides adequate volume for the expansion of liquid fuel volume with temperature change.

Both types of fuel tanks are vented, but the gas caps are nonvented to seal the tank.

Liquid-vapor separator. A liquid separator, Fig. 7-13, as the term implies, separates liquid fuel from vapors. The separator contains a check valve that closes the passage of liquid fuel to the engine by the vapor route. When the separator chamber is temporarily flooded with gas, a *float* rises to close the *valve* to stop the liquid fuel, which flows back into the fuel tank through a drain line.

Carbon canister. The carbon canister is connected to the air cleaner and fuel tank vent line. If the engine is running, most of the fuel vapors are fed directly to the engine; the remainder are absorbed by the charcoal. During periods of engine shutdown, the vapors enter the charcoal canister and are stored until the engine is started. The vapors are then drawn into the engine and burned.

Control valve. A control valve is used to protect the fuel tank by opening the system to the atmosphere when necessary. This action prevents a vacuum or pressure buildup which might damage the main fuel tank. Fuel vapor flows forward from this valve to the carbon canister.

Carburetor. Carburetors are modified to control the vapors given off at the carburetor fuel bowl. Vapor and idle vents are removed to seal the carburetor, and an aluminum heat-dissipating plate is added between the carburetor and the intake manifold. This plate minimizes fuel-bowl vapors by providing maximum heat transfer to the atmosphere. A relatively low fuel temperature is possible when the engine is shut down, resulting in a reduced vapor emission.

Maintenance. Maintenance on the carbon-canister system is limited to the canister itself. The accumulator-purge air filter, an oiled foam filter assembled in the bottom of the canister, should be replaced every 12,000 miles or 12 months, whichever comes first. Under extremely dusty conditions, more frequent attention may be required.

Crankcase Air-Cleaner System

Chrysler Corporation cars equipped with EEC use a closed system that controls fuel expansion and feeds fuel-evaporation emissions from the carburetor or fuel tank to the engine for burning. Fuel vapors are routed through vent lines to the crankcase by way of the crankcase inlet air cleaner, Fig. 7-14. Fuel vapors, which are two to four times heavier than air, settle at the bottom of the crankcase. When the engine is running, these fuel vapors are purged from the crankcase and, together with the normal crankcase vapor, they are drawn into the base of the carburetor to be burned by engine combustion. Vapors are delivered to the carburetor via the crankcase ventilation system.

Fuel tank. The fuel tank is designed with a 1.4-gallon overfill limiter tank located inside the main fuel tank. This tank fills at a much slower rate than the main tank, and when the main tank is filled, it remains practically empty to allow for thermal expansion.

The loss of any fuel or vapor out of the filler neck is prevented by using a filler cap that will open when tank pressure differs from atmospheric pressure by ½ to 1 psi, and when vacuum is ¼ to ½ inch. By opening at the critical time, the tank keeps the fuel tank from becoming deformed. This cap is marked *pressure vacuum* and must, if necessary, be replaced by a similar unit.

Vapor-liquid separator. The fuel tank is flat. A vent is located on each corner of the tank, and these vents are connected to a vapor-liquid separator by rubber hoses.

The liquid-vapor separator is a piece of 2-inch steel tubing mounted at an angle inside the trunk. It is composed of four vent lines from the fuel tank and a vent line connected to the crankcase inlet air cleaner. Referring to Fig. 7-14, you

can see that all vent lines are of a different height in the separator. Thus, the tank is always vented regardless of the vehicle altitude, and fuel vapor is transferred to the crankcase.

Carburetor. Closed ventilation of fuel vapor from the carburetor fuel bowl is included on Chrysler products equipped with an EEC system. On 8-cylinder engines, closed ventilation is provided by a hose connection from the carburetor fuel bowl to the crankcase inlet air cleaner. On 6-cylinder engines the hose from the carburetor fuel bowl is connected to the crankcase by way of a connecting nipple on the fuel pump. Also, the fuel pump has a bleed device which guards against a pressure buildup in the fuel line between the pump and carburetor. A pressure buildup in the fuel line causes problems in hot starting. Six-cylinder engines not equipped with EEC use a fuel pump with a bleed device but without the connecting nipple. If replacement of the fuel pump is necessary, make sure you use the right pump.

Maintenance. The EEC system should not require any maintenance in normal service. In most instances you need only your nose and eyes to tell if the system is working properly. The most common sign of a malfunctioning system is restricted fuel flow to the carburetor. This will result in rough or poor engine performance.

If there is any loss of fuel or vapor from the system, check the following: (1) The seal between the fuel tank cap and the filler neck. (2) The fuel tank cap release valve: place the cap next to your mouth and blow into the valve housing; an immediate leak by blowing lightly, or a lack of valve release by blowing hard, indicates a defective unit. (3) The lines between the fuel tank and the vapor-liquid separator: these should be unobstructed. (4) The fuel-tank expansion-chamber inlet hole: a removable plug is provided in the top surface of the fuel tank for access to the expansion chamber in case the fill-drain hole plugs up; if fuel-tank purging is needed, the expansion chamber must be purged separately through the top access plug hole.

Cylinder Head Cover Design

In the American Motors EEC system, raw fuel vapors go to the cylinder-head cover and through the P.C.V. system before being burned in the engine. The system consists of a *fuel-expansion tank*, Fig. 7-15, and a closed fuel tank vent system. A *fuel-check valve*, and a *pressure and vacuum-relief valve* are also included.

Fuel tank. The fuel tank has an integral expansion tank. Fuel passes through small holes in the expansion tank at a given rate as the fuel volume becomes greater due to an increase in temperature. The fuel level in the expansion tank changes correspondingly with the fuel level in the main tank.

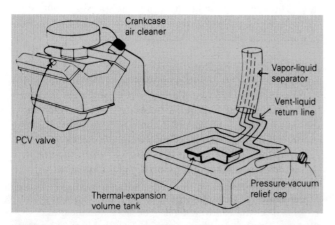

Fig. 7-14. Evaporation emission control system: crankcase aircleaner system. *Courtesy of Chrysler Motors Corporation.*

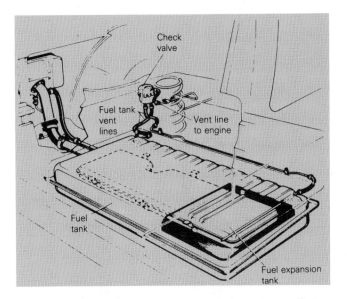

Fig. 7-15. Evaporation emission control system: cylinder head cover design. *Courtesy of American Motors Corporation.*

Fuel tank filler cap. The filler cap is made with a two-way relief valve that is closed to the atmosphere under normal operating conditions. The relief valve opens only when a pressure of ½ to 1 psi or a vacuum of ¼ to ½ inch occurs within the tank. After the pressure or vacuum is released, the valve returns to the normally closed position.

Fuel tank vent. The closed fuel tank vent system routes vapors from the fuel tank, through a check valve and connecting lines, to the cylinder head cover of the engine. The fuel vapors are then drawn into the P.C.V. system and burned in the engine.

The check valve located in the vent system prevents any liquid fuel from entering the engine through the evaporative emission-control system.

EXHAUST CONTROLS

There are a multitude of exhaust controls. It would not, therefore, be feasible to attempt to cover each type of control here. What we shall do, however, is discuss the most common devices and systems.

AIR-PUMP SYSTEMS

Air-pump systems include the General Motors Air Injection Reactor (A.I.R.), the Ford Thermoactor, the American Motors Air Guard, and the Chrysler Corporation Air Injection System. All four are similar. Thus, when we speak of air-pump systems in general, we refer to all four.

All air-pump systems include an air-injection pump, air-injection tubes (one for each cylinder), airdiverter valve (or air-bypass valve), check valve (two for V-8 engines), air-manifold assemblies, and the hoses that connect the components.

Carburetors and distributors that are a related part of the system should not be interchanged with, or replaced by, carburetors or distributors designed specifically for engines that do not have an air-pump system.

Operation of the Air-Pump System

The air-pump system controls exhaust-emitted gases by burning the hydrocarbon and carbon monoxide concentrations in the exhaust ports of the cylinder heads. To burn the contaminants, air under pressure is injected into the exhaust ports near each exhaust valve. The fresh air, plus the heat of the exhaust gases in each exhaust outlet port, promotes the combustion of the unburned portion of the exhaust gases during the exhaust stroke of the piston.

The air-injection pump compresses the air which flows through the bypass valve, Fig. 7-16(a), or a diverter valve, Fig. 7-16(b), to the air manifolds that distribute the air to the air supply tube in each exhaust port. A General Motors A.I.R. System is shown in Fig. 7-17.

The diverter or bypass valve, when activated by a sharp increase in manifold vacuum, shuts off the injected air to the exhaust port areas and prevents backfiring during this rich-mixture period. During periods of deceleration, the air delivery to the manifolds is dumped through the muffler on the diverter or air-bypass valve and into the atmosphere.

At high engine speeds, the excess air is dumped through the pressure-relief valve when the relief valve is part of the air pump, and through the diverter or bypass valve when either has the relief valve as a component part.

The check valve (one on in-line engines, two on V-8 engines) prevents backflow of exhaust gases into the air pump when the exhaust back pressure exceeds the air-pump delivery pressure.

When the air-pump system is properly installed and maintained, it effectively reduces exhaust emissions. If any system component or engine component operating in conjunction with the system should malfunction, however, an increase in exhaust emissions may occur.

Air-Pump System Maintenance

Air-pump driver belt adjustment. The belt drive for the air pump must be correctly adjusted at all times. A loose belt causes improper pump action. A belt that is too tight places a severe strain on the air-pump bearings.

A drive belt adjusted to the correct tension minimizes noise and ensures maximum belt life. A belt-tension gauge, obtainable at auto supply houses, should be used to check and adjust the belt tension. Follow the specific instructions of the auto manufacturer and read the literature of the ten-

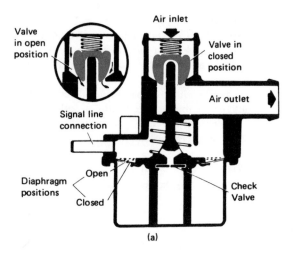

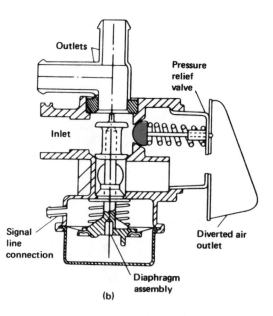

Fig. 7-16 Backfire control valves: (a) Air bypass valve, and (b) diverter valve. *Courtesy of Chevrolet Division, General Motors Corporation.*

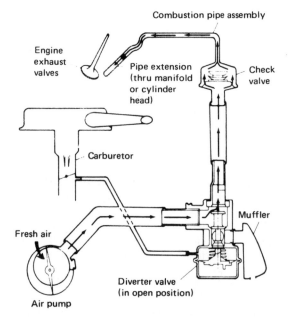

Fig. 7-17 Schematic of A.I.R. System. *Courtesy of Chevrolet Division, General Motors Corporation.*

sion-gauge manufacturer carefully to see precisely how the gauge should be connected and used.

If the belt is obviously in poor shape, or cracked, it must be replaced with a new one.

Air bypass or diverter valve. A defective air-bypass valve or diverter valve should be replaced. Before replacing the valve, however, check the condition and routing of all lines leading to and from the valve, especially the vacuum signal line. All lines must be secure and should be checked for leaks by using a soapy water solution. Disconnect the vac-

uum signal line; with the engine running, a vacuum signal must be detected by placing your finger over the hose opening.

With the vacuum system working, and the engine stabilized at idle speed, no air should be escaping through the valve muffler. Manually open and quickly close the throttle. A blast of air should be discharged through the muffler for at least one second for the valve to be in proper working order.

Be careful when you must replace an air-bypass or diverter valve, as valves may be similar in appearance but designed to meet the particular requirements of various engines. Be sure to install the correct valve, and follow the manufacturer's instructions exactly as given.

Check valve. Inspect the check valve every time the hose is disconnected from it or whenever the check valve appears to be defective. An air pump that has failed and shows indications that exhaust gases have been in the pump, indicates a check valve malfunction.

A check valve can be tested by using your mouth to blow through the valve in a direction toward the air manifold, and then trying to suck back through the valve. Flow should be in only one direction, that is, toward the air manifold.

To remove the check valve, disconnect the pump outlet hose at the valve; remove the valve from the air manifold. Be careful not to bend or twist the air manifold.

Air manifold. If the air manifold must be replaced, the following procedure is recommended. (1) Disconnect the air-supply hose at the check valve and place the hose so that it does not interfere with your work. (2) Loosen all compression fittings between the air manifold and the cylinder head

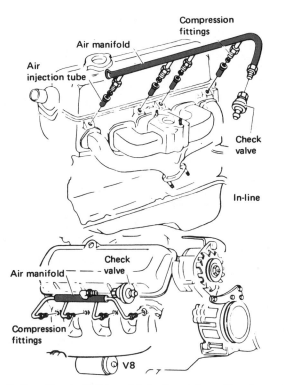

Fig. 7-18 Air manifold and injection tubes. *Courtesy of Chevrolet Division, General Motors Corporation.*

(Fig. 7-18). Then unscrew each fitting until it is free of the cylinder head. Grasp the air manifold at each end and pull it away from the cylinder head. If the engine is a V-8, follow the same procedure to remove the other air manifold.

Air-injection tubes. There is no periodic service schedule for the air-injection tubes. However, when the cylinder head is removed on in-line engines, or when the exhaust manifolds are removed on V-8 engines, check the tubes for carbon buildup, burning, or warping. Carbon deposits can be removed with a wire brush. Replace burned or warped tubes.

Air-injection pump. The major components of the air pump are enclosed in a die-cast aluminum housing. A filter-fan assembly, a rotor shaft, and drive hub are all visible on the outside of the pump. On pumps equipped with a pressure-relief valve, both the valve and the exhaust tube are visible. See Fig. 7-19. The relief valve is pressed into the hole provided in the housing. To remove the air pump, proceed as follows. (1) Disconnect hoses at pump. (2) Keep pump pulley from turning by compressing drive belt. Loosen pulley hub bolts. (3) Loosen adjustment bracket bolt and air-pump mounting bolt. Push air pump toward the cylinder block. Remove drive belt and pulley from the hub. (4) Remove adjustment bracket bolt and air-pump mounting bolt. Remove air pump.

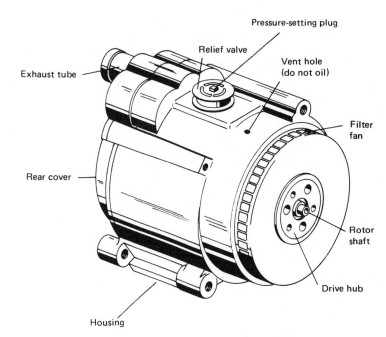

Fig. 7-19 Air pump. *Courtesy of American Motors Corporation.*

The air pump is designed to be relatively service free. The exhaust tube, relief valve (on units so equipped), and the filter-fan assembly require service.

To install an air pump proceed as follows: (1) Position pump assembly on mounting bracket and install bolts, but do not tighten them. (2) Install pump pulley with retaining bolts. (3) Install drive belt over pulley. Keep pulley from turning by compressing drive belt, then tighten bolts. (4) Move pump until belt is tight, then tighten mounting bolt and adjustment bracket bolt. (5) Recheck belt tension and adjust if needed. Do not, under any circumstances, pry on housing.

If the relief valve has to be replaced, it should be removed by using a suitable puller and a steel bridge, as shown in Fig. 7-20. Do not clamp the pump in a vise.

Before installing a new relief valve, check to see if the pressure plug is installed in the valve. If it is, remove the plug before installing the valve. Install the valve into the mounting hole in the pump housing. Place a block of wood over the valve and tap the wood with a hammer until the valve shoulders lightly on the pump housing. Be careful not to distort the housing. After the valve is installed, the pressure plug should be replaced in the valve.

The exhaust tube may be removed, if necessary, by grasping it in a vise or with a pair of pliers and pulling it out, using a twisting motion.

A new exhaust tube is installed by inserting the tube into the hole in the housing and tapping the tube, using a block of wood. Approximately ⅞ inch of the tube should extend above the cover.

A damaged filter fan may be removed by first removing the drive belt and pulley. Then remove the filter by prying

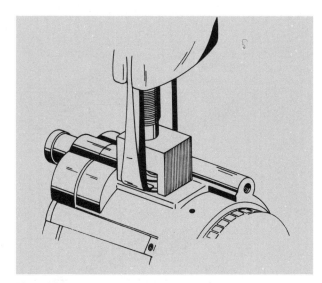

Fig. 7-20 Removing relief valve. *Courtesy of American Motors Corporation.*

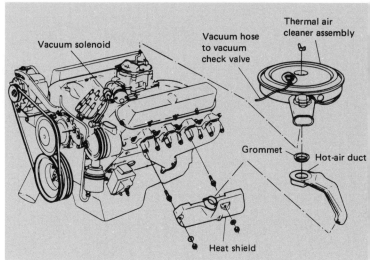

Fig. 7-21 Controlled-combustion system. *Courtesy of Cadillac Division, General Motors Corporation.*

loose the outer disk and pulling off with pliers the remaining portion of the filter. It is seldom possible to remove the fan without destroying it. Be careful to keep any fragments from entering the air-intake hole. The metal drive hub is not serviceable, so do not try to remove it.

To install a new filter fan, place the filter in the housing and, using the pulley and bolts to do so, draw it into position. Do not hammer or press it into place. Draw the filter down evenly by alternately torquing the pulley bolts. The outer edge of the filter must slip into the housing. A slight amount of interference with the housing bore is normal. A new filter may squeal for a while until the outside-diameter sealing lip has worn in.

CONTROLLED COMBUSTION SYSTEM

Introduction

A controlled combustion system (CCS), used by General Motors, has a retarded spark advance at lower engine speeds plus leaner carburetor and choke calibrations.

A full vacuum spark advance at closed throttle normally is used on cars with air conditioning because the engine heat rejection to the coolant is reduced at idle, causing lower radiator temperatures. Thus, a more efficient air-conditioning system is possible. However, with vacuum spark advance at closed throttle, exhaust emissions are very high. These emissions are reduced to a great extent by retarding the idle advance. Although the throttle must be opened slightly more to maintain the same idle speed as with full vacuum spark advance, retarding the idle advance gives better mixture distribution and less exhaust dilution, resulting in more complete combustion.

The CCS has a so-called ported spark advance, with the

vacuum takeoff located just above the throttle valve. There is no vacuum spark advance at closed throttle, but there is vacuum spark advance as soon as the throttle is opened slightly. Ignition timing is set at or near top dead center, and centrifugal advance does not start until approximately 1,000 rpm.

Because the engine may overheat due to greater heat rejection of the coolant during idle with no vacuum spark advance, a thermovacuum switch is used on some engines. This switch, located in the engine cooling system, senses the coolant temperature. When the coolant is at normal operating temperature, the thermovacuum switch is positioned internally to supply *ported* vacuum to the distributor. If the ambient temperature rises above 200°F, the switch supplies full intake manifold vacuum to the distributor, even at closed throttle. An improvement in idle quality results and causes an idling engine to speed up. This improves fan and water pump action and lowers heat rejection to the coolant.

Operation

As noted earlier, the CCS has a leaner carburetor calibration at idle and part throttle in addition to leaner choke calibration. Former carburetor design offered a mixture as lean as possible without interfering with good drivability, and with air-inlet temperatures as low as −20°F. A leaner mixture is possible with the CCS because a heated-air system is incorporated into the overall system. With the heated-air system in operation, the inlet air temperature is at a minimum of 100°F after only a few seconds of operation. The heated air thus makes it possible to have leaner carburetion calibration and still permits the car to function satisfactorily in cold weather.

The heated-air system includes a thermal air cleaner, a temperature sensor, a vacuum motor, control damper, and connecting vacuum hoses. The vacuum motor is controlled by the temperature sensor, and operates the damper to control either the flow of preheated air from a heat shield around the exhaust manifold, or non-preheated air from under the hood.

The *heat shield,* Fig. 7-21, is bolted on the *exhaust manifold.* Air is drawn along the lower edge of the shield and passes across the manifold surface, picking up heat. The heated air is then drawn out from the upper center of the *manifold,* through the hot-air duct, and into the *snorkel* of the air cleaner.

The thermal air cleaner combines exhaust-manifold heated air with cool air from under the hood so that the carburetor inlet air temperature is at least 100°F. The mixing is done by *hot-air* and *cold-air doors* located in the *air-cleaner snorkel.* When the cold-air door is closed, the hot-air door is open, and vice versa. Most of the time, both doors are partly open. When the temperature under the hood reaches a predetermined amount (105°F to 135°F, depending on the automobile), the cold-air door opens wide and the hot-air door fully closes. See Fig. 7-22. When the temperature under the hood is above the predetermined amount, the air cleaner is no longer able to control air temperature, and the inlet air temperature increases with the temperature under the hood.

The *damper* (Fig. 7-22) is moved by a *diaphragm-type vacuum motor.* With no vacuum in the motor, a *diaphragm spring* forces the cold-air door open and the hot-air door closed. When the engine is running, the vacuum present in the vacuum motor depends on a *bimetal temperature sensor,* which is located in the vacuum line between the intake manifold and the vacuum motor. When the temperature in the air cleaner rises above a minimum of 100°F, a spring in the temperature sensor starts to open a valve to bleed more air into the vacuum line. When the temperature drops below the minimum 100°F, the *sensor spring* begins to close the air bleed into the vacuum line, allowing more manifold vacuum to reach the vacuum motor. When the vacuum in the vacuum motor reaches a predetermined amount, the diaphragm spring is compressed, the cold-air is closed, and the hot-air door opened.

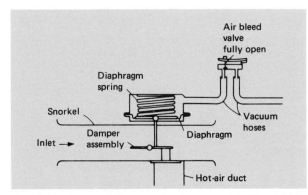

Fig. 7-22   Cold-air delivery mode. *Courtesy of Cadillac Division, General Motors Corporation.*

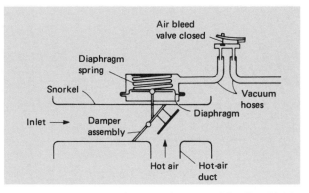

Fig. 7-23   Hot-air delivery mode. *Courtesy of Cadillac Division, General Motors Corporation.*

When the engine is not operating, the diaphragm spring holds the cold-air door open and the hot-air door closed. When the engine is operating, the positions of the doors depend on the air temperature in the air cleaner.

When the air-cleaner temperature is below 85°F and the engine is started, the cold-air door closes and the hot-air door opens immediately. See Fig. 7-23. The cold-air door closes because the air bleed valve in the temperature sensor is closed and full manifold vacuum is applied to the vacuum motor. The cold-air door remains closed only a few seconds, however, because as the air cleaner begins to receive hot air from the heat stove, the temperature sensor causes the cold-air door to open partially. Mixing of the cold air and hot air is necessary to regulate air-cleaner temperature within 20°F of the ideal air-inlet temperature.

If the underhood air temperature reaches the predetermined maximum, the air bleed valve in the temperature sensor is wide open and vacuum to the vacuum motor drops to zero. The diaphragm spring located in the vacuum motor holds the cold-air door wide open and closes the hot-air door tightly. A rise in underhood temperature above the predetermined maximum results in a carburetor inlet air temperature rise of the same amount.

If the engine is accelerated rapidly, the manifold vacuum drops. Whenever vacuum drops below a predetermined level, the diaphragm spring opens the cold-air door wide to obtain the maximum air flow needed for maximum acceleration.

Transmission-Controlled Spark

The CCS on later model automobiles includes a Transmission-Controlled Spark Advance (TCSA). The component parts of the TCSA are a *transmission switch, solenoid valve,* and *temperature switch.* The distributor vacuum advance in low gears is eliminated. See Fig. 7-24. The vacuum advance is controlled by the solenoid valve, which is energized in the low gears by grounding a switch at the transmission. When the transmission is in first or second gear, the solenoid is energized, eliminating vacuum advance to the dis-

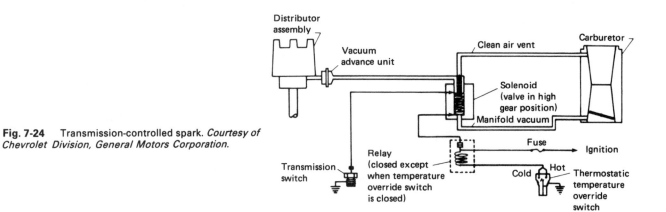

Fig. 7-24 Transmission-controlled spark. *Courtesy of Chevrolet Division, General Motors Corporation.*

tributor and thereby reducing exhaust emissions. The vacuum advance unit is vented to the atmosphere by means of a clean-air connection in the carburetor air hose. This keeps the vacuum advance unit from becoming vacuum locked at some advanced position. When the transmission is shifted from the low forward gears, the solenoid is de-energized, allowing the vacuum advance unit to operate normally for best fuel economy.

The TCSA also includes a temperature override for full vacuum in all gears when the engine is cold. A thermostatic water-temperature switch provides a signal that energizes a normally closed relay, opening the circuit to the solenoid vacuum switch and thereby providing full vacuum.

CCS Service

Thermal air cleaner. If lean operation occurs on an automobile equipped with CCS, always test the thermal air cleaner before working on the carburetor. The following procedure is recommended. (1) Check all hoses for condition and secure connections. If kinked, plugged, or otherwise damaged, replace. (2) With the engine off, check the condition of the cold-air door through the snorkel (a mirror may be needed). If the door is not open, check for binding in the linkage. (3) To see if the cold-air door closes properly, apply vacuum, by mouth, to the diaphragm assembly through the hose when disconnected at the sensor unit. When vacuum is applied, the cold-air door should close the snorkel passage completely. If not, check the linkage, and look for a vacuum leak. (4) With vacuum applied, bend or clamp the hose-to-trap vacuum in the diaphragm assembly. The cold-air door should remain closed. If not, there is a leak in the diaphragm assembly, and the entire assembly should be replaced. Kits are available with instructions from the auto manufacturer. (5) If the diaphragm assembly is O.K., next check the temperature-sensing unit. With the engine off, remove the air-cleaner cover and tape a temperature gauge as close as possible to the air-cleaner sensor. The test must be performed with the air-cleaner temperature below 85°F. If the engine has been run recently, allow

sufficient time for the temperature to drop to the required level. (6) When the engine is cool enough, start it. The cold-air door should close immediately. With the engine idling, the cold-air door should begin to open in a few minutes. Remove the air-cleaner cover and read the temperature gauge. The reading should be as specified by the auto manufacturer. (7) If the cold-air door does not begin to open at the specified temperature reading, the temperature sensor is defective and must be replaced.

Transmission-controlled spark advance. A malfunction in the TCSA system may result in continuous vacuum advance in the low forward gears and the car cannot pass the emission test. No vacuum advance in high gear results in poor mileage.

As part of any tune-up operation, check the TCSA system as follows: (1) With an automatic transmission in drive, check the system with a timing light. Make sure, however, the parking brake is on and block both the front and rear wheels. Increase engine speed to the amount specified by the manufacturer, and check timing. There should be no vacuum advance. (2) Now shift the transmission into reverse, and at the same specified speed, check the timing mark. There should now be full vacuum advance. (3) For cars with manual transmissions, have a helper depress the clutch pedal and shift the transmission into high gear. Observe the timing marks. Timing should advance as the transmission switch for the system is opened whenever shifting into high gear. If the component is not working, it should be replaced.

FORD IMCO SYSTEM

Operation

The Improved Exhaust Emission Control System (IMCO) uses a thermostatically controlled air cleaner, leaner carburetor calibration, and later ignition timing under conditions of closed-throttle operation. Because higher engine op-

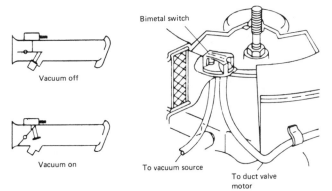

Fig. 7-25 Vacuum-operated duct and valve assembly. *Courtesy of Ford Motor Company.*

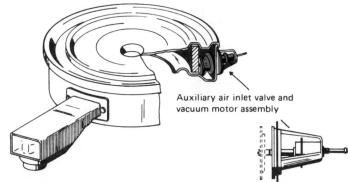

Fig. 7-27 Air cleaner with auxiliary inlet valve. *Courtesy of Ford Motor Company.*

erating temperatures are encountered, some cooling system changes have been incorporated to handle the increased heat rejection at idle and at low speed.

Thermostatically controlled air cleaner. The air cleaner maintains carburetor air temperature at or above 100°F. Preheated air is picked up from the outer surface of the exhaust manifold and is ducted into the carburetor if the underhood temperature is less than 100°F. The operation of the air cleaner on some engines is similar to the operation of the thermal air cleaner used on General Motors cars. A bimetallic switch, Fig. 7-25, controls a vacuum motor which opens and closes a valve plate in the air cleaner snorkel to control entering air temperatures.

On other engine models, as the underhood temperature increases, a thermostatic bulb located in the air cleaner senses the air temperature. A spring-loaded valve plate is connected to the thermostatic bulb through linkage. As the temperature of the air passing the thermostatic bulb rises, the thermostat starts to expand, and through linkage forces the valve plate down. This allows cooler air from under the hood to enter the air cleaner. When the temperature of the air further increases, the valve plate moves to the down position and only underhood air enters the air cleaner.

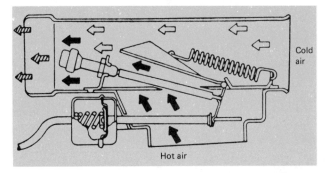

Fig. 7-26 Vacuum override motor controlled. *Courtesy of Ford Motor Company.*

The air cleaner is also equipped with either a vacuum override motor, Fig. 7-26, or an auxiliary air-inlet valve, Fig. 7-27. Both function to provide additional underhood air during periods of cold acceleration. The drop in manifold vacuum during acceleration causes the vacuum override motor to override the thermostat control. This opens the system to both underhood air and manifold heated air. The auxiliary air-inlet valve, which is controlled by a vacuum motor, opens to allow additional underhood air into the carburetor when the intake manifold vacuum drops.

Dual-diaphragm advance distributor. The dual-diaphragm vacuum advance distributor consists of two independently operated diaphragms (Fig. 7-28). The primary diaphragm utilizes carburetor vacuum to advance ignition timing. The second diaphragm is actuated by intake-manifold vacuum to provide additional ignition timing retard during periods of closed-throttle idle. The ignition timing retard helps reduce exhaust system hydrocarbon emissions.

The primary diaphragm is connected to the carburetor above the throttle plate(s), so that when the throttle is opened, timing is advanced. The secondary diaphragm is connected to the intake manifold so that, during closed-throttle operation when manifold vacuum is high, the timing is retarded to provide more complete combustion. This timing retard occurs automatically during periods of engine idle or deceleration, except when a distributor-modulator system is installed in the vacuum supply line.

Distributor modulator system. The distributor modulator system reduces engine emissions by closely controlling the distributor spark advance during specified conditions of acceleration and deceleration. The system, Fig. 7-29, consists of four major components: a speed sensor, thermal switch, electronic control amplifier, and a three-way solenoid valve that controls vacuum applied to the distributor. The electronic control amplifier and the solenoid are an integral unit mounted inside the passenger compartment on the dash panel. The speed sensor is connected to the speedometer

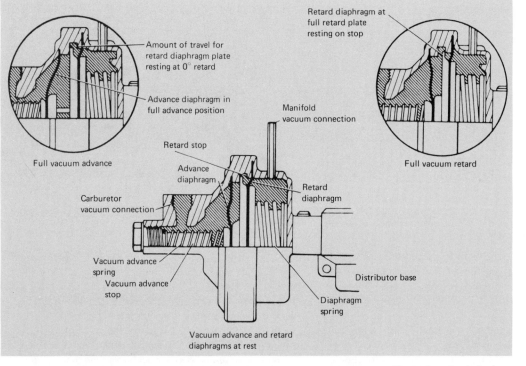

Amount of travel for retard diaphragm plate resting at 0° retard

Advance diaphragm in full advance position

Retard diaphragm at full retard plate resting on stop

Manifold vacuum connection

Retard stop

Advance diaphragm

Retard diaphragm

Carburetor vacuum connection

Full vacuum advance

Full vacuum retard

Vacuum advance spring

Vacuum advance stop

Distributor base

Diaphragm spring

Vacuum advance and retard diaphragms at rest

Fig. 7-28   Dual-diaphragm vacuum advance mechanism. *Courtesy of Ford Motor Company.*

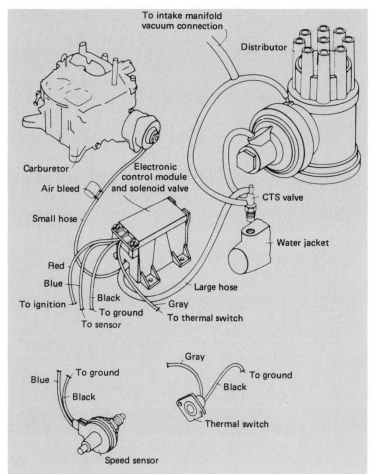

To intake manifold vacuum connection

Distributor

Carburetor

Electronic control module and solenoid valve

Air bleed

Small hose

CTS valve

Water jacket

Red

Blue

Black

To ignition

To ground

Gray

To sensor

Large hose

To thermal switch

Gray

Blue

To ground

Black

Black

Thermal switch

Speed sensor

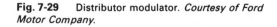

Fig. 7-29   Distributor modulator. *Courtesy of Ford Motor Company.*

cable. The thermal switch is mounted near the front door-hinge pillar on the outside of the cowl panel.

The system prevents spark advance below a specified speed when accelerating, and also prevents advance below a specified value on deceleration. Operating speeds vary according to the engine, and Ford specifications should be checked for the applicable speeds.

Distributor vacuum control coolant temperature sensing valve. The coolant temperature sensing valve is similar to the thermal vacuum switch used on some General Motors engines. The valve is installed on certain engines in the distributor vacuum advance supply line to provide advanced ignition timing under extended idling conditions. The valve is exposed to the engine cooling system to sense engine coolant temperature. Under normal conditions the valve connects two ports—normal source vacuum at the carburetor and the distributor port. During long idle periods, should the coolant temperature exceed normal limits, the valve closes the normal source port and connects the distributor port to the intake manifold vacuum. This vacuum in turn causes the ignition timing to be advanced, which speeds up the engine idle until the coolant temperature returns to normal.

Distributor vacuum deceleration valve. A distributor vacuum deceleration valve is installed on certain engines in the distributor vacuum system to give added control over ignition timing. The valve is installed between the vacuum lines of the intake manifold and carburetor and the primary diaphragm of the dual-diaphragm advance distributor. The primary diaphragm is normally connected to a vacuum port on the carburetor. During these periods of deceleration when intake manifold vacuum rises above a specified value, the valve closes off carburetor vacuum and provides direct intake manifold vacuum to the primary diaphragm of the distributor. This action allows maximum ignition timing advance in order to restrict afterburning in the engine exhaust system. When the automobile slows down and the engine is operating at idle, the valve closes off the intake manifold vacuum and allows carburetor vacuum to be channeled to the distributor.

EXHAUST GAS RECIRCULATION

The Exhaust Gas Recirculation (EGR) system is designed to introduce small amounts of exhaust gas into the combustion cycle, thereby reducing the generation of nitrous oxides (NOx). The amount of exhaust gas introduced and the timing of the cycle varies by calibration and is controlled by various factors including engine speed, altitude, engine vacuum, exhaust system back pressure, coolant temperature, and throttle angle depending on the calibrations. All EGR valves are vacuum actuated.

As shown in Figure 7-30, an EGR valve controls the

flow of exhaust gas into the intake manifold. Several different types of controls (which usually monitor engine temperature) are used to turn the vacuum on and off and thereby open and close the EGR valve.

The simplest EGR system, Figure 7-30(a), is the so-called "ported" variety in which the EGR valve hose connects to the base of the carburetor, either directly or through a temperature-control valve. There is no separate vacuum amplifier and the system is operated by vacuum taken from a port located above the carburetor throttle plate. At idle there is no vacuum and a spring in the EGR valve keeps it closed. Under these conditions, there is no recirculation of exhaust gases. But as the throttle is opened, the port is exposed to vacuum. Consequently, the EGR valve opens and exhaust gases do recirculate.

In the more complicated venturi-vacuum system, Figure 7-30(b), manifold vacuum is applied to a vacuum amplifier and the output vacuum of the amplifier is transmitted to the EGR valve. Venturi vacuum is also applied to the amplifier. At idle there is no venturi vacuum. But as the throttle plate opens, the flow of air through the venturi is

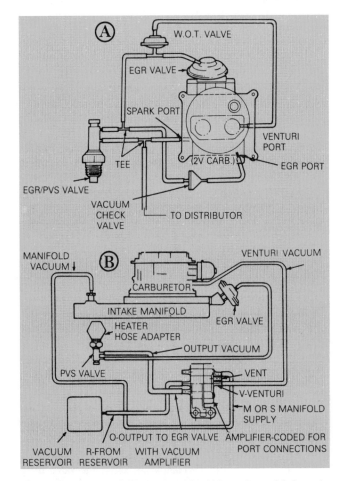

Fig. 7-30. Typical EGR systems for V-8 engines. (a) Ported system. (b) Venturi system.

rapid enough to create a slight vacuum that is adequate to open the amplifier. The amplifier then allows manifold vacuum to open the EGR valve.

All temperature controls used with EGR systems are designed to keep the EGR valve closed when the engine is cold. Once the engine warms up, the temperature controls let the EGR valve operate normally.

Troubleshooting the EGR System

General. When malfunctioning of the EGR system is indicated, the following general procedure is recommended.

1. Check all vacuum lines for proper routing, leaks, or restrictions.

2. Disconnect the vacuum hose at the EGR valve and connect a vacuum gauge to the hose.

3. Connect a tachometer to the engine.

4. Start the engine and operate it briefly at 2000 to 2500 rpm. Repeat eight to ten times and check for consistent response. If the engine is cold and vacuum rises above zero, the temperature vacuum switch (TVS) or the ported vacuum switch (PVS) is leaking and must be replaced. Once the engine is warmed up, the vacuum should rise above 15 in. Hg. and return to zero when the throttle is released. If the vacuum is less than 15 in. Hg., check the vacuum source and service if needed. If the vacuum does not return to zero when the throttle is released, or if the vacuum reading is inconsistent, the PVS or TVS is defective and must be replaced.

5. If satisfactory vacuum readings are obtained in Step 4, be guided by the vehicle systems that follow. Should the EGR dignostics indicate that the EGR system is O.K., investigate possible carburetor or ignition malfunctions. Also keep in mind that excessive exhaust back pressure in vehicles equipped with the integral back-pressure type EGR valve can cause abnormally rough running at part throttle due to excessive EGR. Check for foreign material blocking the exhaust system and/or collapsed exhaust-system components.

Rough idle and/or stall.

1. EGR valve receiving vacuum at idle, vacuum hoses misrouted. Check the hose routing and correct as required. Also check the vacuum supply at idle with the engine at operating temperature.

2. EGR valve not closing fully or stuck open. Inspect the valve for proper closing and seating. Clean or replace as required.

3. EGR valve gasket blown, or hose attachment loose. Check the valve attaching bolts for tightness and inspect the gasket. Tighten valve or replace gasket as needed.

4. EGR valve air bleeds are plugged (back-pressure-type valve only). With the engine off, see if the valve holds vacuum. If it does, replace the valve.

Rough running, surge, hesitation, and generally poor performance at part throttle when the engine is cold.

1. Repeat Steps 1 through 4 shown under "Rough idle and/or stall".

2. TVS or PVS opening too early. Check TVS or PVS at outlet port for vacuum. When the engine is cold, there should be no vacuum. If vacuum is present, the switch is defective and must be replaced.

Rough running, surge, hesitation, and generally poor performance at part throttle when the engine is either hot or cold.

1. Excessive EGR due to the EGR valve being stuck wide open. Remove the valve and inspect all components for freedom of movement. Clean or replace as required.

Engine stalls on deceleration.

1. EGR valve sticking open or not closing fully.

Part-throttle engine detonation. (Note: Detonation can also be due to carburetor or ignition malfunction.) In the EGR system the problem is caused by insufficient EGR which may be due to any of the following causes, or a combination thereof.

1. EGR valve stuck closed. Check valve for freedom of operation by pressing and releasing the valve diaphragm to stroke the valve mechanism. Clean or replace the valve that is not operating smoothly.

2. Leaky valve diaphragm not actuating valve. Check the valve by applying vacuum. (On back-pressure type valves only, block the tailpipe with drive socket of outside diameter approximately $\frac{1}{16}$ inch less than the inside diameter of the tailpipe. DO NOT BLOCK FULLY. Idle engine while applying vacuum to valve. DO NOT RUN THE ENGINE FASTER THAN IDLE OR FOR PROLONGED PERIODS OF TIME. Be sure to remove socket from the tailpipe at the end of this test. If these precautions are not observed, either the engine or the exhaust system, or both, could be damaged.) If the valve leaks vacuum, replace it.

3. Vacuum restricted to EGR valve. Check vacuum hoses, fittings, routing, and supply for blockage.

4. EGR disconnected. Check connections and correct as required.

5. TVS and/or PVS not opening. Check the TVS or PVS at the outlet to the EGR valve for vacuum. There should be vacuum at part throttle when the engine is warm. If not, replace damaged switch. Make sure the vacuum supply is not restricted.

6. Load control valve venting. Check for proper functioning. Vacuum should be present at load-control-valve vacuum port to EGR valve. Replace if damaged.

7. EGR passages blocked. Check EGR passages for restrictions and lockage.

8. Insufficient exhaust back pressure (with back-pressure EGR valve only). Check for vacuum leaks ahead of muffler/catalyst or for blown-out muffler/catalyst. Also check for blockage to EGR valve. Service or replace as required.

9. Vacuum hose leaking (cracked, split, broken, loose connection). Check all vacuum hoses for breaks and all connections for proper fit.

Abnormally low power at wide-open throttle (WOT).

1. Load control valve not venting. Check for proper functioning. Vacuum should not be present at vacuum port to EGR valve at WOT or heavy load. If vacuum is present, the valve is defective and must be replaced.

Engine starts but stalls immediately thereafter when cold.

1. EGR valve receiving vacuum, vacuum hoses misrouted. Check hose routing and correct as required.

2. EGR valve not fully closing. Remove valve and inspect. Clean or replace as required.

3. Carburetor malfunction.

Engine hard to start or will not start.

1. EGR valve receiving vacuum, vacuum hoses misrouted.

2. EGR valve stuck open.

Poor fuel economy.   EGR related if:

1. Caused by detonation or other symptom of restricted or no EGR flow.

CATALYTIC CONVERTERS

A catalytic converter is simply a chamber in the exhaust system that works as a gas reactor. When certain pollutants pass over the catalyst they react with oxygen in the exhaust and are converted into harmless water and carbon dioxide. The catalyst function is to speed up the heat-producing chemical reaction between the exhaust gas components in order to reduce the air pollutants in the engine exhaust.

The engine exhaust consists mainly of nitrogen (N_2), but also contains carbon monoxide (CO), carbon dioxide (CO_2), water vapor (H_2O), oxygen (O_2), nitrous oxides (NOx), hydrogen (H_2) and various unburned hydrocarbons (HC). The major pollutants are CO, NOx, and HC.

The catalyst inside the converter is made in two forms. General Motors and American Motors use a pellet-type catalyst in most (but not all) of their automobiles. Here, loose pellets are packed into a canister and can be emptied and changed. Ford and Chrysler use a monolithic converter. The catalyst material is made of a ceramic substate that is coated with alumina and impregnated with chemically active precious metals. The catalyst in a monolithic converter is not serviceable.

Multiple converters are now common and there are three basic types of catalysts:

1. The *conventional oxidation catalyst* (COC) that contains platinum and paladium and is effective for catalyzing the oxidation reactions of hydrocarbons (HC) and carbon monoxide (CO).

2. The *three-way catalyst* (TWC) that contains platinum and rhodium and catalyzes the oxidation reactions of HC, CO and nitrous oxides (NOx).

3. The *light-off catalyst* (LOC) is used in a single-bed converter that is connected in front of (in series with) COC and/or TWC converters. The LOC provides exhaust emission control during engine warmup when the COC and/or TWC converters have not yet reached the temperature required for maximum efficiency. The LOC operates effectively in the high-temperature environment near the manifold flange.

Although periodic maintenance of the exhaust system is not required, if the car is raised for other service, check the general condition of the catalytic converter, pipes, and muffler.

If a converter overheats, the catalyst may melt and block the exhaust. Sometimes, pieces of the catalyst are ejected from the exhaust pipe when the engine is running. The solution is to replace a monolithic converter or change the pellets in a pellet-type converter.

To prevent overheating of the converter, Ford uses a heat-sensitive switch that controls the vacuum to the air-pump bypass valve in a Thermactor system. When the vacuum is cut off, the bypass valve dumps the pump air into the atmosphere rather than into the exhaust. When this occurs, the converter does not convert and cools off.

To check for exhaust blockage, connect a vacuum gauge to the engine and operate the engine at about 2500 rpm with the shift selector in the P (park) or N (neutral) position. A steady vacuum shows that all is well. But a slowly dropping vacuum indicates a pressure buildup.

DO NOT USE LEADED FUEL in a car equipped with a catalyst converter. After just a few tanks of leaded fuel the catalyst loses its ability to catalyze the oxidation reactions. Eventually the use of leaded fuel can plug the catalyst to the point where the engine cannot operate.

VACUUM OPERATED HEAT RISER VALVES

The exhaust-manifold heat valve (heat riser) was discussed in an earlier section of this chapter dealing with carburetor troubleshooting. Recall that the purpose of this valve is to force part of the engine exhaust through a passageway under the intake manifold in order to preheat the fuel mixture and obtain better fuel vaporization during engine warmup.

Looking Ahead

Emission control systems, like all other major systems in modern automobiles, are usually modified from year to year. In the interest of fuel conservation, however, it is likely that all such systems over the next five years or so will be some version of those described here. Because the presence of such systems often imposes certain requirements in engine tune-up, always read the manufacturer's servicing literature before you attempt any adjustment.

8

ENGINE VALVES

Contents

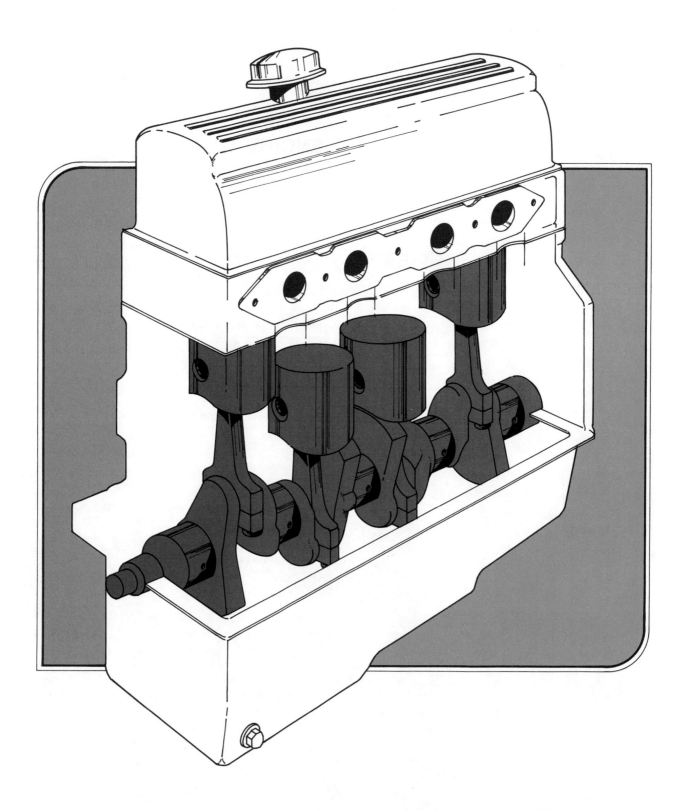

SIMPLE 4cylinder ENGINE

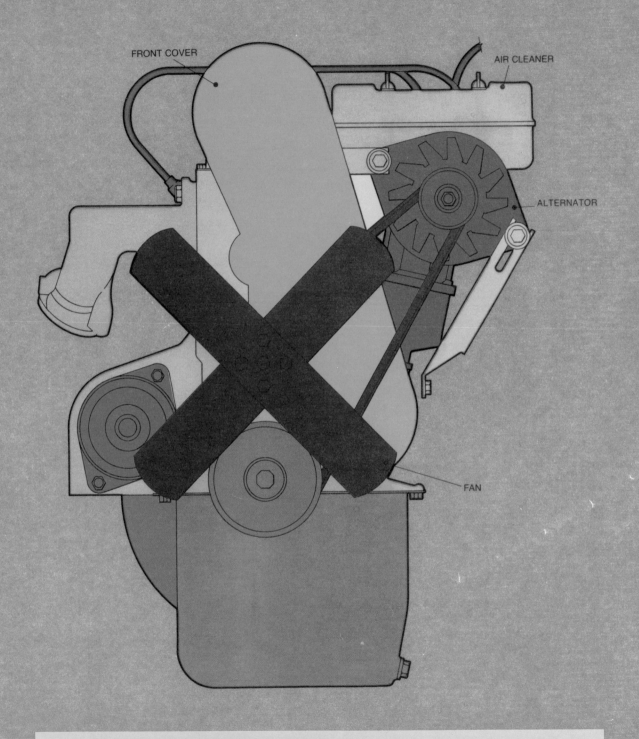

FRONT COVER

AIR CLEANER

ALTERNATOR

FAN

The components which comprise the electrical system are shown in red. The starter motor turns the engine, which starts a series of events. The coil, which is mounted in the engine compartment, takes an electrical current from the battery and increases the voltage and sends it to the distributor. The distributor allots the electrical charge to each spark plug in the correct firing order. The alternator replenishes electricity to the battery.

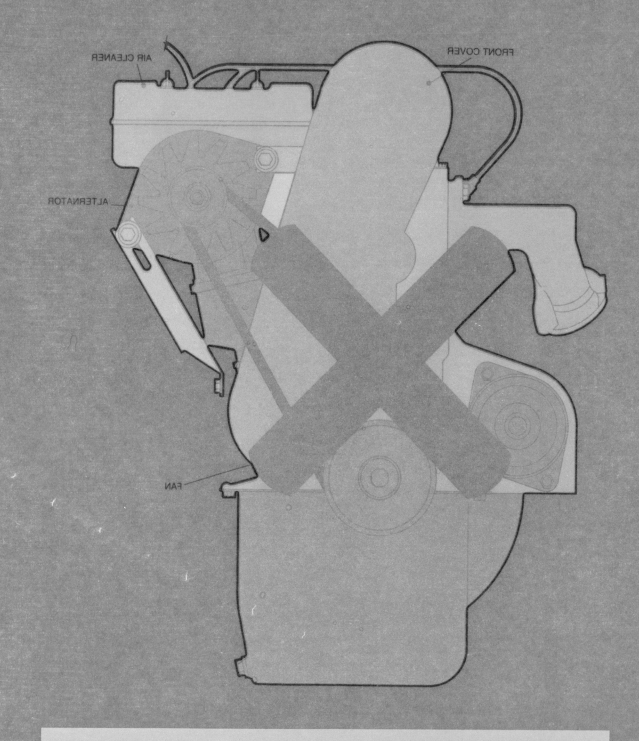

The components which comprise the electrical system are shown in red. The starter motor turns the engine, which starts a series of events. The coil, which is mounted in the engine compartment, takes an electrical current from the battery and increases the voltage and sends it to the distributor. The distributor allots the electrical charge to each spark plug in the correct firing order. The alternator replenishes electricity to the battery.

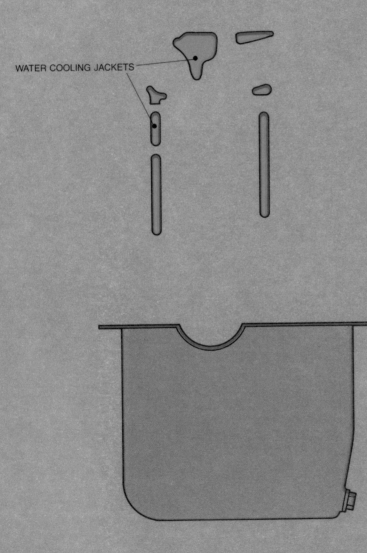

WATER COOLING JACKETS

The automobile engine creates tremendous amounts of heat. Most automotive engines use water and air to dissipate this heat. The water pump is directly behind the fan shown on the previous page. This pump moves water (blue color) around the cylinder walls and valve jackets. The heat created at these critical areas is transmitted to the water. This warm water is pumped to the radiator where it is cooled by air convection. The cooled water is then pumped back into the engine where it repeats the cycle.

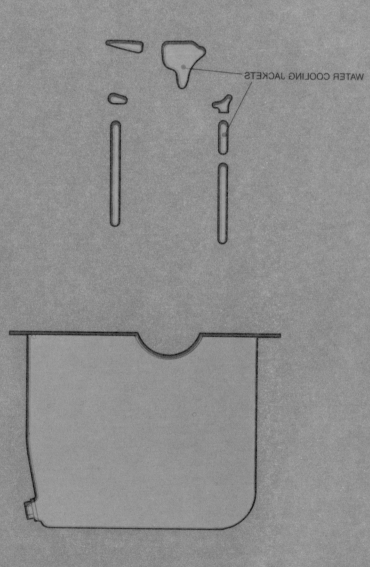

The automobile engine creates tremendous amounts of heat. Most automotive engines use water and air to dissipate this heat. The water pump is directly behind the fan shown on the previous page. This pump moves water (blue color) around the cylinder walls and valve jackets. The heat created at these critical areas is transmitted to the water. This warm water is pumped to the radiator where it is cooled by air convection. The cooled water is then pumped back into the engine where it repeats the cycle.

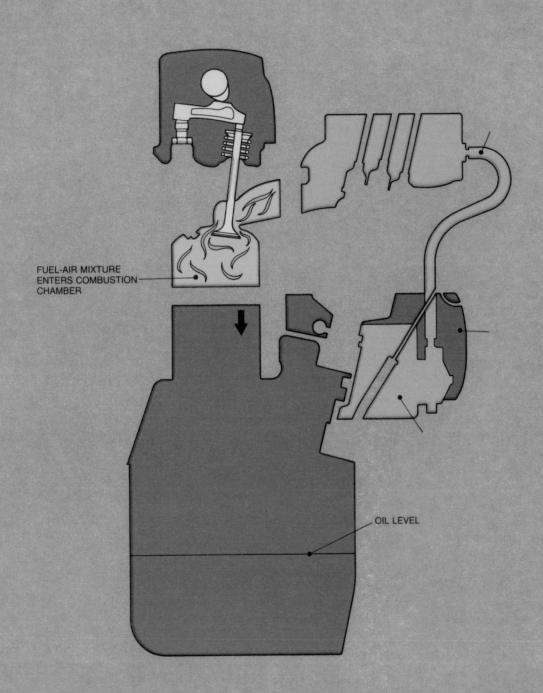

FUEL-AIR MIXTURE
ENTERS COMBUSTION
CHAMBER

OIL LEVEL

Oil is used to decrease friction caused by metal moving against metal. The oil pump circulates the oil to the critical areas of the engine. The oil filter cleanses the oil by removing dirt and foreign particles. The fuel pump pushes gas into the carburetor which introduces air and creates a fuel-air mixture. The mixture is then drawn through the open intake valve into the cylinder chamber. This is known as the intake stroke. Arrow indicates piston travel.

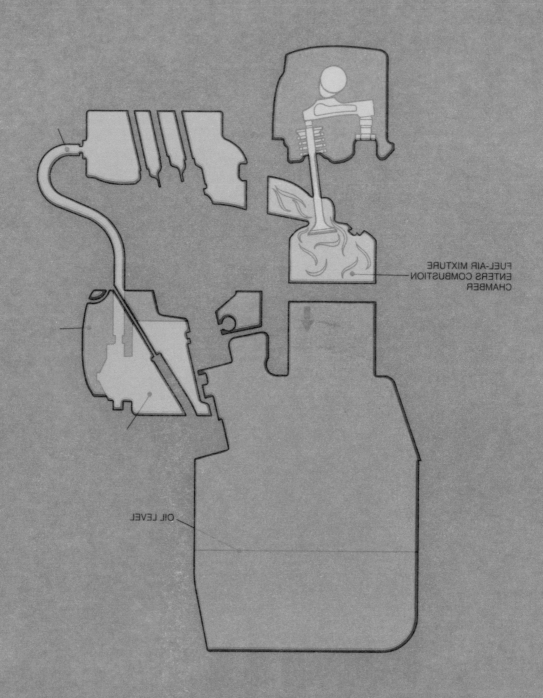

FUEL-AIR MIXTURE

Oil is used to decrease friction caused by metal moving against metal. The oil pump circulates the oil to the critical areas of the engine. The oil filter cleanses the oil by removing dirt and foreign particles. The fuel pump pushes gas into the carburetor which introduces air and creates a fuel-air mixture. The mixture is then drawn through the open intake valve into the cylinder chamber. This is known as the intake stroke. Arrow indicates piston travel.

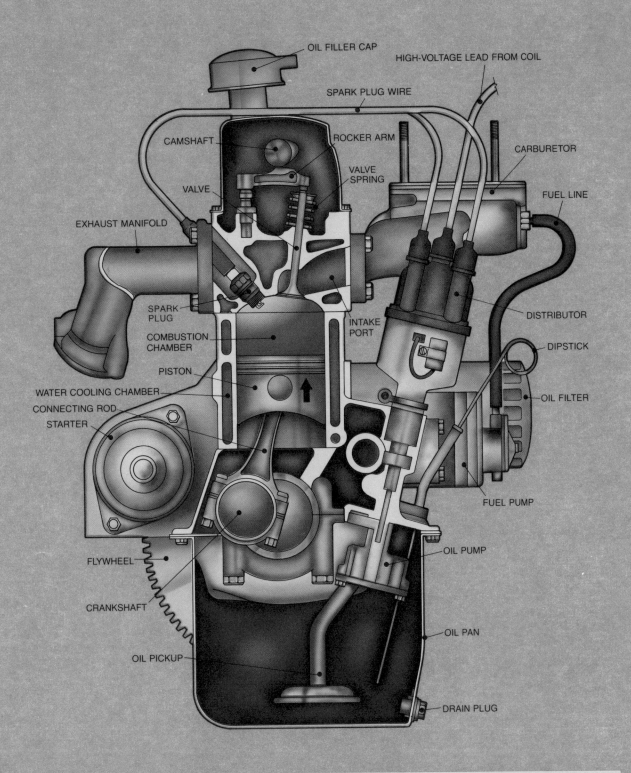

OIL FILLER CAP

HIGH-VOLTAGE LEAD FROM COIL

SPARK PLUG WIRE

CAMSHAFT

ROCKER ARM

VALVE SPRING

CARBURETOR

VALVE

FUEL LINE

EXHAUST MANIFOLD

SPARK PLUG

INTAKE PORT

DISTRIBUTOR

COMBUSTION CHAMBER

DIPSTICK

PISTON

WATER COOLING CHAMBER

OIL FILTER

CONNECTING ROD

STARTER

FUEL PUMP

OIL PUMP

FLYWHEEL

CRANKSHAFT

OIL PAN

OIL PICKUP

DRAIN PLUG

The electrical spark through the spark plug ignites the compressed fuel mixture driving the piston downward. This is called a power stroke. Momentum drives the piston upward expelling the exhausted gases through the open exhaust valve into the exhaust pipe. This is known as the exhaust stroke. These four strokes—intake, compression, power, and exhaust—are basic to the four-stroke engine. This series of actions creates a rotary movement of the crankshaft. The rotary movement is transmitted through the transmission, drive shaft, differential and axle to the wheels of the automobile.

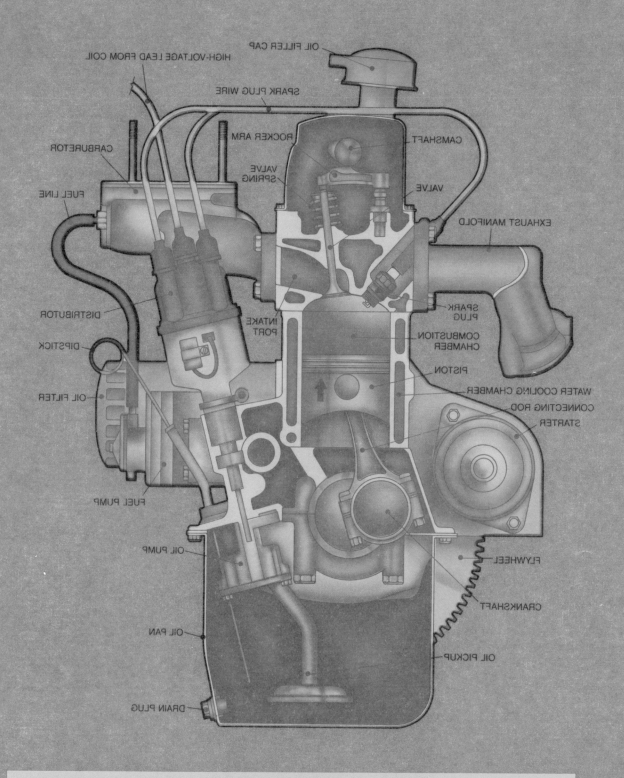

OIL FILLER CAP
HIGH-VOLTAGE LEAD FROM COIL
SPARK PLUG WIRE
CAMSHAFT
ROCKER ARM
CARBURETOR
VALVE SPRING
VALVE
FUEL LINE
EXHAUST MANIFOLD
SPARK PLUG
STARTER
FUEL PUMP
OIL PUMP
FLYWHEEL
CRANKSHAFT
OIL PAN
OIL PICKUP
DRAIN PLUG

The electrical spark through the spark plug ignites the compressed fuel mixture driving the piston downward. This is called a power stroke. Momentum drives the piston upward expelling the exhausted gases through the open exhaust valve into the exhaust pipe. This is known as the exhaust stroke. These four strokes — intake, compression, power, and exhaust — are basic to the four-stroke engine. This series of actions creates a rotary movement of the crankshaft. The rotary movement is transmitted through the transmission, drive shaft, differential and axle to the wheels of the automobile.

OPERATION AND DESIGN

Basic Operation

In a gasoline engine, exhaust and intake manifolds and valve ports are needed to supply air and fuel on the intake stroke of the cylinders, and to expel burned gases on the exhaust stroke. The ports are opened and closed at the proper times by the intake and exhaust valves, which close against the seats (sides) of the ports. See Fig. 8-1.

The intake stroke, (a), occurs as the piston moves downward from top dead center (TDC). This action of the piston creates a partial vacuum in the cylinder. The exhaust valve is closed, and seals the cylinder from the exhaust manifold. The intake valve is open, however, and the partial

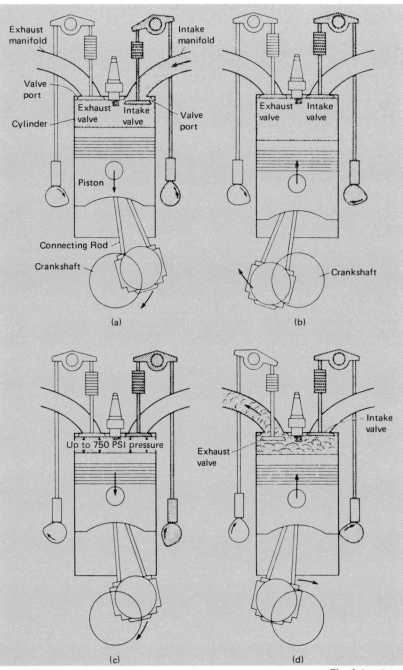

Fig. 8-1   Strokes of four-cycle engine: (a) intake, (b) compression, (c) power, and (d) exhaust. *Courtesy of Chevrolet Division, General Motors Corporation.*

vacuum extends into the intake manifold. As a result, fuel-air mixture is drawn into the cylinder. The intake valve begins to close as the piston passes bottom dead center (BDC). The valve is kept open as long as possible to pull more fuel-air mixture into the cylinder.

As soon as the piston passes BDC, the intake valve closes completely, as shown in Fig. 8-1(b). The exhaust valve remains closed during the compression stroke. Thus, as the piston is forced up by the rotating crankshaft, the fuel-air charge is trapped and compressed. Since compression and power output are directly related, both the intake and exhaust valves must be tightly sealed. Any leakage reduces compression and causes power loss.

The fuel is ignited just before the piston reaches TDC on the compression stroke. The heat generated by combustion causes the gases to expand, creating high pressure in the cylinder, which forces the piston down, as shown in (c). This is the power stroke. The valves still remain fully closed to seal the pressure (about 750 psi).

As the piston reaches the lower half of the power stroke, the thrust from the pressure diminishes. Some pressure remains, but it is of no practical value so far as engine power is concerned. The exhaust valve then begins to open, relieving any remaining pressure that would resist the upward stroke of the piston on the exhaust stroke.

With the exhaust valve open and the intake valve still closed, the piston moves upward and forces hot gases out through the exhaust-valve port, as shown in Fig. 8-1(d). The exhaust valve remains open throughout the exhaust stroke and partly into the intake stroke to make sure all burned gases are removed from the combustion chamber. Even though the piston is starting down again, the gases still have enough momentum from the exhaust stroke to carry them into the exhaust manifold.

The intake valve starts to open just before the beginning of the intake stroke. This period, when both valves are open, is called *valve overlap*. This overlap is necessary to start the fuel-air mixture moving about the intake valve, so that it moves without delay into the cylinder on the intake stroke.

Valve overlap has increased in recent years because of the trend toward higher speed engines. This increase in overlap is necessary to make the engine breathe, that is, get rid of exhaust gases and get a fresh charge into the cylinder quickly. One unfortunate effect of overlap is the need for higher idle speeds.

Valve timing. Valve timing are those points in the cycle when valves open and close. These points are measured in terms of degrees, rather than in piston travel distance. For example, with the intake valve timed to open 15° before TDC on the exhaust stroke and the exhaust valve timed to stay open for 15° into the intake stroke, overlap is measured as 30°.

Design

In an eight-cylinder engine, at turnpike speeds, there are more than one million valve openings and closings per hour. The valves must make a gastight seal, withstand high pressures, and be able to operate at high temperatures and dissipate heat rapidly. The intake valve gets a cool bath each time a fresh charge is admitted to the cylinder, but the exhaust valve is subject continuously to gas blasts of up to 4000°F, and the temperature at the top of the valve may reach as high as 1400°F. Because of the high temperatures involved, engines are designed with the cooling system as close to the exhaust valves as possible.

Poppet valves. Various types of valves have been used in the past. In today's cars, however, the valve in general use is the poppet (mushroom) valve shown in Figure 8-2. In this design, the mushroom-shaped valve end (head) blends into the stem. The valve face is the closely machined, tapered edge that mates with the seat to seal the port. The valves operate in a guide in the cylinder head (block). Either a retainer groove or a slot on the bottom of the valve accommodates the valve retainer.

As shown in Fig. 8-2(b), lift is the farthest distance cov-

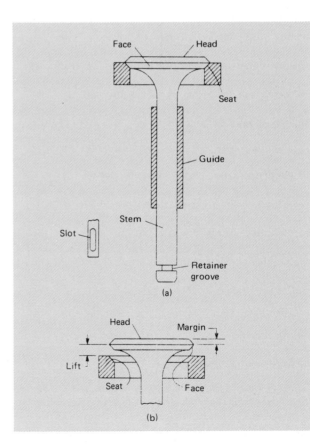

Fig. 8-2 Poppet valve: (a) parts, and (b) lift and margin.

ered by the valve when it opens, and margin is the thickness of the valve head above the face.

Valve-face angles are usually either 30° or 45°, with corresponding angles on the seats. It is not uncommon, however, to find the valve-face angle one degree less than the angle on the seat. Thus, contact is made on a sharp edge rather than on the whole face, providing a wedging action for fast and better sealing.

Valve seats and guides. When the engine block is cast iron, inserts are used to form the seat. Otherwise, the seat is machined directly into the block casting. Inserts are made of cast alloys or steel. When used, inserts are shrunk, pressed into the valve ports, and then ground to the correct angle. Seat inserts are easily replaced.

Valve guides are either machined into the block or arranged as separate inserts. Guides that are machined in transfer heat better, but must be bored out when worn, making necessary the use of valves with oversized stems. Since the guides must maintain squareness of the valves with their seats, guide-to-stem clearance is critical. Intake valves usually operate with 0.0015 to 0.0035 inch clearance, and exhaust valves with 0.0020 to 0.0040 inch clearance, depending upon the size of the stem.

Relative sizes—intake and exhaust valves. When the intake valve opens, atmospheric pressure is the only force that acts to push the air-fuel mixture into the cylinder. But when the exhaust valve is opened, the high pressure created by the upward-moving piston forces exhaust gases through the valve. Thus, the intake valve (and port) is usually larger than the exhaust valve.

Effect of lead-free gasoline. Because lead can cause serious problems in the emission controls, modern engines generally use lead-free gasoline. But the absence of lead creates a problem for valve faces and valve seats. When lead is present in the gasoline, it forms a coating on the valve faces and seats and this coating acts as a lubricant. When the lead is absent, the loss of lubricant increases wear. To overcome this problem, manufacturers now use special coatings on valve faces.

VALVE TRAINS

Valve-Operating Mechanisms

Three basic kinds of engine valve trains are used in American-made automobiles: L-head (flat head), valve-in-head (overhead valve), and overhead cam. Because the L-head arrangement is fast disappearing in American automobiles, only the overhead valve and overhead cam types are considered here.

Overhead valve train. In most engines, the valves are built in the head and are operated by rocker arms. The *cam* is followed by a *lifter*, which raises the *pushrod*. This actuates the *rocker arm* on its pivot, and the arm pushes down against the *valve stem* to open the valve. The spring closes the valve when the lifter is lowered. Clearance adjustment is provided by the adjusting screw in the rocker arm.

Note that the portion of the rocker arm that extends from the pivot to the valve stem is approximately equal in length to the portion that extends from the pivot to the pushrod. With this arrangement, the valve lift is equal to the cam rise. If, on the other hand, the valve end of the rocker arm is 1½ times as long as the pushrod end, the valve lift is 1½ times the cam rise. Conversely, if the pushrod end of the rocker arm is longer than the valve end, valve lift is proportionately less than the cam rise.

Overhead cam train. The overhead cam (OHC) engine is very popular in 4-cylinder cars and has been used in some 6-cylinder models. Different arrangements are used to convey the cam action to the valve stems.

With the ever-increasing popularity of 4-cylinder engines, this arrangement may very well become the most common of all. Here, the cam is mounted overhead.

A rocker arm, actuated by the cam to open and close the valve, is mounted on an automatic lash-adjustment mechanism that operates on the same principle as a hydraulic *lifter* (discussed shortly).

Cam action is carried directly to the valve stem through a cap, called the valve *tappet*, that fits over the stem and spring. Valve clearance is adjusted by turning the screw located in the tappet.

The camshaft is mounted in a special housing on top of the cylinder head. The housing is a die-cast aluminum cover containing seven bearing surfaces that support the camshaft. The cover is assembled on top of the cast iron cylinder head, and the valve guides are an integral part of the casting. The cam lobes on the rocker arms are approximately twice the width of the average cam lobes to promote increased reliability and durability.

The valves are oversized to permit freer breathing. Because a large quantity of oil is needed to lubricate an overhead valve mechanism, the intake valves are equipped with specially designed oil seals.

Notice that two springs are used in the overhead cam train. The outer spring is a conventional round-wire spring, and the inner spring, called a *damper* spring, is a flat-wire spring.

Camshaft Drives

The basic operating principles of the camshaft are always the same regardless of the camshaft location. Since the valves cycle once for every two revolutions of the engine, the camshaft must be driven at one-half the engine speed. This reduction in speed is accomplished either by a gear drive, Fig. 8-3(a), or chain drive, (b). The camshaft gear (or sprocket) has twice as many teeth as the crankshaft gear (or sprocket). The Pontiac overhead cam is driven by sprockets and an oil-resistant belt made of rubber reinforced with fiberglas.

The gears, sprockets, chain, and belt used to drive the camshaft are referred to as the timing gears, the timing chain, and so on. The camshaft must be synchronized with the crankshaft in order to time valve openings and closings properly.

Camshaft Design

Camshaft design is important to the basic valve timing of the engine. A typical cam is shown in Fig. 8-4. The height of the cam nose determines the amount of valve lift, and the ramp taper determines lift duration. Short-duration opening and moderate lift give smooth idling and good low-speed torque. When speed is important, high-lift and long-duration cam designs are used, and smooth idling is sacrificed to some degree.

In the overhead cam engine, a concentric hole is drilled through the camshaft and holes are drilled in the cam heels to provide for lubrication.

Lifters

Solid lifters. The valve lifter shown in Fig. 8-5 is known as the mushroom type because of the shape of that portion of the lifter which contacts (follows) the cam. There is also a roller-type lifter, Fig. 8-6, which, as the name suggests, uses a roller to follow the cam. Both types of lifters operate in guides that are machined in the cylinder block, or in guide brackets attached to the block. The roller-type lifter has a lug that moves in a slot in the guide to keep the roller from turning crosswise on the cam.

Both types of lifter are referred to as *solid, hard,* or *mechanical* lifters to differentiate them from hydraulic lifters; the latter operate on a cushion of oil rather than on solid metal.

Hydraulic lifters. Hydraulic valve lifters automatically take up valve-stem clearance while the valves are closed. Thus the need for adjustment after initial installation, as

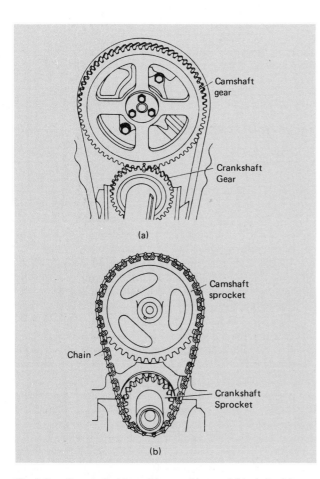

Fig. 8-3 Camshaft drives: (a) gear drive and (b) chain drive.

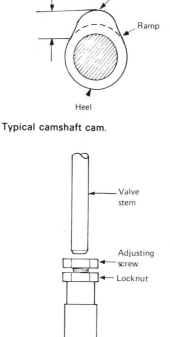

Fig. 8-4 Typical camshaft cam.

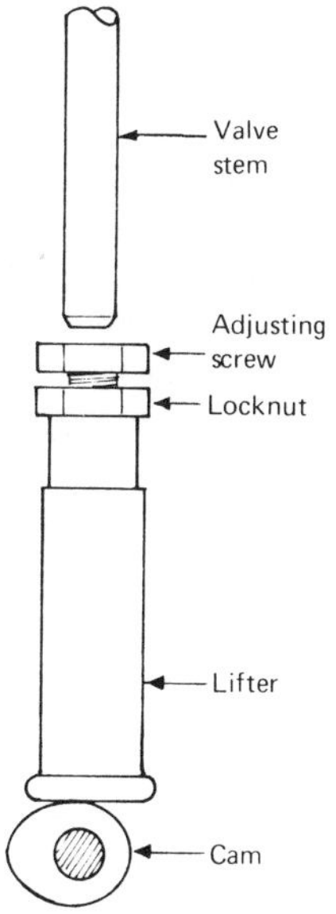

Fig. 8-5 Mushroom-type valve lifter.

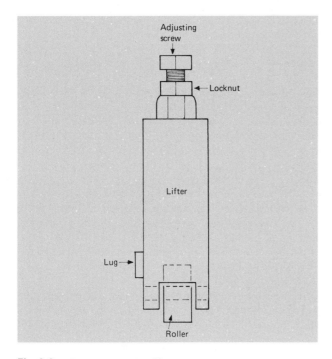

Fig. 8-6 Roller-type valve lifter.

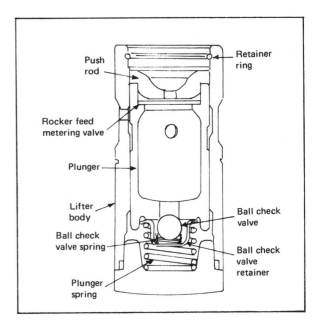

Fig. 8-7 Hydraulic valve lifter. *Courtesy of Pontiac Division, General Motors Corporation.*

well as tappet noise (the annoying clicking sound heard in some engines), is eliminated.

A typical hydraulic lifter, Fig. 8-7, has a body and a *spring-loaded plunger* fitted with a pushrod cup to bear against the *pushrod* or *valve,* depending on the type of engine involved. A *channel* (or hole) in the lifter body matches with an oil-feed hole in the plunger.

When the lifter is lowered to the base circle of the cam, engine oil under pressure enters the body through the channel. It flows through the plunger, around the check valve, and into the cavity below the plunger. At the same time, the plunger spring raises the plunger to take up clearance. The check valve is held in place by the retainer.

When the cam starts to raise the lifter, the oil under the plunger is subjected to high pressure and closes the check valve. Because oil is not compressible, the lifter assembly rises and opens the valve. Oil leakage between the plunger and body, however, lets the plunger drop slightly in the body bore. Because of this leakage, the valve clearance is adjusted to zero each time the valve is opened. Leakage rate is critical, since excess leakage reduces the valve lift.

Engine oil cleanliness is particularly important because contamination may cause a hydraulic lifter to stick and not take up the clearance.

Zero-lash mechanical lifters. Another lifter which takes up valve clearance automatically is the zero-lash mechanical lifter shown in Fig. 8-8. A spring-loaded *eccentric* maintains constant contact between the *rocker arm* and *valve stem.* A spring pushes the *plunger* against the eccentric, which, be-

cause of its shape, eliminates the clearance between the valve stem and the eccentric. Conventional solid lifters are used in the unit shown.

VALVE TROUBLESHOOTING

Valve Faults

Sticking. Sticking may be caused by too little clearance between the valve stem and guide to permit the stem to expand when the valve is hot. Too much clearance also can cause sticking by allowing carbon deposits on the upper portion of the stem to lodge between the stem and guide.

Valve sticking is often due to a warped stem. This results from overheating or pressure on the valve caused by misalignment or an eccentric seat. Also, a spring or keeper incorrectly installed may cock the valve and bend the stem.

Another possible cause of sticking is poor lubrication. In this case, the valve may stick when the engine is cold and become free when the engine is warm. Lack of lubrication hastens valve guide wear and this, in turn, aggravates sticking.

Deposits on the upper portion of the valve stem are the most common cause of sticking. Deposits can be minimized by using high-quality engine oil containing the proper additives, and by changing oil at recommended intervals.

Floating. Sometimes, failure of a valve to close is due to failure of the valve spring to exert enough force to hold the

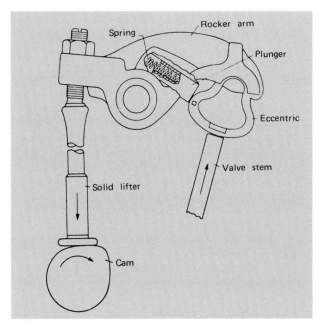

Fig. 8-8 Zero-lash mechanical lifter. *Courtesy of Pontiac Division, General Motors Corporation.*

valve mechanism against the cam. The spring may be weak, or the inertia of moving parts may be too much for the spring to overcome at high speed.

It is not possible always to distinguish between sticking and floating, but floating usually occurs in high-performance, high-compression ratio engines. Until corrected, floating can be avoided by driving at low speeds to guard against serious engine damage resulting from the piston hitting the valve head.

Burning. A burned valve has been so overheated that metal has eroded. This problem usually is encountered with exhaust valves.

Anything that keeps the valve from seating properly keeps the valve from transferring heat from its head to its seat and may lead to burning. Also, if the valve is partly open during the exhaust stroke, some of the gases blow by the valve. The heat concentration in these gases is much higher than during exhaust, and the valve is heated still further. Sticking valves or valves operated without enough clearance are susceptible to burning. Insufficient lash, even though it lets the valve seat properly, may not leave it seated long enough to transfer the heat and eventually burns the valve.

Other causes of burned valves are worn guides, which do not transfer heat readily; clogged passages in the cooling system; and engine overloading. Too lean a fuel mixture, a cool running engine, and detonation and preignition also cause overheating in the combustion chamber and may burn the valves.

Leaking. Leaking valves occur when valves are not sealed tightly on their seats. This condition, if not corrected, often leads to a burned valve. When a valve leaks, engine compression is so reduced that power is lost in the affected cylinder(s). Also, the fuel-air mixture may be blown back into the intake manifold and cause backfiring.

Normal wear may cause a leak, but wear is accelerated by dirt on the seat or by hammering from too much tappet clearance. The carburetor air cleaner must be maintained properly to avoid dirt entering through the carburetor and intake manifold.

Next to wear, insufficient lash is the most common cause of valve leakage. Overheating may cause lengthening of the valve stem, in turn causing insufficient lash, so that the valve will leak only when the engine is hot. Other causes include eccentric seats, misalignment, cocking from excessive wear, or an incorrectly installed spring or keeper.

Valve mechanism noises. Noise usually indicates looseness in valve operating mechanisms. Tappets may be loose in their guides, there may be too much lash, or the rocker-arm bushings may be worn excessively. A worn camshaft drive can cause looseness between the gears or in the sprocket chain.

Tappet noise is a regular clicking sound that increases in intensity with engine speed. Because the valves cycle once for every two revolutions of the engine, the frequency of the noise is half that of engine noises, though this frequency may not readily be discernible. Other engine noises, however, such as rod knock, pin noise, and piston slap, are all heavier and more metallic in sound. Piston-ring rattling resembles tappet noise but is evident only when the engine is accelerated. Any noise that changes with engine load is unlikely to be tappet noise. Worn timing gears produce a humming or knocking sound. The gears chatter sharply at low or idle engine speed, particularly if the idle is rough.

Hydraulic-lifter noise. Noisy hydraulic lifters sound like valve noise. Any of the following may be the cause.

1. Plugged or loaded oil filter.
2. Incorrect oil level: if the oil level in the oil pan is too high, the oil may foam; if the level is too low, air may enter the pump inlet. Either condition may lead to noisy action of the valve mechanism.
3. Incorrect oil pressure.
4. Weak valve-lifter plunger springs: in some cases, the weakness permits excessive plunger movement and wear. The following steps should be taken to check and remedy the trouble: (a) Remove the valve-lifter assemblies. (b) Disassemble and clean each assembly. (c) Dry each part carefully and reassemble the unit. (d) Check the pressure required to compress each plunger spring while dry. If this pressure is less than 6 or 7 pounds, replace the hydraulic unit. The valve cylinder and plunger are mated, and should be replaced as a unit.

5. Dirty, scored, or worn valve-lifter parts: when the tap or click occurs at regular intervals, trouble in a single valve unit is indicated. Since the most likely cause of sticking is dirt, disassemble the defective unit, wash it in gasoline, and wipe with a soft cloth. A stuck check valve may be loosened with a small blunt tool, after which the cylinder should be washed in gasoline. Air pressure may be used to dry parts of the valve mechanism, but the nozzle should be held at least 2 inches from the parts. Always remove and clean the oil pan and flush the engine with clean solvent when valve sticking occurs; otherwise the trouble might reappear almost immediately. Also remove valve lifter brackets and clean out oil passages. Sticking may also be caused by pitting and scoring of the cylinder or plunger resulting from gritty particles, excessive wear, or damage during installation. When this condition is found, replace the cylinder and plunger.

6. Aerated oil: if the crankcase oil level drops below "fill," the oil pump may force air into the lubrication system at high engine speeds. On the other hand, if the oil level is too high, the crankshaft counterweights make the oil foam.

7. Contaminated oil: gum, varnish, water, or antifreeze in the oil are other sources of trouble. Combustion by-products blowing past the piston rings affect the entire lubricating system. Worn out or misfiring spark plugs naturally increase this contamination. Another source of trouble is the oilfilter cap screen, which should be cleaned frequently to help ventilate the crankcase and remove combustion by-products.

8. Dirty oil: this is the most frequent cause of hydraulic valve mechanism troubles. Oil and filter changes always should be made at recommended intervals to provide the greatest protection possible against trouble of this type.

Valve system wear. Wear occurs any time two parts are in contact with each other. Wear is aggravated by foreign particles and by poor lubrication. It is extremely important, therefore, to use high-quality engine oil. In particular, the cam lobes and follower surfaces on the lifters are susceptible to wear, pitting, and scuffing when high valve spring loads cause the film of lubricating oil to break down. Only engine oil rated MS (maximum severity) minimizes this type of wear. Other parts likely to wear because of dirt or inadequate lubrication are lifters and guides, pushrod seats in the rocker arms, rocker-arm bushings, and valve stems and seats. Timing gears, also susceptible to wear, may be more tolerant of dirt than other parts, but they must have adequate lubrication to function properly.

Diagnosis

Excess lash (solid lifters). To determine if valve noise is caused by excessive lash, insert a feeler gauge between the valve stem and rocker arm on overhead-valve engines. If the

noise stops, adjust the lash to eliminate the trouble. If the noise does not stop, push against the side of the spring. If the noise stops, the trouble is a cocked valve spring, worn valve guides, or a worn rocker arm.

Noisy lifters. To check a noisy hydraulic lifter, press down on the rocker-arm end of each pushrod while the engine is running. If a lifter isn't doing its job, you'll feel a mechanical shock. That lifter should then be removed, tested, and repaired. Both hydraulic and solid lifters can become noisy when there is excess clearance in their guides after high mileage. The clearance is checked by removing the access cover and trying to wiggle the lifters by hand. If a lifter can be wiggled, the clearance probably is incorrect and adjustments or repairs should be made.

Rocker-arm wear. Rocker arms are wiggled by hand to determine whether there is excessive wear of shaft bushings. If the arm seems loose, remove it and check its clearance. Wear can also occur in the pushrod sockets. To detect this, try to wiggle the pushrods.

Sticking valves. A sticking valve makes a clicking sound very similar to that made by a loose tappet, but the sound may come and go as driving conditions change. To check, first bring the engine rapidly up to operating temperature, and then allow it to return quickly to idle. If a valve sticks, the clicking sound will decrease in intensity, or perhaps disappear as the engine cools. Also, a jerk will be felt if the cylinder misfires.

Noisy timing gear. Remove one or two spark-plug wires and let the engine idle roughly. If the trouble is in the timing gear, it will chatter sharply.

If the engine has an exposed accessory shaft driven from the timing gears, noise in the gears may be detected by firmly pressing against the shaft with the handle of a hammer. This will vary the intensity of the noise.

Vacuum-gauge testing. A vacuum gauge is very useful in diagnosing engine troubles. The gauge may be connected to the windshield wiper fitting on the intake manifold, a fitting on the carburetor, a fitting on the power brake, or to the intake manifold itself when a pipe plug is removed.

The gauge measures the inches of vacuum created by pistons on their intake strokes. Vacuum fluctuations indicate various engine troubles, including sticking valves, leaking valves, weak springs, and worn guides.

To make the test, run the engine until operating temperature is reached, and make vacuum readings at idle and at 2,000 rpm. A normal vacuum runs from about 18 to 22 inches, but the action of the gauge needle actually is more important than the reading itself.

Vacuum readings tend to fluctuate widely on engines with large valve overlap. To overcome this tendency, the gauge restrictor valve, if provided, is adjusted, or the hose is pinched.

Table 8-1 Vacuum Gauge Readings

Gauge Needle Action	Trouble
	Idle
Needle steady	Valves operating correctly
1- to 7-in. drop at regular intervals	Leaking valve
Rapid drop at regular intervals	Broken valve spring
Rapid intermittent drop	Sticking valve
Low vacuum and slow fluctuation of about 3 in.	Worn valve guides admitting air
Steady, but at 3 to 9 in.	Air leak in intake manifold; ignition or valve timing late
	2000 rpm
Rapid fluctuation from 10 to 22 in.	Weak or broken valve spring

Table 8-1 provides a quick interpretation of gauge needle actions that may be encountered during a vacuum test. The actions noted deal specifically with valve troubles.

If the vacuum test points to a sticky valve, apply a little penetrating oil or lacquer thinner to each valve guide and note the reading again. The condition is remedied temporarily when the oil or thinner reaches the bad valve.

When late timing is indicated, set the ignition timing with a timing light (stroboscope). If the condition persists, valve timing is off.

Compression gauge. To make the compression test, all spark plugs are removed and the accelerator pedal is blocked on the floor. Both wires from the starter relay are removed, and a remote starter button is connected to the starter and battery terminals. The gauge nipple is then inserted into the cylinder and the engine is cranked to get about six power impulses. This is done for each cylinder in the engine, and the final reading for each cylinder is recorded.

Modern engines hold a compression of about 175 psi, but it is the *difference* in readings that is most important. If the variation is not more than 15 psi, everything probably is all right. If all cylinders record low pressure, the engine probably needs a ring job, a valve job, or both. If a low reading is obtained on one cylinder, squirt some oil into the cylinder and crank the engine. If the compression increases, the piston rings are defective; if the compression stays low, the valves are defective. If there are two low readings on adjacent cylinders, the head gasket may be leaking in the area of those two cylinders, and should be replaced.

Pressure leakage tester. If a pressure leakage tester is used to check the cylinders, the gauge readings on the tester will be equal if all cylinders are good. When using the tester, crank the engine until the piston in the cylinder being checked is near TDC before blowing in the air under pressure. If the air passes right through the cylinder, the piston is on the exhaust-intake cycle rather than on the compression-power cycle, and the engine should be turned over one revolution.

If the gauge indicates leakage, various parts should be checked for escaping air. If air escapes through the carburetor, the intake valve is leaking; if it escapes through the exhaust pipe, the exhaust valve is leaking. Ring blow-by lets air out through the breather tube or cap. A leaking head gasket produces either bubbles in the radiator or air loss through an adjacent cylinder.

Adjustments

Feeler-gauge adjustment. Most manufacturers' specifications furnish the proper adjustment for an engine running at normal operating temperature. The radiator coolant, checked to make sure it is at the proper level, can prevent overheating during adjustment.

Except for hydraulic valve lifters, valve lash normally is adjusted with a feeler guage. The locknut on the adjusting screw is loosened, and the feeler inserted between the valve stem and rocker arm. The adjusting screw is then tightened to take up the excess clearance, and the locknut is retightened. The clearance is rechecked after the locknut is tightened.

If, for any reason, an overly tight adjustment is suspected, loosen the adjusting screw until the valve becomes noisy, and then readjust to specifications.

Because the end of the rocker arm can wear until it is grooved, a flat feeler is not a reliable tool for checking the valve gap.

Valve-gapper. A precision instrument used to set the valve gap accurately, even though the rocker arm may be grooved, is the valve-gapper shown in Fig. 8-9. The valve-

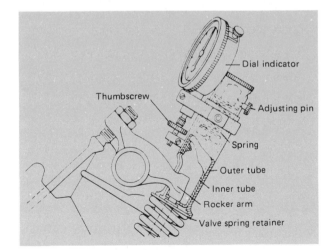

Fig. 8-9 Use of valve-gapper.

gapper is used also to detect noisy or defective hydraulic valve lifters. The illustration shows that the instrument has a *dial indicator*, an *inner tube*, an *outer tube*, and a *spring*. The base of the outer tube fits around and on top of the valve-spring retainer. The base of the inner tube has a U-shaped slot that fits around the valve stem so that the base of the inner tube contacts the lower face of the rocker arm.

With the valve-gapper in place for adjusting valve gap, the upward or downward movement of the rocker arm, when not in contact with the end of the valve stem, moves the inner tube inside the outer tube by the same distance that the rocker arm moves. The distance the inner tube moves is the actual valve gap, and the movement is registered on the dial indicator. When the rocker arm is in contact with the valve stem during the opening and closing of the valve, the downward and upward movements of the rocker arm do not register on the dial indicator, because the inner and outer tubes move the same distance at the same time.

With the engine idling, turn the thumbscrew until the pointer of the dial indicator registers zero when the valve is open. If it is difficult to determine that the pointer is stopping at zero, push upward on the lifter end to close the valve completely while the thumbscrew is being turned. Adjust the valve gap until the pointer of the dial indicator moves back and forth between zero and the clearance desired.

Checking hydraulic valve lifters.   Noisy and defective hydraulic valve lifters are checked with the valve-gapper in the same position used to adjust the valves. Now, however, the adjusting pin is in its upper position. No attempt should be made to determine the condition of the lifters until the valve-gapper has been in place and the engine running for at least 10 seconds.

If the lifters are in good condition, the pointer remains at zero. Sticking lifters are indicated by the pointer fluctuating between zero and 0.010. Badly worn lifters or stuck risers are indicated by the pointer fluctuating between zero and 0.050. Badly worn lifters should be replaced. Sticking lifters should be cleaned; if they are not worn or scored, they may be used again. If after cleaning the lifters show scores or nicks, replace them with new lifters.

VALVE TIMING

Timing Marks

The flywheel of some engines, and the vibration dampers of others, are marked in a number of ways, all of which have a direct bearing on valve timing. The marks correspond in position with those shown on valve-timing diagrams. Such diagrams consider only one cylinder, but the flywheel has marks for all cylinders.

Because the driven gear on the camshaft is twice as large as the driving gear on the crankshaft, the usual valve-

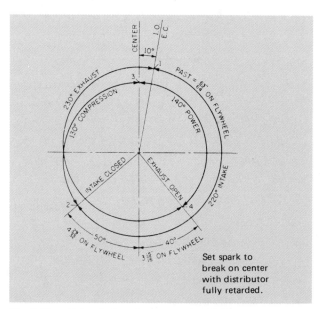

Fig. 8-10   Valve timing diagram marked in degrees.

timing diagram shows a combination of two revolutions of the crankshaft to one of the camshaft.

The valve-timing diagram, Fig. 8-10, is shown as an endless curve; the right portion contains two concentric semicircles, while the left portion has two eccentric semicircles. The starting point of the curve is at 1. At the end of the radial line passing through this point is found the abbreviation I.O., meaning that the inlet valve opens after the flywheel has revolved through an angle of 10°. The next point on the curve is at 2, where the intake valve closes and compression begins, continuing up to 3, where one revolution is completed.

The second revolution begins at point 3, where the charge is exploded. Power is applied to the piston until

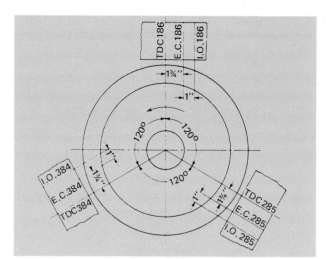

Fig. 8-11   Valve timing diagram marked in inches.

point 4 is reached, where the exhaust valve opens and remains open up to a point 10° past the centerline (point 1). The abbreviation E.C. found at this place means that the exhaust is closed.

Another valve-timing diagram is shown in Fig. 8-11. Here all of the angles, except three, are left out and the corresponding points are set off on the flywheel by giving their distance, in inches, from the top center points, which are spaced 120° apart. In the position shown, the pistons of cylinders 1 and 6 are in their TDC positions.

At a position 1¾ inches to the right is marked the point at which the exhaust valves for these cylinders are closed. At a distance one inch to the right of this point, a mark is made to show where the inlet valves for cylinders 1 and 6 open. The flywheel is marked in a similar manner for other pairs of cylinders.

General Procedure

When a valve-timing diagram for a particular engine is not available, it is best to start the timing where the exhaust valve closes. The position of this point is fairly uniform in timing diagrams.

The exhaust valve usually closes inside an arc beginning at TDC and ending 18° to the right of this point. This corresponds to a maximum piston travel of 1/32 of an inch. Since the average gear or sprocket has a rather coarse pitch, a mistake of one tooth, either way, is readily discovered.

For a six-cylinder engine without flywheel marks or one in which the flywheel is incorrectly bolted to the crankshaft, and for which no diagram is available, the engine may be timed by using the steps given below, in the order of their presentation.

1. Set the tappets to the recommended clearances.

2. Turn the engine over by hand slowly after the spark plugs have been removed.

3. Hold one finger over the hole for the No. 1 spark plug and turn the crank until a pressure is felt against your finger. Continue to turn the crank slowly until the pressure is considerably increased. Then remove your finger and continue the turning until the piston of the No. 1 cylinder reaches its TDC position—that is, until the piston is in its firing position.

4. With the piston in its firing position, examine the tappet clearance of the exhaust valve for cylinder No. 6. This valve should be nearly closed, with the tappet tight against the end of the valve stem, thus showing the valve is being held open.

5. Turn the engine very slowly until the piston in cylinder No. 1 descends not more than 1/32 of an inch. At this point, the No. 6 exhaust valve tappet should be slightly loose (starting to close). The tappet clearance of this valve should then be no more than 0.002 inch. If the piston of the No. 1 cylinder must be moved more than 1/32 of an inch either way from the position just described, the

valves are out of time and the gear-case cover must be removed to allow the position of the camshaft to be changed while the piston in cylinder No. 1 remains stationary. In other words, the camshaft timing gear must be unmeshed and the camshaft moved until the No. 6 exhaust valve is just closed (this must be done without moving the crankshaft).

Make sure that you understand the described method of timing. The essential points of adjustment are stated in the following rule: *When the exhaust valve of the last cylinder has just closed, the piston of the first cylinder should be on the top center of the compression stroke, or not more than 1/32 of an inch below and past this center.*

This rule applies to any four-cylinder or six-cylinder engine, as well as any eight-cylinder engine that has a firing order giving the effect of two four-cylinder engines. After the engine is set running by this rule, obtain the correct timing from the manufacturer and then check it against the timing obtained according to the rule.

It is important to remember that the opening and closing points of a valve are not at the instants when the lifter begins to rise and to come to rest, respectively. On the contrary, the opening point is that point at which the rising lifter makes contact with the end of the valve stem. The closing point is that point at which the descending lifter breaks contact with the end of the valve stem.

Finding TDC and BDC

The tuning operations just described may be simplified if the TDC and BDC positions of the No. 1 piston are found first and marked on the flywheel. Then perform the following operations:

1. Use a depth gauge that will pass through the spark-plug hole and rest on the piston. If a depth gauge is not available, use a piece of round steel stock that will just fit the opening over the piston.

2. Bring the No. 1 piston up to within ¾ of an inch of the top of its stroke. The distance need not be exact, but when it is approximated, make a mark on the gauge or rod at a point flush with the reference line, usually the top surface of the cylinder head.

3. With chalk or with a prick punch, make a mark on the flywheel in line with the pointer. Make sure it will not be confused with other marks on the flywheel.

4. Crank the engine slowly until the mark on the rod shows that the piston is the same distance past TDC as it was when the first mark was made on the rod.

5. Again mark the flywheel in line with the pointer. A point halfway between the two marks on the flywheel indicates the exact TDC position of the No. 1 piston.

6. To find the BDC position, proceed in the same manner as for the TDC position.

If there is no pointer or reference mark on the station-

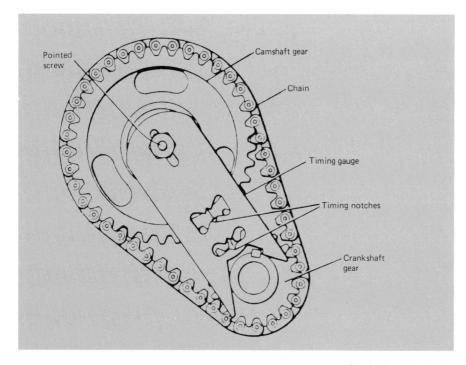

Fig. 8-12   Timing-sprocket gauge for setting gears.

ary part of the engine for the marks on the flywheel, one must be provided. With an unclosed flywheel, it is sufficient usually to make a reference mark on the housing with a prick punch. Or a pointer may be made of sheet metal and attached by the rear cylinder nuts. The punch mark or the pointer need not be directly above the crankshaft if it can be more conveniently located elsewhere.

It is important to remember that in an engine with an offset shaft the piston is in its TDC position when the crank is in line with the connecting rod, and not when both are vertical.

Using a Timing Gauge

Engines with chain drive usually can be timed correctly by placing the chain on the sprockets so that marks on the chain are in exact alignment with corresponding marks on the sprockets. In other engines, the timing marks on the camshaft sprocket should be in exact alignment with those on the crankshaft gear or sprocket, and on the center line of the crankshaft and camshaft.

To ensure absolute alignment of these points when a new chain is installed, some manufacturers provide a timing-sprocket gauge, such as that shown in working position in Fig. 8-12. To set the gears with this gauge, the V-shaped end of the gauge is placed on the protruding end of the crankshaft, and the *pointed screw* is adjusted to fit into the lathe center on the camshaft. The cam sprocket and the crankshaft sprocket then are turned until the timing marks

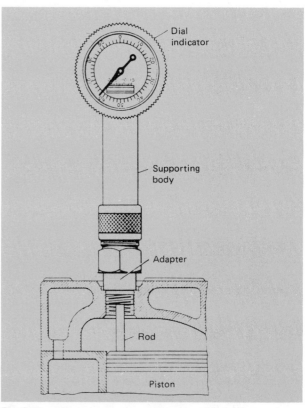

Fig. 8-13   Motor gauge in position for valve timing.

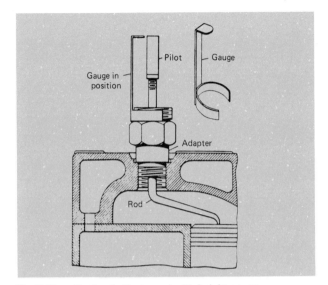

Fig. 8-14 Setting indicator rod with height gauge.

on the sprockets are visible through the *small notches* in the center of the gauge.

Timing With Motor Gauge

The valves can be set accurately by using a precision apparatus that measures the travel of the piston within limits of 0.001 inch.

If a modern engine is to develop its rated horsepower and simultaneously function smoothly at all speeds, the valve and ignition timing must be correct.

A precision instrument used to time both valves and ignition is shown in Fig. 8-13. Known as a motor gauge, this instrument has an accurate *micrometer dial* graduated in thousandths of an inch, a supporting *body*, and *adapters* and *rods*. The adapters and rods are suitable for attachment to any engine either through the spark-plug holes or through special ⅛ inch pipe-sized holes located in some engines for this purpose. The complete assortment of adapters and rods that are available make the gauge universal. The rods are either straight, as shown in Fig. 8-13, or offset, as shown in Fig. 8-14, to ensure that the end of the rod within the cylinder will rest upon the top of the piston.

The pointer of the indicator dial is designed to make six complete revolutions, with each revolution representing 0.10 inch. Thus, the permissible length of rod travel is 0.60 inch. A special height gauge, Fig. 8-14, forms part of the

motor gauge equipment and should always be used in the manner shown before attaching the micrometer indicator to the rod and adapter. This keeps the instrument from being damaged by forcing the indicator beyond its limits. With the piston at TDC, the rod should not project above the top of the height gauge. Threaded pilots are placed on all rods to bring their lengths within the proper limits.

To check valve timing with the motor gauge, proceed as follows:

1. Remove all spark plugs and see that the piston in the cylinder being timed is below TDC.

2. Consult the chart that comes with the motor gauge, and select the adapter and rod specified for the particular engine. Place the rod through the adapter, and screw the pilot to the rod; hand tighten. Pass the rod through the spark-plug hole, and screw the adapter tightly into the cylinder head. If a straight rod is used, be sure it extends into the cylinder bore so that the piston will strike it on its upward stroke.

3. Turn the engine over slowly until the piston is at TDC, and adjust the pilot until its top is flush with the top of the height gauge. Then screw the cylindrical body of the gauge onto the adapter.

4. Turn the engine until the piston in the cylinder is on its compression stroke, as indicated by the escape of air through an opening in the adapter. Continue turning the engine slowly until the piston strikes the end of the timing rod, as indicated by a movement of the indicator. Continue to turn the engine over slowly with the fan blade until the piston reaches TDC, as shown when the indicator hand comes to a full stop and then tends to move backward. Turn the dial until the zero mark is directly under the indicator hand. The gauge is then set in the TDC position.

5. If the manufacturer specifies that the inlet valve should open at, say, 0.014 inch after TDC, turn the gauge dial to the left 14 gradation marks and tap the starting crank or turn the fan blades slowly until the indicator hand moves back to zero.

If the valve should open 0.014 inch before TDC, turn the dial to the left 14 marks as before, but turn the fan blades and engine in a direction opposite to engine rotation until the dial indicator is at least 0.025 inch past the zero position; then turn the engine in the proper direction until the indicator hand is squarely over the zero mark.

9

PISTON ASSEMBLIES

Contents

Connecting Rods

Pistons, Piston Rings, and Piston Pins

Piston Assembly Troubles

Overhauling Piston Assemblies

Detecting and Curing Excessive Oil Consumption

CONNECTING RODS

To change the reciprocating (up-and-down) motion of pistons to rotary (turning) motion, each piston is connected to the crankshaft by means of a connecting rod. See Figure 9-1.

The part of a crankshaft to which a connecting rod is attached is called the *crankpin*. The crankpin end of the connecting rod has a split-type sleeve bearing and is attached to the crankpin by means of a bearing cap, rod bolts, and nuts.

The piston end of the connecting rod is attached to the piston by means of a *piston pin* (also called a *wrist pin*). As shown in Figure 9-2, bosses in the piston have holes into which the wrist pin is inserted. The pin goes through the connecting rod.

Although several different methods are used to attach the piston and rod with the pin, the most common arrangement has the pin press fit in the connecting rod. The press fit is tight enough to keep the pin from moving out of position.

When the pin is to swing back and forth in the rod, a sleeve bearing (bushing) is provided for the pin.

PISTONS, PISTON RINGS, AND PISTON PINS

Piston Nomenclature

The pistons used in automobile engines are called *trunk* pistons because they are made to operate without a piston rod. This allows the designer to develop shorter and more compact engines. A piston rod is not to be confused with a connecting rod, which is one part of the overall assembly.

The various parts of a trunk piston are shown in Fig. 9-2, with (a) being a perspective view and (b) a bottom view.

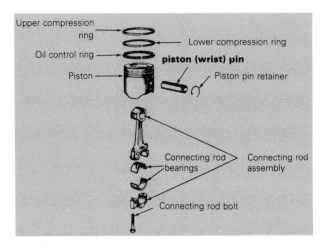

Fig. 9-1. Exploded view of piston and connecting-rod assembly. *Courtesy of Ford Motor Company.*

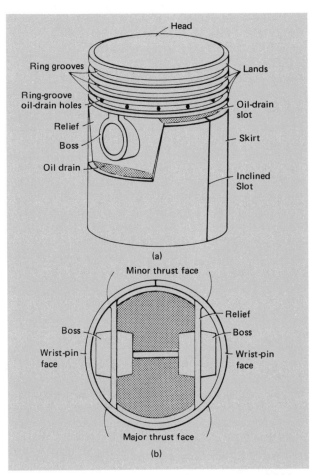

Fig. 9-2 Aluminum alloy piston: (a) perspective and (b) bottom views.

The end wall is known as the *head* or *crown*. Below the head are three ring grooves located between the circular nibs, called *lands*. The top land is designated the *head* land or *first* land, and the others are named by their numerical order. This combination of rings and lands is known as the *ring section*, or *ring belt*. The radial holes in the lower-ring grooves are *ring-groove oil-drain holes*. there are two *wrist pin*, (or *piston pin*,) *bosses*, one on each side of the piston.

Below the ring section is the *skirt*, which is divided into four parts, as shown in (b). The portion below the piston pin is called the *major thrust face* because it receives the major portion of the side thrust imparted by the angularity of the connecting rod and the explosion pressure. The opposite portion is called the *minor thrust face*. The faces at right angles to the thrust faces are known as the *wrist pin*, or *piston pin*, *faces*. Around each pin boss there is a recessed face known as the *relief;* the resulting slot serves as an oil drain. The ring section is separated from the skirt by two horizontal slots, one of which is shown in (a). The slots allow the oil from the cylinder walls to drain through them into the crankcase, which assists in controlling piston expansion. The minor thrust face has a vertical or slightly inclined slot to give the pistons some flexibility and allow for head expansion on the thrust face so that the piston may be fitted with a minimum of clearance when cold.

Piston Metals

It is very unlikely that cast-iron pistons will ever again be popular in automobile engines, simply because aluminum pistons offer too many advantages. Light-weight aluminum permits higher engine speeds, and since doubling the speed doubles the horsepower, more powerful engines can be built with relatively little increase in weight or bulk. Aluminum's high heat conductivity opened the way to higher compressions and greater efficiency.

Aluminum has the disadvantages of high heat expansion and lower strength at all temperatures. However, the hardness and strength needed at high temperatures has been provided by the use of alloys. No alloy of sufficiently low expansion rate has been developed yet. Two piston designs are used to avoid the problem of expansion; namely, the strut design and the T-slot design. The strut design is used almost universally in modern engines.

Strut-Type Piston

The strut-type piston, Fig. 9-3, was an early answer to the expansion problem. Although it almost went out of use in the mid-50's, it has come back big in the modern square-engine design. In this design, the diameter of both the cylinder bore and piston is greater than the length of the piston stroke. In older designs, the opposite was true. This new design reduces the length of the stroke and, therefore, the piston maximum speed and average speed. In other words, the piston moves a shorter distance for each crankshaft revolution. The design also reduces piston and bore wear.

A strut of low-expansion alloy steel is cast into the piston to restrain expansion in a direction at right angles to the piston pin; that is, in the direction of the thrust faces. Most expansion is thus shifted to a direction parallel to the piston pins by the so-called *hatband effect*: if a hatband is com-pressed in its front and rear, it expands at the sides; if it is pulled fore and aft, the sides contract.

The restrained expansion in the direction at right angles to the piston pins and the resultant larger expansion in the direction of the piston pins are compensated by larger clearances in the area of the pin bosses. As a result, the combined expansion of the strut and skirt structure may be made substantially less, depending upon the strut material. A clearance as low as 0.0003 to 0.0009 inch is not uncommon. This, of course, calls for an oval-section, cam-ground piston and is the reason why a new piston must not be machined or ground before installation.

T-Slot Piston

The T-slot design overcomes expansion trouble without the use of a strut. As shown in Fig. 9-4, the name is derived from the T formed by the horizontal and vertical slots in the minor thrust face. The diameter at right angles to the thrust faces is less than the diameter at the thrust faces by as much as 0.007 to 0.012 inch. This results in the hatband effect, which makes the diameter at the thrust faces contract as the pin-area diameter expands.

The major thrust face is complete with the piston head

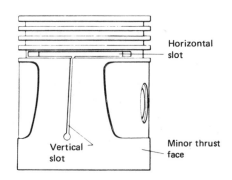

Fig. 9-4 T-slot piston.

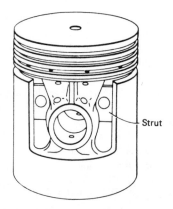

Fig. 9-3 Strut-type piston.

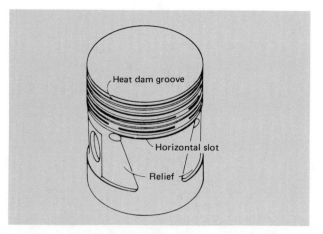

Fig. 9-5 Low-expansion piston. *Courtesy of Sterling Division, Federal-Mogul-Bower Bearings, Inc.*

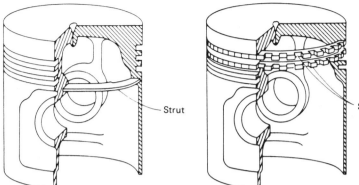

Strut

Steel rings

Fig. 9-6   Strut-type pistons. *Courtesy of Sterling Division, Federal-Mogul-Bower Bearings, Inc.*

and has no slots. There are no openings around the piston bosses. The vertical slot does not extend to the bottom of the skirt, counteracting the tendency of the skirt to collapse. Sometimes this type of piston is factory-machined to a slight taper on the thrust faces, with the slightly larger diameter at the bottom of the skirt. The diameter at the pin hole is about 0.013 inch less than at the thrust face.

An aluminum alloy having a coefficient of expansion 18 percent lower than that of copper-aluminum alloys has been developed. Pistons cast of this alloy can be designed without vertical slots (see Fig. 9-5). As with many other designs, reliefs are built into the piston skirt. The heat-dam groove at the top of the piston protects the top ring from heat and gas pressure.

Other Types of Pistons

Other piston designs are shown in Fig. 9-6. The piston on the left is called the Comformatic and incorporates a specially designed *oval steel strut* to control expansion. The strut is set into the mold before the piston is cast, and this is embedded into the finished piston. The piston on the right, called the Anchortite, contains one or *two serrated steel rings* next to the top compression ring.

Hard-surfaced aluminum pistons.   Aluminum is not as hard as cast iron. As a result, aluminum pistons tend to scuff, especially when the engine is started from cold. To overcome the problem, tin plating and oxidizing are used to give aluminum pistons a hard surface. Tin plating is self-explanatory. Oxidizing is an electrolytic process which forms a hard, smooth (oxidized) surface of aluminum oxide. Aluminum oxide is one of the hardest substances known; sapphire and ruby are forms of this oxide, and they are used for bearings in watches and delicate instruments.

The oxidizing process used on aluminum pistons provides a slight porosity that allows for some oil absorption. Thus, enough oil is retained on the pistons to help with lubrication on a cold start. Wear resistance is also improved. The oxidized surface is made from the aluminum itself; no extraneous substance is added.

Neither the tin-plated piston nor the oxidized piston can be machined or ground after treating. To do so would destroy the hard surface.

Tin-plated iron pistons.   Tin-plated iron pistons permit closer initial clearance and reduce the time needed for wearing in. The tin coating ranges from 0.00075 to 0.001 inch. One distinct disadvantage of this type of piston is that the surfaces of the cylinder bores tend to become glazed after a time; this can prevent the piston rings from seating after a ring job. Therefore, the glaze must be honed off before new rings are installed.

Purpose of Piston Rings

It is impossible to have a solid piston that will provide a gas-tight seal and, at the same time, a free-running fit in a cylinder under the conditions encountered in an automobile engine. Piston rings are used, therefore, literally to fill the gap between the cylinder and piston.

A piston ring is an elastic, expandable element, slightly larger than the cylinder bore, which expands to hug the bore and reduce leakage of combustion gases past the moving piston. The ring is square in cross section and is placed in a square groove around the outside of the piston. The upper rings are known as compression rings. In addition to reducing gas leakage (blow-by), the rings also conduct heat from the piston to the cylinder walls. It is estimated that 60 percent of the heat from the pistons gets out through the piston rings.

One ring, usually the third from the top of the piston, scrapes excess oil from the cylinder walls and returns the oil to the crankcase. Usually, this ring is a composite; that is, it is made in several pieces. It is called the *oil ring*, and various types are discussed shortly.

Piston rings may be made of cast iron, coated cast iron, chrome-plated cast iron, stainless steel, Teflon-coated steel, and spring steel. Teflon-coated rings are not widely used as yet, but the low friction of Teflon makes it very promising. Originally, most rings were made of very close-grained cast iron, which is still a satisfactory material for many installations.

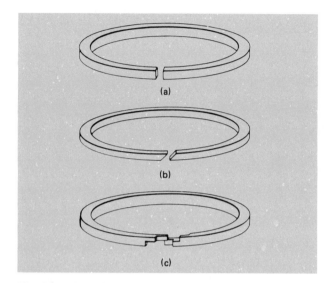

Fig. 9-7 One-piece compression rings. (a) Vertical gap, (b) diagonal gap, and (c) step gap.

Types of Rings

In general, there are two types of piston rings: one-piece and multiple-piece. Compression rings usually are of the one-piece type and oil rings are of the multiple-piece type. One-piece compression rings are shown in Fig. 9-7. Most compression rings in modern automobiles are made with either the vertical gap, (a), or the diagonal gap, (b). The step gap, (c), is rarely used because it is expensive to produce and it is not much better than the straight gaps.

Most one-piece rings are concentric in section; that is, they are of uniform thickness from end to end. A circumferential groove is sometimes cut on the ring face. Other rings may have a groove on the inner face. Unless the compression ring is so marked, one with an inner groove is assembled with the groove upward. If the ring has an outer groove, it is installed with the groove downward. In either case, the groove acts to wipe oil from the cylinder walls; hence, the ring is called a wiper ring, although it is not an oil ring in the strict sense of the word.

The top compression ring on the piston in the hottest spot, exposed both to the most heat and the heaviest expansion loads, receives the least lubrication of any ring. It also is subjected to the brunt of bad conditions, such as incorrect air-fuel ratio, preignition, deterioration. Quite often, this ring is made of chromium-faced cast iron, which helps reduce ring and cylinder wall wear and provides excellent heat resistance. The second compression ring, or even the third, if there is one, may be chromium-faced, plain cast iron, or phosphate-covered.

Obtaining wall pressure. To meet operating requirements the piston ring must exert pressure against the cylinder walls. In a one-piece type ring, this tension or wall pressure

must be built into the ring. One way to build tension into a one-piece ring is called *peening*. A ring is built from individual castings of truly circular shape. The circular casting is machined to the diameter of the cylinder it is to fit, after which the casting is sawed off or milled to form the joint. Up to this time the ring has no tension. To put tension into the ring, some manufacturers hammer (peen) the inside face, which spreads the metal and increases the radius of curvature at the point opposite the joint. To obtain uniformity of tension, the greatest amount of peening is done at the middle of the ring and the intensity is decreased toward the ends. One of the widely used piston rings built by the peening method is called *American hammered*. A variation of the peening method of securing tension is to roll or knurl the inside circumference while the ring is mounted in a die or mold of suitable form.

Ring gap. Ring gap is the space between the ends of the ring after the ring has been installed. The gap should be as small as possible without having the ends of the ring butting. To check the gap, put the ring into the cylinder bore and, with a piston head, push the ring down to about the middle of the bore. Then use a feeler gauge to measure the gap, as shown in Fig. 9-8. The minimum gap should be 0.010 inch for rings measuring from 3 to 3-31/32 inches in diameter and 0.013 inch for rings measuring from 4 to 4-31/32 inches in diameter.

Oil rings. The oil ring is the lowest ring on the piston; it is either the third or fourth ring from the top. It is specially constructed to wipe excess oil from the cylinder wall. The oil drains back to the crankcase through slots or holes in the piston and behind the ring.

Although there are many designs of oil rings, usually

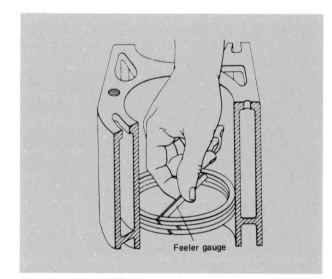

Feeler gauge

Fig. 9-8 Measuring ring gap.

they are made of steel and consist of three parts: top rail, bottom rail, and spacer. Some designs contain a fourth part in the form of a backing ring.

Several designs of oil rings are shown in Fig. 9-9. Those shown in (a) through (d) have a backer (expander) ring that fits inside the oil ring; those in (e), (f), and (g) are made with a spacer (expansion) spring. Oil ring replacements always should be of the type specified by the automobile manufacturer.

Chrome rings. Chrome is the best answer to higher engine speeds and compression. Old-type piston rings that operated at the top of the cylinder where lubrication is poor, pressure greatest, and temperature highest did not give an engine the wear protection it needed. The old-style rings wore more than twice as fast as the chrome rings used in modern engines.

Solid chrome plating on both top and bottom rings gives excellent wear protection, which exists through the entire area of ring travel in the cylinder. The top compression ring usually is a chrome-alloy cast iron with a solid chrome face. Most of the oil rings are the ventilated type. The side rails of the oil rings have solid chrome faces. Both the compression and oil rings are beveled or tapered to thread-line contact for quick seating and blow-by control.

To assist in early break-in, the top rings are preseated by some manufacturers. Preseating is a factory-applied lapping process. This process applied to the chrome-plated surface of the compression ring is equivalent to approximately 400 miles of actual engine operation. Preseated rings have fine grooves, or lands, on the circumference. The smooth, even bearing of the narrow lands on the surface of the cylinder guarantees early break-in and fast oil control. The long-wearing quality of chrome rings assures premium performance and long engine life.

Open-design rings. Another type of chrome ring is the open design which has two and one-half times more open areas than the ventilated types. The ring consists of two steel rails with a corrugated or continuous S-shaped spacer between them. The open design allows almost triple oil drainage and almost entirely eliminates plugging. The faces of the two walls are chrome plated to resist abrasion and scuffing and provide long life. This type of ring uses an expander somewhat different than the hump-type expander shown in Fig. 9-9(c). The new expander has a vertical corrugated design and is truly cylindrical. It applies equal outward pressure to the piston ring around the entire surface and thus assures uniform contact and tension all around the cylinder even in tapered or out-of-round bores.

Piston Pins

The primary function of the piston pin is to couple the connecting rod to the piston. Because there is no piston rod, as

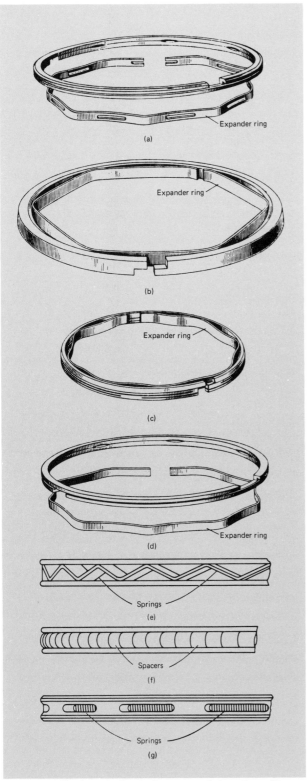

Fig. 9-9 Oil ring designs. *Courtesy of American Motors Corporation.*

such, in an automobile, the connecting rod must be free to oscillate.

The piston pin carries an extremely heavy load—up to two tons per square inch in automobile engines. For this reason, the pins are made of hardened alloy steel. Some pins are chrome plated for extra wear and for protection against etching by the acids that form in the crankcase. The pins are ground after being hardened and may be lapped. To reduce their weight, piston pins are hollow, even though their walls are quite thick.

PISTON ASSEMBLY TROUBLES

Classification of Troubles

Practically all troubles traceable to the piston assembly can be heard, seen, or measured in one way or another. The most important symptoms and the likely causes producing them are as follows:

1. Abnormal engine noises or knocks due to one or more of the following causes: (a) too much diametrical clearance producing piston slap, (b) piston pins loose on their mountings at the piston bosses or upper end of the connecting rod, (c) piston rings loose in their grooves or broken, (d) interference of piston or rings with some part of the cylinder, the cylinder head, the cylinder-head gasket, or a ridge in the cylinder bore near the top of the ring travel, (e) cocking of the piston assembly in the cylinder due to a bent connecting rod or to loose crankpin bearings.

2. Loss of compression or blow-by due to one or more of the following causes: (a) loss of tension in piston rings or insufficient initial tension causing looseness, (b) vibration of ring occurring mostly at high speeds, (c) rings loose in their grooves, (d) rings stuck by sludge or varnish in their grooves, (e) face of rings worn convex by normal cocking of piston at high speeds or excessive piston-to-cylinder clearance, (f) ring faces not conforming to cylinder wall because of worn or distorted cylinders or poorly fitting rings,(g) cracked piston or piston of inadequate design, (h) broken piston rings.

3. Excessive oil consumption or oil pumping may be the result of any of the aforementioned causes or any of the following causes: (a) loose or incorrectly adjusted main, connecting rod, or camshaft bearings, which allow an excessive amount of oil to be thrown onto the cylinder walls, (b) worn valvestem guides, which permit oil to be drawn into the combustion chamber by way of the valve stems and guides, (c) incorrect valve timing, (d) external leakage of oil at the main or accessory shaft bearings, or at the oil-pan joint.

4. Seizing or scoring of pistons. These troubles are usually due to poor design, insufficient clearance, or inadequate lubrication.

Piston Slap

The phenomenon known as piston slap is caused by the piston moving from side to side in the cylinder. A certain amount of such movement cannot be avoided; it may, however, be reduced to an extent that practically eliminates the noise.

For every two revolutions of the crankshaft, each piston moves six times from one side of the cylinder to the other. Fortunately, these motions are rather gradual except for the one occurring at the moment of explosion, when the firing stroke begins. This piston motion is very sudden and really is the one that causes the piston slap in the case of too much clearance.

The amount of clearance that will produce piston slap varies with the size of the engine, the length of the connecting rod, the position of the piston pin, and several other factors. In some engines, the piston pin is mounted to one side of the piston center line. One purpose of this construction is to reduce the tendency for the pistons to slap, but there is no convincing evidence that the results conform to the theory. The same may be said of engines with the crankshaft center line off to one side of the longitudinal center line of the cylinder bores. There is reason to believe that the offset piston pin and the offset crankshaft methods actually do reduce the side thrust loads on the pistons, but their effectiveness in the prevention of piston slap is questionable.

Locating piston slap. Piston slap is loudest usually when the engine suddenly is accelerated, when it is under light load with advanced spark, or when it has just been started from cold. To determine whether an abnormal noise is due to piston slap, short out the spark plug in the suspected cylinder; if the sound cannot be traced to any one cylinder, each cylinder should be treated in the following manner: Remove the spark plug and pour into the cylinder about three or four tablespoonfuls of very heavy engine oil. Allow the engine to stand for about two minutes, then replace the plug and start the engine. Accelerate the speed suddenly by opening the throttle. If the noise disappears, the slapping piston is in the cylinder under test.

The oil introduced serves to reduce, temporarily, the clearance between the cylinder and piston and thus stop the noise. If the oil fails to diminish or stop the noise, it is due to some other cause such as loose piston pins or crankshaft bearings.

Eliminating piston slap. The best way to eliminate piston slap and high oil consumption traceable to the piston assemblies is to install new pistons and rings fitted to the recommended clearance. Sometimes, however, a temporary job must be done either because new pistons are not available or because the cost is prohibitive. The following slap-prevention methods should be viewed as expedients. They do not always constitute an approved reconditioning job. Their effectiveness, however, usually extends over a period of time sufficient to make the necessary expenditure worthwhile.

Remove the piston and rod assembly and check its condition. Piston slap that occurs at low mileage is most often encountered with aluminum-alloy pistons of the split-skirt type. Piston slap in these cases usually is due to partial collapse of the skirt rather than actual wear. Visual examination will provide preliminary clues as to whether the slap is due to wear or skirt collapse. If the slot tapers in width from top to bottom, it is definite proof that the slap is due to collapse. As a further check, measure both the top and bottom skirt diameters at right angles to the piston pin. If the bottom of the skirt is noticeably smaller than the top, it indicates partial collapse. The approved method of correcting this condition on aluminum pistons of the split-skirt type is to install some form of skirt expander.

Although piston-skirt expanders are designed to correct skirt collapse in split-skirt type alloy pistons, they are sometimes used to compensate for skirt wear on all types of pistons. Saw a skirt slot in worn, but originally unslotted, pistons and install an adjustable-type expander. Although this method is not recommended on all pistons, it may be utilized on certain installations approved by the maker of the particular skirt expander.

Use of inner rings. Temporary relief from piston slap may be secured by installing inner rings or ring expanders. The method consists of inserting behind the top piston ring a crimped steel expander of the type shown in Fig. 9-9(a)(b)(c). A similar expander, but of the ventilated type, is inserted behind the lowest piston ring. The crimped expanders apply some support to the regular piston ring and tend to damp out the noise produced by the piston moving from side to side in its cylinder.

When used as the sole means of slap prevention, crimped steel expanders are effective usually for about 4,000 miles if the skirt clearance is not more than 0.004 inch greater than the recommended amount. Best results are obtained when the steel expanders are installed in conjunction with devices such as skirt expanders that help support the lower end of the piston.

Piston Seizure

Piston seizure, the sticking of a piston in its cylinder, is caused by the fusion of piston and cylinder metals. Seizure occurring at low engine speed causes the engine to stop. To free a low-speed seizure, first insert light oil through spark-plug holes and then place the gear lever in direct-drive and rock the automobile back and forth.

High-speed seizure does not cause the engine to stop, but the piston, connecting-rod bolts, and/or the connecting rod are broken. Piston seizure nearly always occurs on new or on recently rebuilt engines with insufficient clearance or failure of the lubrication system. Damage resulting from low-speed seizure of nonoxidized aluminum alloy pistons most usually is confined to the piston and rings. With iron or oxidized aluminum pistons, the damage frequently includes scoring of the cylinder-bore wall.

Cracked or Broken Pistons

A piston head, cracked sufficiently to cause a miss at low engine speed, may be diagnosed by use of a compression gauge. The cylinder with the cracked piston always shows a pressure 10 to 25 psi lower than that of the other cylinders. To pinpoint the trouble, listen for valve leakage at the inlet and exhaust manifolds and check for ring leakage by inserting three spoonfuls of heavy oil on top of the piston. Cracked pistons may result from such causes as chronic preignition, piston seizure, or piston pins fitted too tightly.

Broken pistons result from the same causes as cracked pistons and may be diagnosed by using a compression, or vacuum, gauge. If the break occurs near the center of the head, examine the broken pieces; any sign of melted edges or burned hole in the head indicates the cause as preignition induced by too hot a spark plug, too lean a mixture, or both. Metal fatigue due to age or strain, inadequate design, and improperly adjusted or designed piston skirt expanders are other causes of breakage.

Scored Pistons

Scored pistons have scratched or grooved faces resulting from total or partial seizure. A partial seizure sufficient to cause scoring may occur any time during the life of the engine without outward manifestation of trouble. Major scoring allows some of the fused metal to be deposited on the face of the piston rings, thus causing reduced compression. When scoring is confined to the piston and rings, it is not necessary to replace the piston; a new set of rings and smoothing of the piston faces with a fine file are sufficient.

Minor scratches on piston thrust faces can be caused by scuffing action when the engine is started in very cold weather and the oil is stiff. This trouble is much less frequent since the advent of multiple-viscosity oils with anti-scuffing additives.

Blow-By

Blow-by is the leakage of gas past the piston rings and occurs during the compression and power strokes. Some blow-by is present in all engines because it is impossible to secure a perfectly airtight seal between the piston and the cylinder walls. Some engines in fair to poor condition show practically no blow-by at low speeds but excessive blow-by at high speeds. Excessive blow-by occurring only at low engine speeds results mainly in loss of power, but if the blow-by also occurs at full throttle and high speed, it produces high oil consumption, breakage of piston rings, piston ring noises, and burning or erosion of the piston faces.

A rough test for blow-by can be made by observing the

crankcase breather pipe while the engine is running. If the blow-by is excessive it can be heard, felt as an outward pressure when the hand is held over the breather pipe, or seen in the form of oil vapor issuing from the breather pipe. Excessive high-speed blow-by may be detected by a coating of oil on the engine in the vicinity of the breather and a steady stream of vapor from the breather. These rough tests are dependable only for detecting extremely bad conditions, and cannot be used to compare the sealing qualities of different makes of rings. A quantitative test may be made with an ordinary house gas meter connected directly to the breather pipe. This hookup lets you read the leakage in cubic feet per minute. An engine showing not more than 1 cubic foot of leakage per minute for every 100 cubic inches of total piston displacement, at 3,200 to 3,800 rpm, is considered well sealed; leakage exceeding 4 cubic feet per minute per 100 cubic inches displacement is considered excessive.

The following are the usual causes of blow-by in descending order of their approximate frequency of occurrence:

1. *Piston rings too loose in their grooves.* This is due to natural wear of the rings, grooves, or both, or to careless fitting of the rings. Rings should have not more than 0.004-inch up and down clearance in grooves and not more than 0.035-inch end-gap clearance. If clearances are greater, replace the rings.

2. *Piston too loose in cylinder.* Excessive clearance allows the piston to rock, which causes ring faces to wear barrel-shaped. When ring faces are barrel-shaped (convex) they only make line contact, and this is insufficient to seal the cylinder properly. To correct this condition either replace the piston or expand it by knurling.

3. *Cylinder bores badly out of round or tapered.* Cylinders cannot be sealed with any ring when the out-of-roundness exceeds 0.006 inch, or the taper exceeds 0.010 inch. If worn beyond these limits, the cylinder should be reconditioned and new pistons installed. If wear is less than these limits, the trouble can be partially corrected by using special compression and oil rings and expanding the piston by knurling.

4. *Broken piston rings.* Ring breakage may be due to carelessness at installation, insufficient end-gap clearance, or fluttering. To prevent invisible fractures, which later develop into actual breakage, use ring-replacement pliers for placing the rings on the piston. To prevent breakage during entry of the assembly into the cylinder, use a sleeve-type ring compressor. An end-gap clearance of 0.003 inch per inch of bore diameter prevents breakage due to butting of the ends except when the butting is due to flutter or ring vibration.

An expander or crimped-steel inner ring of very light tension installed under the regular one-piece ring often stops breakage from flutter. Flutter, however, is quite unusual in modern automobile engines.

5. *Rings stuck in grooves.* This condition is most often due to gum or varnish, but may be due to insufficient clearance when fitted. To correct, introduce modern solvents into the lubricating oil. Solvents should be used according to the manufacturer's directions.

Occasionally stuck rings result from squeezing of the top ring because the top groove becomes deformed by the expansion pressure on the piston head. If repeated solvent treatments fail to free stuck rings, it may be necessary to remove the pistons and do a thorough cleanup of the grooves, rings, and related units. After everything has been cleaned, a squeezed ring will usually be evident.

6. *Ring faces do not conform to cylinder walls.* Rings that are either too small or too large are the usual causes of this trouble. Never install a ring that is more than 0.005-inch oversize or undersize, and measure the cylinder bores with a micrometer before ordering new rings.

7. *Cylinder distortion.* Distortion is caused by wear or uneven tightening of the cylinder head hold-down screws or nuts. Uneven tension on one or two of the stud nuts may seriously distort adjacent cylinders. Distortion can also be caused by too much tension, even though the tension is applied evenly. Cylinder distortion may cause the valve seats to become distorted and result in compression loss and burned valves and seats. To avoid distortion troubles, always use a torque wrench to tighten the cylinder head hold-down nuts, the stud nuts that fasten the valve tappet cluster, and the valve cover plate nuts. If a torque wrench is not available, use a wrench with a handle no longer than 10 inches.

Piston-Ring Noises

Broken or partly stuck rings, fluttering rings, or rings that are biting a ridge in the cylinder bore can produce abnormal noises in an engine. Sometimes the top ring strikes the upper ridge in a worn bore. A ridge forms near the top of the bore because the piston does not go all the way to the top, as the bore wears, the ridge is formed. If this ridge is not removed when the bore is reconditioned, new rings or rings on oversized pistons can bump this shoulder.

Piston-Pin Bearing Noises

If a piston-pin (or wrist-pin) bearing has worn and the pin is loose, it will rattle. A pin knock is spotted by grounding the spark plug in the suspected cylinder. Without the sudden pressure of the explosion, the knock disappears. A new, oversized bushing cures the trouble. In a modern engine, however, with the pin press fitted into the connecting rod, the rod eye has to be bored to fit the new bushing.

An alternative procedure is to bore out the piston-pin hole and use a bushing into which the existing pin fits. If the pin is worn, a new standard-sized pin is used. Sometimes after the installation of new piston rings, especially those with expanders or with high wall pressure, pin bearings develop an audible knock. This knock is temporary and stops as soon as the rings are seated to the cylinder walls.

OVERHAULING PISTON ASSEMBLIES

Removal of Assemblies

Pistons are removed from the engine for overhaul. Sometimes they can be removed from underneath the engine by removing the caps from the lower ends of the connecting rods and sliding out both the rods and pistons. It may be necessary to remove the crankshaft also.

Because the cylinder bore is inspected for possible reconditioning, the cylinder head must be removed. This procedure allows the pistons and connecting rods to be removed upward, provided, of course, the lower part of the rod is not too large to pass through the cylinder. If the lower part is too large, it usually is necessary to raise the pistons and rods until the piston pins are above the top of the cylinder block. Then the pins can be pushed out and the pistons lifted out through the top. The rods can then be lowered through the bottom of the engine.

Most modern engines are of the valve-in-head type, and the heads are heavy and bulky. In removing the piston assembly, the oil pan is removed and, if necessary, the cylinder head. The assembly removal procedure is then as follows:

When the caps of the connecting-rod lower bearings are removed, examine them for identification marks. Most factory-installed connecting rods have corresponding numbers marked on the rods and caps. These numbers also indicate the positions of the piston assemblies in the engine.

Next, the engine is removed, placed on a support stand, and the cotter pins are removed from the bolts of all the lower rod bearings. Diagonal or side-cutting pliers are used in this step.

With a socket wrench, the nuts are removed from each of the lower connecting-rod bolts. Before the last nut of each rod is removed, the cap is grasped in one hand and the nut is removed with the other hand.

If shims are used, they are retained in position by reinstalling the nuts. The crank and main bearing inserts are removed and marked, if necessary, for replacement in their original positions. If these bearings are worn, the crankshaft may have to be reground and new bearings installed.

If the piston pin must be pulled before the piston can be removed, make sure the piston head is marked to correspond to the mark on the lower end of the rod.

Pistons usually indicate by markings which side should face the front during reassembly. This mark may be a V mark in the edge of the piston, or the letter F stamped on or cast into the front surface of the piston. If there is no mark, one should be made. Marking will ensure proper orientation of the thrust faces.

If the piston pins are press fitted into the piston holes and the piston rods oscillate on them, the pistons are warmed with a torch to loosen the press fit by expansion; and the pins are then pushed out easily. If the pins are press fitted into the rod eyes, they are pressed out with a pilot driver, as shown in Fig. 9-10. The pins can be reinstalled with the same tool.

After disassembly, all parts should be washed in a cleaning solution or in kerosene.

After the parts of the piston assembly are cleaned, a step-by-step procedure is followed to determine if they can be reassembled without further work:

1. *Rings.* If the face of a ring is bright all over, it usually is considered to be in good condition. Dark spots anywhere on a ring indicate failure of the ring to contact the cylin-

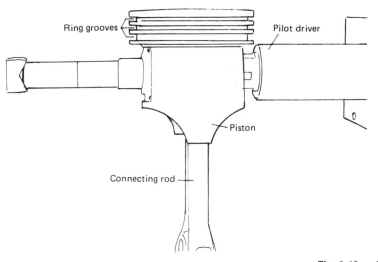

Fig. 9-10 Piston pin being removed with pilot driver. *Courtesy of American Motors Corporation.*

der walls and hence failure in sealing. Such a ring is discarded. A burned oil deposit on the face of the ring near the tip indicates ring collapse at high speeds. Shiny ends of the ring gap may indicate that the ends are making contact somewhere during operation.

2. *Groove clearance.* If, when checked with a feeler gauge, Fig. 9-11, the side clearance is more than 0.004 inch, on engines with up to a 5-inch bore, the loss of compression probably causes oil pumping. Such rings should be replaced.

Whenever the pistons and pins are removed for any reason, it is good practice to replace the rings. If the piston bore is reconditioned, new pistons and new rings are installed.

3. *Bore taper and out of roundness.* The ridge at the top of the cylinder, which marks the upper limit of piston travel, is removed first. Then the bores are measured for taper and out-of-roundness by using an inside micrometer or a telescoping gauge and outside micrometer. If the ridge is removed with a ridge reamer, use a dial indicator.

The first measurement for taper is made at the top of the ring travel, just below the cylinder ridge and at right angles to the length of the block. All measurements are recorded. A second measurement is made just above the lowest point of ring travel. The second measurement is then subtracted from the first, and the difference represents the taper of the cylinder.

A minimum of three measurements is made to determine out of roundness. Again, all measurements are recorded. The first is made, as when measuring the taper, at the top of ring travel and at right angles to the block. The second measurement is made at the same depth in the cylinder, but with the micrometer turned one-third revolution. A third measurement is made with the micrometer turned another one-third revolution. The

smallest measurement is subtracted from the largest to determine the out of roundness.

If any cylinder bore has more than 0.010 inch of taper or is out of round more than 0.006 inch, it is reconditioned and fitted with new pistons. For a first-class job, cylinders are reconditioned if any are more than 0.001 inch out of round per inch of bore diameter or have more than 0.0015 inch of taper per inch of bore diameter.

4. *Piston-skirt clearance.* An outside micrometer is used to measure the skirt diameter of each piston at the thrust faces. The skirt measurement subtracted from the cylinder bore measurement gives the piston-to-cylinder diametrical clearance.

If the piston has a split skirt, the diameter is measured at both top and bottom. If the bottom is more than 0.003 inch smaller than the top, it indicates collapse rather than wear. If the collapse is not too serious, it can be corrected by knurling.

If an aluminum piston clearance is more than 0.003 inch greater than that recommended by the manufacturer, or if the total clearance is more than 0.005 inch between the top of the skirt and the cylinder, the piston is replaced. At one time, skirt expanders were used in such cases, but are seldom used now because they may change the weight of the piston and cause considerable trouble.

In some engines the pistons will stand more clearance than in others. Thus, if there is any probability that a piston is worn to the point of slapping, it should either be replaced or be expanded by knurling.

5. *Bent connecting rods.* If the top of either side and the bottom of the opposite side of a piston look polished, the connecting rod is checked to see if it is bent or twisted. The procedure has been described earlier.

Sometimes a piston rocks in operation, causing bright spots on the lands. Too much clearance or weakened piston rings are the usual cause of this trouble.

6. *Cracked piston.* In order to detect a cracked piston, the piston must be cleaned thoroughly. All carbon should be removed from the top and underside of the piston and from all ring grooves. The grooves can be scraped out with a piece of broken ring or with a special tool made for the job. Then the piston, washed in solvent, is examined for head cracks, cracked bosses, or loose struts. If any of these faults show up, the piston is discarded.

7. *Skirt shoulders.* All portions of the skirt are examined for scratches and scoring. Scratches or deep scoring in the vicinity of the piston-pin bosses show that the pins were fitted too tightly or that insufficient clearance was built into the piston when it was originally machined. Scoring or scratches appearing on the skirt shoulders of a strut-type aluminum piston are smoothed with a file and relieved to a depth of 0.005 to 0.010 inch. The relief is not extended beyond the area where the scratches exist.

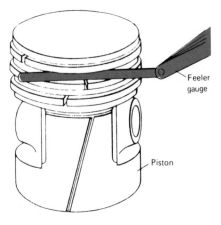

Fig. 9-11 Measuring side clearance in grooves. *Courtesy of Chyrsler Motors Corporation.*

8. *Piston pins.* If there are any visible scratches at the bearing surface, the pin is discarded. If there are no scratches, the amount of wear on the bearing surface is checked with a micrometer. If the wear exceeds 0.002 inch, or if the pin is out of round more than 0.002 inch, it is discarded.

9. *Piston-pin bushings.* The piston-pin bushings are examined in the piston, or in the upper end of the connecting rod, and checked for size. The oil-supply holes must be in register and the bushings must be anchored snugly. If the bushings are scored, they are discarded.

Renewing Pistons

If any pistons are cracked, broken, or too loose in their cylinders, or if they fail to pass any inspection, they are replaced. Do not attempt the repair of cracked or broken pistons.

Because new pistons are available in standard oversizes and cam-ground, they are never machined. The cylinder bores are finished according to piston size plus the manufacturer's recommended clearance. Sometimes this clearance is very small—as little as 0.0005 inch in a 3½-inch cylinder.

To select the proper oversized pistons, the skirt is checked as shown in Fig. 9-12. The illustration shows a typical cam-ground piston at normal room temperature. Measurements at points *a*, *b*, *c*, and *d* are sufficient.

Checking size with a feeler gauge. Because the clearance may be smaller than the thickness of the thinnest feeler stock, the use of feeler gauges is not recommended. Also, the feeler stock is flat and the space to be measured is curved. A dial gauge or a micrometer are much more reliable.

Removing Rings

The quickest way to remove rings is to break them off. To do so, however, may damage the ring grooves. The most common method of removing rings is with specially designed ring-removal pliers. These pliers are a necessity if the rings are to be reused, or for the removal and/or installation of the high-unit pressure, ventilated-type oil ring.

Replacing Rings

Before new rings are ordered, each cylinder and bore is measured carefully. If the selective-fit assembly system is used on the engine, the original bore diameter may be slightly over or under the specified size. Also, the bores may have been reconditioned during a previous overhaul. The importance of careful measurement cannot be overstressed.

Depth of the ring grooves is measured with a tapered bar and either a rule or straightedge, as shown in Fig. 9-13. The tapered strip may be plain steel or it may be marked with various widths. If a strip without markings is used, the place where the straightedge contacts the strip is marked and the width measured at that point. A straightedge is used because the depth of the ring groove is always measured from the thrust face of the skirt, and not from the top of the ring lands, because the diameter of the ring lands is slightly less than the diameter of the skirt.

When reconditioning of the cylinders results in different diameters, each piston and ring must match the diameter, minus the proper clearance of the cylinder in which it is to be installed. Because it is easy to get rings mixed up, set packages are opened and installed one at a time.

Oversized piston rings are usually obtainable in steps of 0.005 inch. When cylinders are rebored, piston weight is of no concern since manufacturers make all pistons for a given engine the same weight, regardless or oversize. This is why pistons are not remachined.

Fitting rings to cylinder. When cylinders are not reconditioned, new rings being installed are checked for end-gap

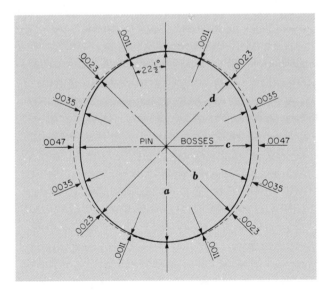

Fig. 9-12   Dimensions of a cam-ground piston.

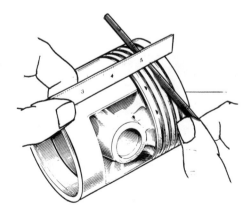

Fig. 9-13   Measuring ring grooves with tapered bar and straightedge. *Courtesy of Chrysler Motors Corporation.*

clearance at the smallest diameter of the bore. Usually, this is at the lowest part of the travel portion of the ring. Most cylinders wear with a taper, with the larger dimensional portion at the top of the cylinder. If the bores have been reconditioned, the ring-gap clearance may be checked at any point. The correct procedure for measuring ring end-gap was described earlier. In this procedure, two or three rings are put into the cylinder and a piston is used to shove them down to the point of measurement. A feeler gauge is then used to check the gap, which should be within the limits of 0.003 to 0.004 inch per inch of cylinder bore. If the gap is less, the rings may jam together at the ends and cause broken rings, scored pistons, scored cylinders, or all three. On the other hand, if the gap is too great, it may cause more blow-by and power loss.

If the end-gap clearance is too small, the rings should not be used unless the ends are filed to the proper gap size. Modern rings are accurately made, and unless sizes become mixed, the end gaps are the same. Thus, if the rings are ordered to the proper size, the gaps are correct. It is good practice, however, to always check the gap before the pistons and rings are locked inside the engine.

If the ring gaps must be enlarged by filing, this is done by first clamping a flat, fine-cut mill file in a vise, as shown in Fig. 9-14. The file should be about an inch wide. The rings are placed over the file as shown, and stroked back and forth. Square-cut rings can be filed two or three at a time, but angle-cut rings must be filed individually. After about a dozen strokes, recheck the gap. Considerable tolerance on the wide side is allowable on new rings. If the gap clearance has been increased too much, the ring need not be discarded unless the clearance is more than 0.025 inch.

Fitting rings to grooves. The rings should have enough side clearance in the grooves to fall to the bottom of the grooves when the piston is held in a horizontal position. This means the clearance must be 0.0015 to 0.003 inch for a top compression ring and for the intermediate ring. Side clearance for a composite oil ring usually should not exceed

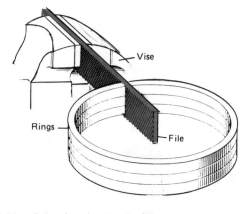

Fig. 9-14   Enlarging ring gap by filing.

0.005 inch. Compression rings are usually marked to indicate the top of the ring, so that in installation the top will face the top of the piston.

A preliminary check of the ring-to-groove clearance is made by setting the outside edge of the ring in the groove and rolling it all the way around the piston taking care that the ring is at full depth all the way. Both the ring and the groove must be clean. A 0.0015-inch feeler gauge, inserted between the ring and groove, should bend noticeably when pulled out. A 0.001-inch feeler gauge that can be pulled out with just the thumb and forefinger indicates an actual clearance of about 0.0015 inch.

If a ring does not enter the groove freely at all points, the ring can be reduced in size by grinding and lapping. A smooth flat board, such as a new kitchen cutting board, with a piece of No. 000 emery cloth tacked to it, is handy for lapping. The board must have a true flat surface. The ring is placed on the emery cloth and moved in a circular path while pressing lightly, but keeping even pressure all around. This is done on each side of the ring for about one minute. The ring is then cleaned and rechecked in the groove. The ring is lapped enough when every part of the ring circumference fits into every part of the groove.

Much less work of this type is needed with modern pistons and rings. Improvements in manufacturing procedures have greatly improved the precision and, hence, the fit of various components.

Mounting rings on pistons.   In mounting rings on the pistons, great care must be exercised to avoid microscopic cracks or breakage. Very fine cracks cause a great deal of trouble. Actual breakage is easy to correct and inexpensive, but microscopic cracks can cause ring breakage after the engine is returned to service. The engine then has to be opened up again and the pistons removed, resulting in additional expense.

Each ring is mounted in its groove and the up and down clearance is rechecked with a 0.001-inch feeler gauge. It should be possible to pass the feeler between the ring and the land all around the ring. Also, the ring should drop as a result of its own weight when the piston is held in a horizontal position. The piston rings make a seal by pressing against the walls of the cylinder bore. Unless they are free to move in their grooves, they cannot make an effective seal.

The foregoing instructions apply to one-piece rings. Manufacturers of multiple-piece rings supply special instructions for installation. Needless to say, these instructions should be followed to the letter.

The ridge in the top of the cylinder was discussed earlier. This ridge should be removed before the piston is removed, since pistons sometimes are broken at the ring lands by being forced past the ridge. In any case, the ridge must be removed before new rings are installed. If it is not, the rings are compressed to get past the ridge. This makes the gap ends touch and may cause ring breakage.

Renewing Piston Pins and Bushings

A piston pin should be renewed whenever wear has increased the clearance between the pin and its bearing to more than 0.002 inch or whenever the pin is badly scratched or scored. Because measurement of that particular clearance is difficult, it is general practice to renew a pin if it shakes noticeably when moved up and down in the piston.

If the pin bearings are in a boss equipped with bushings, reconditioning is simplified. A new set of bushings restores the bearing-bore size and a new set of standard-sized pins completes the job. On the other hand, if the pin bores do not have bushings, they may be reamed to fit oversized piston pins, or they may be relined to accept bronze sleeve bushings.

Fastening the pin.   When the bearing surface is in the piston boss, as in most engines today, the pin has to be fastened in the eye of the rod, usually with a shrink or press fit. The eye of the rod has to be reamed for a press fit with a new oversized pin. An attempt to press in an oversized pin without reaming may result in rupturing the eye of the rod. The pin-to-bore clearance is 0.0003 to 0.0005 inch at room temperature. This is checked by turning the piston on its side with the bore down. The pin should slide out of its own weight.

A drift pin is used to press out a piston pin from the press fit. The piston is placed over a tubular remover so that the pin can be pressed through into the remover. Pins are pressed in by placing the pin pilot in the support, inserting the pin, and pressing.

Renewing pin bushing.   When the connecting rod oscillates on a pin that is fixed in the piston boss, there usually is a bronze bushing in the rod eye. In such cases, an expander bar mounted in an arbor press is needed to press the bushing in place. As shown in Fig. 9-15, the expander bar presses the bushing into such intimate contact with the bore of the rod boss that the bushing is tightly anchored in place. The circular steps on the bar also smooth and compress the metal surface on the inner wall of the bushing. The burnisher is then used to bring the bushing to final size.

Rod alignment.   If a connecting rod is reused, its alignment must be checked to make sure the rod is straight and the pin bore is exactly parallel with the crankpin. Misalignment or twist by 0.002 inch or more should be corrected either by straightening the rod cold or by installing a new rod.

Exchange systems for rods provide a supply of properly reconditioned rods for most engines, so normally it is not necessary to recondition a rod. However, it is good practice to check all rods for straightness and alignment before installing them in an engine. With a bad rod in for a long while, it will manage to slip through. It takes only a few minutes to check these parts, but if there is something wrong with them and it doesn't show up until the engine is reassembled, additional expense is involved.

Alignment of the piston and rod assembly is equally important. Misalignment on the pin sides of the piston should be less than 0.004 inch. To correct misalignment, the pin bores are remachined to bring them to a right angle with the side of the piston. In other words, the piston bore should be exactly parallel with the crankshaft and at right angles to the side of the piston. Although misalignment up to 0.012 inch can be corrected by reboring, it is cheaper usually to buy new pistons.

Installing Piston Assemblies

The cylinder bores, cylinders, pistons, piston rings, ring grooves, bearings, and crankpins should be cleaned thoroughly. The piston and rod assemblies are washed with gasoline or kerosene, and dried with an air jet or a piece of lint-free cloth.

To avoid breaking piston rings when the piston is installed, some kind of ring compressor must be used, regardless of whether the assemblies are installed from above or underneath the engine. Practically any type of compressor is adequate for installing piston assemblies from above, but to be effective for installation from below, the compressor must be specially designed for the job. Such a compressor, shown in Fig. 9-16, is adaptable to installation from below because its maximum extension beyond the piston is only 3/16 inch. When the handle is pushed up, it pulls the band together, compressing the rings so that they will pass into the cylinder bore with the piston.

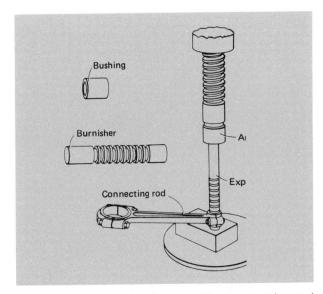

Fig. 9-15   Arbor press for installing connecting-rod bushings.

Before using a compressor, oil the rings thoroughly to make them slide easily into the cylinder bores.

After all assemblies are replaced in their cylinders and the oil pan is installed, the crankshaft is revolved several times. Watch the top of the connecting rod to see that it does not move across the piston and tend to strike the inner ends of the piston bosses. If the top of the rings moves more than 0.0125 inch, the cylinder bore is not at right angles to the crankpin center line.

Starting and running in. An engine prelubricator is the most useful and safest tool for the preliminary running of an engine that has been equipped with new rings or new piston pins and rings. The prelubricator, recall, fills the lubricating system with oil and prevents startup with dry bearings and subsequent burnout.

If a prelubricator is not available, one end of each piston rod is sealed with a nonfluid oil (not ordinary cup grease). The piston is turned over, filled with light oil, and the other end is sealed with the nonfluid oil. The nonfluid oil seals hold the light oil in until the engine heat melts the solidified oil and places the light oil where it is needed most.

A quart of light oil is added to the first five gallons of gasoline. This is good practice whether or not a prelubricator is available. If a prelubricator is not used, the proper amount of SAE 10 viscosity engine oil is put in the crankcase. If a prelubricator is used, the crankcase is filled to the dipstick full reading.

To avoid possible scoring or seizure of tight pins in aluminum pistons, the cooling system is filled with hot water before the engine is started. Heat from the jackets causes the pistons to expand and lets the pins oscillate freely.

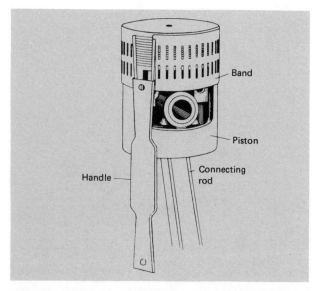

Fig. 9-16 Ring compressor for installing piston assemblies from below. *Courtesy of American Motors Corporation.*

DETECTING AND CURING EXCESSIVE OIL CONSUMPTION

Location of Troubles

Normal oil consumption in a modern automobile engine should not exceed one quart every 1,000 miles. Certain defects or malfunctions, however, can cause oil wastage through any or all of the following paths.

1. Normal leakage, such as the rear or front main bearing, accessory shaft bearings, or inadequately sealed joints such as the oil pan or valve covers.

2. By being passed in excessive amounts from the crankcase into the combustion chamber, or, in other words, oil pumping.

3. Oil working its way into the combustion chamber through the inlet valve ports by way of loose valve-stem guides or a defective vacuum-pump diaphragm.

Corrections

Checking for external leakage. The best way to locate external leaks is to jack up the automobile and look for the leaks. If the leaks are not immediately obvious, put some dye in the oil and drive the automobile with a sheet tied across the frame side rails under the engine. Usually the leak can be found without the sheet. In any case, after the run, check the front and rear bearings, all accessory shaft bearings, oil pan, and valve cover-plate gasket. Any serious leak should be corrected by replacing the offending gasket or packings or by refitting or renewing the bearings.

Oil waste through inlet valve ports. If the valve stems or stem guides are badly worn, suction created by the intake stroke can suck oil through the clearance past them into the combustion chamber. Inability to get an engine to idle properly is reason enough to suspect worn guides. The guides should be renewed, or valve packing should be installed on the valve stems.

Some automobiles with a vacuum-motor drive for the windshield wipers are still around. Usually, the engine has a vacuum-booster pump to assist the vacuum-wiper motor. The assist pump is built into the lower part of the regular diaphragm-type fuel pump. If the booster-pump diaphragm develops a leak, oil can be sucked from the crankcase through the wiper vacuum line to the inlet manifold. This leak may pass more oil than the average worn piston ring.

Oil leakage past piston rings. Any substantial amount of smoke emitting from the exhaust usually indicates oil leakage past the piston rings. If the smoke is accompanied by an increase in oil comsumption, the leakage is further confirmed. It is claimed that oil leakage amounting to four millionths of a cubic inch per stroke will increase oil consumption from the normal one quart per thousand miles to one quart every 400 miles. Such consumption shows the need for new rings, probable reconditioning of the cylinder bore, and, if the condition is bad enough, new pistons.

An additional factor in oil consumption is the amount of oil thrown on the cylinder walls. The best oil rings are limited in the amount of oil they can regulate. Examine the rod bearings. If the crankpins are out of round more than 0.002 inch, they should be reconditioned with a truing tool. Both hand-operated scrapers and power grinders are available for truing a crankpin without removing the crankshaft. If more than one or two crankpins are out of round, it is easier and often more economical to either replace the crankshaft with a reconditioned unit or remove the crankshaft and have it reground. Undersized bearings are then required.

Expanding worn pistons.   A number of methods have been developed to enlarge worn pistons, though many are no longer used. It is entirely practical to enlarge pistons because the diameter of the skirt is slightly larger than the head when the piston is new. The rings in the head provide the seal and also absorb all of the wear. Thus, enlarging operations are confined to the skirt.

The method most used for enlarging the skirt is knurling, which is done by a machine that rolls a serrated wheel over the thrust face of the skirt. The threadlike serrations are pressed into the metal as the wheel is pressed over the skirt. This action forces metal out between the serrations, and thus enlarges the skirt. A piston worn from 0.005 to 0.006 inch may be restored to its original size by knurling.

10

ENGINE BEARINGS

Contents

PURPOSE AND TYPES

Purpose

Engine bearings essentially perform three functions: (1) keep a shaft in proper position with respect to other parts of the engine; (2) prevent wear of expensive parts that are difficult to replace; and (3) transmit power smoothly and with the least possible friction.

Types

The bearings encountered most frequently are *main bearings*, *connecting-rod bearings*, *camshaft bearings*, and *wrist-pin bearings* (bushings). See Fig. 10-1.

The main bearings hold the crankshaft in place and let it rotate. The crankshaft, of course, is connected to the power train that propels the automobile. The connecting-rod bearings, located at the lower end of the connecting rod, encircle the crankpins and allow the connecting rods to move as required. The connecting rods, recall, transmit the thrust of the pistons to the crankpins. The crankpins change

the up-and-down motion of the pistons to the rotary motion of the crankshaft. All main and connecting-rod bearings are made in matching halves.

The camshaft bearings support the camshaft, and the wrist-pin bushings couple the connecting rod to the piston. The camshaft contains a number of cams that directly or indirectly cause the valves to open and close. The wrist pin allows the small end of the connecting rod to rotate, first in one direction and then in the other, as the piston moves up and down. All camshaft bearings and wrist-pin bushings are circular and slide over their respective shafts.

The part of a shaft that rotates in a bearing is called a *journal*.

Bearing Materials

Six types of bearing lining materials are in common use; tin-base babbitt, lead-base babbitt, copper alloys (high lead content), overplated copper alloy, solid aluminum alloy without backing, and overplated steel-backed aluminum alloy.

Although babbitt is an ideal bearing material from the

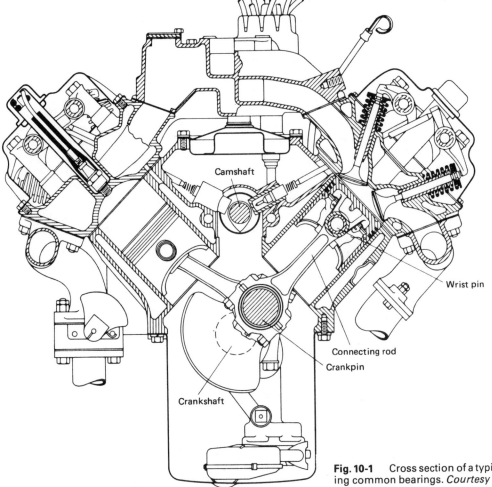

Fig. 10-1   Cross section of a typical modern V-8 engine showing common bearings. *Courtesy of Ford Motor Company.*

standpoint of low friction and wearability, it does not have the strength needed for modern engines, where bearings must resist a thrust of up to three tons psi, and may be subjected to engine speeds as high as 8,000 rpm.

Precision engine bearings are built to absorb punishment and reduce wear. Although it is theoretically possible to produce bearings with virtually unlimited life, such bearings would soon wear out the journals and crankpins. It is much cheaper to replace a set of bearings than to replace a crankshaft or camshaft.

Standardization in Bearings

Modern bearings require no cutting, fitting, scraping, or other work to assure perfect fit. In most cases, the replacement of bearings is fairly easy if the proper bearings are obtained and simple procedures followed.

Replacement bearings will fit accurately if the journals and crankpins of the crankshaft and the journals of the camshaft are in good condition and do not need refinishing. (A crankpin is that part of a crankshaft to which the connecting rod is attached.) If the journals or crankpins need regrinding, however, undersized bearings must be used to compensate for the metal removed from the journals or crankpins in the regrinding process. ("Undersized," in this case, refers to the radius of the bearing as measured from its inner surface.) Undersized bearings are available in standard sizes; journals and crankpins normally are reground to accommodate these sizes.

Differences in Bearings

In older engines, the bearing halves often are separated by shims at the parting faces, as shown in Fig. 10-2. The shims are sheets of thin metal, usually brass, held together by babbitt metal facings. Bearing wear is compensated for by removing one or more shims as needed. As shims are removed, however, the clearances at the top and bottom of the bearing are reduced, but those at the sides remain the same. The effects created by the removal of shims are clearly illustrated in Fig. 10-2. As shown, the shims extend through to contact the shaft. This construction keeps the

bearing shell from turning and seals the bearing in the pressure-lubricated engine. Shim bearings are seldom encountered today.

Modern bearings have no shims; when worn, they are simply removed and replaced. Seal at the parting face of the shells, as well as complete and snug contact with the surface against which the shells rest, is obtained by making the ends of each bearing shell project slightly above the parting surface of the bearing, as shown in Fig. 10-3. This projection may be as little as 0.00025 inch. The two halves are brought together and forced tightly into the bore of the housing when the bearing cap is bolted in place, thus creating an effective seal.

In some older engines, a dowel in the bearing housing fits into a corresponding hole in the bearing shell to hold the shell securely in place. In modern engines, however, a nib (locking lip) fits into a matching recess in the bearing cap or housing. The nib holds the bearing shell securely in place but permits easy removal of the shell.

When it is necessary to regrind the crankshaft, undersized bearings must be used. In such cases, the regrinder automatically furnishes the correct undersize. Bearing manufacturers provide lists of standard undersized bearings as a guide for regrinding.

MINOR OVERHAUL

Introduction

For a major overhaul the engine is removed from the chassis and extensive work is performed on the crankshaft, camshaft, connecting rods, and bearings. In a minor overhaul, the engine is not removed from the chassis and the work may include the replacement, repair, or reworking of bearings, valves, pistons, or piston rings. Our sole concern in this book is with minor overhaul.

Again, the amount of work you can do yourself will depend upon your experience, or lack of it, and the availability of tools.

Bearing Inspection

When an engine is torn down for valve or ring work, the bearings are checked to see if they are in satisfactory condition or need replacement.

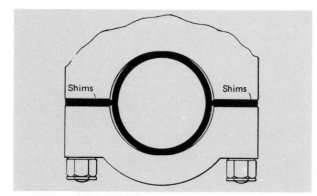

Fig. 10-2   Shimmed bearing.

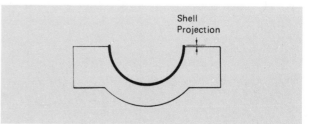

Fig. 10-3   Bearing shell projection for snug fit and seal.

First, the front of the car is raised with a hoist. Then the oil pan is removed. Connect an engine prelubricator and watch the oil dripping from the bearings. Let's assume the prelubricator shows excessive leakage at crankshaft journals and crankpins. This means there is trouble with the journals, crankpins, or bearings. The first step to remedy the problem is to remove the connecting rods and piston assemblies in the manner described previously. Before each part is removed, mark it to permit correct reassembly. Next, remove the bearing caps from all but the front and rear main bearings, again making sure all parts are marked.

The crankpins are now measured with a micrometer to find any out-of-round, uneven wear, or taper. We will assume the crankpins are in good condition and do not need reworking. Next, the crankshaft journals are measured by using a crankshaft gauge, such as that shown in Fig. 10-4. The principal parts of the gauge are the angular pads, plunger, button, and thumbscrew.

Before the gauge is used, clean the journals to be measured. The gauge is also cleaned with particular attention being paid to the angular pads, the plunger tip, and the button. When the gauge is ready for use, the plunger is pushed down into its farthest position and locked into place by turning the thumbscrew. The gauge is then placed on the journal with the angular pads resting against the journal and rocked slightly radially several times. The rocking is important, since it seats the pads firmly against the journal.

With the gauge held firmly against the journal, the thumbscrew is loosened to allow the plunger to butt against the journal. A distinct clicking sound is heard when the plunger hits the journal. The thumbscrew is then turned back and forth several times, and tightened just enough to hold the plunger in position. If the thumbscrew is tightened too much, the position of the gauge may be changed. Proper tightening of the thumbscrew requires some practice, but is necessary to obtain accurate measurements. After the thumbscrew is locked into position, a micrometer is used to

measure the distance between the button and the tip of the plunger. See Fig. 10-5. The measurement obtained is the radius of the journal and is multiplied by two to obtain the diameter. Several measurements are taken with the gauge in various positions on the journal to determine if it is out-of-round, unevenly worn, or tapered. If defects are found, the journal must be reground to the proper undersize. All journals and crankpins are checked in this manner. To check the front and main rear-bearing journals, the other main-bearing caps are replaced and tightened to specified torque. This allows the front and rear bearing caps to be removed and the journals checked.

Replacement Bearings

Let us now assume that all journals and crankpins are in good condition, but some of the bearings are so badly worn as to require replacement. First obtain new bearings of the correct size. To replace the connecting-rod bearings and the lower half of the main bearings, follow the instructions given earlier. The upper half of the main bearings presents another problem, however, since the crankshaft is still in the engine.

The upper half of the main bearings is removed and replaced by using a special tool known as a roll-out pin. In Fig. 10-6, this pin is inserted into the crankshaft oilway, with the head of the pin hugging the crankshaft and butting against the parting face of the bearing. The crankshaft is then turned so that the pin forces the bearing half out of the cylinder-block bore. The crankshaft must be turned in the proper direction so that the nib on the bearing is raised out of the recess in the cylinder block. The same tool and procedure are used to install the new bearing half. Coat the new bearing shaft with oil before it is installed.

Some automotive experts disapprove of this method of installing new bearings. They claim there is no way to know

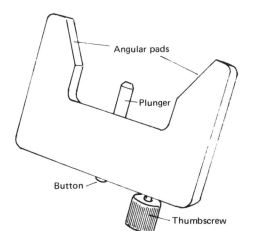

Fig. 10-4 Crankshaft gauge. *Courtesy of Federal-Mogul Division, Federal-Mogul-Bower Bearings, Inc.*

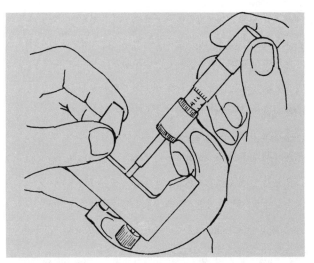

Fig. 10-5 Micrometer used to obtain radius of journal. *Courtesy of Federal-Mogul Division, Federal-Mogul-Bower Bearings, Inc.*

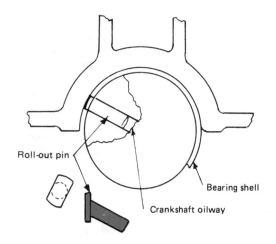

Roll-out pin

Bearing shell

Crankshaft oilway

Fig. 10-6 Roll-out pin used to remove upper half of main bearing. *Courtesy of Federal-Mogul Division, Federal Mogul-Bower Bearings, Inc.*

if the cylinder-block bore is clean and that the new bearing half seats tightly into the bore. Other experts claim that a check of the removed half bearing indicates, to some degree, the condition of the cylinder-block bore. The instructions given here are intended merely to show what can be done and how to do it.

Occasionally, only one or two crankpins are out-of-round or slightly worn. In this case, the crankpins can be reground with a portable grinder, but with care. Take every possible precaution to keep small pieces of metal from falling and becoming embedded in other parts. When the grinding is completed, clean the engine carefully. Otherwise the grinding may prove more costly and troublesome than a major overhaul.

If more than two crankpins need reworking, and the main-bearing journals are in poor condition, a major overhaul of the crankshaft and its bearings by a shop that specializes in this type of work is indicated. Alternatively, you may be able to find a reground shaft on an exchange basis. These shafts are particularly advantageous in that they come with the correct undersized bearings.

BEARING TROUBLESHOOTING

Detecting Bearing Troubles

Engine bearings cannot be inspected or measured without tearing down the engine, at least in part. It is possible, however, to detect bearing trouble by sound.

Certain characteristic sounds indicate loose or defective bearings. With experience, the significance of the sounds is readily understood. A loose connecting-rod bearing, for example, makes a sort of slapping sound as the blade strikes the crankpin. The sound is often loudest when the engine is running at about half its maximum speed. At idling speed, the rod usually emits sharp tapping sounds. A test often

used to pinpoint a defective connecting-rod bearing is to short out the suspected cylinder by disconnecting the spark-plug wire. If the intensity of the sound increases, that bearing is loose.

A loose main bearing emits a heavy thumping sound, particularly if the engine is made to lug (operate under a heavy load). One way to make an engine lug is to drag the brakes while the engine is pulling the automobile along. Suddenly accelerating a standing automobile will also produce the thump.

Not all knocks, however, are caused by loose or worn bearings. The valve tappets, fuel pump, and many other engine parts can cause knocking sounds. Tappet knocks are perhaps the most common. Therefore, the tappets should be checked before the engine is torn down to get to suspected bearings.

There is no substitute for experience in detecting and identifying engine noises, particularly those noises caused by loose or worn bearings. If you lack this experience, visit a shop that specializes in engine overhauls and ask if you can listen, watch, and ask questions while investigation of problems progresses.

Detecting Causes of Bearing Troubles

As mentioned several times, when engine parts are removed they should be marked clearly so that they can be returned to their original positions during reassembly. The best way to mark bearings is to scratch an identifying mark on the backs of the bearing halves, using any sharp-pointed tool. One system of marking is to use 1U to identify the upper half of the first bearing, 1L for the lower half of the same bearing, 2U, 2L, 3U, 3L, and so on. After the bearings are marked, clean them in solvent and examine both the linings and back surfaces.

Examine the bearing linings first by placing the halves, with their linings up, in rows; the uppers in a row, and the corresponding lowers in another row. Both the main and connecting-rod bearings are set up this way. The locking nibs should be in correct position. Use good lighting and a magnifying glass to study fine details.

Bearing damage shows up, of course, in the linings. But the cause of the damage may originate elsewhere in the engine, perhaps even in the backs of the bearings. Thus, when the linings are examined and damage is noted, turn the bearings over and examine the backs for irregularities.

Dirt is the most frequent cause of bearing trouble. Particles of steel and iron are common troublemakers, and usually result from machining where care was not exercised during the cleaning operations. Adverse wear or chippage of front-end gears, cam lobes, oil-pump gears, tappets, rocker arms, push rods, cylinder walls, piston rings, and the like are all potential sources of chips, strings, flakes, or slivers of metal. These fine bits of metal often become embedded in the surface of the bearing lining and are seen easily through a magnifying glass. They sometimes provide a clue to trouble in other parts of the engine. Iron or steel particles are easily identified with a magnet. Scrape the surface of the bearing lining with a sharp knife and let the particles fall on a sheet of white paper. Move the magnet around under the paper. If the particles follow the magnet, they are either iron or steel.

If aluminum particles are suspected, swab the bearing lining surface with a strong solution of lye (sodium hydroxide). Aluminum particles will foam or bubble when treated this way. Since lye is poisonous and a corrosive caustic that can cause serious burns, it should be handled with extreme care and should be put away after each use.

Brass and bronze particles are identifiable by their distinctive yellowish and brownish colors. Presence of these metals usually indicates wear in bushings or main-bearing thrust washers. Sand will show rounded corners when viewed through a magnifying glass, and may be clear or colored. Grinding-wheel grit or honing chips have distinctly sharp edges and irregular shapes. Babbitt or other metals sometimes show up because of the failure of another bearing.

Types of Bearing Damage

There are too many types of bearing damage to be covered in a book of this type, but let's take a look at some of the more common ones.

Scoring and scarring. Damages due to scoring and scarring are detected by a series of scratches, grooves, or scars in the direction in which the shaft turns. This condition shows that some form of hard particles have found their way, usually carried by the oil, into the bearing. Large dirt particles may be compressed by the shaft and, thus, will indent or scar the bearing surface. The coarseness or fineness of the marks indicates the general consistency of the contaminant.

To minimize such scoring and scarring, change the oil and oil filter at conservative intervals. Also check the air filter frequently to make sure it is in good condition. All other inlets to the engine, whether for oil, air, or water should be inspected periodically as well.

A wide and deep score pattern is caused by chips, strings, or flakes of iron or steel. The flakes may be the result of adverse wear and spalling of the front-end gears.

The lower halves of engine bearings often show more scoring or abrasive wear than the upper halves because the shaft usually exerts more pressure on the lower halves. This happens often on main bearings and usually is accompanied by greater wear on the upper halves of the connecting-rod bearings than on the lower halves.

Scoring or dirt pileup may occur in the central area of the surface or between the center and one side of the connecting-rod bearings. In general, this type of scoring is due

to the angular drilling of the crankshaft oilway, and is caused by the centrifugal action of the rapidly turning crankshaft, which tends to move the heavier particles to one side of the bearing.

When bearings are abraded by sand or fine grit, the scored lines are extremely fine, and may be short or intermittent. Short lines occur when the dirt is crushed by shaft pressure and carried for a short distance on the bearing surface. This type of scoring usually results when dirt and sand pass through the air filter.

Irregular pock marks are caused by aluminum flakes resulting from piston failure.

Residue remaining from earlier bearing trouble can cause heavy scarring. Again, this emphasizes the importance of cleanliness during reassembly. Carelessness is the cause of such damage.

Very fine scoring that resembles the grooves on a phonograph record may result from inadequate polishing of the shaft after regrinding. In such cases, the bearings are free or nearly free of dirt.

Wiping, burning, and seizure. Wiping, burning, and seizure always spell lubrication trouble. A bearing not properly lubricated will overheat from friction and the bearing lining might melt. Wiping and burning are easily recognizable, since the lining is heavily smeared. Seizure is a condition in which the bearing literally seizes the shaft and stops the engine.

A common cause of wiping or seizure, particularly during early running of an overhauled engine, is a so-called *dry* start. This occurs when the engine lubrication system has not been primed properly with oil prior to starting. With oil in the oil pan only, sufficient time may elapse before pressured oil reaches the bearings to cause wiping or seizure.

Wiping and burning can also be caused by insufficient oil clearance, low oil level, or even oil dilution. Other causes of wiping, burning, or seizure include misassembly or bad fit. For example, the bearings may be reassembled into oversized, excessively out-of-round, or distorted housings. The damage could also be caused by thermal expansion due to excessive heat from lack of lubrication, by a sudden charge of dirt, or even by extremely hard engine usage.

Corrosion and erosion. Occasionally you will encounter unusual forms of bearing damage. When this happens, contact a bearing specialist instead of attempting to diagnose the probable cause. One example of such damage is caused by corrosion and erosion.

All fossil hydrocarbon fuels—crude oil, fuel oil, natural gas, gasoline, or diesel fuel—contain sulfur and other chemicals in varying amounts. Even highly refined gasoline contains a small amount of sulfur. Hydrocarbons are compounds of hydrogen and carbon.

When the hydrogen burns, it leaves a residue of water, which reacts with any sulfur in the combustion gases to form a weak sulfurous acid. This acid seldom causes trouble in an automobile engine because it is usually vaporized by the heat and blown out with the exhaust gases. When the vaporized acid reaches the muffler, however, the gases may be sufficiently cooled to cause some of the acid-water vapor to condense and attack the muffler metal. This is why steel mufflers tend to corrode so quickly.

Some types of corrosion are caused by organic acids which result from chemical changes in the oil. These types can destroy the lead in copper-lead bearings, leaving only spongy copper, which breaks down in service. They also attack lead-base babbitt bearings, in which the damage appears as a light-gray, chalky residue on the surface of the lining. When probed with a pointed tool, the residue crumbles and can be observed with a magnifying glass.

Other rare causes of corrosion include the following: (1) Antifreeze leaking into the crankcase and contaminating the oil. (2) Excessive blow-by of combination products past the piston rings, thus contaminating the oil. (3) Very cool operation, due to short and long stops (in this case, particularly in cold weather, the engine never gets hot enough to boil off the condensed combustion products, some of which blow by the piston rings; though the contamination of the oil is slight, it forms acids which may cause corrosion—one possible solution to this type of problem is to change oil more frequently). (4) Extremely high-temperature operation, due primarily to prolonged high-speed driving. (This can heat the oil above normal operating temperature, thus causing the oil to break down and form corrosive chemicals). (5) Use of inferior oils, many of which may contain corrosive acids.

Troubles Caused by Defective Bearings

Some of the troubles attributed to loose, worn, or cracked-up bearings include the following: (1) High oil consumption or oil loss: badly worn main, connecting-rod, and camshaft bearings, or any of these with cracks or defects in the lining, or crankshaft journals and crankpins out-of-round permit excessive oil leakage, or throwing of oils from the ends of the bearings. This excessive oil is picked up by the rotating crankshaft and connecting rods and thrown up into the cylinder bore, where it works past the piston rings, into the combustion chamber, and is then burned. External leaks at the front and rear main bearings may be caused by faulty bearings or by defective oil seals. (2) Engine missing: this may be caused by carbon-covered spark plugs—one result of oil pumping induced by defective main, connecting-rod, or camshaft bearings. (3) Engine knocking: this may be caused by excessively worn, or otherwise defective main or connecting-rod bearings, or by too much clearance. It might also result from excessive crankshaft end-play caused by the wear of thrust flanges of the bearing. Knocking also results from sprung or bent connecting rods. (4) Smoking exhaust: bluish-white smoke issuing from the exhaust pipe when the engine is warmed up is indicative of oil pumping. (5) Sluggish performance: a poor engine performance may often be traced to dirty spark plugs, combustion-chamber walls, piston heads, valves, and the like, caused by excessive oil thrown from faulty bearings. (6) Low oil pressure: this condition often is caused by excessive clearance at the main, connecting-rod, or camshaft bearings.

11

OVERHAULING CYLINDERS AND ENGINE BLOCKS

Contents

INTRODUCTION

About the Chapter Content

A quick glance at the chapter content may convey the impression that it is a "catch-all" for topics that should (or could) be presented elsewhere. To some extent this criticism is justified. But the arrangement decided upon has the overriding advantage of making the chapter essentially self-contained in order to minimize the number of costly (and sometimes dangerous) mistakes that new and/or nonprofessional mechanics are most likely to make.

Another characteristic of the chapter is the duplication of certain procedures covered in earlier chapters. Again, the intent is to maximize learning through reinforcement and thereby reduce mistakes. But the duplication is not carried to a ridiculous extreme.

Preliminary Considerations

The inspection of an engine may reveal that one or all of the bores should be reconditioned and new oversized pistons and rings installed, or that cracks or other serious damage exist. The degree of experience possessed by the reader is the major determinant of what should, or should not, be attempted. For example, welding or brazing may be considered. But these are not jobs for the beginner, and serious consideration must be given to the relative economics of new versus repair.

If a decision is made to weld, improved welding rods and welding techniques make it possible for oxyacetylene or electric-arc welding to be done without preheating the block. This means that the block need not be completely stripped for preheating. If, for example, the damage is confined to the outer wall of the water jacket at a point where no severe strain occurs, a simple brazing or welding job may effectively repair the block, and this work can be done with the engine practically intact. If the damage is inside the bore, or around the valve seats, more disassembly and very precise welding is required. Obviously, if the bore must be reconditioned, the piston and connecting-rod assemblies must be removed.

If the piston and connecting-rod assemblies are removed, it is good practice also to remove the crankshaft and camshaft, or at least to inspect them for wear and possible bearing damage. If bearing repairs or renewals are needed, complete the work while the block is stripped.

Piston and Connecting-Rod Removal

As you already know, the method of removal of the piston and connecting-rod assembly is governed by the construction of the crankshaft and the diameter of the cylinder bore compared to the outside measurement of the large end of the rod. An exploded view of a typical piston and rod assembly is shown in Figure 11-1. If the rod will pass through the bore, the assembly is removed from the top. But if the rod is too large, it must come out from the bottom (seldom necessary in modern engines).

In some engines both the piston and connnecting rod can be removed at the bottom of the block without removing the crankshaft. Clearances in some engines may require that the crankshaft be rotated a certain number of degrees

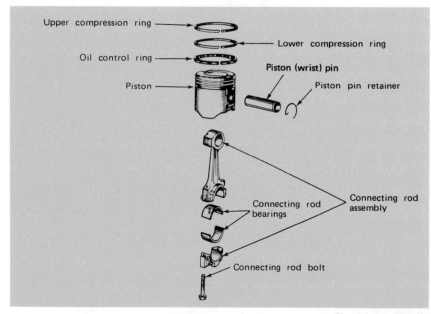

Fig. 11-1 Exploded view of piston and connecting-rod assembly. *Courtesy of Ford Motor Company.*

first and then held stationary in that position. In other engines the crankshaft must be revolved slowly as the piston is withdrawn to keep the piston from becoming jammed between the block and the crankshaft where it can damage the block, the shaft, and the piston.

Sometimes the piston can be removed by disassembling the connecting rod from the crankshaft and pushing up the connecting rod until the piston and wrist pin are above the bore. The pin can then be pushed out of the piston and the rod to separate them. The connecting rod is removed from the bottom of the block and the piston is removed from the top. This procedure, however, can be bothersome, and take almost as much time as removing the crankshaft. If pistons are removed at the top, the wear ridge at the top of each cylinder should be reamed out first to avoid piston-ring breakage.

Whenever a piston and connecting rod are removed as an assembly from the top of the cylinder bore, there is a possibility of damaging the crankshaft journal and cylinder wall with the free end of the connecting rod as the assembly is moved upward in the bore. Disconnected from the crankshaft, a connecting rod is free to swing on the wrist pin; in pushing out the piston, the rod may strike the crankshaft journal or the cylinder bore unless it is guided carefully. A special guide tool, available for removal of a piston and connecting-rod assembly, allows one to proceed with minimum trouble.

Cylinder Castings

In modern engines, the cylinders are cast in a single metal block which includes the supports (housings) for the upper halves of the main bearings. The lower halves of the bearings are carried in caps, which are bolted on.

A bottom view of a typical cast-iron block for a V-8 engine is shown in Figure 11-2. The main-bearing sets are machined in the bulkhead that separates each bank of cylinders.

An aluminum block differs from a cast-iron block in that it usually has nonreplaceable cast-iron cylinder lines and

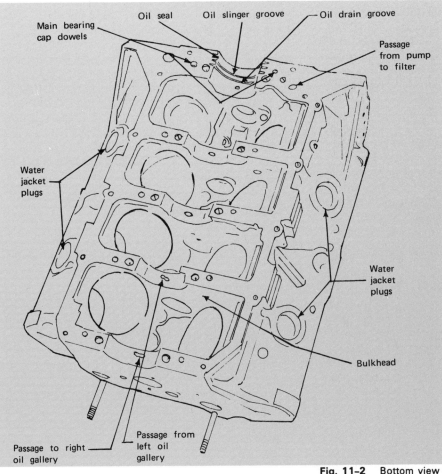

Fig. 11-2 Bottom view of cast-iron engine block. *Courtesy of Pontiac Division, General Motors Corporation.*

valve seats. The valve-stem guides in the block, however, are replaceable. Reconditioning the bores in an aluminum block requires careful preparation of the block.

Method of Repair

Primarily, the method of repair depends on the nature of the problem. For a specific job, however, there may be more than one procedure. If, for example, a bore needs reconditioning, either a portable boring tool or a special grinder may be used. If obstructions do not prevent the use of a hand tool, the portable bore may be entirely satisfactory, and may save the work and expense of pulling the engine. But if grinding is needed, the engine must be removed from its compartment for transport to the grinder. Never attempt the removal of an engine or machining operations unless you have the necessary lifting equipment and are skilled in machine work (as some of you may well be). This means that major repairs should usually be entrusted to specialty shops.

Crankcase Dilution and Formation of Sludge

Poor driver habits, combined with the lack of simple preventive maintenance, are the underlying causes of many expensive repairs. Infrequent oil changes, for example, often causes the formation of sludge—a mixture of water, gasoline and contaminants introduced by the blow-by of exhaust gases past the piston rings—in the crankcase. As a result, engine bearing, cylinder walls, and moving parts are subjected to severe wear and fail prematurely. Sludge is also created when the engine is started and stopped frequently and operated for only short periods of time at low speeds.

When a cold engine is started, the air-fuel mixture admitted to the cylinders contains a greater proportion of gasoline than is needed for normal operation. Consequently, a small amount of the vaporized fuel is unburned. The unburned portion condenses to a liquid where it gets into the cylinders, washes past the piston rings, and enters the crankcase. As the engine warms, moisture in the air is drawn into the crankcase, condenses to water, and gets into the oil. As soon as the engine reaches its normal operating temperature and continues to operate for some time at that temperature, the water and gasoline in the crankcase become hot enough to vaporize and go out the crankcase breather. Hence, the oil in the crankcase is not seriously affected and only normal engine wear takes place.

Under start/stop, slow-speed operating conditions, the engine does not reach normal operating temperature, especially in cold weather, and the oil soon forms a sludge.

Some Simple Mechanical Operations

Water jacket repairs. A cracked water jacket is nearly always caused by freezing of the coolant in the water passages of the block. The frozen coolant expands and exerts sufficient force to crack the metal jacket. Cracked water jackets

are rare today because of the widespread use of dependable permanent antifreeze solutions.

A cracked water jacket usually is repaired by electric-arc or acetylene welding.

Replacing cylinder-head studs. Studs are used extensively for holding the cylinder head and other engine components in place on the block. A stud is similar to a bolt except that it is threaded at both ends. One end of the threaded stud is screwed into a tapped hole in the block until it is tight. The other threaded end extends beyond the surface of the block to receive the cylinder head or other mating component. If, for example, a cylinder head is to be clamped to the block, the head gasket and head are installed with the studs extending through the stud holes in the head. A hexagonal nut is screwed on each stud, and all the studs are tightened in accordance with the manufacturer's torque and sequence specifications.

To replace a cylinder-head stud that has unscrewed with the nut, screw two nuts on the stud. Then, keep the lower nut from turning while the upper nut is tightened until it jams against the lower one. The wrench is applied to the upper nut when the stud is being screwed in, and to the lower nut when the stud is being removed.

Removing broken studs. Occasionally a stud breaks off level with or below the surface of a cylinder block or some other part of the block. If the the broken stud fits loosely in the threaded hole, it is removed by setting a dull chisel at the outer edge of the stud and striking the head of the chisel with a hammer in the direction that unscrews the stud. However, a stud extractor is more likely to be needed because a stud is often rusted (frozen) in the hole. If an extractor is necessary, it should be used as follows:

1. Use a drill that fits the stud hole in the cylinder head and drill only far enough to spot the top of the broken stud with a center.

2. After the center of the stud has been spot drilled, use a ³⁄₁₆-inch drill for a ³⁄₈- or a ⁷⁄₁₆-inch stud, or a ¼-inch drill for a ½-inch stud, and drill vertically down to a depth of at least ½ inch.

3. Turn the extractor into the drilled hole and unscrew the broken piece of the stud by turning the extractor with a wrench in a left-hand direction. The extractor is similar to a spiral tapered reamer, except that the spiral is left-handed instead of right-handed and the taper is greater than that of a conventional reamer. The cutting edges on the tapered end enable the extractor to grip the wall of the hole drilled in the stud as the tool is turned in the direction that unscrews the stud. Some cylinder heads are so deep, it is necessary to remove them in order to insert the extractor.

Drilling out a broken stud. If the threaded end of a broken stud is rusted in the mating threads in the block, or if the threads have been damaged or upset, the broken piece usually cannot be removed with a stud extractor. If either one of these conditions is encountered, the stud may be drilled out as follows:

1. Leave the cylinder head or manifold in place until the drilling is finished.

2. Use a drill size that is the same as the smallest diameter of the broken stud, which will be from $\frac{1}{32}$ to $\frac{3}{32}$ inch smaller than the major diameter of the stud. With the hole in the cylinder head as a guide, center the drill very carefully and drill to the full depth of the screw or stud hole. Maintain sufficient grease or oil on the sides of the drill to keep the drill from cutting or enlarging the hole in the head. After drilling, the broken piece can be removed and a tap of the proper size run through to clean up the threads. A bottoming tap is used because it has threads of full height all the way to its end.

Drilling out for a larger stud or screw. If the method just described is not practicable, the threads may be drilled out of the hole and the hole retapped for a larger stud. With the head in place on the block, use a drill that is the same size as the hole in the head. Drill the threads out of the stud hole, then tap the enlarged hole. Use a tap that will make the hole fit the next larger stud diameter. If the hole was fitted originally with a $\frac{3}{8}$-inch stud or screw, tap it for a $\frac{7}{16}$-inch replacement; if it was originally tapped for a $\frac{7}{16}$-inch stud or screw, a $\frac{1}{2}$-inch stud or screw should be used. Now, using a hand drill or a drill press, ream or bore a hole in the cylinder head to a size $\frac{1}{32}$ to $\frac{1}{16}$ inch larger than the new oversized screw or stud diameter.

Heli-coil screw-thread insert. Sometimes the metal in the head around the stud hole may not be thick enough to permit the use of a larger sized stud. Formerly, if the metal was not thick enough, the only recourse was to weld the original hole closed and then to drill and tap the hole to the original stud size. This repair required much time and work. A more recent development, called the *Heli-coil screw-thread insert,* showed in Fig. 11-3, facilitates repairs of this kind. In some cases the thread insert actually strengthens the section of the casting in which the damaged stud hole is located. It restores the hole to the original stud size and eliminates the need for an oversized stud.

The screw-thread insert is a helical coil of stainless steel with a diamond-shaped cross section in which both the inner and outer surfaces conform to the profile of the American National Thread. When the insert is installed in the threaded stud hole, it provides a hard, smooth, antifriction threaded lining which eliminates galling and seizing of the threads when the stud is screwed into the hole. Also, any tendency to abrasion and stripping of the threads is greatly reduced. In softer metals, such as aluminum, a Heli-coil insert provides a strong protective lining for tapped threads.

To install inserts as a repair for damaged threads, it is necessary to remove all traces of the original threads by using a drill of the proper size. After the threads have been drilled out, a special tap is used to cut the threads for the insert. Drilling out the old thread enlarges the hole slightly, and if the hole is located in a spot that does not permit a larger hole, the Heli-coil repair cannot be used. Where hole size is a critical factor, the original hole can be repaired only by filling, redrilling, and tapping to the desired size.

The inserts are made slightly larger than the tapped holes, so that when they are installed there is a slight springing effect which helps hold them in place. For this reason, a special prewinder tool is needed for inserting the thread insert. An insert is placed on the prewinder; the prewinder in turn is placed against the tapped hole. The insert is turned into the stud hole until the last coil of the insert is below the surface of the casting. The insert thus provides a new thread into which the stud or screw is screwed. The Heli-coil thread insert offers a quick, easy, and economical repair.

Cleaning the cylinder block after completing repairs. After the repair work on a cylinder block and cylinder head is completed, both are thoroughly cleaned. A good cleaning solvent and brush should be used. A high-pressure hose is used to rinse all traces of the cleaning solution from the block and head. After rinsing, a light coating of ordinary

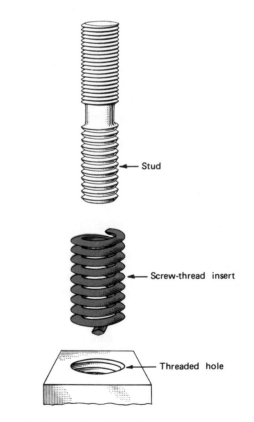

Fig. 11–3 Heli-coil screw-thread insert.

machine oil is applied to machined surfaces, and the block and head are covered with a lint-free cloth, paper, or plastic wrapper.

Replacing the Cylinder Head

Warping of the cylinder head and burring of the metal near the head studs are usually caused by improper installation of the cylinder head. To avoid trouble, the following suggestions should be kept in mind:

1. Always clean the top of the block and the face of the head thoroughly before placing the head on the block.

2. Always see that the gasket is properly seated on the face of the block before installing the head.

3. See that the gasket openings line up with all water passages in the block and on the head before applying the gasket because, sometimes, the gasket will be defective in this respect. Check this point carefully, since it is a common cause of overheating.

4. If the copper-asbestos gasket has a lapped edge, place the lapped-edge side of the gasket toward the cylinder block whenever possible.

5. After the gasket has been properly applied, place the cylinder head on the block. Then crank the engine to see that there is no interference between the pistons and the gasket. Interference will be indicated by a slight knock, and by possible movement of the loose head while cranking.

6. Use a high-quality gasket-sealing compound, and apply it evenly and sparingly to both sides of the gasket.

7. When tightening the head, follow the correct nut-tightening sequence. Do not overtighten one particular stud. Instead, tighten all the studs evenly, alternating from one side to the other, using a torque wrench.

8. Be extra careful when tightening the nuts on the studs in the vicinity of the valves. If the nuts on these studs are tightened to the straining point, there is a chance of distorting the valve seats in the block or head, so that there will be leakage past the valves. Cylinder-head tightening has become such an important operation that special wrenches, which indicate on a scale the tightness in foot-pounds or inch-pounds, are now considered necessary for satisfactory results.

Tightening cylinder-head nuts. Cylinder-head nuts must be tightened in the proper sequence and to a prescribed tightness. The sequence for tightening is illustrated usually in the manufacturer's service manual as a guide to the mechanic when replacing a cylinder head. A general tightening sequence is illustrated in Fig. 11-4. The nuts are tightened in numerical order as indicated by the encircled numbers. Failure to tighten the cylinder-head nuts in the proper order may result in a warped block or head, distorted valve

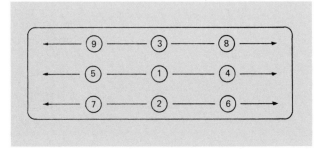

Fig. 11-4 Typical cylinder head nut-tightening sequence.

seats, gasket leakage, or bolt failure. The nuts on the center row of studs should be tightened first, and the nuts on the remaining rows of studs should then be tightened from the center row to each end. If the nuts on the end studs are tightened first, a lever effect may be set up in the head in which the end studs act as a pivot. Tightening the nuts at the opposite ends of the head may develop sufficient transverse stresses in the metal at the center of the head to cause it to crack.

Each nut on a stud should be tightened in several steps. The complete sequence should be followed through several times, with each nut being drawn down a little each time around. When all the nuts for a cast-iron cylinder head have been tightened, the engine should be run until it reaches operating temperature, after which the tightness should be checked again. On engines that have aluminum heads the tightness of the nuts should be checked after the engine has been run and then allowed to cool.

Need for torque wrench. The tightness of any nut or threaded fastener is determined by means of a torque wrench. Automobile manufacturers furnish torque-wrench specifications for the tightness of cylinder-head nuts, bearing caps, and other threaded fasteners to ensure that the proper force is applied to the threads. Too little tightening usually results in parts working loose or in the malfunctioning of parts from misalignment. Too much tightening can warp or crack an assembly or a component, or it can stretch and deform the threads of a screw or bolt so much that the desired clamping effect cannot be obtained. Always follow the torque specifications and use an accurate torque wrench to do the tightening. Dirty threads will cause a false reading on the torque wrench.

Torque wrench. All conventional torque wrenches are based on the principle of the lever. The torque about a given point is equal to the torque exerted on the lever multiplied by the length of the lever. The lever length of a torque wrench is the distance between the centerline of the drive square and the pivot point of the handle. The wrench is designed so that the force exerted on the handle is concentrated at the pivot point, which enables the lever length of the wrench to be accurately measured. If the lever length is measured in feet, the torque is measured in foot-pounds; if the lever length is measured in inches, the torque is measured in inch-pounds. If the torque-wrench scale reads in inch-pounds and the torque-tightening specifications are given in foot-pounds, multiply the foot-pounds value by 12 to obtain inch-pounds. Conversely, if the torque-wrench scale reads in foot-pounds and the torque-tightening specifications are given in inch-pounds, divide the inch-pounds value by 12 to obtain the foot-pounds.

Calculating torque when an adapter (extension) is used. Adapters, or extensions, are often used with a torque wrench to gain access to a nut or bolt or to increase the capacity of the wrench. An adapter or extension, if it doubles the lever length of the wrench, doubles the capacity of the wrench. Therefore, if an extension is used, the lever length of the wrench is increased, and the wrench capacity is proportionately affected. Because the scale on a torque wrench is calibrated (marked) on the basis of the original length of the wrench, the use of an adapter or extension affects the accuracy of the scale reading. The amount of error is directly proportional to the added length of the adapter or extension. The formula used to determine torque is

$$T = L \times F$$

where T is the torque in foot-pounds or inch-pounds, L is the lever length in feet or in inches, and F is the force in pounds.

Example 1. To tighten a nut, a force of 40 pounds is applied to the handle of a torque wrench having a lever length of 12 inches (1 foot). What is the torque in foot-pounds on the nut?
Solution. The torque is the product of lever length and the force. The lever length is 1 foot and the force is 40 pounds. Therefore, the torque on the nut is

$$T = 1 \times 40 = 40 \text{ foot-pounds.}$$

If an adapter or extension is used with a torque wrench, as shown in Fig. 11-5, the torque indicated on the scale is

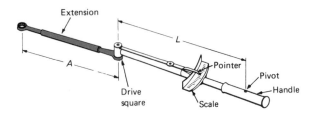

Fig. 11-5 Torque wrench with extension.

not the true torque value, because the original lever length of the wrench has been increased. The difference between the observed torque reading and the actual torque at the end of the adapter or extension is directly proportional to the added length of the lever. When the lever length of a torque wrench is increased, the torque exerted at the end of the extension can be determined by the formula

$$T(\text{ext}) = \frac{T(L+A)}{L}$$

in which $T(\text{ext})$ is the torque exerted at the end of the extension, T is the torque-wrench scale reading, L is the nominal lever length of the wrench, and A is the length of the extension.

Example 2. A 4-inch extension is added to a torque wrench that has a nominal lever length of 10 inches. If the scale reading is 40 foot-pounds, what is the torque in foot-pounds exerted at the end of the 4-inch extension?
Solution. The values to be substituted in the formula are $T = 40$, $L = 10$, and $A = 4$. The torque exerted at the end of the extension is

$$T = \frac{40(10+4)}{10} = \frac{40 \times 14}{10} = 56 \text{ foot-pounds.}$$

Thus, the 4-inch extension adds 16 foot-pounds of torque to the scale reading of 40 foot-pounds.

Torque and tension. Some people mistakenly refer to a torque wrench as a tension wrench. Since a torque wrench imparts a twisting or turning motion to a threaded fastener by means of a force applied to a lever arm, the force it exerts is torque. The standard unit of measurement for torque is the foot-pound. Tension, on the other hand, is a straight pull or a force applied in a straight line which tends to stretch the body to which it is applied. The standard unit of measurement for tension is the pound.

Torque-tightening specifications. Torque-tightening specifications for cylinder heads, bearings, screws, and bolts are available in chart form for all makes of automobiles. The specifications are usually given in foot-pounds, but in some cases the manufacturer may use inch-pounds to express torque. The torque wrench then becomes an important precision instrument for properly tightening to the manufacturer's specifications the many threaded fasteners found on an automobile.

All cylinder-head nuts, for example, should be tightened to the same torque value so that each stud receives its proper share of the load to hold the cylinder in place on the engine block. In general, cylinder-head nuts on ⅜-inch studs are tightened to a torque of 45 to 50 foot-pounds. On ⁷⁄₁₆-inch studs, the nuts are tightened to a torque of 55 to 60 foot-pounds, and on ⅝-inch studs, between 95 and 100 foot-pounds. If the studs or bolts thread into aluminum, the torque should be about half the values of those given above.

Crankshafts and Flywheels

Crankshaft construction.   Crankshafts are made of special grades of alloy steels or cast steels to provide the best combination of strength and lightness. Since the crankshaft changes the reciprocating motion of the pistons into rotary motion, the entire power output of the engine is handled by the crankshaft. Therefore, the crankshaft must be strong enough to withstand the downward thrusts of the pistons on each power stroke without becoming distorted, and to resist the bending and twisting action to which it is subjected. The journals and bearings are made large enough to distribute crankshaft loads and to withstand wear during continuous rotation at high speed.

Automobile engine crankshafts usually are made in one piece and are machined from drop-forged blanks. Where it is not possible to make drop-forged blanks without considerable removal of metal, the crankshaft is made of cast steel. Because of the speed at which a crankshaft revolves, it must be balanced very carefully to eliminate vibration resulting from the weight of the offset cranks and the attached connecting rods and pistons. To provide the necessary balance, counterweights are used.

Counterbalancing.   Considered by itself, a finished crankshaft is in perfect static and dynamic balance. When the crankshaft is installed, however, the weight of the connecting rods and pistons and the centrifugal force during rotation require counterweights on the shaft to compensate for the unbalanced condition. At low speeds of rotation, the distorting forces and the bending stresses of the crankshaft are negligible. But modern automobile engines rotate at more than 6,000 rpm. Each time the rotative speed is doubled, the centrifugal force acting on the crankshaft is increased four times. Therefore, an unbalanced crankshaft cannot obtain comparatively high rotative speeds without setting up severe and destructive vibration.

To permit high rotative speeds, crankshafts are counterbalanced very carefully by means of counterweights lo-

cated at the proper points so that the various forces tending to cause vibration are balanced. These counterweights are comparatively large, and most of their weight is positioned as far as possible from the axis of the crankshaft.

As shown in Fig. 11-6, the counterweights attached to the crank flange are directly opposite the crankpins to which are attached the connecting rods and pistons.

Purpose of flywheels.   In the four-cycle automobile engine, only one of the four strokes is a power stroke. In a single-cylinder four-cycle engine, turning effort is exerted on the crankshaft on only one stroke, and there are three idle strokes before the next working stroke occurs. Even in a four-cycle engine, where the power strokes of the different cycles are timed to give an impulse to the crankshaft every half-revolution, the connecting rod and crank throw are in a straight line in each cylinder at the end of each power stroke and there is no tendency for the crankshaft, in itself, to rotate further. In order to have a practical working engine, some means must be provided for storing the mechanical energy developed in the crankshaft during the power stroke, and for using this energy to maintain a uniform motion of the crankshaft between power strokes. In a gasoline engine a flywheel is used to fulfill this function.

The flow of power from a gasoline engine is not smooth. While the power strokes on a six- or eight-cylinder engine overlap, the power delivered to the crankshaft is not uniform. This variation in power impulses tends to make the crankshaft go faster and then slow down. When a flywheel, which has most of its weight in its rim, is bolted to the crankshaft and rotates with it, the inertia of the flywheel tends to keep the crankshaft turning at a constant speed. Thus the flywheel absorbs power when the crankshaft tries to speed up and gives back power when the crankshaft tries to slow down.

In addition to giving uniform rotation to the crankshaft, a flywheel has gear teeth around its outer rim that mesh with the starting motor drive pinion for starting the engine. Also, the rear face of the flywheel serves as the driving member of the clutch on automobiles equipped with manual-shift transmissions.

The front end of the crankshaft has the gear or sprocket

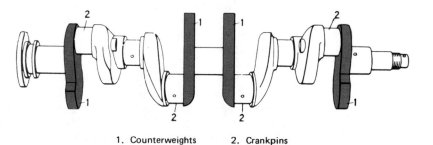

1. Counterweights   2. Crankpins

Fig. 11-6   Location of counterweights on crankshaft. *Courtesy of Ford Motor Company.*

that drives the crankshaft, the vibration damper, and the fan-belt pulley. The pulley drives the engine fan, the generator, and the water pump with a V-belt.

Vibration damper. Each time a piston moves downward on its power stroke, the power impulse transmitted to the crankshaft through the connecting rods tends to set up torsional vibration in the crankshaft. This force, which may exceed two tons, acting against the crankpin, exerts a twist on the crankshaft at the moment it is applied. At the end of the power stroke the thrust against the crankpin ceases, and the crank untwists and assumes its original relationship with the rest of the crankshaft. This twist and untwist, repeated with every power stroke, sets up an oscillation in the crankshaft which is called *torsional vibration.* If this vibration were not controlled, the oscillations could break the crankshaft at certain speeds. To control torsional vibration, a vibration damper, sometimes called a *harmonic balancer,* is used. The vibration damper usually is mounted on the front end of the crankshaft, and the fan-belt pulley is integral with the damper.

One type of damper consists of a small damper flywheel and the pulleys. These are bonded to each other by a rubber insert about one-quarter of an inch thick. Any tendency for the crankshaft to suddenly gain speed on a power stroke, and then slow down at the end of the power stroke, is controlled by the damper flywheel. The inertia of the damper flywheel imposes a dragging effect on the crankshaft, and when this happens the rubber insert flexes slightly and holds the crankshaft to a constant speed. The damper checks the slight twist and untwist of the crankshaft and relieves the stresses in the crankshaft by canceling the torsional vibrations. Also, distortion of the rubber insert causes friction among the molecules of rubber. This friction generates some heat and thus energy is absorbed.

A vibration damper of the type described is shown in Fig. 11-7. The hub of the *fan-belt pulley* is keyed to the *crankshaft* and is held in place by the *nut.* The *inertia member* is fastened to a *pressed-steel cup* by the *rubber,* which is bonded to both the inertia member and the cup. The cup is attached to the pulley hub by the *cap screw.*

LATE MODEL, 4-CYLINDER OHC ENGINES

We shall now look at representative 4-cylinder engines produced by American manufacturers. Certainly the most unique of these engines is the Compound Valve Hemispherical (CVH) engine developed for use in the Ford Escort and Lynx and special attention is given to this type of engine.

The three major sections that follow, Engine Diagnosis and Testing, Overhaul, and Cleaning and Inspection, are generally applicable to any engine, but portions are specifically applicable to the CVH engine.

Chrysler Omni and Horizon

This is a conventional 4-cylinder engine with a displacement of 104.7 cubic inches (1.7 liter). The block is cast iron and the head is aluminum. A forged steel crankshaft is rotated by cast-aluminum piston. Five main bearings support the crankshaft, but there is no vibration damper. The oil-filter base and the intake manifold are aluminum.

Chrysler Aries and Reliant

The standard engine for these two models is a 135 CID (2.2 liters) but is very similar in most other respects to the 1.7 liter engine. One major difference, however, is the use of hydraulic-lash adjusters in place of the shim-type adjusters used on the smaller engine.

A larger 155.9 CID (2.6 liters) engine is optional. Certainly its most unusual feature is a "jet valve" located inside the intake valve of each cylinder. Operated by the intake valve rocker arm, this valve admits a swirl of air into the combustion chamber, resulting in more complete combustion.

GMC Chevrolet Monza and Vega

From 1975 through 1977, the Monza and Vega were equipped with 4-cylinder single OHC engines. The cylinder block is cast aluminum and the head is cast iron. The valve train is completely contained in the head, in a straightline vertical configuration. In a manner typical of most other OHC engines, the camshaft is driven by a timing belt which is driven in turn by a front-camshaft pulley.

In 1978-1980 models, Monza has the 151 CID engine described under Astre and Sunbird.

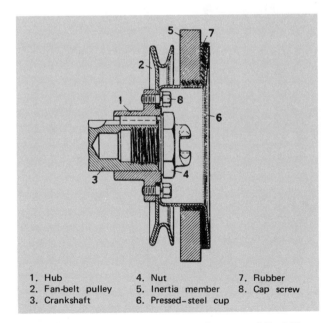

1. Hub	4. Nut	7. Rubber
2. Fan-belt pulley	5. Inertia member	8. Cap screw
3. Crankshaft	6. Pressed-steel cup	

Fig. 11-7 Typical vibration damper. *Courtesy of Ford Motor Company.*

Pontiac Astre and Sunbird

The 151 CID engine (designed and manufactured by Pontiac) is used in the Astre, Sunbird, 1978-1980 Monza and the current model AMC Gremlin.

This engine has a so-called crossflow-design cylinder head. There are two overhead cams and each cylinder is serviced by two intake and two exhaust valves located in manifolds placed on opposite sides of the head. The distributor is located at the rear left-hand side of the block. The dual overhead cams, water pump, and fan are belt driven in a manner similar to most 4-cylinder designs.

Ford Escort and Lynx

Developed jointly by Ford of Europe and Ford of North America, the Compound Valve Hemispherical (CVH) engine is available in models having 1.3 and 1.6 liter displacements. Cylinder bore size is the same, but the 1.6 liter en-

gine has a longer stroke and therefore requires a block with a somewhat higher deck height.

A cutaway view of the CVH engine is shown in Figure 11-8.

All valve components are located in or on an aluminum alloy cylinder head having a hemispherically shaped combustion chamber that provides the highest power, lowest fuel combustion, and lowest level of engine emissions of all existing engine designs.

To avoid the use of dual overhead cams, the valve axis is rotated around the combustion chamber and the valves are canted (tilted) at a *compound angle* so that each valve and port is offset from the longitudinal and transverse center lines of each cylinder bore. Angling the valves in this manner has permitted their size to be maximized for improved air flow. Head-installed tappets allow the valves to be operated through hydraulic lash adjusters and rocker arms, thereby eliminating the need for push rods. The spark plug

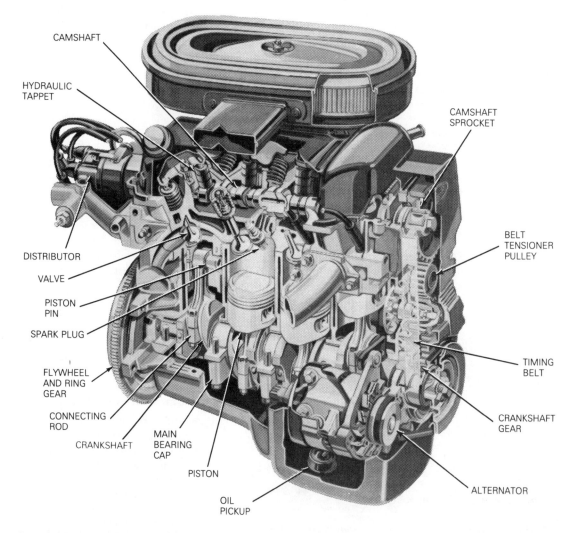

Fig. 11-8. Cutaway view of CVH engine. *Courtesy of Ford Motor Company*

is centrally located in the combustion chamber. To further increase efficiency, a crossflow induction system, with intake and exhaust manifolds on opposite sides of the engine, is used in conjunction with the hemispherical combustion chamber.

The camshaft is supported in the cylinder head by five bearing surfaces. To absorb camshaft thrust, a thrust plate is installed over the cam at the forward end of the cylinder head. The ignition distributor is located at the rear end of the cylinder head. The shaft that turns the ignition rotor is tanged directly to the end of the camshaft to eliminate the need for a drive gear or additional drive mechanism.

The camshaft is rotated by a belt that fits over gears located at the ends of the crankshaft and camshaft. Tension on the belt is maintained by a spring-loaded pulley located about midway between the belt spans. The belt tension is not adjustable and tension should not be relieved from the belt unless required by a service procedure. A new belt must then be installed.

In addition to driving the camshaft, the belt also drives the water pump, eliminating the need for another drive belt and pulley on the front of the engine.

The oil pump is bolted to the front of the cylinder block with the pump drive gear positioned directly over the crankshaft. Thus, the pump is driven directly by the crankshaft.

The crankshaft is also supported by five main bearings, with the center bearing providing the crankshaft thrust surfaces. The pistons, attached to the crankshaft through connecting rods, are domed and relief-cut to match the valve and combustion chamber configuration.

ENGINE DIAGNOSIS AND TESTING

Some portions of the information presented in the following sections are a repeat (or near repeat) of earlier topics. They are of such great importance, however, as to justify repetition. Moreover, not everyone will have either the equipment or experience to handle some of the work described. But an awareness of one's own limitations is very often just as important as the ability to do a given job.

PCV System.

A malfunctioning closed crankcase ventilation system may cause loping or rough idle. Do not attempt to compensate for the idle condition by disconnecting the PCV system and making carburetor adjustments. Removing the PCV system will adversely affect fuel economy and engine ventilation with a resulting shortening of engine life.

Engine Oil Leaks.

The following procedure is effective and requires a minimum of equipment. Prior to starting work, clean the cylinder block, cylinder head(s), rocker cover(s), oil pan, and fly-wheel housing areas with a suitable solvent to remove all traces of oil.

To perform the oil-leak diagnosis without the use of a special tool, you will need the following items: (1) air supply and air hose; (2) air pressure gauge that registers pressure in one-psi increments; (3) air-line shut-off valve; (4) appropriate fittings to attach the above parts to the oil fill, PCV grommet holes and rocker-arm cover tube; (5) appropriate plugs to seal any openings leading to the crankcase; (6) a solution of liquid detergent and water to be applied with a suitable applicator, such as a squirt bottle or brush.

Fabricate the air-supply hose to include the air line shut-off valve and the appropriate adapter to permit the air to enter the engine through the rocker-arm cover tube. Fabricate the air-pressure gauge to a suitable adapter for installation on the engine at the oil-fill opening. Now, follow this testing procedure.

(1) Open the air-supply valve until the pressure gauge registers 5 psi (maintain this pressure).

(2) Inspect the sealed and/or gasketed areas for leaks by applying a solution of liquid detergent and water. The formation of bubbles will indicate leakage. Under the hood examine the rocker-cover gasket, cylinder front-cover gasket, intake-manifold gaskets, front and rear intake manifold and seals, cylinder-head gasket, fuel-pump and/or mounting gasket, distributor 0-ring, auxiliary driveshaft cover gasket, oil-level indicator (dipstick) tube connection, oil-pressure sending unit, and cup plugs and/or pipe plugs at the end of oil passages.

Next, with the vehicle raised on a hoist, check under the engine at the oil-pan gasket, oil-pan front and rear end seals, and crankshaft front and rear seals.

Then, with the transmission and flywheel removed, inspect the crankshaft rear seal. Air leakage in the area around the seal does not necessarily indicate a leak. But if no other cause can be found for oil leakage, assume that the rear seal is faulty. Continue by inspecting the rear main bearing-cap parting line, rear main bearing cap and seals, flywheel-mounting bolt holes, and the rear cup and/or pipe plugs at the ends of oil passages. Oil leaks at crimped seams in sheet-metal parts and cracks in cast or stamped parts can be detected when pressurizing the crankcase. Note: Light foaming equally around rocker-arm cover-bolts and crankshaft seals is not detrimental and no corrections are required.

Compression Test

First make sure that the oil in the crankcase is at the proper level and the battery is properly charged. Operate the engine until it is at normal operating temperature. Then turn the ignition switch off and remove all the spark plugs. Set the carburetor throttle plates and choke plate in the wide-open position and install a compression gauge in the No. 1 cylinder. Insert an auxiliary starting switch in the starting circuit. With the ignition switch turned off, use the auxiliary switch to crank the engine for at least five compression strokes and record the highest compression reading. Also make note of the approximate number of compression strokes required to obtain the highest reading. Repeat this test on each cylinder using the same number of compression strokes.

The indicated pressures are considered to be within specification if the lowest reading cylinder has a pressure equal to at least 75 percent of the highest reading recorded.

If one or more cylinders read low, squirt about one tablespoon of engine oil on top of the pistons in those cylinders and repeat the test procedure described above.

If the pressure improves considerably, the piston rings are at fault. If it does not, the valves are either sticking or seating poorly. If two adjacent cylinders indicate low compression pressures, and squirting oil on the pistons does not increase the compression, the cause may be a cylinder-head gasket leak between the cylinders resulting in the presence of engine oil and/or coolant in the cylinders.

Static Valve-Train Analysis (Engine Off)

Start by checking the individually mounted rocker-arm assemblies for loose mounting studs and nuts or plugged oil feed in the rocker arm. Then inspect the valve-spring assembly for broken or damaged parts. Continue by checking the valve stem retainer and keys (both one-piece and two-piece retainers). The keys must be seated properly on the valve stem and in the retainer. Also look for proper seating of the keys on the valve stem in the positive rotator. On the valves and cylinder head, ascertain that the cylinder head gasket is installed properly and that there are no plugged oil drain-back holes or worn or damaged valve tips. Also look for missing or damaged valve-stem oil seals, or a collapsed tappet gap. Finally, check the installed spring height. On the camshaft check for plugged oil feed, correct cam lift, and the presence of the camshaft oil plug.

Dynamic Valve-Train Analysis

After the static checks are completed, start the engine and while running at idle, check the individually mounted rocker-arm assemblies for plugged oil feed in the rocker arm. If a condition of insufficient oiling is suspected, accelerate the engine to 1200 rpm ± 100 rpm with the transmission in neutral and the engine at normal operating temperature. Oil should squirt from the rocker-arm oil holes so that valve tips and rocker arms are well oiled and/or, with the rocker-arm cover off, oil splash may overshoot the rocker arm. If oiling is insufficient for this condition to occur, examine the oil passages for blockage.

Next, check the valves and cylinder head for plugged oil drain-back holes, missing or damaged valve-stem oil seals or guide-mounted oil seals.

Camshaft Lobe Lift

Check the lift of each lobe in consecutive order and make a note of the readings.

1. Remove the air cleaner and the valve rocker-arm cover.

2. Remove the rocker-arm fulcrum nut, rocker arm, and fulcrum guide.

3. Make sure the tappet is seated against the cam. Install a dial indicator in such a manner as to have the ball socket adapter of the indicator on the top of the tappet and in the same plane as the tappet movement.

4. Connect an auxiliary starter switch in the starter circuit. (If checking during engine assembly, use a socket and ratchet to turn the crankshaft.) Crank the engine with the ignition switch off. "Bump" the crankshaft over until the tappet is on the base circle of the camshaft lobe. At this point, the tappet is in its lowest position.

5. Zero the dial indicator. Continue to rotate the crankshaft slowly until the tappet is in the fully raised position (highest indicator reading). The total lift recorded on the indicator should be at least 0.229 inch (5.806 mm).

6. To check the accuracy of the original indicator reading, continue to rotate the crankshaft until the indicator reads zero. If the lift on any lobe is below 0.229 inch, the camshaft and the tappets operating on the worn lobe(s) must be replaced along with any tappet showing pitting or having its contact face worn flat or concave. (Refer to camshaft and hydraulic-lash adjuster inspection.)

7. Remove the dial indicator and auxiliary starter switch. After installing the rocker arms, do not rotate the crankshaft until the tappets have had sufficient time to drain down. To do otherwise may cause serious valve damage. Manually bleeding down will reduce the waiting time.

8. Install the valve rocker-arm cover and the air cleaner.

Hydraulic Tappet Leakdown Test

A hydraulic tappet is a zero-lash hydraulic device, similar in construction and operation to the hydraulic tappets used on push-rod engines. They are cleaned, inspected, and checked in the same manner.

Hydraulic tappet noise may be caused by excessive collapsed tappet gap, sticking tappet plunger, tappet check valve not functioning properly, air in the lubrication system, leakdown rate too rapid, or excessive valve guide wear.

Excessive collapsed tappet gap may be caused by loose rocker-arm fulcrum nuts, incorrect initial adjustment, or wear of the tappet face, rocker arm, rocker-arm fulcrum, or valve tip. With the tappet collapsed, check the gap between the valve tip and the rocker arm to determine if any other parts are damaged, worn, or out of adjustment.

A sticking tappet plunger may be caused by dirt, chips, or varnish inside the tappet. The sticking can be corrected by disassembling the tappet and removing the particles causing the condition.

A tappet check valve that is not functional may be caused by dirt or chips that keep it from closing when the lobe is lifting the tappet. It may also be caused by a broken check-valve spring.

Air bubbles in the lubrication system will prevent the tappet from supporting the valve-spring load and may be caused by too high or too low an oil level in the oil pan, or by air being drawn into the system through a hole, crack, or leaking gasket on the oil-pump pickup tube.

The tappet leakdown rate should be 15 to 75 seconds for 0.100 inch (2.5 mm). A lower leakdown time may cause noisy operation. If no other cause for noisy tappets can be found, check the leakdown rate. Tool 6500-E or its equivalent is needed to perform this test, and only the special fluid provided with the tool will give accurate results.

First disassemble and clean the tappets to remove all traces of engine oil. Do not mix parts from different tappets. They are not interchangeable.

Next, place the tappet in the tester, with the plunger facing upward. See Figure 11-9. Pour the hydraulic tester fluid into the cup to a level that covers the tappet assembly.

To facilitate timing as the pointer passes the "start-timing" mark, adjust the length of the ram so that the pointer is 1/16-inch below the starting mark when the ram contacts the tappet plunger.

The center mark on the scale should be used as the "stop-timing" mark rather than the original mark at the top of the scale.

Work the tappet plunger up and down until the tappet fills with fluid and all traces of air bubbles have disappeared. This places a 50-pound load on the plunger.

Let the ram and weight force the plunger downward. Measure the exact time it takes for the pointer to move from the "start-timing" mark to the "stop-timing" mark. The leakdown rate must be within the range of 15 to 75 seconds.

Any tappet that does not meet specifications must be replaced. To facilitate testing, new tappets contain the proper test fluid.

To help depress tappet plungers when checking the valve clearance, remove the fluid from the cup and bleed the fluid from the tappet by working the plunger up and down.

Camshaft End Play

Push the camshaft toward the rear of the engine. Install a dial indicator so that the indicator point is on the camshaft-sprocket attaching screw. Zero the dial indicator. Pull the camshaft forward and release it. The camshaft end play should be from 0.002 inch to 0.006 inch (0.050-0.15 mm). If the end play is excessive replace the thrust plate. See Figure 11-10. Remove the dial indicator.

Crankshaft End Play

See Figure 11-11. Force the crankshaft toward the rear of the engine. Install a dial indicator so that the contact point rests against the crankshaft flange and the indicator axis is parallel to the crankshaft axis. Zero the dial indicator. Push the crankshaft forward and note the reading on the dial. If the end play exceeds 0.008 inch (0.200 mm), replace the

Fig. 11-10. Thrust plate replacement. *Courtesy of Ford Motor Company*

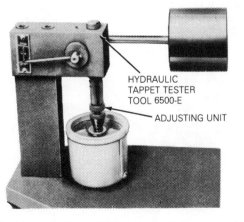

Fig. 11-9. Hydraulic tappet leakdown test. *Courtesy of Ford Motor Company*

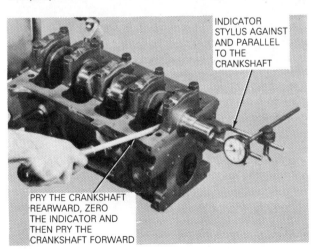

Fig. 11-11. Measuring crankshaft end play. *Courtesy of Ford Motor Company*

thrust bearing. If the end play is less than 0.004 inch (0.100 mm), inspect the thrust-bearing faces for scratches, burrs, nicks, or dirt.

Flywheel Runout

Remove the spark plugs and install a dial indicator so that the indicator point rests on the face of the ring gear adjacent to the gear teeth. See Figure 11-12. Hold the flywheel and crankshaft forward or backward as far as possible to prevent crankshaft end play from being indicated as flywheel runout. Set the indicator dial to zero. Turn the flywheel one complete revolution and note the total indicator reading. If it exceeds 0.007 inch (0.180 mm), the flywheel and ring gear assembly must be replaced.

OVERHAUL

Service Limit Specifications

These specifications are intended to be a guide only when overhauling or reconditioning an engine or engine component. A determination can be made whether a component is suitable for continued service or should be replaced for extended service while the engine is disassembled.

In the case of "valve-stem to valve-guide clearance," the "service clearance" is intended as an aid in diagnosing engine noise only and does not constitute a failure or indicate need for repair. However, when overhauling and reconditioning a cylinder head, the service clearance should be regarded as a practical working value, and used as a de-

terminant for installing the next oversize valve to ensure extended service life.

Cylinder Head

Replace the head if it is cracked. Do not plane or grind more than 0.010 inch from the original cylinder head gasket surface. Remove all burrs or scratches with an oil stone.

Reaming Valve Guides

If it is necessary to ream a valve guide to install a valve with an oversize stem, a Rotunda 14-0224 or equivalent hand-reaming kit contains the following reamer and pilot combinations: a 0.003-inch OS reamer with a standard diameter pilot, a 0.015-inch OS reamer with a 0.003-inch OS pilot, and a 0.030-inch reamer with a 0.015-inch OS pilot.

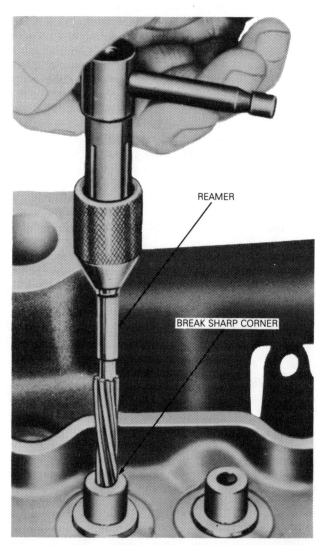

REAMER

BREAK SHARP CORNER

Fig. 11-13. Reaming valve guides. *Courtesy of Ford Motor Company.*

DIAL INDICATOR STYLUS CONTACTS FLYWHEEL APPROXIMATELY ONE INCH FROM EDGE

HOLD FLYWHEEL AND CRANKSHAFT FORWARD OR BACKWARD WHILE CHECKING RUNOUT

Fig. 11-12. Measuring flywheel runout, CVH engine with manual transmission. *Courtesy of Ford Motor Company.*

When replacing a standard size valve with an oversize valve always use the reamer in sequence (smallest oversize first, and then next smallest, etc.) so as not to overload the reamers. Always reface the valve seat after the valve guide has been reamed, and use a suitable scraper to break the sharp corner (ID) at the top of the valve guide. See Figure 11-13.

Refacing Valve Seats

Refacing of the valve seat should be closely coordinated with the refacing of the valve face so that the finished seat and valve face will be concentric and the specified interference angle will be maintained. This will ensure a compression-tight fit between the valve and seat. Make sure the refacer grinding wheels are properly dressed.

Grind the valve seats to a true 45° angle. Remove only enough stock to clean up pits and grooves or to correct the valve-seat runout. After the seat is refaced, use a seat-width scale, Figure 11-14, or a machinist scale to measure the seat width. Narrow the seat, if necessary, to bring it within specifications.

If the valve-seat width exceeds the maximum limit, remove enough stock from the top and/or bottom edge to reduce the width to specifications.

Refer to Figure 11-15. On intake seats, use a 77° angle grinding wheel to remove stock from the bottom of the seats (raise the seats). Use a 70° wheel when removing stock from the bottom of an exhaust seat. An 18° angle wheel is used to remove stock from the top of the seats (lower the seats).

The finished valve seat should contact the approximate center of the valve face. It is good practice to determine where the valve seat contacts the face. To do this, coat the seat with Prussian blue and set the valve in place. Rotate the valve with light pressure. If the blue is transferred to

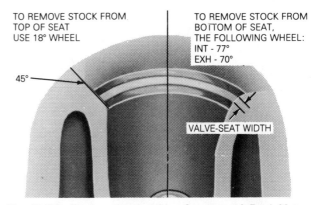

Fig. 11-15. Stock-removal guide. *Courtesy of Ford Motor Company.*

the center of the valve face, the contact is satisfactory. If the blue is transferred to the top edge of the valve face, lower the valve seat. If the blue is transferred to the bottom edge of the valve face, raise the valve seat.

Refacing Valves

Minor pits, grooves, etc. may be removed. Discard valves that are seriously damaged if the face runout cannot be corrected by refinishing or if stem clearance exceeds specifications. Discard any excessively worn or damaged valve-train parts.

If the valve-face runout is excessive and/or if you want to remove pits and grooves, reface the valves to a true 44° angle. Remove only enough stock to correct the runout or to clean up the pits and grooves. See Figure 11-16. If the

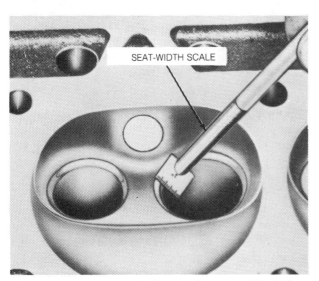

Fig. 11-14. Using a seat-width scale. *Courtesy of Ford Motor Company.*

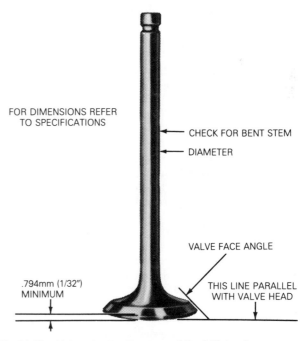

Fig. 11-16. Valve checks. *Courtesy of Ford Motor Company.*

edge of the valve head is less than $\frac{1}{32}$-inch (0.794 mm) thick after grinding, replace the valve. Otherwise, it will run too hot in the engine. The interference angle of the valve and seat should not be lapped out. Remove all grooves or score marks from the end of the valve stem, and chamfer it as necessary. Do not remove more than 0.010 inch from the end of the valve stem.

If the valve and/or valve seat has been refaced, check the clearance between the rocker-arm pad and the valve stem with the valve-train assembly installed in the engine.

Select Valve Fittings

If the valve stem-to-valve-guide clearance exceeds the service clearance, ream the valve guide for the next oversize stem. Valves with oversize stem diameters of 0.003, 0.015, and 0.030 inch are available for service in diameters of 0.008, 0.016, and 0.032-inch oversize. Always reface the valve seat after the valve guide has been reamed.

Camshaft Service

Clean and inspect the camshaft as described earlier. Remove light scuffs, scores, or nicks from the camshaft machined surface with a smooth oilstone.

Fitting Pistons

The standard-size pistons are color coded red or blue, or have 0.003 OS stamped on the dome. The diameters are 3.1466 to 3.1461 inches for red, 3.1478 to 3.1472 inches for blue, and 3.1506 to 3.15 inches for the oversize.

Measure the cylinder bore and select the piston to assure the proper clearance (0.008 to 0.016 inch). When the bore diameter is in the lower one-third of the specified range, use a red piston. When the bore diameter is in the middle one-third, use a blue piston. And when the bore diameter is in the upper one-third, the 0.003 OS piston should be used.

Measure the piston diameter to ensure that the specified clearance is obtained. It may be necessary periodically to use another piston (within the same grade size) that is either slightly larger or smaller to achieve the specified clearance. If none can be fitted, refinish the cylinder to provide the proper clearance for the piston. When a piston has been fitted, mark it for assembly in the cylinder to which it was fitted. If the taper, out-of-round, and piston-to-cylinder-bore clearance conditions of the cylinder bore are within specified limits, new piston rings will give satisfactory service. If new rings are to be installed in a new cylinder that has not been refinished, remove the cylinder-wall glaze using only a spring-loaded cylinder hone and only if there is no visible sign of cross-hatch markings on the cylinder walls. Be sure to clean the cylinder bore thoroughly.

After any refinishing operation, allow the cylinder bore to cool and make sure the piston and bore are clean and dry before the piston fit is checked.

Fitting Piston Rings

1. Select the proper ring set for the size cylinder bore.
2. Position the ring in the bore in which it is to be used.
3. Push the ring down into the bore area where normal ring wear is not encountered.
4. Use the head of a piston to position the ring in the bore so that the ring is square with the cylinder wall. Use caution to avoid damage to the ring or cylinder bore.
5. Measure the gap between the ends of the ring with a feeler gauge. (0.012 to 0.020 inch for the top and bottom compression rings and 0.034 to 0.037 inch for the oil ring.) If the ring gap is less or greater than the specified limits, try another ring set.
6. Check the ring side clearance of the compression rings (0.001 to 0.003 inch for the first ring and 0.002 to 0.003 inch for the second ring) with a feeler gauge inserted between the ring and its lower land. The gauge should slide freely around the entire ring circumference without binding. Any wear that occurs will form a step at the inner portion of the lower land. If the lower lands have high steps, replace the piston.

Refinishing Journals

Dress minor scores with an oilstone. If the journals are severely marred or exceed specifications, they should be refinished to give the proper clearance with the next undersize bearing. If the journal will not clean up to the maximum undersize bearing available, replace the crankshaft.

The same journal shoulder radius that existed originally should always be reproduced. If the radius is too small it will cause fatigue failure of the crankshaft. If it is too large, there will be bearing failure due to radius ride of the bearing.

After journals are refinished, the oil holes should be chamfered and the journal should be polished with a No. 320 grit polishing cloth and engine oil. Crocus cloth may also be used as a polishing agent.

All oil passages must be cleaned thoroughly after chamfering and polishing, using a suitable bristle brush and solvent.

Fitting Main or Connecting Rod Bearings with Plastigage

1. Clean the crankshaft journals. Inspect the journals and thrust faces (thrust bearing) for nicks, burrs, or bearing pickup that would cause premature bearing wear. When replacing standard bearings with new bearings, fit the bearings to minimum specified clearance. If the desired clearance cannot be obtained with a standard bearing, try one 0.0005-inch or 0.001-inch undersize in combination with a standard bearing to obtain the proper clearance.
2. If fitting a main bearing in the vehicle, position a jack under the counterweight adjoining the bearing checked. Support the crankshaft with the jack so its weight will not compress Plastigage and provide an erroneous reading.

3. See Figure 11-17. Place a piece of Plastigage on the bearing surface across the full width of the bearing cap and about ¼ inch off center.

4. Install the cap and torque the bolts to specifications. Do not turn the crankshaft while the Plastigage is in place.

5. Remove the cap. Using the Plastigage scale, check the width of the Plastigage at its widest point to get the minimum clearance. Check the Plastigage at its narrowest point to get the maximum clearance. The difference between readings is the taper of the journals.

    The bearing clearances should be: 0.0002 to 0.0025 inch (desired) or 0.00016 to 0.00028 inch (allowable) for the connecting rod and 0.0004 to 0.002 inch (desired) or 0.007 to 0.0067 inch (allowable) for the main journal.

6. If clearance exceeds the specified limits, try 0.001- or 0.002-inch undersize bearings in combination with the standard bearings. Bearing clearance must be within specified limits. If 0.002-inch undersize main bearings are used on more than one journal, they must all be installed in the cylinder-block side of the bearing. If 0.002-inch undersize bearings do not bring the clearances within the desired limits, the crankshaft journal must be refinished before undersize bearings are installed.

7. After the bearings have been fitted, apply a light coat of engine oil to the journal and bearings. Then install the bearing cap and torque the cap bolts to specification.

8. Repeat the procedure just described for any remaining bearings that require replacement.

Refinishing Cylinder Walls

Honing is recommended for refinishing cylinder walls only when no cross-hatch pattern is visible on the cylinder walls,

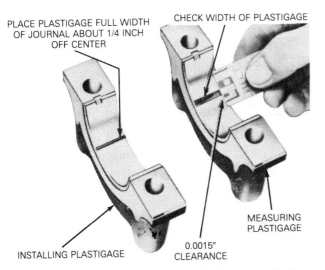

Fig. 11-17. Fitting main or connecting-rod bearing with Plastigage. *Courtesy of Ford Motor Company.*

or for fitting pistons to the specified clearance. The grade of hone to be used is determined by the amount of metal to be removed. Follow the instructions of the hone manufacturer. If coarse stones are used to start the honing operation, leave enough material so that all honing marks can be removed with the finishing hone which is used to obtain the proper piston clearance. After honing, thoroughly clean the cylinder bores with a detergent and water solution.

Cylinder walls that are severely marred and/or worn beyond the specified limits must be refinished. Before any cylinder is refinished, all main bearing caps must be in place and tightened to the proper torque so that the crankshaft bearing bores will not become distorted from the refinishing operation. Hone only the cylinder or cylinders that require finishing. All pistons are the same weight, both standard and oversize; therefore, various sizes of pistons can be used without upsetting engine balance. Refinish the cylinder with the most wear first to determine the maximum oversize. If the cylinder will not clean up when refinished for the maximum oversize piston recommended, the block must be replaced.

Refinish the cylinder to within approximately 0.0015 inch of the required oversize diameter. This will allow enough stock for the final step of honing so that the correct surface pattern and finish are attained. For the proper use of the refinishing equipment, follow the instructions of the manufacturer. Do not attempt this work unless you have had previous experience and know what you are doing. Use a motor-driven, spring pressure-type hone at a speed of 300 to 500 rpm. Hones of grit sizes from 180 to 220 grains will normally provide the desired bore surface finish.

In honing cylinder bores use a lubricant mixture of equal parts of kerosene and SAE No. 20 motor oil. Operate the hone in such a way as to produce a cross-hatch finish on the cylinder bore. The cross-hatch pattern should be at an angle of approximately 30 degrees to the cylinder bore.

After the final operation in either of the two refinishing methods described and prior to checking the piston fit, thoroughly clean the bores with a detergent and water solution and oil the cylinder walls. Mark the pistons to correspond to the cylinders in which they are to be installed. When all required refinishing is completed and all pistons are fitted, carefully clean the entire block and oil the cylinder walls.

Servicing Sand Holes or Porous Engine Castings

Porosity or sand holes that will cause oil seepage or leakage can occur with modern casting processes. Make a complete inspection of the engine and *transaxle* (name used on product for transmission and differential). If the leak is attributed to the porous condition of the cylinder block or sand holes, repairs can be made with metallic plastic. Cracks are not to be serviced with this material. Service must be confined to those cast-iron engine-component surfaces where the inner wall surface is not exposed to engine coolant, coolant pressure, or oil pressure. The shading in Figure 11-18 indicates serviceable areas and includes the following: cylinder-block

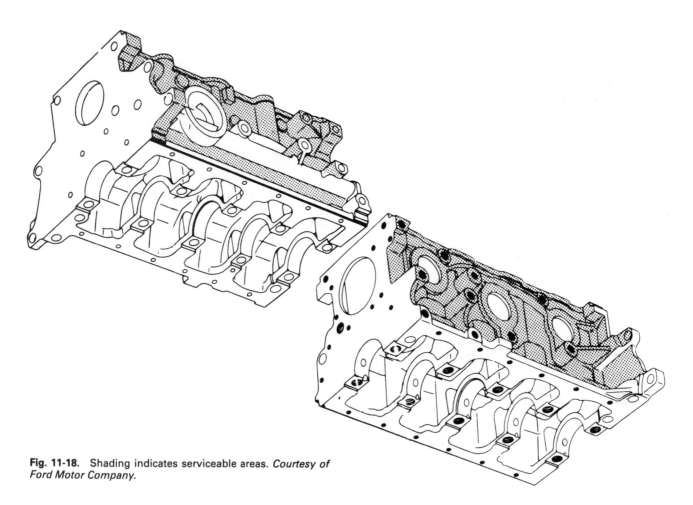

Fig. 11-18. Shading indicates serviceable areas. *Courtesy of Ford Motor Company.*

surfaces extending along the length of the block, upward from the oil-pan rail to the cylinder water jacket but not including machined areas; lower rear face of the cylinder block; intake-manifold casting (not the exhaust crossover section); and the cylinder head along the rocker-arm cover-gasket surface.

The procedure for servicing porous areas or sand holes is as follows:

1. Clean the surface to be serviced by grinding to a clean bright metal surface. Chamfer or undercut the hole or porosity to a greater depth than the rest of the cleaned surface. Solid metal must surround the hole. Openings larger than ¼ inch should not be repaired with metallic plastic. Instead, they should be drilled, tapped, and plugged using common tools. Metallic plastic will not stick to a dirty or oily surface.

2. Mix the metallic-plastic base and hardener as directed on the container. Stir thoroughly until uniform.

3. Apply the mixture with a clean putty knife or wooden spoon, forcing the epoxy into the hole or porosity.

4. Let the mixture harden. This can be done by two methods. Heat cure with a 250-watt lamp placed 10 inches

from the surface, or air dry for 10 to 12 hours at temperatures above 50°F.

5. Sand or grind the serviced area to blend with the general contour of the surrounding surface and paint the surface to match the rest of the block.

CLEANING AND INSPECTION

The instructions given here apply to a complete engine overhaul. For a partial overhaul or parts replacement, simply follow the pertinent procedures.

Intake Manifold

Cleaning. Remove all gasket material from the machined surfaces of the manifold. Clean the manifold in a suitable solvent and dry it with compressed air.

Inspection. Inspect the manifold for cracks, damaged gasket surfaces, or other defects that would make it unfit for further service. Replace all studs that are stripped or otherwise damaged. Clean the EGR exhaust passages. Remove all filings and foreign matter that may have entered the manifold as a result of repairs.

Exhaust Manifold

Cleaning.   Remove all gasket material from the manifolds.

Inspection.   Examine the cylinder head joining flanges of the exhaust manifold(s) for evidence of exhaust gas leaks. Look for cracks, damaged gasket surfaces, or other damage. Replace warped or cracked manifolds.

Cylinder Heads

Cleaning.   With the valves installed to protect the valve seats, remove deposits from the combustion chambers and valve heads with a scraper and a wire brush. Be careful not to damage the cylinder head-gasket surface. After the valves are removed, clean the valve-guide bores. Use cleaning solvent to remove dirt, grease, and other deposits. Clean all bolt holes. Remove all deposits from the valves with a fine wire brush or buffing wheel.

Cylinder Head Flatness

When a cylinder head is removed because of gasket leaks, use a straightedge and feeler gauge to check the flatness of the cylinder-head gasket surface for conformance to specifications. The gasket surface flatnesses should be 0.0016-inch/ 1-inch; 0.0030-inch/6-inches; 0.0059-inch total. If the cylinder-head gasket surface must be refinished, do not remove more than 0.010 inch.

Valve-Seat Runout

Check the valve-seat runout with an accurate gauge. It should not exceed 0.003 inch. Follow the instructions of the gauge manufacturer. If the runout exceeds the wear limit, the valve and valve seat must be refaced.

Valve-Seat Width

Using a seat-width scale, measure the valve-seat width. It should be from 0.069 inch to 0.091 inch. If the width is not within specifications, reface the valve seat.

Check the cylinder head for cracks and inspect the gasket surface for burrs and nicks. Replace the head if it is cracked.

The following inspection procedures are for a cylinder head that is to be completely overhauled. For individual repair operations, use only the pertinent procedures.

Valve Stem-to-Guide Clearance

Check the valve stem-to-guide clearance of each valve in its respective valve guide with the tool shown in Figure 11-19. Use a flat end indicator point. The clearances should be

VALVE STEM
CLEARANCE
CHECKING TOOL
TOOL-6505-F

Fig. 11-19. Measuring valve stem to guide clearance. *Courtesy of Ford Motor Company.*

0.008 inch to 0.0027 inch for the intake valve and 0.0018 inch to 0.0037 inch for the exhaust valve.

Install the tool on the valve stem until it is fully seated, and tighten the knurled set screw firmly. Permit the valve to drop away from its seat until the tool contacts the upper surface of the valve guide.

Position the dial indicator with its flat tip against the center portion of the tool's spherical section at approximately 90° to the valve-stem axis. Move the tool back and forth in line with the indicator stem.

Take a reading on the dial indicator without removing the tool from the valve-guide upper surface. Divide the reading by two, the division factor for the tool. The resulting measurement is the valve-stem clearance.

Valve-Spring Tension

Inspect the valve spring, valve-spring retainer, locks, and sleeves for wear or damage. Discard any damaged parts.

Using the tool shown in Figure 11-20, check the springs for proper pressure at the specified spring lengths (180 pounds at 1.09 inches). Weak valve springs cause poor engine performance. Replace any spring not within specifications. Manually rotating the valve-spring assemblies while they are installed in the engine will not indicate the condition of the springs.

Valve-Spring Squareness

Check each spring for squareness, using a steel square and a flat surface as shown in Figure 11-21. Stand the spring and square on end on the flat surface. Slide the spring up to the square. Remove the spring slowly and observe the space

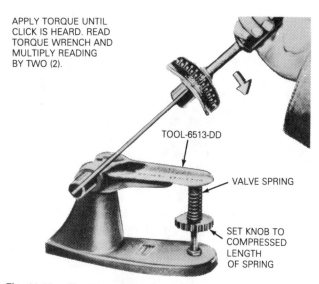

APPLY TORQUE UNTIL
CLICK IS HEARD. READ
TORQUE WRENCH AND
MULTIPLY READING
BY TWO (2).

TOOL-6513-DD

VALVE SPRING

SET KNOB TO
COMPRESSED
LENGTH
OF SPRING

Fig. 11-20. Checking valve spring tension. *Courtesy of Ford Motor Company.*

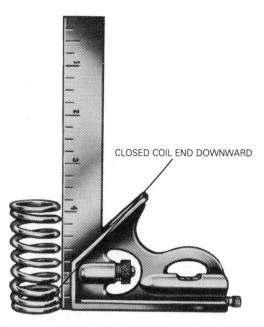

CLOSED COIL END DOWNWARD

Fig. 11-21. Checking valve spring out-of-square. *Courtesy Ford Motor Company.*

between the top coil of the spring and the square. Valve spring out-of-square should not be more than 0.060 inch.

Follow the same procedure to check new valve springs before installing them in the engine.

Hydraulic Tappets

The tappet (lash-adjuster) assemblies should be kept in proper sequence so that they can be installed in their original position. Inspect and test each tappet separately and do

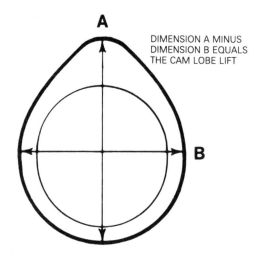

A

DIMENSION A MINUS
DIMENSION B EQUALS
THE CAM LOBE LIFT

B

Fig. 11-22. Determining camshaft lobe lift. *Courtesy of Ford Motor Company.*

not mix the internal parts. If any part of the assembly needs replacing, replace the entire assembly.

Camshaft

After cleaning the camshaft in solvent and wiping it dry, inspect the lobes for scoring and signs of abnormal wear. Lobe pitting in the general area of the lobe toe is not detrimental to the operation of the camshaft; therefore, the camshaft should not be replaced unless the lobe lift is less than 0.229 inch.

The lift of the lobes can be checked with the camshaft in the engine or on centers. To measure the lift, use a vernier caliper to measure the distance between the major (A) and minor (B) diameters, as shown in Figure 11-22. Record the readings. The difference in the readings on each cam diameter is the lobe lift.

If the readings do not meet specifications, replace the camshaft and all rocker arms.

Oil Pump

Cleaning. Wash all parts in a solvent and dry them thoroughly with compressed air. Use a brush to clean the inside of the pump housing and the pressure-relief valve chamber. See Figure 11-23. Be sure all dirt and metal particles are removed.

Inspection. The outer race-to-housing clearance (diametral) should not be more than 0.0027 inch to 0.0055 inch.

Check the inside of the pump housing and the outer race and rotor for damage or excessive wear.

Check the mating surface of the pump cover for wear. Minor scuff marks are normal, but if the cover mating surface is worn, scored, or grooved, replace the pump. Inspect the rotor for nicks, burrs, or score marks. Remove minor imperfections with an oilstone.

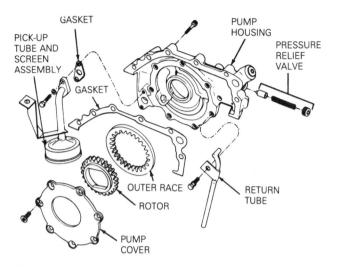

Fig. 11-23. Exploded view of oil pump. *Courtesy of Ford Motor Company.*

Fig. 11-24. Using a ring groove cleaner. *Courtesy of Ford Motor Company.*

Measure the outer race-to-housing clearance. With the rotor assembly installed in the housing, place a straightedge over the rotor assembly and the housing. Measure the clearance (rotor-end play) between the straightedge and the rotor and outer race. Inspect the relief valve spring to see if it is collapsed or worn. Check the relief valve spring tension. Check the relief valve piston for free operation in the bore.

Internal components are not repaired or replaced. If any component does not meet specifications, replace the complete pump.

Connecting Rods

Cleaning. Remove the bearings from the rod and cap. Identify the bearings if they are to be reused. Clean the connecting rod, rod bore, and back of the inserts in solvent. Do not use a caustic cleaning solution. Blow out all passages with compressed air.

Inspection. Inspect the connecting rods and related parts for conformance to specifications. Various forms of engine wear caused by these parts can be readily identified.

A shiny surface on either pin-boss side of the piston usually indicates that a connecting rod is bent.

Abnormal connecting rod bearing wear can be caused by either a bent connecting rod, a worn or damaged crankpin, or a taped connecting-rod bore.

Twisted connecting rods will not create an identifiable wear pattern, but badly twisted rods will disturb the action of the entire piston, rings, and connecting-rod assembly and may be the cause of excessive oil consumption.

Inspect the connecting rods for signs of fractures and the bearing bores for out-of-round and taper. If the bore exceeds the recommended limits and/or if the connecting rod is fractured, it should be replaced. Check the ID of the connecting rod and piston pin bore. If the pin bore in the connecting rod is larger than specifications, install a 0.001-inch oversize piston pin. First, pre-fit the oversize pin to the bore by reaming or honing the piston to provide 0.0002-inch to 0.0004-inch clearance (light slip fit). Then assemble the piston, piston pin, and connecting rod. It is not necessary to ream or hone the pin bore in the connecting rod. Replace damaged connecting rod nuts and bolts. Check the connecting rods for bend or twist on a suitable alignment fixture. Follow the instructions of the fixture manufacturer. If the bend and/or twist exceed specifications, replace the connecting rod.

Pistons, Pins, and Rings

Cleaning. Remove deposits from the piston surfaces. Clean gum or varnish from the piston skirt, piston pins, and rings with solvent. Do not use a caustic cleaning solution.

Clean the ring grooves with a ring-groove cleaner, as shown in Figure 11-24.

Inspection. Carefully inspect the pistons for fractures at the ring lands, skirts, and pin bosses, and for scuffed, rough, or scored skirts. If the lower inner portion of the ring grooves has a high step, replace the piston. The step will interfere with ring operation and cause excessive ring-side clearance.

Sprongy, eroded areas near the edge of the top of the piston are usually caused by detonation or preignition. A shiny area on the thrust surface of the piston, offset from the centerline between the piston pin holes, can be caused by a bent connecting rod. Replace pistons that show signs of excessive wear, wavy ring lands or fractures or damage from detonation or preignition.

Check the piston-to-cylinder-bore clearance by measuring the piston and bore diameters. Measure the OD of the piston with micrometers at the centerline of the piston pin bore and at 90 degrees to the pin bore axis. Check the ring side clearance.

Replace piston pins showing signs of fracture, etching or wear. Check the piston pin fit in the piston and rod.

Check the OD of the piston pin and the ID of the pin bore in the piston. Replace any pin or piston that is not within specifications.

Replace all rings that are scored, broken, chipped or cracked. Check the end gap and side clearance. Rings should never be transferred from one piston to another regardless of mileage.

Main and Connecting-Rod Bearings

Cleaning.   Clean the bearing inserts and caps thoroughly in solvent, and then dry them with compressed air. Do not scrape gum or varnish deposits from bearing shells.

Inspection.   Inspect each bearing carefully. Bearings that have a scored, chipped or worn surface should be replaced. The copper lead bearing base may be visible through the bearing overlay. This does not mean that the bearing is worn. It is not necessary to replace the bearing if its clearance is within recommended limits. Check the clearance of bearings that appear to be satisfactory with Plastigage as detailed earlier.

Crankshaft

Cleaning.   Handle the crankshaft with care to avoid possible fracture or damage to the finished surfaces. Clean the crankcase with solvent, then blow out all oil passages with compressed air.

Inspection.   Inspect the main and connecting-rod journals for cracks, scratches, grooves, or scores. Inspect the crankshaft oil seal surface for nicks, sharp edges, or burrs that might damage the oil seal during installation or cause premature seal wear.

A vs B = VERTICAL TAPER
C vs D = HORIZONTAL TAPER
A vs C and B vs D = OUT OF ROUND

CHECK FOR OUT-OF-ROUND AT EACH END OF JOURNAL

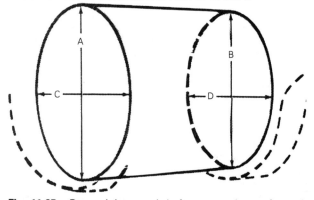

Fig. 11-25. Determining crankshaft taper and out-of-round. *Courtesy of Ford Motor Company.*

Measuring the diameter of each journal in at least four places, determine an out-of-round, taper, or undersize condition. See Figure 11-25. The crankshaft taper should not exceed 0.0003 inch per inch. The crankshaft out-of-round should be no greater than 0.002 inch.

Flywheel

Manual transmission.   Inspect the flywheel for cracks, heat check, or other damage that could make it unfit for further service. If the friction surface of the flywheel is scored or worn, it must be machined. In no case should more than 0.045-inch material be removed. If it is, the flywheel must be replaced.

Inspect the ring gear for worn, chipped, or cracked teeth. If the teeth are damaged, replace the ring gear.

With the flywheel installed on the crankshaft, check the flywheel face runout following the procedure described earlier.

Automatic transmission.   Inspect the flywheel for cracks or other defects that would make it unfit for further service. Inspect the flywheel ring gear. If any teeth are damaged, replace the ring gear and flywheel assembly.

With the flywheel installed on the crankshaft, check the gear face runout.

Cylinder Block

Cleaning.   After any cylinder-bore repair operation, such as honing or deglazing, clean the bore(s) with soap or detergent and water. Then rinse the bore(s) with clean water to remove all traces of the soap or detergent, and wipe the bore(s) dry with a clean, lint-free cloth. Finally, wipe the bore(s) with a clean cloth dipped in engine oil. If these procedures are not followed, rusting of the bore(s) may occur.

If the engine is disassembled, clean the block with solvent. Remove old gasket material from all machined surfaces. Remove all pipe plugs that soil oil passages and clean out the passages. Blow out all passages, bolt holes, etc. with compressed air. Make sure the threads in the cylinder heat-bolt holes are clean. Dirt in the threads may cause binding and result in a false torque reading. Use a tap to true up threads and to remove all deposits. Thoroughly clean the grooves in the crankshaft bearing and bearing retainers.

Inspection.   After the block has been thoroughly cleaned, check it for cracks. Tiny cracks not visible to the naked eye may be detected by coating the suspected area with a mixture of 25 percent kerosene and 75 percent light engine oil. Wipe the part dry and immediately apply a coating of zinc oxide dissolved in wood alcohol. If cracks are present, the coating will become discolored at the defective area. Replace any cracked block.

Check all machined gasket surfaces for burrs, nicks,

scratches, and scores. Remove minor imperfections with an oilstone.

Replace all expansion type plugs that show evidence of leakage.

Inspect the cylinder walls for scoring, roughness, or other signs of wear. Check the cylinder bore for out-of-round and taper. Measure the bore with an accurate bore gauge following the instructions of the manufacturer. Measure the diameter of each cylinder bore at the top, middle, and bottom with the gauge placed at right angles and parallel to the centerline of the engine. See Figure 11-26. Cylinder bore out-of-round should not exceed 0.001 inch and the cylinder-bore taper should be no more than 0.001 inch per inch. Use only the measurements obtained at 90° to the engine centerline when calculating the piston or cylinder-bore clearance.

When cylinders are deeply scored or when out-of-round and/or taper exceed specifications, the cylinders must be refinished. But if the wall imperfections are minor, and the out-of-round and taper are within limits, it may be possible to remove the imperfections by honing the cylinder walls and installing new piston rings providing the piston clearance is within specified limits.

ADJUSTMENTS

Tappet-Valve Clearance

The 1.3 and 1.6 CVH engines are OHC engines with hydraulic-lash adjusters.

Valve-stem to rocker-arm clearance should be within specifications with the tappet completely collapsed. Repeated valve reconditioning operations (valve and/or valve-seat refacing) will decrease the clearance to the point where, if not compensated for, the tappet will cease to function and the valve will be held open.

To determine the rocker-arm to tappet clearance, make the following check:

1. Connect an auxiliary switch in the starting circuit. Crank the engine with the ignition switch OFF until the No. 1 piston is on TDC after the compression stroke. See Figure 11-27.

2. With the crankshaft in the position designated in Steps 3 and 4, position the hydraulic-lifter compressor tool on the rocker arm, as shown in Figure 11-29. Slowly apply pressure to bleed down the tappet until the plunger is completely bottomed. Hold the tappet in this position and check the available clearance between the rocker arm and the valve-stem tip with a feeler gauge. The feeler-gauge width must not exceed ⅜-inch in order to fit between the rails on the rocker arm. If the clearance is less than specifications, check the fulcrum, tappet and cam lobe for wear.

3. With the No. 1 piston on TDC at the end of the compression stroke, check No. 1 intake and No. 1 exhaust valves and No. 2 intake and No. 3 exhaust valves.

4. Rotate the crankshaft to Position No. 2 (Fig. 11-28) and check the following valves: No 2 intake, No. 3 exhaust, No. 4 intake, and No. 4 exhaust.

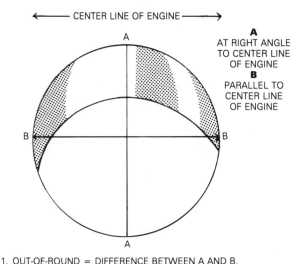

1. OUT-OF-ROUND = DIFFERENCE BETWEEN A AND B.
2. TAPER = DIFFERENCE BETWEEN THE A MEASUREMENT AT TOP OF CYLINDER BORE AND THE A MEASUREMENT AT BOTTOM OF CYLINDER BORE.

Fig. 11-26. Determining cylinder bore out-of-round and cylinder bore taper. *Courtesy of Ford Motor Company.*

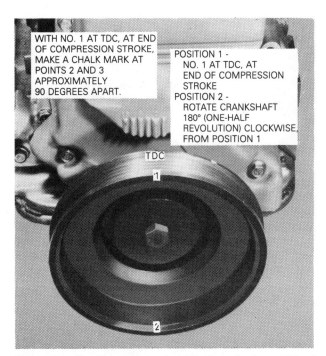

Fig. 11-27. Checking tappet valve clearance. *Courtesy of Ford Motor Company.*

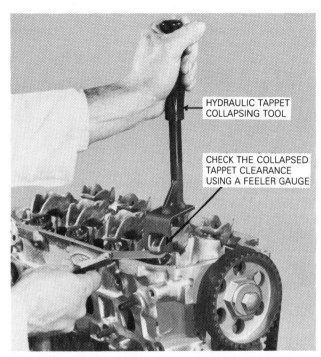

Fig. 11-28. Using the hydraulic lifter compression tool. *Courtesy of Ford Motor Company.*

HYDRAULIC TAPPET COLLAPSING TOOL

CHECK THE COLLAPSED TAPPET CLEARANCE USING A FEELER GAUGE

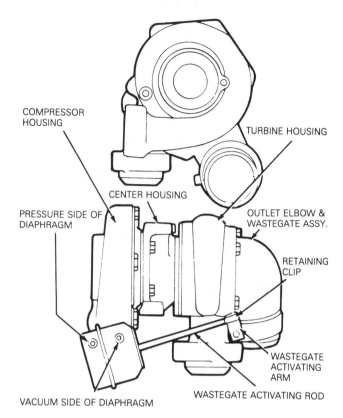

COMPRESSOR HOUSING

TURBINE HOUSING

CENTER HOUSING

PRESSURE SIDE OF DIAPHRAGM

OUTLET ELBOW & WASTEGATE ASSY.

RETAINING CLIP

WASTEGATE ACTIVATING ARM

WASTEGATE ACTIVATING ROD

VACUUM SIDE OF DIAPHRAGM

Fig. 11-29. Front and side views of a typical turbocharger. *Courtesy of Ford Motor Company.*

TURBOCHARGED ENGINES

General Features

In a conventionally aspirated engine, the energy contained in the exhaust gases is wasted. But in turbocharged engines this energy is used to pressurize the intake charge. Consequently, a greater than normal charge is drawn into a cylinder, with a resultant improvement in volumetric efficiency and a significant boost in engine power—typically, 30 percent or more.

Because turbocharging is not mechanically coupled to the engine and does not operate at low engine-speed and/or low engine-load conditions, engine losses associated with the use of a turbocharger are minimal.

Moreover, a turbocharger does not seriously increase the engine size, weight, or operating load. Thus fuel economy is much the same as on a conventionally aspirated engine of the same CID. Turbocharging does, however, increase cylinder pressure, necessitating the use of fuel having a higher octane rating in order to prevent detonation (spark knock).

A Typical Turbocharger

See Figure 11-29. A typical turbocharger contains two vaned wheels called the *compressor wheel* and the *turbine wheel*, connected by a common shaft. The inlet housing surrounds the compressor wheel and is joined to the air inlet and the intake manifold. An outlet housing encloses the turbine wheel and, in the Ford and GMC systems, a so-called *wastegate* assembly. This housing is connected to the exhaust system. A center housing surrounds and supports the shaft that joins the compressor and turbine wheels and connects the inlet and outlet housings.

The wastegate is a bypass valve that opens when the pressure reaches a predetermined value (about 5 psi in the Ford and GMC systems) and shunts some of the exhaust gases around the turbine wheel. Without the wastegate, compressor pressure, called *boost*, would increase beyond the design limits of the engine and cause serious damage to engine components.

Operation

Exhaust gas pressure and heat energy cause the turbine wheel to rotate. This rotation is transferred to the compressor wheel via the common axle. When the air-fuel mixture from the carburetor strikes the spinning compressor wheel, the mixture is packed into a dense mass and conveyed to the combustion chamber where it delivers greater horsepower during the compression cycle. The exhaust gases pass through the turbine and the operation cycle just described is repeated.

Controlling Spark Knock

Ford controls spark knock by limiting boost to 6 psi through wastegate operation and by including two spark-retardation points in the electronic ignition system. When boost pressure reaches about 1 psi, a switch in the intake manifold closes and transmits a signal to the ignition module that causes the ignition timing to be retarded by 6°. When the boost pressure reaches approximately 4 psi, a second switch in the manifold closes. The resulting signal from the ignition module causes an additional 6° of spark retard.

On GMC products the wastegate limits boost to 6 psi, but spark retardation is accomplished by installing a detonation sensor in the block of V-6 engines and the intake manifold of V-8's. When the sensor picks up the vibrations caused by detonation, it sends a signal to the Electronic Spark Control (ESC) module. After processing this signal, the ESC module sends a signal to the High Energy Ignition (HEI) distributor where the spark retard may reach as much as 22° on V-6's and 15° on V-8's.

Lubrication

Because the turbocharger shaft rotates at high speeds (20,000 to 40,000 or more rpm), adequate lubrication of the shaft bearing by clean engine oil is critical. If the oil supply is interrupted, inadequate, or contaminated, both the turbocharger and engine will be damaged.

When starting the engine, always allow time for oil pressure to build up before accelerating heavily. In addition, when the engine is stopped after high-speed operation, allow enough time for the turbine wheel to stop spinning before shutting off the engine (and oil supply). A quick shutdown after high-speed operation also lets the air-fuel mixture become very lean and this causes detonation and high engine temperatures with resultant damage.

After an oil and filter change, or after any operation that causes oil drainage or loss, do not start the engine immediately. Instead, momentarily disconnect the distributor (by removing the ignition lead) and crank the engine for several short intervals (15 to 20 seconds) in order to let the oil pressure build up.

Troubleshooting

No boost. Exhaust leakage or blockage; throttle opening incompletely; dirty air filter or blocked air intake; worn rings or valves; defective seals.

Detonation. Low octane fuel; faulty detonation sensor; improper operation of ignition retard system; no circulation of coolant; defective thermostat; low coolant level.

Ignition miss. Low ignition-coil output; excessive resistance in the ignition wires; excessive spark-plug gap.

Oil leaks into turbine. Blocked oil-return hose.

12

COOLING SYSTEMS

Contents

INTRODUCTION

Cooling Methods

For an automobile engine to run at maximum efficiency and provide the most power from a given amount of fuel, the explosive charges must be of the correct composition and the explosions must be properly timed. Also, the temperature of the cylinders and the adjoining parts must be within a specified range. Above all, the cooling system must not remove (dissipate) any more heat than is absolutely necessary.

Two methods are used to cool automobile engines: forced-circulation water cooling and air cooling. As the name implies, the forced-circulation water-cooling system used in the vast majority of automobiles, either domestic or foreign makes, uses water as the cooling medium. Circulation is maintained by a pump that forces the water through the system.

The most efficient temperature of the coolant used in the forced-circulation water-cooling system depends on the design of the particular engine. Generally, for automobiles built before 1968, the best range is between 175°F and 180°F. Temperatures exceeding 190°F may cause these engines to ping. Engines designed to reduce exhaust emissions, however, are operated at much higher temperatures. In some cases, 205°F is the design goal. Special carburetor and ignition systems are combined with carefully designed combustion chambers and valves to accommodate such high-temperature operation. Under some conditions, the coolant may reach 250°F and still be within operating limits. Obviously, water alone cannot be used as the coolant because it boils at 212°F. Therefore, an antifreeze solution, with a higher boiling point than water, must be added. A pressure radiator cap (explained later) is a vital part of the cooling system.

On the other hand, temperatures below 150°F must be avoided. Low-temperature operation causes valve burning, contamination of the oil in the crankcase, and increases exhaust emissions.

In an air-cooling system, of course, air is the cooling medium. This system is not nearly as common as the forced-circulation water-cooled system, but has been used in several cars. Here, circulation is maintained by a blower in conjunction with shrouds, shields, panels, and other devices. A thermostat controls the air flow.

Because the Chevrolet Corvair was the only American-made car to use air cooling, and this engine has now been discontinued, our only concern here will be with the water-cooled systems.

Typical Forced-Circulation Water-Cooled System

A diagram of a typical forced-circulation water-cooled system is shown in Fig. 12-1. The illustration shows the arrangement of the parts used in an engine with cylinders cast in the block.

The cooling water passes from the cylinder-head jacket,

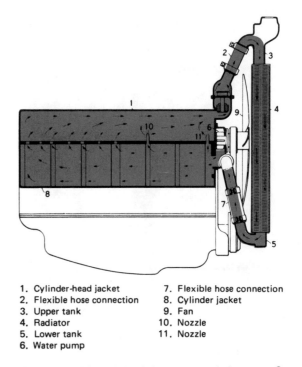

1. Cylinder-head jacket
2. Flexible hose connection
3. Upper tank
4. Radiator
5. Lower tank
6. Water pump
7. Flexible hose connection
8. Cylinder jacket
9. Fan
10. Nozzle
11. Nozzle

Fig. 12-1 Typical forced-circulation water-cooled system. *Courtesy of Chrysler Motors Corporation.*

which surrounds the combustion chambers of the cylinders, through the first flexible hose connection to the upper tank of the radiator. The water then passes downward through the radiator tubes or between cells, depending on the type of radiator, to the lower tank of the radiator. This tank is connected to the casing of the circulating water pump by another flexible hose connection. The pump is driven by the engine and delivers the cooling water to the cylinder jacket.

The radiator is filled with water through an opening in the upper tank, which is closed by a pressure cap. The fan, as it is driven at a high speed by the engine, draws air around the radiator tubes or cells, and thus removes excess heat from the water.

The overhead valve Chevrolet engine uses nozzles to spray water on the exhaust-valve port castings in the cylinder-head jacket to keep the temperature of the exhaust ports and valves from becoming too high. These nozzles, two of which are shown diagrammatically in Fig. 12-1 and in perspective in Fig. 12-2, are pressed into the lower part of the cylinder head. There are two types of nozzles used. One type, which has a single opening as shown in Fig. 12-2, is used to spray water on the single exhaust valve at each end of the cylinder block. The other type has two openings and is used to spray water on the middle pairs of exhaust valves.

In Chrysler Corporation automobiles, water is sprayed on the exhaust-valve ports through small openings in a distribution tube that carries the water directly from the water pump.

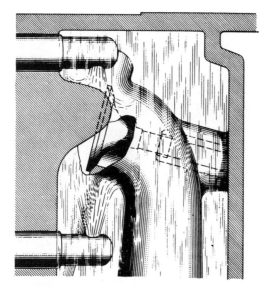

Fig. 12–2 Spray nozzles. *Courtesy of Chrysler Motors Corporation.*

Radiator Pressure Caps

Most American-made automobiles use a pressure cap on the radiator to improve the efficiency of the cooling system and to prevent evaporation and surge losses. Water boils at 212°F at sea level; at higher elevations, the boiling point is less than 212°F. The purpose of the pressure cap is to increase the pressure within the cooling system, and thereby increase the boiling temperature of the water. The water entering the radiator is thus at a much higher temperature than the air surrounding the radiator. This difference in temperature causes the heat to be more quickly transferred to the air thus improving the overall efficiency of the cooling system. For each pound of pressure increase on the coolant, the boiling point is raised three degrees. Thus, a radiator pressure cap rated at 10 lbs. raises the boiling point of water from 212°F to 242°F, a total increase of 30°F.

Details of an automobile radiator pressure cap are shown in Fig. 12-3. The pressure cap fits over the radiator filler tube and seals the tube tightly. The cap consists of two valves: *a blowoff valve* and *a vacuum valve*. The blowoff valve is held against the *valve seat* by the pressure exerted by a *calibrated spring*. The valve remains on its seat until the pressure in the cooling system exceeds the pressure that the spring in the cap is designed to exert. The cooling-system pressure then forces the blowoff valve upward, allowing steam to escape through the *overflow tube*.

The vacuum valve prevents a vacuum from forming in the cooling system after the engine is shut off and the system begins to cool and condense. If a vacuum forms, the atmospheric pressure causes the vacuum valve to open and allow air to enter the cooling system and equalize the pressure.

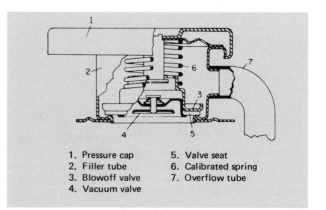

1. Pressure cap	5. Valve seat
2. Filler tube	6. Calibrated spring
3. Blowoff valve	7. Overflow tube
4. Vacuum valve	

Fig. 12–3 Radiator pressure cap. *Courtesy of Chrysler Motors Corporation.*

The amount of pressure needed to raise the blowoff valve from its slot is given in psi and usually is stamped or printed on the pressure cap.

Extreme care must be taken when removing a pressure cap with the engine at operating temperature; the escaping steam or hot water may cause serious burns. The cap should be turned slowly to the left until the vent is uncovered, and then allowed to remain in this position until all the pressure or steam has been released through the vent. The cap can then be turned farther to the left and removed. If the engine has been running for some time, the cap will be hot. For that reason, it is good practice to wear gloves or use some type of protective material when touching and turning the cap. When the cap is put back on, it should be turned to the right as far as it will go in order to seal the cooling system.

The high temperature to which the pressure cap is subjected causes the sealing gasket to wear rapidly. Also, since the cap is located above the normal liquid level, it is not protected by the inhibitors in the cooling system. As a result, the valves and the inside of the cap are exposed to the extremely corrosive effects of hot steam and air in the upper radiator tank. Since only a small amount of rust, scale, or dirt can interfere with the operation of the blowoff and vacuum valves, the cap is not likely to maintain the pressure in the tank. Further, frequent removal and replacement of the cap for checking the water level, or for other purposes will result in leakage of coolant and loss of pressure due to wear of the gasket and locking mechanism.

An air leak above the water level in the radiator will offset the advantages of the pressure cap. On the other hand, if the blowoff valve rusts in place and fails to open under the required pressure, the pressure in the system is likely to build up to a point where the radiator will crack or the hose connections will be blown off.

To avoid damage to the cap gasket, as well as its seat on the filler neck, the cap should always be removed and replaced carefully. Metal spouts or nozzles should never be allowed to come into contact with the filler-neck gasket and seat when either water or antifreeze is being poured into the radiator.

The pressure cap, its seat, and gasket should be inspected regularly; the gasket should be replaced if it is not in good condition. Also, the cap should be cleaned at regular intervals and the valves checked for proper operation. The valves and the cap seal should be checked for tightness.

Sealed cooling systems. In the normal pressured cooling system, a considerable amount of coolant is lost from the overflow tube at the top of the radiator as engine heat expands the coolant. As a result, some automobile manufacturers are now using a cooling system, known as a *sealed* system, in which coolant overflow is trapped in an auxiliary reservoir outside the radiator.

When the engine reaches its operating temperature, the expanding coolant forces the blowoff valve in the radiator pressure cap off its seat and allows the coolant to flow from the radiator, through the overflow tube, into a transparent reservoir where it is retained. As the engine cools, the coolant in the radiator and water jacket contracts and the change in coolant volume creates a partial vacuum beneath the vacuum valve in the radiator cap. Atmospheric pressure causes the vacuum valve to open, but instead of air being admitted to the space below the cap, the coolant trapped in the transparent reservoir is drawn back into the top of the radiator and returns to the cooling system.

In the sealed cooling system, the radiator cap need not be removed to add coolant or to check the level of the coolant in the radiator. Instead, the level can be checked by noting the gradation marks on the auxiliary reservoir. Additional coolant, if needed, is added by removing the non-pressurized cap on the reservoir. After a major servicing of the cooling system, refill the system by adding coolant through the radiator in the usual way and replace the pressure cap on the radiator. All subsequent checks of the coolant level then are made at the overflow reservoir.

Testing pressure caps. Pressure caps should be tested at least twice each year, at the beginning of summer and winter, to ensure proper functioning of the cooling system. The tester consists of a *cylinder* to which a pressure cap can be attached; a *pressure gauge,* which indicates the amount of pressure applied; an *air bulb,* which is used to build up the desired pressure in the gauge; and a *hose,* which transmits the air from the bulb to the gauge.

Vacuum adapters (not shown in the illustration) are available to allow the tester to be used on all sizes of pressure caps and all sizes of radiator filler tubes.

Two tests can be made on a pressure cap. The first is a check of the point at which pressure is released. To do this, first attach the pressure cap to the tester, using the proper adapter. Apply maximum air pressure by squeezing the bulb

of the tester until the needle on the pressure gauge will not go any higher. The gauge should indicate a reading of plus or minus one pound of the cap rating. As mentioned earlier, the rating of a cap usually is stamped or printed on it. For example, if a cap is rated for 15 psi, the gauge reading can range from 14 to 16 psi. A reading outside this range shows that the cap is defective and should be replaced.

The second test is a check of the pressure-holding capability of the cap. The cap is tested as just explained, and the gauge needle should be watched to see if it holds the range limit for a reasonable period of time. If the cap is in good condition, the needle should remain steady for at least several minutes. If the needle drops rapidly, the cap is defective and should be replaced.

Wipe all surfaces of the cap and its seals before performing the tests. Dirt on these surfaces and seals may cause the valve to leak and make the test results invalid.

Testing Cooling Systems for Leaks

The pressure tester can also be used to check the cooling system for leaks. To perform this check, the cooling system must be filled to within ½ inch of the neck of the radiator filler tube. The sealing surface of the neck should then be wiped clean, the tester attached, and the pressure built up to 15 psi. If the needle of the pressure gauge holds steady, the cooling system is not leaking. If the needle drops, a leak is indicated.

To find the leak, follow this procedure: Check the hose connections, engine expansion plugs, water pump, and radiator for any visible external leaks. If no leaks are visible, remove the tester and start the engine, running it until the normal operating temperature is reached. Then put the tester back on, build up the pressure to 15 psi, and increase the engine speed to half throttle. If the gauge needle fluctuates, the trouble is likely to be a combustion leak probably caused by a damaged cylinder-head gasket.

If the gauge needle holds steady, accelerate the engine quickly a few times and check the exhaust tail pipe to see if water is coming out. If it is, the trouble could be a cracked block or head or a damaged head gasket.

OVERHEATED ENGINE

Tests

Two common complaints that indicate trouble in the cooling system are slow warm-up and overheating. Slow warm-up may be caused by a thermostat that fails and remains open. When this occurs, water circulates between the radiator and engine block even when the engine is cold. Thus, the engine must run for a considerably longer period of time before it reaches its efficient operating temperature. This condition is more properly known as overcooling and is covered thoroughly in a later section of this chapter.

When overheating takes place, the cooling system should be gone over thoroughly, but it is advisable also to check the following points, one or more of which could conceivably cause overheating:

1. The fan belt may be slipping.

2. The carburetor may be supplying too lean a mixture.

3. Preignition may be taking place.

4. Circulation of the water may be hampered by an improperly installed cylinder-head gasket.

5. There may not be enough water in the system.

6. The exhaust system may be clogged.

7. The head gasket may be leaking, forcing water from the overflow.

8. Any one of the many water passages may be clogged by rust or scale.

9. The water distribution tube, if one is used, may be rusty and blocked.

10. One or more of the cylinders may be overheating because of heavy rust deposits.

11. The thermostat may be defective and fail to open.

12. Any of the flexible connecting hoses may have collapsed because of inner liner failure. Pieces of the liners may have broken away, blocking water passages.

13. The radiator tank baffle may be bent, restricting the flow of water.

14. The radiator may be clogged with rust or scale.

15. The radiator cooling fins may be clogged with leaves or other debris, causing poor air circulation.

16. The water pump may be defective. The impeller may be loose or broken.

17. The water may contain alcohol. This can cause overheating in mild weather.

18. The automatic transmission may be slipping badly, particularly if it is of the water-cooled type. A slipping transmission will result in excessive engine speeds. The trouble may also be in the transmission cooler, which is located in the lower part of the radiator. Because of the high temperature at which a transmission normally operates, the oil level, transmission pump, and converter sprag bearings or turbine should be checked. Also, the band or clutches may be slipping.

19. In cars equipped with air conditioning, the condenser may be installed improperly, blocking air circulation.

20. When air conditioning was installed, a heavy-duty radiator or fan may not have been installed.

All of the foregoing points should be checked before further work is done on the engine. When an automobile engine overheats, look first for the most frequently occurring troubles that are most easily corrected. Make sure the cooling system is full of water, the fan operates properly, the mixture is right, and the spark is set correctly. Remove the radiator cap when the engine is running and observe whether the water seems to be circulating.

Testing a Forced-Circulation System

If general investigation shows that water is not circulating properly, the cooling system should be checked completely.

The degree of overheating should first be determined. If the cooling water begins to boil after a ten-minute drive, serious trouble is indicated. However, if only a drive at high speed, the steady pulling of a full load, or a long drive on a hot day produces the boiling, the trouble usually is local and easy to repair.

If soon after the engine is started the water begins to boil, proceed as follows: Grasp the upper radiator hose tightly with your hand while the engine speed is being accelerated. If the water pump is circulating the water properly, the hose will bulge noticeably as engine speed is increased. If no outward pressure is felt, either the pump is defective or the passages are badly clogged. For engines in which the hose cannot easily be squeezed, a test may be made by first draining the water from the system, removing the upper hose connection and substituting a longer hose. Then connect the longer hose to the cylinder-jacket outlet only. Insert a plug in the end of the upper hose fitting, or nipple, of the radiator, and place a large funnel in the filler opening. Refill the cooling system with water. The hose substituted should be about one foot longer than that disconnected at the header, and its upper end should be held over the funnel. With the engine running at a speed corresponding to 20 mph, a steady stream should flow from the hose and, as the engine speed is momentarily accelerated, a full, solid stream should flow into the funnel.

If a good stream of water flows into the funnel, the pump is in working order and the trouble lies in the radiator itself or in the fittings of the engine. While this test is progressing, it is advisable to cover the upper end of the hose with your hand to see if the pump creates a pressure against your hand. The object of this test is to detect a possible slipping of the pump impeller.

If no pressure is felt against the hand, or if the circulation seems to be below normal, the trouble may be in the thermostat or the pump. To check the operation of the thermostat, remove the screws holding the cylinder-jacket outlet in place and remove the outlet. The thermostat can then be lifted out. With the thermostat removed, replace the water outlet and repeat the test. If the water now flows freely, the thermostat is defective and should be replaced. If there is no improvement with the thermostat out of the engine, the trouble may be in the pump, which should be removed and examined carefully. If the impeller is loose on the shaft, or the pump otherwise is defective, make necessary repairs and replacements and reassemble the pump to the engine. If the water still fails to circulate freely, the passages through the engine block or the radiator itself are blocked up.

By testing the cooling system in the manner described, you should be able to determine the exact cause of noncirculation of water in the system. With a pump system, once circulation has been verified, the next step is to check whether the engine itself overheats. A preliminary check may show the circulation to be normal, yet the engine may still overheat. In this case, the cause of overheating must be found by the process of elimination: by checking every part of the system until the source of trouble is located.

Hose connections. The water hose connections are the most likely sources of trouble. Even the best quality hose deteriorates at its inner lining in time, often without showing any sign of this condition on the outside. The hose is lined with a layer of rubber to make it waterproof; this rubber lining gradually peels off and can obstruct the circulation. When a hose has deteriorated internally, it will feel soft and flabby when squeezed, and will often collapse in service. On inspection, a collapsed hose shows almost complete deterioration of its inner walls. Its collapse severely restricts the flow of water and causes engine overheating.

Suction created by the water pump often contributes to the collapse of a hose. This suction is sufficient to produce a partial vacuum in the hose. If the hose is not in excellent condition, this vacuum will cause the sides of the hose to bend inward and eventually to remain collapsed. It is possible for a bend in the sides to restrict the flow of water, particularly at high engine speeds. Therefore when checking a system for overheating, it is advisable to observe the action of the pump hose while the engine is running at high speed.

To check most reliably the inner condition of the hose, disconnect and inspect it.

When a new hose is installed, it must be long enough to cover at least one inch of the pipes or nipples at each end. Before the hose is placed in position, the nipples should be checked to make sure that they are circular and not badly dented. To correct nipples that are only slightly out of round or dented, insert a round piece of metal into the nipple and tap the nipple lightly on the outside with a hammer. If the nipple is inaccessible, or if it is badly out of round, the unit to which it is attached must be removed, placed on a work bench and the nipple straightened. This correction is required only on sheet-metal type connections. Do not attempt this correction on cast-metal types.

To install the hose, one end is pushed over the first nipple, and both hose clamps are slid on loosely. Then the other end of the hose is pushed onto its nipple and the clamps are positioned and tightened. Some mechanics use a sealing compound on that part of the inside of the hose that fits over the nipples. Shellac produces a leakproof joint but dries the lining, rendering the hose unfit for reuse once it is removed. If the nipples are round and the hose is a good fit, the joints can be made tight without the use of a sealer or shellac, and the hose may, if needed, be removed and reinstalled.

Hose clamps. The purpose of hose clamps is simply, to draw the hose tightly around the pipe or nipple and thus form a firm and leakproof joint. Four types of clamps are found on American-made automobiles: corbin, aeromotive, screw, and squeeze. The squeeze type is comparatively new. It consists of a circular band with a neck that can be squeezed to tighten the clamp around the hose. A special plier is needed to install this clamp. One distinct disadvantage of the squeeze type is that it is not reusable.

The corbin clamp requires a special plier for installation and removal. Occasionally this clamp loses some of its tension and must be replaced. For this reason, the corbin clamp is being replaced by the aeromotive and screw types.

The aeromotive clamp is easy and quick to install with only a screwdriver. A special screw in the unit contacts and rides on threads or slots in the band. The aeromotive clamp is advantageous particularly because it can be used over and over again, and one size accommodates various sized hoses.

The screw clamp, like the aeromotive clamp, is easily and quickly installed or removed with a screwdriver. Made of sturdy double-wire construction, it is standard equipment on many new automobiles. The screw, which rides in a firmly held nut, causes the ends of the clamp to be pulled apart, thus tightening the clamp around the hose. Here again, one size clamp can accommodate various sized hoses. Another version of the screw clamp works in the opposite manner from that shown in the illustration; that is, tightening the screw causes the ends of the clamp to be drawn together, thus tightening the clamp around the hose.

Regardless of its make or style, a clamp is intended to draw tightly all around the hose. If, when the clamp is tightened, the hose seems to pucker at one point, either the clamp does not fit properly or the inside diameter of the hose is too big for the nipple. If the hose is too large for the nipple, a layer of friction tape wrapped around the nipple can make a better fit but should be resorted to only in an emergency. It is far better to replace the hose with one of proper size.

Cylinder-head gasket. Improper water circulation in a cooling system can be caused by either an imperfect or an improperly installed cylinder-head gasket. If a check of the water pump, hoses, and hose connections does not locate the difficulty, the cylinder head and head gasket should be removed and checked. The gasket should be examined carefully to make sure that each water hole or space in the block has a corresponding hole or space in the gasket. If the gasket is cracked or deteriorated, it should, of course, be replaced.

The gasket for some automobiles is marked *FRONT* at one end. This end should be next to the radiator. Such a gasket is used in Ford V-8's. If the gasket is installed in the reverse position, the water will not circulate freely.

While the cylinder head is off, all water passages should be checked and cleaned of all obstructing matter that can be reached. A piece of wire or strap iron properly bent will help in reaching inaccessible openings. In some instances it may be necessary to remove the core plugs from the engine block and clean the block by means of a steam cleaner.

Automatic transmission cooler. Most American automobiles are equipped with automatic transmissions. The torque converter unit of the transmission becomes very hot when the automobile is driven in hilly country or is accelerated rapidly. The heat is caused by the friction of the oil between the valves in the converter.

In some instances, a transmission cooler is used. The cooler usually is located in the lower tank of the radiator and is connected to the transmission by oil lines. Because of the high operating temperatures, a malfunction or improper adjustment will often cause the transmission to overheat the engine coolant or water. For this reason, the transmission cooler should be checked when all other possible causes of overheating have been eliminated. In this case, a blocked oil line is the most likely fault.

With a transmission converter equipped with fins for air cooling, the settings of the fins should be checked. The use of fins, however, is declining and they are being replaced by the more dependable and positive cooler-type system.

Fan assembly. Another possible cause of engine overheating is the fan assembly. Look for a slipping fan belt at the first sign of overheating. If the belt is in good condition and simply slipping, it should be adjusted. If the belt is defective in any way, it should be replaced.

Defective fan belts may be frayed, glazed, or stretched, and should be examined for these defects. A frayed belt is likely to break loose at any time, whereas a belt that is glazed or stretched will lack sufficient traction to drive the fan, water pump, and generator. It has been estimated that seven horsepower is required to drive the average four-blade fan at a car speed of 60 mph, exclusive of water pump, generator, or other load that the fan belt may carry. Obviously a certain amount of slippage will occur unless the belt is in very good condition and properly adjusted.

Mechanical means are provided on all automobiles for adjusting belt tension, but occasionally a belt otherwise in good condition may be found to be stretched to a point where the extreme adjustment will not provide sufficient tension in the belt to prevent slippage. In such cases the only remedy is to install a new belt. The replacement must be of the proper length and width and must fit the grooves in the pulleys. Otherwise it will not make the proper contact with the pulley and soon will slip in service.

The fan belt is driven from the pulley made fast on the crankshaft of the engine, and in turn drives the fan, water pump, and generator. The fan and its pulley are made fast to the shaft of the water pump. Because of the work the belt must do, it is of utmost importance that proper tension be maintained on the belt at all times. If the tension is too low, the belt will slip and not function properly. If, on the other hand, the tension is too high, the generator and water-pump

bearings will wear quickly, making necessary extensive repairs and parts replacement.

Fan belt tension may be checked in two ways, depending upon the make of the automobile. Some manufacturers express the belt tension as its torque in foot-pounds while others measure tension by the amount of belt deflection in inches. Still others will use both torque and belt deflection to measure the tension.

Table 12-1 shows typical belt tensions for late-model automobiles. Unless otherwise noted, the tension is for new belts and is expressed as torque in foot-pounds. The torque can be measured with a belt-tension gauge and the reading compared with that specified by the automobile manufacturer. Belt deflection can be measured by using a straightedge and rule. The straightedge is placed across the top of the belt, from the water pump and fan pulley to the alternator or generator pulley. The belt is then pressed down with the thumb or with a rule and the amount of deflection is measured. This measurement should be compared with the manufacturer's specifications and adjusted if necessary.

Adjusting or removing fan belt. The generator or alternator is supported in a bracket. To adjust the belt tension, the nut is loosened, the generator or alternator is moved inward or outward as needed, and the nut is then tightened. Needless to say, the tension should be rechecked after the adjustment has been made. To remove the belt, the nut on the bracket is loosened, the generator or alternator is moved inward toward the block, and the belt is removed from the generator or alternator pulley, the crankshaft pulley, and finally the fan pulley. A new belt may be installed simply by reversing the procedure.

Fan blades. The fan should also be checked for broken or bent blades. If the blades are bent, the cooling effect of the fan may be reduced to a point where the engine will overheat. The contour of the blades is worked out carefully by the manufacturers to give just the right amount of air circulation, and the fan is balanced at the factory to prevent vibration. Slightest distortion of the fan blades, therefore, reduces the volume of air drawn through the radiator and throws the fan out of balance, causing severe vibration which is sometimes accompanied by a shrill whistling sound. If blades are broken, they must be replaced or a new fan must be installed. If the blades are bent so as to reduce their effectiveness but are otherwise satisfactory, they usually can be restored to their original shape and normal efficiency.

No accurate methods exist for determining the exact cooling efficiency of a fan but, for all practical purposes, a fan may be considered as meeting the requirements if it is in good mechanical condition and if it throws a good stream of air. The suction of a normal fan, while the engine is run at a speed equivalent to 25 mph, should be strong enough

Table 12-1 Typical belt-tension data for representative late-model automobiles.

Make of Car	Belt	Tension (ft-lb. or in.)
American Motors	All	125-145
Buick	Alternator	80
	Power Steering	90
	Air Cond.	100
Cadillac	All	100
Chevrolet	Alternator	120-130
	Power Steering	120-130
	Air Cond.	135-145
	Air-Injection Reactor	70-80
Chrysler	Alternator (no air cond.)	3/32
	Alternator (with air cond.)	3/16
	Power Steering	3/32
	Fan Idler	1/16
Dodge	Alternator (no air cond.)	3/32
	Alternator (air cond.)	3/16
	Power Steering	3/32
	Fan Idler	1/16
Ford	Generator or alternator (1 belt)	110-140
	Generator or alternator (2 belts)	
	Front	110-140
	Rear	105-155
	Power Steering	120-150
	Air Cond.	120-150
Imperial	Alternator (no air cond.)	3/32
	Alternator (air cond.)	3/16
	Power Steering	3/32
	Fan Idler	1/16
Mercury	Gen. or Alt. (1 belt)	110-140
	Gen. or Alt. (2 belts)	
	Front	110-140
	Rear	105-155
	Power Steering	120-150
	Air Cond.	120-150
	Air Cond.	120-150
Oldsmobile	All	Use special tension gauge BT-33-70M. This gauge has special calibration marks for all Olds belts.

Make of Car	Belt	Tension (ft-lb. or in.)
Plymouth	Alternator (no air cond.)	3/32
	Alternator (air cond.)	3/16
	Power Steering	3/32
	Fan Idler	1/16
Pontiac	Generator	100-125
	Power Steering	135-150
	Air Cond.	135-150
	80-ampere Gen.	135-150

to draw a piece of newspaper about the size of the front of the radiator firmly against the face of the radiator core.

Variable-speed fans. Variable-speed fans are now used on late-model automobiles, especially those equipped with air conditioning, to conserve power and reduce fan noise at higher engine speeds. This type of fan has six blades bolted to a central fan drive attached to the belt-driven water-pump pulley.

The drive clutch for a variable-speed fan is simply a fluid coupling that contains silicone oil. Because of the high viscosity of the silicone oil, this type of drive is sometimes called a *viscous drive*. Fan speed is regulated by the torque-carrying capacity of the silicone oil and the amount of oil in the coupling. Higher fan speeds require more oil to be admitted to the fluid coupling from the oil reservoir in the fan hub. Lower fan speeds require less oil in the fluid coupling.

Two types of drive clutches are used. In one type a heat-sensitive, flat, bimetal thermostatic spring is connected to a control piston that allows oil to enter the fluid coupling from the oil reservoir. In the other type, a coiled bimetal thermostatic spring, connected to an opening plate on the reservoir, accomplishes the same result. Both units cause fan speed to increase as the temperature increases and to decrease as the temperature decreases.

Drive-clutch operation. Since both types of fan-drive clutches depend either on a heat-sensitive bimetallic strip or a thermostatic coil spring for their operation, it is the expansion or contraction of the bimetallic element that controls the amount of silicone oil admitted to the fluid coupling. On fans equipped with the flat, bimetal thermostatic spring and piston, the spring expands and bends outward as the temperature increases. This bending allows the control piston to move outward and open the valve that regulates the flow of silicone oil from the oil reservoir to the fluid coupling. As more fluid enters the fluid coupling the fan speed increases to provide faster cooling of the engine.

When the temperature decreases the bimetal spring contracts and closes the control piston, and oil in the fluid coupling goes back to the reservoir through a bleed hole in the piston.

On fans equipped with the thermostatic coil spring that is connected to an opening plate on the oil reservoir, the operation is similar to that described above. A temperature increase, however, unwinds the thermostatic coil spring and causes it to open the plate on the oil reservoir and allow oil to enter the fluid coupling to increase the speed of the fan. A decrease in temperature contracts the coil spring and closes the opening plate on the oil reservoir. From the coupling, oil then returns to the reservoir through a bleed hole in the coupling and the fan speed is reduced.

Fan-drive clutch test. To test the fan-drive clutch (fluid coupling) the engine should be run until it reaches its normal operating temperature. Stop the engine, use a cloth or glove to protect your hand, and check the effort required to turn the fan. If considerable effort is required, the coupling can be assumed to be in good operating condition. If the fan turns easily, the coupling is likely to be defective and should be replaced.

Service procedure. If the fan clutch or coupling must be removed, it should be supported vertically on the car to prevent the leakage of silicone oil.

The removal procedure for either type of bimetal element is the same. Merely unfasten the unit from the water pump and remove the assembly from the car. The variable-speed unit with the flat spring can be partially disassembled for cleaning and inspection. Unscrew the cap screws that hold the assembly together and separate the fan from the drive clutch. Remove the metal strip on the front of the unit by pushing one end of it toward the clutch body. Then push the strip to one side until the opposite end springs out of place. The control piston beneath can then be removed.

Check the piston for free movement of the coupling. If the piston is sticking, clean it with fine emery cloth. If the bimetal strip or spring is damaged, replace the entire unit. The bimetal strips are not interchangeable.

To reassemble, install the control piston so that the projection on the piston contacts the bimetal spring. Install the spring with any identification letters or numbers facing the clutch. After reassembly, clean the clutch drive with a cloth soaked in solvent. Do not dip the clutch assembly in any type of cleaner or solvent. Reinstall the assembly on the car in the reverse order of its removal.

The coil-spring type of fan clutch cannot be disassembled, serviced, or repaired. If it does not function properly, replace it with a new unit.

Miscellaneous Causes of Overheating

It is possible that excess heating may be caused by either a too lean or too rich fuel mixture, by a retarded spark, by wrong or insufficient oil in the crankcase, by a blocked exhaust pipe or muffler, by improper valve action, or by binding brakes. In these cases, however, the general performance of the automobile will give other clues. If the mixture is so lean or so rich as to cause overheating, the car will lack speed and power; this will also hold true if the engine is run on a retarded spark. A badly carbonized engine can also cause overheating. Other possible causes include sticking of the manifold heat valve due to a seized shaft and failure of the heat valve to close because of a defective thermostatic unit. These points should be checked on all overheating cars before extensive examination of the pump, fan, or gaskets is started. If the car passes all of the tests previously described and still overheats, the radiator probably is at fault.

Before the radiator is checked for possible obstructions, it is well to know how long the radiator has been on the car, and if recently installed, whether the overheating occurred before its installation. Many mysterious cases of engine overheating have been traced to a replacement radiator.

Troubleshooting Sequence

Cooling-system troubles are always caused by definite parts or assemblies, some of which are at fault more often than others. For this reason, troubleshooting a cooling system should follow a definite pattern, as given below:

1. Check the fan belt for slippage or a break.
2. Check coolant level in radiator. Loss of water may be due to a broken hose or a blown-out soft plug. During the winter months, check for a frozen radiator caused by lack of sufficient antifreeze.
3. Check the thermostat to see if it is stuck closed.
4. Check the radiator for clogging.
5. Make sure the radiator pressure cap is in good condition.
6. Check the valve timing chain. It may be jumping teeth on its sprocket. If the chain is O.K., check for late ignition timing. A check of these systems would be indicated by power losses and hard starting.
7. Check the brakes to see if they are dragging or not releasing. Hand-brake cables may be stuck or, in cold weather, frozen. The master cylinder may be defective, or its linkage to the brake pedal may not be set properly.
8. Check the transmission. An automatic type may be slipping because of lack of fluid, or slipping bands or clutch; a standard transmission may have a slipping clutch.
9. Check the smog-control system. The vacuum-control valve for the ignition system may be inoperative or defective.

Overcooling

The effect of running an engine at too low a temperature is not as immediately apparent as running it at too high a temperature, but it can be just as serious. When an engine is run at lower than normal temperatures, especially during freezing weather, excessive fuel consumption, dilution of the engine oil, and sludge formed by water condensation are likely to result. The formation of sludge may cause lubrication failure and result in serious damage to the engine. Corrosive acids that attack engine parts are also likely to be formed by burned fuel vapors mixing with water in the crankcase.

The symptoms associated with operation at below normal temperatures are easily recognized and commonly include the following:

1. The needle of the temperature gauge stays near the cold end of the scale. If an indicator light is used in place of a gauge, the light may remain on at all times or take a very long time to go off.

2. The engine seems to be unusually sluggish on pickup, or sputters considerably during acceleration.

3. Frequent stalling in traffic.

4. The heater does not operate satisfactorily, but emits cold or only slightly warm air.

5. The engine oil becomes very sludgy between changes, or gasoline is mixing with and diluting the oil.

Causes and remedies. Overcooling may be caused by any of the following conditions:

1. Thermostat not closing; if the thermostat is defective and does not remain closed until the engine warms up, it should be replaced by a new one.

2. Operating conditions; if the car is operated for short distances, especially during cold weather, the engine never has time to warm up adequately. Stopping for intervals long enough to let the engine cool off, driving at low speeds, and excessive idling are other possible causes of overcooling.

When overcooling is found to be caused by operating conditions, a higher reading thermostat may solve the problem quickly. With a higher reading thermostat the engine heats quickly to the desired temperature and remains at that level as long as the engine is running.

CARE OF THE COOLING SYSTEM

Scale Prevention

A major cause of overheating is partial obstruction of the radiator passages by rust and scale, which allows little heat transfer between the water and the engine. In a new car, the formation of rust and scale can be prevented or reduced to a minimum by using a suitable rust-resisting agent twice each year. Soluble oil may be employed for this purpose. Addition of the oil to the water produces a white emulsion. This solution, in passing through the cooling system, coats all metal surfaces with which it comes in contact. The coating looks soapy but is harmless and does not interfere with the transfer of heat. It prevents the formation of rust by keeping the oxygen in the water from acting on the metal and resists the adherence of lime particles to the metal, thus preventing a buildup of scale.

The soluble oil also reduces the rate of evaporation of the cooling water. Because, since the need for fresh water is reduced, fewer foreign substances are entered into the cooling system when water is added.

Most antifreeze solutions now contain soluble oil. If the antifreeze is drained during periods of warm weather, a small amount of rust inhibitor should be added to the water. For best results, however, the antifreeze solution should be used year around.

Never pour rust inhibitor into a hot radiator. Heat may cause the emulsifying agent to evaporate and prevent a complete emulsion of the oil with the water. Once the emulsion is formed it is unaffected by heat. A safe solution is to mix the soluble oil with cold water in a separate receptacle and then pour it into the radiator.

Cleaning

Cooling systems, because of the narrow passages through which the water circulates, have a tendency to become clogged. Of course, rust and scale accumulate but are not likely to interfere seriously with water circulation until the automobile has been in service for some time. Commonly radiators become clogged by an accumulation of oil and grease in the cooling system. This accumulation may be caused by use of an improper lubricant in the water pump, or by the leakage of oil from a cylinder-head gasket that is not bolted down properly. In passing through the cooling system the lubricant is deposited on the inside of the radiator tubes and the water jacket where it catches and holds particles of dust, dirt, or other solid materials.

To remove the accumulation of oil and grease before it causes cooling difficulties, the cooling system should be flushed out periodically. A good time for such flushing is just before the introduction of an antifreeze solution or just after its removal. For best results, the flushing solution should be circulated through the system in a reverse direction from the normal flow of water. The reversed flow is quite effective in dislodging and carrying away the dissolved grease and any foreign substances. A pressure flushing gun is the only special equipment needed to do a satisfactory job. To prepare the cooling system for the flushing operation, proceed as follows:

For an engine with a cast-iron head, fill the radiator with a solution consisting of a half-pound of washing soda and one quart of kerosene mixed with water. First dissolve the soda in a pail of hot water. Pour the kerosene directly into the radiator. Then add the soda solution and complete filling with clear water. Run the engine for about twenty minutes to get the cleaning solution hot but not boiling. In cold weather, it may be necessary to cover the radiator core to generate sufficient heat. Disconnect the lower hose connection, drain the solution, and then reverse flush both the engine block and radiator.

Commercial cleaning compounds are available. Because they are prepackaged, they are somewhat easier to work with, but may be considerably more expensive.

Use of flushing gun. Before flushing the cooling system with a flushing gun, disconnect the upper radiator hose. Refer to Fig. 12-4. The flushing gun is equipped to inject both hot water and air into the flushing system. To flush the radiator, attach a hose to the *upper radiator fitting (nipple).* Put the radiator cap in place on the filler opening, insert the flushing gun into a second hose, which is connected to the lower radiator opening, and turn on the water. When the water begins to flow freely from the upper hose, apply the air cautiously in short spurts to create a pulsing action. If the radiator is clogged, apply water and air gradually since the radiator core will stand only a limited pressure. To help loosen rust, hold a board against the face of the radiator core and strike the board lightly with a hammer. Place the board in several positions and repeat this part of the operation.

The method used to flush the engine block is illustrated in Fig. 12-5. After removing the thermostat, attach the flushing gun to the upper hose connection. Turn on the water and allow the block jackets to fill. Then apply air in short spurts to loosen scale and dirt and force them out through the lower connection.

The cleaning solution must not be allowed to remain in the cooling system for any appreciable length of time before the entire system is drained and flushed. No soda solution should be used in engines having aluminum cylinder heads or pump parts, since it will cause corrosion.

Before the thermostat is put back in place, it should be checked for correct opening and closing temperatures. If operation is improper, replace the thermostat.

Removal of rust and scale. For engines with aluminum heads, lye, powerful alkaline cleaning solutions, or acids must never be used to clean the cooling system. When in doubt about the material used in the cylinder head, scratch the surface lightly with a knife or scraper. Aluminum scratches easily, and has a light silver color. Cast iron is not easily scratched and has a dark gray color. The same precautions must be observed when the car is equipped with an aluminum water pump.

When the head or water pump are aluminum, use a commercial cleaning compound that carries the manufacturer's guarantee that it will not damage such parts.

To determine if a radiator is clear after cleaning, proceed as follows: If the radiator is cold, fill the system with hot water and feel the core with your hand. A cold spot on the core marks a point where clogging still exists. If the radiator is fairly hot when the test is made, fill the system with cold water and look for hot spots on the core.

Cleaning a plugged core. If a partly plugged radiator core is found in the test described above, more drastic treatment is in order. Remove the radiator from the car, and plug up the top and bottom openings and the overflow pipe. With the radiator in an upright position, fill it about three-quarters full with a solution consisting of one pound of lye or caustic soda to five gallons of water. After the filler opening is closed with its cap, place the radiator on a bench and rock it back and forth for a while to circulate the solution. Then remove the plugs and drain the solution. A stream of water from a hose is then sent into the radiator through the lower opening to reverse the normal direction of flow.

Some radiator repairmen use a solution of muriatic (hydrochloric) or oxalic acid to remove stubborn scale from radiators with zigzag passages. If muriatic acid is used, the proportion should be one part acid to ten parts water. Oxalic acid should be used in the proportion of one pound of acid to three gallons of water. When the acid is used, the upper and lower hose connections should be closed by soldering a sheet of brass over the openings, and the solution should be poured into the radiator. The radiator is then placed over a

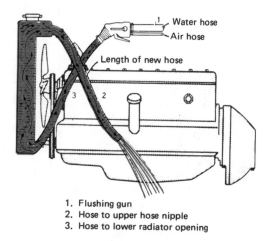

1. Flushing gun
2. Hose to upper hose nipple
3. Hose to lower radiator opening

Fig. 12-4 Reverse flushing of radiator.

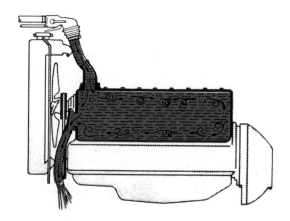

Fig. 12-5 Flushing of engine block.

gas flame to heat the lower tank, and the solution is allowed to boil for two to three hours with water being added from time to time to maintain the original level in the radiator. After this, the solution is poured out and the radiator is neutralized with a soda solution. Finally, the radiator is flushed with clear water.

When a radiator has been removed for cleaning, it should be placed in a test tank and checked for leaks before being reinstalled.

When rust and scale cannot be removed from the cylinder-block jackets by the use of cleaning solutions and flushing, the cylinder head and water-jacket plates (if used) should be taken off and the water passages scraped, as far as possible, with a screwdriver or similar tool.

Draining. When it is necessary to drain a cooling system completely, it is imperative that the engine block as well as the radiator be emptied. This is done by opening the drain plugs located at the bottom of the radiator and underneath the engine block. Six-cylinder engines have one drain plug at the lower rear part of the block; V-8s have two drain plugs at the lower rear part of the block, one on each side.

Winter Care

To prepare a cooling system for winter driving involves a number of procedures and precautions. It is necessary, for instance, to make sure the cooling system is watertight. Small leaks in the radiator, hose connections, or water pump may not be very important in the summer because they usually cause nothing more serious than the need for frequent replenishment of the water. Antifreeze mixtures, however, are expensive, and their loss is both costly and dangerous. The loss must be replaced, and if only water is used for the replacement, the solution is weakened and the freezing point raised. The entire cooling system, therefore, should be gone over carefully to see that all hose connections are tight and that the hoses are in good condition. If the rubber on any hose is cracked, swollen, or porous, it should be replaced since it probably will leak before the winter is over.

Also check the water pump. Although the pump is a relatively simple mechanism and normally needs very little service, it can cause a lot of trouble. A leaking water pump usually is the result of a defective seal. The pump must be removed for repair or replacement. Some pumps require lubrication, but others in which the bearings are sealed need no lubrication. If a noise develops in the pump bearing, available additives may remedy the trouble. Replacing a pump with either a rebuilt or new unit is often more practical and economical than repair.

Other points of possible leakage are at the cylinder-head gasket and the various plugs and connections around the water jackets. Leaks in the radiator core or header must be repaired. The fan belt should also be checked since it drives the water pump in most cars; any slippage of the belt will cause overheating and evaporation in the cooling system.

The external air openings in the radiator core often become partially clogged by leaves and bugs during the summer and should be cleaned before the onset of cold weather. To clean the openings, apply a pressure gun at the rear of the radiator and force air and water through the core openings. If no gun is available, a garden hose may do the job.

Perhaps the most important step in preparing for winter driving is the addition of antifreeze. More is said about this subject at a later point in this chapter.

Steaming radiator. A steaming radiator in cold weather usually results from water freezing because of insufficient antifreeze or from mechanical troubles that cause overcooling. Test the strength of the antifreeze solution by means of a hydrometer and make any adjustment that may be necessary. Mechanical defects should be checked and any defective parts repaired or replaced.

Formation of steam in the cooling system causes loss of the antifreeze solution either by evaporation or through the overflow pipe.

The automobile should not be parked headed downward on a hill, especially with the engine running. Under these conditions, steam pockets may form in the cooling system, siphon off the cooling solution, and cause engine damage.

Frozen radiators. When a radiator is only slightly frozen, it is common practice to block off air by covering the front of the radiator, and then run the engine. The best plan, however, is to move the car into a warm garage and let it stay there until the radiator thaws out. The cooling water usually freezes at the bottom of the radiator. Thus, if the lower hose connection is cold when the upper hose connection is hot, freezing at the bottom is indicated. Very often the radiator can be thawed by first opening the drain cock and then pouring hot water on the lower end of the radiator. When circulation is indicated by dripping at the drain cock, close the cock, fill the radiator with warm water, and run the engine until complete circulation is restored. A blanket thrown over the radiator may also thaw the frozen portion. The engine should not be run when the radiator freezes and steams, since cold air drawn through the radiator by the fan can keep the radiator frozen.

If an automobile has been standing in a cold place long enough for the entire cooling system to freeze, the radiator and engine will probably be damaged before the ice liquifies. When frozen solid, the radiator should be removed and immersed in warm water. The water must not be too hot or it will damage the radiator finish. When the radiator is finally thawed, it should be checked for leaks.

A number of round openings, sealed with metal plugs, are usually found on each side of a cylinder block. These holes serve no useful purpose in cooling, but are needed to cast the block at the foundry. The metal plugs are often called *freeze plugs*, because it is believed that they will be forced out when a solid freeze occurs and prevent cracking of the cylinder block. While it is true that the plugs probably would be forced out, engine damage will not necessarily be prevented.

WATER PUMPS

Typical Water Pump

A typical water pump is shown disassembled in Fig. 12-6. Principal parts of the pump include the *body, impeller, seal, shaft, bearing, slinger, hub,* and *gasket.* Most water pumps are of the impeller pump type and are installed at the front end of the cylinder block. As shown in the illustration, the impeller is a flat plate with a series of curved blades. As the impeller turns, the blades force the water through the pump outlet and into the cylinder block. After returning to the radiator and being cooled, the water is drawn through the opening in the bottom of the pump. This opening is connected by a hose to the bottom of the radiator. The impeller is supported by the shaft, which is supported in turn by the bearing. The pump, of course, is driven by the same belt that drives the generator and fan. The fan and its pulley usually are bolted fast to the hub of the water pump; consequently, the fan pulley actually drives the pump.

The water pump shown in Fig. 12-6 is but one of many types used. However, all water pumps, regardless of their construction, operate on the same principle. You should, therefore, have little trouble in removing, repairing, or replacing any water pump.

Disassembly

To remove and disassemble a typical water pump, use the following procedure as a guide:

1. Disconnect the battery cable.
2. Loosen the nut that holds the generator in place, swing the generator toward the engine, and lift the belt off all pulleys.
3. Remove the shield, fan, and spacer.

4. If the car is air conditioned, also remove the power-booster clutch and compressor drive pulley.
5. Remove the radiator supply tank.
6. Remove the clamp that secures the bypass hose to the water pump.
7. Remove the generator splash guard.
8. Remove the belt.
9. Remove the hose from the pump.
10. Remove the bolts used to mount the pulley on the engine block. Reposition any obstructing parts and remove the water pump.
11. Place the body of the pump in a press or vise, and remove the impeller cover plate and gasket at the rear of the pump.
12. Use a suitable puller to remove the hub from the front of the pump.
13. Use a suitable press to force out the seal and impeller.
14. If the slinger is damaged, mark its position on the shaft and then remove the slinger.
15. Check all parts for wear and replace worn parts as needed.

Reassembly

The following steps should be used as a guide in reassembling a typical water pump.

1. Remove all gasket material from the mounting faces of the water pump and engine block.
2. If the slinger was removed, use the position marks made previously as a guide to install a new unit.
3. Coat the outer diameter of the bearing lightly with grease, and press the shaft and bearing assembly into the body of the pump.
4. Apply a thin film of waterproof sealer on a new seal and press the seal into the housing.
5. Check the seal-rubbing face of the impeller for grooves. If the impeller is worn or damaged, replace it. Put a light coat of grease on the rubbing face.
6. Press the impeller onto the shaft. There must be a

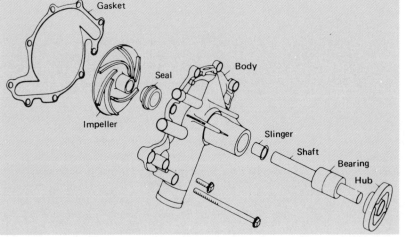

Fig. 12-6 Disassembled water pump.

clearance of 0.030 to 0.040 inch between the impeller and the surface of the impeller cover gasket.

7. Press the hub onto the shaft.

8. Put a new gasket on the impeller cover and install the cover.

9. On pumps that have ceramic seats, use ethylene glycol antifreeze to lubricate the seat before the pump is installed on the engine block.

10. Mount the water pump on the engine block, reversing the first nine steps of the disassembly procedure.

11. After the installation is completed, fill the radiator with water, and run the engine until it is warm. Check the pump carefully to make sure there are no leaks.

THERMOSTATIC TEMPERATURE CONTROL

General Information

Before an engine is warm, only a part of the gasoline vaporizes and burns in the combustion chamber and this causes high fuel consumption. In addition, the unburned fuel works past the piston rings and down into the crankcase where it dilutes the oil.

To lessen the time required for the engine to reach its normal operating temperature, a thermostat is used to restrict the circulation of water until a certain temperature is reached. The thermostat then opens and restores normal circulation.

Water circulation through the cylinder jackets is continued by the pump until a predetermined temperature is reached and the thermostat opens. During the warm-up period, the water pump circulates the cooling solution through the engine but not through the radiator. A radiator bypass is included either as part of the original engine or as part of the thermostat itself. When the thermostat opens, the radiator bypass is closed.

A thermostat contains a thermostatic device and a valve. The bellows type has a springlike bellows and a valve. The bellows contains a liquid that evaporates as the temperature increases. This evaporation causes the bellows to expand and raise the valve, thus opening the water passage to the radiator.

Some thermostats, like the sleeve type and the butterfly type contain a wax pellet inside a liquid. As the pellet expands, the sleeve or butterfly is opened to allow water to circulate between the engine and the radiator.

All thermostats are designed to open at a specific temperature. A 160°F thermostat, for example, starts to open between 157°F and 162°F, and is fully open at 182°F. A 180°F thermostat operates at 20°F above these temperatures; that is, it starts to open between 177°F and 182°F, and is fully open at 202°F.

The type of thermostat to be used depends on the operating requirements of the engine and the type of antifreeze used in the cooling system. Most automobile manufacturers recommend a 160°F thermostat with permanent-type antifreeze, and a 180°F thermostat with alcohol. On vehicles equipped with exhaust-emission controls, a thermostat that operates at a much higher temperature is used. Thermostats for such vehicles are rated at 205°F. Always follow the manufacturer's recommendations.

Bypass Control

Some automobile manufacturers install small bypass valves between the engine block and water pump. A bypass valve allows the engine to reach its efficient operating temperature more quickly. The use of a bypass valve is illustrated in Fig. 12-7. Part (a) of the illustration shows circulation during the warm-up period, and part (b) shows normal circulation. When the engine is below normal operating temperature, the cooling liquid is blocked from circulating

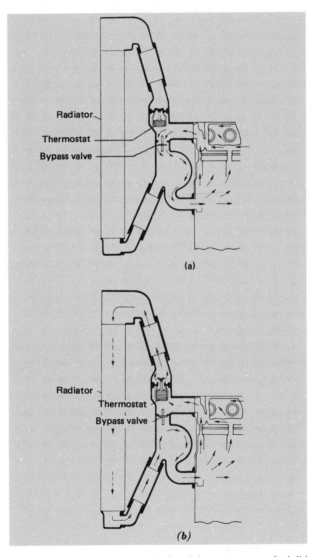

Fig. 12-7 Bypass control during (a) warm-up period (b) normal circulation.

through the radiator by the thermostat, which is held on its seat by the bellows. The pump pressure forces the bypass valve off its seat, and water circulates through the cylinder-block jackets and cylinder head. When the liquid reaches its proper temperature, the thermostat opens and circulation proceeds through the radiator in the normal manner, as shown in (b). The passage of liquid through the upper radiator hose relieves the pump pressure on the bypass valve, causing it to close.

Installation and Testing

A thermostat should always be installed with the bellows or spring toward the engine. A pinhole is provided at some point in the thermostat to prevent the trapping of air in the cooling system, and to permit water to drain from the upper radiator when the system is drained. Rust, scale, grease, or bits of rubber hose may obstruct this pinhole and cause trouble. When checking the cooling system, it is advisable, therefore, to remove the thermostat and make sure the pinhole is open.

When the cooling system is being refilled, the water should be poured very slowly, with the engine running, to make sure the thermostat opens. After the system is filled, let the engine run for a while to be sure it is indeed filled. If the rated capacity is, say, 4½ gallons, and the system fails to take this much coolant, an air pocket exists in the system and the trapped air must be released. If operating the engine at normal temperature fails to release the air, remove and test the thermostat. Also make sure the valves for the heater lines are open to ensure complete filling of the system.

A simple way to check the operation of a thermostat is shown in Fig. 12-8. After removal, the thermostat is suspended by a rod in a container of water. The water is heated, and the opening and closing of the thermostat is checked with an accurate thermometer. The temperature at which the thermostat begins to open should be within two or three degrees of the designated temperature, which is stamped on the thermostat. If the thermostat does not function within a few degrees of the designated temperature, it should be replaced with a new one.

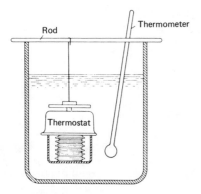

Fig. 12-8   Testing thermostat.

ANTIFREEZE SOLUTIONS

Requirements and Types

Most automobiles require an antifreeze solution in the cooling system to prevent the water from freezing when the temperature drops below 32°F. If the water does freeze, its expanding force may crack the radiator, the cylinder block, or both. An antifreeze solution, when used in the proper amount and when thoroughly mixed with the water, will prevent damage by lowering the freezing temperature of the coolant.

A good antifreeze solution must mix readily with water, prevent the coolant from freezing at the lowest temperature expected, circulate freely, not damage the cooling system through corrosion, not lose its properties after being used over an extended period of time, and raise the boiling point of the coolant for high speed and high temperature engine operation.

After an antifreeze solution is added to the cooling system, run the engine long enough to assure a good mixture, and then have the solution tested at your local service station just to make sure everything is in good shape.

Some Final Suggestions for Cold-Weather Driving

1. On cars equipped with a manual clutch, shove the clutch in when starting; this frees the engine from the transmission.

2. If the engine does not start after a short period of cranking, let it stand a few minutes to allow the gasoline to vaporize before trying again. Do not choke the engine.

3. Do not race the engine to warm it. Racing is always bad, but considerably worse in cold weather.

4. If an alcohol-base antifreeeze is used, remember it is highly inflammable. For the sake of safety, pour the solution into the radiator while the car is out-of-doors.

5. Always run the engine for a short time after adding antifreeze or filling the storage battery with water. Otherwise, freezing may occur.

6. Be careful in removing the cap from a boiling radiator. The escaping steam and water can give you a nasty burn.

7. Change oil more frequently than in the summertime and use a lighter grade of oil.

8. Do not pour water into the radiator of an overheated engine, since a cracked cylinder head or cylinder jacket might result. Let the engine cool down until you can place your hand on it without getting burned. Then refill the radiator.

9. With an alcohol-base antifreeze, never run the engine after steam starts to issue from the overflow pipe. The steam will cause the radiator solution to run out of the overflow pipe until the radiator is empty, and scored cylinders or burned pistons are likely to result.

10. Make sure the engine is running at its normal temperature when the antifreeze solution is checked. The solution occupies more space when hot than it does when cold.

Many materials, such as oil, calcium, chloride, denatured alcohol and methanol, wood alcohol, distilled glycerine, and ethylene glycol, have been tested and used in antifreeze solutions. Of the materials listed, only two are in common use today; alcohol (or alcohol-base) materials and ethylene glycol. The alcohol-base materials actually make temporary antifreeze solutions since they evaporate at temperatures below the boiling point of water. Thus, periodic additions have to be made to keep the solution at the proper strength for adequate protection. The ethylene glycol (permanent) antifreeze solutions, on the other hand, remain liquid at the boiling point of water. Accordingly they can be used for the entire season without the need for additions. All late model automobiles are equipped with thermostats that operate at temperatures considerably above the boiling point of alcohol. Thus, ethylene glycol is the only practical antifreeze solution for these automobiles.

Adding Antifreeze Solutions

Before pouring an antifreeze solution into a radiator, drain off enough water to make room for the solution and to provide for expansion in the upper radiator tank. Alternatively, drain all water from the cooling system, close the petcocks, and then pour in water to about one-third the capacity of the cooling system. In either method, run the engine until it is hot enough to assure the opening of the thermostat. Then add the amount of antifreeze and water necessary to fill the system.

Table 12-2 shows the amount of antifreeze to be added to a cooling system of given capacity to achieve protection at a specified temperature. For example, if the capacity of the system is eighteen quarts, and protection is required down to $-10°F$, seven quarts of permanent antifreeze must be added.

Table 12-2 Permanent-type antifreeze.

Cooling System Capacity (quart)	Quarts of Antifreeze Needed for Protection to Temperatures Shown Below													
	1	2	3	4	5	6	7	8	9	10	11	12	13	14
5	16	−12	−62											
6		0	−34											
7		6	−18	−54										
8		11	−8	−34										
9		14	0	−21	−50									
10		16	4	−12	−34	−62								
11		18	8	6	−23	−47								
12		19	10	0	−15	−34	−57							
13		21	13	3	−9	−25	−45							
14			15	6	−5	−18	−34							
15			16	8	0	−12	−26							
16			17	10	2	−8	−19	−34	−52					
17			18	12	5	−4	−14	−27	−42					
18			19	14	7	0	−10	−21	−34	−50				
19			20	15	9	2	−7	−16	−28	−42				
20				16	10	4	−3	−12	−22	−34	−48			
21				17	12	6	0	−9	−17	−28	−41			
22				18	13	8	2	−6	−14	−23	−34	−47		
23				19	14	9	4	−3	−10	−19	−29	−40		
24				19	15	10	5	0	−8	−15	−23	−34	−46	
25				20	16	12	7	1	−5	−12	−20	−29	−40	−50
26					17	13	8	3	−3	−9	−16	−25	−34	−44
27					18	14	9	5	−1	−7	−13	−21	−29	−39
28					18	15	10	6	1	−5	−11	−18	−25	−34
29					19	16	12	7	2	−3	−8	−15	−22	−29
30					20	17	13	8	4	−1	−5	−12	−18	−25

Figures preceded by a minus sign (−) indicate freezing points below zero.

13

CLUTCHES AND UNIVERSAL JOINTS

Contents

CLUTCH FUNDAMENTALS

Introduction

When an automobile equipped with a standard transmission—that is, a transmission requiring manual shifting of the gears from low to high speed—is operated, a device called a *clutch* must be used. The clutch, when disengaged (released by pressing down on the clutch pedal), separates the transmission from the engine drive shaft. When the clutch is disengaged, the gears in the transmission are shifted to their neutral position or from one gear ratio to another and the clutch prevents damage to the gears. The neutral position is used when the automobile is not moving.

Shortly after World War II it was predicted that the automatic transmission (one not requiring the use of a manual clutch) would replace the standard transmission. However, the steadily increasing demand for automobiles with standard transmissions produced outside the United States proved the predictions to be wrong. The demand further pointed to the continued need for better clutch designs.

Clutch classification. In order to provide different power requirements for automobiles with various gross weights, several versions of the so-called *plate* clutch have been designed. The proper performance of the entire power train in an automobile depends on sufficient friction being produced in the clutch. This friction must be produced in the contact area between the *driving* and *driven* plates of the clutch. The manner in which the friction is produced determines the classification of each clutch design. The various clutch designs include the single-plate clutch, double-plate clutch, cone clutch, disk clutch, expanding clutch, and contracting clutch. Of all these designs, only the single-plate clutch has survived in passenger-car service.

The type "S" clutch, produced by Borg-Warner Corporation, is a variation of the single-plate clutch and is especially suited to use in low, compactly designed automobiles. The importance of the type S clutch is that it reduces the force the operator must apply to disengage the clutch.

Plate-clutch requirements. Some of the most important plate-clutch requirements for satisfactory operation include the following: (1) It must engage without seizing to keep the automobile from being jerked into operation; (2) once the car is accelerated, it must hold without slipping; (3) it must release instantly without dragging around the driven member—no more than 25 to 35 pounds of foot pressure should be required to release the clutch; (4) it should be of such form that the driven member will have the minimum tendency to keep rotating of its own momentum once the pressure plate is released. This tendency usually is referred to as the *centrifugal effect;* (5) it should not require constant adjustment to perform properly; and (6) all parts of the clutch should be of high mechanical strength and possess lasting qualities.

In operation, the driving plates and the driven member of a plate clutch are normally engaged fully, being held together firmly by the force of coiled steel springs or a spring diaphragm, both of which are discussed later.

Disengagement of the engine from the change-gear mechanism of the clutch is brought about by depressing the clutch pedal. The pedal, through flexible linkage or a flexible cable, disengages the driven member from the driving plates, thereby compressing the pressure springs or the spring diaphragm, as the case may be. The engine remains disconnected from the transmission so long as the clutch pedal is depressed. As soon as the pedal is released, the pressure springs or the spring diaphragm presses the driving and driven members together, once again connecting the engine to the transmission.

Operating Principles of the Plate Clutch

The simple form of plate clutch shown in Fig. 13-1 illustrates the operating principle of all plate clutches. The clutch has a *driving shaft* and a *driven shaft* through which power is transmitted by the friction between the *driving plate* and the *driven plate* when their flat adjacent surfaces are forced together.

When the friction surfaces are entirely flat, so that the entire face of one plate is in contact with the entire face of the other plate, there is a great difference in the circular motion of parts located at various distances from the center. The maximum motion (speed of rotation) exists at the circumference. It follows that, with two plates in contact, one revolving and the other stationary, the relative motion (slippage) between the plates must be at a maximum near the periphery (outer edge). Accordingly, most wear must occur at the outer edge.

To minimize the effect of this wear, which reduces the amount of torque (turning effort) that can be transmitted from one plate to another, each plate is recessed so as to leave only a narrow ring-shaped contact surface at the outer edge. Since the diameter at the inner edge of this narrow

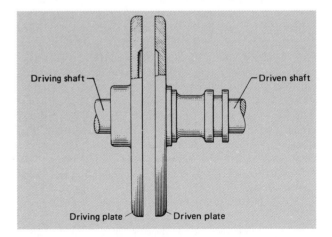

Fig. 13-1 Simple plate clutch.

ring is very little less than at the outer edge, the wear is distributed fairly evenly.

Because the contact surfaces are flat and at right angles to the direction of the force applied to close them, the pressure between the surfaces is equal to the amount of the closing force. As a rule, the frictional force of the clutch is numerically equal to the cubic-inch displacement of the engine cylinder. For example, the clutch for a 400 cubic inch engine displacement develops a 400-pound frictional force. This amount of force, then, is able to transmit the full power of the engine to the drive shaft without slippage.

Features of dry plate clutches. In the plate clutch, which must be completely dry at all times, the necessary friction is obtained either by facing one or both plates with asbestos fabric or by using special molded facing on both plates. Both of these materials have good frictional qualities when used against steel. The asbestos fabric is composed of asbestos fiber and woven wire and is riveted to the plates. The asbestos is used for its good frictional qualities and its resistance to heat, and the wire is used to bind the asbestos together and give it strength. Molded lining is hard and dense, has high mechanical strength, and engages smoothly.

Various methods are used to produce a smooth and gradual clutch engagement. In one method, helical springs are used to force a cushion between the driven disk and its hub. In another method, the disk is divided into sectors or has segments riveted on it, and the ends are sprung outward so that the part of the lining over these ends will come in contact first. A combination of these two methods is also used.

Clutch pedal travel. The travel of the clutch pedal is the total distance in inches of down and up movement of the pedal as the operator releases and engages the clutch when shifting gears. During this complete clutch pedal cycle of travel, two other significant terms connected with pedal travel are encountered: *free travel* and *reverse travel.*

As the clutch pedal is slightly depressed in the engaged position, the pedal moves freely for a small distance. Very little effort is required to move the pedal through the first inch of travel.

The free travel in the pedal represents the distance between the tips of the release levers in the clutch mechanism and the bearing surfaces that are attached to the driving-plate assembly. For proper clutch operation, free travel must always be present in the clutch pedal. When a driver "rides" a clutch, depressing the pedal to the limit of free travel, the weight of the foot on the pedal effectively reduces the amount of friction between the driving and the driven plates. When this practice is followed, the clutch will slip, wear excessively, and permit loss of power transmission to the wheels. These conditions lead to poor gas mileage and early clutch failure.

At a point about three-quarters of an inch from the floorboard of the automobile, the clutch should be released cleanly. This distance is the reverse travel. At the end of reverse travel the driven plate is completely disengaged from the driving plate. When the operator fails to depress the clutch pedal sufficiently to disengage the clutch, a fault known as gear stripping occurs. This same effect is experienced when the clutch drags and makes it difficult (and sometimes impossible) to shift gears.

Plate load. Plate load is the force in psi applied to the driven and driving plates by the pressure springs in the clutch assembly. One pressure spring is shown in Fig. 13-2. In some maintenance instructions the driven plate may be called a clutch disk or a driven member. Additional plate load occurs as the engine speed increases because of the inherent design features of the clutch system. This additional plate load permits the efficient transmission of increased power as the engine is accelerated. In general, poor clutch operation results when the pressure springs become overheated for appreciable periods of time.

Driving plates. As shown in Fig. 13-2, the (pressure) plate is attached to the clutch cover plate which, in turn, is bolted to the flywheel. The pressure plate is free to move as the clutch is disengaged.

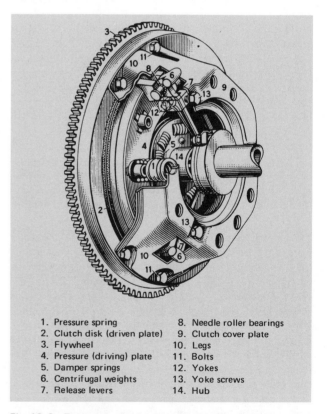

1. Pressure spring
2. Clutch disk (driven plate)
3. Flywheel
4. Pressure (driving) plate
5. Damper springs
6. Centrifugal weights
7. Release levers
8. Needle roller bearings
9. Clutch cover plate
10. Legs
11. Bolts
12. Yokes
13. Yoke screws
14. Hub

Fig. 13-2 Typical single-plate clutch assembly. *Courtesy of Borg-Warner Corporation.*

Driven plate. Details of the driven plate are shown in Fig. 13-3. By comparing Figs. 13-2 and 13-3 you can get a fuller understanding of the principles involved in the operation of the clutch.

The clutch disk (driven plate) is designed to absorb sudden rotational shock caused by engaging the clutch. The damper springs shown in Fig. 13-2 are provided for this purpose. When the clutch is engaged, the pressure springs cause the clutch disk to be squeezed in a vise-like grip between the pressure plate and the machined face of the flywheel. A splined connection is made at the hub of the disk so that the disk may slide when the clutch is engaged.

Typical Single-Plate Clutch

The clutch illustrated in Fig. 13-2 is a typical single-plate clutch with centrifugal weights on the release levers.

At zero speed, the only load on the pressure plate is that created by the pressure springs. But, as the engine is started and the speed increased, the centrifugal weights on the outer ends of the release levers increase the load on the pressure plate. The initial pressure-spring load provides more than ample torque to get the automobile moving and permits a low clutch-pedal pressure at the lower speeds. At higher speeds, however, the pressure required to depress the pedal is increased.

The release levers are mounted on needle roller bearings at their connection to the pressure plate. One of these bearings is shown in Fig. 13-2. This type of mounting reduces friction and permits smoother and easier pedal operation.

The clutch cover, triangular in shape, has three legs extending down to meet the flywheel. The cover is attached to the flywheel by six alloy-steel bolts. If the bolts are removed for any reason, they should never be replaced by ordinary cap screws. Forged steel yokes, one of which is shown in Fig. 13-2, are fastened to the cover by yoke screws at the point where the levers are mounted.

The clutch disk is of the two-part spring-and-friction type. Damper springs in the hub (Fig. 13-2) cushion the load in either direction, and stop pins limit the movement of the hub in relation to the clutch disk. Four friction studs located on each side of the hub flange introduce a friction between the hub and disk and thus dampen out torsional vibrations from the engine.

As shown in Fig. 13-4, a hardened steel screw contact (there are three such contacts in the clutch) is provided on the inner end of the release lever. The same contact can be

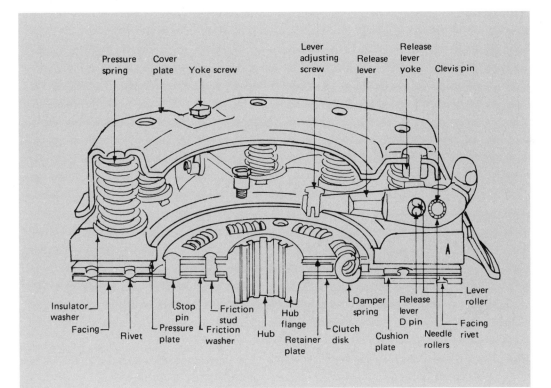

Fig. 13-3 Sectional view of typical clutch. *Courtesy of Borg-Warner Corporation.*

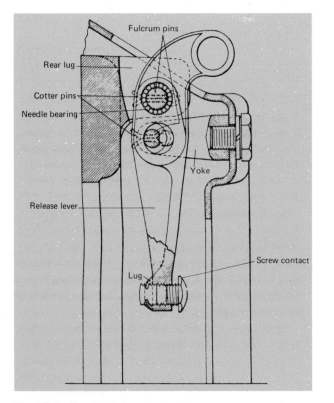

Fig. 13–4 Sectional view of release-lever construction. *Courtesy of Borg-Warner Corporation.*

seen in Fig. 13-3. The contact is locked in place by the clutch manufacturer by bending the lug (Fig. 13-4) into the slots in the screw, and needs changing only when a new or rebuilt clutch is installed.

A needle bearing is used at the pivot point of the lever. The bearing is located only in the lever; the rear lug and the ear of the yoke are shown cut away in Fig. 13-4 to make the bearing visible.

The only clutch adjustments recommended by the manufacturer are for clutch-pedal position. However, if it is desired to disassemble the release levers, remove the cotter pins from the end of the fulcrum pins, pull out the fulcrum pins, and then lift out the lever with the needle bearing.

Diaphragm Spring Clutch

The diaphragm spring clutch, one type of which is shown disassembled in Fig. 13-5 and diagrammatically in Fig. 13-6, is designed around a diaphragm spring shaped like a thin dished washer. The diaphragm spring, which contains eighteen integral fingers tapering toward the center, is fulcrumed on the clutch cover by two ⅛-inch round wire rings. As shown in Fig. 13-6, the rings are held to the cover by bolts and special washers. The bolts go through holes in the diaphragm close to its outer ring, and thus also serve to hold the diaphragm in place. The holes are slightly elongated to allow for movement of the diaphragm, which is centered on the clutch shaft by the inner ends of the radial fingers.

When the clutch cover plate is tightened down on the flywheel, Fig. 13-5, the fulcrum ring forces the outer rim of the diaphragm spring against the pressure plate and holds the clutch disk in contact with the flywheel. The clutch is

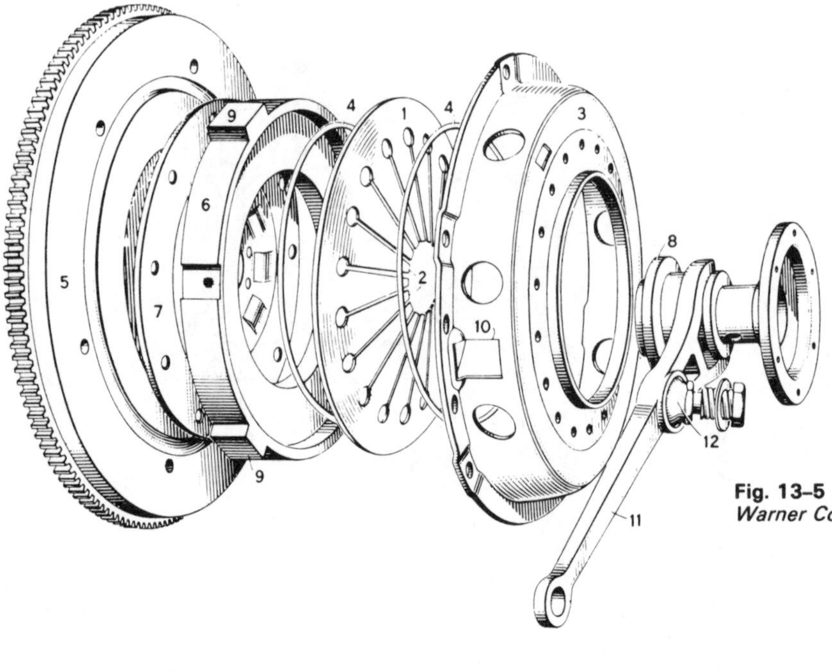

1. Diaphragm spring
2. Fingers
3. Clutch cover
4. Fulcrum rings
5. Flywheel
6. Pressure plate
7. Clutch disk
8. Release bearing
9. Lugs
10. Slot
11. Release fork
12. Fulcrum ball

Fig. 13–5 Diaphragm spring clutch. *Courtesy of Borg-Warner Corporation.*

then in the engaged position, as shown in Fig. 13-6(a). When the clutch pedal is depressed, the pressure of the release bearing on the inner ends of the fingers moves the ends of the fingers toward the flywheel and causes the outer ends of the fingers near the rim to pivot on the inner fulcrum ring. This action causes the rim of the diaphragm spring to move outward. Then, by means of the so-called retracting springs, Fig. 13-6, the pressure plate is moved away from the clutch disk, Fig. 13-5, disengaging the clutch. This position is shown in Fig. 13-6(b).

The three retracting springs, one of which is shown in Fig. 13-7, hold the pressure plate against the diaphragm spring and keep the plate centered. Compare Fig. 13-7 with Figs. 13-5 and 13-6 to locate the various parts. When the clutch pedal is released, and the release bearing no longer makes contact with the inner ends of the fingers, the spring on the diaphragm causes the fingers to pivot around the rear fulcrum spring and makes the outer rim of the diaphragm bear against the pressure plate.

The pressure plate carries three lugs that engage slots, one of which is visible in the clutch cover plate, Fig. 13-5. The retracting springs are bolted to the pressure plate.

The release bearing is a sealed ball bearing, and the release mechanism is positively operated by the release fork so that no pullback spring is needed.

With the engine idling, a rattling noise when the diaphragm spring clutch is released may be caused by insufficient tension in the retracting springs or by excessive clearance between the lugs on the pressure plate and the slots in the clutch cover plate. A rattle in the clutch release fork may result from a loose fulcrum ball in the fork.

Type S Clutch System

The type S clutch, Fig. 13-8, as compared to the single-plate clutch already described, is more compact, has fewer parts, and is easier to produce and maintain.

In a type S clutch the load is applied through the linkage from an externally mounted *main load spring*. See Fig. 13-8(a). The linkage system includes seven parts that connect the pedal with the *release lever*. The *flexible cable* affords certain design freedom and allows the pedal pressure to be determined without adding parts to the complex linkage system used with single-plate clutches.

The *spring moment arm* oscillates on a sealed Oilite bushing or on *needle bearings* on the larger V-8 engines,

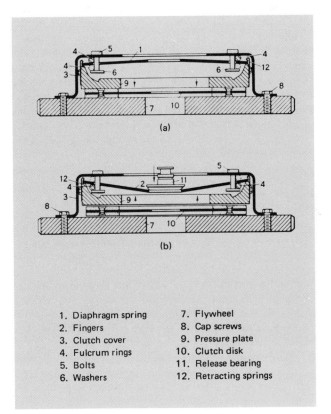

1. Diaphragm spring
2. Fingers
3. Clutch cover
4. Fulcrum rings
5. Bolts
6. Washers
7. Flywheel
8. Cap screws
9. Pressure plate
10. Clutch disk
11. Release bearing
12. Retracting springs

Fig. 13-6 Diagrammatic view of diaphragm spring clutch: (a) engaged; (b) disengaged. *Courtesy of Borg-Warner Corporation.*

1. Slot
2. Lug
3. Retracting spring
4. Retracting spring cap-screw hole
5. Retracting spring cap screw

Fig. 13-7 Installing retracting spring. *Courtesy of Borg-Warner Corporation.*

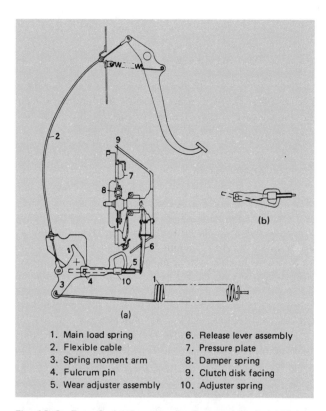

1. Main load spring
2. Flexible cable
3. Spring moment arm
4. Fulcrum pin
5. Wear adjuster assembly
6. Release lever assembly
7. Pressure plate
8. Damper spring
9. Clutch disk facing
10. Adjuster spring

Fig. 13-8 Type S clutch system by Borg and Beck. (a) Linkage system. (b) Automatic wear adjuster assembly. *Courtesy of Borg-Warner Corporation.*

and is supported on a fulcrum pin attached to the engine or clutch housing. The moment arm transmits motion through an *automatic wear adjuster* assembly, Fig. 13-8(b), to the *fork* and in turn to the *cover* assembly, thereby engaging and releasing the clutch. The cable assembly acts as a pantograph to eliminate the effect of the engine on clutch operation.

The externally mounted spring is attached to the engine and transmission structure, and the other end is attached to the moment arm. The spring load is applied through the moment arm, wear adjuster, fork, and release lever assembly to the pressure plate, which carries the engine torque. When the clutch pedal is depressed to release the clutch, the spring load is transferred from the clutch to the clutch pedal via the cable. The clutch-pedal effort is determined by the position of the spring mounting points, the spring load and rate, the angular rotation of the spring moment arm, and the spring rate of the damper spring in the driven member.

The operation of the cable, the wear adjuster, and the spring pivot points at the spring moment arm is based on a D-hole design, which permits a rolling contact at these points. The D-hole is self-cleaning and offers very little friction and wear. The single hazard in operation is

that, if the D-hole is left uncovered, slush and ice may freeze the joint.

The externally mounted main-load spring is the feature that permits the pedal effort reduction needed for efficient, compact installations. The pivoting spring on the spring moment arm allows about a 3 to 1 reduction in the rotation of the spring moment arm as the clutch is released. This means that if 25 pounds is applied to the foot pedal, the effective force actuating the release levers is 75 pounds.

In the linkage system an automatic wear adjuster compensates for plate facing wear. This eliminates any initial adjustment on the manufacturer's production line. Operating the clutch pedal will automatically position the wear adjuster, when necessary, to the correct operating position of the spring moment arm.

Wear adjuster operation. The wear adjuster is an integral part of the spring moment arm and is positioned between the main load spring and the release-lever assembly. In this position, the adjuster maintains constant plate load and pedal effort during the life of the clutch. The adjuster senses and maintains a specific angular travel of the spring moment arm.

Since the angular travel of the moment arm determines the pressure plate travel, the wear adjuster is able to maintain the desired plate travel. As the clutch disk facing (Fig. 13-8) wears, the angular travel of the moment arm increases, causing the fork assembly on the moment arm to contact the adjuster spring. The spring acts as a one-way clutch on a threaded pushrod. With the fork assembly pushing on the spring when the clutch is released, the spring rotates the rod and increases the overall length of the adjuster portion of the fork assembly that contacts the release lever. The actuating arm also repositions the spring on the rod when the clutch is engaged. This sequence of events during clutch operation reduces the angular travel of the moment arm to the desired rotation.

About Troubleshooting

During the initial planning of this manual, we contacted the Borg and Beck Division of the Borg-Warner Corporation to obtain certain information relating to clutch repair. In their reply, the engineering department noted that today's high-powered engines pose especially critical design problems in the areas of materials specifications, concentricity, and balance, to name the most prominent. The operation of the clutch makes it particularly susceptible to malfunction when improperly repaired due to the above requirements.

That manufacturer recommended that we advise against all attempts to repair clutches and urge instead replacement with either a new original-equipment clutch or a clutch rebuilt by a quality rebuilder who will adhere to manufacturers' specifications and use only quality replacement parts.

As responsible publishers, we must endorse this recommendation.

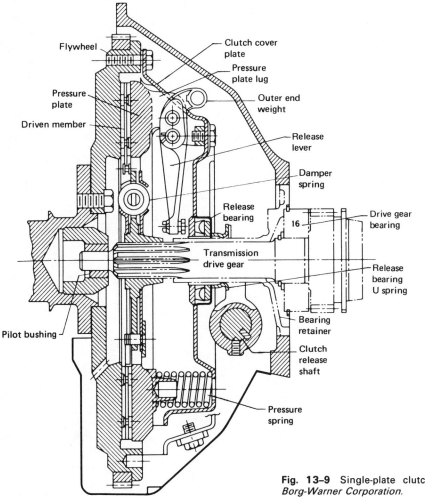

Fig. 13–9 Single-plate clutch. *Courtesy of Borg-Warner Corporation.*

Application of a Single-Plate Clutch

The single-plate clutch illustrated in Fig. 13-9 is used in many General Motors automobiles equipped with synchromesh transmissions. The clutch is of conventional design, having *coiled pressure springs* and *three adjustable release levers.*

The *clutch cover plate* is bolted to the *flywheel; three lugs* on the *pressure plate engage slots* in the cover plate to transmit torque to the plate.

Pressure springs (only one is shown) are located between the cover plate and the pressure plate. The *release lever* is located so that its inner end is in position to be engaged by the *clutch release bearing.* The release lever is pivoted on a *fulcrum* which is bolted to the cover plate and is mounted in the pressure plate lug.

The *outer end weight,* an integral part of the release lever, is included so that at higher engine speeds where slippage may occur, the centrifugal force developed by the weight causes more pressure to be applied on the pressure plate. The faster the rotation of the clutch by the engine, the greater the pressure exerted against the clutch plate, and the greater the torque-transmitting ability of the clutch. This additional pressure allows the use of a clutch, which requires less foot pressure at the pedal for normal clutch operation.

When the clutch is engaged, the release lever is clear of the release bearing, and the pressure spring causes the pressure plate to clamp the *driven plate* against the flywheel with sufficient force to transmit power from the engine without slippage. The power drive is from the flywheel to the cover plate, then to the pressure plate, and finally to the driven member.

When the clutch is disengaged, the release bearing is pressed forward on the inner ends of the release lever. The release lever than pivots and forces the pressure plate backward against the pressure spring, thereby disengaging the driven member.

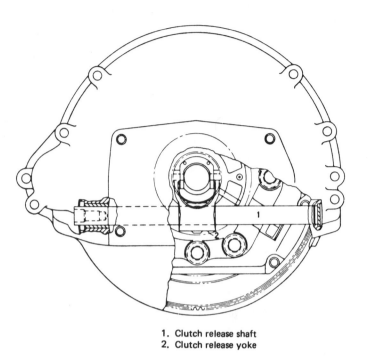

1. Clutch release shaft
2. Clutch release yoke

Fig. 13–10 Driven-member assembly. *Courtesy of Borg-Warner Corporation.*

Driven member.   The driven-member assembly, Fig. 13-10, is mounted with a free-sliding fit on the transmission drive gear and is keyed to the gear by ten splines. The front end of the drive gear is piloted by a bushing pressed into a recess in the rear end of the engine crankshaft.

The outer area of the driven member is divided into segments which are formed in low waves. These waves form a rippled-spring effect between the plate facings to cushion the engagement of the clutch. The waved cushion plate is in the same position as the cushion plate in Fig. 13-3. A molded facing is riveted to each side of every plate segment. When the clutch is fully released, the segments cause the facings to spread approximately 0.055 inch to assure full release of the driven member.

The driven member is designed to prevent the rattle-causing torsional periods of the engine from being transmitted to the transmission gears. This is accomplished by the *coiled damper spring* and the frictional dampening effect of *molded friction washers.* See Fig. 13-3.

The clutch is actuated through the linkage system that connects to the clutch release shaft. The clutch yoke is positioned so that it pushes forward on the release bearing when the clutch pedal is depressed. A *U-shaped spring,* Fig. 13-10, riveted to the *release bearing* holds the bearing in contact with the clutch release yoke.

The release bearing is mounted over the *front bearing retainer,* which retains the drive gear bearing of the transmission. The release bearing is filled with a permanent lubricant during production. The inside diameter of the re-

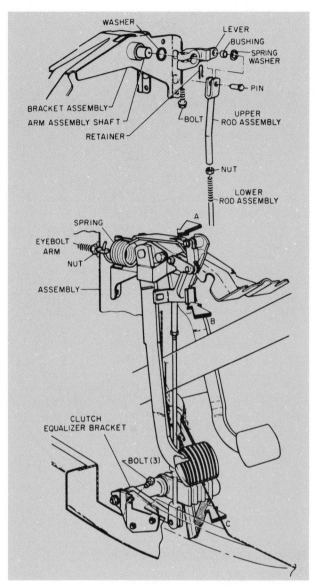

Fig. 13–11 Clutch-linkage system. *Courtesy of Borg-Warner Corporation.*

lease bearing is lightly lubricated with wheel-bearing lubricant or with heavy grease before it is installed.

Clutch linkage.   A typical clutch-linkage system is shown in Fig. 13-11. The clutch pedal is suspended, as shown at arrow *A,* and pivoted on a *shaft* which extends through the *clutch-pedal bracket.* Upon its return from a depressed position, the clutch pedal stops against a nonadjustable pedal stop, shown at arrow *B,* on the bracket assembly.

The *upper rod assembly* extends through the floor to connect the *lower rod assembly pedal linkage* to the *clutch equalizer.* The equalizer pivots between a ball stud located at the *upper flywheel housing* at one end and at the frame of the automobile at the other end. This pivoted area is

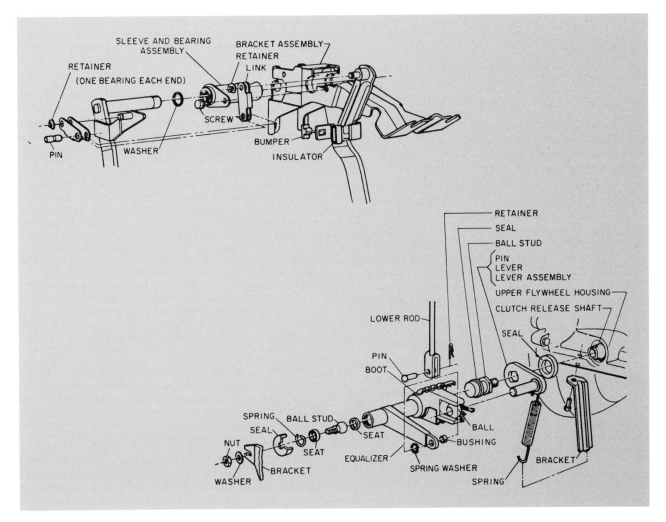

Fig. 13–12 Exploded view of clutch-linkage system. *Courtesy of Borg-Warner Corporation.*

shown more clearly in Fig. 13-12. The lower end of the release rod is fastened to the *clutch equalizer,* shown near arrow *C* in Fig. 13-11, with a clevis pin and a *retainer snap pin.*

Adjustment of the clutch is made on the lower rod assembly by adjusting the threaded rod and tightening the *nut* that is shown at the base of the *upper rod assembly.* The release-rod length must be adjusted to provide clearance between the *release bearing* and the *release levers.* As mentioned previously, the clutch release shaft pivots in the upper flywheel housing. The clutch is retained in this housing by the clutch release-lever assembly and clutch equalizer.

Lubrication. Lubrication of the clutch release equalizer in the linkage is required only when the clutch is overhauled. If lubrication becomes necessary between overhauls, in order to eliminate squeaks or excessive pedal pressure, the clutch must be removed from the automobile and lubricated as follows:

1. Very sparingly apply wheel-bearing lubricant in the pilot bushing to the engine crankshaft. If too much lubricant is used, it will heat up and run out onto the face of the flywheel, ruining the driven-member facings. Make sure the surface of the flywheel is clean and dry. Facings with grease stains should be replaced.

2. Make sure the splines in the hub of the driven member are clean. Apply a light coat of wheel-bearing lubricant to the splines. Slide the release bearing over the retainer several times, and then wipe off all excess lubricant pushed up by the bearing hub.

3. If the pressure plate driving lugs are dry, brush a small amount of lubricant between the clutch cover plate and the driving lugs and between the driving lugs and the release levers. Any excess lubricant must be wiped clean.

UNIVERSAL JOINTS

Basic Concepts

Purpose. The propeller shaft of an automobile is made in sections which must be coupled together without the use of a rigid coupling. To permit the use of a rigid coupling the propeller shaft would have to be absolutely straight from the transmission to the differential joint.

In many automobiles the propeller shaft has two halves which are joined at an angle with a center bearing support and constant-velocity joint. A universal joint is used at each end of the complete assembly. See Fig. 13-13. The universal joints compensate for any lack of alignment between the engine and axle during manufacture, and for any disturbance of the alignment due to road shock and bounce. The construction of a universal joint permits a certain slip within itself, as in a ball-and-trunnion joint or by providing the joint with a sliding connection. This latter type of slip joint, usually made as an integral part of the universal joint, is identified later by the term *splines*. Also, a constant-velocity joint is necessary to eliminate any variation in the turning rate of the propeller shaft.

Drive classification. The universal joints used in automobiles are classified according to the two general types of drive systems in which they are used—the Hotchkiss drive and the torque-tube drive. A Hotchkiss drive has an exposed shaft with a universal joint at each end. See Fig. 13-13. A torque-tube system has a single, enclosed universal joint at the front end of the shaft.

Propeller-shaft speed variation. A single universal joint transmits motion at a variable speed during each revolution.

This speed variation is inherent in most universal joints which connect two shafts that are out of alignment. The speed variation increases with an increase in the angle that the propeller shaft makes with the driving shaft.

Refer to Fig. 13-14. Suppose the main drive shaft from the transmission and the differential pinion shaft are connected by the propeller shaft, and that the change-speed gears are located at the forward end of the propeller shaft. The angle through which the motion is transmitted is made large in order to show clearly the relative positions of the universal joints.

Considering only the universal joint connecting the main drive shaft and the propeller shaft, if the main drive shaft turns at a uniform speed, the propeller shaft will not; instead, the speed of the propeller shaft will increase and decrease four times during each revolution, as shown in Fig. 13-15. The range of speeds indicated in Fig. 13-15 is from a minimum of 850 rpm to a maximum of 1150 rpm.

The alternate increase and decrease in propeller-shaft speed is due to the similar variation in radii through which the forks of the joint rotate. These changes in radii are indicated in Fig. 13-15 by the relative positions of point A. Initially, point A is at a certain perpendicular distance from the centerline of the driving shaft. As the propeller shaft turns through the first quarter-revolution, however, this distance increases gradually. Thus, the linear velocity of point A also increases since the speed of the driving shaft is uniform. During the second quarter-revolution, the distance of point A from the centerline decreases, so its linear velocity also decreases. The cycle is then repeated in the opposite direction during the next half-revolution. The table at the base of Fig. 13-15 shows the variations in propeller-shaft speed as a percentage of the driving-shaft rpm for 30° deviations in universal joint shaft angles.

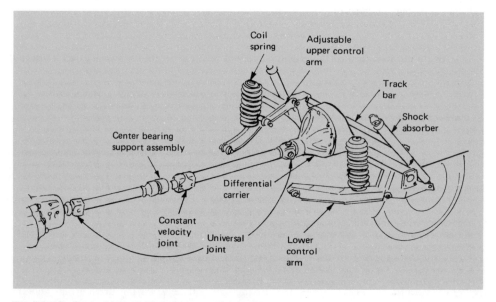

Fig. 13-13 Typical Hotchkiss Drive propeller-shaft installation. *Courtesy of General Motors Corporation.*

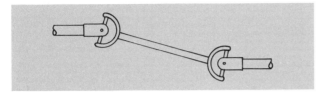

Fig. 13–14 Simplified view of propeller-shaft installation.

Types of Universal Joints

Various types of universal joints are available to connect the transmission of an automobile with its differential drive. The propeller shaft, whether solid or tubular, is connected at each end to a universal joint. As noted earlier, when an enclosed ball-and-trunnion universal joint is used, the joint is known as a torque-tube installation. Hotchkiss-drive installations have similar but exposed universal joints called

cross, spider, or needle-bearing joints, all of which are synonymous. The trunnion-and-bearing cap assembly is also called by various names, such as cross-and-bearing assembly, spider-and-bearing assembly, and needle-bearing assembly. The term cross type will be used here. The Hotchkiss drive system is most common.

Torque-tube universal joint. In the universal joint of Fig. 13-16 there are two bearing rings. These rings are similar and are fastened together by bolts. Each ring has four ears. In the assembled rings these ears form hubs into which the bushings are clamped.

The front and rear yokes have a pair of trunnions which project through corresponding bushings in the rings. The rings connect the yokes, but permit them relative motion in planes at right angles to each other.

In (a) the speedometer drive gear is shown attached to

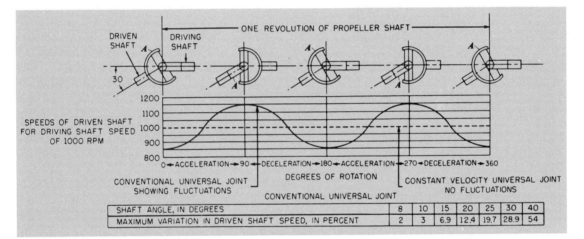

Fig. 13–15 Speed variations in conventional universal joint.

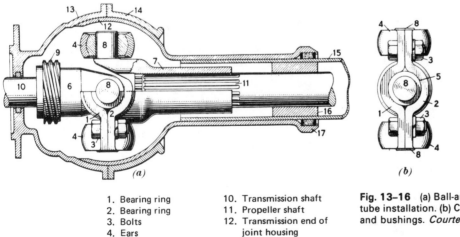

1. Bearing ring	10. Transmission shaft
2. Bearing ring	11. Propeller shaft
3. Bolts	12. Transmission end of joint housing
4. Ears	13. Slip coupling, or rear end of joint housing
5. Bushings	14. Retainer collar
6. Front yoke	15. Torque tube
7. Rear yoke	16. Bearing
8. Trunnions	17. Packing
9. Speedometer drive gear	

Fig. 13–16 (a) Ball-and-trunnion universal joint torque-tube installation. (b) Close-up of bearing rings, trunnions and bushings. *Courtesy of Borg-Warner Corporation.*

the hub of the yoke which is keyed to the end of the transmission shaft. The rear yoke fits the splined end of the propeller shaft.

The transmission and rear ends of the joint housing are semispherical and are joined by means of a retainer collar. A flange on the retainer collar is bolted to a similar flange on the front part of the housing by four cap screws (not shown). The retainer collar permits freedom of motion of the rear part of the housing, with the center of the housing as the center of motion.

The tubular extension of the rear housing fits over the front end of the torque tube. The *torque tube* encloses the propeller shaft, which is supported by a bearing. The packing prevents oil leakage along the propeller housing. The housing of the universal joint is connected directly to, and receives its lubrication from, the transmission case.

Hotchkiss-drive universal joints.   The universal joints we have selected for discussion are representative of joints used in Hotchkiss drive systems. Remember, however, many different universal joints are found in different makes of automobiles. The representative universal joints discussed here include the so-called Detroit joint and the Mechanics joint. The Detroit joint is produced by the Detroit Universal Division of the Chrysler Corporation, and the Mechanics joint is made by the Borg-Warner Corporation.

Detroit universal joint.   The Detroit universal joint, Fig. 13-17, features *needle bearings*, *centering caps* for centering the *pin* in the housing, and a combined *spring seat* and *grease-retainer cover*. There is no spring guide. *Thrust washers* are located between the end of the propeller shaft and the needle bearings.

As in other types of similar joints, the *front yoke* of the *front joint* is bolted to the transmission companion flange. A *dust boot*, clamped to the rear of the housing, keeps road dirt and moisture away from the splines.

The disassembly, reassembly, and lubrication instructions for the Detroit joint are as follows:

The first step in disassembly is to remove the bolts that hold the transmission adapter-flange assembly and the hous-

ing together and let the propeller shaft down carefully. To release the spring seat, gasket, and spring, break the flange connection and bend up the tabs on the grease-retainer cover. Lay these parts aside where they will not be lost. The housing should then be pushed back over the propeller shaft far enough to expose the joint assembly. After this, the centering cap and washers are removed, and the trunnion pin is pressed out of the end of the propeller shaft. Be careful not to lose any of the needle bearings (rollers) or the thrust washers during disassembly.

Wash all parts in clean gasoline and inspect them thoroughly for wear. No adjustment is provided for wear, and if excessive radial movement exists between the balls and the pin, replace the parts. A repair kit includes a boot, housing, spring seat and grease-retainer cover, spring, centering caps, gasket, balls, thrust washers, and needle bearings.

In some cases the housing may be worn to the extent that replacement is needed. A new boot can be installed by threading it over the trunnion pins and ballhead (flanged section of the propeller shaft) and through the housing. The inside of the body, ballhead, and boot must be covered with a light coating of grease before the new boot is installed. Be sure the small end of the boot is positioned properly after the boot is in place, and then clamp the large end of the boot to the housing. Assemble the thrust washers, balls, and centering button, and then clamp the small end of the boot to the ballhead.

For reassembly, reverse the disassembly instructions. It is necessary to slip the housing over the end of the propeller shaft before pressing the trunnion pin into place, as the opening in the outer end of the housing is too small to go over the pin.

Before reassembly the universal joint should be given two ounces of special universal or long fiber grease distributed evenly and equally in the two raceways. Replace the grease cover and gasket and bend the lugs into the notches in the body. Slide the body back and forth to distribute the grease.

Mechanics universal joints.   A typical Mechanics universal joint is shown in Figs. 13-18 and 13-19(a). The disassembly

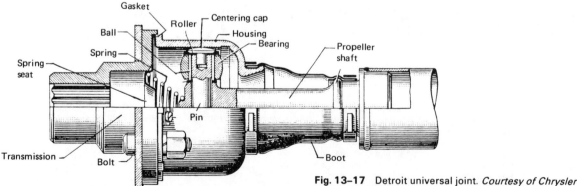

Fig. 13–17   Detroit universal joint. *Courtesy of Chrysler Motors Corporation.*

of the right-end companion flange, with the cross, bearing, lug, and washer is shown in Fig. 13-19(b). The joint consists of two flanges, Fig. 13-18, joined to a central unit, which consists of a steel-forged cross and four needle-bearing assemblies. The cross contains four trunnions, which are clearly visible in Fig. 13-19(b). The bearings (one of which is visible in Fig. 13-18) are sealed against the leakage of lubricant and the entry of dirt or water. A stamped metal retainer is pressed into the bearing housing and retains the cork washers and roller bearings in place.

The companion flange on the rear-axle pinion and the transmission shaft are provided with grooves. When the parts are assembled, lugs on two of the bearing housings fit into these grooves. Lugs from the other two bearing housings fit into similar grooves of the yoke on the universal joint. The companion flanges and yokes are undercut to ensure accurate centering of the bearing housings. Each bearing housing is fastened to the companion or yoke flanges by means of two bolts that are locked into place by a lock plate.

The instructions for the disassembly, assembly, and lubrication of the Mechanics universal joint are as follows: If the Mechanics universal joint shown in Figs. 13-18 and 13-19 is to be disassembled, it is not necessary to remove the propeller shaft since each joint may be disassembled sepa-

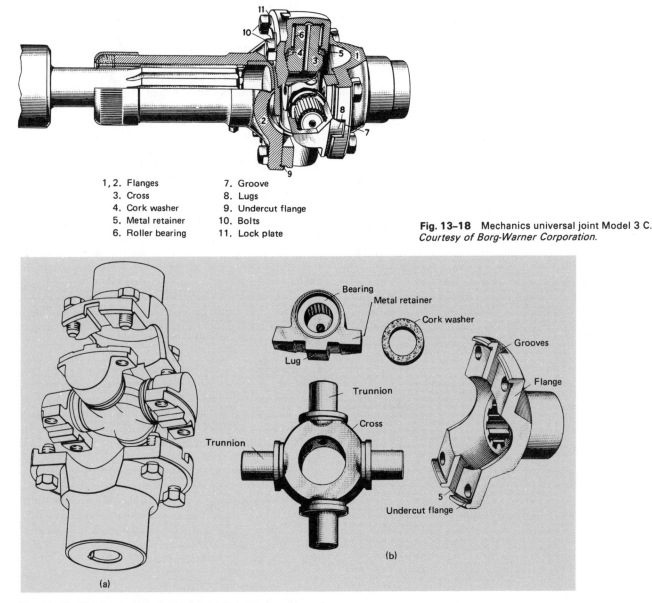

1, 2.	Flanges	7.	Groove
3.	Cross	8.	Lugs
4.	Cork washer	9.	Undercut flange
5.	Metal retainer	10.	Bolts
6.	Roller bearing	11.	Lock plate

Fig. 13-18 Mechanics universal joint Model 3 C. *Courtesy of Borg-Warner Corporation.*

Fig. 13-19 Mechanics universal joint. (a) Unit disassembly and (b) detail dissasembly. *Courtesy of Borg-Warner Corporation.*

rately. To disassemble a joint, it is necessary to remove only the eight retaining screws, pull the cross and bearing assemblies away from the flanges, and slip the bearing assemblies off the arms of the cross. Further disassembly is done by pulling off the retainers and the cork gaskets. If a joint is removed but is not to be disassembled, the bearing assemblies opposite each other should be clamped or tied together to keep them in place on the journals of the cross.

To disassemble the types of universal joints having cylindrical bearings locked by snap rings or clamps in one yoke, and wing-shaped bearing caps connected to the companion flange, first separate the joint by removing the four cap screws that hold the bearing caps to the companion flange, and remove the propeller shaft. If the bearings in the joint yoke are held in place by clamps, straighten out the prongs of the lock plates that hold the cap screws, unscrew the cap screws, and remove the clamps. If the bearings are held by lock rings, mount the universal joint in a vise and drive the lock rings out with a punch and a hammer.

With the clamps or lock rings removed, disassemble the remainder of the joint as follows: (1) Place the joint assembly in a brass or copper-jawed vise with the trunnions of the cross resting on the edges of the vise, as shown in Fig. 13-20. (2) Strike the suspended yoke with a babbitt hammer, and drive the yoke down until it makes contact with the cross; this will leave the upper bearing protruding as shown. (3) Turn the assembly over, and repeat the process on the other side, so that both bearings will be projecting beyond the ends of the yoke. (4) Using brass or copper jaws in the vise, clamp the projecting end of a bearing in the vise, and drive off the bearing with a babbitt hammer. Repeat the operation on the other bearing.

All parts of the universal joint are washed in clean gasoline and inspected for wear. If the trunnions of the cross show signs of wear, replace the complete cross assembly, including the gaskets, retainers, and snap rings or clamp plate.

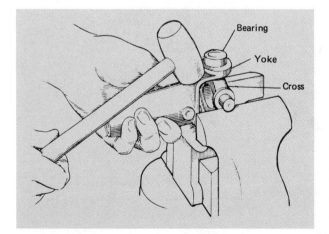

Fig. 13–20 Method of disassembling universal joint.

When reassembling cylindrical bearings in their yoke, place the cross in the yoke and partially assemble the bearings on the cross with new seal washers in place. Rest one of the bearings on a flat plate and strike the end of the upper bearing with a babbit hammer until both bearings are about flush with the ends of the yoke. Then lock the bearings in place with clamps or snap rings. Always use new snap rings, and make sure they are securely seated in the grooves in the bearings and against the inside surface of the yoke. If clamps are used, new lock plates should also be used. Be sure the lugs are bent up around the cap screws.

When reassembling the universal joint to the companion flange, make sure all screws are drawn up tight, and that the ears of the lock plates are turned up to lock the screw caps in place. Always use new lock plates.

The wing-shaped bearing caps are attached with heat-treated alloy-steel screws, having small heads for wrench clearance. Inferior screws should not be substituted for the original ones, and the screws must be tightened securely.

The Mechanics universal joint is generally packed with lubricant and sealed at assembly. Most often, no provision is made for later lubrication.

When a universal joint requiring lubricant must be serviced, use a good grade of "0" chassis lubricant. Grades 1 and 2 may be needed in hot weather and for heavy-duty service. These lubricants should have a high melting point and a fine fiber.

The interval between lubrications depends on the types of service. In general, an interval of 400 hours is satisfactory for normal service, but a 100-hour interval is recommended for heavy-duty service. When a joint is subjected to extremely severe operating conditions, more frequent lubrication may be needed.

CAUTION: Lubrication must be done with a low-pressure hand-type grease gun or with a high-pressure gun fitted with a low-pressure adapter. High pressure will rupture the front seals.

Constant velocity joint and center-support bearing. The constant velocity universal joint shown in Fig. 13-21 has *two single joints* connected with a special *link yoke*. A *center ball and socket* in the yoke maintains the relative position of the two universal joints. In other words, the center ball joint permits constant angles to exist between both universal joints. As a result, each universal joint operates through exactly half of the complete cycle *a* between the front and rear propeller shafts, respectively. Because the two joint angles *b* and *c* are the same, even though the universal joint fluctuation is present with the assembly, the acceleration of the front joint is compensated for by deceleration of the rear joint. Thus, a constant rpm and torque from the propeller shaft drives the rear wheels of the car.

The center support bearing is sealed and its inner race is held in place by a locknut against a shoulder at the rear end of the front propeller shaft. The outer race is set in a metal container to which is bonded a rubber support cush-

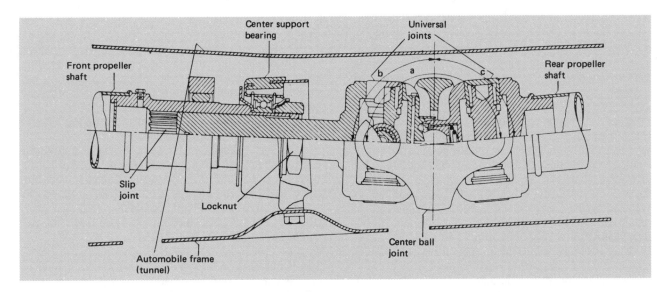

Fig. 13–21 Constant velocity joint and center-support bearing.
Courtesy of General Motors Corporation.

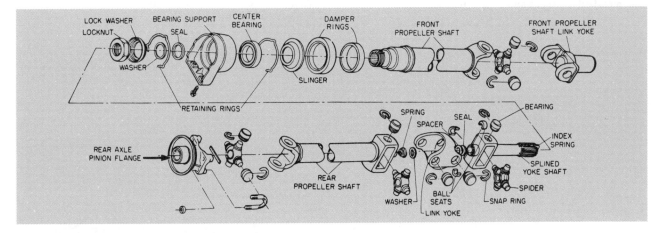

Fig. 13–22 Exploded view of typical propeller-shaft assembly.
Courtesy of General Motors Corporation.

ion. The cushion in turn is bonded to a support bracket bolted to the frame tunnel. The locknut, which keeps the center bearing in place, prevents the slip joint from separating. The seal that retains the lubricant in the splined slip joint is located inside the locknut.

The propeller shaft assembly requires little or no servicing, and the center support bearing never needs additional lubrication because it is given lifetime lubrication during production. The universal joints, also lubricated for life, cannot be lubricated while in the automobile. If a joint becomes worn or noisy, a service kit containing complete cross and bearing assemblies and snap rings is available.

The front and rear propeller shafts are available as com-

plete assemblies to permit balancing by the manufacturer. If the automobile is undercoated, care must be taken not to spray the propeller shaft, bearing, and joints. Undercoating of these parts will upset the balance and may cause serious vibration.

Propeller-Shaft Assemblies

A typical unit. The propeller shaft assembly, Fig. 13-22, includes front and rear shafts, a standard universal joint at each end, and a double, constant-velocity universal joint in the center.

A center support bearing secures the rear end of the

front propeller shaft to the frame tunnel. A splined front yoke on the front end of the rear propeller shaft extends to make up a slip-joint coupling in the rear end of the front propeller shaft. This slip joint permits a slight lengthening and shortening of the propeller shaft to accommodate road bounce.

Vibration. Vibration in a propeller shaft will occur from either an imbalance or an uncompensated joint angularity. Vibrations due to imbalance have a frequency equal to the number of revolutions of the propeller shaft and are called *first-order vibrations*. This means one vibration is produced during each revolution. When two pulses are produced, as indicated by the sine wave in Fig. 13-15, the vibrations are called *second-order vibrations*. The vibrations may be either torsional or transverse in nature. An unbalanced shaft produces only torsional vibration. Joint angularity produces both torsional and transverse vibrations.

The causes of vibration include the following: (1) imbalance in the propeller shaft; (2) excessive clearance due to wear in component parts; (3) runout in parts that support the shaft; (4) excessive speed, which causes the shaft to run at its so-called critical range; and (5) secondary forces due to joint angularity. Except for the last, the vibrations are of the first order, and their frequencies are the same as the frequency of the propeller shaft rpm.

To check for transverse vibration, accelerate the vehicle to high speed and then put the transmission in neutral. Since most states have laws that prohibit coasting, this test should be conducted on a roadway designed for testing and racing.

First-order vibrations are emphasized during coasting because the engine and transmission noises are absent.

Torsional (second-order) vibration is dependent on the joint angularity and the torque of the propeller drive shaft. Torsional vibration is identified by driving on a smooth road and working the throttle from high acceleration to zero acceleration. If torsional vibration is present, clicks and backlash will be heard during the load-to-no-load shift. The common cause for this condition is worn parts.

Troubleshooting guide. Table 13-1 lists the most common propeller shaft complaints, their causes, and remedies.

Shaft alignment. The alignment of the complete propeller shaft assembly is extremely important. Misalignment causes vibration and passenger annoyance. Always follow the manufacturer's specifications when aligning a propeller shaft.

Table 13-1 Propeller Shaft Troubleshooting Chart.

Complaint	Possible Cause	Remedy
Shudder as car accelerates from stop or low speeds	Incorrect plan view joint angles	Use alignment gauge cable and weighted strings from engine pulleys and propeller shaft to align shaft in plan view.
	Loose or missing bolts at center bearing support to frame tunnel	Tighten bolts.
	Incorrectly set front joint angle	Shim under transmission support mount to decrease front joint angle.
	Improperly adjusted joint angle	Check and adjust according to alignment gauge.
	Improper yoke phasing	Check for correct yoke phasing and correct if necessary.
Roughness or vibration at any speed	Bent shaft	Replace.
	Improper yoke phasing	Check for incorrect yoke phasing and correct if necessary.
	Cut center bearing support rubber	Replace.
	Dented shaft	Replace. Check to see if sufficient clearance exists between rear frame tunnel and propeller shaft if car is raised on a frame hoist. Grind out frame for sufficient clearance if necessary.
	Tight universal joints	Impact yokes with hammer to free up. Replace joint if unable to free up or if joint feels rough when rotated by hand.
	Improperly aligned support	Align or check for proper installation of mountings.

Table 13-1 Continued

Complaint	Possible Cause	Remedy
	Undercoating on shaft	Clean shaft.
	Worn universal joints	Replace.
	U-joint retainer bent against bearing cup	Replace.
	Incorrect rear joint angle (usually too large an angle)	Check and adjust according to alignment gauge.
	Tire unbalance	Balance wheel and tire assembly or replace from known good car.
	Burrs or gouges on companion flange snap ring location surfaces	Clean flange if possible, replace if necessary.
	Incorrect U-bolt torque	Check and correct (12 to 15 ft-lb.).
Roughness on heavy acceleration (short duration)	CV joint ball seats worn	Replace with ball seat repair kit.
	Seat spring set or broken	Replace with ball seat repair kit.
Roughness or vibration at any speed	Shaft or companion flange unbalance combination	1. Check for missing balance weights. 2. Remove and reassemble shaft to companion flange 180 deg. from initial location 3. Remove and replace companion flange on transmission output shaft or rear axle pinion 180 deg. from initial location. 4. Rebalance.
Whine or whistle	Center support bearing	Center support bearing may be noisy. Place car on hoist so rear wheels rotate, and replace if this is noise source.
Knock or click	Joint hitting frame tunnel	Shim up or replace center bearing mount.
	Worn CV joint centering ball	Replace with splined yoke or ball seat replacement kit.
	Loose upper or lower control arm bushing bolts	Tighten bolts.
	Broken or cut center-bearing support rubber	Replace center bearing support.
	Stones or gravel in frame tunnel	Remove foreign matter.
Boom period (30 to 40 mph) carrying heavy loads or hauling trailer	Excessive rear joint angle	Reduce angle.
Squeak	Lack of lubrication or worn CV joint centering ball	Lubricate, but replace with ball socket kit if squeak continues.
Scraping noise	Parking-brake cable interference in frame tunnel	Correctly route cable.
	Slinger on companion flange rubbing on rear axle carrier	Straighten out slinger to remove interference.
Roughness usually at low speeds, light load, 15 to 35 mph	Improperly adjusted joint angles	Check and adjust rear joint angle, decrease front angle by shimming transmission support.

14

MANUAL TRANSMISSIONS

CONSTRUCTION AND OPERATION

Why a Transmission is Needed

If you have ever set a car into motion without shifting from first, into second, and then into high gear, you know without my telling you why a transmission is required. Starting in high gear places a tremendous strain on the engine and, unless you are on a flat road, the engine will probably stall. To get a smooth start, some means is needed to multiply the torque (turning effort) of the engine. This is the job of the transmission.

Application of torque. With a shaft, such as an extension on an engine crankshaft, rotating at a given speed, different sized gears can be mounted on the shaft and produce varying results. A large gear will give more speed and less power at the rim of the gear than a smaller one.

A second shaft operating in parallel with the drive shaft, with the gears meshing on the two shafts, can attain practically any desired combination of speed and power (within the capability of the engine). This may be done simply by changing the sizes of the gears on either or both shafts. An automobile transmission operates in exactly this manner by using selected gear combinations.

Gears simply apply leverage to rotating parts and are an application of the lever and fulcrum principle. An ordinary lever has more power if the fulcrum is moved closer to the load to which power is applied. In Fig. 14-1(a), the fulcrum is placed very close to the load, and the lever must be moved a considerable distance to raise the load by an appreciable amount. In (b), the fulcrum is farther from the load and the lever must move a shorter distance than in (a) to raise the load to a given height. The distance between the fulcrum and the load, and the distance between the center and rim of a gear, are comparable. Thus, a small gear will drive a large gear more slowly but with greater power.

In an automobile the gear sizes are selected to give the best performance under a variety of driving conditions. Power may be sacrificed for greater speed, or vice versa. The final choice of gears is a compromise that provides sufficient power and speed to satisfy the needs and desires of the driver.

Reversing gear. A four-cycle automotive engine cannot be reversed. To drive the car backward, therefore, it is necessary to change the direction of rotation of the driving wheels by reversing the direction of rotation of the propeller shaft. The mechanism that accomplishes this reversal is called the *reversing gear* and is used in all transmissions.

Transmissions. The model-T Ford was the first car to be equipped with a planetary-gear transmission that provided a two-speed shift. Next came the sliding-gear transmission. Today, the synchromesh transmission is used exclusively. In the synchromesh transmission, the gears are brought to the same speed, that is, they are *synchronized*. The use of synchromesh transmissions eliminates the irritating clashing of gears associated with the older forms of transmissions.

Although the great majority of manual transmissions are of the three-speed variety, four-speed transmissions have become quite popular on cars made in the United States. The four-speed transmission is similar to the three-speed variety but another gear is added between second and high.

Gear Ratios

Gear ratios can be determined by counting the number of teeth on a pair of meshing gears. If the drive gear has 20 teeth and the driven gear has 40 teeth, the gear ratio is 2 to 1. If the drive gear has 40 teeth and the driven gear has 20 teeth, the gear ratio is 1 to 2. The transmission gear ratio should not be confused with the final drive ratio, which refers to the overall ratio between engine revolutions and the rear wheel revolutions. The overall ratio includes the ratio between the drive pinion on the propeller shaft and the ring gear in the differential, as well as the transmission gear ratio.

Any discussion of transmissions involves reference to gear ratios and rear-axle ratios. The gear ratio in any type of transmission (manual or automatic) indicates how many times the engine revolves while the propeller shaft, which drives the rear axle, revolves once. The propeller shaft, of course, completes the power link between the transmission and rear axle. The rear-axle ratio is the number of times that the propeller shaft turns for each revolution of the rear axle (or rear wheels).

For example, a typical three-speed transmission has the following gear ratios: low (first) gear, 2.605 to 1; second gear, 1.630 to 1; third (high) gear, 1 to 1 (direct drive); and reverse gear, 3.536 to 1.

Thus, when the engine makes 2.605 rpm with the transmission in low gear, the propeller shaft makes one revolution. In second gear, the engine makes 1.630 rpm to one revolution of the propeller shaft. In high gear the engine turns once for each turn of the propeller shaft.

The propeller shaft drives the rear axle through a bevel-gear set, or the equivalent. The small gear on the propeller shaft is called the *pinion*, and the larger gear on the rear axle is called the *ring gear*. Because the ring gear is larger than the propeller-shaft gear, another change in ratio, called the *axle ratio*, is present. A typical axle ratio is 3.08 to 1, which means that the propeller shaft turns 3.08 times for

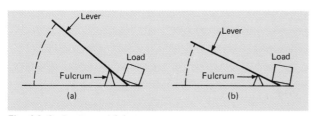

Fig. 14–1 Lever and fulcrum.

each turn of the rear axle. Generally, in speaking of any gear ratio in a car, the word one is omitted because the ratios are based on one turn. Thus, instead of saying the ratio is 3.08 to 1, you can simply say the ratio is 3.08.

Rear-axle speed.   To know the number of revolutions an engine makes for each turn of the rear wheels, simply multiply the gear ratio by the axle ratio. Using the typical ratios given above, when the transmission is in low gear the engine must turn $2.605 \times 3.08 = 8.0234$ (approximately 8) revolutions to one for the wheels. With the transmission in high, the gear ratio is 1, so the engine turns $1 \times 3.08 = 3.08$ (approximately 3) for every turn of the rear axle.

SYNCHROMESH TRANSMISSIONS

Introduction

In a synchromesh transmission the gears are in constant mesh but can run free until a shift is made. The gear selected is locked in the gear train by a positive clutching device after the gear is brought to the same (synchronous) speed.

Synchromesh transmissions employ helical gears for easier shifting and quieter in-mesh operation.

Operation

The simplified diagram of Fig. 14-2 shows how a synchromesh transmission operates. For the sake of clarity, only the *second-* and *high-speed gears,* the *countershaft,* and the *clutching mechanism* are shown. When the transmission is in neutral, there is no power flow; the engine clutch is depressed and the *main drive shaft* is disconnected from the engine. The driven shaft is connected to the propeller shaft, which drives the rear axle. The propeller shaft is turned by the momentum of the car once the vehicle is in motion. The driven shaft is not connected to the main drive shaft. Instead, it turns freely in a bearing located between those two shafts. In the illustration, this bearing is hidden by the *high-speed gear,* which is part of the main drive shaft and in constant mesh with the high-speed gear on the countershaft.

High-speed and second-speed gears are keyed to the countershaft and are integral with it. The second-speed gear on the countershaft is in constant mesh with the second-speed gear on the driven shaft, but is separated from it by a bearing so that it rotates freely in the neutral position.

When a shift is made to second gear, the gearshift lever moves the synchromesh clutch to the right where it locks the second-speed gear to the driven shaft. This is accomplished by means of splines on the driven shaft which carries the synchromesh clutch. The high-speed gear on the main drive shaft meshes with, and drives, the high-speed gear on the countershaft. The second-speed gear on the countershaft drives the second-speed gear on the driven shaft. The second-speed gear is now locked on the driven shaft by the synchromesh clutch. This completes the transmission of power from the main drive shaft to the driven shaft. Because the high-speed gear on the main drive shaft is smaller than the high-speed gear on the countershaft, and the second-speed gear on the countershaft is smaller than the second-speed gear on the driven shaft, the speed of the driven shaft is slower than that of the drive shaft. As a result, torque is increased.

In high speed, the synchromesh clutch moves to the left and locks the driven shaft to the high-speed gear. The flow of power then goes directly from the main drive shaft to the driven shaft, and both shafts turn at the same speed. Although the countershaft and its gears continue to spin, no power is transmitted through them.

The operation just described is typical of all synchromesh units. Although such units vary in design, all of them depend on the locking or unlocking of gears by the clutching mechanism for their operation. Additional speed combinations are obtained with additional locking devices and gear combinations.

Identifying Component Parts

Figure 14-3 shows an assembled view of a Pontiac three-speed transmission (minus the casing). The important parts and subassemblies are identified. Study this illustration carefully. Unfortunately, the same name is not always used to identify a component that does a particular job. For this reason, a short glossary of transmission terms is given here:

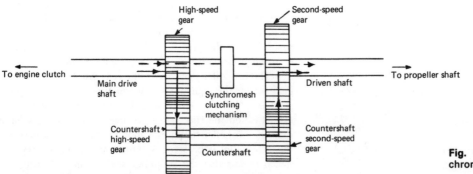

Fig. 14–2 Simplified view of synchromesh transmission.

blocking ring – This ring, also called a *stop ring*, synchronizes the speed of a synchromesh unit and the gear selected. Internal cones on the rings contact external cones on the extensions of the second- or high-speed gears. Friction between the cones causes the gear and synchromesh unit to turn at the same speed.

countergear – A gear mounted on the countershaft that is driven by the main drive gear. Other gears on the countershaft drive gears on the main shaft when the main-shaft gears are shifted. This reduces the speed of the vehicle and increases power.

countershaft – The shaft in the transmission that is driven by the main drive gear.

dummy shaft – A shaft, or arbor, used to hold the rollers of a needle bearing in place when disassembling transmissions that contain needle bearings.

drift – A metal rod or pin used to drive out or reseat a gear or shaft. A drift is usually struck with a hammer and is made of metal that is softer than the parts it comes in contact with.

main drive shaft – A short shaft with splines on one end and a helical gear on the other, which drives the countershaft. The gear end of this shaft is bored to receive the end of the main shaft inside the transmission and has needle bearings on which the main shaft turns. This shaft is also called the clutch shaft, input shaft, and drive pinion and clutch gear.

main shaft – The shaft located inside the transmission case on which is mounted the synchromesh units, the second-speed and high-speed gears, and the speedometer drive gear. This shaft is supported at one end by a recess in the main drive shaft and by a ball bearing at the other end. It extends into the transmission extension housing and is attached to the propeller shaft.

reverse idler gear – Usually a sliding gear mounted on a short, separate shaft below or behind the countershaft.

When this gear is brought into mesh in the gear train, it reverses the direction in which the main shaft turns and, therefore, the direction in which the rear wheels rotate.

shifting plates – Also called *inserts* or *keys*. Rectangular steel plates that are held outward by a spring. Plates are installed in the synchronizer hub. When a shift is made, the plate acts as a detent to lock the selected gear into slots in the blocking ring.

spline – A slot or goove cut into a shaft or a bore. Also, a splined shaft onto which a hub or gear, with matching splines in its bore, is assembled so that the two splined parts must rotate together.

synchromesh clutch – Synchromesh unit assembly.

synchromesh clutch gear – The gear on which the synchronizing sleeve (clutch gear) rides.

synchronizing sleeve – A sleeve having internal splines which slide over the synchronizer hub to lock the gear in the synchronizing operation. Also called a clutch sleeve or a clutch-sleeve gear.

synchronous – Occuring at the same time. For example, gears that are about to mesh and are rotating at the same speed to avoid gear clashing, are synchronous.

The component parts of a typical four-speed transmission are shown in Fig. 14-4. The only significant difference between a three-speed and four-speed transmission is that an additional gear is added for the high speed. This and similar illustrations are used later to identify the parts discussed in repair procedures. Become familiar now with the name, location, and function of the parts, and you will find it easy to follow the later discussions.

The parts shown in Fig. 14-4 are typical of those found in all manual transmissions. The transmission case and extension housing contain all of the parts shown beneath them when the transmission is in operating condition. The input shaft and main drive gear are connected to the engine clutch assembly and are driven by the engine. The input shaft turns in a ball bearing mounted in the front wall of the transmission case and held in place by a retaining nut and a front bearing retainer which is bolted to the case. A gasket is used between the retainer and the case. The main shaft extends from the input shaft, through the transmission case, and into the extension housing.

A detailed view of the input shaft is shown in Fig. 14-5. The shaft is bored concentrically to accommodate the end of the main shaft. The bore contains the bearing rollers that make up the needle bearing into which the main shaft fits. The bearing rollers are shown in place in the bore. In Fig. 14-4 the roller bearings are shown disassembled. The main drive gear, Fig. 14-5, is shown in place on the input shaft.

When assembled, the main shaft of a three-speed transmission carries the second-and-high-speed synchronizer, the second-speed gear, first-speed gear, low-and-reverse gear, and speedometer gear. The main shaft of a four-speed transmission, such as that shown in Fig. 14-4, carries the third-

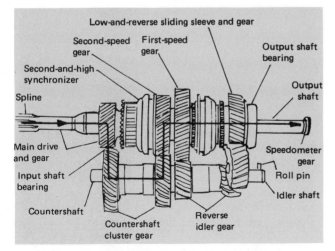

Fig. 14–3 Assembled view of a Pontiac three-speed transmission (minus the casing).

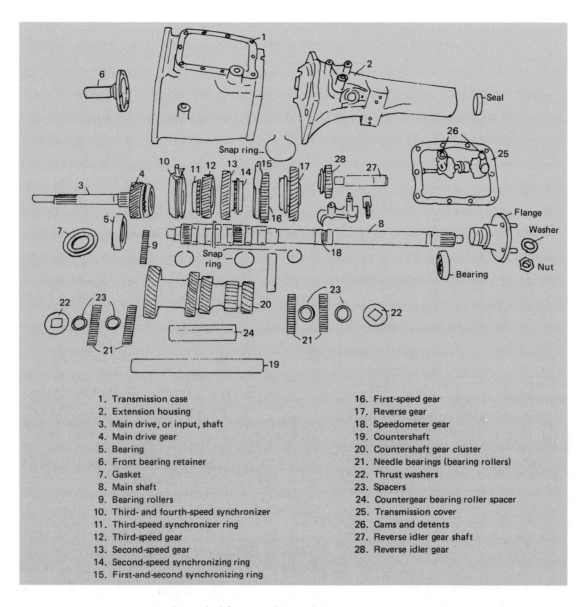

1. Transmission case
2. Extension housing
3. Main drive, or input, shaft
4. Main drive gear
5. Bearing
6. Front bearing retainer
7. Gasket
8. Main shaft
9. Bearing rollers
10. Third- and fourth-speed synchronizer
11. Third-speed synchronizer ring
12. Third-speed gear
13. Second-speed gear
14. Second-speed synchronizing ring
15. First-and-second synchronizing ring
16. First-speed gear
17. Reverse gear
18. Speedometer gear
19. Countershaft
20. Countershaft gear cluster
21. Needle bearings (bearing rollers)
22. Thrust washers
23. Spacers
24. Countergear bearing roller spacer
25. Transmission cover
26. Cams and detents
27. Reverse idler gear shaft
28. Reverse idler gear

Fig. 14–4 Component parts of a typical four-speed transmission. *Courtesy of Pontiac Division, General Motors Corporation.*

and-fourth-speed synchronizer, third-speed synchronizing ring, third-speed gear, second-speed gear, second-speed synchronizing ring, first-and-second-speed synchronizer, first-speed gear, reverse gear, and the speedometer gear.

In Fig. 14-4 the countershaft carries the countershaft gear cluster for second, third, low, and reverse speeds. Each end of the countershaft is supported by a needle bearing. A thrust washer and spacer are also placed on each end of the countershaft. The countergear bearing roller fits over the countershaft. The cover, which fits the top of the transmission case, has been turned over to show the cams and detents that operate the shift rails and shift forks. The reverse idler gear shaft and the reverse idler gear are a separate assembly located beside the countershaft. The reverse

shifter fork and reverse lever are mounted in the transmission case.

Shift rails, forks, and detent plugs. The cams and detents, Fig. 14-4, require linkages to operate them. The linkages attached to the cams connect with the steering wheel shift lever or with the shift lever located on the floor. In other transmissions, shifting cranks are used to operate the rails and forks. If the shift lever is located on the steering wheel (remote-control shifting), the linkages are comparatively long and somewhat complicated. Those connected to a floor shift are shorter and less complicated.

Figure 14-6 is an exploded view of the shifting mechanism of a three-speed transmission. In this illustration, the

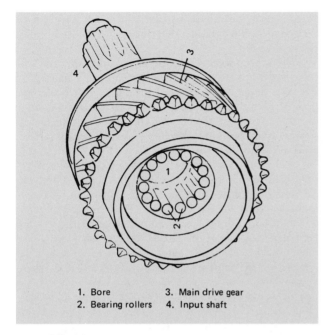

1. Bore 3. Main drive gear
2. Bearing rollers 4. Input shaft

Fig. 14–5 Main drive assembly of three-speed synchromesh transmission, simplified. *Courtesy of Pontiac Division, General Motors Corporation.*

front of the transmission case faces to the right. The shift forks are identified as the *second-and-third shift fork* and the first-and-reverse shift fork. The second-and-third shift fork is mounted on the *second-and-third shift rail* and is held in place on the rail by a *setscrew*. The first-and-reverse fork is mounted on the first-and-reverse shift rail and is also held in place by a setscrew. Each rail has a detent spring and plug which locks the rail in place.

When the second-and-third shift rail is installed, the detent plug and spring are inserted in the detent bore in the transmission case. The rail is inserted through the hole in the front of the transmission and through the hole in the fork and is aligned with the hole inside the case as indicated by the dashed line. The rail is turned until the notch is aligned with the detent bore into which the detent plug fits. The fork is then secured to the rail by the setscrew.

The first-and-reverse shift rail is inserted from the back of the transmission. The interlock plug is then inserted in the detent bore. Again the low-and-reverse rail is inserted in the back of the transmission case and through the hole in the low-and-reverse shift fork and aligned with the hole inside the case. The rail is turned until the center notch in the rail is aligned with the detent bore. The detent plug and spring are then inserted in the bore. The plug fits into the notch in the first-and-reverse shift rail. With the rails and forks in place, the slotted head setscrew is installed in the detent bore and tightened until the head is flush with the edge of the transmission case. Whenever the rails are removed, the expansion plugs are driven out. At reassembly, new plugs should be used. An expansion plug is shown near the end of the second-and-third shift rail.

Pontiac Transmissions

Three-speed synchromesh. The Pontiac three-speed synchromesh transmission utilizes the shifting-plate type of synchromesh unit, and all forward speeds are synchronized. The reverse gear is a sliding gear.

Before the transmission can be disassembled, it must be removed from the car. Refer to Figs. 14-3, 14-5, and 14-6 throughout the discussion.

To remove the transmission, raise the front of the car

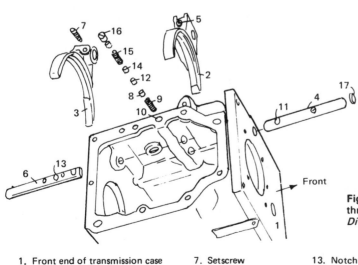

Front

Fig. 14–6 Exploded view of shifting mechanism of Pontiac three-speed synchromesh transmission. *Courtesy of Pontiac Division, General Motors Corporation.*

1. Front end of transmission case
2. Second-and-third shift fork
3. First-and-reverse shift fork
4. Second-and-third shift rail
5. Setscrew
6. First-and-reverse shift rail
7. Setscrew
8. Detent plug
9. Spring
10. Detent bore
11. Notch
12. Interlock plug
13. Notch
14. Detent plug
15. Spring
16. Setscrew
17. Expansion plug

to provide working room underneath. Place a floor jack under the lower control arm of each front wheel. Disconnect the universal joint, speedometer cable, shift linkages, and wires leading to the backup light switch. Remove the upper screws that attach the transmission case to the clutch housing and insert guide pins in the screw holes to take the weight off the main drive shaft. Place a support under the engine before removing the lower screws. Now remove the lower screws and slide the transmission back to free the input shaft from the clutch housing. Lower the transmission to the floor, and then move it to a work bench.

After draining the lubricant and removing the case cover and gasket, remove the input shaft bearing retainer and gasket and the extension housing and gasket. The retaining pin that holds the countershaft to the case is driven out by inserting a drift pin through the filler hole cover in the transmission case. At the top of the transmission case, Fig. 14-6, there is a setscrew which must be removed. Remove this setscrew and take out the spring, detent plug, and interlock plug. Shift the transmission to neutral and remove the shift forks from the rails. Push the first-and-reverse shift rail off of the rear of the case. A special tool is needed to rotate by 90° the second-and-third shift rail to disengage the detent plunger. With a brass drift pin, drive the rail and expansion plug out of the front of the transmission case. The expansion plug fits the hole in the transmission case through which the shift rail is removed.

By using a dummy shaft, drive the countershaft out of the rear of the case. Hold or support the cluster gear with a hook to keep it from dropping into the case. After removing the countershaft, lower the countergear to the bottom of the transmission case. Remove the speedometer drive gear, snap ring, drive gear, and retaining ball. Then remove the snap ring and the rear bearing. Slide the input shaft forward until the main drive gear rests against the transmission case. Remove the shift forks and the main shaft assembly through the top of the case.

Take out the large snap ring from the input shaft and remove the countergear and thrust washers. With a brass drift and a hammer, drive the reverse idler gear out of the transmission case and lift out the gear and thrust washers. Starting with the front blocking ring, Fig. 14-7, disassemble the main shaft.

Clean the transmission case thoroughly with a suitable solvent and then dry the case with compressed air. Inspect the case for cracks or stripped threads in bolt holes, and examine all machined mating surfaces for burrs and nicks or any other condition that renders the case unfit for further service. If any burrs are present on the front mating surface, remove them with a fine mill file.

Ball bearings should be washed in a clean solvent and dried with compressed air. Do not spin the bearings with air pressure, since spinning unlubricated bearings may cause damage to the races and balls. Turn the bearing slowly by hand during drying. Now lubricate the bearings with a light grade of engine oil. Also, inspect the bearings for roughness by turning the outer race slowly by hand. Measure the fit of bearings on their respective shafts. Where needle bearing rollers and spacers are used, inspect the bearing rollers for flat spots or damage. Inspect all bearing roller spacers for signs of wear (galling). Defective rollers should be replaced with new ones.

Inspect the gear teeth on the synchronizer clutch gears and stop rings for chipped or excessively worn teeth. Replace any defective units. Be sure the clutch sleeve slides easily on the clutch gear. Also, inspect the countershaft gear and all sliding gears for chipped, broken, or worn teeth. Remove small nicks or burrs with a fine abrasive stone. If the teeth on the main drive pinion are worn excessively, broken, or chipped, install a new pinion.

Test the interlock sleeve and the pin for free movement in the bore of the shift housing. The detent balls should show no sign of damage. If the lever detents are worn to where they will not lock in gear, install a new part. Inspect the shift forks carefully.

Examine the gear teeth and the threads on the synchronizer inner stop rings for broken teeth or worn threads. Look at the shifter plates on the synchronizer outer stop ring assembly, Fig. 14-7, to make sure they are straight and securely attached. Replace defective parts as required.

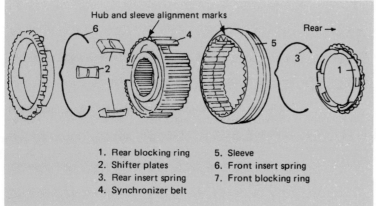

1. Rear blocking ring
2. Shifter plates
3. Rear insert spring
4. Synchronizer belt
5. Sleeve
6. Front insert spring
7. Front blocking ring

Fig. 14-7 Component parts of the Pontiac main shaft. *Courtesy of Pontiac Division, General Motors Corporation.*

If the contact surfaces of the main gear shaft show signs of excessive wear, install a new main shaft. Use a very fine abrasive such as crocus cloth to smooth any rough or burred edges in the snap ring grooves. Also, look for burrs on the synchronizer clutch gear teeth.

To reassemble the main shaft, first install the rear insert spring in the groove in the low-and-reverse synchronizer hub. Make sure the spring covers the entire insert groove. If the tips of the insert spring are less than 0.120 inch apart, replace the spring.

When indexing the alignment marks on the hub and sleeve, start the hub into the sleeve and position the three shifter plates in the hub with the small end of the plate over the spring and the shoulder of the plate on the inside of the hub. Now slide the sleeve over the hub until the detent takes hold and install the front insert spring in the hub.

The assembly of the second-and-third-speed synchronizer is similar to that of the low-and-reverse gear. Install one insert spring in the hub groove, making sure all three slots for the shifting plates are covered. Match alignment on hub and sleeve and start the hub into the sleeve.

Put the three shifting plates in the slots on top of the retaining spring and push the assembly together. Place the remaining insert spring so that the spring ends cover the same slots as the other spring. Do not stagger the springs. Now place a blocking ring on each end of the synchronizer sleeve. Refer to Fig. 14-7.

Lubricate the main shaft splines and other machined surfaces with an approved transmission lubricant and slide the low-and-reverse gear and sleeve onto the main shaft with the toothed end of the gear facing toward the rear (right end) of the shaft. Fasten the gear with the snap ring.

Coat the tapered machined surface on the first-speed gear with cup grease and place the blocking ring on the greased surface. Slide the gear onto the main shaft with the blocking ring toward the rear. Rotate the gear until the three notches in the blocking ring engage the three synchronizer shifter plates. Fasten the first gear with a thrust washer and snap ring.

Grease the second-speed gear in the same manner and slide the blocking ring onto it. Slide the blocking ring, the gear, and the second-and-high-speed gear synchronizer onto the main shaft with the tapered machined surface toward the front of the shaft. Make sure the notches in the blocking ring engage the inserts.

To reinstall the transmission, first place the reverse idler gear, with a thrust washer on each end of the idler shaft, in the transmission case. A roll pin at one end seats in a slot in the back of the case.

Assemble the countergear with the dummy shaft, bearings, and thrust washers and place it in the bottom of the case until the main and input shafts have been installed.

Coat the bore of the input shaft and the main drive gear with a thin film of grease. Be sure the film is thin; a thick grease coating may block the lubricant holes and keep lubricant from reaching the bearings. Install the fifteen bearing rollers in the bore. Since these bearing rollers have no cage or special races, they are held in place by the so-called *keystone effect*. To insert them, hold the shaft in a vertical position with the bore up. The light layer of grease in the bore will prevent the rollers from moving until the keystone effect takes place. Insert the input shaft and the bearing through the top of the transmission case and into the hole in front of the case. Secure the shaft with a large snap ring. Position the main shaft assembly in the case and install the second-and-high shift fork on the second-and-high synchronizer. Insert a detent plug and spring in the detent bore of the case and move the second-and-high synchronizer to second-speed position (toward the rear of the case).

Align the second-and-high shift fork to install the second-and-third shift rail. To install this rail into the bore, depress the detent spring by inserting a drift pin into the bore. Then push the detent rail in until the detent plug engages the forward notch on the rail. Now secure the shift fork to the shift rail with the setscrew in the fork. After moving the synchronizer to the neutral position, install the interlock plug in the case. When the second-and-third shift rail is in neutral, the top of the interlock will be slightly below the surface of the first-and-reverse shift rail bore.

After moving the first-and-reverse synchronizer forward, place the corresponding shift fork in the groove in the sleeve of the synchronizer. Align the shift fork and install the first-and-reverse shift rail. Move the rail until the center notch is aligned with the detent bore, and then install the remaining detent plug and spring. Secure the spring with the slotted head setscrew by turning it until the head is flush with the edge of the case. Position the shift fork on the shift rail and tighten the setscrew. Finally, install a new shift rail expansion plug in front of the case. While holding the blocking ring and input shaft in position, move the main shaft forward until it is seated in the needle bearing in the bore of the input shaft.

Tap the input shaft bearing into its socket in the case and at the same time hold the main shaft in place to prevent the rollers in the bore from dropping out. Install the front bearing retainer and new gasket, making sure that the oil return slot faces to the bottom of the case. Tighten the attaching screws with a torque wrench (19 to 25 foot-pounds). Fasten the large snap ring on the rear bearing. Position the bearing on the output shaft with the snap ring toward the rear of the shaft, and install the speedometer drive gear.

Now lift the countergear from the bottom of the case and align it and the thrust washers with the bore in the case. Insert the countershaft from the rear of the case and push the dummy shaft out of the countergear. Be sure the locking pin hole in the shaft lines up with the locking pin hole in the case. Drive the shaft into place and lock it with the locking pin. Of course, make sure that all gears that should mesh are actually in mesh. Coat a new extension housing gasket with sealer and install it on the transmission case. Also dip the threads of the attaching screws in sealer. Torque the screws to between 40 and 50 foot-pounds. Install the filler and drain plugs, making sure the magnetic drain plug is in the bottom of the case. Fill the case with approved lubricant to the correct level and install the transmission in the vehicle.

Four-speed synchromesh. The Pontiac four-speed synchromesh transmission is similar to the three-speed one. All forward speeds have synchromesh operation. This transmission usually has a floor shift lever.

The disassembly and reassembly sequences are very similar to those followed for the three-speed transmission except that this transmission has three shift forks instead of two. Also, one synchromesh unit handles third and fourth speeds and another unit handles first and second speeds. A separate fork is used for reverse.

The following suggestions should be considered before overhauling the four-speed transmission.

1. Use new snap rings, oil seals, and gaskets.
2. Remove the speedometer drive gear from the main shaft with a special gear puller. Consult the manufacturer's shop manual for detailed instructions.

3. The clutch hubs and sliding sleeves of the synchromesh units are a selective fit. These parts should be kept together as originally assembled to avoid unnecessary refitting. The three shifting plates and the two springs may be replaced if worn or broken.

4. The reverse idler gear bushings are pressed into the gear, peened, and then bored in place to ensure proper alignment and proper gear meshing.

5. Use a narrow feeler gauge to check for excessive wear between the shaft and the bushing. This clearance should be between 0.003 and 0.005 inch.

6. The snap ring installed in the main shaft behind the rear bearing is a selective fit. The rings are made in diameters of 0.087, 0.090, 0.093, and 0.096 inch. To obtain the proper sized ring, measure the clearance. It should run between 0.003 and 0.005 inch.

A cutaway view of the transmission is shown in Fig. 14-8.

To remove the transmission, first disconnect the speedometer cable, shift control rods, and wire to the backup

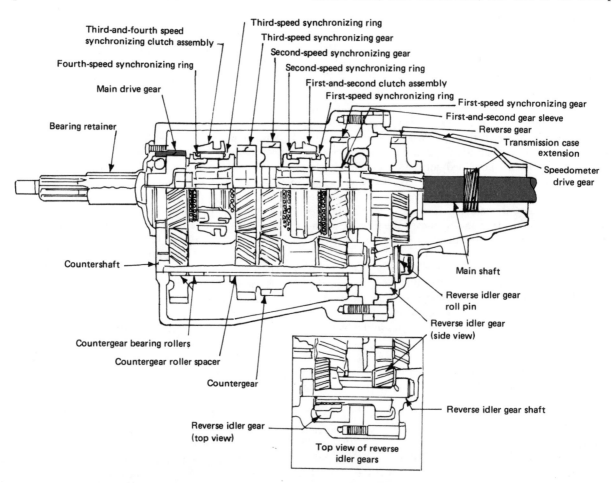

Fig. 14—8 Cutaway view of Pontiac four-speed synchromesh transmission. *Courtesy of Pontiac Division, General Motors Corporation.*

light switch. Remove the transmission drain plug and drain the case. Then remove the manual shift lever and bracket. Disconnect and remove the propeller drive line assembly. Remove the U-bolt nuts, the lock plates, and the U-bolts from the rear axle drive pinion flange and secure the bearings to their journals with a heavy rubber band. Now slide the drive line assembly rearward to disconnect the yoke from the splines on the end of the main shaft.

With an adequate support at the rear of the engine, remove two transmission extension housing insulator crossmember retaining bolts. Remove the two top bolts that hold the transmission housing to the clutch housing and insert two aligning studs in the bolt holes to support the transmission and prevent springing of the clutch disk. The two lower bolts can now be removed and the transmission pulled from the chassis.

Prior to disassembly, note that the shifting mechanism for the forward speeds is in the side cover of the transmission case. Remove the cover. The forks, levers, detent cams, cranks, and detent spring are disassembled readily. Take off the snap ring from the rear spline of the main shaft with a pair of snap ring pliers. With a special wrench available at supply houses, remove the main drive gear retaining nut after locking the transmission by shifting into two gears. This particular nut has a left-hand thread, and it must be turned clockwise (as viewed from the front) to remove it.

Now shift the gears into neutral and drive out the lockpin from the bottom of the reverse shift lever boss. Removing the pin disengages the reverse shift fork from the reverse gear.

Notice in Fig. 14-8 that the reverse gear, idler gear, shaft, and reverse shift fork (not shown) are in the extension housing of the transmission case. Unbolt the case extension and tap it with a soft hammer to loosen it. As the extension housing is pulled off, move it to the right so that the reverse fork disengages and clears the reverse gear. Then remove the reverse idler gear and the tanged thrust washer. To remove the speedometer drive gear, use a gear puller since this gear is pressed on the main shaft.

After moving the third-and-fourth synchromesh clutch sleeve to fourth-speed position, which is to the left in Fig. 14-8, remove the rear bearing retainer and the complete main shaft assembly by tapping the bearing retainer with a soft hammer.

Remove the seventeen bearing rollers from the bore in the input shaft, and disengage the fourth-speed synchronizing ring. Lift out the reverse idler gear and the thrust washer. After removing the main drive gear retaining nut, tap out the main drive gear by using a soft hammer to hit the front of the shaft. Then tap out the bearing and the snap ring from inside the transmission case. To remove the countershaft use an arbor; tap it with a hammer to drive out the shaft while working from the front of the case. The arbor (dummy shaft) holds the bearing rollers in the countergear. Remove the 80 rollers, the 0.050-inch spacers, and the roller spacer from the countergear.

Remove the snap ring from the front of the main shaft and slide the third-and-fourth-speed synchromesh clutch assembly, the third-speed gear, and the synchronizing ring from the front of the shaft. Spread the main shaft rear bearing retainer ring and, by means of an arbor press, push the main shaft out of the retainer. The synchromesh clutches are disassembled and reassembled in the same manner described for the three-speed transmission.

Clean all parts with solvent and inspect all parts, especially the ball bearings, for breakage or excessive wear. Replace parts as necessary.

The first step in reassembly is to place the second-speed gear on the main shaft from the rear with the hub to the rear of the transmission. Next, the first-and-second-speed synchronizer clutch assembly is assembled from the front of the transmission with the sleeve taper to the rear. The keyways must line up with the shifter keys. Press the first-speed gear sleeve onto the main shaft. A piece of pipe of proper length and with an inside diameter of 1¼ inches is a handy tool, and it can be tapped with a hammer if no arbor is available. A piece of pipe with an inside diameter of 1⅝ inches is useful for installing the rear bearing. The snap ring groove should be toward the front of the transmission.

Obtain the correct selective-fit snap ring for the groove in the main shaft behind the rear bearing. If the distance from the snap ring to the rear face of the bearing is between zero and 0.005 inch, then the proper snap ring is being used. Always use new snap rings and do not expand them more than necessary to avoid deforming them.

Next, install the third-speed gear with its hub to the front, the third-speed synchronizing ring with its notches to the front, and the third-and-fourth gear synchronizing unit with the hub and bolt sleeve taper toward the front. Make sure the shifter plates line up with notches in the blocking ring. Secure them with the snap ring on the main shaft in front of the synchromesh unit.

Install the rear bearing retainer and secure it with a snap ring that is spread until it drops around the rear bearing. Then press on the main shaft until the ring engages the grooves in the bearing.

Press on the speedometer drive gear and install the roller spacer in the countergear. Replace the 80 rollers and the spacers in the countergear. Use grease to hold the rollers in place, but make sure the lubricating holes are not blocked by the grease before inserting the dummy shaft.

To start the countergear assembly, place the countergear tanged thrust washers in the case with the tangs resting in the notches. A little heavy grease applied to the washers will hold them in place. Set the countergear in the bottom of the case and lubricate the countershaft before inserting it through the hole in the rear of the case. By inserting the countershaft, the dummy shaft is pushed out the front of the case. Turn the countershaft so that the flat spot is horizontal and facing the bottom of the case. In this position it lines up with the rear bearing retainer. Check the end play of the countergear with a dial indicator. If the end play is greater than 0.025 inch, use new thrust washers.

Install the bearing rollers in the bore of the main drive gear by using a heavy grease to keep the rollers and cage from moving. Put the gear into place through the side opening in the case. The fourth-speed synchronizing ring goes on the main drive gear with the notches toward the rear.

Place the reverse idler gear thrust washer (which is tanged on the machined face of the gear case) in the case for the reverse idler shaft and hold it in place with grease. Install the front reverse idler gear next to the washer with its hub to the rear of the case. Move the third-and-fourth synchromesh clutch sleeve to the fourth-speed detent position (forward). Turn the case so that it rests on its front face. Lower the main shaft with assembled gears and synchromesh units into the case with the front of the shaft entering the bearing in the main drive shaft. The shifting plates should enter the notches in the synchronizing ring. Install the rear bearing retainer and align the guide pin with the hole in the rear of the case before tapping the retainer into place. Insert the rear reverse idler gear by engaging its splines with the internal splines of the front gears.

Apply heavy grease to the rear face of the rear bearing retainer and place a new gasket in position. Install the remaining flat thrust washer on the reverse idler shaft. Push the reverse idler gear, roll pin, and thrust washer into the gears and the front boss of the case. The shaft should then align with the front tanged thrust washer.

The reverse gear is now installed on the end of the spline. Move the reverse shifter shaft to the left of the extension and rotate it to bring the shifter fork to the rear of the extension housing onto the transmission case and, at the same time, ease the shift fork into engagement with the reverse shift collar. Guide the reverse idler shaft into the extension housing so that the extension housing will slide onto the main case. Attach the extension housing to the case with the six bolts. Tighten the upper three bolts to a torque between 15 and 25 foot-pounds and the lower three to a torque between 25 and 35 foot-pounds. Align the groove in the reverse shifter shaft with the hole in the boss and drive the lockpin through the hole. Press the bearing on the main drive gear with the snap ring facing the front of the case and far enough into the case to clear the retaining nuts for the bearing retainer.

After locking the transmission by shifting it into two gears, screw the main drive gear retainer nut on the gear shaft and tighten it to a torque of 40 foot-pounds. Make sure the bearing seats squarely on the gear shoulder. The main nut has a left-hand thread and must be turned counterclockwise to tighten. Attach the bearing retainer and new gasket to the transmission case with the bolts provided and tighten them to a torque of 14 to 22 foot-pounds.

Shift the third-and-fourth synchromesh clutch to neutral and the first-and-second clutch to second gear, which is in the forward detent position. Move the third-and-fourth shifter to the neutral detent position and the first-and-second lever to the second-gear detent. Place the side cover gasket on the case and install the side cover. A dowel pin in the transmission cover serves as a guide for correct alignment. Tighten the cover bolts even to a torque of 14 to 22 foot-pounds.

Install the insulator assembly on the rear extension housing. Torque the bolts to between 25 and 35 foot-pounds. If the lever and bracket support to the extension

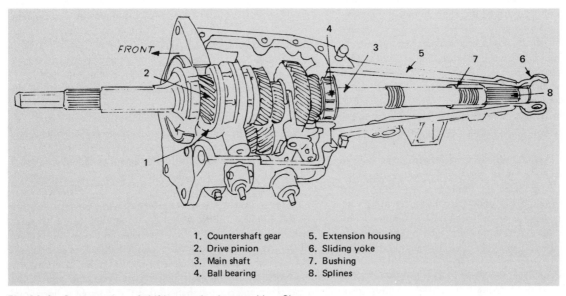

1. Countershaft gear
2. Drive pinion
3. Main shaft
4. Ball bearing
5. Extension housing
6. Sliding yoke
7. Bushing
8. Splines

Fig. 14–9 Cutaway view of shifting mechanism used in a Chrysler three-speed synchromesh transmission. *Courtesy of Chrysler Motors Corporation.*

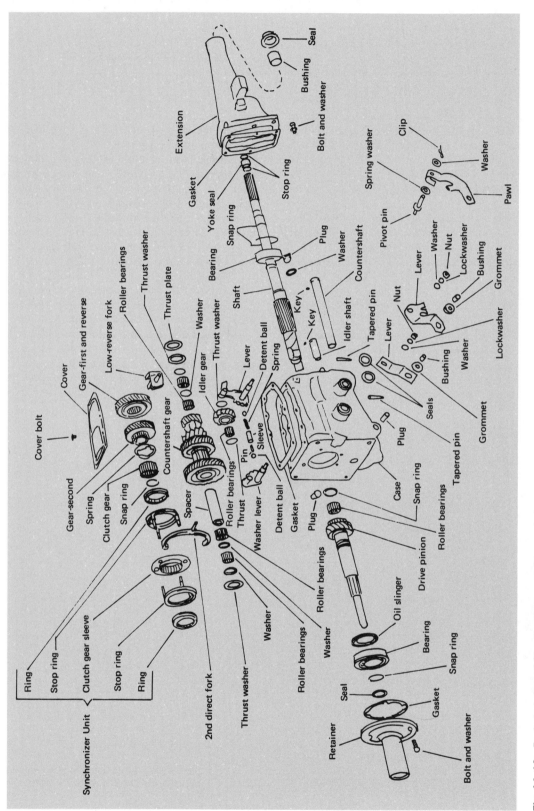

Fig. 14–10 Exploded view of Chrysler three-speed transmission. *Courtesy of Chrysler Motors Corporation.*

housing were removed, replace them and tighten the bolts to a torque between 20 and 35 foot-pounds.

After the transmission is completely assembled on the bench, the installation procedure is the reverse of that described for removal.

When the transmission has been bolted to the clutch housing, remove the filler plug at the side of the transmission case and add 2½ pints of SAE 90 multipurpose gear lubricant. This should fill the transmission case up to the bottom of the filler hole. Replace the filler plug and connect the shift linkages to the transmission. Adjust the shift linkages, if necessary.

Chrysler Transmissions

Three-speed. Figure 14-9 shows a cutaway view of a Chrysler three-speed synchromesh transmission. Synchromesh operation is used on all forward speeds, and helical gears are employed for quiet operation. The *countershaft gear* is in constant mesh with the drive *pinion*, and the countershaft is supported by roller bearings at each end. The front end of the main shaft turns in a *roller bearing* in the bore of the main drive pinion and is supported by a ball bearing at the rear of the case. The part of the main shaft that extends into the extension housing is supported at the rear end by a sliding yoke and bushing. Whenever the propeller-shaft sliding yoke is removed from the transmission, it should be cleaned and relubricated. The yoke, shown at

the extreme right in Fig. 14-9, slides on the splines of the main shaft when the propeller shaft is connected to the transmission.

Figure 14-10 shows an exploded view of the transmission. Disconnect all parts connected to the transmission and drain the case.

Disconnect the propeller shaft at the rear of the transmission extension housing. Be careful not to scratch the precision-ground surfaces on the sliding spline yoke. Then disconnect the speedometer cable and the wires that lead to the backup light switch.

During removal of the transmission, the engine should be supported on a Chrysler engine-support fixture. Raise the engine slightly to remove the support cross-member attaching bolts. Use a jack to support the transmission, and remove the bolts that attach the case to the engine clutch housing. To prevent damage to the clutch disk, slide the transmission back until the input shaft clears the clutch disk before lowering the transmission to the floor.

The synchromesh unit differs from those described previously. See Fig. 14-11. Instead of having ball and spring detents and shifting plates, this unit has *two outer synchronizer stop rings,* each equipped with three pins. The third-speed gear outer stop ring and the second-speed gear outer stop ring are assembled with the pins in alternating positions in the six holes in the clutch sleeve gear.

In operation, the shifting fork moves the clutch gear sleeve so that either cone on the inner ring stops will mate

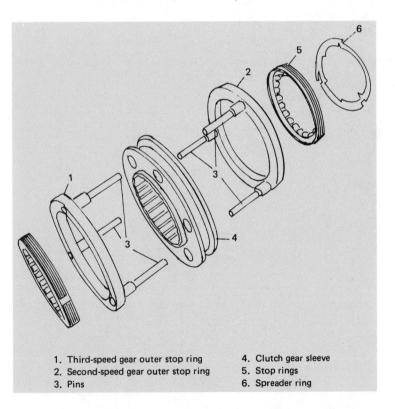

1. Third-speed gear outer stop ring
2. Second-speed gear outer stop ring
3. Pins
4. Clutch gear sleeve
5. Stop rings
6. Spreader ring

Fig. 14-11 Exploded view of synchromesh unit. *Courtesy of Chrysler Motors Corporation.*

with the gear selected to bring the gear to the same speed. As the movement continues, the inner stop ring meshes with the clutch gear and locks together the gear and the shaft. The spreader ring acts as a spring between the second-speed gear and the stop ring.

To start the disassembly of the transmission, unbolt and remove the cover and discard the gasket. Use a new gasket during reinstallation.

With the cover removed, measure the amount of travel between the *synchronizer outer rings* and the *end of the pins* with a pair of feeler gauges placed 180° apart, as shown in Fig. 14-12. This distance should measure between 0.050 and 0.090 inch. If the travel exceeds 0.090 inch, shims must be installed to reduce the travel. If the travel is less than 0.050 inch, an equal amount of material must be removed from the ends of the six pins to make the measurement somewhat greater. This adjustment is made when the main shaft is being assembled, and it is referred to later.

Remove the speedometer pinion adapter in the extension housing. Remove the bolts and one nut and slide the extension housing off the case. Unwind and slide the yoke seal at the rear of the stop ring from the main shaft. Slide from the shaft the seal and the front stop ring.

Unbolt and remove the input shaft bearing retainer and discard the gasket. Drive out the seal by using a suitable drift pin. Pull the shaft assembly slightly out of the case and slide the synchronizer front inner stop ring off the short splines as the input shaft assembly is being removed from the case. Remove the snap ring that locks the main drive gear on the input shaft. After removing the bearing washer, press the input shaft out of the bearing with an arbor press,

and then remove the oil slinger. Remove the snap ring and the bearing rollers from the bore in the end of the main drive gear.

With the transmission shifted to reverse, remove with a hook or a flat blade the main shaft outer snap ring for the rear bearing and then partially remove the main shaft. Cock the main shaft and remove the clutch sleeve rear bearing, the outer synchronizing rings, front inner ring, and the second-and-third shifting fork. The shifting fork is shown in detail in Fig. 14-13. Remove the synchromesh clutch gear retaining snap ring by using a pair of snap ring pliers. Slide the synchromesh clutch gear off the end of the main shaft. Remove the low-and-reverse sliding gear and the shift fork as the main shaft is withdrawn from the case.

With a feeler gauge, check the end play of the countershaft gear. The play should be between 0.0045 and 0.028 inch; if it is greater, install new thrust washers at reassembly. By using a countershaft bearing arbor, drive the countershaft toward the rear of the case until the key can be removed from the countershaft. Now drive the countershaft all the way from the case, taking care to hold the arbor tight against the end of the countershaft to avoid losing the bearing rollers. Remove the countershaft gear, the thrust washers, and the thrust plate from the case. Now remove the bearing rollers, washers, and center spacer from the countershaft gear.

With a suitable drift pin, drive the reverse idler gear shaft toward the end and out of the case far enough to remove the Woodruff key from the end of the shaft. Lift the gear, thrust washers, and bearing rollers from the case. Then remove the bearing rollers from the idler gear. With

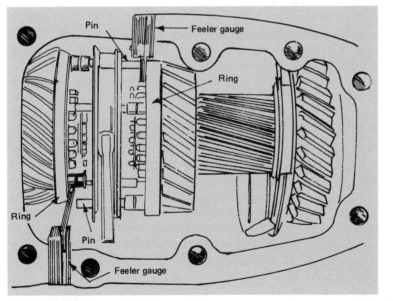

Fig. 14–12 Cutaway view of Chrysler standard model three-speed transmission. *Courtesy of Chrysler Motors Corporation.*

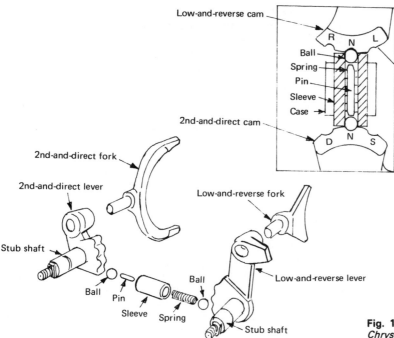

Fig. 14-13 Detail of Chrysler shifting fork. *Courtesy of Chrysler Motors Corporation.*

the removal of the reverse idler gear and shaft, disassembly is completed.

Cleaning and inspection of the transmission is done in the same general manner as described for the Pontiac three-speed transmission.

To start reassembly, slide the bearing roller spacer over an arbor. Coat the bore of the gear with lubricant and slide the spacer and arbor tool into the gear house. For the standard transmission, Fig. 14-9, lubricate the bearing rollers with heavy grease and install the 22 rollers in each end of the gear around the arbor. Coat the bearing spacer rings with heavy grease and install them in each end of the gear. For the heavy-duty transmission used in eight-cylinder cars, place another row of 22 rollers in each end of the gear after installing the spacer rings.

When countershaft end play is found to exceed 0.028 inch during disassembly, install new thrust washers. Coat the washers with heavy grease and install one at each end of the countershaft gear by sliding it over the arbor. Install the gear and arbor in the case, making sure the tabs on the thrust washers slide into the grooves in the case (six-cylinder model). For the eight-cylinder model, coat the washers with heavy grease and install the front washer on the countershaft gear with the tabs outward. The tabbed rear washer goes over the arbor at the front of the countershaft gear with the tabs positioned in grooves in the gear. Install the remaining rear thrust washer plate over the arbor at the rear of the gear so that the step on the plate will engage on the ledge inside the rear of the case to keep the plate from rotating.

Install the countershaft gear and the arbor in the case so that the front thrust washer tabs slide into grooves in the

case and the rear thrust washer step engages on the ledge.

Using the countershaft and a soft hammer, drive the arbor forward out of the countershaft gear and out through the bore in front of the case. Before driving the countershaft all the way into the case, check that the keyway is positioned in line with the key recess in the rear of the case. Insert the shaft key and continue to drive the countershaft forward into the case until the key is bottomed in the recess.

Position a suitable arbor in the reverse idler gear and install the 22 bearing rollers in the gear. Use a heavy grease to hold the rollers in place when assembling them. Place the front and rear thrust washers at the ends of the reverse idler gear and install the assembly in the transmission case with the chamfered end of the gear teeth to the front. Insert the reverse idler shaft into the bore at the rear of the case, threading it into the gear and pushing the arbor out toward the front of the transmission. With the keyway aligned with the recess in the case, drive the shaft forward. Continue until the key seats in the recess.

The main reason for using an arbor in this assembly is to provide a means of placing the bearing rollers in the gear, because the rollers must be in place before the shafts are inserted. Without an arbor, the rollers fall out as fast as they are inserted. A suitable arbor for this job is a short length of round steel rod slightly smaller in diameter than the reverse idler shaft.

An exploded view of the shifting mechanism was shown in Fig. 14-13. The supplementary cross section of the detent mechanism shows the assembly in place with the spring-loaded balls and pin in the neutral (N) position between the shaft cams. When the low-and-reverse cam is moved, the ball enters either the reverse (R) position or the low-speed (L) position on the cam, depending on the gear selected. Likewise, when the second-and-direct cam is moved, the ball enters either the direct drive (D) or second-speed (S) position, depending on the gear selected.

All parts shown in Fig. 14-13 except the shafts are inside the transmission case when the shifting mechanism is assembled. The stub shafts extend through the case, and the operating levers are attached to them. Before the stub shafts are installed, new grease seals should be inserted in the case to keep lubricant from leaking out and around the shafts. Place a seal protector on the end of each of the stub shafts and slide the shafts into the bosses on the case (the bosses extend outward on the side of the transmission case); push each one through the grease seal.

Place the low-and-reverse lever on the stub shaft inside the case and turn it until the center detent is aligned with the interlock bore inside the transmission case. Insert the interlock sleeve in the bore inside the case, and insert the interlock ball, spring, and pin inside the sleeve.

Before installing the second-and-high lever, insert the remaining interlock ball on the top of the spring already in place. Then install the second-and-direct lever in the same manner as the low-and-reverse lever.

The center detent on the second-and-direct lever is now aligned with the bore in the interlock case. A special tool holds the ball and spring in the interlock bore until the neutral detent on the low-and-reverse lever is aligned with the bore. With levers aligned, attach them to the stub shafts by tapered pins and tighten the retaining nuts securely.

The main shaft and rear bearings are inserted through the rear of the case and into the low-and-reverse sliding gear. This gear, in the heavy-duty transmission, should have the hub extension facing to the rear of the case to prevent interference with the straddle-type shifting fork. Place the synchronizer spreader ring, Fig. 14-11, and the rear stop ring on the synchronizer splines of the second-speed gear. Install the second-speed gear on the main shaft, adding shims, if necessary, for spacing.

Adjustment for synchronizer travel was discussed previously. The travel should not exceed 0.090 inch or be less than 0.050 inch. These measurements are obtained before the transmission is disassembled. Shims must be inserted to reduce the travel to less than 0.090 inch, or an equal amount must be removed from the end of each synchronizer pin if the travel is less than 0.050 inch.

Install the synchronizer clutch gear on the main shaft and fasten it with a snap ring. Make sure the ring is bottomed in the ring groove for its entire circumference. Measure the clearance between the clutch gear and the second gear. This clearance should be between 0.004 and 0.014 inch. If the play exceeds 0.014 inch, the second-speed gear may slip out of mesh.

In the standard transmission for six-cylinder cars, install the second-and-direct fork in the lever shift with the offset in the fork toward the rear of the transmission. In the heavy-duty transmission, simply install the second-and-direct fork in the lever shaft.

Hold the synchronizer clutch gear sleeve and the two outer rings together with pins properly entered in the holes in the clutch gear sleeve. While holding the synchronizer parts and the fork in position, slide the main shaft forward so that the synchronizer clutch gear enters the clutch gear sleeve and, at the same time, the main shaft enters the rear bearing in the case bore. If the synchronizer parts are not positioned in this manner, it will not be possible to position them after the main shaft is in place because there will be interference with the countershaft gear. Continue to hold the synchronizer parts in position and tap the main shaft forward until the rear bearing bottoms in the case bore. Install the snap ring in the groove in the case bore for the main shaft rear bearing. This snap ring is a selective fit.

Slide the oil slinger, if it was removed, over the main drive shaft against the main drive gear. Slide the bearing over the input shaft with the snap ring groove away from the gear end, and then seat the bearing on the shaft. Use an arbor press for this purpose. For the standard transmission, install the keyed washer between the bearing and the retaining snap ring. Secure the bearing and washer with a selected-thickness snap ring. Four snap rings are available to eliminate end play. If a large snap ring was used for the bearing when it was disassembled, use the same size ring for reassembly.

Place the pinion shaft in a soft-jaw vise and install the bearing rollers in the main shaft bore. There are fourteen rollers for the standard transmission and fifteen for the heavy-duty version. Coat the rollers with heavy grease to hold them in place and then insert the bearing retainer ring into its groove.

Install the third gear inner stop ring in the third gear outer stop ring. Guide the main drive gear through the front of the case and engage the inner stop ring with the clutch teeth and then seat the main drive gear bearing. When the snap ring makes full contact with the case, the main drive shaft is fully seated. Mount a new seal in the main drive bearing retainer and install the main drive gear and bearing retainer in the case. Use a new gasket between the retainer and the case. Install the bolts and tighten them with a torque wrench to 35 foot-pounds.

If the extension housing bushing needs replacement, drive out the oil seal but be careful not to damage the oil-seal seat. Drive out the bushing and slide a new bushing on the installing tool. Align the bushing oil hole with the oil slot in the housing and drive in the bushing. Install a new cover gasket on the case and place the cover on the gasket. Screw in the cover bolts and tighten them to a torque of 15 foot-pounds. Install the transmission in the car.

Four-speed. The Chrysler four-speed synchromesh transmission, Fig. 14-14, is of much heavier construction than either the three-speed standard or heavy-duty units.

The gears are much stronger and the bearings are

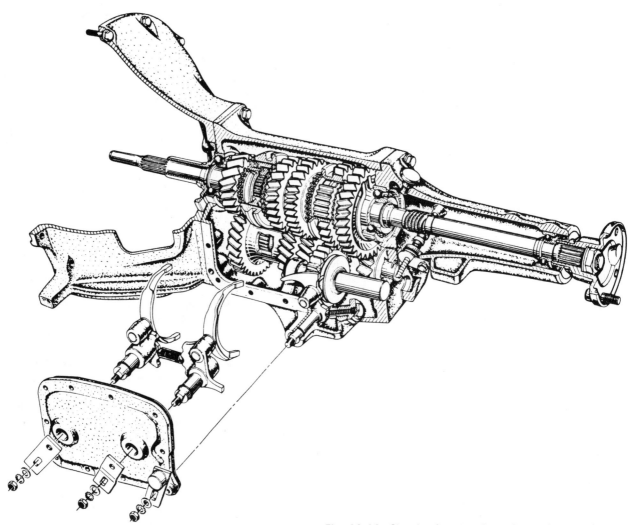

Fig. 14–14 Chrysler four-speed synchromesh transmission. *Courtesy of Chrysler Motors Corporation.*

larger. A torque-lock feature, which does not affect normal shifting, is included to prevent any tendency of the first-and-second-speed gears to slip out of mesh during deceleration. The coast slides of the clutch teeth are undercut sufficiently to form a ridge which prevents the shift sleeve from moving into the neutral position. Also included is a reverse gear interlock which prevents accidental shifting of the first-and-second-speed gears while the car is moving in reverse.

The four-speed synchromesh transmission is made in two sizes. The smaller unit is used in the Plymouth Valiant, Dodge Dart, and Plymouth Barracuda. The larger unit is installed in the Chrysler Imperial and Dodge.

The gear ratios for the smaller unit are as follows: First gear, 3.09 to 1; second, 1.92 to 1; third, 1.40 to 1; fourth (direct) 1 to 1; and reverse, 3.00 to 1.

The gear ratios for the larger transmission are: First, 2.66 to 1; second, 1.90 to 1; third, 1.39 to 1; fourth, 1 to 1; and reverse, 2.58 to 1.

The component parts of the four-speed transmission are much the same as those of the standard three-speed variety except for the synchronizer and clutch sleeve. Shifting plates are used in place of the pins used in the three-speed transmission.

The disassembly and assembly procedures are practically the same as those already described, but an extra gear, another synchromesh unit, and three shifting forks must be considered.

Ford Transmissions

Three-speed. A typical Ford three-speed transmission has synchromesh on all forward speeds, and the synchromesh unit uses shifting plates. Thus, the synchromesh clutches are disassembled and assembled in the same way as those already covered.

Transmission assembly and disassembly procedures, in general, follow those given for the Pontiac transmissions.

Dagenham four-speed. The Ford Dagenham transmission (used on the Mustang and some other models) has synchromesh on all forward speeds and a sliding reverse gear. In the shifting pattern, reverse is in the far upper left position, except on the Mustang, where it is in the far lower left position.

The transmission uses a shifting-plate synchromesh unit, but the plates are called *hub inserts.*

The shifter forks are operated by cams mounted in the transmission cover on the side of the case. The interlock mechanism consists of a detent ball and spring. Disassembly and assembly procedures are the same essentially as for other four-speed units already discussed.

Ford-design four-speed. The Ford designed four-speed transmission also has synchromesh on all forward speeds and a sliding reverse gear. The shifting-plate type synchromesh unit is conventional and shift cams and rails are used to control the shifting of gears.

Disassembly and assembly procedures are conventional, but wear and looseness in the countershaft gear and reverse idler gear should be checked with a feeler gauge during reassembly. Countershaft gear end play should be between 0.004 and 0.018 inch. If the end play is not within these limits, use new thrust washers. The same comments apply to the reverse idler gear.

Warner four-speed. The Warner four-speed, which is optional on certain Ford automobiles, has synchromesh on all four forward gears, a sliding reverse gear and a conventional shifting pattern, except in the Mustang.

A finger-operated release slider on the gearshift lever keeps the transmission from being thrown accidentally into reverse.

The shift forks are controlled by cams that have interlock detents to prevent accidental shifting into more than one gear at a time. The camshafts are extended through the transmission case cover on the side of the transmission.

Assembly and disassembly procedures require no special comment.

TRANSAXLES

Many of the newer American-built compacts combine a four-speed transmission and differential into a single compact unit called the Transaxle. The Transaxle is mounted in a two-piece housing that is bolted to the back of the engine. The Transaxle and engine assembly is mounted transversely, with the engine on the right and the Transaxle on the left.

A typical mounting arrangment is shown in Figure 14-15; a cutaway view of the Transaxle is shown in Figure 14-16.

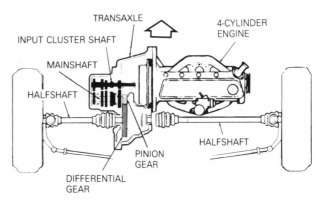

Fig. 14-15. A typical Transaxle mounting arrangement. *Courtesy of Ford Motor Company.*

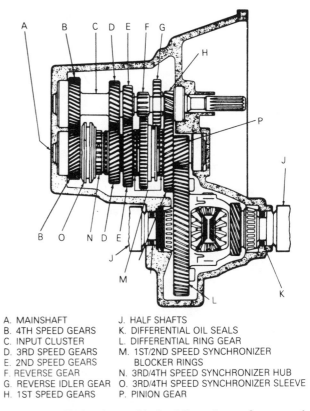

A. MAINSHAFT	J. HALF SHAFTS
B. 4TH SPEED GEARS	K. DIFFERENTIAL OIL SEALS
C. INPUT CLUSTER	L. DIFFERENTIAL RING GEAR
D. 3RD SPEED GEARS	M. 1ST/2ND SPEED SYNCHRONIZER
E. 2ND SPEED GEARS	BLOCKER RINGS
F. REVERSE GEAR	N. 3RD/4TH SPEED SYNCHRONIZER HUB
G. REVERSE IDLER GEAR	O. 3RD/4TH SPEED SYNCHRONIZER SLEEVE
H. 1ST SPEED GEARS	P. PINION GEAR

Fig. 14-16. Transaxle used in Ford Escort/Lynx. *Courtesy of Ford Motor Company.*

From the clutch, engine torque is transferred to the main shaft through the input cluster gear. Each gear on the input cluster is in constant mesh with a matching gear on the main shaft. These matching gear sets provide the four forward gear ratios. The transmission gear ratio is determined, of course, by the number of teeth on the input cluster gear and the number of teeth on the main-shaft gear with which it meshes. On the Ford engine, the four forward-gear ratios are 3.58:1 (first gear), 2.05:1 (second gear), 1.23:1 (third gear), and 0.81:1 (fourth gear).

Reverse gear is accomplished by sliding a spur gear into mesh with the input-cluster shaft gear and the reverse sliding gear. The sliding gear acts as an idler and reverses the direction of main-shaft rotation. The reverse-gear ratio is 3.46:1.

Whenever the engine is running and the clutch is en-

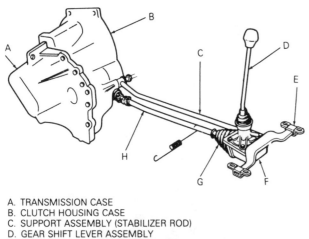

A. TRANSMISSION CASE
B. CLUTCH HOUSING CASE
C. SUPPORT ASSEMBLY (STABILIZER ROD)
D. GEAR SHIFT LEVER ASSEMBLY
E. STABILIZER (TO FLOOR PAN RUBBER
    MOUNTING)
F. CONTROL SELECTOR HOUSING
G. GEAR SHIFT TUBE RETAINING SPRING
H. SHIFT ROD AND CLEVIS ASSEMBLY

Fig. 14-17. External gearshift mechanism in Ford Escort/Lynx. *Courtesy of Ford Motor Company.*

gaged, the input cluster shaft turns with the engine. However, the main-shaft gears merely freewheel unless locked to the shaft through one of the synchronizers. With the gears freely turning on the main shaft, engine torque is not transmitted to the pinion and the Transaxle is in neutral. If one of the synchronizers is shafted, the gear becomes locked to the main shaft and the shaft will rotate at a speed determined by engine rpm and the gear ratio selected. With the main shaft rotating, engine torque has been transmitted as far as the pinion gear.

The pinion gear, located at the end of the main shaft, is in constant mesh with the differential ring gear. Because it is part of the main shaft, the pinion has to rotate whenever the main shaft rotates.

With the pinion rotating, engine torque has flowed through the transmission to the differential, where it flows out to the wheels.

The external gear-shift mechanism, Figure 14-17, consists of a gear-shift lever, transmission selector rod, stabilizer rod, and shift housing. The shift housing provides a gear-shift lever mounting and connection to the selector rod. The housing is bolted to the stabilizer, which is rubber mounted and fitted to the floor pan. On the Transaxle end, the stabilizer rod is mounted through a rubber insulator to a boss on the clutch housing. The stabilizer rod equalizes the movement of the engine with the shift mechanism and prevents the engine movements from causing the gearshift to pull the Transaxle out of gear. Rubber boots are provided for the protection of the shafts and for sound insulation. Adjustment of the external linkage is not necessary and no provisions are made for adjustment.

Internally, Figure 14-18, the gear-shift mechanism be-

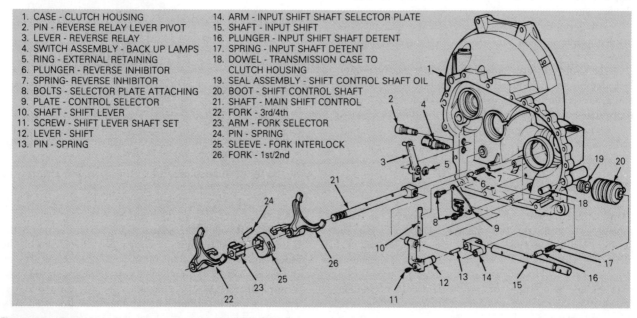

1. CASE - CLUTCH HOUSING
2. PIN - REVERSE RELAY LEVER PIVOT
3. LEVER - REVERSE RELAY
4. SWITCH ASSEMBLY - BACK UP LAMPS
5. RING - EXTERNAL RETAINING
6. PLUNGER - REVERSE INHIBITOR
7. SPRING- REVERSE INHIBITOR
8. BOLTS - SELECTOR PLATE ATTACHING
9. PLATE - CONTROL SELECTOR
10. SHAFT - SHIFT LEVER
11. SCREW - SHIFT LEVER SHAFT SET
12. LEVER - SHIFT
13. PIN - SPRING
14. ARM - INPUT SHIFT SHAFT SELECTOR PLATE
15. SHAFT - INPUT SHIFT
16. PLUNGER - INPUT SHIFT SHAFT DETENT
17. SPRING - INPUT SHAFT DETENT
18. DOWEL - TRANSMISSION CASE TO
    CLUTCH HOUSING
19. SEAL ASSEMBLY - SHIFT CONTROL SHAFT OIL
20. BOOT - SHIFT CONTROL SHAFT
21. SHAFT - MAIN SHIFT CONTROL
22. FORK - 3rd/4th
23. ARM - FORK SELECTOR
24. PIN - SPRING
25. SLEEVE - FORK INTERLOCK
26. FORK - 1st/2nd

Fig. 14-18. Exploded view of internal mechanisms in Ford Escort/Lynx gearshift arrangement. *Courtesy of Ford Motor Company.*

gins with the input shaft which is connected to the external linkage. Attached to the input-shift shaft is the shift-shaft selector arm. The selector arm and its associated selector plate act together to transmit the inward, outward, and rotational movement of the input-shift shaft to the internal-shift lever. The shift lever in turn transmits these motions to the main shift-control shaft to which the shift forks are attached.

An interlock is provided on the main shift-control shaft to allow the shifting of only one synchronizer at a time. This prevents the engagement of the transmission in two gears simultaneously.

Chrysler has experienced some difficulty, however, with failure of the interlock blocker on its A-412 manual transmission. Thus it is possible for the Transaxle to become locked into two gears at once. This will occur if the interlock blocker on the gearshift selector lever has spread apart. The result of operating like this will be clutch failure at the least, and driveline failure at the worst. To correctly diagnose the problem, the interlock, Figure 14-19, should be checked using the following procedure.

1. Disconnect the shift linkage operating lever from the Transaxle selector shaft.

2. Remove the Transaxle-detent spring assembly and selector-shaft boot.

3. Remove the aluminum shaft selector plug.

4. Place the Transaxle in neutral and pull the selector-shaft assembly out of the case.

5. Measure the interlock blocker gap. If it exceeds 0.330 inch, replace the gearshift selector-shaft assembly.

6. Apply a thick coating of chassis grease to the selector-shaft shoulder at the threaded end and carefully insert the shaft through the selector-shaft oil seal. Reverse steps 1 to 4 to install and adjust the shift linkage.

Returning to the shift assembly shown in Figure 14-18, the reverse sliding gear is shifted into position when a pin on the main shift-control shaft engages the reverse lever. The pin moves the gear on the reverse-idler shaft into engagement with the input cluster and main-shaft gears. The pin also actuates the backup-lamp switch.

A Five-Speed Manual-Overdrive Transmission

A typical five-speed manual-overdrive transmission is basically a four-speed transmission with an overdrive gear located in the extension housing at the back of the transmission case.

All five forward helical-gear assemblies are in constant mesh. They are activated by first/second speed synchronizer clutches. Each synchronizer is activated by its own shift fork. All three shifter forks slide along the transmission's single shifter rail. Only the reverse-idler spur gear slides along a rail to engage the reverse spur gear.

The main-shaft assembly (input and output shafts together) includes the first/second, third/fourth, and fifth speed synchronizers.

Although the input and output shaft fit together, fourth gear is direct—input to output. This means that a countershaft gear is needed in order to transfer power from the input-shaft gear through the transmission to the output-shaft gears.

TROUBLESHOOTING MANUAL TRANSMISSIONS

Sticking in low gear.

1. Clutch does not release completely.

2. Shift-rail plunger jammed.

3. Gearshift-lever binding shift rail.

4. Defective transmission main shaft.

5. Improper lubrication or lack of lubrication.

6. Defective transmission parts.

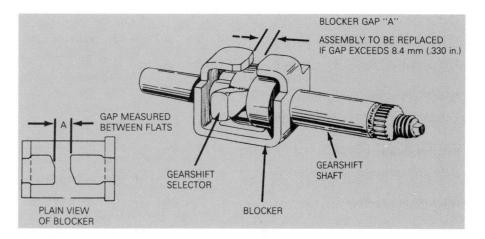

Fig. 14-19. The interlock blocker on the Chrysler Corp. A-412 manual Transaxle. *Courtesy of Chrysler Corporation.*

Jumping out of low gear.

1. Gears do not engage properly.
2. Distorted shift fork.
3. Defective bearings on transmission main shaft.
4. Defective bearings on countershaft.
5. Defective main shaft pilot bearing.
6. End play in transmission main shaft or in countershaft.

Sticking in second gear.

1. Clutch does not release fully.
2. Damaged teeth on sliding sleeve.
3. Damaged transmission main shaft.
4. Shift-rail plunger is stuck.
5. Gearshift lever binding shift-rail.
6. Improper lubrication or lack of lubrication.
7. Synchronizer clutch frozen.
8. Defective transmission parts.
9. Locked second-speed transmission gear bearings.

Jumping out of second gear.

1. Bent or loose shift fork.
2. Gears do not engage completely.
3. Loose transmission gear bearing.
4. Damaged main-shaft pilot bearing.
5. Bent transmission shaft.
6. Not enough spring tension on shift-rail plunger.
7. End play in transmission main shaft.
8. Loose or worn bearing on transmission main shaft.
9. End play in countershaft.
10. Damaged teeth on second-speed sliding gear or sleeve.

Sticking in high gear.

1. Clutch not releasing fully.
2. Synchronizing clutch is frozen.
3. Gear-shift lever jamming shift rail.
4. Defective teeth on high speed sliding gear or sleeve.
5. Defective main-shaft pilot bearing.
6. Improper lubrication or lack of lubrication.
7. Defective transmission parts.
8. Shift-rail plunger is stuck.
9. Defective teeth on clutch shaft.

Jumping out of high gear.

1. Either the transmission case or clutch housing mis-aligned.
2. Bent or loose shift fork.

3. Gears not engaging fully.
4. End play in clutch shaft.
5. Loose or worn bearings on clutch shaft or main shaft.
6. Worn high speed sliding gear.
7. Defective teeth in clutch shaft.
8. Bent transmission shaft.
9. Not enough spring tension on shift-rail plunger.
10. Worn pilot bearing in crankshaft.

Sticking in reverse gear.

1. Clutch not releasing fully.
2. Shift-rail plunger is stuck.
3. Improper lubrication or no lubrication.
4. Defective transmission parts.
5. Gear shift lever jamming shift rail.
6. Defective teeth on transmission main shaft.

Jumping out of reverse gear.

1. Worn gear teeth.
2. Gears do not engage fully.
3. End play in transmission main shaft.
4. Loose or worn bearing on transmission main shaft.
5. Defective main-shaft pilot bearing.
6. Loose or worn bushings on idler gear.
7. Bent or loose shift fork.
8. Insufficient spring tension on shift-rail plunger.

Gears spin when shifting from neutral into gear.

1. Clutch not releasing fully.
2. Binding pilot bearing in crankshaft.
3. Transmission lubricant is too light.

Gears will not synchronize.

1. Clutch not releasing fully.
2. Worn gear teeth.
3. Binding pilot bearing on main shaft synchronizes in high gear only.
4. Weak or broken detent springs.
5. Weak or broken springs under balls in sliding gear sleeve.
6. Binding countershaft.
7. Binding pilot bearing in crankshaft.
8. Binding bearing on clutch shaft.
9. Improper lubrication or no lubrication.
10. Defective cones.
11. Constant-mesh gear does not turn freely on main shaft.

15

AUTOMATIC TRANSMISSIONS

Contents

AUTOMATIC TRANSMISSION FUNDAMENTALS

Introduction

Detailed coverage of all automatic transmissions currently in use would require a separate and large volume. Because we are more concerned with the basic principles of operation than with step-by-step disassembly and assembly instructions, only one automatic transmission, the Ford Model C6, is discussed here. Once you have acquired this background, you should experience no difficulty in understanding the operation of other units and in following manufacturers' troubleshooting adjustments.

The Basic System

All Ford automatic transmissions have a torque converter, planetary gear train, and hydraulic control system.

The torque converter has two functions. First, it acts as a hydraulic clutch (fluid coupling) to connect the engine to the gear train, provide the necessary slip when the engine is running with the transmission in gear and the car standing still, and to absorb shock in the drive line (components that transmit power from the engine to the rear wheels).

Second, the converter multiplies torque (gear reduction) automatically when needed. Most Ford converters provide the equivalent of about 2 to 1 torque multiplication at full stall; that is, when the vehicle is in gear but not moving, and the engine is operating at maximum output. When the engine is not under load, the converter reverts to a direct coupling between the engine and the gear train.

The planetary gear train includes the input and output shafts, gear sets, and the clutches and bands that control the gears.

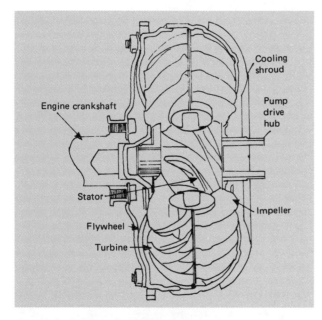

Fig. 15-1 Torque converter.

Each transmission has its own distinctive gear train, but the basic components are similar.

Primarily, the hydraulic system supplies oil under pressure to operate the bands and clutches that control the gear train. It also provides oil to the transmission, torque converter, and, in some transmissions, circulates fluid through a cooler to prevent excessive operating temperatures.

Torque Converter

As shown in Fig. 15-1, the torque converter has three members: an *impeller (pump)*, a *turbine*, and a *stator*. All are encased in a *welded housing*.

The impeller drives the converter and forms the outer shell. The cover is bolted to a driving plate, which is attached to the engine crankshaft. Thus, the *impeller* turns at engine speed.

The turbine is coupled to the gear train input shaft and is the driven member of the converter. The input shaft always turns at turbine speed.

The stator is a central, bladed member, and is supported on a one-way clutch. It is used to direct fluid from the turbine back to the impeller when the converter is in operation.

Fluid coupling. As the impeller turns with the engine, fluid fed to its center is thrown outward by centrifugal force. An inner ring in the impeller guides the fluid to the openings at the front of the impeller blades. The blades are curved to direct the fluid at the turbine and make it turn in the same direction as the impeller.

The curve of the turbine blades is opposite to that of the impeller blades. If the gear train offers too much resistance to the turning effort, the turbine stands still and the converter slips. When the push of fluid leaving the impeller overcomes the resistance of the gear train, the turbine turns. This is the principle of fluid coupling (clutch action).

Installing the stator as shown in Fig. 15-1 completes the torque-multiplication flow path, known as the *vortex flow*. The blades of the stator again reverse the fluid leaving the turbine. The fluid is returned to the center of the impeller, accelerated again, and then discharged to push on the turbine blades with more force. Thus, torque is multiplied whenever the turbine turns slower than the impeller.

To keep the fluid that is leaving the turbine from making the stator turn backward (in a direction opposite to that of the turbine and impeller), the stator has a one-way clutch. Rollers in the clutch are wedged in slots to prevent backward movement. When the rollers are not wedged in the slots, the stator can turn in the same direction as the impeller and turbine. This free rotation allows the stator to play its part in the coupling phase.

Coupling phase. As the turbine picks up speed, centrifugal force pushes the fluid outward and keeps it from being returned to the impeller. When the turbine speed is about nine-tenths the speed of the impeller, fluid leaving the turbine strikes the backs of the stator blades and vortex flow ceases. The one-way clutch is unlocked, and the impeller, turbine, and stator turn together. This condition is known as the *coupling phase.*

Automatic torque adjustment. Since torque multiplication takes place when the speed of the turbine is less than nine-tenths the speed of the impeller, the converter provides more torque when the engine is under load. The impeller runs faster than the turbine, vortex flow ceases, and the converter automatically matches the engine torque to the needs of the wheels. If the initial increase in torque does not meet the demand, further reduction occurs automatically in the gear train.

Fluid cooling. Recirculating vortex flow during the reduction process generates heat that can break down the transmission fluid. Therefore, most Ford automatic transmissions continually circulate the fluid through a cooler located in the bottom of the engine radiator. This cooler circuit is discussed later.

Converter malfunctions. Basically, the converter is a trouble-free unit. The part most likely to fail is the one-way clutch. Without the clutch, converter reduction is not possible, and the vehicle does not accelerate as well as it should in low speed. High-speed operation is not affected since converter reduction is not required.

If the one-way clutch seizes up and the stator cannot turn, the converter stays in reduction. Acceleration is good, but top speed is limited to about 50 mph.

Dirt in the converter causes wear and results in noisy operation and mechanical failure. Most current models are welded units and must be cleaned by agitation and flushing.

Planetary gear construction. The simple planetary gear set shown in Fig. 15-2 has a *ring (internal) gear,* a *central sun gear,* and a number of *planet pinions* (planet gears). Ford transmissions have either three or four planet pinions in each gear set. These pinions are mounted on shafts on a

pinion carrier; thus, they may turn either on their own axes or around the sun gear when the carrier is free to turn.

Unlike manual shift gear sets, a planetary unit is in constant mesh. Gear combinations are obtained by holding one member stationary and driving another member. The third member then becomes the output. It is possible to obtain both reduction and reverse gear.

During reduction, the sun gear is held stationary. The ring gear is driven clockwise by the transmission input shaft. As the ring gear turns, the planet pinions are forced to turn clockwise around the stationary sun gear. The reduced-speed, increased-torque output is from the pinion carriers.

Reverse reduction occurs when the pinion carriers are held stationary and another member is driven. The third member is driven in reverse and represents the output.

In reverse, the input is to the sun gear and the output is through the ring gear. The pinion carriers are held so that the planet pinions can turn only on their shafts. Driving the sun gear clockwise turns the pinions counterclockwise. The pinions then make the ring gear turn counterclockwise.

When any two members of the planetary gear set are locked together, the whole set is automatically locked up. Then, if any one member is driven, the complete set turns as a unit.

Suppose, for example, the sun gear and ring gear are locked together. The input shaft is driving the ring gear, and its output is from the pinion carriers. Everything must turn together.

In neutral, none of the members are locked together or held in any way.

Clutch operation. Hydraulically operated clutches and servo-applied bands are used to lock members of the gear set either together or to the transmission case. (A servo is any driven mechanism that supplements a primary control operated by a comparatively feeble force.)

A clutch normally is used to connect one member to another (with one exception in the C6 transmission). A servo is used to lock a member to the case.

Figure 15-3 shows the simple diagram of a piston-operated clutch. One set of *clutch plates* is externally splined to the *clutch cylinder.* A second set of plates is internally splined to the *clutch hub.* The plates are installed alternately, and the *clutch pack* is flanked by a *hydraulic piston* and a *backing plate.*

When fluid under pressure is forced in behind the piston, the piston moves to squeeze the engine clutch pack against the backing plate. This locks the clutch cylinder and hub together. The parts of the gear train to be locked together are then connected to the hub and cylinder.

Release springs are provided in the clutch assemblies to return the piston when pressure is released.

Band and servo operation. The operation of a typical band and servo is shown in Fig. 15-4. The *band* is tightened

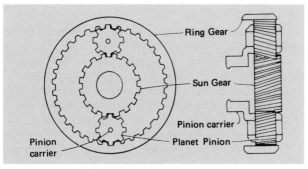

Fig. 15-2 Simple planetary gear set.

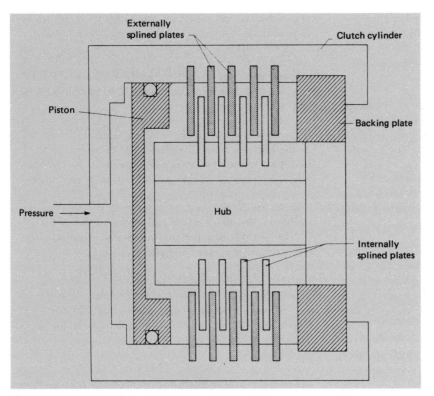

Fig. 15–3 Simple diagram of a piston-operated clutch.

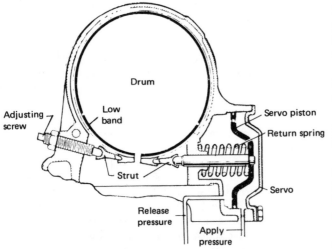

Fig. 15–4 Typical band and servo operation.

around a *drum* and holds the drum stationary. Tightening force is applied to one end of the band by the *servo* which, in the C6 transmission, is built into the case. The other end of the band is anchored to the case.

When the apply side of the *servo piston* is pressurized, the band is squeezed around the drum, holding it stationary. The *return spring* releases the band when the pressure is released. (Some servos are released by pressurizing the opposite side of the piston.)

The C6 gear train. The C6 gear train, Fig. 15-5, has *two planetary gear sets* which can operate either separately or in series through a common sun gear. There are *three friction clutches, one band,* and a *one-way clutch.*

The *reverse-and-high clutch locks* the *input shaft* (splined to the *clutch hub*) to the common sun gear through the *input shell* (splined to the clutch cylinder and sun gear).

The *forward clutch locks* the *input shaft* (splined to the *clutch cylinder*) to the *forward unit ring gear,* which is cut into the *clutch hub.*

The intermediate band tightens around the *reverse-and-high clutch cylinder* to hold the common sun gear stationary through the input shell. The *band servo* is built into the case and is pressure-applied and pressure- and spring-released.

The low-and-reverse clutch locks the reverse planetary-unit ring gear to the case.

The one-way clutch performs the same function as the low-and-reverse clutch in D range low gear only.

In the next few paragraphs the various power flows in the gear train are described briefly by stating which units are involved. The manner in which these units are applied is covered later. Note particularly gear turning directions.

First gear involves both planetary gear sets in what is sometimes called a *double reverse reduction.* As shown in Fig. 15-6, input to the forward unit is reversed to the *sun gear,* which is the output. However, it is also the input to the *reverse planetary unit,* where a second reverse reduction is obtained. The *output shaft* ends up turning in the

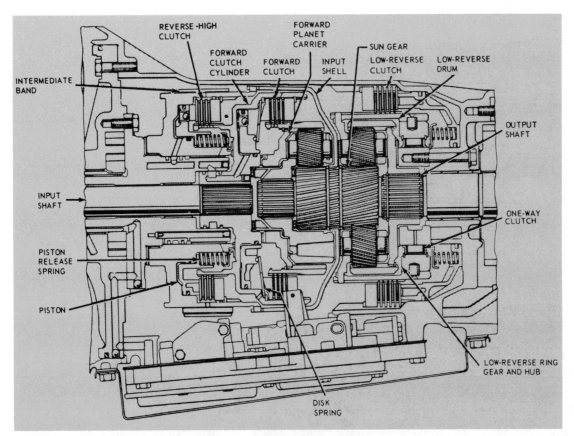

Fig. 15–5 C6 gear train.

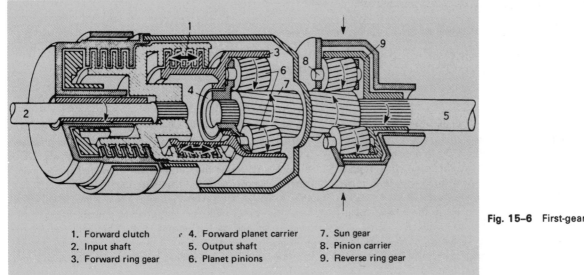

Fig. 15–6 First-gear power flow.

1. Forward clutch
2. Input shaft
3. Forward ring gear
4. Forward planet carrier
5. Output shaft
6. Planet pinions
7. Sun gear
8. Pinion carrier
9. Reverse ring gear

same direction as the *input shaft*, with the combined reduction of the two units.

The forward clutch is applied so that the input shaft drives the *forward-unit ring gear*. The forward-unit planet carrier is splined to the output shaft. Since the output shaft is turning slower than the input shaft, the carrier is, in ef-

fect, being held. The planet pinions thus act as idlers, and the *sun gear* is driven in reverse (counterclockwise).

In the reverse unit, the pinion carrier is locked to the case. Pinion idler action is again obtained. The counterclockwise input of the sun gear is changed to clockwise output of the ring gear, which drives the output shaft.

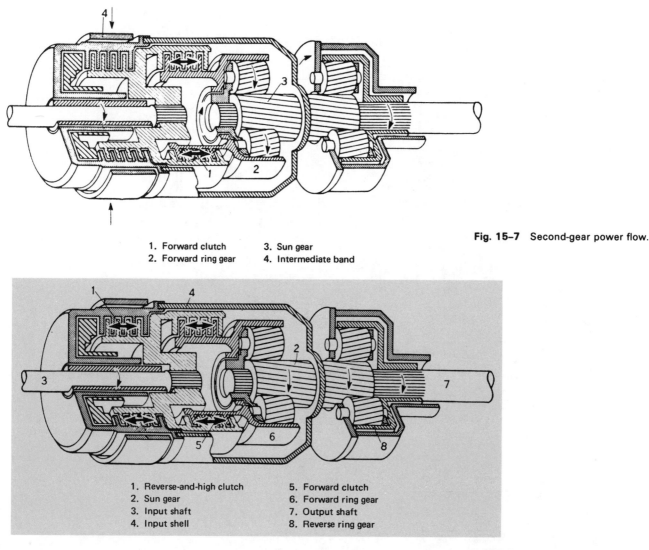

Fig. 15–7 Second-gear power flow.

1. Forward clutch   3. Sun gear
2. Forward ring gear   4. Intermediate band

1. Reverse-and-high clutch   5. Forward clutch
2. Sun gear   6. Forward ring gear
3. Input shaft   7. Output shaft
4. Input shell   8. Reverse ring gear

Fig. 15–8 High-gear power flow.

In D range, the *reverse-unit pinion carrier* is held in one direction only by a one-way clutch. This arrangement lets the transmission "free wheel" in the first gear. In other words, the output shaft can overrun the input. In L range, however, the clutch or band prevents the carrier from turning either way, thus providing engine braking.

Second-gear reduction takes place in the forward planetary gear set. The reverse unit is not involved.

As shown in Fig. 15-7, the *forward clutch* is applied and drives the *forward-unit ring gear*. The *sun gear* is locked to the case by the *intermediate band*. As the ring gear turns, it causes the planet pinions to walk around the sun gear. The pinion carrier, which is splined to the output shaft, is driven clockwise at reduced speed.

In high gear the forward planetary unit is locked up by applying two clutches, as shown in Fig. 15-8. The *reverse-and-high clutch* locks the *sun gear* to the *input shaft*

through the *input shell*. The *forward clutch locks* the *forward ring gear* to the *input shaft*. With two of its members locked to the input shaft, the forward unit must revolve as a solid part. Since the output shaft is splined to the planet carrier, it turns with the planetary unit.

Although the *reverse planetary unit* is not involved, its *sun gear turns* with the output shaft and the reverse ring gear is splined to the output shaft. Therefore the reverse unit is also locked up.

Reverse gear is handled by the reverse planetary unit, as shown in Fig. 15-9.

The reverse-unit planet carrier is locked to the case by the *low-and-reverse clutch*. The *reverse-and-high clutch* is applied, and drives the *sun gear* clockwise. The *planet pinions* act as idlers and drive the *ring gear* counterclockwise. The ring gear is splined to the *output shaft*, which also turns counterclockwise.

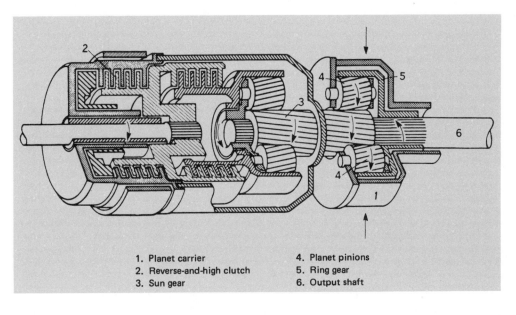

1. Planet carrier
2. Reverse-and-high clutch
3. Sun gear
4. Planet pinions
5. Ring gear
6. Output shaft

Fig. 15-9 Reverse-gear power flow.

Although the sun gear is being driven, the other two members remain loose so that the front planetary unit is in neutral.

In neutral only the output shaft is driven. No clutch is applied and neither of the planetary gear units turn unless the rear wheels are turning the output shaft.

Park is the same as neutral with but one exception. A pawl engages a gear on the output shaft and keeps the shaft and rear wheels from turning.

Gear train malfunctions. Mechanical failure in the gear train is rare when the transmission is properly maintained. The planetary gears, which are in constant mesh and arranged to eliminate side loads, virtually can last forever. However, foreign material in the fluid or lack of lubrication will cause wear and eventual failure of all parts that run together, particularly the bearings, thrust washers, shaft wearing surfaces, and the like.

Band and clutches are made of friction material that is subject to wear. Adjustments to compensate for band wear usually are made at specified intervals. Incorrect pressures, or operation of the vehicle with a low fluid level or an inferior oil, can burn out the clutches and bands.

The seals in the clutch and servo circuits can lose their sealing capability at high mileage and cause pressure loss. If the cause of the pressure loss is not corrected as soon as it is noticed, it can lead to more serious malfunctions.

It is important to remember that the operation of constantly meshed gears is automatic so long as the gears are not damaged and the clutches and bands operate properly. It is not necessary, therefore, to memorize each gear turn in every situation. What you do need to know is which clutches and bands should be applied and when they should be applied. If troubles in the clutches and bands are corrected promptly, the gears will take care of themselves.

HYDRAULIC CONTROL SYSTEM

An Overall Look at the C6 Hydraulic Control System

Let's begin our study of the C6 hydraulic control system by looking at the system in its entirety. Refer to Fig. 15-10. The names and functions of the various components are as follows:

converter – fluid clutch and torque multiplier.

pump – circulates and pressurizes the fluid (oil).

check valve – keeps the converter from draining through the cooler when the engine stops.

cooler – prevents excessive oil temperature.

drain-back – prevents the cooler from draining through the front lube passages when the engine stops.

forward clutch – locks the input shaft to the forward-unit ring gear in all forward gears.

reverse-and-high clutch – locks the input shaft to the sun gear in reverse and high gears.

intermediate servo – applies intermediate band in second gear only.

low-and-reverse clutch – locks the reverse planetary-unit ring gear to the case in L and R ranges only.

primary and secondary governor valves – provide a pressure signal proportional to road speed to help control shift points and pressures.

cutback control – reduces the control pressure as road speed increases.

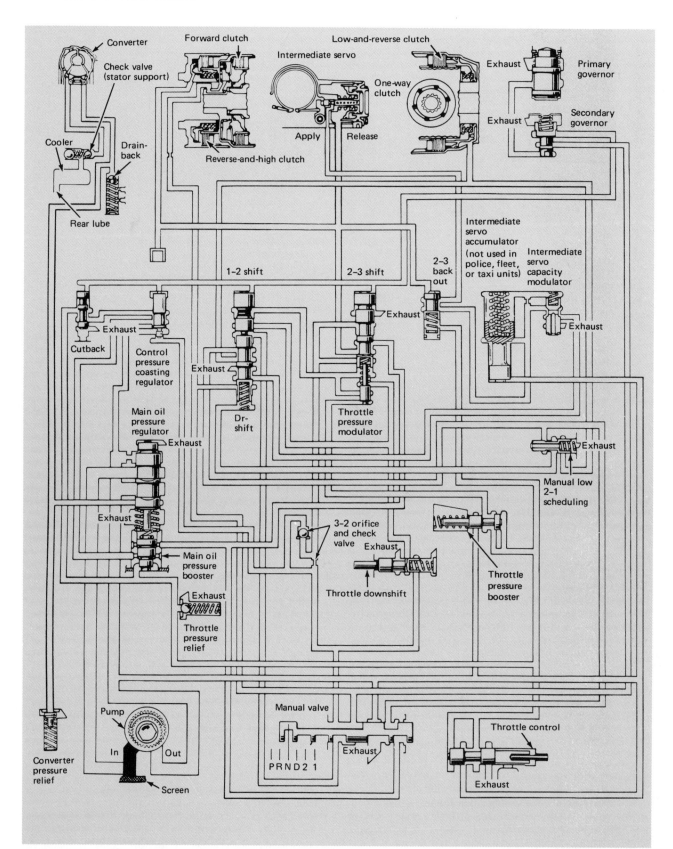

Fig. 15–10 C6 hydraulic control system.

coasting control-pressure regulator – boosts the control pressure when the transmission is shifted to L range at closed throttle.

1-2 shift and DR2 valves – causes 1-2 upshift and 2-1 downshift.

2-3 shift – causes 2-3 upshift and 3-2 downshift.

2-3 back-out – prevents a clutch band from tightening up if the driver releases the accelerator during the 2-3 upshift.

intermediate servo accumulator and intermediate servo capacity modulator – cushions the band applications for smooth 1-2 upshift.

throttle pressure modulator – provides a decreased throttle pressure to the shift valves to delay upshifts.

manual low 2-1 scheduling – shifts the transmission to second gear instead of first when the selector is moved to the L position at speeds above 10 mph.

3-2 orifice and check valve – cushions the servo application on a coasting 3-2 shift.

converter pressure relief – limits the maximum pressure in the converter to about 90 psi.

main oil pressure regulator – regulates the control pressure.

main oil pressure booster – increases the control pressure when the output torque is high (engine under load).

throttle downshift – overrides automatic upshifts and causes forced downshift.

throttle pressure booster – increases the throttle pressure above 50 per cent throttle opening.

manual valve – directs the control pressure to various systems for automatic control of gears and shift quality.

throttle control – provides an engine load pressure signal to control the shift points and the pressure.

Pressure Supply System

The pressure supply system includes a pump to keep the oil in motion, a pressure-regulating valve, and oil supply circuits.

Enough oil must be supplied to keep the torque converter full at all times, operate the hydraulic clutches, servo, and controls, and lubricate the working parts of the transmission. A reservoir of oil, usually referred to as the *sump*, is maintained in the transmission pan and the bottom of the case.

Automatic transmission oil is specially compounded, and you should always use the type recommended by the transmission manufacturer.

Pump operation. As shown in Fig. 15-11, the C6 transmission has *one pump*. The *drive gear,* which engages with *flats on the hub* of the *converter impeller,* turns with the engine. An *internal-tooth driven gear,* which is *eccentric* to the *drive gear,* meshes with the *drive gear* at the bottom, so that both gears revolve together. Spaces are provided between the gears to carry oil from the inlet to the outlet.

The *inlet port* is located where the gears just begin to

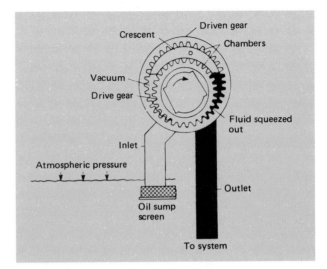

Fig. 15-11 Oil pump.

separate. A partial vacuum is created here, and atmospheric pressure in the sump pushes oil into the inlet.

At the top of the pump a *crescent* is fitted closely between the *gear teeth.* The crescent and the spaces between the teeth form *pumping chambers.* Fluid is trapped in these chambers as the teeth pass the inlet.

Beyond the crescent, the gears start to close and compress the oil. The crescent prevents the compression from pushing oil back to the inlet. Thus the fluid must flow through the outlet.

The pump is designed to deliver more oil than the system needs, and the excess is returned to the sump by the main oil-pressure regulator valve.

Main oil-pressure regulator valve. The main oil-pressure regulator valve bypasses excess oil and regulates system pressure to suit transmission operating requirements.

Refer back to Fig. 15-10. The upper passage to the valve is the controlling passage where oil is routed into a groove between two valve lands. Since the upper land has a smaller diameter than the lower, any pressure in the groove exerts a downward force which opposes the upward push of the valve springs.

In the lower passage leading to the valve, oil pressure is exerted against equal areas, so neither an upward- or downward-acting force results.

When the oil pressure rises to approximately 60 psi, the valve opens the passage leading to the converter. Once the converter is charged (filled with oil), further pressure increases push the regulator valve down far enough to open the sump passage, and all oil not needed in the transmission is returned via the sump to the pump inlet.

Pressure in the supply system is regulated by the force of the spring balancing the downward-acting hydraulic force created in the upper passage of the valve. If the pressure drops, the spring shifts the valve up and cuts off the sump passage (and even the converter passage, if necessary) to maintain the regulated pressure.

Notice that the pump outlet also leads to the manual valve, throttle control, throttle pressure booster, and the intermediate servo accumulator. Control pressure is present at these points whenever the main regulator valve is functioning properly.

Converter and Cooler System

A passage leads from the body of the main oil pressure regulator up to the converter impeller. From the converter turbine, the oil passes through a check valve to the cooler. From the cooler, the oil lubricates the rear parts of the gear train and returns to the sump. A branch circuit from the passage leading to the converter passes through the drainback valve and is used to lubricate the front parts of the transmission. When the engine is stopped, a spring seats the drain-back valve to keep the converter from draining to the sump through the front lube passages.

The converter pressure relief valve limits converter pressure to about 90 psi regardless of how high the control pressure rises. If the converter pressure tries to rise above 90 psi, this valve opens and drains some oil to the sump.

The check valve in the cooler rear lube circuit operates in the same way as the drain-back valve, and is set to open at 10 psi. Thus, it always maintains 10-psi pressure in the converter when the engine is running.

Gear-Train Control

The manual valve is operated by mechanical linkage from the shift selector and directs control pressure to the holding members (clutch and band) involved in starting out in each range, and then to valves involved in automatic shifting to each range.

The pump supplies pressure to two ports of the manual valve. Depending upon the position of the shift selector, the manual valves then direct control pressure to five other passages. Each passage leads to a separate subsystem.

One passage leads directly to the forward clutch, which is applied in all forward gears. Branches of this passage also lead to the DR2 shift and the secondary governor. The governor operates in all forward ranges.

When starting in D1, the holding members are the forward clutch and the one-way clutch. The one-way clutch is not hydraulically operated; therefore, when the forward clutch is applied, you have all the hydraulics needed for a first-gear start in D1.

Now let's go back to the manual valve and build up to a second-gear start in D2.

Again refer to Fig. 15-10; notice that one passage starts at the manual valve and terminates on the combination valve labeled 1-2 shift and DR2 shift. The control pressure exerted between these two valves forces the DR2 shift down against its spring. When the DR2 shift is down, the inter-

mediate servo apply becomes charged and first gear lockout system is always charged.

With the DR2 shift down, the passage from the forward clutch and governor system continues around a groove in the DR2 shift to the intermediate servo capacity modulator, around a groove in this valve, past the intermediate servo accumulator, and through a groove in the 2-3 backout to the apply side of the servo. The servo piston moves to apply the band. The flow ends at the coasting boost valve, and thus keeps the first gear lockout system charged.

Now let's look at the low-and-reverse clutch apply system. First, note that a passage runs from the manual valve to a port on the 1-2 shift. With the 1-2 shift up (as it is in either low-or-reverse gear), oil flows around a groove in the valve and then branches off in two directions. In one direction it applies the low-and-reverse clutch; in the opposite direction it exerts pressure under the DR2 shift, 2-3 shift, and 1-2 shift valves. Thus, all the shift valves are held in the downshift position (that is, the valves are held upward), and no shift can occur while the low-and-reverse clutch is applied. This system is sometimes called the *second-and-third gear lockout system*.

Now, to start in L range (manual low), the low-and-reverse clutch and the forward clutch must be applied. In L range, therefore, the manual valve charges the forward clutch and governor system and the low-and-reverse clutch apply system. An upshift is impossible, because the low-and-reverse clutch apply keeps the shift valves from moving.

In reverse, both the low-and-reverse and the reverse-and-high clutches are applied.

As shown in Fig. 15-10, one passage from the manual valve leads to the 2-3 shift valve. From the 2-3 shift valve, another passage applies the reverse-and-high clutch and pressurizes the release side of the intermediate servo.

When oil from the manual valve enters the pressure booster, it exerts an upward force which compresses the regulator spring. To operate in a balanced condition, the regulator must then maintain a higher pressure in reverse gear. As a result, the clutches are applied with more force to compensate for the higher torque obtained in reverse.

Now that you have seen how the clutches and servo are pressurized when starting out in each range, let's see how upshifts and downshifts are obtained.

The 2-3 shift valve is a single unit, but the 1-2 shift valve train contains the 1-2 shift and the DR2 shift valves. These three valves open and close passages to accomplish the shifts, and are controlled by pressure signals from the governor, throttle pressure booster, and throttle downshift. In the absence of controlling pressure, the shift valves are held up (downshifted) by their springs.

An important point to remember in considering upshifts and downshifts is that the forward clutch stays applied in all forward ranges; only the servo and other clutches are involved in shifting.

A 1-2 shift occurs only in the D1 (normal driving) range. In first gear, the reverse-unit planet carrier is held by the one-way clutch. The 1-2 upshift occurs when the servo applies the band. The one-way clutch then begins to "freewheel" as the planet carrier turns clockwise.

To make the 1-2 shift, the servo must be applied (that is, the servo apply system must be charged). This system is charged in the second-gear start (D2) range. For the 1-2 upshift, the entire 1-2 shift valve train is moved downward by governor pressure, and the servo apply system is charged through the DR2 valve.

If governor pressure falls off during second-gear operation, the 1-2 shift train moves upward. The servo apply system is then open to sump at the DR2 valve. The servo spring releases the band, and the transmission downshifts to first gear.

When governor pressure pushes the 2-3 shift valve down, pressure is exerted at the reverse-and-high clutch apply and at the intermediate servo release. Release pressure plus spring force overcome the apply pressure and therefore the band comes off.

In D2 range the transmission downshifts to second when the governor pressure drops off. The 2-3 shift valve moves upward and blocks pressure to the reverse-and-high clutch apply system. This system is then connected to the sump through a passage at the manual valve.

In D1 range the downshift from high gear is directly to first. When governor pressure falls off, both shift valves move upward simultaneously and this releases both the reverse-and-high clutch and the servo.

Governor System

It has been shown that governor pressure (or its absence) has some control over the operation of the shift valves. Now let's see where and how governor pressure is obtained. Then throttle pressure, which is also involved in the automatic control of gear shifting, will also be explained.

The governor is a device that feeds road speed input to the transmission. Of course, as speed increases a shift to a higher gear is required. Thus, the governor puts out a signal, proportional to engine speed, which attempts to move the shift valves to their upshifted position. In the C6 design there is no governor pressure below 10 mph. The transmission, then, always downshifts at this speed if it is in second or high gears.

Governor pressure is also required to help regulate control pressure and shift smoothly.

Governor operation. The governor has a primary valve and a secondary valve. Both are contained in a housing which is splined to the output shaft. Thus, the valves are driven in rotation and are acted upon by centrifugal force when the car is in motion.

At speeds below 10 mph, the primary governor valve keeps governor pressure from building up. The secondary valve acts as a balanced valve to furnish a pressure proportional to the speed of the output shaft.

With the transmission in neutral, the front clutch system is not charged, so there is no pressure applied to the governor. With the vehicle stopped, the primary valve is held in by its spring, and the secondary valve is held out by its spring.

In any forward gear, control pressure is routed to the governor. See Fig. 15-12. With the automobile at a standstill, control pressure acts on the face of the large *land* of the *secondary valve* and pushes the *valve* in. The inward movement of the secondary valve opens the passage to the *primary valve*. Control pressure applied against the *small land of the secondary valve* holds the valve in against its *spring*. The secondary valve stays fully in at speeds below 10 mph.

When the speed of the automobile reaches 10 mph, centrifugal force acts on the primary governor valve and moves it outward against the force of the spring. See Fig. 15-13. The passage between the two valves is then vented to the *sump*. The removal of pressure from the small land of the secondary valve permits the valve to move outward and connects the supply passage to the governor pressure passage. The governor then acts as a balanced valve, with pressure being balanced against spring force and centrifugal force.

As road speed increases, the valve moves farther out and increases governor pressure. If road speed decreases, the valve moves to decrease the opening and governor pressure. At about 10 mph governor pressure is cut off as the process reverses and the transmission downshifts.

You have already seen that governor pressure is directed to the shift valves to force them to the uplifted position. The passage involved terminates above the cut-back valve and control pressure coasting regulator, as shown in Fig. 15-10.

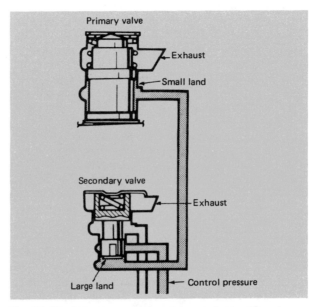

Fig. 15-12 Governor operation at speeds below 10 mph.

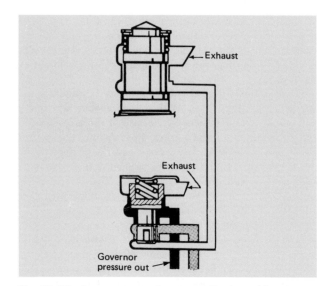

Fig. 15-13 Governor operation at speeds above 10 mph.

Throttle Pressure System

Throttle pressure is a signal to the transmission of how large a load the engine is pulling, that is, the torque demand on the engine.

Throttle pressure opposes governor pressure and either delays an upshift or causes an automatic downshift. Throttle pressure also acts to increase control pressure and thereby permits the handling of a high torque demand.

Throttle-valve operation. The throttle control, which is located in the transmission case, is another balanced valve. Supply pressure always is furnished directly from the pump. To control throttle pressure, a vacuum diaphragm is connected to the engine intake manifold and a spring inside the diaphragm balances the forces acting on the diaphragm. Throttle pressure output is inversely proportional to engine vacuum. Thus, at high vacuum (no load), throttle pressure is low; under load, vacuum drops and throttle pressure increases.

Throttle pressure is routed to two faces of the oil pressure booster valve to provide the extra pressure needed to handle high torque demands. The pressure booster is forced up and adds to the force of the springs of the main oil pressure regulator. Then, more control pressure is needed to balance the main regulator.

Throttle pressure is routed also to two ports on the throttle pressure booster and from there to the throttle pressure modulator; this produces a modulated throttle pressure to control the shift valves. Modulated throttle pressure is used to oppose governor pressure on the shift valves. It is produced by balancing the 2-3 shift valve spring against the throttle pressure in the passage leading from the throttle pressure booster.

To get to the upper port of the throttle pressure booster, throttle pressure must pass the cut-back valve. This valve produces a lower control pressure at higher road speeds by cutting off the passage leading to the throttle booster.

Somewhere between 10 and 30 mph, depending on engine load, governor pressure on top of the cut-back valve overcomes throttle pressure. The cut-back then shifts down and keeps throttle pressure from reaching the booster.

It has been noted that throttle pressure increases as vacuum drops. Unfortunately, above about one-half opening of the carburetor throttle, this relationship is no longer maintained. To compensate for this, the throttle pressure booster increases throttle pressure in the passage leading to the throttle pressure modulator.

Kickdown System

Up to this point, the discussion of upshifts and downshifts has been confined to automatic shifts; that is, shifts that result from the opposition of governor pressure (road speed) to modulated throttle pressure (torque demand).

The driver, however, can override this automatic control with the accelerator and thereby force a downshift. The throttle downshift, also known as the *kickdown valve*, is operated mechanically. Normally, the spring holds it in the position shown in Fig. 15-10. However, when the accelerator is "floorboarded," a mechanical linkage shifts the valve to the right. With the valve shifted, full control pressure is directed into the passages leading to the shifting valves. This pressure moves the shift valve up against the force of the governor pressure and causes a downshift. Hence, the expression "kickdown."

Other Refinements

Basic operation of the hydraulic control system has now been covered. Without certain refinements, however, the shifts would be very harsh.

Intermediate servo capacity modulator and accumulator. The intermediate servo capacity modulator and accumulator valves are placed in the servo supply system to cushion the 1-2 upshift.

These two valves operate to control the rate at which the band applies, in much the same way as a manual clutch pedal is let out rapidly until the clutch starts to apply and then slowly to cushion the final lockup.

Before the servo apply system is charged, control pressure from the manual valve holds the accumulator valve up against spring force. When the DR2 shift moves to charge the servo system, control pressure is routed through the intermediate servo capacity modulator to apply the servo. Control pressure is also routed through a drilled passage to the bottom of the servo capacity modulator, between two lands of the accumulator, and to the tops of both valves via an orifice.

Until the band contacts the drum, no pressure is transmitted through the orifice. But as pressure builds up on the orifice, it forces the accumulator valve downward. As the valve moves down, oil flows through the orifice. This produces a lower pressure above the valve than in the passage between the valves, but only while the accumulator is moving down.

With decreased pressure above it, the capacity modulator becomes a balanced valve. Passage pressure under the valve is balanced against the spring and lowers pressure above the valve. The modulator thus sends a regulated power pressure to the servo until the accumulator valve bottoms.

When the accumulator valve bottoms, no oil flows through the orifice, pressure equalizes throughout the passages, and full control pressure is applied to the servo.

2-3 back-out. The 2-3 back-out valve presents a clutch-band "fight" if the driver releases the accelerator (backs out) in the middle of a 2-3 upshift. Releasing the accelerator lowers pressure, and although enough pressure may remain in the system to apply the reverse-and-high clutch, there may not be enough to release the band. Let's see how this is prevented.

When the driver releases the accelerator, throttle pressure in the passage under the back-out valve drops to zero. Pressure from the clutch apply servo release forces the back-out valve down. This cuts off the servo apply passage at the back-out valve and interconnects the servo apply and release passages. With equal pressure on both sides of the servo piston, the spring releases the band while the clutch is applying.

3-2 orifice and check valve. The 3-2 orifice and check valve provides alternate paths to exhaust servo release pressure on the 3-2 downshift.

During a forced downshift, the vehicle speed is more than 10 mph and governor pressure holds the control pressure coasting regulator down. The release side of the servo is then vented through a passage leading from the back of the control pressure coasting regulator, through the 2-3 shift valve, manual valve, and sump. There is no restriction, and the servo can apply quickly.

In a coasting condition, governor pressure drops off and the spring of the coasting regulator shifts the valve up. This blocks the passage from the secondary governor and oil must flow through the 3-2 orifice to get back to the venting passage. Thus, when coasting, the orifice cushions band application.

Manual-low 2-1 scheduling valve. If the transmission were to shift directly from high speed to low speed, a severe jolt

would be felt. To prevent this, when the selector is moved from D1 or D2 to L at a speed above 10 mph, the downshift is to second rather than to first. The manual-low 2-1 scheduling valve causes this downshift.

In high gear, the 2-3 back-out normally is forced down by control pressure in the servo release passage. When the selector is moved to L, however, control pressure moves the back-out valve up. At the same time, the shift control supply system is vented, thereby relieving pressure in the venting passages and permitting a downshift from high.

With the 2-3 back-up valve up, the servo apply system remains charged and the downshift is to second. If the back-out valve were down, the servo apply system would also be vented and the shift would be to first.

Coasting boost valve. On the manual downshift to L range, a very high control pressure is needed to hold the band on. Drum rotation on this shift has a tendency to loosen the band. Unfortunately, this shift is usually a coasting shift and there is little or no throttle pressure to boost control pressure. Therefore, the coasting regulator takes over the function of applying the pressure needed to hold the band on.

Control pressure is directed to the coasting regulator from the servo apply system. On the coasting downshift from high gear to L, governor pressure pushes the coasting regulator valve down. Servo apply pressure is then routed to the main oil pressure booster to increase control pressure.

HYDRAULIC SYSTEM MALFUNCTIONS

Common Faults

Sticking valves. A sticking valve is probably the most common malfunction in a hydraulic system, and usually is caused by dirt in the oil or by a burr raised in careless assembly. If you know what each valve is supposed to do, this type of problem may be diagnosed by road testing the car. You may not always trace the problem to one valve only, but merely tracing it to the valve body is sufficient. It is common practice when disassembling a valve body for cleaning to remove all valves.

In general, sticking shift valves or a sticking governor will cause either no shifts or shifts at incorrect speeds. Sticking throttle valves tend to cause harsh shifts (pressure too low). Of course, the throttle valve also affects the speed at which the shift occurs.

The manual valve is not likely to shift since it is controlled by linkage. The downshift valve may stick in its "in" position and prevent upshifts, except at very high speed.

Sticking regulator valves affect pressure and, therefore,

the feel of the shift; that is, the shift may feel either harsh or mushy.

When any valves involved in a shifting operation tend to stick, that particular shifting operation will be rough; if the 1-2 shift valve sticks, for example, the shift from first to second will be rough.

Erratic operation. Erratic operation is caused usually by incorrect oil level. A delayed, mushy shift usually is the result of a low or high oil level, and the oil may appear foamy.

Pump wear. Pumps lose efficiency as they wear. With less volume, delay in engagement occurs when the transmission is put in gear, particularly reverse. Where clearance specifications for mating parts are available, it is easy to check a pump. If the pump turns and is not too worn, it will still pump. A pump that is not scored, seized, or otherwise damaged should never be replaced unless it is worn excessively.

Oil leaks. External oil leaks usually occur in the speedometer cable connection, output shaft oil seal in the extension housing, oil pan gasket, or servo covers. Internal leaks from blown or broken seals frequently cause a holding member (clutch or servo) to lose pressure and slip.

Burned clutches and bands. Incorrect pressures, oil foaming, or a loss of pressure may cause burned clutches and bands. Inspection of the oil may show when a friction member is burned out, since there will be particles in the oil. In extreme cases the oil will be black and have a distinct burned odor.

When clutches and bands are burned, always find out what caused the burning and correct the fault before putting the unit back in service.

Troubleshooting and Adjustment Procedures

Like all other manufacturers of automatic transmissions, Ford recommends that a definite troubleshooting and adjustment procedure be followed before dismantling any transmission.

This procedure, often called a *transmission tuneup*, includes the following: a check of the fluid level and condition, engine idle, manual valve linkage, throttle (downshift) linkage, stall test, road test, bands, and pressure test.

Oil level. To check the oil level, first warm up the transmission. Then, just before the check, move the selector through all ranges to fill all clutches and servos. With the engine running and the shift selector in P (Park), remove and wipe the transmission oil dipstick, insert it fully into its tube, again remove it, and note the oil level. It should be at the full (F) mark, but never higher. Add or remove oil to correct the level.

Also note the condition of the oil. It should be clean. A sticky, golden-brown varnish on the dipstick shows that the oil has broken down. All internal parts of the transmission will be similarly coated and a complete disassembly and cleaning are required. Black oil with a burned odor means a clutch or band is burned out and the oil has become overheated. Friction material in the oil means that a band or clutch either has failed or is in the process of doing so. When the oil is milky looking, the cooler is leaking into the radiator and engine coolant is in the transmission. This leak, if not corrected immediately, will damage the seals. If the seals have already been damaged, an overhaul is needed. Before an overhaul is undertaken, however, change the oil and check it at frequent intervals for some time afterward.

Engine idle. Incorrect idle speed is a frequent cause of transmission complaints. With the engine idling too fast, the engagement of transmission tends to be harsh. A fast idle also increases throttle pressure which, in turn, increases control pressure and adds to the harshness.

Ford usually specifies the idle speed with the shift selector in the D (Drive) range, so set the parking brake before any adjustment is attempted. The headlights should also be turned on to place a load on the alternator. In an air-conditioned car, run the air conditioner for twenty minutes before making an adjustment.

Use a tachometer to adjust the idle speed to specifications.

Antistall dashpot. Many Fords with automatic transmissions have antistall dashpots on the carburetors to keep the transmission load from stalling the engine when the accelerator is released. The dashpot is checked by measuring the clearance between its plunger and the throttle lever with the plunger bottomed and the throttle lever at hot idle (off the fast idle cam). If necessary, adjust the clearance to specifications.

Manual valve linkage. Improper operation of the manual valve linkage seldom causes improper transmission operation in a Ford. In every range the manual valve is retained by a spring-loaded ball or plunger falling into a groove inside the transmission. If the detents do not match the selector positions, the detents usually fall in place but the selector points between positions. However, if the detents do not fall in place, the manual valve can be between positions, causing cross leakage, erratic operation, and slippage.

Check the adjustment of the manual valve linkage as follows: (1) Move the shift selector from N (Neutral) to D1 and then to D2. There are no stops in the selector between these positions, so you should be able to feel the detent holding in D2. Make sure the detent corresponds to the small dot on the drive selector indicator. (2) If the detent is on the dot, try to move the shift lever into all other ranges. If the lever can be shifted, the adjustment is off by less than a full notch. If the detent does not correspond with the dot, or if you cannot shift to one of the extreme ranges, (P or L), the linkage must be adjusted.

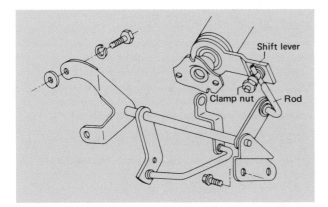

Fig. 15–14   Adjusting column shift linkage.

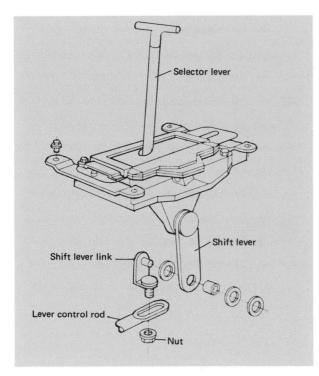

Fig. 15–15   Adjusting console shift linkage.

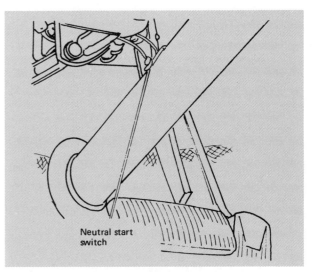

Fig. 15–16   Column mounted neutral start switch.

Adjusting console shift linkage.   To adjust the console shift linkage, proceed as follows: (1) Move the shift selector to position D1. (2) Loosen the *nut* holding the *lever control* to the *shift lever link*, as shown in Fig. 15-15. (3) Move the shift lever to position D1. (4) Tighten the nut to the specified torque. (5) Check to make sure the engine cranks in the N and P positions. If necessary, adjust the neutral start switch.

Adjusting neutral start switch.   If the neutral start switch is column mounted, as shown in Fig. 15-16, loosen the switch-attaching screws. Position the switch so that the engine cranks in neutral, then tighten the screws. With the transmission in neutral, rotate the switch until you can insert a No. 43 gauge pin or drill shank into the gauge pin holes. Make sure the drill shank goes a full $^{31}/_{64}$ inch into each of the three holes in the switch. Then tighten the attaching bolts to the specified torque and remove the pin.

Adjusting throttle linkage.   There are two basic arrangements of throttle linkage to consider.

If the switch is transmission mounted, as shown in Fig. 15-17, loosen the switch-attaching bolts. In these transmissions, throttle linkage must be adjusted with a pressure gauge.

On later units, the throttle linkage operates only the downshift valve, and a stop is provided in the transmission to make the adjustment. The adjustment must be made only after the engine idle and antistall dashpot have been adjusted and with the carburetor throttle lever in its hot idle position.

To adjust the throttle linkage of a late-model Thunderbird, proceed as follows: (1) With the engine idle and dashpot adjusted, the throttle lever should be in the hot idle position. (2) Adjust the height of the *accelerator pedal* (Fig.

Adjusting column shift linkage.   To adjust the column shift linkage, proceed as follows: (1) Move the selector to D1. (2) As shown in Fig. 15-14, loosen the *clamp nut* on the *shift rod* and *trunnion* to let the *shift lever* slide freely from the rod. (3) Move the lever to position D1. (4) Pull the lever against the *gate stop* on the *steering column* and tighten the *clamp nut* to the specified torque. (6) Check the other shift position. Make sure the engine cranks in both the N and P positions. If necessary, adjust the neutral start switch (discussed shortly).

15-18) to specifications at the *carburetor connecting link*. (3) Position the *speed nut* exactly 1¼ inches from the forward face of the *bushing* in the *downshift lever*.

To adjust the throttle linkage of a Ford or Mercury, proceed as follows: (1) With the engine stopped, disconnect the throttle return spring, as shown in Fig. 15-19. (2) Loosen the *control cable conduit clamp*. (3) Block the accel-erator pedal fully on the floor. (4) Pull on the cable conduit until the throttle lever on the carburetor is against its wide-open stop. Tighten the control cable conduit clamp. (5) Push the downshift rod down until the lever on the transmission is against its stop. Hold the rod down and turn the down-shift lever adjusting screw to take up the clearance at the carburetor throttle lever. (6) Lock the adjusting screw, re-lease the pedal, and connect the return spring.

The throttle linkage for the Ford Fairlane is shown in Fig. 15-20. The adjusting procedure is as follows: (1) Dis-connect the *bellcrank-to-carburetor rod* and the accelerator connecting link. Disconnect the stabilizer rod from the bell-crank lever. (2) Insert a ¼-inch-diameter alignment pin through the bellcrank and bracket. (3) Adjust the length of the stabilizer rod so that its trunnion enters the bellcrank freely. Install the retaining clip. (4) Attach the carburetor rod to the bellcrank. (5) Adjust the length of the accelerator rod to obtain a pedal height of 4¼ inches. Connect the ac-celerator rod to the accelerator shaft. (6) Remove the align-ment pin.

A typical Lincoln throttle linkage is shown in Fig. 15-21. The adjustment procedure is as follows: (1) Adjust the height of the accelerator pedal to specifications. (2) Loosen the locknut on the downshift rod. Disconnect the rod from the bellcrank. (3) Check to make sure the movable outer bracket on the bellcrank is against the stop pin on the inner bracket. (4) Pull on the downshift rod to hold it against the stop. Adjust the rod length to line up the hole in the rod with the stud on the bellcrank. (5) Lengthen the rod one turn and reattach it. Tighten the locknut securely. (6) Check

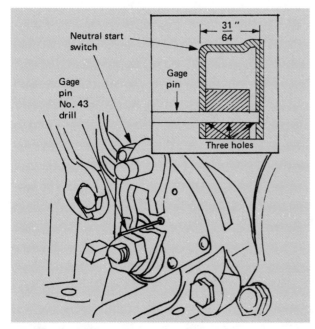

Fig. 15–17 Adjusting transmission mounted neutral start switch.

Fig. 15–18 Throttle linkage for Thunderbird.

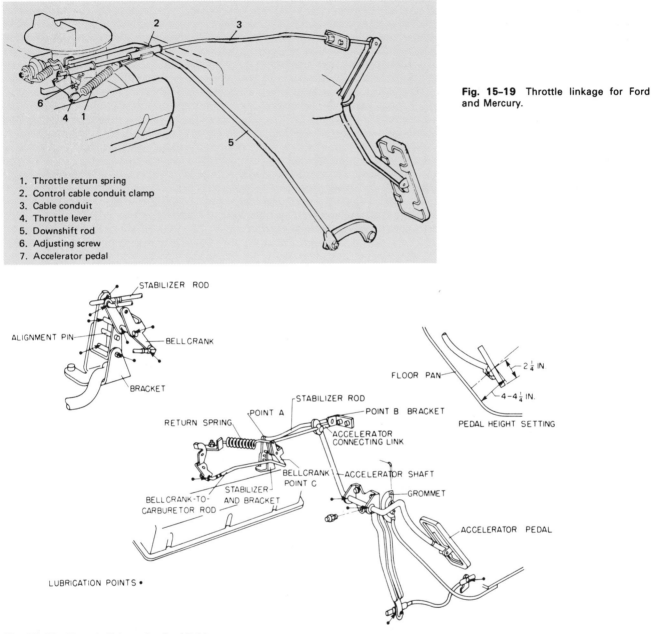

Fig. 15-19 Throttle linkage for Ford and Mercury.

1. Throttle return spring
2. Control cable conduit clamp
3. Cable conduit
4. Throttle lever
5. Downshift rod
6. Adjusting screw
7. Accelerator pedal

Fig. 15-20 Throttle linkage for Ford Fairlane.

again to make sure the bellcrank outer bracket remains against the stop pin. If it does not, lengthen the rod one more turn.

The adjustments just described cover the full line of Ford automobiles, although every model has not been mentioned. Also, design change may cause a different linkage to be used from one year to the next. A check of the actual linkage against the illustrations will show which adjusting procedure should be followed.

For early transmissions with linkage control of the throttle valve, first make the preliminary adjustments described above. Then make a final check with a pressure gauge as follows: (1) Set the parking brake firmly. (2) Install a pressure gauge in the control pressure takeoff (near the control levers) on the transmission case, positioning the gauge so that it can be read from the driver's seat. (3) Mount a tachometer so that it can be read from the driver's seat. (4) Start the engine and shift the selector to the normal driving range. (5) Push down firmly on the foot brake, operate the engine at the specified rpm and note the reading of the pressure gauge. Make the check quickly so that operation at stall does not last more than a few seconds. (6) If it is necessary to increase pressure, lengthen the throttle lever control; shorten the throttle lever control to reduce pressure.

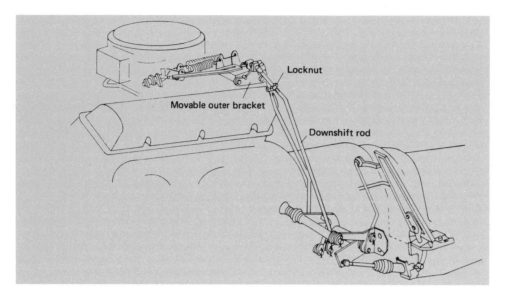

Fig. 15–21 Throttle linkage for Lincoln.

Stall Test

A stall test shows the maximum rpm obtainable in each driving range. It is used to troubleshoot clutch and band slipping, torque converter operation, and overall engine performance.

The test procedure is as follows: (1) Make sure the radiator is full of coolant, that the transmission oil level is correct, and that the engine is at normal operating temperature. (2) Connect a tachometer to the engine, positioning it so that it can be read from the driver's seat. Use a grease pencil to mark the maximum specified rpm on the dial for easy reference. (3) Apply both the parking and foot brakes firmly. (4) In each range, push the accelerator pedal steadily to the floor, holding it there just long enough for the tachometer reading to stabilize—usually no more than five seconds. Record the reading. (5) Return the selector to neutral and run the engine at 1,000 rpm for 60 seconds between tests in each range. This allows the oil in the converter to cool.

A high rpm means either clutch or band slippage. If this is indicated, release the accelerator immediately to prevent damage.

The holding member that is slipping can be determined by knowing which member is applied in each range. Table 15-1 shows the clutch and band applications for each driving range. Since no upshifts occur in the stall test, the members involved in starting in each range provide a clue to the trouble.

Refer to the table and note that a slipping forward clutch would show up at a high rpm in all forward ranges. A slipping one-way clutch would result at high rpm in D1 only. Other members are diagnosed in the same way, simply by noting in which range slippage occurs. In some cases, such as the intermediate band, however, a road test must

be used to detect slippage. In these cases, the band may not hold on the stall test, but the one-way clutch will, and this will give a normal rpm reading.

When the rpm meet specifications, the holding members for that particular range are O.K. The only exceptions are the intermediate and front bands.

A good stall test in any range shows that the converter one-way clutch is holding and engine performance is acceptable.

Low-stall rpm shows either that the one-way clutch on

Table 15–1 Clutch and Band applications.

Range and Gear	Holding Members C4 and C6	
R Reverse	Low-and-reverse clutch or band	Reverse-and-high clutch
2	Forward clutch	Intermediate band
D First	Forward clutch	One-way clutch
D Second	Forward clutch	Intermediate band
D High	Forward clutch	Reverse-and-high clutch
1	Forward clutch	Low-and-reverse clutch or band
	FMX	
R Reverse	Rear clutch	Rear band
2	Front clutch	Front band
D First	Front clutch	One-way clutch
D Second	Front clutch	Front band
D High	Front clutch	Rear clutch
1 First	Front clutch	Rear band

the converter stator is slipping and return flow from the turbine is opposing the impeller or that engine performance is below standard.

To determine which fault is causing the trouble, road test the vehicle. If the one-way clutch is not holding, acceleration will be poor at low speed and normal at higher speed. Poor engine performance will result in poor acceleration at any speed.

Road Testing

Road testing confirms the diagnosis of any holding member that might be slipping and shows if all transmission valves are operating properly.

A road test should be performed after correction of any known faults. Drive the car through all gears in each range and check the shift points and shift feel. To analyze results of the road test, the findings for each shift should be recorded and then related to the operation of the various clutches, bands, or valves.

When the converter one-way clutch is seized so that the stator cannot turn, the stall test will be normal. However, top speed in the road test will be limited to about 50 mph because the converter is always in reduction. If this problem is encountered, remove the converter and test the clutch. Ford has a special tool for making this test. A welded converter, of course, must be replaced if defective. Also

Table 15–2 Troubleshooting automatic transmissions.

Operating Conditions	Components to Check
Rough initial engagement in D or 2	2, 5, 6, 11, 23
Rough initial engagement in 2 only	7, 10
1-2 or 2-3 shift points incorrect	1, 2, 3, 4, 5, 12, 23
Rough 2-3 shift	2, 5, 6
Engine overspeeds on 2-3 shift	2, 5, 6, 7, 23
No shift points	3, 4, 5
No 2-3 shift	3, 4, 5, 18
No forced downshifts	5, 12, 23
Runaway engine on forced downshift	2, 5, 6, 7, 10
Rough 3-2 or 3-1 shift at closed throttle	2, 5, 11
Shifts 1-3 in D and 2	7, 10
No engine braking in first gear—manual low range	8, 9
Creeps excessively in D or 2	11
Slips or chatters in first gear, D	1, 2, 5, 6, 23
Slips or chatters in second gear	1, 2, 5, 6, 7, 10, 23
Slips or chatters in R	1, 5, 6, 8, 9, 23
No drive in D only	3, 5
No drive in 2 only	3
No drive in R only	3, 5, 8, 9, 18
No drive in D, 2, or 1	4, 18, 23
No drive in any selector lever position	1, 3, 5, 6, 18, 23
Lockup in 2 only	8, 9
Lockup in R only	20, 22
Parking lock binds or does not hold	3
Transmission overheats	1, 6, 15
Maximum speed too low, poor acceleration	25
Transmission noisy in N	6
Transmission noisy in first, second, and reverse gear	6
Transmission noisy in P	6
Fluid leak	13, 14, 15, 16, 17, 19, 21, 24

1. Fluid level
2. Vacuum diaphragm unit or tubes
3. Manual linkage
4. Governor
5. Valve body
6. Control pressure regulator valve
7. Intermediate band
8. Low-reverse band (clutch) or rear band
9. Low-reverse servo (clutch) or rear servo

10. Intermediate servo or front servo
11. Engine idle speed
12. Downshift linkage
13. Converter drain plugs
14. Oil pan gasket, or filler tube
15. Oil cooler and connections
16. Manual or downshift lever shaft seal
17. ⅛-in. pipe plug in side of case
18. Perform air-pressure check

19. Extension housing to case gaskets and lockwashers
20. Forward clutch
21. Extension-housing rear oil seat
22. Parking linkage
23. Perform control pressure check
24. Speedometer driven-gear adapter seal
25. Converter one-way clutch

check the transmission oil for evidence of breakdown from overheating.

Ford specifications for minimum throttle shift points occur when the foot pedal is depressed just enough to accelerate the car. Make the following checks: L range—shift to L from high gear in drive and check the point of the 2-1 downshift; D1 range—check the 1-2 and 2-3 shift points and the coasting 3-1 shift speed; D2 range—check the coasting 3-2 shift point.

In each instance, note how the shift feels—harsh, mushy, or normal. Refer to Table 15-1 to see which clutches and bands are released or applied on each shift. This should help to locate the cause of the trouble.

Torque demand shifts, which occur with the carburetor throttle fully open but without actuating the kickdown value, are called "to detent" shifts. It is difficult to feel the "detent" point, where the downshift rod begins to travel. The "detent" shift can be made much more noticeable by installing a moderately heavy spring on the downshift rod during the road test.

Check the 1-2 and 2-3 upshifts with the accelerator held "to detent." Also check the highest speed at which you can force a 3-2 downshift.

So-called "through detent" shift points are specified with the accelerator on the floor and the downshift valve shifted. Again check the 1-2 and 2-3 upshift points and the highest speeds at which you can force 3-1 and 3-2 downshifts.

To see if the valves operate properly, think about which valves are involved in each shift. If the shift points are correct, the governor, shift valves, and throttle valves should all be operating. If there is no harshness or mushiness in shifting, the regulator valves are operating freely. Diagnose "shift feel" valve troubles by creating the condition under which the valve is supposed to operate and then see if the shift is smooth.

Troubleshooting Guide

Table 15-2 lists the various operating conditions that may be encountered, and each condition is keyed to one or more code letter(s), which identify the components to be checked.

Band Adjustments

A slipping low-and-reverse band causes slip in reverse gear only and no downhill braking in L range.

A slipping intermediate (front) band is evident on the 1-2 upshift. The transmission will probably slip momentarily and then engage in second gear with a bump. With bad slippage, you will get a first-gear start in D2.

With two exceptions, both of which are concerned with internal adjustments, Ford has standardized the procedure for tightening the band adjusting screws. The screws are first tightened to a specified torque and then backed off by a certain amount. Tightening is done with a torque wrench or with a special wrench provided by Ford. The special

wrench is designed to slip at 10 ft-lb. of torque (or at the specified torque for the internally adjusted bands).

Refer to Ford maintenance manuals for the procedure to be followed in adjusting the bands on a particular make and model of car.

Pressure Test

Pressure tests are helpful to try to find the cause of slippage or harsh shifting.

Connect a tachometer to the engine, a pressure gauge to the transmission control pressure outlet, and tee a vacuum gauge into the diaphragm vacuum line, as shown in Fig. 15-22. Place all three instruments so they can be read

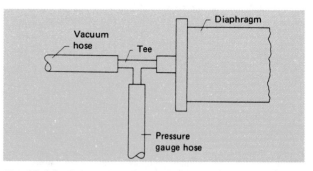

Fig. 15–22 Connections for testing vacuum-actuated throttle-valve units.

Table 15–3 Pressure test interpretations.

Results of Tests	Causes
All readings slightly high or low	Diaphragm improperly adjusted
Pressure increase not to specifications	Throttle valve stuck Pressure booster valve stuck Regulator valve stuck Compensator valve stuck
High idle pressure	Diaphragm leaks (To test, connect the gauge directly to the vacuum hose to see if the vacuum is higher without the diaphragm. Replace the hose if necessary.)
No rise in pressure as vacuum drops	Mechanical connection between the diaphragm and throttle valve disconnected Throttle valve frozen in bore
Low idle pressure at idle in all gears	Low pump output Excessive internal leakage in pump, case, or valve body Sticking regulator or compensator valve
Low idle pressure in certain gear or gears	Hydraulic leak in a system charged in the gear or gears

from the driver's seat. Special automatic testers combining all three instruments are also available.

With the engine idling, and with the vacuum gauge reading at least eighteen inches of vacuum, note the pressure reading. If the vacuum is less than eighteen inches, crack the throttle just a bit to see if it rises. If the vacuum does not rise, locate and correct the leak before continuing. (*NOTE:* In some high-altitude areas, a vacuum reading of eighteen inches may not be possible. Special pressure specifications are available from Ford for this condition.)

Press and release the accelerator to be sure the vacuum changes with the throttle setting. If there is a lag, look for a restriction in the diaphragm vacuum line.

Record the idle control pressure in all transmission ranges and check it with the specifications.

Ford recommends using a stall test to pull the vacuum down in order to test the pressure rise. Pressure specifica-tions are furnished for the various vacuum conditions, depending upon the particular unit being tested. The procedure is as follows: (1) Set the parking brake and firmly apply the foot brake. (2) Depress the accelerator until the vacuum is pulled down to the specified value in each range; record the pressure readings. (3) Between tests, operate the engine in neutral at 1,000 rpm for a full minute to ensure cooling.

The results of the idle and pressure tests can be interpreted by referring to Table 15-3.

The diaphragm is preset at the factory and seldom needs adjustment. If adjustment is needed, however, the adjusting screw can be made accessible by removing the vacuum line.

Insert a thin screwdriver in the end of the diaphragm. Turn it inward to increase the pressure and outward to decrease the pressure. One full turn in either direction produces a pressure change of approximately 3 psi.

16

REAR AXLES

Contents

Introduction

Differential Carriers

Rear-Axle Housing

Axle Shafts

Diagnosis, Testing, and Lubrication

In-Car Repairs

INTRODUCTION

Final Drives

Types. All automobiles use a *final drive* to transmit the power output of the engine to the wheels. Currently, most cars use a *rear-wheel* (conventional) drive, but a *front-wheel* drive is becoming increasingly popular, particularly on the new compacts. For the most part, *four-wheel* drive is confined to heavier vehicles intended for use in open country. Thus, the discussion of four-wheel drives is rather brief.

Rear-wheel drive. Figure 16-1 shows a typical rear-wheel drive system. The propeller shaft, turned by the engine, is equipped with a pinion that meshes with a ring gear inside the differential housing to drive the rear wheels. Leaf springs, attached at their center to the rear-axle housing, are connected to the automobile frame by spring mounts. The rear of each leaf spring is attached to the automobile frame by a movable shackle, and the front of each rear spring is solidly attached to the frame. This construction allows the driving force applied to the rear wheels to be transmitted through the leaf springs to the frame to propel the vehicle.

A cutaway view of a typical rear-axle assembly is shown in Fig. 16-2. When torque is applied to the propeller shaft by the transmission, the shaft turns the drive pinion, and the pinion turns the ring gear with which it is meshed. Since the ring gear is bolted to the differential case, the ring gear drives the differential case. Within the differential case there are two differential side gears, and a set of differential

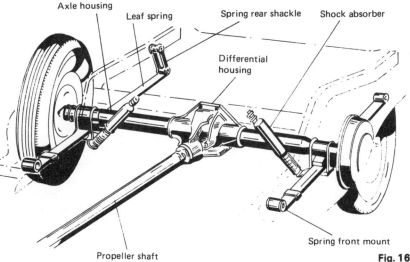

Axle housing

Leaf spring

Spring rear shackle

Shock absorber

Differential housing

Propeller shaft

Spring front mount

Fig. 16–1 Typical rear-wheel drive. *Courtesy of Chevrolet Division, General Motors Corporation.*

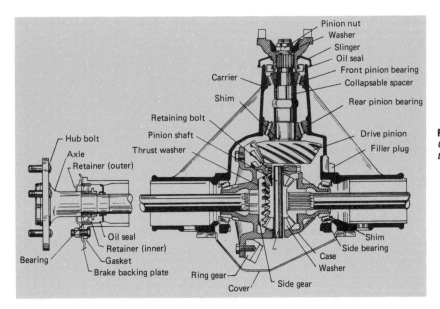

Pinion nut
Washer
Slinger
Oil seal
Front pinion bearing
Collapsable spacer
Rear pinion bearing
Carrier
Shim
Retaining bolt
Pinion shaft
Thrust washer
Drive pinion
Filler plug
Hub bolt
Axle
Retainer (outer)
Oil seal
Retainer (inner)
Gasket
Bearing
Brake backing plate
Ring gear
Cover
Side gear
Case
Washer
Side bearing
Shim

Fig. 16–2 Internal view of typical rear axle. *Courtesy of Oldsmobile Division, General Motors Corporation.*

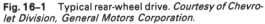

pinions and gears which are mounted on a pinion shaft. The axle shafts are splined to the differential side gears. As the differential case rotates, it turns the axle shaft through the differential pinion shaft, the differential pinion, and the side gears. Thus, power flows from the propeller shaft through the drive pinion, ring gear, differential, and axle shafts to the wheels. The differential also allows the wheels to turn at different rates. The operation of these and other parts shown in Fig. 16-2 is explained shortly.

Rear-end torque.   As the drive pinion rotates, resistance to turning is offered by the ring gear, then transferred to the drive pinion bearings and from there to the axle housing. This force tries to turn the axle housing in a direction opposite to that in which the rear wheels are turning.

When the brakes are applied, however, the opposite effect takes place, because the axle housing becomes frictionally connected to the drive wheels by the brakes. The turning motion of the drive wheels now tends to rotate the axle housing in the same direction as the rear wheels are turning.

The force that tends to rotate the rear-axle housing around the axle shafts is known as *rear-end torque*. Several methods have been used to overcome this torque and maintain the axle in alignment with the automobile frame.

Torque-tube drive.   An early method used to overcome rear-end torque is *torque-tube drive*. Here the propeller shaft rotates inside a housing called a *torque tube*. One end of the torque tube is attached to the transmission case and the other end to the rear-axle housing. Slip-type coupling connects the propeller shaft to the transmission and rear end, and truss rods are attached to a bracket at the front end of the torque tube to maintain axle alignment with the automobile frame. Improved drive-line designs and im-

provements in rear suspension systems have made torque-tube drive obsolete.

Hotchkiss drive.   Another method of absorbing rear-end torque is the *Hotchkiss drive*, Fig. 16-3, which incorporates semielliptical, long leaf springs. The center of each leaf spring is attached to the axle housing. The front end of each spring is rigidly attached to the car frame, while movable shackles connect the rear of each spring to the frame. In this way, rear-end torque is absorbed and, since the springs connect the rear-axle assembly to the frame, any movement of the drive wheels causes the vehicle to move.

Modified Hotchkiss drive.   Today many cars have coil springs instead of leaf springs; control arms (links) are needed to absorb rear-end torque. Since this new design retains some of the features of the Hotchkiss drive, it is called a *modified Hotchkiss drive* (or, sometimes, a *link-type drive*).

In one modification of the Hotchkiss drive, a rubber-insulated upper control arm and a lower control arm are placed on each side of the differential housing to connect the housing to the vehicle frame. These control arms (links) maintain the correct relationship of the rear axle to the car frame and, in addition, absorb rear-end torque.

One variation of the modified drive, shown in Fig. 16-4, has a fixed differential carrier attached at three points by rubber-insulated mountings to the car frame. Strut rods, universal-jointed drive axles, and torque-control arms form three links at each rear wheel. A transversely mounted multileaf spring supports the rear end of the differential carrier.

Front-wheel drive.   The front-wheel drive halfshaft design used in the Ford Escort/Lynx, Figure 16-5, uses constant-velocity (CV) joints at both the differential and wheel ends

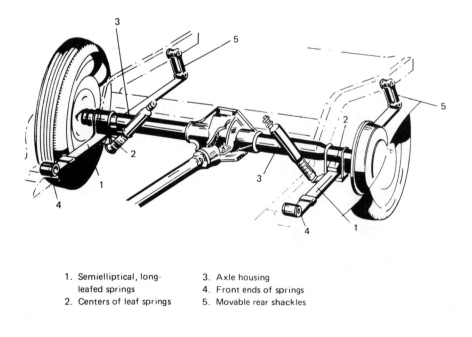

Fig. 16–3   Hotchkiss drive. *Courtesy of Chevrolet Division, General Motors Corporation.*

1. Semielliptical, long-
   leafed springs
2. Centers of leaf springs
3. Axle housing
4. Front ends of springs
5. Movable rear shackles

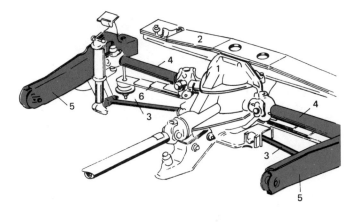

Fig. 16–4 Modified Hotchkiss drive with universal jointed drive axle. *Courtesy of Chevrolet Division, General Motors Corporation.*

1. Fixed differential carrier
2. Automobile frame
3. Strut rods
4. Universal-jointed drive axles
5. Torque-control arms
6. Transversely mounted multileaf spring

for vehicle operating smoothness. The CV joints are joined by an interconnecting shaft. The right-hand and left-hand interconnecting shafts are splined at both ends and are retained in the wheel and differential CV joints by circlips. The halfshaft on the driver's side is of solid steel construction and is shorter in length than the opposite halfshaft. The passenger-side halfshaft is made from tubular steel.

The differential CV joint stubshaft is splined and held in the differential side gear by a circlip. The wheel CV joint stubshaft is splined to accomodate a splined hub which is pressed on and secured with a staked nut. The CV joints are lube-for-life with a special CV joint grease and require no periodic lubrication. The CV joint boots, however, should be periodically inspected and replaced immediately when damage or grease leak is evident. Continued operation will result in CV joint failure due to contamination or loss of the CV joint grease.

The halfshaft design is identical for both automatic and manual Transaxle applications. Halfshaft removal procedures do differ, however, between automatic and manual Transaxles. With the manual Transaxle the halfshaft is removed by applying a load on the back face of the differential CV joint assembly. With the automatic Transaxle the right-hand halfshaft assembly must be removed from the Transaxle in order to remove the left-hand halfshaft assembly. Performing this procedure in any other manner will damage the left-hand differential CV joint.

The front-wheel drive CV joints and halfshaft assemblies rotate at approximately one-third the speed of conventional rear wheel drive driveshafts and do not contribute to rotational vibration disturbances.

The Chrysler Corporation model 44FBJ front-driving axle is composed of the outer drive assemblies, the differential carrier and tube assembly (axle housing), and the differential case and drive-pinion assembly.

Ball joints are preloaded at manufacture and any looseness or end play necessitates replacement.

The axle is of the integral carrier-housing hypoid gear type in which the centerline of the drive pinion is mounted below the centerline of the ring gear.

The axle housing is an iron casting with tubular legs pressed into and welded to the carrier to form a carrier and tube assembly.

The drive pinion is supported by two preloaded taper roller bearings. The pinion bearing cone is a light press-fit on the pinion stem. The outer pinion bearing is a light-press fit to close sliding fit on the pinion stem. The outer and inner bearing cups are a press-fit against a shoulder recessed in the carrier. The drive-pinion depth of mesh adjustment is controlled by locating shims, which are installed between the inner-pinion bearing cup and the carrier casting.

Drive pinion bearing preload is maintained by using different thicknesses of shim packs between the drive-pinion bearing shoulder and the outer-pinion bearing cone.

The differential case is supported by two taper roller-bearing cones which are a press-fit on the differential case hubs. Shims installed between the bearing cone and shoulder of the hub of the differential case perform three functions: eliminate differential-case sideplay, adjust and maintain the backlash between the ring gear and drive pinion, and establish a means of obtaining differential bearing preload.

On some models each front wheel is equipped with a manually operated locking hub, which permits the operator to lock the front wheels in either neutral or drive positions. See Figure 16-6.

Ring Gear and Drive Pinion Sets

Spiral bevel gears. For many years, the ring gear and drive pinion set was designed as shown in Fig. 16-7. In this design, called a *spiral bevel gear,* the centerline of the pinion gear passes through the center of a circle that describes the ring gear. Both the ring gear and drive pinion gear have

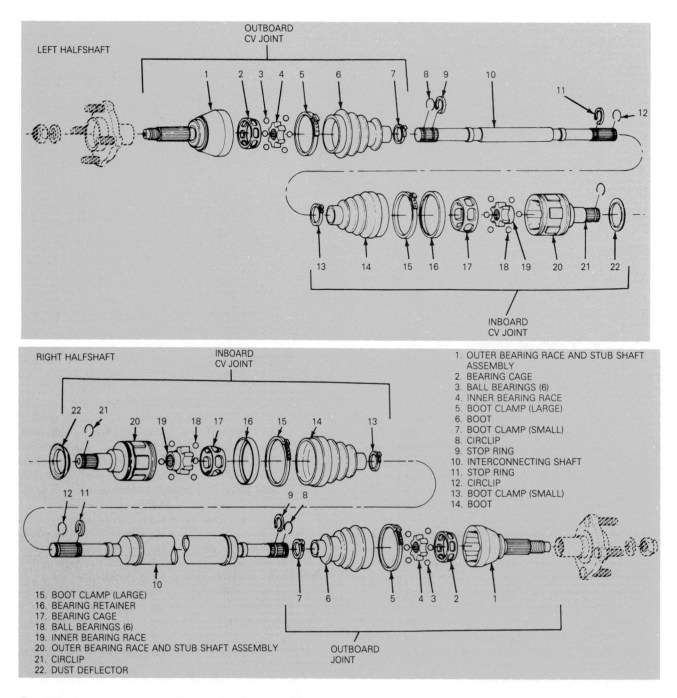

Fig. 16-5. Disassembled view of halfshafts. *Courtesy of Ford Motor Company.*

curved teeth to permit contact between several teeth at a time, to provide more even wear on the teeth and to produce less noise.

Hypoid gears. As automobile body styles changed from the high, boxlike construction to the longer, lower style, automobile manufacturers had to lower the propeller shaft to keep it from interfering with the floor of the car. To lower the propeller shaft, the manufacturers placed the drive pinion below the center of the ring gear, as shown in Fig. 16-8. This change resulted in greater curvature of the teeth and further reduction in noise. However, the sliding-tooth operation also resulted in greater tooth pressures and a corresponding increase in frictional heat. As a result, new lubri-

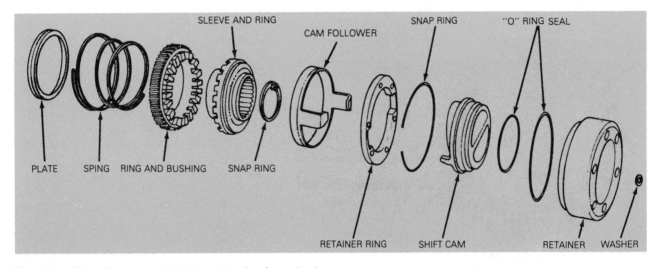

Fig. 16-6. Manually operated locking hub for four-wheel drive.

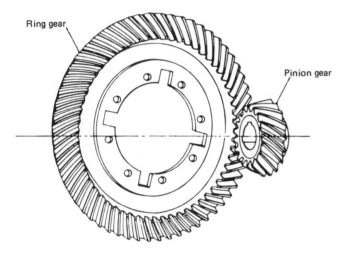

Fig. 16-7 In a spiral bevel gear the centerline of the pinion gear passes through the center of the ring gear.

cants had to be developed for the new gears, commonly referred to as *hypoid gears.*

Because the drive pinion has fewer teeth than the ring gear, it turns more often than the ring gear. The axle ratio on most American cars varies between about 2.5 to 1 and 5 to 1.

Standard Differentials

Need for differentials. When an automobile rounds a curve, the outer drive wheel must turn a greater distance than the inner drive wheel in the same amount of time. On a 90° curve, the outer wheel, on a car with a turning radius of 25 feet, travels about five feet more than the inner wheel. If no provision was made for this difference in wheel travel, true rolling motion could not be achieved, since the front

wheels would drag around a turn. To eliminate skidding and poor handling, a differential is used to let the rear-drive wheels turn at different speeds.

Simple differential. The sectional view of a simple differential is shown in Fig. 16-9. The two rear wheels are attached by axle shafts to bevel gears (differential side gears). A differential case placed around the left side is supported so that it can turn independently of the left axle shaft. A third bevel gear, called a *differential pinion gear,* meshes with the two differential side gears and is supported by a pinion shaft which passes through the pinion gears and the differential case. A ring gear, bolted to the differential case, is turned by the drive pinion.

When the differential gear is turned by the ring gear, torque is transmitted to the differential case, and from there through the differential pinion shaft to the differential pinion. The differential pinion then exerts torque on the two differential side gears to turn the axle shafts and wheels.

When an automobile is being driven straight ahead and the road resistance is equal on both drive wheels, the torque transmitted through the drive pinion to the ring gear moves the pinion shaft. The pinion shaft then exerts force on the differential pinion gear which turns the differential side gear. The differential gears are splined to the axle shafts and turn the shafts at equal speeds. The differential gears are said to be in balance, and the differential turns as if it were a solid unit.

On a curve, the outer drive wheel must turn faster than the inner drive wheel since it travels a greater distance in the same amount of time. The same relationship holds true for the inner and outer side gears. To compensate for these differences, the differential pinion gears turn on the pinion shaft and drive the outer wheel faster than the inner wheel. Although the axle speeds vary, it must be remembered that the torque in each axle shaft is always the same, and the

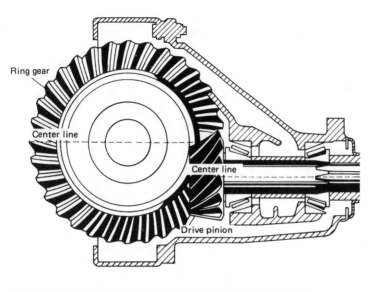

Fig. 16-8 Hypoid ring gear and drive pinion. *Courtesy of Chrysler Motors Corporation.*

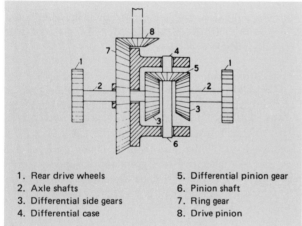

1. Rear drive wheels
2. Axle shafts
3. Differential side gears
4. Differential case
5. Differential pinion gear
6. Pinion shaft
7. Ring gear
8. Drive pinion

Fig. 16-9 A simple differential.

torque delivered to the rear axle by the propeller shaft is equal to that of the easiest-to-turn axle.

When one wheel is spinning, it requires only a small amount of torque. Since this small amount of torque delivered to both wheels is not enough to turn the nonspinning wheel, the vehicle does not move. However, a modified differential, called a *limited-slip differential*, overcomes this difficulty.

Standard differential with one-piece case. The standard differential is manufactured with either a one-piece or a two-piece case, but operation of either is the same as that already described.

A standard differential with a one-piece case is shown in Fig. 16-10. The case houses the two side gears and the two differential pinions, which operate on a press-fitted pinion shaft. The pinion shaft is secured in the differential case by a lockpin. In some other standard axles, a threaded bolt

or screw is used to secure the shaft. A hardened-steel thrust block is mounted on the pinion shaft to absorb the axle shaft thrust. Thrust washers are placed behind both side gears and differential pinions to absorb thrust and minimize wear on the differential case.

Standard differential with two-piece case. A standard differential with a two-piece case is shown in Fig. 16-11. The case and cap, held together by bolts, secure the ring gear to the differential case. Two side gears are splined to the axle shafts, and two differential pinions operate on the pinion shaft. The pinion shaft is held in the differential case by a tight-fitting pin. Thrust washers are placed between the side gears and the differential case and between the differential pinion and differential case to minimize wear.

Limited-Slip Differential

As previously mentioned, a rear axle equipped with a standard differential will be unable to propel an automobile forward if one wheel is spinning. To overcome this difficulty, automobile manufacturers have developed a special differential which transfers torque from the spinning wheel to the nonspinning wheel. If the nonspinning wheel has enough traction, it will propel the automobile. However, if neither wheel has traction, the automobile will not move, even though both drive wheels turn. This type of differential is called a limited-slip differential.

A rear axle equipped with a limited-slip differential is identical in construction to the conventional unit except that it has two sets of clutch plates. In fact, a limited-slip differential can be used in place of a standard differential without any modification of the rear-axle system.

From a convenience standpoint, the limited-slip differential greatly reduces the possibility of stalling. From a safety standpoint, it reduces the possibility of a dangerous steering reaction due to unequal traction of the rear wheels.

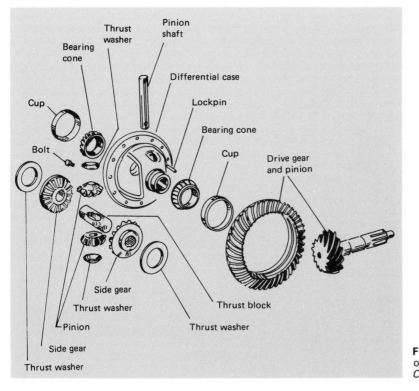

Fig. 16-10   Standard differential with one-piece case. *Courtesy of Chrysler Motors Corporation.*

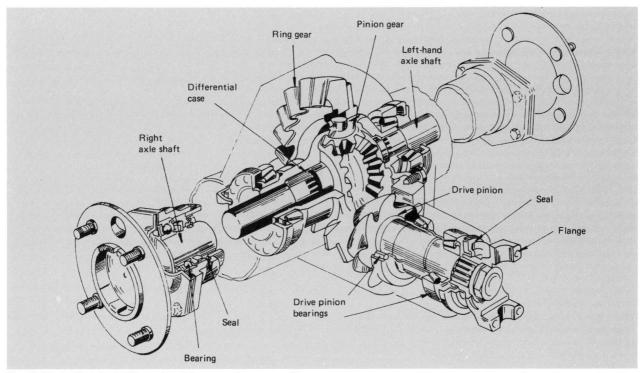

Fig. 16-11   Standard differential with a two-piece case. *Courtesy of Ford Motor Company.*

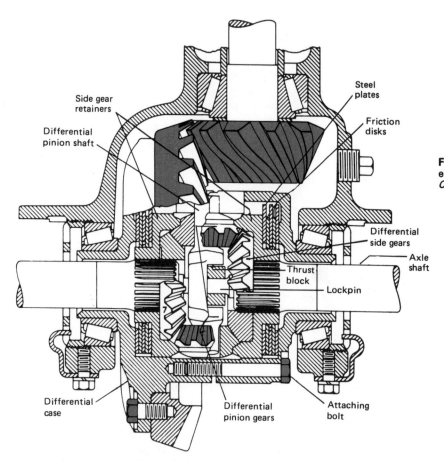

Side gear
retainers

Differential
pinion shaft

Steel
plates

Friction
disks

Fig. 16-12 Dual-clutch, limited slip differential with a two-piece case. *Courtesy of Chrysler Motors Corporation.*

Differential
side gears

Axle
shaft

Thrust
block

Lockpin

Differential
case

Differential
pinion gears

Attaching
bolt

Slight wheel spin may occur if sudden acceleration is attempted on a slippery surface. But, if spin does not occur at one wheel, the major driving force is transmitted to the nonspinning wheel.

Types of limited-slip differential. The two basic types of limited-slip differential are the *clutch type* and the *cone-brake type*. The clutch type uses either one or two clutch packs that are made up of friction disks and steel plates. These disks and plates control differential action. The clutch packs usually are mounted between the differential side gears and the differential case. The cone-brake type uses clutch cones mounted between the differential side gears and the differential case to control differential action.

The clutch-type limited-slip differential comes with either a one-piece or a two-piece case. The cone-brake differential comes only with a two-piece case.

Dual clutch two-piece case limited-slip differential. A dual clutch two-piece case limited-slip differential is shown in Fig. 16-12. The two halves of the differential case are held together by eight bolts. Four differential pinion gears operate on two pinion shafts which are at right angles to

each other. A lockpin and thrust washer maintain the pinion shafts in proper position. The two side gears, which are splined to the axle shafts, operate in retainers that act as thrust members. An equal number of steel plates and friction disks are placed in the hubs of the retainers. The arrangement of the plates and disks is shown clearly in Fig. 16-13. The dished plates and disks exert pressure on the flat plates and disks to keep the clutches engaged at all times. It is to be noted, however, that the arrangement of the plates and disks may vary from that shown, depending on the size of the rear-axle assembly.

A diagram of the torque flow present in an automobile, moving straight ahead, and equipped with a limited-slip differential, is shown in Fig. 16-14. As shown by the solid arrows, torque is transmitted from the drive pinion to the ring gear, differential case, differential pinion shaft, differential pinion, differential side gears, axle shafts, and drive wheels, in turn.

The clutch plates maintain pressure on the clutches. The clutches frictionally connect the differential side gears (which are splined to the axle shaft) to the differential case. The differential case is geared through the ring gear to the drive pinion. Consequently, when the vehicle moves

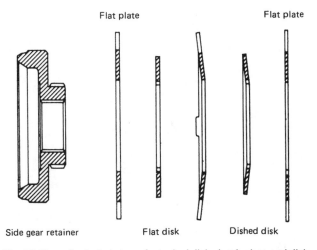

Flat plate   Flat plate

Side gear retainer   Flat disk   Dished disk

Fig. 16-13 Exploded view of a typical disk clutch plate and dish arrangement for a limited slip differential. *Courtesy of Chrysler Motors Corporation.*

straight ahead, the limited-slip differential rear axle operates as a solid axle without a differential.

When the car moves around a curve, the axle shaft connected to the outer wheel begins to turn faster than the axle shaft connected to the inner drive wheel. The torque developed breaks the frictional bond of the clutches and allows the differential pinions to turn. See Fig. 16-15. Because of the slipping clutches, most of the power is applied to the left-hand axle shaft. As soon as the differential resumes a straight-line curve, the resistance to turning each wheel is again equal, and the differential case is again frictionally locked to the differential side gears.

If one rear wheel loses traction, the other rear wheel receives enough torque to move the automobile, because it is frictionally connected to the differential case by the clutch pressure.

Dual clutch one-piece case limited-slip differential. A dual clutch one-piece case limited-slip differential is shown in Fig. 16-16. Here a single differential case holds two differential side gears, two differential pinions, and two thrust washers which are placed on the differential pinion shaft.

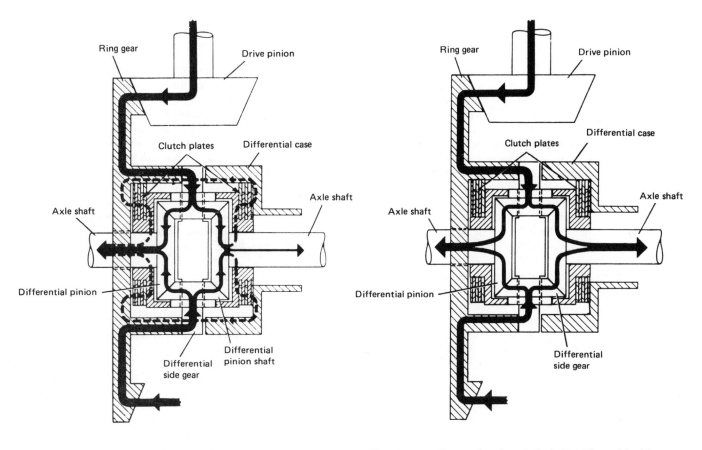

Fig. 16-14 Torque flow in a limited slip differential with car moving straight ahead. *Courtesy of Chrysler Motors Corporation.*

Fig. 16-15 Torque flow in a limited slip differential with car rounding a curve. *Courtesy of Chrysler Motors Corporation.*

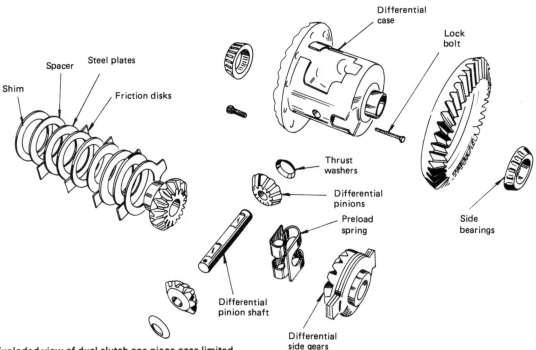

Fig. 16-16   Exploded view of dual clutch one-piece case limited slip differential. *Courtesy of Oldsmobile Division, General Motors Corporation.*

The pinion shaft is secured in the differential case by a lock bolt. The two clutch packs, one on each side gear, are a series of steel plates and friction disks similar to those used in the one-piece case differential. Tangs on the steel plates fit into slots in the differential case, and internal teeth on the friction plates mate with splines machined into the hubs of the side gears. A shim and spacer are placed between the clutch pack and differential case. A single spring-steel preload spring is placed between the two side gears to maintain constant pressure on the two clutches. The side bearings are tapered roller bearings and are used to take up end thrust. The operation of the one-piece case differential is similar to its counterpart described earlier.

Single clutch two-piece case limited-slip differential.   A single clutch two-piece case limited-slip differential is shown in Fig. 16-17. It has a case and cap, held together by special bolts, which attach the ring gear to the differential case. The differential case houses the two side gears and thrust washers, two pinion gears and thrust washers, and the pinion gear shaft. The differential case also has a clutch hub and plates which form the clutch assembly. Three bonded friction plates, mounted between the steel plates, are splined to the clutch hub. A concave (dished) washer, called a *Belleville spring,* is placed against the outer steel plates to keep the clutches engaged.

Operation of this unit is similar to that of the dual clutch limited-slip differential. A lockpin secures the pinion gear shaft, and a washer fits over the bolt.

Cone-brake two-piece case limited-slip differential.   See Fig. 16-18. This unit has a differential case and cap secured by bolts and lock washers. Two cone brakes, housed within the differential case, are located behind the side gears. Two differential pinion gears and thrust washers operate on the pinion shaft. The cone brakes are splined internally to fit the splines on the axle shafts. Internal friction surfaces have a coarse spiral thread that permits passage of a lubricant and the cones seat in the tapered cavities in the two case halves. Six coil springs, held by two clamps, preload the cones in the differential case to provide the internal resistance to differential action. The locking operation of the cone-brake unit is similar to that of the disk type.

Front-Wheel Drive Differentials

Front-wheel drive is used on the Oldsmobile Toronado and Cadillac Eldorado automobiles. The differential is either a standard or a planetary gear type, depending on the age of the car.

Planetary gear front-wheel drive differential.   Two types of differentials are used on front-wheel drive vehicles; the planetary gear type and the standard type. The planetary gear set has a planetary pinion carrier, three pairs of planetary pinions, a sun gear, and an internal ring gear. The internal ring gear is part of the differential case and is driven by the drive pinion. The right-hand drive axle is splined to the sun gear. The planetary pinion carrier fits into the dif-

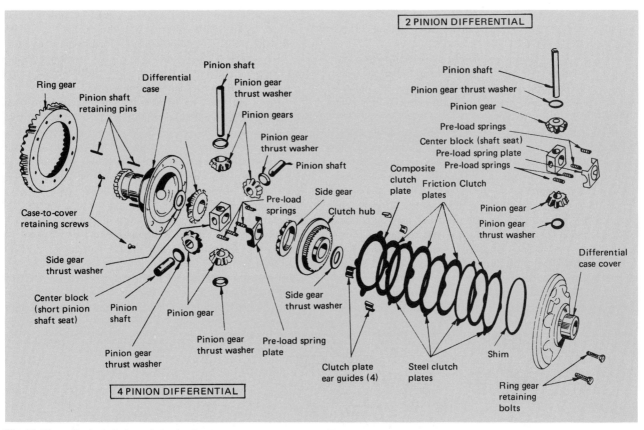

Fig. 16-17   Exploded view of single clutch two-piece case limited slip differential. *Courtesy of Ford Motor Company.*

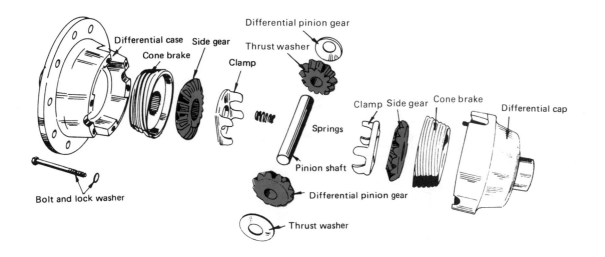

Fig. 16-18   Cone-brake two-piece case limited-slip differential. *Courtesy of Oldsmobile Division, General Motors Corporation.*

ferential case so that the outer planetary pinion meshes with the internal gear. The left-hand drive axle is splined to the planetary pinion carrier.

When the car is moving straight ahead and both drive wheels have equal traction, the ring gear and planetary gear train turn in the same direction, at the same speed, and the entire differential and carrier assembly rotates as one solid unit.

When the automobile turns right, the left front wheel turns faster than the right front wheel. Torque from the drive pinion is transmitted to the ring gear, as shown in Fig. 16-19. The black arrows indicate the faster turning axle and related gears, and the white arrows indicate the components driven by the drive pinion. Since the integral internal gear and the ring gear are bolted together, they may be considered as a unit. Consequently, as the ring gear turns, it rotates the integral internal gear at the same speed. The outer pinions, in mesh with the internal gears, are turned by the internal gears and drive the inner pinions, which drive the sun gear. Three inner pinions (only one is shown in the illustration) try to turn the sun gear at the same speed as the

pinion carrier and outer wheel. However, the sun gear cannot turn as fast as the internal gear due to the friction between the right front wheel and the road surface. In order for both wheels to turn at different speeds, the inner pinions move around the sun gear to allow the left-hand axle shaft to turn faster than the right-hand axle shaft.

For a left turn, the right front wheel turns faster than the left front wheel. Torque again is transmitted to the drive pinion, as shown in Fig. 16-20, and then to the ring gear and differential case. The internal gear drives the outer pinions and the outer pinions drive the inner pinions. Three inner pinions then turn the sun gear and the right-hand output shaft to which the sun gear is splined. As a result of friction between the left-hand tire and the road surface, the planetary pinion carrier cannot turn at the same speed as the sun gear. To let the right-hand wheel turn faster, the planetary pinion moves around the internal gear.

Standard-type front-wheel drive differential.   See Figure 16-21. The final drive gear is riveted to the differential case. Inside the case two differential pinion gears are mounted on

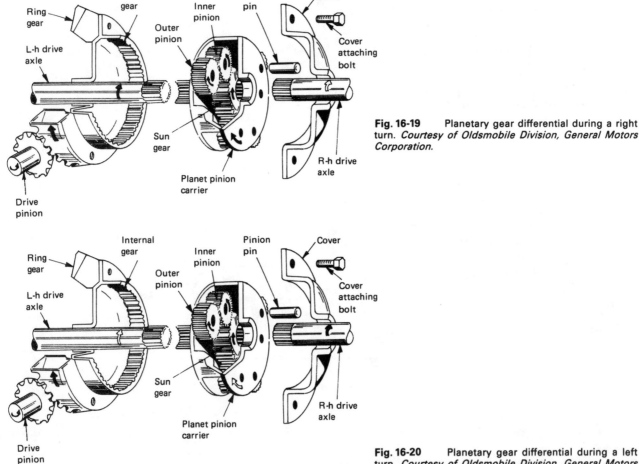

Fig. 16-19   Planetary gear differential during a right turn. *Courtesy of Oldsmobile Division, General Motors Corporation.*

Fig. 16-20   Planetary gear differential during a left turn. *Courtesy of Oldsmobile Division, General Motors Corporation.*

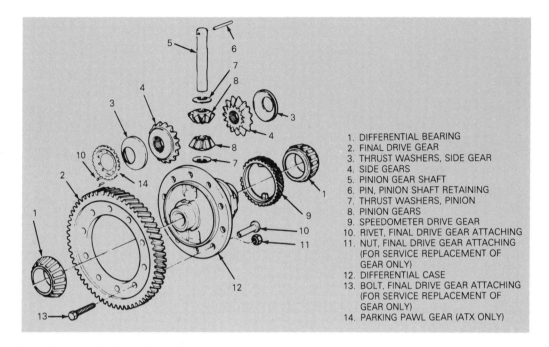

1. DIFFERENTIAL BEARING
2. FINAL DRIVE GEAR
3. THRUST WASHERS, SIDE GEAR
4. SIDE GEARS
5. PINION GEAR SHAFT
6. PIN, PINION SHAFT RETAINING
7. THRUST WASHERS, PINION
8. PINION GEARS
9. SPEEDOMETER DRIVE GEAR
10. RIVET, FINAL DRIVE GEAR ATTACHING
11. NUT, FINAL DRIVE GEAR ATTACHING
   (FOR SERVICE REPLACEMENT OF
   GEAR ONLY)
12. DIFFERENTIAL CASE
13. BOLT, FINAL DRIVE GEAR ATTACHING
   (FOR SERVICE REPLACEMENT OF
   GEAR ONLY)
14. PARKING PAWL GEAR (ATX ONLY)

Fig. 16-21. Exploded view of a standard-type front-wheel drive differential. *Courtesy of Ford Motor Company.*

the differential pinion shaft which is pinned to the case. These pinion gears are engaged with the side gears to which the stubshafts are splined. Therefore, as the differential case turns it rotates the constant velocity joints and the front wheels. When it is necessary for one wheel and shaft to rotate faster than the other, such as in turning a corner, the faster turning side gear causes the pinions to roll on the slower turning side gear to allow the differential action between the two CV joints.

DIFFERENTIAL CARRIERS

Types of Differential Carriers

A differential carrier is a device used to hold the differential and ring-gear assembly in place within the rear-axle housing. The two types of differential carriers in common use are the *removable* differential carrier and the *integral* differential carrier. The removable device is used with the one-piece housing and is a separate casting on which the differential, ring gear, and drive pinion are mounted. The integral-type carrier is forged as part of the rear-axle housing and is used on the integral-carrier type housing. Integral differential carriers are used with front-wheel drive differentials and on the Chevrolet Corvette.

Removable differential carrier. An exploded view of a removable differential carrier, with its ring gear, drive pinion, differential assembly, and various other parts, is shown in Fig. 16-22. The carrier is bolted to the front face of the axle

housing for easy removal. A gasket (not shown) is placed between the axle housing and the carrier to prevent oil leakage. The differential is supported on two bearing cones bearings which are held in the two carrier pedestals by bolted-on caps. Two threaded adjusters, placed between the tapered roller bearings, provide for adjustment of the ring gear-to-drive pinion backlash and the side bearing preload. Backlash is the clearance (lost motion) between the meshing teeth of two gears which allows an appreciable backward and forward rotation of the drive shaft without movement of the drive wheels. Preload is the load imposed on a bearing before any operating loads. Preloading ensures alignment and minimum looseness of the parts.

To hold the adjusting screws in position, locks are engaged in openings in the adjusters. The ring gear is bolted to the flange of the differential case and the drive pinion is held in the nose of the carrier by two tapered bearing cones. A solid spacer and shims, located on the pinion shaft between the pinion bearings, permit adjustment of the pinion bearing preload. An oil seal and a guard retain the axle lubricant and keep dirt out of the axle. To provide for the pinion depth-of-mesh adjustment, an adjusting washer is placed between the pinion gear and the front pinion bearing cone.

Either a one-piece or two-piece differential case can be used on the removable differential carrier. The differential itself may be either the standard or limited-slip type.

Integral differential carrier. The integral differential carrier, Fig. 16-23, a relatively new rear-axle design, is now

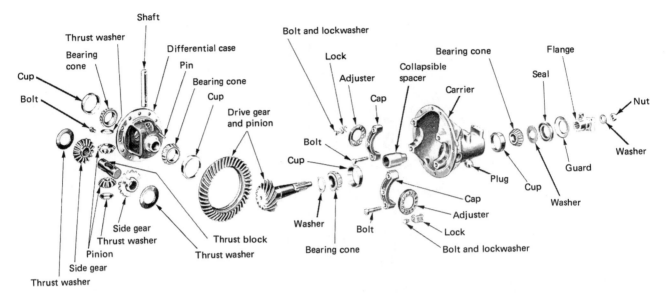

Fig. 16-22 Removable differential carrier. *Courtesy of Chrysler Motors Corporation.*

used by most automobile manufacturers. The one-piece differential case is supported by two tapered bearing cones, mounted on pedestals and cast as part of the carrier. The bearings are retained in the carrier by bolted-on caps. To permit adjustment of the differential bearing preload, shims are placed between the bearings and the carrier pedestals. The drive pinion is supported in the nose of the carrier by front and rear tapered roller bearings and their races (bearing cups). To control the depth of mesh between the drive pinion and ring gear, shims are placed between the rear bearing and the carrier shoulder. To adjust the drive-pinion bearing preload, shims are placed between a shoulder on the drive-pinion shaft and the front bearing.

On some other models, the drive-pinion depth-of-mesh adjustment shim is placed between the front face of the rear pinion bearing and the carrier shoulder. A collapsible spacer, located between the front face of the rear pinion bearing and the shoulder, is used to adjust the pinion bearing preload. Because there are several variations in the devices used to adjust the depth of mesh and preload, the instructions given in the shop manual for a specific make and model of automobile should be followed.

Front-wheel drive differential carrier. As noted earlier, the front-wheel drive differential carrier has a housing which encloses the differential, ring gear, and drive pinion. The differential is supported by two opposed conical thrust bearings and their cups; the bearings and cups are supported by two pedestals and are held in place by bolted-on caps. To adjust the preload of the side bearings, shims are inserted between the side bearing races and the final drive housing (the front-axle housing).

The drive pinion is supported by two opposed adjustable roller bearings and their races. To adjust the drive pinion depth of mesh, a shim is installed between the front edge of the drive pinion and the rear of the front pinion bearing. To adjust the pinion bearing preload, a shim is installed between the bearing housing and the rear pinion bearing race.

The front-wheel drive differential carrier is exactly the same whether the differential is the planetary gear type or the standard type.

Because there is a great deal of similarity between the two types of carriers, only the repair of the integral type is discussed later.

REAR-AXLE HOUSING

Types of Axle Housings

A typical rear-axle housing has a center section that encloses the ring gear, drive pinion, and differential, and two tubular sections which enclose the axle shafts. Special attachments hold the housing to the vehicle. Two types of rear-axle housings used on modern American automobiles are the one-piece (banjo) housing, and the integral carrier housing.

One-piece (banjo) housing. The one-piece housing, Fig. 16-24, is steel pressed in one piece for strength and minimum weight. The banjo design permits removal from the housing of the differential carrier for inspection, adjustment, or repair without removing the complete rear-axle assembly. A pressed-steel cover is either bolted or welded to the rear

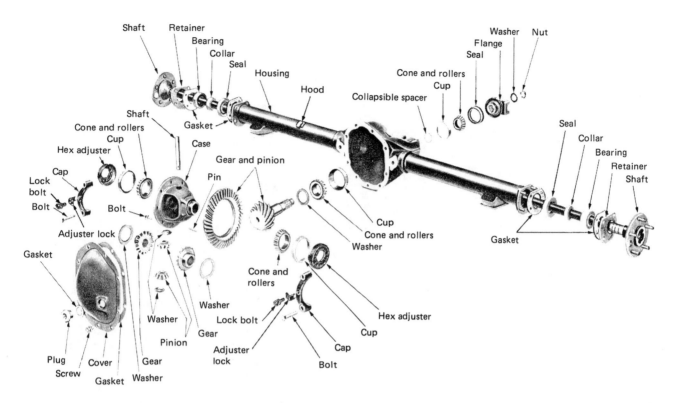

Fig. 16-23 Integral differential carrier. *Courtesy of Chrysler Motors Corporation.*

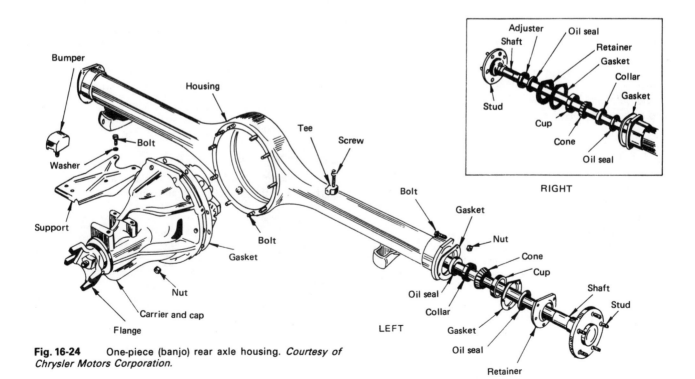

Fig. 16-24 One-piece (banjo) rear axle housing. *Courtesy of Chrysler Motors Corporation.*

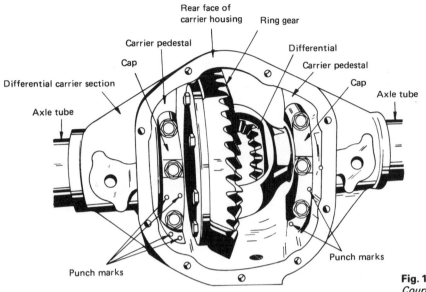

Fig. 16-25 Integral carrier rear axle housing. *Courtesy of Chrysler Motors Corporation.*

face of the housing to complete the enclosure of internal parts. As noted earlier, a removable differential carrier is used with the one-piece housing.

Integral carrier housing. The integral carrier rear-axle housing, Fig. 16-25, has a center differential carrier section that houses the differential, ring gear, and drive pinion (not shown). Steel axle tubes are pressed into the hubs of the carrier section and welded to form a complete housing. The entire differential assembly is mounted on two pedestals which are cast as part of the carrier section. Two bolted-on caps hold the differential assembly in place. A pressed-steel removable cover and gasket are bolted to the rear face of the housing to provide access to the differential assembly for inspection and minor servicing or removal and installation of the differential assembly and drive pinions. The integral carrier housing is used with the integral differential carrier.

Axle-housing attachments. During operation, oil pressure tends to build up in the rear-axle housing. This oil-pressure build-up could result in oil leaking past the pinion shaft and the rear-wheel bearing seals. Air vents are provided to let the rear-axle housing breathe and prevent this from happening.

In some axle housings, a loosely capped tubular vent, Fig. 16-26, is either pressed or threaded into the tubular section of the axle housing. In other axle housings, a small hole, drilled into the tubular section, serves as a vent.

To permit a check of the oil level and the addition of oil, threaded plugs are installed in the rear-axle housing. In some axles, the plug is placed in the rear cover; in others, the plug is placed in the front of the carrier casting.

Automobiles equipped with a Hotchkiss drive have spring perches welded to the axle housing for attaching the semielliptical springs that connect the rear-axle assembly to the frame. A modification of the conventional Hotchkiss drive is shown in Fig. 16-27. Coil springs, instead of semielliptical springs, are mounted between the axle housing and rear cross member of the chassis to cushion road shock. The lower end of each coil spring is supported by a metal pad welded to the rear-axle housing. The lower control arms, which are attached to the frame as shown, allow for the up-and-down movement of the frame. The upper control arms maintain the position of the rear axis in relation to the frame, and resist the tendency of the rear-axle assembly to rotate around the axle during acceleration and deceleration. The forward end of each control arm is attached to the rear cross member of the frame, and the rear ends of the arms are pivoted to brackets on the differential housing. Shock absorbers, mounted at an angle, soften rear-wheel rebound.

AXLE SHAFTS

Semifloating Rear Axle

A semifloating rear axle, used on almost all newer cars, supports part of the weight of the auto and also turns the rear

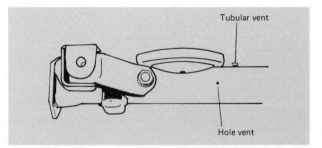

Fig. 16-26 Typical axle housing vents. *Courtesy of American Motors Corporation.*

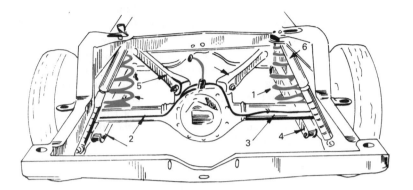

1. Coil springs
2. Axle housing
3. Rear cross member
4. Lower control arms
5. Upper control arms
6. Shock absorbers

Fig. 16-27 Typical axle housing attachments on automobile equipped with modified Hotchkiss drive. *Courtesy of Chevrolet Division, General Motors Corporation.*

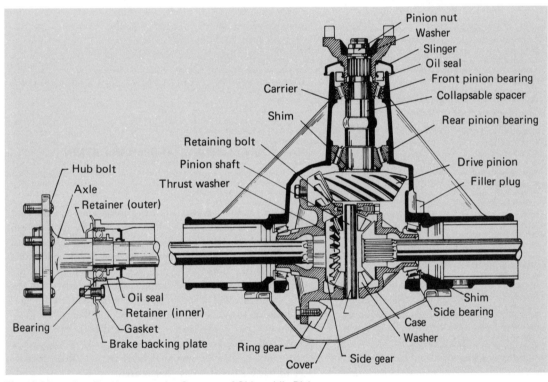

Fig. 16-28 Semifloating rear axle. *Courtesy of Oldsmobile Division, General Motors Corporation.*

wheels. See Fig. 16-28. Bolts with fluted shoulders are pressed into holes in the axle-shaft flange to attach the brake drum. The outer ends of the left-hand and right-hand axle shafts are supported by bearing cones which are pressed onto the axle shafts. After each axle is installed in its housing, the bearings are held in place by a steel ring (inner retainer), which is also pressed against the bearing on the inboard side of the axle. A gasket and outer retainer secure the bearing in the end of the housing. The inner ends of the axle shafts are splined to mate with the corresponding splines in the two differential side gears. The differential assembly and ring gear rotate on adjustable bearing cones which are pressed onto the hubs of the differential case.

The axle shafts pass through the hubs of the differential case and are relieved of the weight of the differential, but the inner ends of the shafts are subjected to driving stresses. The axle-housing tubes support part of the weight of the vehicle. Since the inner ends of the shafts do not support the differential and are not subject to severe binding stresses, these ends are said to float. Because only one end of the axle shaft floats while the other end supports some of the vehicle's weight, the axle is called a *semifloating* rear axle.

Variations of the semifloating axle. Although all semifloating rear axles are basically similar, certain variations deserve additional comment.

Instead of inner and outer retainers, some axles use a C-lock, which is inserted into a slot in the splined end of each axle shaft. The C-lock fits into a machined recess in each differential side gear. As a result, the axles are not held in the housing by the retainer at the wheel hub, but are locked in place within the differential.

On other axles, the shaft is not flanged. In Fig. 16-29, for example, the axle shaft and rear-wheel hubs have splines that fit together on the axle shaft. In addition, a key installed in the keyway (not shown) ensures correct alignment of parts if it becomes necessary to remove the hubs, axle shafts, or both.

End play in the nonflanged axle shafts may be adjusted by one or more shims placed on the left side of the axle. A combination oil seal and retainer is placed between the axle tube flange and the brake support plate to help retain the axle shaft and lubricant. On some nonflanged axles, end play is regulated with an adjuster nut. After the correct amount of end play is determined, special tools are used to turn the adjuster nut and lock it in place.

On the flanged axle shaft no provision is made for end-play adjustment. The axle must be disassembled and all parts checked for excessive wear.

Normally, rear-axle shafts are of slightly different lengths and are not interchangeable. In most cases, the left axle shaft is the shorter one.

Front-Wheel Drive Axle Shafts

Although front-wheel drive axle assemblies may differ in some details from car to car, the Oldsmobile axle assembly described here is very representative of all arrangements. The front-wheel drive axle system has inner and outer constant-velocity universal joints on each axle shaft. The inner joint is flexible; the outer joint is not.

Refer to Fig. 16-30. The inner constant-velocity joint has two main parts, the spider and the housing. The spider has three small projecting posts each of which is filled with a spherical ball. Needle bearings fit between each ball and the post to reduce friction. The spider-ball assembly fits into the housing. The splined axle shaft is inserted into corresponding splines in the center of the spider and is held in place by two retaining rings. A rubber seal fits over one end of the spider housing and is clamped to the axle shaft. A cover and an O ring are fitted over the other end to seal the joint completely.

The outer constant-velocity joint has three main parts; an inner race, a ball cage, and an outer race. A splined stub shaft is attached to the outer race. The front-drive wheel hub is attached to the stub shaft. The inner race has six cavities which hold six steel balls. A ball cage is fitted over the inner race, and the whole assembly is inserted in the outer race assembly and held in place by a retaining ring. The axle shaft is inserted into the splined center of the inner race. A rubber seal is clamped over the outer race and onto the axle shaft to retain the lubricant.

The right-hand axle assembly is exactly the same as the left-hand assembly, except that the axle shaft is formed by two short shafts connected by a torsional damper (see Fig. 16-31).

DIAGNOSIS, TESTING, AND LUBRICATION

Noise

Noise due to insufficient or contaminated lubricant. Check for this condition as follows: (1) Remove the lubricant plug and check the lubricant level in the differential housing; if satisfactory, check for consistency and/or contamination. (2) If the lubricant level is very low, look for causes of loss, such as worn wheel-bearing seals, leaking housing gaskets, loose housing cover bolts, or, in a banjo housing, check for leaks at the differential carrier bolting flange. (3) If the lubricant looks contaminated, replace; if both low and contaminated, remove the old lubricant, make necessary repairs, and refill with specified lubricant. (4) Road test the car to make sure the noise has ceased.

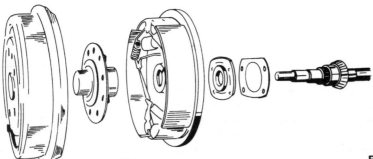

Fig. 16-29   Nonflanged semifloating rear axle shaft.
Courtesy of American Motors Corporation.

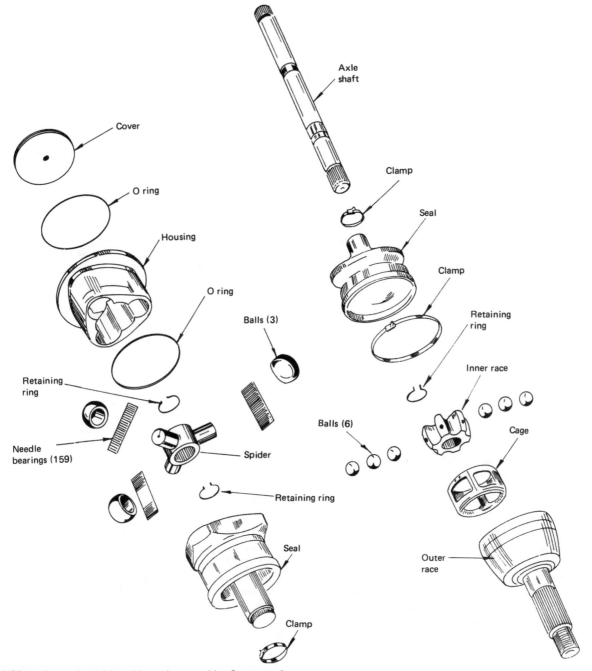

Fig. 16-30   Front-wheel drive, drive axle assembly. *Courtesy of Oldsmobile Division, General Motors Corporation.*

Side gear and pinion noise.   Side gear and pinion noise is rare, since movement of the pinion is negligible during straight-ahead driving. The pinion may be faulty, however, if noise occurs only when rounding a corner.

Tire noise.   Tire noise is often mistaken for axle noise. To eliminate the tires as a cause of noise, proceed as follows:

(1) Inflate all tires to about 50 psi. (2) Drive the car on a smooth macadam road. If the noise is changed, the tires probably are the cause; if the sound does not change, there is trouble in the rear axle.

Types of noise.   Drive noise, coast noise, and float noise may be caused by a defective rear axle. Drive noise is con-

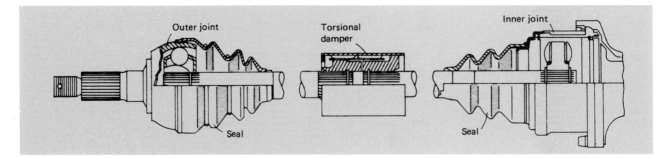

Fig. 16-31 Right-hand axle assembly, viewed from front. *Courtesy of Oldsmobile Division, General Motors Corporation.*

tinuous and occurs on constant acceleration through all speed ranges. However, the tone of the noise may change with speed. Coast noise occurs when the car is decelerating through a speed range with the transmission in gear. Float noise is heard when the car is held at different but constant speeds. The usual fault of noise is improper gear adjustment. The gears must be inspected to determine the exact nature of the trouble.

Sources of noise. Noise sources include defective shaft bearings, drive-pinion shaft bearings, differential case bearings, or excessive backlash between parts.

Shaft-bearing noise is a growling sound which continues when the car coasts with the transmission in neutral.

Drive-pinion shaft bearing noise is also a growling sound which starts at a relatively low speed. It may be most noticeable when the car is pulling lightly at a speed of 18 to 25 mph. Because the pinion shaft bearings turn faster than the pinion ring gear and axle shafts, the pinion bearings produce a more rapid sound than the axle-shaft bearings.

One way to distinguish between axle-shaft bearing noise and drive-pinion shaft bearing noise is as follows: (1) Drive the car on a smooth macadam road. (2) Apply the brakes with the vehicle in gear. If the noise level changes, the axle-shaft bearings are most likely at fault.

Differential case bearing noise is a constant, rough noise, which is usually slower than drive-pinion bearing noise because of the slower turning rate of the differential case. Differential case bearing noise will not change during the axle-shaft bearing test described above.

Noise due to excessive backlash may be caused by loose axle-shaft flange bolts, loose propeller-shaft joint flange bolts, worn axle-shaft splines, or excessive backlash between the ring gear and drive pinion or between the side gears and pinions, due to worn thrust washers or worn or improperly adjusted bearings.

Testing a Typical Limited-Slip Differential

Rear axles equipped with a standard differential are not checked unless noise is heard while the vehicle is in operation. However, a limited-slip differential may not provide torque to the nonslipping wheel even though no noise is heard. The following test is typical of those used to check the limited-slip differential when improper operation is suspected. (1) With the engine stopped, place the transmission in neutral. (2) Raise one rear wheel off the ground, and block the other wheel so that it cannot turn. (3) Install a special axle-shaft puller, an adapter, and a high-capacity torque wrench on the brake drum. (4) Rotate the torque wrench continuously and smoothly, and note the torque reading. For a reading less than that specified, the differential should be removed for inspection and any necessary repairs made.

Axle Lubrication

New and more durable lubricants make periodic changing of the rear-axle lubricant unnecessary. The factory-installed lubricant may safely remain in the axle for the life of the vehicle. Since leaks may occur, however, periodic checks of the lubricant level are recommended.

Whenever an axle is disassembled for repairs, the old lubricant should be discarded and replaced with new lubricant of the specified type. If the vehicle is to be operated for long periods in extremely cold temperature, the lubricant should be drained and a light lubricant installed.

Rear-axle lubricants are produced in several viscosity (thickness) grades, namely, SAE 90, 80, and 75, to allow for different temperature ranges. Although some automobile manufacturers recommend SAE 90 for year-round operation, a change to SAE 80 is recommended when extremely low temperature ranges are experienced for long periods. One manufacturer recommends the use of SAE 90 at temperatures above $-10°F$, SAE 80 down to $-30°F$, and SAE 75 below $-30°F$.

If an automobile is used to tow a boat trailer, and the rear axle is submerged when the boat is launched, water may enter the rear axle and damage the bearings and gears. When this happens, change the lubricant immediately.

Limited-slip differentials use a special lubricant with additives which effectively lubricate and protect the bonded friction disks and cone brakes. The lubricant is available in two viscosities, SAE 90 and SAE 80. If lubricant other than that specified is used, chatter will develop in the clutches. If the wrong lubricant is used by mistake it should be drained and replaced immediately to avoid damage to the disks and cones.

Rear-wheel bearings are permanently lubricated. If they are ever removed, they should be cleaned with a good solvent and relubricated with the recommended lubricant. Never mix lubricants.

IN-CAR REPAIRS

Replacement of Axle Shaft Bearings and Oil Seals

Removal of axle shaft. The procedure for removal of the axle shaft is much the same for most automobiles. Here is a typical procedure:

1. Raise the rear of the automobile until the rear wheels are suspended. Use safety stands to hold the automobile in the raised position.
2. Remove the wheel from the axle that needs repair.
3. Remove the brake drum.
4. Remove the nuts holding the outer brake retainer plate.
5. Loosen the nuts holding the brake backing plate, but leave them in far enough to hold the backing plate in place and to protect the brake liner.
6. Attach a special puller and slide hammer to the flanged end of the axle and withdraw the axle shaft. Be careful not to damage the splines and oil seals. If C-locks are used, they must be removed before the shaft can be withdrawn.

Removal of inner retainer and bearing. After the axle shaft is removed, the inner retainer and bearing may be removed as follows:

1. Lay the axle assembly on an anvil.
2. With a chisel, notch the retaining collar (which is pressing on the axle) in four places. Do not nick the axle shaft. Notching will spread the retainer and make the removal of the axle shaft easier. Discard the retainer.
3. Press the bearing from the axle shaft.

Removal and installation of oil seal. The oil seal for the rear-axle housing tube is replaced as follows:

1. Use a special puller and remove the oil seal.
2. Clean all old grease from the inside of the housing bore.
3. Inspect the housing bore and axle shaft for burrs or other irregularities that may affect the sealing quality of a new seal.
4. If a leather seal is used, soak it in SAE 10 engine oil for one-half hour. A synthetic rubber seal does not need soaking.

5. Place a light coat of oil-resistant sealer on the outside of the new seal.
6. Use a special tool to install the new seal in the housing bore.
7. Coat the lip of the seal with axle lubricant to provide initial lubrication.

Assembly and Installation of Axle Shaft

The procedure for assembling and installing the axle shaft is as follows:

1. Examine the splines on the axle shaft and the bearing surfaces. If either are damaged, replace the axle.
2. Place the outer bearing retainer on the axle shaft.
3. Press the bearing on the axle shaft. Use an arbor press.
4. Press the inner retainer on the axle shaft tightly against the inner cone.
5. Install the inner retainer gasket on the axle.
6. Pack the shaft with a good grade of wheel-bearing lubricant.
7. Apply a coat of rear-axle lubricant on the spline end of the axle shaft.
8. Insert the axle into its housing and guide it carefully into the differential side-gear splines. When the axle is engaged, gently drive it in with a soft-faced hammer.
9. Install the outer retainer, the nuts, and lock washers. Tighten the nuts to the specified torque.
10. Install the brake-support plate, and tighten the nuts to the specified torque.

Checking axle-shaft end play. Axle-shaft end play should be checked before the brake drum and wheel are reinstalled. On a nonflanged axle, end play must be checked before the axle is installed. A typical procedure for checking end play is: (1) Mount a dial indicator on a stud of the axle flange. The stem of the dial indicator should barely touch the brake-support plate. (2) Move the axle flange in and out of the rear-axle housing and check the dial reading. The distance the shaft is able to move should be compared with specifications. If the end play is excessive, shims may be used to meet the specification. (Some vehicles use adjusting nuts to adjust the axle end play.) (3) Install the brake drum and wheel and lower the car to the floor. When C-locks are used to retain the shaft to its housing, all axle lubricant must be drained before an axle shaft is removed.

Pinion Shaft Oil Seal Replacement

Removal of seal. Whether the pinion shaft has a collapsible or solid bearing spacer, the same procedure is used to replace the seal.

1. Raise the rear of the vehicle until the rear wheels are clear of the floor.

2. Remove the rear wheels and brake drums (some cars do not require this step).

3. Mark the propeller shaft and companion flange to permit proper alignment during reinstallation.

4. Disconnect the propeller shaft at the companion flange, and wire the shaft out of the way.

5. Place a torque wrench, with an inch-pound scale, on the pinion shaft nut.

6. Rotate the torque wrench a few times and record the readings.

7. Mark the companion flange, pinion shaft threads, and pinion nut, so that they can be returned to their original positions.

8. Use a special tool to remove the pinion nut and washer.

9. Use a special puller tool to remove the companion flange.

10. With a blunt chisel, pry the seal from the carrier.

Installation of seal.   The pinion shaft oil seal is reinstalled as follows:

1. Examine the companion flange and surface for nicks or other damage that may have caused the seal to leak. If the companion flange is damaged, replace it.

2. Examine the seal bores for burrs that may have caused the seal to leak.

3. Apply a light coat of sealing compound to the outside of the new seal.

4. With a special seal installer, drive the new seal into the seal bore.

5. Apply a coat of sealing compound to the lip of the seal and the seal surface of the compression flange.

6. Install the companion flange and secure it with washer and nut.

7. Torque the pinion shaft nut to 5 inch-pounds beyond the reading recorded in step 6 of the seal removal procedure.

8. Install the propeller shaft, brake drums, and wheels, and lower car to floor.

Servicing of Front-Wheel Drive Axle Shaft

Axle removal.   Since both shafts on a front-wheel drive are similar, only the servicing of the right-hand shaft is given here. When the constant-velocity joints are serviced, remember that they are disassembled only for repacking and resealing. If any parts are damaged, replace the entire joint. Proceed as follows to remove the right-hand axle shaft:

1. Raise the front of the vehicle until the wheels are clear of the floor.

2. Remove the drive axle cotter pin, wheel nut, and washer.

3. Take off the oil filter.

4. Remove the inner constant-velocity joint attaching bolts.

5. Push the inner constant-velocity joint outward far enough to disengage it from the right-hand final-drive output shaft.

6. Remove the right-hand output shaft support bolts.

7. Remove the right-hand output shaft.

8. Remove the drive-axle assembly.

Disassembly of outer constant-velocity universal joint

1. Clamp the midportion of the axle shaft in a vise.

2. Cut the inner and outer seal clamps off with a pair of diagonal cutters.

3. Slide the seal down the axle shaft.

4. Spread the retaining ring until the joint can be removed from the axle.

5. Take off the retaining ring, and slide the seal off the axle shaft.

6. While holding the joint with one hand, tilt the cage and inner race until one ball can be removed. Then remove the remaining balls in the same way.

7. Rotate the cage one-quarter turn, and move the cage around until it can be lifted from the outer race.

8. As shown in Fig. 16-32, remove the inner race from the ball cage.

Cleaning and inspection.   After the outer constant-velocity joint has been disassembled, all metallic parts should be washed in cleaning solvent and dried with compressed air. Replace the rubber seal. Inspect each of the following: (1) the outer race, for wear or scoring in the ball splines; (2) shaft splines and threads; (3) balls and cage for nicks, cracks, or any other damage; and (4) the retaining ring for breaks.

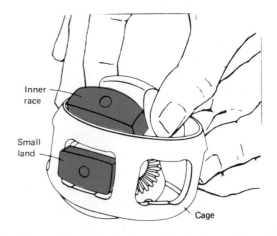

Fig. 16-32   Removing inner race from ball cage. *Courtesy of Oldsmobile Division, General Motors Corporation.*

If a defect is found in any part other than the retaining ring, replace the entire joint. The retaining ring may be replaced separately.

Assembly

1. Insert short land of inner race through bore of cage and pivot to install in cage.

2. Insert outer race in vise, clamping on shank. Protect the shank from damage. Do not tighten too much.

3. Insert cage and inner race into outer race by aligning windows on cage with lands on outer race. See Fig. 16-33. Pivot cage and inner race 90°, making sure the step on the cage is positioned to the inside of joint and the snap-ring groove in the inner race is facing outward.

4. Insert balls into outer race one at a time by rocking assembly to each subsequent ball groove until all six balls are installed. If a brass drift is used to install the sixth ball, make sure metallic chips from the drift do not enter the assembly.

5. Pack constant-velocity joint full with specified lubricant.

6. Pack inside of seal with specified lubricant or equivalent until folds of seal are full.

7. Place service band on axle shaft. Two wraps of band are required.

8. Install seal onto axle shaft.

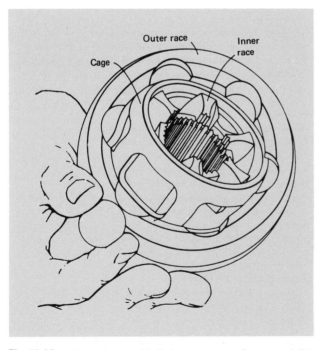

Fig. 16-33   Inserting steel balls in outer race. *Courtesy of Oldsmobile Division, General Motors Corporation.*

9. Install retaining ring into inner race with tangs protruding into relieved area.

10. Insert axle shaft into splines of outer constant-velocity joint until retaining ring secures shaft in second snap-ring groove.

11. Position seal in groove of outer race bell.

12. Position small end of seal in nearest joint groove on axle shaft.

13. After the seal is in position on the shaft, make sure no lubricant is in the grooves of the seal.

14. Using a special tool, install the seal clamp band.

Disassembly of inner constant-velocity joint

1. With axle assembly on a bench, pry up staked areas on seal retainer and drive seal off housing with hammer and chisel.

2. Grasp axle assembly with one hand and joint housing with the other; stand both vertically on the bench. Carefully withdraw axle from housing, making certain not to lose the balls and needles from the axle. Place a rubber band over the ends of the spider to retain the three balls and needle bearings. Wipe all excess grease from the joint. Remove housing O ring seal and discard. Set the housing aside.

3. Insert axle assembly in a vise. Clamp on mid-portion of axle shaft and protect against jaw marks.

4. Using a special tool, remove the retaining ring from the end of the axle shaft.

5. Slide spider assembly from axle shaft.

6. Remove inner retaining ring from axle shaft. Another special tool is required for this step.

7. Remove small seal clamp.

8. Slide boot seal off axle shaft and discard seal. If there is no leakage or apparent damage to rear cup, it is not necessary to remove it from housing.

9. If necessary to remove cover, proceed as shown in Fig. 16-34.

10. Remove O ring from housing and discard.

11. Remove three balls from spider, being careful not to lose any of the 53 needle bearings in each of the balls.

Cleaning and inspection. Wash all metallic parts thoroughly in a cleaning solvent. Dry with compressed air.

Replace the rubber boot, O rings, and clamp. The housing may show a definite polished area where the balls travel, but the joint need not be replaced. However, if this wear pattern is suspected of being the cause of a noisy or vibrating joint, then the housing should be replaced.

1. Inspect the housing for excessive wear, cracks, or chips in the ball grooves.

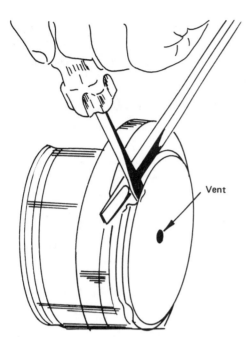

Fig. 16-34   Removing cover from housing of inner constant velocity joint. *Courtesy of Oldsmobile Division, General Motors Corporation.*

2. Inspect the retaining rings for damage.

3. Inspect the three balls for nicks, cracks, scores, or excessive wear.

4. Inspect the needle bearings for wear, breakage, or bending.

5. Inspect the ball washers for wear or bending.

6. Inspect the spider for excessive wear, chips, or cracking.

Assembly

1. Pack a new seal clamp on the axle shaft. This clamp is used later to clamp the small end of the seal to the shaft.

2. Pack the new seal with lubricant until the folds of the seal are full.

3. Place the inner retaining ring on the axle shaft in the inner slot.

4. Load the needle bearings back into the balls, using a special lubricant to hold them in place.

5. Place one washer on each of the spider journals, with the washer groove facing the center of the spider.

6. Carefully install the balls on each of the spider journals. Place a rubber band over the balls to keep them from sliding off the spider.

7. Place the spider assembly on the axle shaft, and install the retaining ring.

8. Install a new lubricated O ring in the outer groove of the housing.

9. Remove the rubber band and place the spider assembly in line with the housing assembly. Then push the spider into the housing.

10. Lubricate the O ring in the outer housing groove with a special seal lubricant.

11. Lay the housing on a flat surface, as shown in Fig. 16-35, and tap the seal into place. Then, with a center punch, mark the axle shaft at six evenly spaced intervals around the housing.

12. Place the seal in the axle-shaft groove and install the clamp that was placed on the shaft in step 1.

13. Extend the axle shaft until the seal expands to its maximum length.

14. Fill the housing with special ball-joint lubricant.

15. Install a new O ring on the housing and lubricate the ring with the recommended seal lubricant.

16. Install the housing cover into the housing, using a special tool for this operation.

Installation of right-hand drive axle assembly.   Whenever a drive axle of a front-wheel drive vehicle is removed or installed, the seals of both the inner and outer constant-velocity universal joints should be protected from possible damage. The joints should not be allowed to turn when they are at the maximum extremes of their movement. In addition, take care not to let the joints strike the shock absorber or stabilizer bar.

The drive-axle assembly is attached to the final drive output shaft, which is also removed during disassembly. Therefore, the first step is to reinstall the output shaft. Figure 16-36 shows the right-hand output shaft, its support, and the brace that attaches to the shaft. Figure 16-37 shows

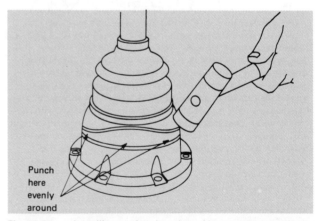

Fig. 16-35   Installing seal on housing of inner constant velocity joint. *Courtesy of Oldsmobile Division, General Motors Corporation.*

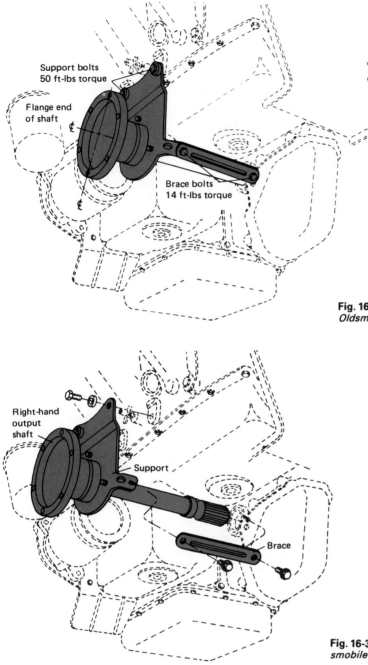

Fig. 16-36   Right-hand output shaft attachment. *Courtesy of Oldsmobile Divison, General Motors Corporation.*

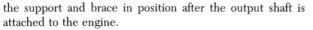

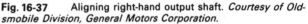

Fig. 16-37   Aligning right-hand output shaft. *Courtesy of Oldsmobile Division, General Motors Corporation.*

the support and brace in position after the output shaft is attached to the engine.

When the right-hand output shaft is being attached to the engine, it should not be allowed to hang free; this will avoid damage to the splines on the shaft and to the final drive seal. Assemble the support bolts loosely, and by moving the flange end of the shaft up and down and back and forth, find the center location. Hold the shaft in this position to maintain alignment, and then tighten the support bolts to

50 foot-pounds torque. Attach the brace as shown in the illustration and tighten the brace bolts in 14 foot-pounds torque. To install the axle, proceed as follows:

1. Carefully place the drive-axle assembly into the lower control arm and turn the axle until the outer splined end of the shaft goes into the steering knuckle.

2. Lubricate the seal on the output shaft with a special seal lubricant.

3. Install the output shaft into the final-drive assembly and align the shaft in the manner described above.

4. Move the drive-axle assembly toward the front of the car and align it with the right-hand output shaft.

5. Bolt the drive axle to the flange on the output shaft and tighten the attaching bolts to the specified torque.

6. Install the oil filter.

7. Install the washer and nut on the wheel end of the drive axle.

8. Lower the automobile to the floor.

9. Check the engine oil and add oil if necessary.

Servicing of Locking Hub (Four-Wheel Drive)

Removal and disassembly.

1. Place the hub in lock position. Using an allen wrench, remove the six socket head screws and washers from the retainer. Remove the retainer and shift cam. Separate the shift cam from the retainer and discard the O rings.

2. Pry snap ring from hub internal groove. Slide retainer ring and cam follower from hub. Figure 16-38.

3. While pressing against the sleeve and ring, remove snap ring from axle shaft. Remove sleeve and ring, ring and bushing, spring and spring plate. Figure 16-39.

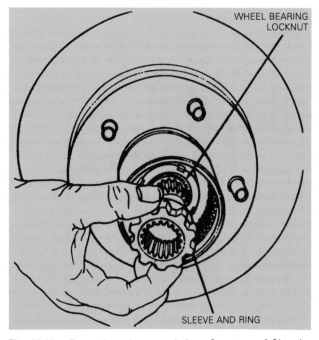

Fig. 16-39. Removing sleeve and ring. *Courtesy of Chrysler Corporation.*

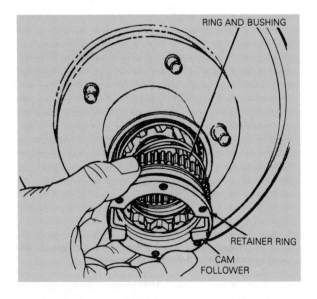

Fig. 16-38. Removing retaining ring and cam follower. *Courtesy of Chrysler Corporation.*

4. Wash all parts in a suitable cleaning solvent and inspect them for nicks, burrs, or wear. Replace all parts that look questionable.

Assembly and installation.

1. Refer back to Fig. 16-6. Insert the spring plate and spring (large coils first) into the wheel hub housing.

2. Assemble ring and bushing, and sleeve and ring, into one assembly and slide into housing.

3. Install snap ring in axle shaft groove.

4. Position cam follower and retainer ring into housing and with the large internal snap ring lock it into position.

5. Place small O ring seal in shaft-cam groove, lubricate with MOPAR Multi-Purpose Lubricant or equivalent and install in retainer at lock position.

6. Lubricate and place large O ring seal in retainer groove. Position groove in assembly. Install washers and socket head screws. Use an allen wrench to tighten screws. Check hub operation.

17

SUSPENSION SYSTEMS

Contents

FUNDAMENTALS OF WHEEL SUSPENSION

New Terminology

Our study of suspension systems will begin with the definition of certain new terms.

Caster. Caster is the backward or forward tilt of the ball joint from the vertical, as shown in Fig. 17-1. When the ball joint steering support arm is tilted backward from true vertical, as shown in (a), we have *positive caster*. When the ball joint steering support arm is tilted forward from true vertical, we have *negative caster*. Both positive and negative caster are found in modern passenger cars.

Caster is used to offset road crown, and to gain directional control when coming out of a turn.

Camber. As shown in Fig. 17-2, camber is the inward or outward tilt of the wheel at the top. When the wheel is tilted outward at the top from true vertical, as shown in (a), we have *positive camber*. When the wheel is tilted inward at the top from true vertical, as shown in (b), we have *negative camber*.

Excessive camber, either positive or negative, creates varying diameters of the tire, and the smaller diameter slips

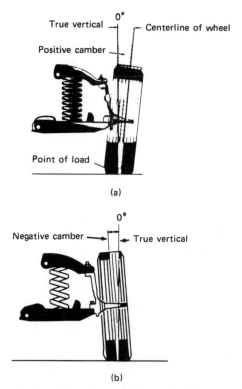

(a)

(b)

Fig. 17-2 Camber: (a) positive and (b) negative. *Courtesy of Bear Manufacturing Corporation.*

and slides to equal the speed of the largest diameter. Incorrect camber results in excessive wear on one side of the tread.

The purpose of camber is to bring the road contact of the car more nearly under the point of load, to provide easy steering (weight of vehicle borne by inner wheel bearing and spindle), and prevent tire wear.

Steering-axis inclination. As shown in Fig. 17-3, steering-axis inclination, also called the directional control angle, is the inward tilt of the ball joint at the top. Steering-axis inclination reduces the need for excessive camber, distributes the weight of the vehicle more nearly under the road contact of the tire, and provides a pivot point about which the wheel turns and thereby ensures easy steering.

The steering-axis inclination angle is nonadjustable, and any variation from the manufacturer's specifications is caused by a bent spindle-support arm (ball joint).

The steering-axis inclination angle and the camber angle, taken together, are called the *included angle*. Thus, the camber angle is included in the measurement of true steering-axis inclination, with positive camber being added to, and negative camber subtracted from, the steering-axis inclination angle.

Turning radius. As shown in Fig. 17-4, the wheels turn about a common center determined by the wheelbase of a

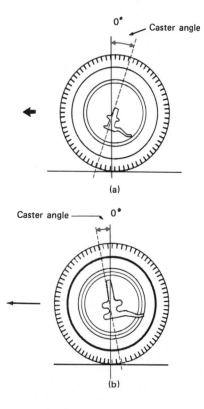

(a)

(b)

Fig. 17-1 Caster: (a) positive and (b) negative. *Courtesy of Bear Manufacturing Corporation.*

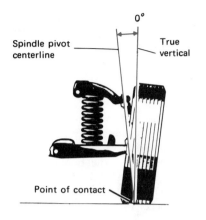

Fig. 17–3 Steering-axis inclination. *Courtesy of Bear Manufacturing Corporation.*

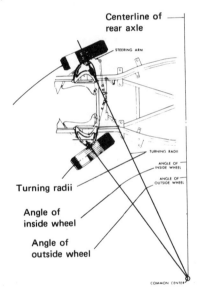

Fig. 17–4 Turning radius. *Courtesy of Bear Manufacturing Corporation.*

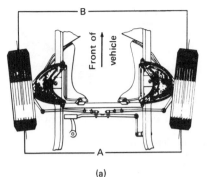

(a)

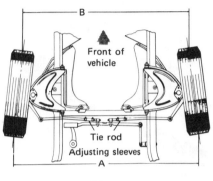

(b)

Fig. 17–5 (a) Toe-out and (b) toe-in. *Courtesy of Bear Manufacturing Corporation.*

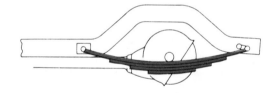

Fig. 17–6 The semielliptic spring.

vehicle. Note that with respect to the common point, the inside wheel, ahead of the outside wheel, makes the sharper angle.

Turning radius is the amount the front wheels toe out on turns; it is controlled by the angle of the spindle steering arms.

As shown in Fig. 17-5(a), when the front of the wheels, line B, are farther apart than the rear of the wheels, line A, they are said to be toed out. As shown in (b), when the front of the wheels are closer together than the rear of the wheels, they are said to be toed in. The purpose of toe-in is to compensate for tolerances in the steering linkage.

Springs

The semielliptic spring, Fig. 17-6, is used on many modern automobiles. Either multileaf or single-leaf semielliptic springs may be encountered. Multileaf springs have several individual leaves of flat, high-quality alloy steel, and each leaf is graduated in length. Figure 17-7 shows a rear semielliptic spring. The leaves are bolted together with a center bolt, and spring clips keep the ends of the leaves from spreading. When the spring is bent, the individual leaves slip on each other and it is necessary to use a lubricant between leaves.

To maintain a more constant interleaf friction, interliners made of various materials are used between the spring leaves.

The single-leaf (tapered plate) spring, Fig. 17-8, is made from a single steel plate which is thick at the center and tapers down at each end.

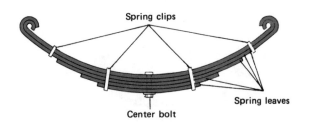

Fig. 17–7 A rear semielliptic spring.

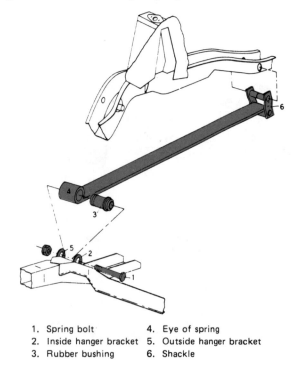

1. Spring bolt
2. Inside hanger bracket
3. Rubber bushing
4. Eye of spring
5. Outside hanger bracket
6. Shackle

Fig. 17–8 A single-leaf spring.

Both multileaf and single-leaf springs are mounted in the same manner. One end of the spring, usually the front, is attached to the spring hanger, as shown in Fig. 17-8. The spring bolt passes through one side of the hanger bracket, a bushing in the eye of the spring, and the other side of the hanger bracket. The rear of the spring is connected to the frame by a shackle.

Torsion bar springs and coil springs. Torsion bar springs and coil springs are used in the front and rear suspension systems of many automobiles. These springs require little maintenance and eliminate the disadvantages of leaf springs, such as interleaf friction, leaf breakage, and looseness or breakage of shackles, pivots, or U-bolts. Also, the amount of space required for torsion bars and coil springs is much less than that required for leaf springs.

The trend is to use coil springs mounted between the rear axle and the frame. Coil springs on rear suspensions act only as springs and do not absorb any torque applied to the rear-axle housing. The power drive and rear-suspension alignment are provided for by control arms and various types of stabilizers.

Coil springs and torsion bar springs mechanically are identical but differ in physical appearance. The torsion bar spring, Fig. 17-9, is a straight piece of spring steel. One end is anchored to the car frame restraining member to keep it from twisting, while the other end is twisted by the up and down movement of the control arm. The twisting action (torsion) stores energy that is released when the spring unwinds. The coil spring, Fig. 17-10, acts in exactly the same manner, but is made from a piece of spring steel formed into a coil.

Shock Absorbers

The springs need some device to reduce flex (compression) and rebound (recoil). When a spring is compressed, it stores energy momentarily. With no restraint placed on it, the spring releases this energy, rebounding in an attempt to regain its original shape. Before this happens, however, the

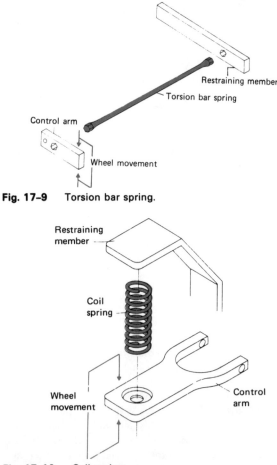

Fig. 17–9 Torsion bar spring.

Fig. 17–10 Coil spring.

spring very rapidly continues to flex and rebound, a motion called *oscillation*.

The device used to slow down (dampen) spring oscillations when a wheel passes over a hole or bump in the road is the hydraulic shock absorber.

Direct double-acting shock absorber. A direct-acting shock absorber displaces fluid in one chamber and forces it to flow through a restricted opening into another chamber. Resistance to the flow of liquid through the restricted opening enables the shock absorber to control the compression and recoil of a spring. Figure 17-11 shows a direct double-acting shock absorber of the type found on the front- and rear-suspension systems of all modern automobiles. It has a stone and dust shield, cylinder tube, reservoir tube, check-valve orifice, fluid reservoir, piston, upper mount, and piston rod.

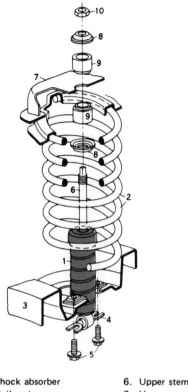

1. Shock absorber	6. Upper stem
2. Coil spring	7. Upper support
3. Lower control arm	8. Retainers
4. Lower pivot	9. Rubber grommets
5. Bolts	10. Retaining nut

Fig. 17-12   Mounting of front shock absorber and coil spring between lower control arm and frame.

Mounting shock absorbers. Figure 17-12 shows one method of mounting a shock absorber in a car having a coil spring front suspension. The absorber is placed inside the coil spring through the opening in the lower control arm. The lower pivot is then secured to the lower control arm with bolts. The upper stem is fastened to the upper support by retainers, rubber grommets, and a retaining nut.

Figures 17-13 and 17-14 show shock absorbers installed in front torsion bar suspension and rear leaf (or coil spring) suspension, respectively. Notice that the shock absorber is always mounted between the moving member, such as the axle housing or control arm, and the frame.

The direct double-acting shock absorber has three concentric tubes, a piston valve, various gaskets, and other related parts. Refer back to Fig. 17-11 and note that the outer tube (stone and dust shield) protects the working parts of the unit from dirt and stones which may be thrown up from the road by the wheels. The cylinder and reservoir tubes are sealed from each other except for a valve at the lower end. The space between the two tubes acts as a fluid reservoir. The piston, which is attached to the upper shock mount by a heavy piston rod, moves up and down as the length of the shock absorber changes.

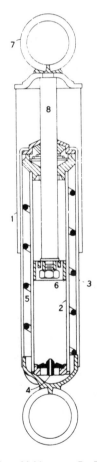

1. Stone and dust shield	5. Fluid reservoir
2. Cylinder tube	6. Piston
3. Reservoir tube	7. Upper mount
4. Check valve orifice	8. Piston rod

Fig. 17-11   Direct-acting shock absorber.

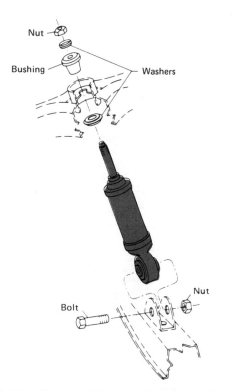

Fig. 17-13 Mounting of front shock absorber with torsion-bar springs.

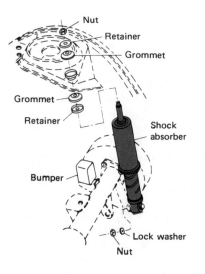

Fig. 17-14 Rear shock-absorber installation.

Operation. Figure 17-15(a) shows what happens when the wheel hits ruts in the road. As the wheel moves upward, the spring is compressed and the shock absorber is shortened. This makes the piston move downward, exert pressure on the fluid in the bottom of the cylinder, and create a vacuum in the section of cylinder above the piston. Thus, fluid is forced through the orifices in the piston and into the space above the piston. At the same time, the piston also

displaces liquid through the check valve to the reservoir between the inner and outer tubes. If the spring movement is very rapid, or if the pressure is excessive, as when a large bump is hit, the relief valve flexes away from the upper face of the piston and opens the inner piston passage to allow fluid to flow more rapidly. Even with the opening of additional passages, however, the fluid flow is restricted and the movement of the piston is slowed down. Since the piston is connected to the spring by the piston rod, spring action is held to a minimum.

On rebound, the shock absorber is extended, as shown in Fig. 17-15(b). As the piston moves to the upper part of the cylinder, fluid flows through the orifices to the lower part of the cylinder. At the same time, the check valve is lifted off its seat and fluid also flows from the reservoir into the lower section of the cylinder.

During both the compression and rebound strokes, the relief valves open varying amounts to prevent excessive pressure buildup, which might damage the shock absorber.

Testing. To test a shock absorber mounted on a car, grasp the bumper and jounce the automobile up and down. If the absorbers are in good condition, the car will stop the up and down movement immediately and settle to its normal posi-

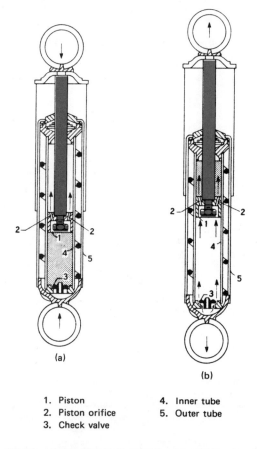

1. Piston	4. Inner tube
2. Piston orifice	5. Outer tube
3. Check valve	

Fig. 17-15 Operation of direct-acting shock absorber: (a) compressed, (b) extended.

tion when the bumper is released. If the car continues to move up and down, the shock absorbers are faulty. This test should not be made on a vehicle having leaf-spring suspension since interleaf friction produces the same effect as good shock absorbers.

To test a shock absorber with the unit off the car, push and pull the shock absorber while it is clamped in a vertical position in a vise. If the action is not smooth, replace the unit. During this test, do not operate the absorber in a horizontal position, because air will become trapped in the unit and may cause a good absorber to appear defective.

Unless shock absorbers have been in use for only a thousand miles or so, both front or both rear units should be replaced at the same time.

Pneumatic Tires

The pneumatic tires in current use cushion the ride of a vehicle and provide the necessary friction between the power train and the road to operate the vehicle. Both tubed and tubeless tires are in use. In the tubed type, a rubber innertube contains the air. Innertubes usually are made of synthetic rubber, either butyl or GR-S (Government rubber-styrene), or natural rubber. Innertubes made of butyl synthetic rubber have a blue identication stripe; those made of GR-S synthetic rubber have a red identication stripe; and those made from natural rubber have no identifying stripe.

A seal-sealing innertube has an inner coating of plastic sealing material to keep air from escaping. If the tube is punctured, the sealing material, under the pressure of air in the tube, is forced into the hole and closes it. Upon hardening, the sealing material closes the hole.

The tubeless tire is constructed so that air will not leak through any part of the tire itself or between the tire and rim. The rim has airtight welds to prevent leaks.

Tire construction. At present, there are three basic types of tire construction available for passenger cars: conventional bias ply, bias-belted ply, and radial.

The conventional bias-ply tire, Fig. 17-16(a), has two or more cord plies that run at opposing angles of about 35°. This type of tire provides fairly strong sidewalls, good handling, comfortable riding at all speeds, high rolling resistance, and usually is low priced. Tread wear is greater, however, than with either of the other two constructions.

The bias-belted ply tire, Fig. 17-16(b), also has corded plies that run at opposing angles of about 35°. In addition, it has a two-ply belt under the tread. The bias-belted tire provides longer tread wear, fair handling, a fairly soft ride, and is usually medium priced.

In a radial tire, Fig. 17-16(c), the cord plies run vertically between the tire beads, and a belt of two or more plies is added under the tread. Radial tires provide a smooth ride at only high speed and are high in price. However, they have a high resistance to scuffing and lateral movement and, under normal driving conditions, their tread life is longer than that of any other tire.

At one time, all cord plies were made of cotton. New

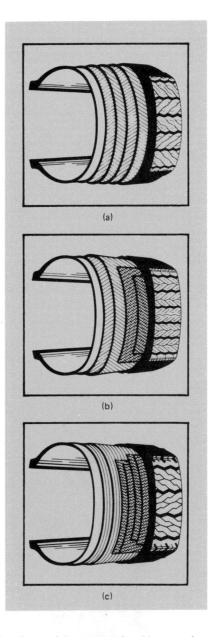

Fig. 17-16   Types of tire construction: (a) conventional bias ply, (b) bias-belted ply, and (c) radial ply. *Courtesy of Firestone Tire and Rubber Company.*

cord plies are made of rayon, nylon, polyester, and fiberglas. These synthetic fibers, along with steel wire or mesh, are also used in the tread belts. Each synthetic has its own qualities, and each is used extensively. Because they provide extra safety, steel-belted tires are becoming very popular.

Sidewall information.   Refer to Fig. 17-17. The load and inflation limits show that this tire will support a maximum load of 1,620 lbs. when inflated to a maximum air pressure of 32 psi.

The load range replaces the ply rating formerly used and identifies the load and inflation limits of the tire. Code letter B is used for any four-ply rating, C for any six-ply rating, and D for any eight-ply rating. The tire shown is, therefore, a four-ply rated tire.

The tire construction is radial ply.

The number assigned to Firestone by the Department of Transportation (DOT) is 147.

A coding system now is used for size information. The tire shown is labeled GR70-15. The G represents the load-carrying limit (1,620 lbs. at 32 psi air pressure), R represents radial-ply construction, 70 is a series number indicating the height-to-width ratio (in this case, height is 70 percent of width), and 15 represents the rim diameter in inches.

At one time, all tires were sized according to their circumference, from bead to bead, and the diameter of the rim. For example, if a tire was marked 7.35:14, its circumference was 7.35 inches from bead to bead, and the tire fit a rim having a diameter of 14 inches. The adoption of series

coding caused considerable confusion and led to the use of conversion charts, such as that shown in Table 17-1. Always use the same load range on both front or both rear tires.

The tread on the tire shown in Fig. 17-17 is six-ply rayon cord and the sidewalls are two-ply rayon cord. In this particular tire, the tread cords have four so-called stabilizer belts and two radial body plies (6 in all).

Snow tires. For winter driving, rear wheels usually are equipped with snow tires. Originally this type of tire had only large rubber cleats in the tread for better traction, but now many are made with carbide studs. Studded tires cannot be used in all states, and some states require their removal by a specified date.

Tire retreading (recapping). If the original tread is worn to a smooth surface, but the tire casing is good, new tread can be applied. This process is called *recapping*.

Before a tire is recapped, the old tread is ground off

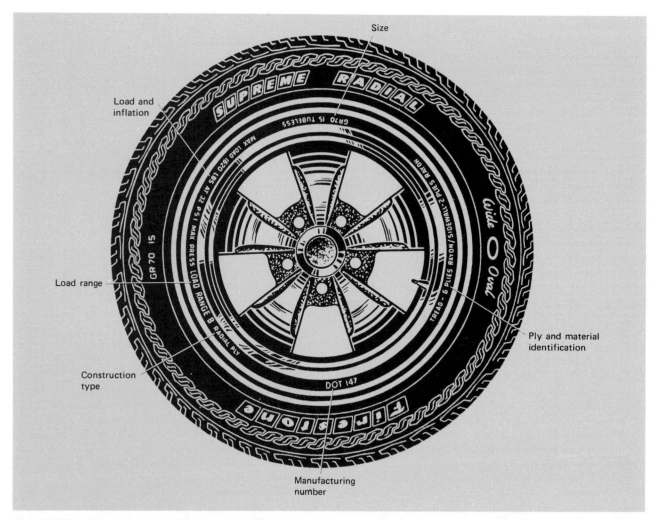

Fig. 17–17 Sidewall information. *Courtesy of Firestone Tire and Rubber Company.*

Table 17–1 Tire Size Conversions, *Courtesy of Firestone Tire and Rubber Company.*

Convention Bias Ply		Bias and Belted-Bias Ply				Radial Ply	
1965 On	Replaces Pre-1965	78 Series	70 Series	60 Series	Metric, or 80, Series	78 Series	70 Series
6.00-13					165R13		
		A78-13	A70-13			AR78-13	AR70-13
6.50-13		B78-13	B70-13		175R13	BR78-13	BR70-13
7.00-13		C78-13	C70-13		185R13	CR78-13	CR70-13
			D70-13			DR78-13	DR70-13
			E70-13		195R13	ER78-13	ER70-13
			A70-14		155R14		AR70-14
6.45-14	6.00-14	B78-14	B70-14		165R14	BR78-14	BR70-14
6.95-14	6.50-14	C78-14	C70-14		175R14	CR78-14	CR70-14
		D78-14	D70-14			DR78-14	DR70-14
7.35-14	7.00-14	E78-14	E70-14		185R14	ER78-14	ER70-14
7.75-14	7.50-14	F78-14	F70-14		195R14	FR78-14	FR70-14
8.25-14	8.00-14	G78-14	G70-14		205R14	GR78-14	GR70-14
8.55-14	8.50-14	H78-14	H70-14		215R14	HR78-14	HR70-14
8.85-14	9.00-14	J78-14	J70-14		225R14	JR78-14	JR70-14
			K70-14				KR70-14
			L70-14				LR70-14
	6.00-15				165R15	BR78-15	
6.85-15	6.50-15	C78-15	C70-15		175R15	CR78-15	CR70-15
		D78-15	D70-15			DR78-15	DR70-15
7.35-15		E78-15	E70-15	E60-15	185R15	ER78-15	ER70-15
7.75-15	6.70-15	F78-15	F70-15	F60-15	195R15	FR78-15	FR70-15
8.25-15 (8.15-15)	7.10-15	G78-15	G70-15	G60-15	205R15	GR78-15	GR70-15
8.55-15 (8.45-15)	7.60-15	H78-15	H70-15		215R15	HR78-15	HR70-15
8.85-15	8.00-15	J78-15	J70-15		225R15	JR78-15	JR70-15
9.00-15	8.20-15		K70-15				KR70-15
9.15-15		L78-15	L70-15		235R15	LR78-15	LR70-15
	8.90-15	N78-15					

until the carcass is of a uniform diameter. The old tread area is thoroughly cleaned and roughened before a strip of new rubber tread, called *camelback,* is placed around the tire casing. The casing and new tread are then placed in a recapping machine and clamped together. Heat, applied for a specified period of time, vulcanizes (bonds) the new tread onto the casing.

A recapped tire usually will provide many more miles of service if good materials are used and proper procedures are followed. At sustained high-speed operation, however, a recapped tire is dangerous since the tread might peel from the casing.

Tire inspection. Take the time to examine your tires at frequent intervals. Steering and braking depend on the ability of the tire to grip the road. Of course, badly worn tires should be replaced (or recapped). Overinflated tires cause a harsh ride, wear excessively in the center, and are susceptible to rupture when the wheel hits a hole or bump. Underinflated tires make steering difficult, cause a car to sway on curves, increase gasoline consumption by increasing rolling friction, and the shoulders wear faster than the center.

FRONT-WHEEL SUSPENSION SYSTEMS

Independent Front-Wheel Suspension

The design details of independent front-wheel suspensions vary in automobiles of different manufacture, but all such systems have the same basic elements. As shown in Fig. 17-18, the wheel is connected to the frame by a steering knuckle which has a spindle to hold the wheel assembly, an upper ball joint, and a lower ball joint. Upper and lower control arms are connected to the frame. A spring (coil or torsion bar) and a direct-acting shock absorber control and dampen wheel bounce, which normally is limited to the vertical plane. A stabilizer bar, links, and strut rods are used to control the sideward and fore-and-aft motions of the front wheels and the front suspension. Pivot points and other points of motion are equipped with grease fittings for regular lubrication.

Typical independent front-wheel suspensions. A coil spring may be mounted between the spring housing and upper control arm, Fig. 17-19, or between the lower control

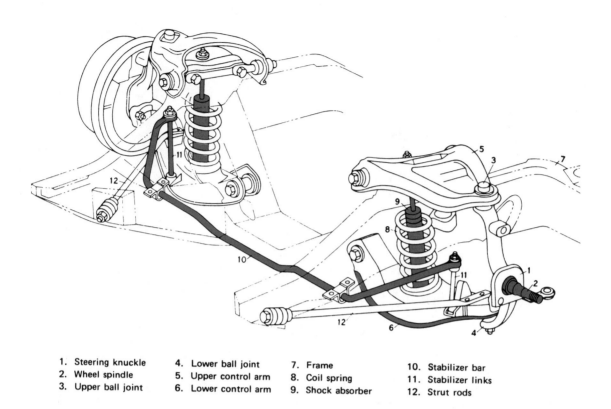

1. Steering knuckle
2. Wheel spindle
3. Upper ball joint
4. Lower ball joint
5. Upper control arm
6. Lower control arm
7. Frame
8. Coil spring
9. Shock absorber
10. Stabilizer bar
11. Stabilizer links
12. Strut rods

Fig. 17–18 Typical independent front-wheel suspension system. *Courtesy of Chevrolet Division, General Motors Corporation.*

arm and frame, Fig. 17-20. Mounting on the lower control arm is most common. Direct-acting shock absorbers are mounted inside the coil springs. Neither front-end nor rear-end absorbers can be serviced in the field; instead, they are replaced as complete units when defective. It is advisable to replace coil springs in pairs (both springs on a rear suspension) to ensure uniform spring action and front-end height.

Removal and installation of coil springs. Although the exact spring-removal procedure for a given make and model of automobile may differ somewhat from that presented here, all involve the use of spring-compression tools. Here is a typical front-spring removal.

1. Raise the car on a hoist and remove the wheel and tire assembly.

2. Disconnect the stabilizer bar link from the lower arm.

3. Remove the bolts that attach the shock absorber to the lower arm assembly.

4. Remove the upper nut, retainer, and grommet from the shock absorber. Remove the shock.

5. Remove the steering center link from the pitman arm.

6. Support the vehicle with safety stands under the jacking pads and lower the hoist for working room.

7. Using the spring-compressor tool shown in Figure 17-

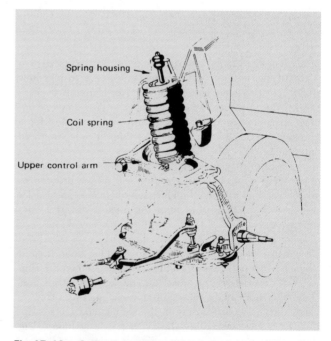

Fig. 17–19 Coil spring mounted above upper control arm. *Courtesy of Ford Motor Company.*

Spring housing

Coil spring

Upper control arm

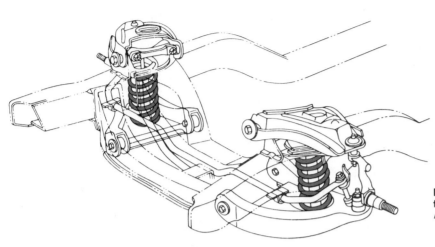

Fig. 17–20 Coil spring mounted between frame and lower control arm. *Courtesy of Chevrolet Division, General Motors Corporation.*

21 (or equivalent), install one place with the pivot-ball seat facing downward into the coils of the spring. Rotate the plate, so that it is flush with the upper surface of the lower arm.

8. Install the other plate with the pivot-ball seat facing upward into the coils of the spring. Insert the upper ball nut through the coils of the spring, so that the nut rests in the upper plate.

9. Insert the compression rod into the opening in the lower arm through the upper and lower plate and upper ball nut. Insert the securing pin through the upper ball nut and compression rod.

10. With the upper ball nut secured, turn the upper plate, so that it walks up the coil until it contacts the upper spring seat. Then back off one-half turn.

11. Install the lower ball nut and thrust washer on the compression rod and screw on the forcing nut. See Figures 17-22 and 17-23.

12. Tighten the forcing nut, Figure 17-24, until the spring is compressed enough to be free in its seat.

13. Remove the two lower arm-pivot bolts, disengage the lower arm from the frame cross member, and remove the spring assembly.

14. If a new spring is to be installed: (a) Mark the position of the upper and lower plates on the spring with chalk. Figure 17-25. (b) As a guide to assist you in compressing a new spring for installation, measure the compressed length and the amount of curvature of the old spring.

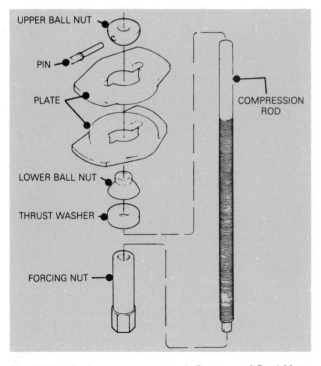

Fig. 17-21. Spring-compressor tool. *Courtesy of Ford Motor Company.*

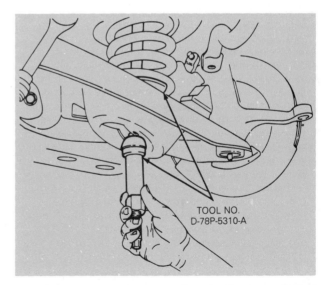

Fig. 17-22. Coil spring removal tool. *Courtesy of Ford Motor Company.*

15. Loosen the forcing nut to relieve spring tension and remove the tools from the spring.

16. To install the new spring, first assemble the spring compressor and locate in the positions indicated by the chalk marks (Step 14).

17. Before compressing the coil spring, be sure that the upper ball nut-securing pin is inserted properly.

18. Compress the coil spring until the spring height reaches the dimensions obtained in Step 14(b).

19. Position the coil-spring assembly into the lower arm. See Figure 17-26.

20. Now reverse the removal process. The tail of the coil spring must be positioned as shown in Figure 17-27.

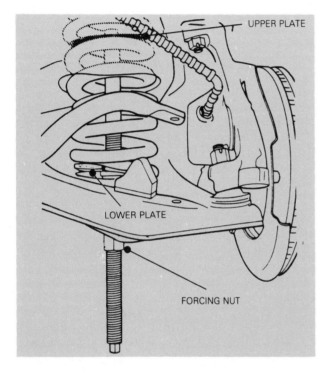

Fig. 17-23. Compressor tool forcing nut. *Courtesy of Ford Motor Company.*

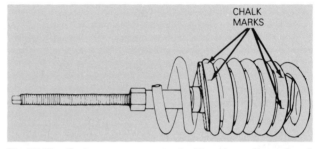

Fig. 17-25. Spring compressor tool with spring collapsed and removed from vehicle. *Courtesy of Ford Motor Company.*

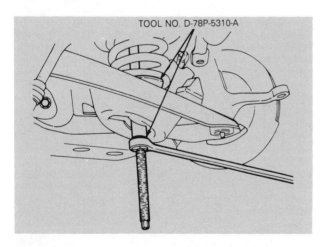

Fig. 17-24. Spring compressed for removal. *Courtesy of Ford Motor Company.*

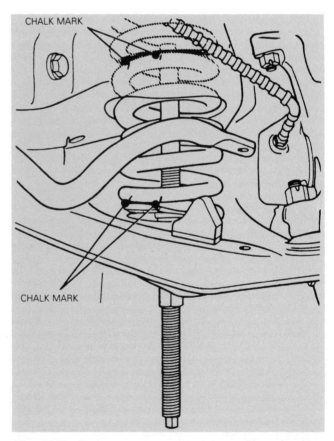

Fig. 17-26. Spring compressor tool in position showing marks on spring where plates are located. *Courtesy of Ford Motor Company.*

Fig. 17-27. Exploded view of typical spring on lower arm. *Courtesy of Ford Motor Company.*

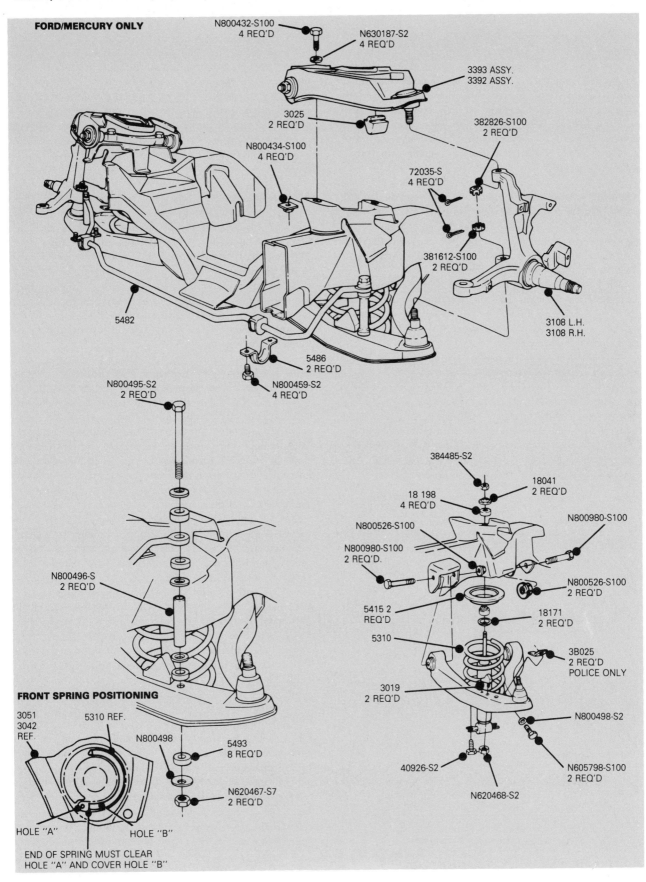

FORD/MERCURY ONLY

N800432-S100
4 REQ'D

N630187-S2
4 REQ'D

3393 ASSY.
3392 ASSY.

3025
2 REQ'D

N800434-S100
4 REQ'D

382826-S100
2 REQ'D

72035-S
4 REQ'D

381612-S100
2 REQ'D

5482

5486
2 REQ'D

N800459-S2
4 REQ'D

3108 L.H.
3108 R.H.

N800495-S2
2 REQ'D

N800496-S
2 REQ'D

384485-S2

18041
2 REQ'D

18 198
4 REQ'D

N800526-S100

N800980-S100
2 REQ'D.

N800980-S100

N800526-S100
2 REQ'D

5415 2
REQ'D

18171
2 REQ'D

5310

3B025
2 REQ'D
POLICE ONLY

3019
2 REQ'D

N800498-S2

N605798-S100
2 REQ'D

40926-S2

N620468-S2

FRONT SPRING POSITIONING

3051
3042
REF.

5310 REF.

N800498

5493
8 REQ'D

N620467-S7
2 REQ'D

HOLE "A"

HOLE "B"

END OF SPRING MUST CLEAR
HOLE "A" AND COVER HOLE "B"

A torsion bar suspension system. A basic front torsion bar suspension system is shown in Figure 17-28. The front of the torsion bar is attached to the lower control arm, and the rear of the torsion bar is attached to the frame cross member in the manner shown in the inset. The rear anchor is adjusted by turning the threaded bolt. This bolt also regulates the front height of the vehicle. The active section of the torsion bar must be protected from nicks, scratches, and corrosion, any of which could lead to premature weakening of the spring.

Removing a torsion bar spring. To remove a torsion bar spring, first hoist the automobile and place jack stands under the frame. Next, release the tension on the torsion bar by loosening the anchor adjusting bolt. Remove the lock ring, the plug (if one is used), and the balloon-type seal. Withdraw the torsion bar from the rear.

Do not apply heat to the anchor to aid in removal, because heat may destroy the temper of the torsion bar. Be careful not to mar or scratch the surface of the bar, because a deep scratch or an indented spot may lead to a fatigue crack in the torsion bar.

New torsion bars are stamped L (for left) and R (for right) and are not interchangeable.

Installing a torsion bar spring. To install a torsion bar spring, first clean the hexagonal openings in the anchors and the hexagonal ends of the torsion bars. Insert the torsion bar through the rear anchor, and over the bar slide the balloon-type seal with the large cupped side of the seal facing rear-

ward. Next, coat each end of the torsion bar with chassis lubricant before inserting an end into its respective anchor in the lower control arm. Install the plug and lock ring and then move the torsion bar rearward until it contacts the lock ring. Pack the anchor until the lip of the seal is seated in its groove. Tighten the adjusting bolt until approximately an inch of the thread shows. This setting is used as a starting point for suspension height adjustment. It is also used to get a load on the torsion bar before lowering the vehicle to the floor.

Front suspension trim height. The front suspension must be a uniform height above ground on both sides to ensure safe control, proper wheel alignment, good braking, extended tire life, and proper operation of suspension parts. The exact trim height varies from car to car and is specified in the manufacturers' manuals. The trim height is adjustable in autos equipped with torsion bar springs. If the vehicle has coil springs, devices such as spacers (shims) may be used to correct the trim height. The installation of new coil springs is advisable, however, since a loss of trim height indicates a worn spring.

Trim height–Chrsyler products and Oldsmobile Toronado. To check front suspension trim height, place the car on a level floor. Inflate the tires to the recommended pressure with the auto standing at full curb weight (full gas tank, spare tire and tools, but no passengers or driver). Grasp the front bumper and jounce the vehicle up and down several times to settle the suspension system. Then proceed as follows: (1) *On Chrysler products*, measure from the lowest point of the lower ball joint to the floor. Then measure from the underside of the lower control arm bushing, at the centerline of the bushing housing, to the floor. Due to the weight of the automobile, the last measurement will always be the greater of the two. The difference between readings should be within the limits specified. If the difference between the readings is less than 0.125 inch, and the measurements are within specs, the height is correct. If not, adjust the torsion bar for correct height. (2) *On the Oldsmobile Toronado*, the front height is measured from the front of the rocker panel to the ground. This distance should be 8 inches. The side-to-side height should not vary by more than 0.625 inch; if it does, adjust the torsion bars for correct height.

Ball Joints

All ball joints are similar in design and operation. The ball joint shown in Fig. 17-29 has a ball that rides on a Teflon seat. Because the ball has a tendency to rattle and become battered if the socket fit is too loose, a preload rubber, or in some instances a spring, maintains the proper bearing clearance. The steel socket and cap enclose the ball and ball seat and are used to mount the entire assembly. The seal retainer holds the rubber seal in position. The seal keeps the

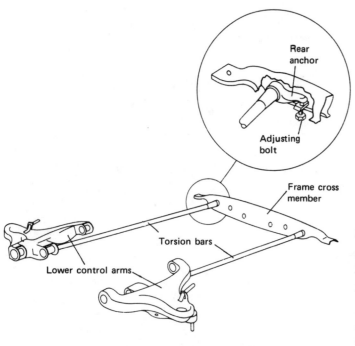

Fig. 17-28 Front torsion bar suspension system.

lubricant in and dirt and moisture out. The stud is used to attach the ball joint to the steering knuckle.

Lubrication of ball joints.   Lubricant for ball joints is introduced through the grease fittings, Fig. 17-29, under high pressure. It is forced around the joint, and excess lubricant is retained by the rubber seal. Newer automobiles have a threaded plug that must be removed in order to install the grease fitting in a ball joint. When the grease job is completed, the grease fittings should be removed and the plug reinstalled. The period of time between lubrication jobs is usually 36,000 miles or 36 months, whichever comes first.

Inspection of ball joints.   Ball joint seals should be inspected every six months and at any other time the auto is being serviced on a rack. If the seals are cracked or split, install new ones because dirt, moisture, and corrosive materials may get into the space between the ball and seat and cause rapid wear of the joint.

The ball joints themselves are also checked when the seats are inspected. Begin by jacking up the car as shown in Fig. 17-30. Next, grasp the tire at top and bottom and try to move the wheel back and forth. If the wheel moves more than 0.05 inch, check to see which ball joint has the greatest amount of play and replace it. When the play is still excessive, the other ball joint must be checked and replaced if necessary. Do not mistake wheel bearing looseness for ball joint looseness.

During assembly, ball joints are riveted in place. Because ball joints are not adjustable and must be replaced when worn, it is necessary to drill out the attaching rivets in order to remove worn joints. To remove the rivets, first drill in the center of each rivet a hole of 0.125 inch in diameter and 0.25 inch in depth. Then, with a 0.5-inch twist drill, drill only deep enough to remove each rivet head. If necessary, drive out the shank of the rivet with a hammer and drift pin and remove the ball joint.

The new ball joint is attached by nuts and bolts. First, the nuts are drawn up finger tight; then each nut is tightened to a torque of 8 foot-pounds. Front-wheel alignment should always be checked after new ball joints are installed, because of the reduced clearance in new parts.

Front-Wheel Bearings

Assembled wheel bearings and related parts are shown in Fig. 17-31. The wheel is attached to the hub and brake drum assembly by hub bolts and nuts. (In some instances, the bolts screw into the hub.) The complete assembly is then mounted on the spindle. Tapered roller bearings are used to reduce friction between the hub and spindle. The grease retainer keeps lubricant from escaping from the hub and coating the brake drum friction surface. The bearings roll on the outer bearing races (cups), which are hardened steel inserts in the hub. The washer and adjusting nut hold the bearings and hub on the spindle. The cotter pin prevents the nut from turning and possibly coming off the spindle. The grease cap prevents loss of grease from the outside of the assembly.

Lubrication and servicing of front-wheel bearings.   Wheel bearings should be repacked with grease at the mileage in-

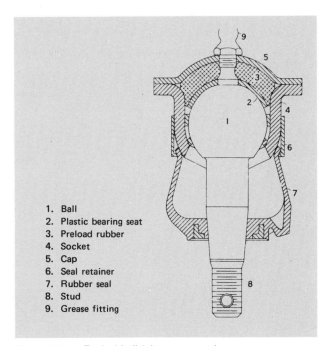

1. Ball
2. Plastic bearing seat
3. Preload rubber
4. Socket
5. Cap
6. Seal retainer
7. Rubber seal
8. Stud
9. Grease fitting

Fig. 17-29   Typical ball joint cross section.

Fig. 17-30   Checking ball joint condition. *Courtesy of Bear Manufacturing Corporation.*

tervals recommended by the manufacturer. To repack a wheel bearing, remove the cotter pin, adjusting nut, and washer from the wheel spindle. Pull the hub and drum assembly off the spindle, taking care not to damage the bearings or the bearing races. Wash all parts except the roller and the roller separator assemblies in clean solvent. The rollers and roller separator assemblies should be washed in clean gasoline.

Front-wheel bearings are precision parts and must be handled with care. When dry, they should not be spun and handling should be kept to a minimum.

Inspect the bearing assemblies for worn or pitted rollers and cracked separators, and the bearing races for scores, cracks or surface chipping. If any of these defects are evident, new parts should be installed. Before the outer races of either the inner or outer bearings can be replaced, the race must be driven out with a hammer and a brass drift rod.

To install new races, use a brass drift rod and a steel washer slightly smaller in diameter than the inside of the hub. See Fig. 17-32. Insert the race in the hub, place the washer and drift rod on the race, and strike the drift rod with a hammer. Make sure the bearing race is fully seated.

On assembly, the inner bearing must be installed first. Lubricate the bores of the inner races and pack the roller and separator assemblies with EP (extreme pressure) wheel-bearing grease. Install the inner bearing and separator assembly into the outer race. Next, install the inner race and carefully tap the grease seal into the hub. Make sure the brake linings and brake drum inner surfaces are clean before positioning the hub and drum assembly on the spindle. Place the outer bearing roller and separator assembly into the hub and install the outer bearing inner race over the spindle. Place the washer and adjusting nut on the spindle, and adjust the nut to a torque of 17 to 25 foot-pounds to seat the bearings. Install the locknut so that the grooves are

aligned with the cotter pin hole. Back off the adjusting nut one groove and install the cotter pin. Install the grease cap and wipe off excess grease.

REAR-WHEEL SUSPENSION SYSTEMS

Leaf-Spring Suspension

Although the weight on the front wheels of an automobile remains fairly constant, the weight on the rear axle is subject to wide variations. Consequently, the semielliptic

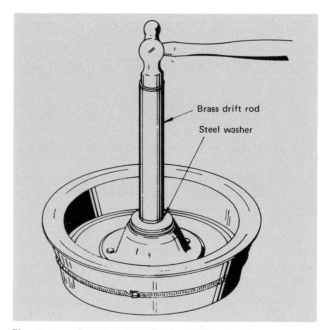

Fig. 17-32   Installing inner bearing outer race. *Courtesy of Oldsmobile Division, General Motors Corporation.*

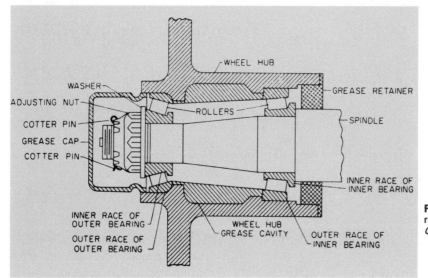

Fig. 17-31   Assembled wheel bearings and related parts. *Courtesy of Plymouth Division, Chrysler Motors Corporation.*

spring, because of its adaptability to varying loads, is still used for the rear suspension of some automobiles.

The usual rear semielliptic spring, shown in Fig. 17-33, has a number of plates (leaves) fastened together at or near the middle by a center bolt for ease in handling and positioning the spring on the rear-axle housing. The head of this bolt fits a recess in the axle and helps keep the spring in position; main dependence, however, is placed on the U-bolts, which clamp the spring to the axle housing. In routine spring service make sure the U-bolt nuts are tight. The spring is weakened at the middle because of the bolt hole, but the tendency to break at this point is eliminated by keeping the U-bolts so tight that the spring is clamped to the axle as though in a vise. The tie bolt is not always located at the middle of the spring, and care must be taken to replace a spring properly.

The importance of tight U-bolts cannot be overemphasized. Fleet operators have found that the center breakage of springs is greatly reduced by retightening U-bolts after the first day of running after a spring has been repaired or replaced. A rubberized fabric pad sometimes is placed between the spring and axle of passenger cars, and there are a number of surfaces between the spring leaves that bed down a little in use. Consequently, it is good practice to tighten the U-bolt nuts of new cars after the first thousand miles of use. A torque wrench should be used to draw up the U-bolt nuts to the recommended torque.

Worn spring pads on the axle housing will keep the spring from seating firmly even after the U-bolt nuts are tightened.

A spacer is used with the U-bolts to hold them parallel with each other and directly in line with the pull on them. Without the spacer, long U-bolts may be tilted at a slight angle when the nuts are drawn up and seem to be tight. However, the flexing of the spring will soon cause the U-bolts to assume their proper position, and they may become loose enough to let the spring break at its middle. Spacers are shaped to fit the contour of the U-bolts so that the bolts can be drawn up square and tight. The spacer should never be omitted when installing springs.

Spring clips. When a car wheel strikes a bump, the leaves tend to separate and let the main leaf absorb most of the rebound. Leaf separation actually would occur if the leaves were not bound together by means of spring clips (rebound clips), such as those shown in Fig. 17-33. The spring clips also maintain more constant interleaf friction, and this friction acts as a dampener (shock absorber) in controlling spring action.

Broken clips should be replaced as soon as possible with clips of the proper size. The width of the clip should be 0.0625 inch more than the width of the spring leaves; the spacer tube that fits over the spring clips bolt maintains this clearance. In addition, the spacer tube permits free lengthwise movement of the ends of the leaves as the spring flexes. Clearance between the clip spacer tube and the top of the main leaf also allows spring twist to be distributed over a greater length of the main leaf, thus reducing the likelihood of breakage.

Spring clips should be assembled with the head of the bolt away from the tire to avoid possible tire damage.

Spring shackles. Spring shackles have rubber bushings that fit the shackle pins. See Fig. 17-34. The bushings act as insulators to keep wheel noise from being transmitted to the chassis frame. To prevent wear, the bushing is made to flex rather than to rub on the shackle pin. Therefore, the nuts on the shackle bolts should be tightened only when the shackles are under normal load. This keeps the bushings from being overstressed in either the bound or rebound positions and gives the shackle free action as the spring deflects. Rubber bushings should never be lubricated.

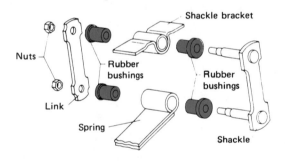

Fig. 17-34 Spring shackle with rubber bushings.

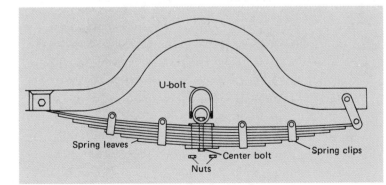

Fig. 17-33 Rear semielliptic leaf spring.

Spring Faults

Broken springs. In most cases, initially only one or two leaves of a semielliptic spring break. The remaining leaves usually provide enough strength for the vehicle to be driven for some time. However, this safety factor should not be overworked, because the adjacent leaves eventually will break.

In most cars and trucks the end of the second leaf partly or entirely surrounds the eye of the main leaf. With this construction, if the main leaf breaks, the second leaf supports the vehicle for some time if the vehicle is driven carefully.

Causes of premature spring failure. If a spring breaks before its normal life is achieved, it should be examined carefully, because the position and nature of the break often indicate the source of the trouble. If possible, the cause should be determined and eliminated before a new spring is installed. For instance, loose U-bolt nuts or worn spring pads often will cause a spring to break at the center bolt hole. Breakage of the main leaf about halfway between the U-bolts and the end of the leaf may be caused by loose or broken spring clips, which result in the failure of adjacent leaves to take their share of the stress during rebounds. Breakage near the eye of the main leaf may indicate that the rubber bushings are defective and the shackle bolts are rusted (frozen) in the spring eyes.

Leaf spring replacement. The first step in replacing a rear leaf spring is to raise the vehicle by means of a chain hoist, frame lift, or jacks to a comfortable working level and high enough so the wheels are off the floor and the rear springs hang free. Disconnect the shock absorber at the lower

mount and support the rear-axle housing in this position. Next, remove the front-hanger bolt, U-bolts, and spacer plate. Unfasten the rear shackle and remove the spring from the vehicle.

To install a rear spring, reverse the procedure given above. After the spring is installed, jounce the automobile several times and then compare spring heights. If the automobile now sags on the side having the old spring, that one should be replaced also.

Coil-Spring Suspension

In coil-spring rear-suspension systems, the rear springs simply support the weight of the vehicle and absorb road shocks. Direct-acting shock absorbers are used to provide greater rear-end stability. With coil springs, radius rods (control arms) are often used between the rear-axle housing and frame to absorb the torque applied to the housing.

Figure 17-35 shows a typical installation of upper and lower control arms for absorbing torque. These arms also keep the axle housing aligned with the frame while allowing up-and-down movement of the axle. With the upper control arms attached at an angle to the axle housing, as shown, side sway of the housing is prevented. If the control arms are perpendicular to the axle housing, a track bar similar to that shown in Fig. 17-36 is needed.

Coil springs may also be mounted on either the rear-axle housing, as shown in Fig. 17-37, or the lower control arm, as shown in Fig. 17-38. In either location the operation of the spring is the same.

Fatigued and broken coil springs. A coil spring acts by torsion rather than by bending and is coiled only to obtain greater compactness, so it would seem desirable to preset

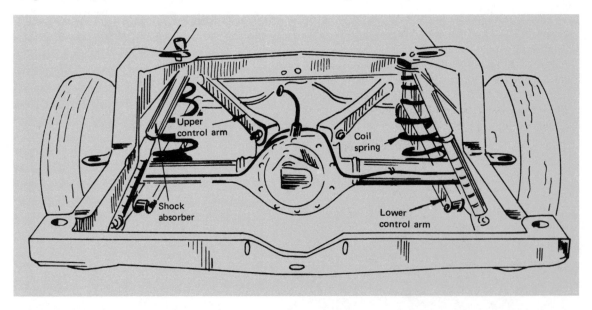

Fig. 17-35 Typical installation of axle housing control arms.
Courtesy of Chevrolet Division, General Motors Corporation.

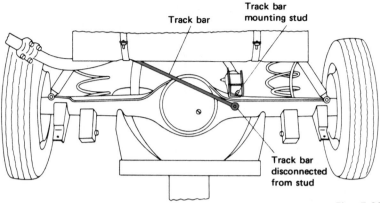

Fig. 17-36 Using a track bar in the rear-suspension system. *Courtesy of Ford Motor Company.*

coil springs. Presetting is not feasible, however, because the adjacent coils make contact with each other before the elastic limit of the spring is reached. Stretching coil springs to restore them to their normal length does no good because it presets the spring in the wrong direction and the spring soon sags again.

To check the rear coil spring height, measure from the underside of the body to the axle housing at each side. If the difference in measurements is greater than 0.25 inch, the spring is removed from the lower side of the car and a spacer placed on the lower spring pad to make up the difference in spring lengths. The spring is then replaced.

When a coil spring breaks, it must be replaced. The replacement of a coil spring on a front suspension requires realignment of the front wheels.

Replacing rear coil springs. To replace the rear coil springs, the automobile is raised until the wheels are at least 8 inches from the floor. Floor stands are then placed under the frame rails to support the vehicle safely. With a jack,

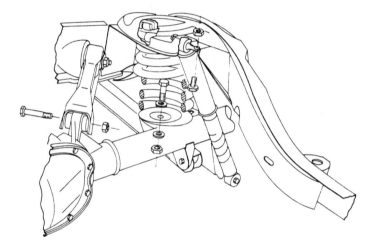

Fig. 17-37 Coil-mounted spring on rear-axle housing. *Courtesy of Pontiac Division, General Motors Corporation.*

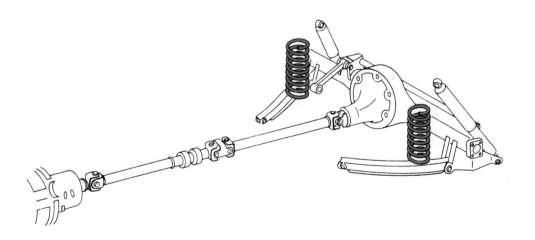

Fig. 17-38 Coil springs mounted on lower control arm. *Courtesy of Buick Division, General Motors Corporation.*

raise the axle housing until all weight is off the shock absorbers, and then disconnect the shock absorber lower studs. (On some automobiles it may be necessary also to disconnect the track bar and loosen the horizontal arm bolts.) Now lower the axle housing on the jack until the coil springs are free. The springs and spring pads can now be removed. To install new coil springs, simply reverse the directions for their removal.

AUTOMATIC LEVEL CONTROL SYSTEM

Introduction

An automatic level control system keeps the frame and body in a level position even when loads up to 500 pounds are either added to or removed from the vehicle directly above the rear axle. The system, which operates by compressed air, is available as optional equipment on some vehicles and is standard equipment on others.

The automatic level control system includes a compressor, air reservoir tank, pressure regulator valve, height control valve and link, two Superlift shock absorbers, and flexible air lines.

Air Compressor

The air compressor is a two-stage vacuum-actuated type that requires no lubrication. Refer to Fig. 17-39. The vacuum

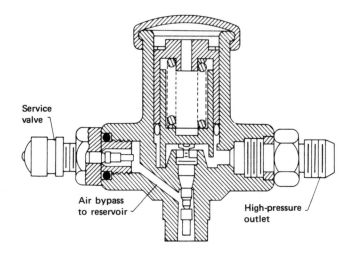

Fig. 17-40   Air pressure regulator valve. *Courtesy of Buick Division, General Motors Corporation.*

line is connected to the engine positive crankcase vent hose. The difference in pressures between the manifold vacuum and the atmosphere acting on a diaphragm causes the piston to move toward the side of the diaphragm having the lower pressure.

On the first-stage intake stroke, air is drawn in at at-

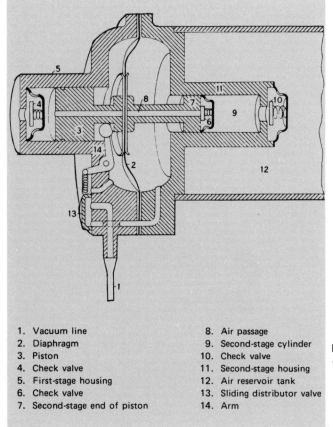

1. Vacuum line	8. Air passage
2. Diaphragm	9. Second-stage cylinder
3. Piston	10. Check valve
4. Check valve	11. Second-stage housing
5. First-stage housing	12. Air reservoir tank
6. Check valve	13. Sliding distributor valve
7. Second-stage end of piston	14. Arm

Fig. 17-39   Compressor. *Courtesy of Buick Division, General Motors Corporation.*

mospheric pressure through a one-way check valve located at the left end of the first-stage housing. On the first-stage compression stroke, this check valve is closed, and another one-way check valve in the second-stage end of the piston is opened. Air from the first stage then flows through the air passage into the second-stage cylinder where it is subjected to further compression. The second-stage compression stroke closes the check valve in the second-stage end of the piston, and opens the check valve in the end of the second-stage housing, forcing air into the air reservoir tank.

The intake and compression strokes are controlled by the sliding distributor valve. The arm is tripped by the piston as it nears the end of each stroke. Each time the arm moves, the distributor valve moves up or down and covers a different set of holes in the first-stage housing. By this arrangement, the valve controls the flow of air under atmospheric pressure and the manifold pressure, alternately directing the unequal pressure to opposite sides of the diaphragm. As the compressor operates, the air pressure in the

reservoir tank gradually increases and exerts a back pressure on the second-stage piston until the air pressures exerted on the diaphragm by the piston and reservoir are equal. At this point, the compressor and regulator unit stops operating because of the balance in pressure. It remains inoperative until air is needed in the level control system. The reservoir pressure then drops, and the operation just described is repeated.

Since manifold vacuum and atmospheric pressure are both affected by altitude, a pressure balance may vary from 150 to 275 psi.

Pressure Regulator Valve

The air pressure regulator valve, Fig. 17-40, is preset to regulate air pressure from the reservoir to the height control valve and shock absorbers at approximately 125 psi, regardless of reservoir pressure.

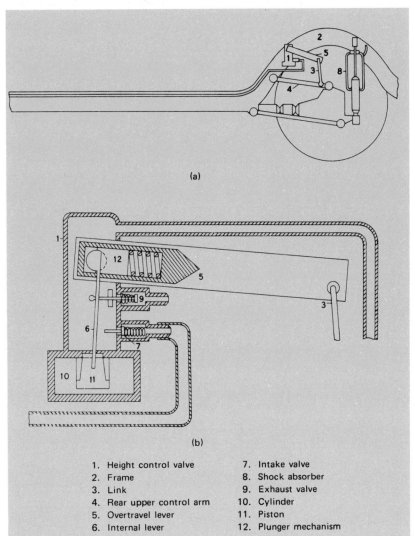

(a)

(b)

Fig. 17-41 Level control system. *Courtesy of Buick Division, General Motors Corporation.*

1. Height control valve	7. Intake valve
2. Frame	8. Shock absorber
3. Link	9. Exhaust valve
4. Rear upper control arm	10. Cylinder
5. Overtravel lever	11. Piston
6. Internal lever	12. Plunger mechanism

The regulated air pressure is supplied to the height control valve and shock absorbers via flexible air lines. These lines must be free of kinks and must be located far enough away from the exhaust system to prevent heat damage. The regulator valve is not adjustable and must be replaced if air pressure is less than 100 psi or more than 130 psi, as determined by an air-pressure gauge.

Height Control Valve

Figure 17-41 shows a level control system. View (a) shows the parts that make up the system and their relative locations on an automobile. View (b) shows the details of the height control valve. This valve, mounted on the car frame, senses rear height by means of a link attached to the rear-upper control arm on the rear-axle housing. When enough weight is added to move the rear frame downward, the link forces the overtravel lever upward, and an internal lever opens the intake valve. When the intake valve opens, high-pressure air is admitted to the shock absorbers, which extend and raise the vehicle to a level position. When the car is level, the intake valve shuts off.

When a load is removed from the vehicle, the overtravel lever is forced downward by the link and connects to the upper control arm. The internal lever then opens the exhaust valve and allows air to escape from the shock absorbers. As air escapes, the shock absorbers retract and lower the frame to a level position. As soon as the frame is level, the overtravel arm rises, and the internal lever allows the exhaust valve to close.

To keep the level control mechanism from responding to variations in road level, the height control valve includes a time-delay piston. When the overtravel lever is suddenly forced up by the link, fluid in the cylinder resists sudden motion of the piston. Torque exerted by the overtravel lever is absorbed by the plunger mechanism and the internal lever returns to normal without any transfer of air from or to the height control valve.

When the overtravel lever is in the offset position long enough for the piston to displace the fluid in the cylinder, air is admitted to the shock absorbers. Torque is then absorbed in the time-delay cylinder, which allows the internal lever to operate the air-transfer valve.

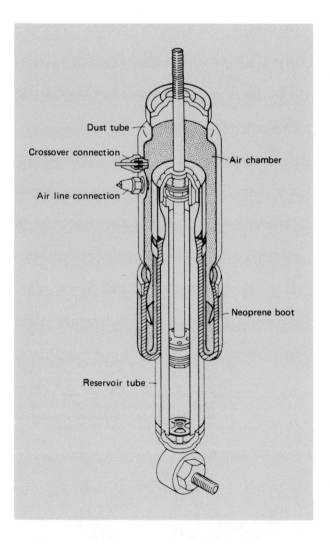

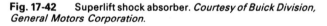

Fig. 17-42   Superlift shock absorber. *Courtesy of Buick Division, General Motors Corporation.*

Superlift Shock Absorbers

The shock absorbers used in the level control system are essentially conventional hydraulic shock absorbers with an added nylon-reinforced neoprene (synthetic rubber) boot to form an air chamber. Figure 17-42 shows a Superlift shock absorber in which the neoprene boot forms an airtight seal between the dust tube and reservoir tube to provide an air chamber around the shock absorber.

The air chamber is connected to the air line from the height control valve. When compressed air enters the air chamber it makes the shock absorber extend. When air escapes from the air chamber, the shock absorber retracts. A crossover air line between the two Superlift shock absorbers equalizes the pressure in these units.

To minimize boot friction, 8- to 15-psi pressure is maintained in the air chamber at all times. A check valve inside the exhaust valve on the height control unit keeps the chamber from becoming entirely deflated when no air is needed by the shock absorbers.

WHEEL BALANCE

Importance of Balanced Wheels

The importance of balanced wheel assemblies cannot be overemphasized. Imagine a wheel to which has been fastened a heavy weight. As the wheel revolves, centrifugal force would try to throw the weight off the wheel. Centrifugal force always acts outward from the center of the wheel, and tends to pull the wheel upward, forward, downward, and backward as the wheel revolves. The result of this force is a rapid flexing of the chassis spring and an up and down movement of the front suspension. When a wheel is completely balanced, however, there is an equal distribution of weight. Although centrifugal forces are still present, they cancel one another.

The centrifugal force of an unbalanced wheel usually causes the end of the wheel spindle to travel in a circle, and this in turn makes the wheel swing from side to side and up and down—a condition known as *shimmy*. Although any wheel misalignment aggravates shimmy, its principal cause is unbalanced wheels.

Wheel unbalance creates heavy stresses on front-end parts, abnormal wear on front-end parts, passenger discomfort, extreme tire wear, and shimmy.

Static and Dynamic Wheel Balance

There are two kinds of wheel balance: static (at rest) and dynamic (in motion). A wheel is in static balance when it has the weight distributed around the circumference in such a manner that there is no tendency for the wheel to rotate by itself. Static imbalance results in vertical oscillations (hop) of the wheel assembly.

A wheel at rest that is unbalanced due to a heavy spot will tend to rotate by itself until the heavy portion of the assembly is down. To correct the static imbalance, compensating weight is added at the top.

It is possible for a wheel to be in balance statically (at rest) and out of balance dynamically (in motion). Once the wheel is in motion, static weights try to reach a point exactly perpendicular to the true plane of rotation due to the action of centrifugal force. See Fig. 17-43(a). At 180° of wheel rotation, static weights, in attempting to reach the true plane of rotation, kick the spindle in the opposite direction. See Fig. 17-43(b). Severe vibration and shimmy result.

To eliminate the shimmy, dynamic compensating weights are placed 180° opposite each other, as shown in Fig. 17-43(c). Dynamic balance is obtained while static balance remains unaffected.

Other names used in place of shimmy are wheel wobble and wheel runout.

Checking static balance with wheels off car. A wheel-balancing machine checks both static and dynamic balance.

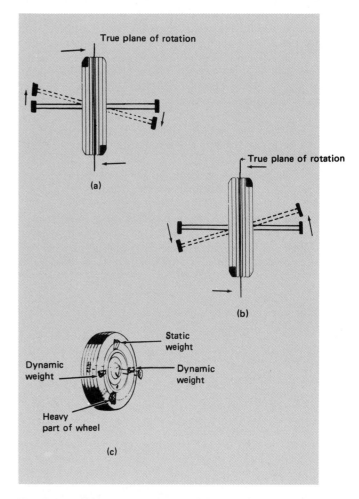

Fig. 17-43 Dynamic unbalance. (a) Static weights try to reach a point exactly perpendicular to true plane of rotation. (b) At 180° of wheel rotation, static weights attempt to reach true plane of rotation. (c) Use of dynamic compensating weights.

The wheel assembly is mounted vertically on the spindle of the balancing machine and spun rapidly by a wheel-driving drum. After rotation stops, the heaviest part of the wheel and tire is at the bottom. Static balance is achieved by attaching equal weights on both sides of a heavy spot. The weights are attached to the rim by spring clips.

Checking dynamic balance with wheels off car. Dynamic balance can be checked on the same machine. The wheel is spun, and an indicating device shows where and by approximately how much the wheel is unbalanced dynamically. Balance is again achieved by the use of weights.

There is also another form of static-balance checker. The wheel and tire assembly is placed on the top of the pedestal and is supported by a flange. A circular line, concentric with the rim, is scribed on a cylindrical spirit level. When the bubble is centered within the scribed circle, the wheel and tire assembly is in static balance.

If the bubble is off center, the operator sets wheel weights on the lighter side of the rim until the bubble becomes centered within the scribed circle. As soon as the bubble remains centered, the weights are hammered onto the rim.

The handle moved to the *on* position locks the flange and spirit level in place; this allows the operator to add the required weights. This type of balancer is not as accurate as the wheel-spinner type discussed earlier.

Wheel balancing on car. Wheel and tire assemblies can also be balanced without removing them from the automobile.

Equipment for spinning the front wheels is shown in Fig. 17-44. First, the front wheels are raised clear of the floor and any small stones or other objects embedded in the tread are removed. A vibration indicator (not shown) is then placed under the bumper and is adjusted in height with its pointer set in a horizontal position. The wheel-spinning unit has a foot switch to start and stop the motor, which spins

the wheel, and to raise a braking device that stops wheel rotation.

The spinner rotates the wheel at a steadily increasing speed until the top speed is reached or until the pointer on the vibration indicator shakes to indicate imbalance. A special adapter (for that particular wheel) is then installed as shown in Fig. 17-45. The locating stops are positioned on the wheel rim, and the wing nuts are tightened to hold the adapter in place on the rim. The milled-edge disks (pads) provide contact surfaces for the balancer unit shown in Fig. 17-46, and they are adjustable.

The balancer unit is attached to the adapter by a threaded screw that passes into the adapter hub. When the rim of the balancer is tight against the four disks, the balancer is in a vertical plane parallel to a vertical plane through the wheel.

The balancer has two knobs. The outer knob controls the amount of weight that must be added to the wheel rim for balance, and the inner knob controls the position around the wheel rim where the unbalanced weight should be applied. Thus, when the wheel is spun, the operator, by manipulating the knobs, can add or subtract unbalanced weight and move this weight around the rim until the exact amount of weight and its position for balance are determined. Then, with the wheel stopped, the amount and position of the weight are noted on the scale.

Balancing Rear Wheels

Rear wheels can be balanced with the same equipment used to balance front wheels. However, only one wheel at a time is raised from the floor, unless the car has a no-slip (positive traction) differential. On such cars, both wheels are raised and the one not being checked is removed from the car.

With the rear wheels raised, the engine is used, instead of a spinner, to turn the wheels. Excessive wheel spinning should be avoided since driving the wheels at high speed for more than two minutes will damage the differential.

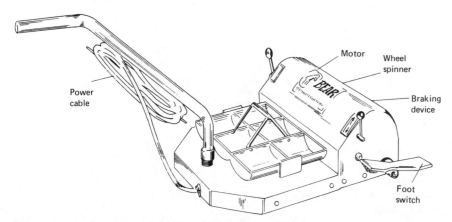

Fig. 17-44 **Wheel spinner.** *Courtesy of Bear Manufacturing Corporation.*

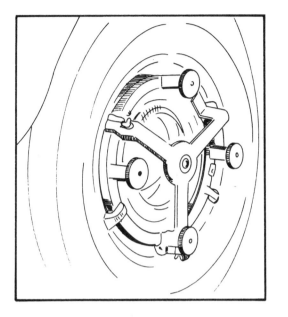

Fig. 17-45   Adapter installed on wheel preparatory to checking dynamic balance. *Courtesy of Bear Manufacturing Corporation.*

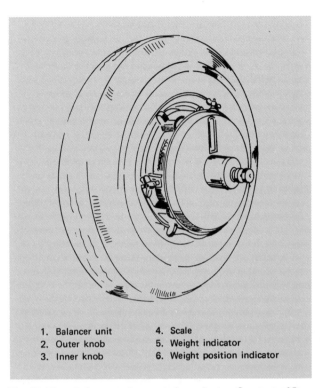

1. Balancer unit	4. Scale
2. Outer knob	5. Weight indicator
3. Inner knob	6. Weight position indicator

Fig. 17-46   Balancer unit mounted on adapter. *Courtesy of Bear Manufacturing Corporation.*

Other Factors Affecting Wheel Balance

Brake drums, wheel wobble due to a bent rim, or a wheel and tire assembly that is not centered about the wheel spindle should be considered when wheel balance is checked. A wheel that does not run true is said to have *runout*. If the wheel and tire are off center and are out-of-round, the runout is called *radial runout*. If the wheel wobbles from side to side, the runout is called *lateral runout*.

A brake drum is considered to be part of the wheel assembly when the wheel is bolted to the hub. Because the drum has a comparatively small diameter, however, its effect on static wheel balance is negligible. Moreover, the brake drums are balanced during manufacture to minimize any such condition.

Checking radial runout.   An out-of-round wheel and tire assembly causes continuous up and down motion of the wheel spindle as the wheel turns. If an off-center wheel and tire assembly is mounted on a fixed spindle and spun, the tire tread appears to move up and down. The amount of this movement is the radial runout (wheel hop) and, if excessive, causes tire tramping, which is felt as a thump each time the high portion of the circumference meets the road surface.

Radial runout is measured by using the dial-indicator arrangement shown in Fig. 17-47. The wheel and tire assembly is raised off the floor. A dial indicator, attached to a special support, is adjusted to make the pointer on the indicator dial swing through nearly a complete revolution. The zero mark on the dial is then made to line up with the pointer. As the wheel turns, the radial runout causes the contact point to move back and forth while the pointer swings in one direction and then the other to indicate the amount of runout in thousandths of an inch.

Checking lateral runout.   Lateral runout (side-to-side wobble) occurs as the wheel rotates. This form of runout, if accompanied by shimmy, is strictly a front-wheel condition. However, lateral runout may be present in both front and rear wheels, especially if a wheel is bent or if the tire has a construction defect. Worn front-wheel bearings and looseness in the suspension and steering linkages can make lateral runout in front wheels a serious safety hazard even at moderate speeds.

Lateral runout may be checked by spinning the wheel and holding a piece of chalk against either the wheel rim or the tire sidewall. If the wheel has runout, the chalk mark will not be uniform. On areas where the wheel moves out, the mark will be wide; on areas where the wheel moves in, the mark will either be narrow or completely missing.

For a more precise measurement of lateral runout, a dial indicator and support may be used as described above. In this instance, the contact point of the dial indicator is adjusted to touch the sidewall of the tire. The side-to-side movement of the wheel and tire assembly moves the contact point and causes the pointer to swing back and forth. If the runout exceeds 0.0625 to 0.125 inch, depending on the make and model of car, either the tire should be replaced or the wheel should be straightened or replaced.

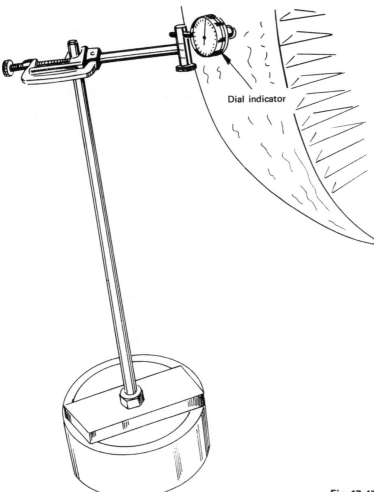

Dial indicator

Fig. 17-47   Checking radial runout with dial indicator. *Courtesy of Cadillac Division, General Motors Corporation.*

Before wheel runout is checked, the wheel bearings must be in proper adjustment and the tires should be inflated to the recommended pressure. Make runout measurements immediately after the car has been driven to minimize the possibility of a tire having a flat spot from being parked for several hours.

FRONT-WHEEL ALIGNMENT PROCEDURES

Caster and Camber

Preliminary tests.   Before the front wheels of an automobile are aligned, a complete check should be made of the wheel bearings, wheel and tire assembly, steering and suspension linkages, and springs to determine if they are in good operating condition. The automobile should be at normal curb weight.

Front-wheel caster, camber, and toe-in are adjustable on all automobiles that have independent front-wheel suspension systems. However, steering-axis inclination and toe-out are not adjustable; if either of these does not meet specifications, the steering knuckles are bent and should be replaced.

Camber and caster testers.   One tester used to check camber and caster, Fig. 17-48, has three curved spirit levels mounted inside the case. The hub end of the tester has a magnetic attachment which holds the tester in place when it contacts the wheel hub. A template is installed over the four stud screws. Each template is calibrated (marked) for specific makes and models of automobiles. A setup of the wheel and tire assembly is shown in Fig. 17-49.

Before the caster or camber is checked, possible errors caused by lateral runout should be eliminated by marking the point of maximum runout with chalk on the sidewall of each front tire. If the wheels are set with the chalk marks at

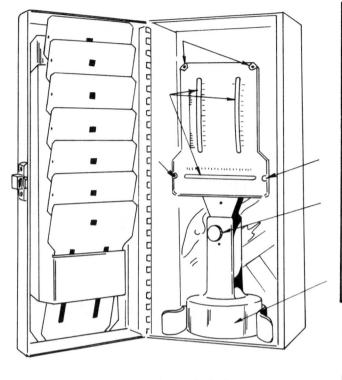

1. Curved spirit levels
2. Magnetic attachment
3. Template
4. Stud screws
5. Thumbscrew

Fig. 17-48 Camber and caster tester. *Courtesy of Bear Manufacturing Corporation.*

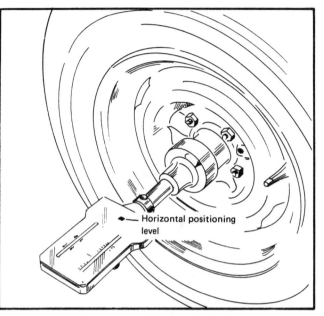

Fig. 17-49 Alignment tester in position on wheel and tire assembly. *Courtesy of Bear Manufacturing Corporation.*

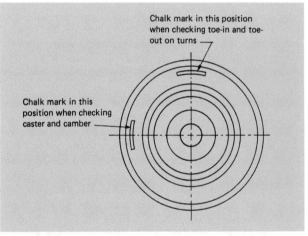

Fig. 17-50 Location of points of greatest lateral runout in front wheel when checking caster, camber, toe-in, and toe-out on turns. *Courtesy of Ford Motor Company.*

the level of the hub, as shown in Fig. 17-50, lateral runout will not affect the alignment accuracy.

To use the tester, roll the car forward until the front wheels are centered on the turning radius gauges. The point of maximum runout (marked on the tire sidewall) should be level with the hub. The turning radius gauges measure the number of degrees a front wheel moves in or out when the steering wheel is turned.

Checking camber. With the front wheels in a straight-ahead position, remove the hub cap and grease cap on each wheel. Wipe all grease from the end of the wheel spindle and carefully clean the face of the wheel hub. To prevent the wheels from turning, use a brake-pedal depressor to lock all four wheels. Make sure the tires are inflated to their recommended pressure.

Select the correct template and install it over the four stud screws on the tester. Attach the tester to the left wheel hub, centering it on the spindle so that it is in a horizontal position as indicated by the bubble at the end of the tester nearest the hub (see Fig. 17-49).

Note the location of the bubble on the outer camber scale. See Fig. 17-51. If the bubble rests entirely within the solid black mark, as shown, camber is correct. If the bubble

is not in the position shown, the amount and direction (positive or negative) of the required correction is indicated on the scale. For example, if the tip of the bubble lies two marks above the solid black stripe (in the direction of the wheel hub), and if the camber adjustment is made by means of shims, it is necessary to add (positive) two shims, each shim being 0.0625 inch thick. (Various methods of camber adjustment are discussed later.)

The procedure described above is then repeated for the right wheel.

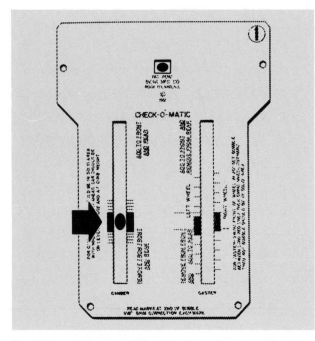

Fig. 17-51 Correct camber at left wheel. *Courtesy of Bear Manufacturing Corporation.*

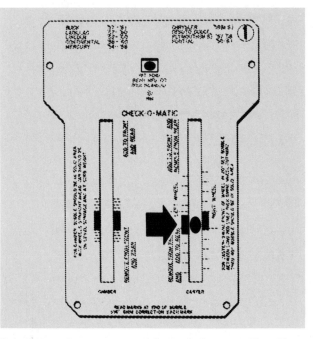

Fig. 17-52 Correct caster at left wheel. *Courtesy of Bear Manufacturing Corporation.*

Checking caster. Set the pointer to zero on the turning radius gauge when the wheels are pointing straight ahead.

Caster is checked by swinging the wheels 40° in either direction. However, whether the reading obtained is positive or negative depends on the direction of swing as noted on the scale. For simplicity, therefore, it is recommended to start the caster check by turning the front of the left wheel in toward the center of the car until the turning radius gauge reads 20°. Adjust the tester thumb screw, Fig. 17-48, until the bubble is centered between the two solid black marks on the caster scale.

Turn the left wheel outward until the turning radius gauge again indicates 20° (a total movement of 40°). If the left-wheel caster is correct, the bubble will be centered on the solid black mark of the inside caster scale. See Fig. 17-52. Negative caster is indicated if the tip of the bubble is below the solid black marker; positive caster is indicated if the tip of the bubble is above the solid black marker.

The same procedure is repeated on the right front wheel. See Fig. 17-53 for the indication of correct caster.

Caster and Camber Adjustments

The method of adjusting camber and caster on a specific automobile depends on how the control arms are attached to the frame. Some cars have shim-type adjustments, and others have eccentric pins (bushings) which are turned to move the upper control arm. When shims are added or re-

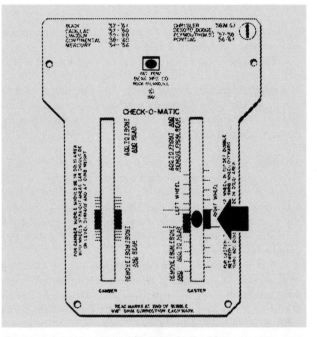

Fig. 17-53 Correct caster at right wheel. *Courtesy of Bear Manufacturing Corporation.*

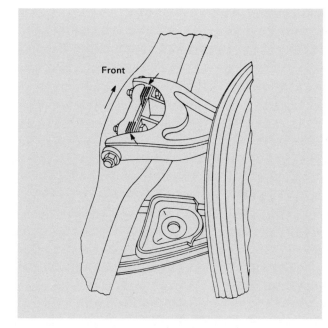

Fig. 17-54 Location of shims for adjusting camber and caster when shims and upper control arm shaft are inside frame bracket. *Courtesy of Bear Manufacturing Corporation.*

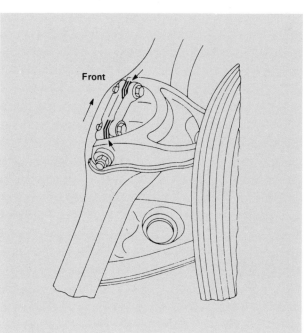

Fig. 17-55 Location of shims for adjusting camber and caster when shims and upper control arm shaft are outside frame bracket. *Courtesy of Bear Manufacturing Corporation.*

moved from between the upper control arm shaft and the frame bracket, the upper control arm is moved in relation to the frame. This changes the position of the upper ball joint and thus changes the caster and camber.

Shims adjustments. On most General Motors and Ford automobiles, shims are used to adjust camber and caster. Figure 17-54 shows the location of the shims and upper control arm shaft when both are inside the frame bracket. Adding shims moves the upper control arm and the top of the front wheel inward and decreases camber.

In Fig. 17-55 the shims and upper control arm are outside the frame bracket. Adding shims moves the upper control arm outward, tips the top of the front wheel outward, and increases camber.

Caster is adjusted by adding shims to one end of the attachment bolts on the upper control arm and removing shims from the other end. If a shim is removed from the front attachment bolt, and added to the rear attachment bolt, the outer end of the upper control arm moves forward and decreases positive caster (backward tilt of steering axis from the vertical).

Adjusting caster and camber with cams. Several types of eccentric bushing arrangements are used to adjust the caster and camber of front wheels. One arrangement, found on late-model Chrysler products, is shown in Fig. 17-56. The two bushings at the inner end of the control arm are attached to the frame brackets by bolt-and-cam assemblies. If

these cam assemblies are turned, caster and camber are changed.

Turning both cam assemblies by the same amount and in the same direction moves the control arm in or out to change camber. If only one cam is turned, or if the two assemblies are turned in opposite directions, the outer end of the control arm is moved backward or forward to change the caster.

After the direction and type of correction is determined, the adjustment is made by loosening the nuts on the cam bolts and turning the bolts. Adjust the caster first. Camber is then adjusted by turning both bolts by the same amount. One complete rotation of the cam bolt represents the greatest adjustment possible. Always recheck the setting after tightening the nuts on the cam bolts to see that no change occurred during the tightening.

Use of elongated bolt holes for caster and camber adjustment. Some suspension systems have elongated holes in the frame at the two points where the inner shaft of the upper control arm is attached to provide caster and camber adjustments. The attaching bolts, elongated bolt holes, and inner shaft are shown in Fig. 17-57. The bolts are loosened to let the control arm attachment shaft move. Moving the shaft inward or outward changes the caster and camber because the upper control arm also moves. A special tool is needed for this job. If both ends of the shaft are moved in or out together, the camber is changed; if only one end is moved, the caster is changed.

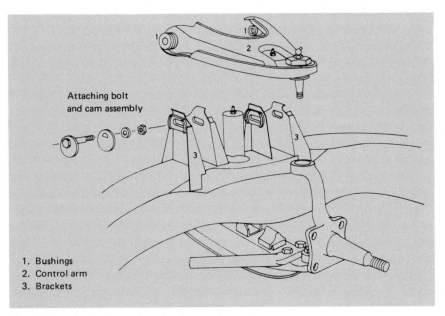

Attaching bolt
and cam assembly

1. Bushings
2. Control arm
3. Brackets

Fig. 17-56   Bolt and cam for adjusting camber and caster.

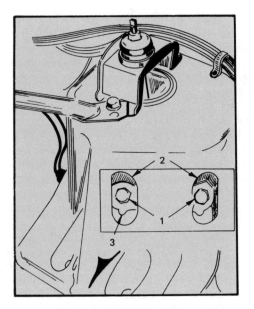

1. Attaching bolts
2. Elongated hole bolts
3. Inner shaft

Fig. 17-57   Use of elongated bolt holes to adjust caster and camber. *Courtesy of Ford Motor Company.*

Toe-In Adjustment

Measuring toe-in.   Toe-in is adjusted after the camber and caster. To measure toe-in, first raise the front wheels off the floor. Spin each wheel by hand and, with a piece of chalk, mark a circumferential line in the center of the tire tread. Then lower the wheels to the floor and roll the automobile forward to settle the linkage in the running position with the wheels pointing straight ahead. The point of maximum lateral runout, indicated by the chalk mark on the sidewall of the tire, should be vertically above the wheel hub, or at the top of the tire, as shown previously in Fig. 17-50. Next measure the distance between the chalk marks on the treads at the front of the wheels at hub height, and the distance between the chalk marks on the treads at the rear of the wheels at hub height. The difference between these two measurements is toe-in.

Adjusting toe-in.   Toe-in is adjusted by shortening or lengthening the tie rods. A typical tie rod arrangement, Fig. 17-58, is comprised of a right-hand tie rod, left-hand tie rod, clamps and clamp bolts, and tie rod sleeves. If the toe-in is not correct, loosen the clamp bolt on the sleeve of each tie rod and turn the sleeves as required. Turning the sleeve in one direction increases the effective length of the rod, and turning it in the opposite direction decreases its effective length.

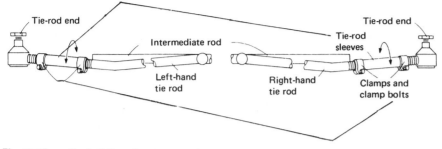

Fig. 17-58 Typical tie-rod arrangement.

TIRE WEAR

Speed as a Factor in Tire Wear

Driving habits of an individual directly affect tire wear. Even if tires are inflated to the recommended pressures and the front-end suspension system of the vehicle is in proper alignment, excessive speed on curves, severe braking, over-acceleration from standing starts, and sustained high-speed driving shorten the life of tires. The driver is the only one who can prevent excessive tire wear due to these factors. High-speed operation causes tire treads to wear rapidly because of the continual flexing and scuffing to which the tires are subjected and the resultant frictional heat developed in the tires.

Abnormal Tire Wear

There are various types of abnormal tire wear; the manner in which the tread is worn often shows a defect in the suspension or steering systems or improper vehicle operation. Wear due to underinflation, improper toe-in, improper camber, or a combination of these causes usually can be identified by observing the tread wear.

Underinflation. The sidewalls of a tire operated with insufficient air pressure bulge under the weight of the car. As a result, the outer edges of the tread wear excessively while the center of the tread, which is lifted clear of the road surface by the arching of the bulged sidewalls, is scarcely worn.

This type of uneven tire wear shortens the life of the tread and weakens the sidewalls. The repeated flexing as the tire rolls on the road surface eventually causes the fabric in the sidewalls to crack and the plies to become separated. The weakened sidewalls soon lead to complete tire failure.

Overinflation. Overinflation causes the tire tread to be higher at the center than at the edges. As the tire rolls, only the center of the tread is in contact with the road.

Uneven tread wear shortens tire life, and an overinflated tire does not absorb road shocks well. Instead of spring (giving), the tire fabric takes the major shock of each bump, and this may cause the fabric to break.

Excessive toe-in or toe-out. If toe-in or toe-out on turns is excessive, the tire is, in effect, dragged sidewise while it is moving forward. The sidewise drag scrapes the rubber from the tread and leaves featheredges of rubber on one side of the tread design.

When both front tires show this type of wear, the front suspension system is misaligned. However, if only one tire is worn, and both tires have been on the automobile for the same length of time, a bent steering arm, causing one wheel to have more toe-in than the other, is indicated.

Excessive wheel camber. Excessive camber of the front wheels will cause the tire treads to wear more rapidly on one side than on the other. If the tires tilt outward at the top (positive camber), the heavy tread wear is on the outside of the tread. If the tires tilt inward (negative camber), the heavy wear is on the inside of the tread.

Uneven tire tread wear. Uneven tread wear of this type can result from a number of mechanical conditions, such as misaligned wheels, improperly adjusted brakes, unbalanced wheels, overinflated tires, incorrect linkage adjustments, or out-of-round brake drums.

Cornering wear. Cornering wear on tires is caused by rounding corners at high speeds. The centrifugal forces then acting on the vehicle cause the tires to roll beneath the wheel rims and to slide on the road surface. Tires subjected to this treatment show diagonal tread wear which rounds off the outside shoulder of the tires and roughens the surface of the tread along the outside edge. Cornering wear can be avoided by slowing on curves.

TIRE SERVICE OPERATIONS

Wheel Removal

Wheels can be hard to remove from a car due to rusting on a tight fit between the wheel center hole and the axle or rotor. These wheels can be removed without damage by following this procedure:

1. Retighten all lug nuts on the affected wheel, then loosen each nut two turns.

2. Lower vehicle to ground.

3. Rock the car from "drive" to "reverse," allowing the car to move several feet in each direction. Apply quick, hard jabs on the brake pedal to loosen the wheel.

4. Raise the car. Remove the lug nuts and wheel.

Penetrating oil has been found to be effective in removing tight wheels. If it is used, however, it should be applied only to the hub surface. Do not allow the oil to get on the vertical surfaces between the wheel and the drum (or rotor) because penetrating oil in this area could cause the wheel to work loose as the car is driven and cause loss of control.

Never use heat to loosen a tight wheel because the application of heat to the wheel can shorten the life of the wheel and damage to the wheel bearings.

Wheel nuts must be tightened in sequence and to proper torque to avoid bending the wheel, brake drum, or rotor. See Figure 17-59.

Before reinstalling wheels, remove any buildup of corrosion on the wheel mounting surface and brake drum or disc mounting surface by scraping and wire brushing. Installing wheels without good metal-to-metal contact at the mounting surface can cause the wheel nuts to loosen and later allow the wheels to come off while the vehicle is moving.

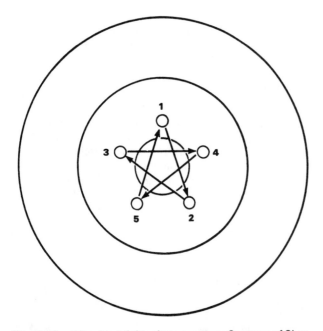

Fig. 17-59. Wheel nut tightening sequence. *Courtesy of Chevrolet Division, General Motors Corporation.*

Tire Mounting and Demounting

Use a tire changing machine to mount or demount tires. Follow the equipment manufacturer's specifications. Do not use hand tools or tire irons alone to change a tire since they may damage the tire beads or wheel rim.

Rim head seats should be cleaned with a wire brush or coarse steel wool to remove lubricants, old rubber, and light rust. Before mounting or demounting a tire, the bead area should be lubricated with an approved tire lubricant.

After mounting, inflate the tire to 40 psi so that the beads are completely seated. Do not stand over the tire when inflating. Beads may break when they snap over the safety hump, causing serious personal injury.

Do not exceed 40 psi pressure when inflating. If 40 psi pressure will not seat beads, deflate, relubricate, and reinflate. Overinflation may cause the bead to break and cause serious personal injury.

Install valve core and inflate to proper pressure. Check the tire locating rings, Figure 17-60, to be sure that they show around the rim flanges on both sides.

Tire Repair

There are many materials and techniques available on the market for the repair of tires. But not all of these work on all types of tires. Consequently, tire manufacturers publish detailed instructions on how to repair their tires. These instructions should be followed.

Puncture-Sealing Tires

Some tires have a puncture-sealing feature. Such tires are designed to seal permanently most of the tread punctures up to about 3/16 inch in diameter, so that the tire remains inflated. The actual sealant is made of a special rubber compound which is applied to the tire at the manufacturer's facility. The sealant only covers the inside of the tire under the tread area and is designed to surround the embedded object and seal the puncture at the inner surface of the tire below the tread. If a nail or other puncturing object penetrates the tire tread into the sealant layer, the object picks up a coat of the sealant. As the puncturing object is either removed or thrown from the tire by centrifugal force, the sealant adheres to it and is pulled into the puncture opening in the tread. When the object is completely removed, the

Fig. 17-60. Tire locating rings. *Courtesy of Chevrolet Division, General Motors Corporation.*

sealant fills the entire puncture opening. This keeps the tire inflated and forms a permanent seal.

Puncture sealing tires are identified by a distinctive marking on the sidewall and carry a special warranty. Such tires can be serviced with current tire changing and wheel balancing equipment.

High-Pressure Spares

Some new cars are equipped with a high-pressure spare that has a narrow 4-inch wide rim, although the wheel diameter is one-inch larger than the road wheels.

The spare wheel should not be used with standard tires, snow tires, wheel covers, or trim rings. If such use is attempted, damage to these items or other parts of the car may occur. A spare of this type should be used only on cars that offer it as original equipment.

Inflation pressure must be periodically checked and maintained at 60 psi. The tire can be mounted and dismounted from its wheel with current tire-changing equipment and procedures. The bead should seat at 40 psi.

Do not exceed 40 psi when initially inflating the tire. If 40 psi will not seat the beads, deflate, relubricate, and reinflate.

Matched Tires and Wheels

The tires and wheels on some cars are match mounted at the assembly plant. This means that the radially stiffest part of the tire, or "high spot," is matched to the smallest radius or "low spot" of the wheel. This is done to provide the smoothest possible ride.

The "high spot" on the tire is originally marked by a white paint dot on the outboard sidewall. This paint dot will eventually wash off the tire.

The "low spot" of the wheel can be marked by several different methods, such as the following:

1. Most standard wheels will have an arrow stamped into the metal in the bolt circle area of the wheel. This arrow, always on the outboard side, will point to the wheel's "low spot" and, when properly assembled, should point to the paint dot on the car.

2. If no arrow is present, look for a paint dot or adhesive dot on the outboard side of the tire. This method of marking the wheel's "low spot" will be most often found on styled wheels. When properly assembled the paint dot or adhesive dot should line up with the paint dot on the tire. Some styled wheels may have the paint dot in their drop center.

3. If no arrow is stamped on the wheel, and no paint dot or adhesive dot can be found on the wheel, line the valve stem up with the paint dot on the tire. Some styled wheels will have their valve stems located at the "low point".

Whenever a tire is dismounted from a wheel, it should be remounted so that the tire and wheel markings are matched. If one or both marks cannot be found, a line should be scribed on the tire and wheel before dismounting to assure that it is remounted in the same position. Replacement tires and wheels that are of original equipment quality will be marked in the same manner.

Cast-Aluminum Wheel Hubs

To remove and install cast aluminum wheel hubs, follow this procedure:

1. Remove wheel and tire assembly from car.

2. Place a block of wood 2.5 inches in diameter with a squared-off end against the back surface of the cap. A sharp hammer blow on the block of wood will remove the cap.

3. To install, place cap into position at wheel opening and place a block of wood at least three inches in diameter against the cap face. Install the cap by striking the block of wood with a hammer.

4. Install the wheel and tire assembly.

Failure to hit the cap squarely without the load distributed evenly may result in permanent damage to the cap.

Inflation of Tires

The pressure recommended for any model car is carefully calculated to give a satisfactory ride, stability, steering, tread wear, tire life, and resistance to bruises.

Tire pressure, with the tires cold (after the car has sat for three or four hours or more, or after it has been driven less than one mile) should be checked monthly or before any extended trip and set to the specifications on the tire placard located on the rear face of one of the car doors (often the driver's door).

Tire pressure may increase as much as 6 psi during hot weather. Higher than recommended pressure may cause any of the following:

1. Hard ride.

2. Tire bruising or carcass damage.

3. Rapid tread wear at center of tire.

Lower than recommended tire pressure may cause:

1. Tire squeal on turns.

2. Hard steering.

3. Rapid and uneven wear on the edges of the tires.

4. Tire rim bruises and rupture.

5. Tire cord breakage.

6. High tire temperatures.

7. Reduced handling.

8. High fuel consumption.

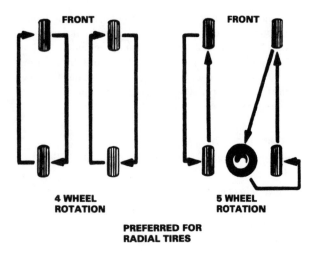

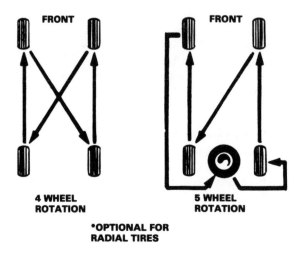

Fig. 17-61. Tire rotation for radials. *Courtesy of Chevrolet Division, General Motors Corporation.*

Uneven pressure on the same axle may cause:

1. Uneven braking.
2. Steering lead.
3. Reduced handling.
4. Swerve on acceleration.

Tire Rotation

To equalize wear, tires should be rotated periodically. Refer to the manufacturer's specifications. As shown in Figure 17-61, the X-method of rotation is allowed with radial tires if necessary.

Due to their design, radial tires tend to wear faster in the shoulder area, particularly in front positions. This makes regular rotation especially necessary.

Always use 4-wheel rotation unless the car is equipped with a full-size standard tire.

After rotation, be sure to check the wheel nut tightness.

18

STEERING SYSTEMS

Contents

MANUAL STEERING SYSTEMS

Introduction

American manufacturers currently employ two types of manual steering; namely, *rack and pinion* and *circulating ball*.

Before any adjustments are made to the steering gear in an attempt to correct such conditions as shimmy or loose or hard steering, a careful inspection should be made of front-end alignment, shock absorbers, wheel balance, and tire pressure for possible cause. All such defects must be corrected before the steering shaft can be made to operate properly.

Although power steering is found on the majority of automobiles sold in this country, manual steering has found greatly increased popularity with the advent of late-model compacts and sub-compacts. Although servicing procedures may differ somewhat from model to model and among different makes of cars, a typical procedure is presented in the sections that follow.

RACK AND PINION STEERING GEAR

Description

A typical rack and pinion steering gear is shown in Figure 18-1. The input shaft is connected to the steering shaft through a U-joint shaft and flexible covering. A steel tube encloses the toothed rack. A pinion gear, machined on the input shaft, engages the rack, and the rotation of the input-shaft pinion causes the rack to move laterally.

Tie rods, attached at each end of the rack joint, move with the action of the front suspension. The gear is sealed at each end with rubber bellows. The steering gear lubricant is a fluid grease type.

The ball housings and tie rods are not adjustable for preload. They feature a simple tightening and set screw serviced procedure, and must be serviced as a sub-assembly.

Do not turn the steering wheel quickly or forcefully from lock to lock when the front wheels are off the ground. This could cause a build-up of hydraulic pressure within the gear, which could damage or blow off the bellows.

With the front suspension and linkage in good condition and the gear in proper adjustment, there should be no more than $\frac{3}{8}$ inch of free play at the rim of the steering wheel.

In a stationary vehicle, there should be no knock in the steering gear when the steering wheel is turned from stop to stop. If a knock is experienced, check the adjustment of the rack preload and pinion bearing preload. A faint knock produced by the steering gear while driving on an extremely rough road is acceptable, and does not indicate a defect in the gear.

Adjustments

The rack and pinion gear provides two means of service adjustment. The gear must be removed from the vehicle to perform both adjustments.

Support yoke to rack adjustment.

1. Clean exterior of steering gear thoroughly and mount the gear in a vise, gripping it near the center of the steel tube. Do not overtighten the vise or damage to the tube may result.

2. Remove the yoke cover, gasket, shims, and yoke spring as shown in Figure 18-2.

3. Clean the cover and housing flange areas thoroughly. Then reinstall the yoke and cover, but omit the gasket, shims, and spring. Tighten the cover bolts lightly until the cover just touches the yoke.

4. Measure the gap between the cover and the housing flange. With the gasket, add selected shims to give a combined pack thickness 0.005 to 0.006 inch greater than the measured gap.

5. Again remove the cover. Assemble the gasket next to the housing flange, then the selected shims, spring, and cover.

6. Install the cover bolts, sealing the threads with an approved sealer, and tighten the bolts to specification. (Typical torque is 5 to 8 foot-pounds.)

7. Check to see that the gear operates smoothly without binding or slackness.

Pinion bearing preload adjustment

1. After cleaning the exterior of the gear, place the gear in a vise, as described earlier.

2. Loosen the bolts of the yoke cover to relieve spring pressure on the rack.

3. Remove the cover and gasket and clean the cover flange area thoroughly. Then remove the spacer and shims, as shown in Figure 18-3.

4. Install a new gasket and fit shims between the upper bearing and spacer until the top of the spacer is flush with the gasket. Check with a straightedge, using light pressure.

5. Add one 0.005 inch shim to the pack in order to preload the bearings. The spacer must be placed next to the pinion cover.

6. Remove the oil seal from the cover and install the cover using a special centering tool. See Figure 18-4. Tighten bolts to specifications (typically, 12 to 18 foot-pounds).

7. Install the pinion oil seal.

Tie Rod Articulation Effort

1. Loop a piece of wire through the hole in the rod end stud. Insert the hook of a pull scale through the wire loop, as shown in Figure 18-5. The effort to move the rod should be 1 to 5 foot-pounds. Be careful not to damage the tie-rod neck.

2. If the pull effort falls outside the specified range, replace

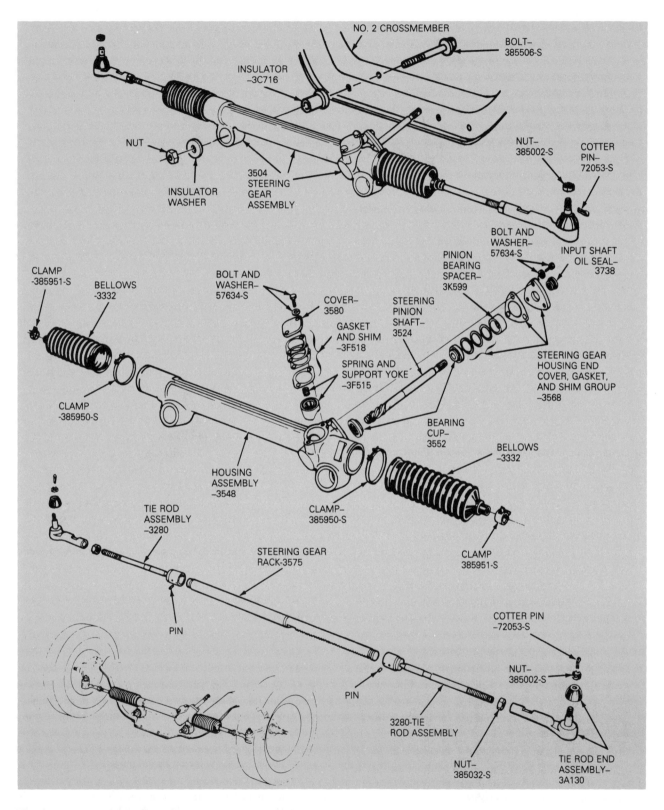

Fig. 18-1. A typical rack and pinion steering gear and linkage.
Courtesy of Ford Motor Company.

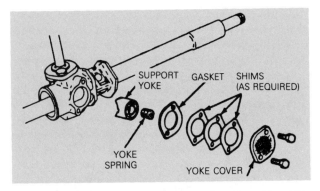

Fig. 18-2. Support-yoke arrangement. *Courtesy of Ford Motor Company.*

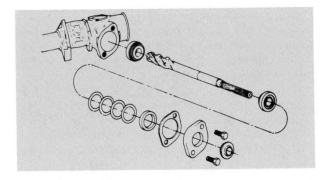

Fig. 18-3. Pinion, bearing cover, and shim. *Courtesy of Ford Motor Company.*

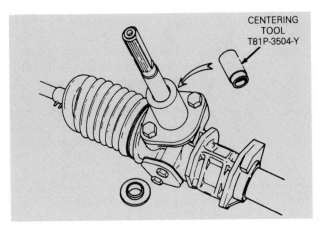

Fig. 18-4. Pinion-cover installation. *Courtesy of Ford Motor Company.*

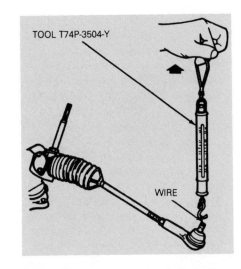

Fig. 18-5. Tie rod articulation check. *Courtesy of Ford Motor Company.*

the ball-joint/tie-rod assembly. Save the tie-rod end for use on the new tie-rod assembly.

Tie-Rod End Replacement (Gear in Vehicle)

1. Remove and discard the cotter pin and nut from the worn tie-rod end ball stud.

2. Using a tool equivalent to that shown in Figure 18-6, disconnect the tie-rod end from the spindle.

3. Holding the tie-rod end with a wrench, loosen the rod jam nut.

4. Grip the rod with locking pliers and remove the rod-end assembly from the tie rod. Using the jam nut as a marker, note the depth to which the tie rod was located.

5. Thread a new tie-rod end on the tie rod to the same depth as the one that was removed and tighten the jam nut.

6. Place the tie-rod end stud into the steering spindle.

7. Install a new nut on the tie-rod end stud. Tighten the nut to the minimum specified torque (typically about 35 foot-pounds), and continue tightening the nut to align the next castellation with the cotter pin hole in the stud. Install a new cotter pin.

8. Set toe to specifications (23-35 foot-pounds) and tighten jam nut to proper torque (50 foot-pounds).

Removal and Installation of a Typical Manual Steering Gear

Removal. Disconnect the negative (−) cable from the battery, turn the ignition key to the ON position and remove the access panel from the dash below the steering column. A typical procedure is then as follows:

1. Remove the intermediate shaft bolts at the gear-input shaft and at the steering-column shaft.

2. Using a wide-blade screwdriver, spread the slots enough to loosen the intermediate shaft at both ends. DO NOT REMOVE THE INTERMEDIATE SHAFT AND GEAR-INPUT SHAFT AT THIS TIME.

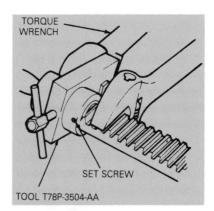

Fig. 18-7. Removing and installing the tie-rod ball-housing assembly. *Courtesy of Ford Motor Company.*

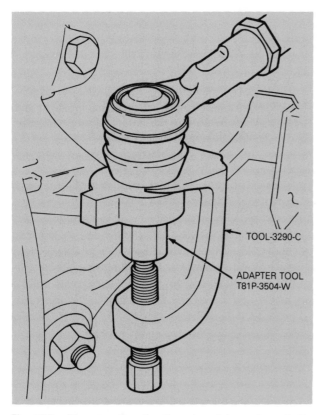

Fig. 18-6. Disconnecting the tie-rod end from the spindle. *Courtesy of Ford Motor Company.*

3. Turn the steering wheel full left so that the tie rod will clear the shift linkage for removal (Step 11).

4. Using the special tool and adapter shown in Figure 18-7 (from under the car) separate the rod ends from the steering knuckles and turn the right wheel to the full left-turn position.

5. Remove the left tie-rod end from the tie rod.

6. Disconnect the secondary air tube at the check valve. Disconnect exhaust system at exhaust manifold. Support the exhaust system with a wire or a stand in a position to allow enough clearance for gear removal. Alternatively, the exhaust may be removed entirely. DO NOT let the exhaust hang by the rear hangers since it may fall to the floor.

7. Remove the exhaust hanger bracket from below the steering gear.

8. Remove the gear mounting brackets and insulators. See Figure 18-1.

9. Separate the gear from the intermediate shaft, with an assistant pulling up on the shaft from inside the car.

10. Rotate the steering gear forward and down to clear the input shaft through the dash-panel opening.

11. Make sure the input shaft is in the full left-turn posi-

tion. Move gear through right (passenger) side apron opening until the left tie rod clears the shift linkage and other parts so that it may be lowered.

12. Lower the left side of the gear and remove gear out of the vehicle.

Care should be taken during the gear removal and installation to prevent tearing or damaging the steering-gear bellows.

Installation

1. Rotate the input shaft to full left-turn stop.

2. Position right road wheel to full left turn.

3. Start right side of gear through the opening in the right apron. Move gear in until the tie rod clears all parts so that it may be raised up to the left apron opening.

4. Raise gear and insert left side through apron opening.

5. Rotate gear so that the input shaft enters the dash-panel opening.

6. With an assistant guiding the intermediate shaft from outside the car, insert the input shaft into the intermediate-shaft coupling. Insert intermediate-shaft clamp-bolts finger tight. DO NOT TORQUE AT THIS TIME.

7. Install the gear mounting insulators and brackets. Make sure the flat in the left mounting area is parallel to the dash panel. Tighten the left mounting bracket first to locate the gear properly and then tighten the right bracket.

8. Install left tie-rod end on tie rod.

9. Attach tie-rod ends to steering knuckles. Tighten the castellated nuts to the minimum specified torque, then tighten nuts until a slot aligns with the cotter pin hole. Insert a new cotter pin.

10. Install exhaust hanger bracket.

11. Connect exhaust system.

12. Tighten coupling clamp bolt at gear input shaft first. Then tighten the other (intermediate) shaft clamp bolt.

13. Install access panel below the steering column.

13. Turn ignition key OFF.

15. Connect negative cable to battery.

17. Check and adjust toe. Tighten tie-rod end jam nuts.

Assembly and Disassembly of a Typical Manual Steering Gear

Disassembly. Tie-rod ends, bellows and tie-rod ball-joint sockets.

1. Clean exterior of gear thoroughly and place gear in a vise.

2. Loosen jam nuts on outer ends of tie rods.

3. Remove tie-rod ends and jam nuts.

4. Remove two wires and two clamps, retaining bellows to gear housing and tie rods. Drain the lubricant and remove bellows. Use care to prevent damage or contamination to the inside of the bellows.

5. Remove set screw from ball housing with an allen wrench.

6. Install ball-housing torque-adapter tool on ball housing. Locate the point of the locking screw in the large hole midway along length of housing. Tighten firmly. Use care not to place point of locking screw into tapped set-screw hole.

7. Attach a standard ½-inch drive ratchet handle to the tool. Expose enough rack teeth to install an adjustable wrench over the flat formed by the top of the rack teeth. Loosen the ball housing tie-rod assembly by holding the adjustable wrench and turning the ball-housing torque-adapter tool. See Figure 18-7. CAUTION: If the rack is not restrained by the adjustable wrench, the pinion will be damaged.

Assembly. Tie-rod ends, bellows and tie-rod ball-joint sockets.

1. Clean and inspect the condition of threads on the rack and in the ball-housing socket. Lubricate the inner seat with an approved multi-purpose lubricant.

2. Be sure that the ball housing is seated firmly into the ball-housing socket and on the tie-rod ball. It is important that the back of the inner seat and the face of the rack are wiped clean of grease to avoid a hydraulic lock and improper assembly.

3. Thread the tie-rod assembly into the end of the rack.

4. Install the ball-housing torque-adapter tool on the ball housing. Locate the point of the locking screw in the large hole midway along the length of the housing and tighten firmly. Use care not to place the point of the locking screw into the tapped set-screw hole.

5. Hold the rack with an adjustable wrench on the flat of the rack teeth, as near the end of the rack as possible. If the pinion has not been removed, use care not to load the pinion during tightening. Holding the rack with the adjustable wrench, tighten the ball housing to 40 to 51 foot-pounds by turning the torque adapter tool with a ½-inch drive-torque wrench. (Figure 18-7).

6. Rotate the tie rod at least 10 times (without forcing the rods against the limits of articulation travel) before measuring articulation effort. If articulation effort is not to specification, replace with a new tie-rod assembly.

7. Install set screw in the ball housing and tighten to specification.

8. Apply specified lubricant to tie rods in undercut where bellows will be clamped. This will prevent bellows from twisting during toe adjustment. Install small bellows clamps. Install the large bellows clamp on the right side only (opposite end from pinion). Use service, screw-type clamps. Do not re-use original production wire retainers.

9. Place gear in a vertical position with the pinion end of the gear facing up. Fill housing with approved fluid grease. Install left large bellows clamp, fastening bellows to the gear housing. Do not re-use original production-wire retainers.

10. Install jam nuts and tie-rod ends on the tie rods.

Disassembly and assembly of input-shaft seal.

1. Clean input shaft seal area thoroughly. Do not scratch or damage the pinion shaft. Pry the pinion seal from its bore and discard.

2. Check to be certain that the pinion cover is centered with the center tool (Figure 18-4). If the cover is not centered, loosen the bolts, center the cover, and tighten bolts to specifications.

3. Lubricate a new pinion seal with approved lubricant and install the seal over the shaft.

4. Use a piece of tubing to engage the outer flange of the seal and press or tap seal into bore until flange is flush with the shoulder of the bore. If the outer edge of the seal is not engaged when assembling, the seal will be damaged.

Disassembly. Rack-support yoke, spring, gasket, shims, and cover.

1. Clean the exterior of the gear thoroughly and place the gear in vise.

2. Remove the yoke cover, shims, gasket, and yoke spring. (Figure 18-3).

3. Discard gasket.

Assembly. Rack-support yoke, spring, gasket, shims, and cover.

1. Clean cover and cover-flange areas thoroughly.

2. Assemble yoke and yoke spring. (Figure 18-3).

3. Assemble a new gasket next to the housing flange. If new shims are to be installed, refer to the previous section on adjustments.

4. Assemble shim pack and cover.

5. Add an approved sealant to the cover bolt threads and tighten the bolts to specifications.

Disassembly. Pinion cover, gasket, pinion shaft, spacer, shims, upper bearing, rack, lower bearing, and housing.

1. Clean exterior of the gear thoroughly and place the gear in vise.

2. Remove bolts, yoke cover, gasket, shims, spring, and yoke from the housing.

3. Remove the right-ball housing and tie-rod assembly from the rack. Be sure the rack is restrained with an adjustable wrench during removal or damage to the pinion could result.

4. Move rack to the right-turn stop and note the position of the flat on the input shaft. It is important that the flat be in the same position in subsequent assembly. Otherwise, the steering gear will not be centered; that means unequal numbers of turns in right and left directions.

5. Remove pinion, cover bolts, pinion cover gasket, pinion shaft, spacer, shims, and upper housing.

6. Remove pinion seal from cover and discard.

7. Remove rack from the housing.

8. Remove the lower bearing through the pinion shaft bore. Access to the bearing is easiest through the support-yoke bore.

Assembly. Pinion cover, gasket, pinion shaft, spacer, shims, upper bearing, rack, lower bearing, and housing.

1. Clean the interior of the gear thoroughly.

2. Install lower bearing in pocket at bottom of housing.

3. Coat the entire length of the rack with fluid grease.

4. Install rack in the housing.

5. With the rack moved to the right lock (Step 5 under disassembly), install the pinion shaft. Be sure that the pinion-shaft gear end is engaged in the lower bearing inside diameter.

6. Install the upper bearing. Turn pinion from lock to lock, counting the turns. Turn pinion back from one of the locks exactly half the total turns with the gear on center. The flat must be in the 3 o'clock position as viewed from the driver's seat. Adjust the pinion position to the rack if it is not centered. If not on center, remove the pinion

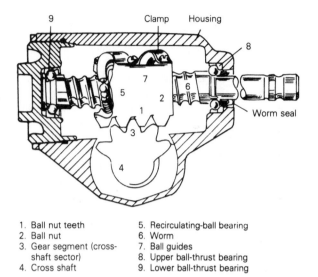

1. Ball nut teeth
2. Ball nut
3. Gear segment (cross-shaft sector)
4. Cross shaft
5. Recirculating-ball bearing
6. Worm
7. Ball guides
8. Upper ball-thrust bearing
9. Lower ball-thrust bearing

Fig. 18-8. Saginaw ball-nut-and-worm steering gear. *Courtesy of Buick Division, General Motors Corporation.*

and rotate one tooth in the proper direction to center it. Repeat check.

7. Install shims, spacer, gasket, pinion cover, and bolts. Center the pinion cover with the centering tool and tighten the bolts to specification. If the bearing preload needs to be altered or a new shim pack is to be installed, refer to the adjustments section.

8. Install new pinion seal in cover and right ball-housing tie-rod assembly on the end of the rack. (Figure 18-9.)

9. Install support yoke, spring, shims, gaskets, yoke cover, and bolts. Tighten bolts to spec. Adjust yoke preload (see adjustments section).

RECIRCULATING BALL-NUT-AND-WORM STEERING GEAR

Description

In the recirculating ball-nut-and-worm steering gear, Figure 18-8, a ball nut rides on ball bearings which circulate between the nut and the worm. Teeth on the ball nut operate a gear segment which is mounted on the cross shaft (also called the pitman-arm shaft or pitman shaft). The bore of the ball nut is drilled to a greater diameter than the worm and is threaded with a helical groove that corresponds to the helical groove in the worm. The teeth on the ball nut are made so that a "high point" or tighter fit exists between the ball nut and gear segment (pitman-shaft sector) teeth when the front wheels of the automobile are in the straight-ahead position.

Within the length of the ball nut, the helical grooves are filled with steel ball bearings. The helical grooves form two complete circuits through which the balls circulate. To complete the circuit and keep the ball from running out of the ends of the grooves, the nut has tubular guides at each end.

The worm shaft is supported by ball thrust bearings. Because the operating thrust must be absorbed by these bearings, they are mounted with their thrust faces opposite each other.

When the steering gear is turned to the right, the ball nut moves down the worm and pushes against the pitman-shaft sector. This makes the cross shaft and attached pitman arm (not shown in illustration) move through a circular arc. The pitman arm then moves the steering linkage so that the front wheels are turned to the right.

The opposite action occurs when the steering wheel is turned to the left.

The teeth on the pitman-shaft sector are slightly tapered so that a proper preload may be obtained by moving the pitman shaft midway by means of a preload adjuster screw that extends through the gear housing side cover. See Figure 18-9. The head of the preload adjuster and a selectively fitted shim fit snugly into a T-slot in the end of the pitman shaft, so that the screw also controls the end play of the shaft.

Maintenance and Adjustments

Although the following information is generally applicable, some differences will be encountered on different makes and models of automobiles. Thus the manufacturer's instructions should be read carefully before proceeding.

Lubrication.   The steering gear is factory filled with steering-gear lubricant. Seasonal change of this lubricant should not be performed and the housing should not be drained. No lubrication is required for the life of the steering gear.

At intervals specified by the manufacturer, the gear should be inspected for seal leakage (actual solid grease, not just film). If a seal is replaced or the gear is overhauled, the gear housing should be refilled with the lubricant specified by the manufacturer.

Adjusting the steering gear.   Note: The fasteners are important attaching parts in that they could affect the performance of vital components and systems, and/or could result in major repair expense. They must be replaced with fasteners bearing the same part number or with equivalent parts if replacement becomes necessary. Do not use a replacement part of lesser quality or substitute design. Torque values must be used as specified during reassembly to ensure proper retention of parts.

Correct adjustment of the steering gear is very important. The sequence presented here is very typical of that followed with most circulating-ball units.

1. Disconnect the battery ground cable.

2. Raise the wheel.

3. Remove the pitman-arm nut. (A special tool is generally required for this purpose.) Mark the relationship of the pitman arm to the pitman shaft.

4. Loosen the steering-gear adjuster-plug locknut, Figure 18-10, and back the adjuster plug off one-quarter turn.

5. Remove the steering-wheel horn-button cap or shroud.

6. Turn the steering wheel gently in one direction until stopped by the gear. Then turn the wheel back one-half turn. Do not turn the steering wheel hard against the steps when the steering linkage is disconnected from the gear as damage to the ball guides could result.

7. Measure and record "bearing drag" by applying a torque wrench with a ¾-inch socket on the steering wheel and rotating through a 90° arc. The torque wrench should have a *maximum* torque of 50 lb-in.

8. Adjust the thrust-bearing preload by tightening the adjuster plug until the preload is obtained (typically 5 – 8 inch-pounds). When the proper preload is obtained, tighten the adjuster plug locknut to specifications (typically 85 foot-pounds). Recheck torque. If the gear feels "lumpy" after adjustment, there is probably damage in

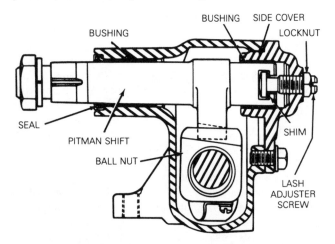

Fig. 18-9.   Gear cross section. *Courtesy of Chevrolet Division, General Motors Corporation.*

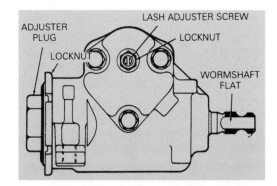

Fig. 18-10.   Typical adjustment points for a circulating ball steering gear. *Courtesy of Chevrolet Division, General Motors Corporation.*

the bearings due to severe impact or improper adjustment. The gear must be disassembled for replacement of damaged parts.

9. To adjust "over center preload" four steps are necessary: (a) Turn the steering wheel gently from one stop all the way to the other while carefully counting the total number of turns. Then turn the wheel back exactly half-way to its center position. (b) Turn the lash-adjuster screw (Fig. 18-10) clockwise to take out all lash between the ball nut and the pitman-shaft selector teeth. Then tighten the locknut. (c) Check the torque at the steering wheel, taking the highest reading as the wheel is turned through center position. Compare with specified over-center preload. (d) If necessary, loosen the locknut and readjust for proper torque. After tightening the locknut to spec., recheck the torque through center-of-travel.

   If maximum specification is exceeded, turn the over-center adjuster screw counter-clockwise, then come up on adjustment by turning the adjuster locknut in a clockwise motion.

10. Reassemble the pitman arm to the pitman shaft, lining up the marks made during diasassembly. Torque the pitman shaft nut to specification (typically 25 foot-pounds).

11. Install the horn button cap or shroud and connect the battery ground cable. Lower the vehicle to the floor.

Replacing pitman-shaft seal. A faulty seal may be replaced without removing the steering gear from the car by removing the pitman arm.

1. Rotate the steering wheel from stop to stop, counting the total number of turns. Then turn back exactly half-way placing the gear on center (the worm-shaft flat should be at the 12 o'clock position).

2. Remove the three self-locking bolts attaching side cover to the housing and lift the pitman shaft and side cover assembly from the housing.

3. Pry the pitman-shaft seal from the gear housing. Use a screwdriver to do so, but be careful not to damage the housing bore. Inspect the lubricant in the gear for contamination. If the lubricant is contaminated in any way, the gear must be removed from the vehicle for a complete overhaul or damage may occur.

4. Coat the new pitman-shaft seal with the specified lubricant. Position the seal in the shaft bore and tap into position using a suitable size socket.

5. Remove the lash-adjuster locknut. Remove the side cover from the pitman-shaft assembly by turning the lash-adjuster screw clockwise.

6. Place the pitman shaft in the steering gear so that the center tooth of the shaft sector enters the center tooth space of the ball nut.

7. Fill the steering-gear housing with approved lubricant.

8. Install a new side-gasket cover onto the gear housing.

9. Install the side cover onto the lash-adjuster screw by reaching through the threaded hole in the side cover with a small screwdriver and turning the lash-adjuster screw counter-clockwise until it bottoms and turn back one-quarter turn.

10. Install the side cover bolts and torque to specification.

11. Install the lash adjuster-screw locknut, perform the steering-gear adjustment and install the pitman arm using the procedures described earlier.

POWER STEERING SYSTEMS

Hydraulic Principles Used in Power Steering

Two basic principles are used in all hydraulic power steering systems: (1) Liquids can be compressed very little. (2) Pressure applied to a liquid makes it act equally in all directions, so liquids can be used to transmit a force.

Pressure can be multiplied into a force. For instance, connect two cylinders, one ten times as large in area as the other, by a tube or pipe, as shown in Fig. 18-11. Apply 100 pounds of pressure to the liquid in both cylinders and it will produce a force ten times greater (1,000 pounds) in the piston with the larger area. The pressure will be the same in both cylinders, but in the larger cylinder, as a result of greater area, it produces a force greater than the pressure.

These basic hydraulic principles are applied to provide hydraulic power steering. A pump is used to develop pressure and a cylinder to develop force. The pressure at the pump and in the cylinder, for all practical purposes, is the same but in the cylinder it is multiplied into a work force. The work force is reduced when pressure is reduced. Oil is the liquid used in hydraulic power steering systems.

Basic Power Steering Systems

The primary purpose of a hydraulic power steering system is to provide power assistance for the driver. All such systems consist of the same principal components (see Fig. 18-

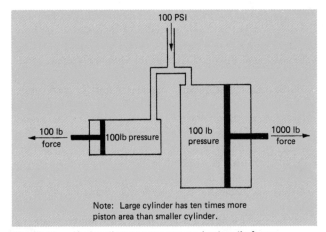

Note: Large cylinder has ten times more piston area than smaller cylinder.

Fig. 18-11 Hydraulic pressure versus hydraulic force

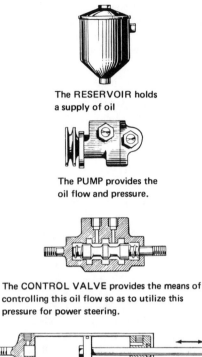

The RESERVOIR holds
a supply of oil

The PUMP provides the
oil flow and pressure.

The CONTROL VALVE provides the means of
controlling this oil flow so as to utilize this
pressure for power steering.

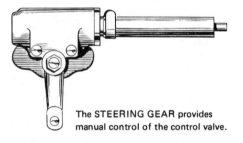

The POWER CYLINDER provides
the steering force.

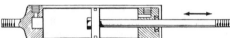

The STEERING GEAR provides
manual control of the control valve.

Fig. 18-12 Principal components of hydraulic power-steering system.

12). Interconnecting hoses and a means of driving the pump are also needed. A V-belt (or belts) is the usual pump drive, and all components are interconnected to form an oil circuit. Circulation of the oil is continuous when the engine is running.

Basically, the pump supplies hydraulic fluid under pressure to the control valve, which directs the fluid to the right or left side of the power cylinder piston, depending upon the direction of turn being made. The power cylinder, when actuated by this applied pressure, reduces the amount of effort required at the steering wheel.

Arrangement of the principal components differs according to installation requirements. Some of these are shown in the following illustrations.

In the so-called *linkage* type, the control valve and

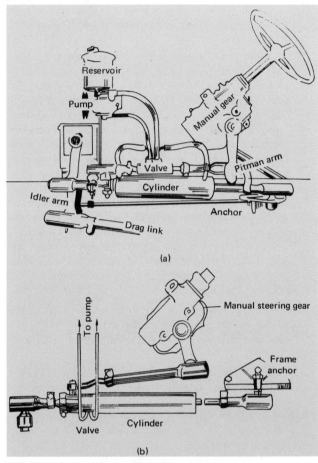

Fig. 18-13 Linkage types. (a) Valve and cylinder mounted separately. (b) Valve and cylinder in single in-line unit.

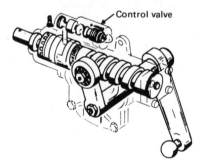

Fig. 18-14 Semi-integral steering; cylinder mounted in linkage (not shown).

power cylinder may be separate parts and mounted separately in the linkage, Fig. 18-13(a), or they may be in a single unit known as an *in-line unit,* Fig. 18-13(b).

In the *semi-integral* type (Fig. 18-14) the control valve is assembled on the steering gear, and the power cylinder is mounted in the linkage. In the *integral* type (Fig. 18-15) the control valve and power cylinder are an integral part of the steering-gear assembly.

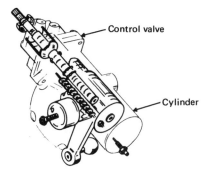

Fig. 18-15 Integral steering gear; valve and cylinder integral with gear.

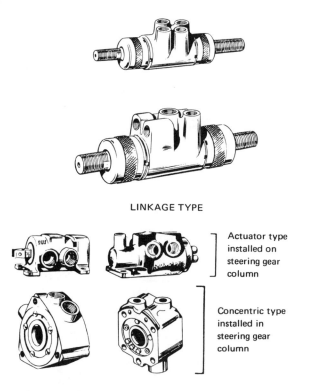

LINKAGE TYPE

Actuator type installed on steering gear column

Concentric type installed in steering gear column

Fig. 18-16 Linkage- and column-type control valves.

Basic Components

Control valve. The control valve is of the type through which there is a continuous flow of oil. The valve is actuated to change the direction of oil flow as required for power steering.

There are many types of valves, but all of them do the same job. See Fig. 18-16.

Except in in-line units, Fig. 18-13(b), the valve housing has four ports to which hydraulic hoses are connected; one port carries oil from the pump to the control valve, one carries oil from the valve to the reservoir, and two carry oil

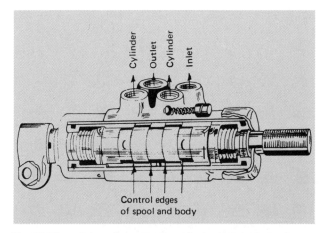

Fig. 18-17 Internal construction of a typical control valve.

from the valve to the cylinder. Hoses are not needed between the valve and cylinder in the in-line units.

The control valves described here are of so-called linear design. Located inside the valve housing (body) is a valve spool which is moved back and forth by the driver's steering action. The spool and the body have similar control edges. See Fig. 18-17.

When there is no steering action by the driver, the spool is centered and oil flows through the valve to the reservoir; however, pressure is maintained at the two cylinder ports. This pressure is low and equal at each port and produces ineffective forces in the cylinder. As a result, there is no movement of the cylinder piston and no circulation of oil in the lines to the cylinder. The spool is centered by centering springs, hydraulic pressure, or a combination thereof; centering force requirements vary.

When the driver turns the steering wheel, the valve spool is actuated and the fluid is channeled to one end of the cylinder where the force is applied to turn the front wheels. At the same time, another channel in the valve allows oil from the opposite end of the cylinder to flow to the valve and then to the reservoir. When the steering wheel is turned in the opposite direction, the flow to and from the cylinder is reversed.

The valve action and change of oil flow for four different types of valves is shown in Figs. 18-18 and 18-19.

Cylinder. Cylinders for installation in the linkage are made in several sizes, but are of two general types: single wall, and double wall, Fig. 18-20.

A hydraulic hose connects to a port in each end of the single-wall cylinder. In the double-wall type, the two ports are in one end and both hoses connect to the cylinder at that end. Fluid flows internally to the opposite end between the double wall and through a flow opening in the other end. In either case, hydraulic fluid flows in one end, pushing the piston and forcing fluid out the other end.

As shown in Fig. 18-21, some linkage cylinders have a shuttle valve in the piston. The shuttle valve is held closed

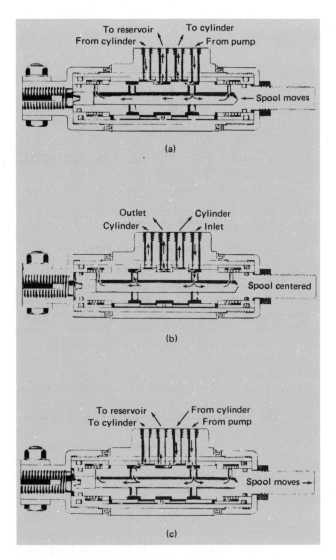

Fig. 18-18   Fluid flow in linkage-type valve.

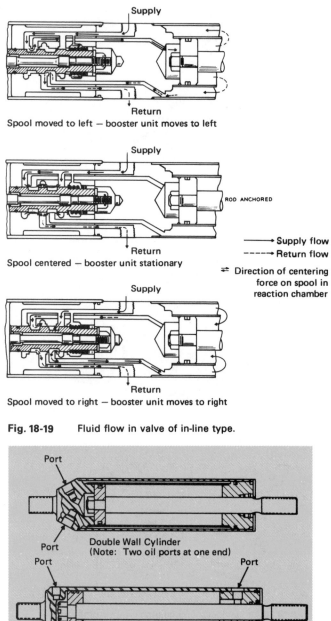

Fig. 18-19   Fluid flow in valve of in-line type.

Fig. 18-20   Double- and single-wall cylinders.

by the hydraulic pressure acting on the piston. At the end of its stroke, the shuttle contacts the end of the cylinder and is pushed open. This allows fluid to flow through the piston and prevents full hydraulic force at the end of the stroke. Thus, it is an "unloading" valve. The shuttle valve will not operate as an unloading valve if the cylinder is too long for the stroke used.

The in-line valve-cylinder unit (valve and cylinder in a single unit) is for linkage installations. See Fig. 18-22. The only hoses needed are one from the pump to the valve and one to the reservoir.

The cylinder is of the double-wall type and fluid flows from valve to cylinder through internal channels.

Pump.   Hydraulic pressure pumps are manufactured in different sizes and types, but all do the same job—they create pressure in the system to transmit the steering force.

Pumps use rotors, vanes, or gear teeth to do this. The pump, usually driven by a V-belt, operates whenever the engine is running.

Pumps must supply the necessary gallonage of oil for desired speed of steering, and must deliver at a maximum pressure when required. Two types of hydraulic pumps are shown in Fig. 18-23.

The oil flow from the pump is at low pressure until steering effort is applied by the driver at the steering wheel. When this effort is applied and the engine is revved, the

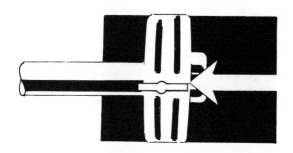

Fig. 18-21   Shuttle valve in piston.

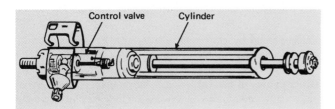

Fig. 18-22   In-line valve-cylinder unit.

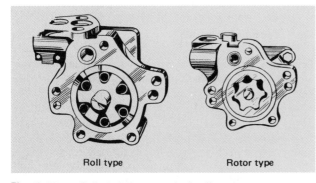

Fig. 18-23   Roll- and rotor-type hydraulic pumps.

pump may build up excessive pressure which results in excessive oil flow; therefore, pressure-relief and flow-control valves are needed in the system. These valves, usually inside the pump, are set to open at a predetermined pressure and flow. Maximum pressure and flow requirements vary. The pressure maximum usually is specified in the service manuals.

When the pressure-relief valve opens, it bypasses some of the fluid to limit the pressure at the outlet port. The bypassed fluid either recirculates in the pump or returns to the reservoir. Full pressure for longer than approximately fifteen seconds may overheat the oil and cause damage to the pump and other units of the system.

The flow-control valve operates in a similar manner, controlling the amount of oil flow through the system to prevent overheating and possible other undesired conditions.

Pump pressure can be checked with a gauge in the pressure line. Oil flow is not easily checked, but if the flow-control valve is not sticking open or closed, it is likely the flow is being controlled, unless the pump is not producing full flow.

Reservoir. Most pumps, but not all, have the reservoir mounted integral with the pump. A filter, usually located at the reservoir, should be included in the system. Oil is returned to the supply chamber of the reservoir through the filter.

The filter also serves as a baffle, to "break up" the stream of oil coming into the reservoir from the system. A filter that is displaced, or charred brittle by heat, is apt to allow oil to spill out of the reservoir. Filters must be checked regularly. The specified amount of oil must be kept in the reservoir at all times.

Hoses. High-quality hoses should be connected securely at their ends so that leaks do not occur and so that air is not vacuumed (sucked) into the oil circuit.

Manual section of steering. The manual section, usually a steering gear, of the hydraulic power steering system provides the driver the usual means of controlling steering. The action of the hydraulic system blends in with the manual section. Steering gears, covered in the first part of this chapter, vary in design and size, but all can be adjusted to eliminate binding. In a power steering system, the effect of a bind in the steering gear may be amplified.

Troubleshooting

Power steering systems, for the most part alike in operation, share common troubles regardless of how the basic units are arranged.

Trouble shows up in various ways, of course, but by following orderly procedures, you can eliminate many possible causes and find the real cause quickly.

Complaints usually are in three general areas: hard steering, external leakage, and undesired steering actions other than hard steering, such as shimmy, wander, oversteer, etc.

Detailed instructions for repair and adjustment of specific power steering systems are not given here. Always consult the manufacturer's service manual.

General diagnosis. The first step is to drive the vehicle a reasonable distance and answer these questions. How does the steering act? Does it act this way all the time? Does it occur in only one direction? Under what conditions does it usually occur? Is it accompanied by an unusual noise?

Some steering actions that may help you get a complete definition of the trouble include the following: (1) Turn steering wheel with car at rest or moving slowly; (2) steer in both directions while moving; (3) turn steering wheel rapidly one or two turns in both directions; and (4) note action when traveling straight ahead.

Now you should have a thorough understanding of the complaint.

General inspection. For common trouble symptoms, check for conditions such as low oil supply in reservoir, air in oil circuit as evidenced by bubbling or foaming, loose or defective belt, linkage binding or loose (sockets and connections), and improper tire pressure. *Look for the simple things first.*

Hard steering. Make sure hard steering actually exists, and that you are not expecting easier steering than the system was designed to produce.

Hard steering means either the hydraulic power section is not creating sufficient steering force, or the driver must overcome excessive friction (binding) in the mechanical section to actuate the control valve and apply hydraulic power.

If the hydraulic section is not creating sufficient force, it may be because (1) it does not develop maximum pressure; (2) too much friction (binding) in the system beyond the point of power application (the valve) must be overcome by the power force; or (3) troubles in the front end, such as excessive weight, low tire pressure, and so forth.

The more common causes of hard steering are (1) pump belt slipping or broken; (2) low fluid level; (3) insufficient oil pressure; (4) insufficient oil flow; (5) air in oil circuit; (6) low tire pressure; and (7) binding friction in the system (anywhere between the steering wheel and front wheels). This binding may be caused by linkage (bent, loose, or tight connections), steering knuckles, spindles, pins and bushings, lack of lubrication (linkage, steering gear, spindles), steering-gear column misaligned, and steering-gear adjustments too tight.

Hard Steering Occurrences and Causes

While parking. Belt slippage, insufficient hydraulic pressure, insufficient oil pressure, low tire pressure, lack of lubrication at some point in the system, or overload on front wheels.

Existing at all times. Causes are the same as those listed for while parking, but more severe.

Occurring only part of the time. Belt slippage, lack of hydraulic pressure, air in oil circuit, loose or tight linkage connections, improper steering-gear adjustment, changes in load, tires, road surface, or temperature of oil, or parts shifting in their mounting to new locations.

Noticeable when trying to steer fast. Low oil flow for the speed of steering attempted—low engine rpm or belt slippage could be the cause.

Occurrence in one direction, either right or left. Bent cylinder piston rod, bind in mechanical section, off-center adjustment of control valve (when normal spool travel is the same in each direction), or mechanical interference preventing valve-spool travel in one direction (such as jacket tube ends interfering with axial movement of wheel tube).

Noticeable at certain steering-wheel positions. Mechanical binding. May be in steering-gear adjustment or elsewhere in linkage.

Lumpy feeling (momentary spots of hard steering). Indicates a delay in power application. (Can be caused by excessive free play in mechanical parts.) Air in the oil (aeration) is the first cause to suspect. Other causes include loose joints or linkage connections, insufficient oil flow, or low oil supply.

Jerks or surges in steering action. Loose belt (slipping momentarily) or insufficient oil flow.

Accompanied by abnormal noises—growl. Air in the circuit, mechanical trouble in pump, or low oil supply.

Other causes of hard steering. Valve spool sticking, valve out of adjustment, valve loose on mounting, bind in power (bent rod, broken piston, or piston rings), insufficient lubricant in valve-actuator unit, steering wheel tube bent or sprung, or bind in wheel tube bearing caused by tight clamp.

Hard Steering Remedies

Belt slippage. Belt squeal is evidence of belt slippage. The belt may be so loose that the pump output is very low. The belt may only be semiloose and fail to turn the pump only when there is a heavy demand for hydraulic force. Belt and pump pulleys often can be seen to stop momentarily, when someone steers. A belt in good condition and properly tensioned can be made to slip if the engine is accelerated rapidly while steering pressure is maintained. This action usually causes belt stretching and glazing. Belt glazing can cause slippage, but may be reduced by using an antiglaze application. To cure belt slippage, it may be necessary to replace the belt and check its tension regularly.

Lack of sufficient hydraulic pressure. Do not trust the pump pressure unless it is checked with a gauge. First make sure the reservoir oil supply is not low. Then install a pressure gauge in the line from the pump to the control valve. Make sure the gauge can withstand the maximum pressure the pump can produce.

Do not disconnect any hoses until you have thoroughly cleaned all dirt off the assembly and have plugged the portholes to keep dirt from entering.

With the engine running at recommended idle, watch the pressure develop as efforts are made to steer first in one direction and then in the other with the car standing still. Refer to the manufacturer's service manual to determine the maximum pump-relief pressure.

If the maximum relief valve pressure is reached before the piston rod reaches the end of its travel, the pump obviously is developing full hydraulic power and the control valve is operating properly; therefore, the trouble is not in the hydraulic circuit. Check the other causes of hard steering listed earlier.

If, however, the maximum relief valve pressure is not reached and steering is hard, the system is not developing full power. This may indicate a defective pump, valve, or cylinder.

First check the pump. Install a shutoff valve in the pump-to-valve outlet line. Locate it between the pressure gauge and the valve.

The shutoff valves must be a high-pressure type to withstand the maximum pressure the pump produces. Ordinary plumbing valves are not satisfactory for this purpose.

With the shutoff valve open, there should be no restriction in flow from the pump. With the engine running at recommended idle speed, gradually close the shutoff valve. Do not leave the valve closed for more than fifteen seconds to avoid quick heating of the oil, which may damage the pump, oil seals, hoses, or filter.

The pump is doing its job if the gauge shows the specified maximum pressure. If not, the drive belt may be loose, the pressure relief valve may be sticking open, or the pump may need repairs. If the belt is loose or glazed, the pump should be disassembled and inspected (described shortly).

When the pump is producing the required maximum pressure, next test the valve for pressurizing the cylinder. Disconnect a hose at one of the cylinder ports, cap the end of the hose, and plug the cylinder port. First, however, remove all dirt and make sure none gets into the valve ports. Have the shutoff valve open.

To test pressure in both hoses connecting the valve to the cylinder, apply steering effort at the steering wheel. Then, with the engine running at its recommended idle speed, check the pressure as someone tries to steer in both directions while the auto is standing still. Remember, do not hold at maximum pressure for very long; otherwise, the pump may be damaged by overheating.

If maximum pressure is not obtained, there is either internal valve leakage past the restricting control edges of the valve spool, or severe external leakage past the seals. The valve should be disassembled and inspected.

A scored or seized valve should be replaced. Polishing will simply destroy the very close fit required between the spool and body. A valve spool must move freely and without sticking; dirt, burrs, and other foreign particles cannot be tolerated in a valve.

If the valve tests satisfactorily, there may be internal leakage or binding in the power cylinder, binding in the steering system, or low oil flow.

The cylinder should then be disassembled and inspected. Look for scored walls, broken piston ring, bent or scored piston rod, and linkage binding.

Insufficient oil flow. In most systems, a flow only slightly in excess of barely maintaining pressure is needed for desired speed of steering. If it is possible to steer slowly and

with enough hydraulic power to do it easily, but the auto lacks power and hard steering is experienced when trying to steer faster, the problem may be one of insufficient oil flow. Always check the supply to make sure it is not too low.

Before trying to find the cause of insufficient oil flow, make sure the expected speed of steering is within the capability of the system.

A pinched intake (reservoir-to-pump) hose can starve a pump and limit its flow and pressure. Internal breakdown of the hose may also be the fault.

Remove and inspect the flow control valve. In particular, check for weak or sticking springs.

If the flow control valve is not at fault, disassemble and inspect the pump. High-pressure pumps depend on closely fitted and finely finished mating parts to maintain the sealing needed for pumping.

Worn parts may be the cause of insufficient oil flow. Refer to the manufacturer's servicing information.

Air in oil circuit. Air in the circuit can be caused by a low oil level in the reservoir. This causes the pump to suck in air with the oil. A leaky pump-shaft seal may also allow air to enter the system.

If the reservoir is mounted separately, look for a kinked intake hose, which will cause excessive vacuum pull on the pump intake seal.

The procedure for bleeding air from the oil is described shortly. If the air cannot be bled out, its cause must be determined and corrected.

Loose or tight linkage connections. Loose ball joints (sockets) are associated with hard steering because they unseat under load. This causes a lag in the application of the hydraulic power and a momentary feel of hard steering.

With the front wheels on the ground and normally loaded, inspect the linkage for looseness and unseating of joints as someone steers rapidly one-half turn in each direction. When improperly adjusted or worn, some shafts snap in and out of their seats. This can cause erratic and "jerky" steering.

Tighten ball sockets until the parts are compressed solidly, then back off to the nearest lock point.

Improper steering-gear adjustment. Make sure all adjustments are within the manufacturer's specifications.

In some steering gears a shim pack is used between the inner lever and housing to prevent a bind by the tapered stud being pulled into the cam groove by external forces on the lever shaft.

Other steering gears use a threaded stud assembly, with screws through the side cover into the end of the lever shaft, to keep the tapered stud from binding by being pulled into the cam groove by external forces on the lever shaft.

Binding. This may be difficult to locate. For cars with either manual or power steering, first jack up the front end and turn the front wheels in both directions. Look for binding. Check all brackets for tightness, interference of operating parts, or a cracked or broken frame.

Hydraulic Oil Leakage—External

Extra care must be used in checking for oil leakage; some leaks are misleading. The symptoms to look for include oil-wetted areas, dirty oil accumulation, oil dripping on floor, reservoir spilling, and a noisy pump caused by air in the circuit that results from a loss of oil.

Pinpoint and make sure of the place where a leak occurs before you look for the reason. Clean and dry all exterior surfaces since wind and fan draft sometimes make the oil spread from the point of leakage. This makes it difficult to locate the origin of the leak. Also keep in mind that some oil leaks do not occur under pressure; instead, they are static, and occur when the system is not in operation. A likely cause of such leakage is worn, heat-damaged, or cut O-ring seals.

Common causes of external oil leakage include fitting leaks at seats, threads, or seals; hose leaks; defective O-ring seals; or reservoir spilling. In case of reservoir spillage, examine the filter. A swinging dipstick may have rubbed the opening in the filter elements and allowed an unbaffled stream of oil to shoot directly at the filter cap and out the breather. A swinging dipstick may also loosen the rivet that holds the vent baffle and dipstick in the cap. In time, the rivet, baffle, and dipstick fall into the reservoir and leave a hole in the cap from which oil can spill readily. As oil is sprayed out of the reservoir, the reservoir level drops sufficiently to let the pump outlet be only partially covered as the oil sloshes around. This produces aeration and foaming and forces more oil from the cap. Replace the filter as often as necessary to be sure it is doing its job correctly. Also, be sure the spring remains in place and holds the filter in its correct position.

CAUTION. Do not disconnect any hose connections until you have thoroughly cleaned off all dirt. Cleanliness is essential. After reconnecting the hose, run the engine for a while and then recheck the oil supply.

Undesired Steering Actions Other Than Hard Steering

Wander. This is an abnormal tendency to stray away from the course set by the driver. Common causes include the following: (1) incorrect front-end alignment; (2) broken springs; (3) tight steering gear or linkage; (4) loose spring shackles; and (5) unequal tire pressure.

Drift. This is a tendency for an automobile to self-steer toward right or left on a flat road with no crown or cross wind. Common causes include the following: (1) dragging brake; (2) tight or dry wheel bearing; (3) unequal tire pressure; (4) incorrect front-end alignment; (5) steering control valve not centering; and (6) bent frame.

Oversteer. This is a tendency to get more steering action than required. Probable causes include (1) excessive friction in the steering system, and (2) the steering control valve not centering.

Shimmy. This refers to the front wheels vibrating wildly and without control. Sometimes it occurs only at certain speeds or after striking a hard bump. (System chatter is sometimes started by front-wheel shimmy.) Common causes include: (1) low-speed shimmy—incorrect front-end alignment, loose linkage connections, loose wheel bearings, worn knuckle pins or bushings, or weak or broken springs; and (2) high-speed shimmy—unequal tire pressure, wheels or tires either eccentric or out of balance, or badly worn and uneven tires.

System chatter. System chatter, as noted above, is sometimes caused by front-wheel shimmy. When chatter is apparent, first make sure the system is stable by checking every connecting part of the steering system for correct adjustment, tightness, and lack of lash. Check for front-end stability, particularly if shimmy also occurs. The front end must be stable.

When the system and front end are stable, and chatter persists, replacement of the control valve may correct the condition.

Recovery. In so-called recovery, the front wheels return to the straight-ahead position after a right turn or left turn is completed. On some power-steering installations, the recovery may be slower than for manual steering.

In a power-steering system, any friction that tends to keep the valve spool from returning to center or resists the return of parts to the straight-ahead position can keep enough hydraulic power applied to slow or stop recovery unless manually helped by the driver.

Possible points of friction include tight ball sockets and other linkage connections, bent piston rod, broken piston or rings, tight knuckle pins or bushings, bind in the wheel tube or wheel-tube bearing, sticking valve spool (not centering), excessively tight steering-gear adjustments, or insufficient caster.

Filling and Bleeding Hydraulic Power Steering Systems

If sufficient oil is available to replace the air, most power steering systems are self-bleeding. However, when bleeding is required, use the following procedures:

System completely drained of oil. (1) Completely fill the reservoir. (2) Start the engine, but be ready to add oil as soon as it is started and running at idle. (3) Maintain a full reservoir by adding oil as necessary for a minute or so without turning the steering wheel. This allows air to escape. (4) Slowly steer wheels, with no abrupt changes of speed or pressure. (Keep engine idling.) Add oil needed to keep reservoir full. Four or five complete turns of the wheels usually is enough to eliminate air from the system.

At this point, some systems will have eliminated practically all air; however, others will retain a great deal of air in the oil, and the oil will look cloudy or creamy. In the latter case, let the engine run at 1,000 to 1,500 rpm for a few minutes, and steer the system from stop to stop every minute until the oil is clear and steering is normal. Then adjust the oil level in the reservoir to the recommended level and secure the system.

System partially drained. (1) Fill reservoir to recommended level; (2) start engine and run at idle, adding oil to reservoir to maintain recommended level; (3) after several minutes, steer gently and slowly from stop to stop, slowly increasing and maintaining a moderate speed; and (4) when oil clears, adjust oil to recommended level and secure system.

Troubleshooting Chart

A troubleshooting chart for hydraulic power steering systems is shown in Table 18-1. Remember, ball socket adjustment is more critical for power steering than for manual steering.

Tips for Maintenance of Steering Gear Systems

1. Always check for wear in steering linkage and other system components before making adjustments to steering-gear assembly.
2. Prevent internal bottoming of steering gear. Carefully check axle stops.

3. Make periodic checks of lube levels.
4. Make periodic checks for front-end alignment.
5. Maintain properly inflated tires.
6. Always use a puller to remove steering arms. Never use a hammer or torch.
7. Always examine steering parts that have been subjected to impact, and replace any that are questionable.
8. Immediately correct any play, rattle, or shimmy in linkage or steering mechanisms.
9. Correct steering-column misalignment. If necessary, elongate support-bracket holes at dash.
10. Make note of any malfunction or accident that may damage the steering mechanism.
11. Never weld any broken steering component. Always replace with original equipment.
12. Never cold-straighten any part of the steering-mechanism.
13. Never hot-straighten any part of the steering-mechanism.
14. Always use new seals and O rings during repairs and overhauls.
15. Never replace single bearing assemblies or balls in a set.
16. Never hold the steering wheel to either extreme right or extreme left for more than a few seconds.
17. Keep dirt out of hydraulic steering system.
18. Never permit minor hydraulic leaks to continue.

Table 18-1 Troubleshooting

Symptoms	Causes	Remedies
Car pulling left or right	Front end misaligned	Adjust to specifications.
	Worn or damaged valve shaft assembly	Replace.
Steering wheel hard to turn to left or right or back to center when driving	Lower coupling flange rubbing against adjuster plug	Loosen and reposition bolt for clearance.
	Tight steering-shaft bearings	Replace bearings.
	Steering wheel rubbing against turn signal collar	Adjust mast jacket endwise.
	One or more tires not properly inflated to specs	Check manual and inflate to specifications.
	Steering gear misaligned	Align at frame.
	Thrust-bearing adjustment too light	Adjust to specifications.
	Steering-linkage tie-rod joints misaligned	Loosen tie-rod sleeve and center ball joint.
	Tight overcenter adjustment	Adjust to specifications.
	Loose pump belt	Adjust to specifications.
	Ball preload too tight	Adjust to specifications.
	Sticky valve spool	Remove and clean valve or replace valve assembly.
	Sticking pump-flow control valve	Remove valve and clean.
	Lack of lubrication in steering linkage	Check for foreign particles, then lubricate.

Table 18-1 (continued) Troubleshooting

Symptoms	Causes	Remedies
Momentary increase in effort required when steering fast to right or left	Pump belt slipping	Tighten or replace belt.
	Low fluid level in pump	Check fluid level and refill.
	Excessive internal leakage	Replace rack piston seal and O-ring and/or replace valve spool.
External oil leaks	Reservoir fluid level too high	Remove excess fluid.
	Loose hose connections	Tighten connections.
	Defective housing	Replace housing.
	Worn or damaged torsion bar seal	Replace valve shaft assembly.
	Worn or damaged side-cover O-ring seal	Replace.
	Damaged hose	Replace.
	Damaged reservoir cap	Replace.
	Worn or damaged adjuster plug seals	Replace.
	Worn or damaged housing-end-cover O-ring seal	Replace.
	Worn or damaged pitman shaft seals	Replace.
Loose steering	Lash in steering linkage	Replace parts affected.
	Lash between pitman shaft and rack piston	Make overcenter adjustment.
	Incorrect ball nut-and-worm preload	Remove rack piston and worm, and change balls for correct preload.
	Loose thrust-bearing adjustment	Adjust to specifications.
Gear noise (hissing sound)	Hiss may be expected when the car is not moving, especially during tight parking situations	Slight hissing does not affect steering. Any metal-to-metal contact through the flexible coupling will cause valve hiss. Check clearance around safety drive bolts in flexible coupling. Make sure steering shaft and gear are aligned so that the flexible coupling rotates in a flat plane and is not distorted as the shaft rotates.
Gear noise (rattle, creak, chucking)	Loose gear on frame	Tighten mounting bolts.
	Loose overcenter adjustment	Adjust to specifications.
	Loose steering linkage	Tighten linkage pivot points.
Tight steering when parking	Low fluid in reservoir	Fill to proper level. Then check for leaks often.
	Low pressure due to restriction in hose	Clean or replace.
	Lack of lubricant in ball joints and steering linkage	Lubricate.
	Low pressure due to steering-gear assembly	Remove steering gear for disassembly.
	a) Pressure loss in cylinder due to worn rack piston seal, damaged O-ring, or scored housing bore	a) Inspect rack piston seal, O-ring and bore. Replace seal or housing.
	b) Leakage at valve rings, valve body-to-worm seal	b) Replace rings.
	c) Loose-fitting spool in valve body or leaky valve body	c) Replace valve shaft assembly.
	Tire not properly inflated	Check manual and inflate to specifications.
	Insufficient hydraulic fluid pressure	Check pump and line for leaks. Repair or replace defective parts.
	Loose pump belt	Tighten to specifications.
Pump noise	Loose belt	Tighten bolt.
	Low fluid level in reservoir	Add fluid.
	Hose touching part of car	Adjust hose position.
	Scored rotor	Remove light scoring by lapping, but replace heavily scored part.
	Extreme wear of pump ring	Replace.

Table 18-1 (continued) Troubleshooting

Symptoms	Causes	Remedies
	Face of thrust plate scored	Remove light scoring by lapping, but replace heavily scored part.
	Vanes (or similar pump components) sticking in slots	Remove burrs or dirt.
	Vanes (or similar pump components) not installed properly	Re-install.
	Excessive back pressure caused by hoses or steering gear	Locate restriction and correct.
	Scored pressure plate	Remove light scoring by lapping, but replace heavily scored part.
	Air in fluid	Bleed system, check fluid level, and fill.
No effort required to turn steering wheel	Broken torsion bar	Replace valve shaft assembly.
Valve squawk when turning	Cut or worn dampener O-ring on spool valve	Replace dampener ring.
	Loose or worn valve	Replace valve shaft assembly.
Pump inoperative or provides little steering assist	Faulty flow-control-valve assembly	Clean and free parts; replace as necessary.
	Loose drive belt or pump	Tighten belt.
	Air in fluid	Bleed system, check fluid level, and fill.
	Low fluid level	Add fluid.
	Vanes sticking in rotor slots	Remove burrs or dirt.
	Flow control valve stuck	Remove burrs or dirt.

19

BRAKE SYSTEMS

Contents

DRUM BRAKES

A modern drum brake is self-energizing, self-adjusting, and hydraulically activated.

An increasingly common arrangement is to use drum brakes on the rear wheels (to facilitate attachment of the parking brake) and disc brakes, with their superior braking action, on the front wheels. This is the arrangement that we shall assume throughout this chapter. Disc brakes are discussed after drum brakes and the chapter concludes with an examination of power-braking systems.

Construction

Refer to Figure 19-1 as necessary. The *backing plate*, as its name implies, is simply the support on which all of the remaining parts are mounted. To keep it from moving when the brakes are applied, the backing plate is attached to the rear-axle housing.

Bosses (raised sections), located around the outer edge of the recessed portion of the backing plate, serve as mounts for the *brake shoes*.

Holes are provided in the backing plate to permit attachment to the rear-axle housing, the insertion of *shoe hold-down spring pins*, and (in most, but not all, cases), access to the *adjuster assembly*.

The *anchor*, located at the top of most brake drums, serves a dual purpose: as an attachment for the *brake-shoe return springs* and as a stop for the brake-shoe mounting. The anchor may be fixed (most common) or adjustable. The fixed anchor is bolted to the backing plate and permits no adjustment in the position of the brake shoes. On adjustable-anchor assemblies, the most common arrangement is to have the *anchor pin* inserted in a slotted hole. Depending on the locked position of the pin, the position of the brake shoes is variable.

The brake shoes are of metal construction. The outer rim serves as a foundation for the brake lining while the

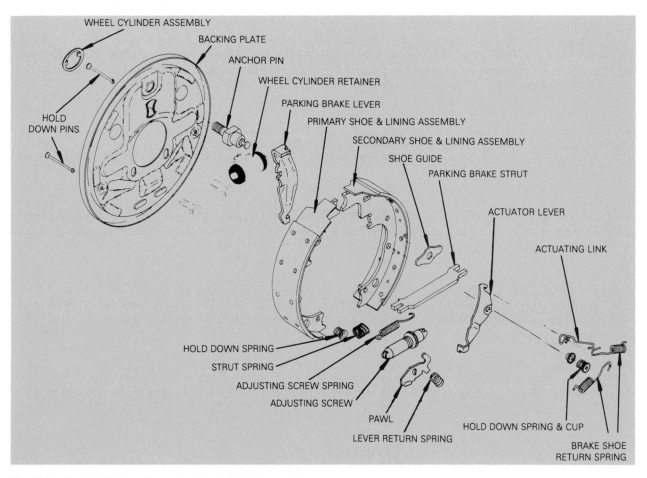

Fig. 19-1. Exploded view of a typical drum-brake assembly. *Courtesy of Chevrolet Division, General Motors Corporation.*

inner *web* provides needed mechanical strength and a place for the shoe return-springs to be mounted. One end of the web snugs around the anchor pin and keeps the brake shoe from turning with the drum. The front brake shoe is called the *primary* shoe and the rear brake shoe is known as the *secondary* shoe.

Providing it is in satisfactory condition, a brake shoe may be used repeatedly simply by installing new *brake linings*. When a brake lining comes into contact with a turning brake drum, kinetic energy (the energy of movement) is converted to heat energy by means of friction, causing the automobile to slow or stop. Thus, the most important characteristic of a given brake lining is its frictional quality. When the frictional quality is excessive, the brake pedal will be very "sensitive." On the other hand, when the frictional quality is too low, the brake pedal will be very "unsensitive" and slowing down or stopping may be very difficult.

Brake linings may be bonded or (more often) riveted to the shoe.

On manually adjusted drum brakes (as distinguished from the self-adjusting type), you will find four types of springs: shoe hold-down springs, shoe-return (retraction) springs, adjuster-screw springs (also called star-adjuster springs), and parking-brake springs.

Hold-down springs are color coded by the manufacturer for certain specific uses. The correct replacement is essential since the springs vary in length and strength. Moreover, the spring for primary and secondary shoes may be completely different.

Shoe-return springs are also color coded and replacements must be selected with care. All shoe-return springs attach to a brake-shoe web at one end and to the anchor pin at the opposite end and bring the shoes back into position when the foot brake is released.

The adjuster screw provides a means of expanding the shoes as the lining wears in order to maintain the correct lining-to-drum clearance for proper braking action. The screw assembly fits between the webs at the bottom of the two brake shoes. The adjuster-screw spring is hooked into the webs of the shoes, thereby holding the shoes together against the ends of the adjuster screw. (The adjuster screw is shown very clearly in Figure 19-1.) On manually adjusted brakes, the spring rides on the adjuster screw and provides enough drag to keep the adjuster assembly from expanding or contracting on its own.

The points (teeth) on an adjuster used with manually adjusted brakes are larger and spaced farther apart than on self-adjusting brakes. In addition, manually operated adjuster screws almost always have right-hand threads. But the self-adjusting screws usually have either right-hand or left-hand threads to allow for placement of the screw in the same position on either side of the car.

The parking-brake assembly on each rear wheel consists of a cable and return spring, a lever, strut, or link, and a retaining clip.

When the emergency brake is activated the cable pulls the lever forward at the bottom; the lever pivots at the top and applies pressure via the strut to the primary shoe and through the lever to the secondary shoe.

The retaining clip attaches the parking-brake lever to the secondary shoe. A spring on the end of the strut holds the strut in place between the two shoes.

Self-Energizing and Servo Actions

All modern brakes allow the shoes mechanically to increase the force applied through the wheel cylinder and thereby assist braking action. The increase in force occurs because the shoes are mounted to the backing plate in such a way as to take advantage of the frictional force that occurs when the brake linings come into contact with the rotating brake drum.

To clarify this idea, think about what happens to the shoes when they contact the drum. Friction between the two parts tends to rotate the shoes around the anchor pin in the direction of drum rotation. But hydraulic pressure, exerted by the wheel cylinder, forces the top of the primary (front) shoe outward while the bottom of the shoe is anchored. Consequently, the rotational force causes the primary shoe to be dragged hard against the drum and this increases the braking action to a greater extent than would otherwise be the case. For this reason, the primary shoe is said to be self-energizing.

But what is happening to the rear shoe? Here, the friction of the rotating drum pushes the brake shoe away from the drum, effectively reducing the force applied by the wheel cylinder.

Servo action, by which force is transferred from one to another, is used to overcome the problem existing at the rear shoe.

Assume a single-anchor brake shoe with an adjuster assembly located between the bottoms of the two shoes. When the brakes are applied, both shoes move outward toward the rotating brake drum. But if the primary shoe is installed properly, its outward movement is faster than that of the secondary shoe, and when it contacts the drum, friction tends to drag the primary shoe around with the drum. This force then pushes the secondary shoe against the anchor pin and wedges it against the drum. Now, pressure applied by the wheel cylinder is significantly increased by servo action and the entire assembly is self-energizing.

In a servo brake, the secondary shoe ends up doing most of the work (about 70 per cent). To compensate for this condition, the secondary-shoe lining is larger and more wear resistant than the primary-shoe lining.

All late-model cars have so-called duo-servo brakes in which servo action occurs when the car is moving either forward or backward. When the car moves forward, the secondary shoe again does the bulk of the work. But with the car in reverse, the primary shoe becomes the "work horse."

Self-Adjusting Drum Brakes

The difference between the duo-servo, self-adjusting drum brake and a manually adjusted brake is in the adjuster assembly.

Notice that the top end of the adjuster cable fits over the anchor pin, then wraps around a guide (mounted on the web of the secondary shoe) and extends down to the adjuster lever. The adjuster spring then attaches to the adjuster lever. (On a manually adjusted brake the adjuster spring is attached to the web of the secondary shoe.)

The self-adjuster mechanism attaches to the secondary shoe. It operates *only* when the vehicle is moving in reverse, and then *only* when the brake lining is worn enough to let the secondary shoe move far enough away from the anchor pin to actuate the self-adjuster lever.

When the car is in reverse and the brakes are applied, the secondary shoe moves away from the anchor pin. When brake adjustment is needed, this movement of the shoe is sufficient to pull the adjuster lever up and over one of the points on the star wheel of the adjuster assembly. When the brakes are released, the automatic-adjuster spring pulls the adjuster lever down. This movement turns the adjuster star wheel, thereby increasing the length of the adjuster assembly and moving the brake lining closer to the drum.

When the vehicle is moving in a forward direction and the brakes are applied, the secondary shoe is held against the anchor pin and the adjuster lever does not operate.

A lever-type of self-adjusted brake (GMC), known as a "self-adjusting standard duo-servo self-energizing brake with a single fixed anchor," is shown in Figure 19-2.

Again, the self-adjuster mechanism does not operate except when the car is in reverse and the shoe linings have worn enough to require adjustment.

In operation, as the secondary shoe moves out, the link pulls on the adjuster lever. The edge of the lever turns the star wheel on the adjuster assembly and moves the shoes closer to the brake drum.

SERVICING SELF-ADJUSTING DRUM BRAKES

Duo-servo self-adjusting drum brakes (both cable and lever operated) have been used on virtually all American cars produced since 1974. Thus, we shall confine our servicing procedures to this type of brake.

First, however, a word of caution. A very common practice around brake-repair shops is to use compressed air to blow asbestos dust (from linings) from brake parts. Asbestos is known to cause cancer! Play it safe and use either a damp cloth or a well-filtered vacuum cleaner to remove the dust and seal the bag before you dispose of it.

Star and Screw Adjustment and Testing

1. Remove the access plug from the backing plate (or front of drum on GMC cars). If the access slot has been filled in, punch it out and, when the adjustment is completed, insert a plug in the slot to keep out dirt and water.

2. With a screwdriver, move the star teeth up to tighten the brakes or down to loosen them. If necessary, use another small screwdriver to hold the adjuster lever away from the star wheel.

3. Tighten the brakes until they are nearly locked. Then loosen the brakes until the wheel can be rotated freely. To prevent side-to-side brake pull, the star wheel must be backed off the same number of turns on both rear wheels. (If drum brakes are also used on the front wheels, the same remark applies.)

4. After all brakes are adjusted, check the brake-pedal travel. Then, place the car in reverse and make several stops in order to equalize all four wheels.

When proper star adjustment cannot be achieved, an adjuster component is either broken, worn, or improperly installed. To inspect these components, it is necessary to remove the drum. To avoid any unnecessary work, first check the operation of the adjuster assembly (using the procedure that follows) and make sure that your adjustments were made properly.

1. With an assistant in the car to operate the brake pedal, raise the vehicle on a hoist.

2. Loosen the brakes by turning the star wheel down about 30 notches.

3. Spin the wheel and drum in reverse and have your assistant apply the brakes. If all is well, movement of the secondary shoe should pull the adjuster lever up. When the brakes are released, the lever should drop down and turn the star wheel up to tighten the brakes.

Removing Brake Shoes

NOTE: Work on one wheel at a time. You may have to refer to the other wheel with all parts in place. You must also have a brakespring service tool (available at most parts-supply houses).

1. Place the hollow end of the spring service tool on the brake shoe anchor pin. Twist the tool to disengage *one* shoe-retracting spring. Then remove the other shoe-return spring in the same manner.

2. On GMC automobiles, grasp the secondary shoe return spring with a pair of pliers and lift up on the spring to detach it from the automatic-adjuster link.

NOTE: When removing any spring, be very careful not to let the spring slip off the tool. A flying spring can be lethal. At best, the spring will probably be ruined.

3. Reach behind the backing plate and place a finger on the hold-down pin of either brake shoe. Using pliers, clamp

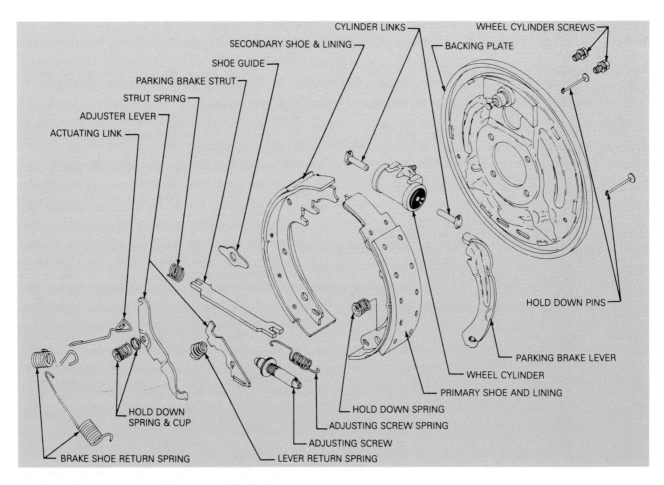

Fig. 19-2. Exploded view of lever-type self-adjusting brake. *Courtesy of Chevrolet Division, General Motors Corporation.*

the washer on the top of the pin being held from behind. Push down on the pliers and turn them 90 degrees. A slot in the washer will then be aligned with the head of the mounting pin. Remove the spring and washer. Repeat operation on the remaining brake shoe.

NOTE: Select the appropriate Step 4.

4. **Ford and AMC.** Using a tip of a screwdriver, lift up on the adjuster lever. When there is enough slack in the adjuster cable, disconnect the cable from the anchor. While still holding the adjuster lever away from the screw, back off on the screw. Grasp the tops of the brake shoes and move them out until they disengage from the wheel cylinder and parking-brake link. Lift the shoes from the backing plate. Twist the shoes slightly and the adjuster assembly will come completely apart.

4. **Chrysler (except Omni and Horizon).** Remove the adjuster cable from the anchor pin and detach it from the adjuster lever. Remove the cable, overload spring, and cable guide. Disengage the adjuster-lever return spring and remove the lever and spring. Move the tops of the shoes out far enough to clear the cylinder pins and parking-brake

link. Lift the brakes from the backing plate and remove the adjuster screw.

4. **Chrysler Omni and Horizon.** Unhook the parking-brake lever and the bottom shoe-to-anchor spring. Remove the clips and pins that hold the shoes to the backing plate. Spread the shoes apart. Back off and remove the adjuster assembly. Pull the bottom of the secondary shoe away from the backing plate in order to release the spring tension. Remove the shoe. Repeat procedure for removal of primary shoe.

4. **General Motors.** First remove the automatic-adjuster link. Then remove the adjuster lever, pivot (pawl) and lever return spring from the secondary shoe-return spring as an assembly. Move the top of both shoes outward far enough to clear the cylinder pins and parking-brake link. Lift the shoes off the backing plate and remove the adjuster screw.

5. Using pliers, clamp the end of the brake cable and, using the brake cable as a fulcrum, pull the end of the spring away from the lever. Disconnect the cable from the brake lever.

Brake-Shoe Installation (except Chrysler Omni and Horizon)

1. Connect the brake cable to the secondary shoe before that shoe is installed on the backing plate. To transfer the brake lever from the old shoe to the new one, spread the bottom of the horseshoe clip and disconnect the lever. Position the lever on the new shoe and install the spring washer and horseshoe clip. Close the bottom of the clip. Using pliers, clamp the metal tip of the parking-brake cable. Grasp the end of the coil spring with a pair of side cutters. Using the pliers as a fulcrum, pull the coil spring back with the side cutters. Position the cable in the parking-brake lever.

2. Apply a light coating of high-temperature grease to the backing plate at the points of contact with the shoes. Place the primary shoe on the front of the backing plate. Install the hold-down spring and washer over the shoe-mounting pin. Install the secondary shoe.

3. Install the parking-brake link between the primary shoe and the secondary shoe.

NOTE: Use the appropriate Step 4.

4. **Ford and AMC.** Place the automatic-adjuster cable loop on the anchor pin with the crimped side of the loop facing the backing plate.

4. **Chrysler.** First install the adjuster lever and return spring, then the adjuster overload spring and cable. One end of the cable attaches to the adjuster lever and the other end goes over the anchor pin.

4. **General Motors.** Assemble the adjuster lever, pivot, and override spring. Join the secondary spring as an assembly.

5. Install the primary shoe return spring. Using the tapered end of the brake-spring-service tool, slide the top of the spring onto the anchor pin.

6. Install the automatic-adjuster-cable guide in the secondary shoe. Make sure the flared hole in the guide fits inside the hole in the brake shoe. Fit the cable into the cable-guide groove.

7. Install the secondary shoe return spring through the hole in the cable guide and the brake shoe. Using the spring tool, slide the top of the return spring onto the anchor pin.

8. Clean the threads of the adjuster screw and apply a light coating of high-temperature grease to the threads. Screw the adjuster closed, and then open it one-half turn.

9. Install the adjuster screw between the brake shoes. The star wheel should be nearest to the secondary shoe. Make sure the star wheel can be adjusted through the hole in the backing plate.

10. Install the short, hooked end of the automatic-adjuster spring in the proper hole in the primary shoe.

11. Connect the hooked end of the automatic-adjuster cable and the free end of the adjuster spring in the slot at the top of the adjuster lever.

12. Pull the adjuster lever (with attached cable and spring) downward and to the left. Engage the lever pivot hook in the hole in the secondary shoe.

13. Make sure of the following: shoes engage the wheel cylinder properly and are flush on the anchor pin; the adjuster cable is flat on the anchor pin and in the back slot of the cable guide; the adjuster lever rests on the star wheel. Then pull up on the adjuster cable until the lever is free of the star wheel. Release the cable. The lever should snap back into place on the star wheel and turn the wheel one notch.

14. Expand the brake adjusting screw until the brake drum just fits over the brake shoes. Install the wheel and drum and adjust the brakes.

Brake-Shoe Installation—Chrysler Omni and Horizon

1. With the primary shoe return spring in position on the shoe, install the shoe at the same time as the return spring is engaged in the end support.

2. Position the end of the shoe under the anchor.

3. With the secondary shoe return spring in position, install the shoe at the same time as the spring is engaged in the support.

4. Position the end of the secondary shoe under the anchor.

5. Spread the shoes and install the adjuster assembly. Make sure that the fork end that enters the shoe is curved down.

6. Insert the shoe hold-down pins and install the hold-down springs.

7. Install the shoe-to-anchor springs.

8. Install the parking-brake cable into the parking-brake lever.

9. Replace the brake drum and tighten the nut (240-300 inch-pounds) while rotating the wheel.

10. Back off the nut enough to release the bearing preload and position the locknut with one pair of slots aligned with the cotter-pin hole.

11. Install the cotter pin. (End play 0.001-0.003 inch)

12. Install the grease cap.

HYDRAULIC SYSTEM

For many years, a single-piston master cylinder was standard equipment on automobiles. For safety reasons, however, the single-piston cylinder has been replaced with a tandem master cylinder that provides two completely separate hydraulic systems, one for the front brakes and one for the rear brakes. With this arrangement, the loss of pressure in one system does not result in the loss of pressure in the other system.

Although the single-piston cylinder is now considered to be obsolete, a brief discussion of this mechanism should make it easier to understand the operation of the tandem variety.

Single-Piston Master Cylinder

Refer to Figure 19-3. When the brake pedal is depressed, the operating linkage moves the piston and forces brake fluid through the piston-cylinder outlet and tubing connections (not shown) into the four wheel cylinders, thereby moving the brake shoes against the drum. When pressure on the foot pedal is released, the shoe-return springs return the shoes to their normal (off) position and force fluid back to the master cylinder.

The piston and primary cup return to the release position much faster than fluid can return to the master cylinder through the piston-cylinder outlet. A momentary vacuum is thus created in the piston chamber, and additional fluid is drawn into the chamber, and past the lip of the primary cup from the main reservoir through holes drilled in the piston. Any excess fluid returning from the wheel cylinders is by-passed through the compensating port into the main reservoir. Thus, the piston cylinder is always full of fluid for the next brake application.

The operating rod must be adjusted for clearance where it seats in the piston. There should be one-half inch free movement of the brake pedal before the pressure stroke begins. Should the linkage be adjusted tightly against the piston, the piston-cylinder outlet may be blocked by the primary cup and the compensating action of the master cylinder destroyed. The primary cup must be clear of the compensating port when the piston is in its normal (returned) position. The clearance can be determined by assuming that there is a slight amount of free movement of the brake pedal before the piston starts to move. Blocking

the compensating port causes the brake shoes to fail to release fully, and may even make the brakes lock.

The secondary cup keeps fluid from leaking out of the master cylinder and into the boot.

Wheel Cylinders

Compensation for the wrapping action of the primary brake shoes is accomplished by either of two methods. In one, longer linings are used on the secondary shoes than on the primary shoes and the shoes are operated by a wheel cylinder having pistons of equal diameter at each end, as shown in Figure 19-4. In the second method, Figure 19-5, a step-

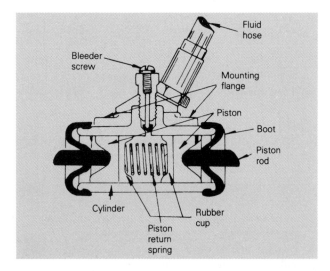

Fig. 19-4. Wheel cylinders with pistons of equal diameter at each end.

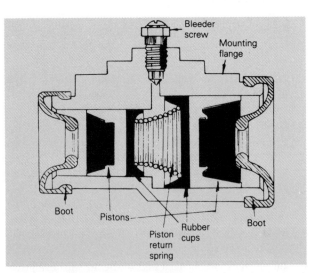

Fig. 19-5. A step-cut wheel cylinder.

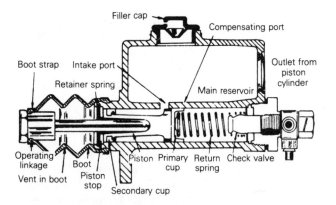

Fig. 19-3. A single-piston master cylinder.

cut wheel cylinder is used. Notice that these cylinders have a smaller diameter piston in one end than in the other. Consequently, such cylinders must be installed in the proper position. On some cars the larger bore is assembled toward the front, on others toward the rear. The brake cylinders for front wheels, regardless of their design, have different diameters than those for the rear wheels to compensate for load transfer when the brakes are applied sharply. Thus, front and rear cylinders are not interchangeable.

Wheel cylinders of the step-cut type are not interchangeable from the right to the left side of the chassis. Those used on the right side have the letter R cast on their upper surfaces; those for the left side have the letter L.

In another type of wheel cylinder, Figure 19-6, the cylinder is mounted on the web of the secondary shoe and contains a single piston against which rests a rod from the primary shoe. The piston return spring, mounted between the piston and the rear cylinder wall, returns the piston to its former position when cylinder fluid pressure is released.

The wheel cylinder illustrated in Figure 19-6 is, by far, the most common in current usage and is the only type for which maintenance procedures are given.

The following is a typical procedure for the removal, disassembly, assembly, and installation of a wheel cylinder having pistons of equal diameter at each end.

1. Remove the wheel, drum, and brake shoe, being careful not to get grease or dirt on the brake lining.

2. Clean all dirt and foreign material around the cylinder at the brake line and disconnect the line from the cylinder.

3. Remove the wheel cylinder from the backing plate. To do so, insert pins (⅛-inch diameter or less) into access slots between the wheel-cylinder pilot and the retainer locking tabs. Then bend both tabs away simultaneously until they spring over the abutment shoulder, releasing the wheel cylinder. See Figure 19-7.

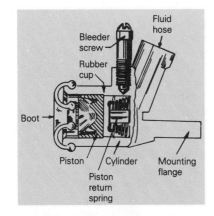

Fig. 19-6. Wheel cylinder mounted on web of secondary shoe. A rod from the primary shoe rests against the single piston.

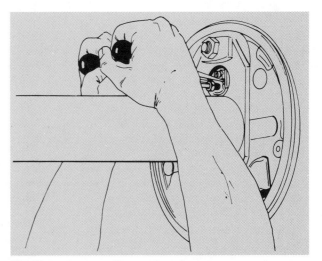

Fig. 19-7. Removal of a typical wheel cylinder. *Courtesy of Chevrolet Division, General Motors Corporation.*

The disassembly procedure is as follows:

1. Inspect the cylinder bore for scoring or corrosion. Replace a corroded cylinder.

2. Polish any discolored or stained area with a crocus cloth by revolving the cylinder on cloth supported by a finger.

3. Rinse the cylinder in clean brake fluid.

Shake excessive rinsing fluid from cylinder. Do *not* use a rag to dry the cylinder since lint from a rag cannot be kept off the cylinder bore surfaces.

To reassemble the cylinder, proceed as follows:

1. Lubricate the cylinder bore and counterbore with clean brake fluid and insert spring-expander assembly.

2. Install new cups (lint and dirt free). Do not lubricate cups prior to assembly.

3. Install pistons.

4. Press new boots into cylinder counterbores by hand. Do not lubricate boots prior to assembly.

Here is the installation procedure:

1. Install the wheel cylinder on the brake backing plate. Hold the wheel cylinder against the backing plate by inserting a block between the cylinder and axle flange. Install new retaining spring over wheel cylinder, lining up the retainer tabs with the cylinder tab grooves. Drive the retainer into position using a 1⅛-inch socket and 10-inch extension. The retainer is in place when the tabs are snapped under the retainer abutment. Make sure both tabs are properly engaged.

2. Connect the brake pipe. Torque the cylinder to 100 inch-pounds.

3. Install brake shoes, drum, and wheel. Then flush and bleed the hydraulic system (see next section).

Brake Bleeding

The process of bleeding the hydraulic brakes is simply the removal or purging of any air trapped in the brake lines or cylinders. Always bleed the brakes after doing any brake job or after any part of the hydraulic system has been opened.

The quickest and easiest way to bleed a brake system is to externally pressurize the system. But this method requires special equipment. Gravity bleeding, on the other hand, requires no special equipment and is, therefore, the method described here.

NOTE: AMC cars for 1974 use drum brakes on all four wheels. When bleeding, it is necessary to remove a warning light switch terminal and plunger (see next section, "Three-Way Control Valve–Disc/Drum Brakes").

1. Clean the bleeder screw at each wheel.

2. Attach a small rubber hose to the bleeder screw on the selected wheel and place the end in a container of clean brake fluid.

3. Fill the master cylinder with brake fluid and keep it at least half full during the bleeding process.

4. Have an assistant work the brake pedal.

5. Open the bleeder screw about one-quarter turn, press the brake pedal to the floor, close the bleeder screw and release the pedal slowly. Repeat this process until no air bubbles are forced from the cylinder when the brakes are applied.

6. If a dual master cylinder (described soon) is bled, cap one reservoir section while bleeding the other in order to prevent the loss of pressure through the cap vent hole.

Disc brakes may be bled in the same manner as drum brakes except that it takes longer to complete the job. Also, rotate the disc to make sure the piston has returned to its unapplied position when the bleeding is completed and the bleeder screw is closed.

Three-Way Control Valve Assembly–Disc/Drum Brakes

Working in unison with a tandem master cylinder, the brake-control valve assembly performs three separate brake functions through its three related valves: a pressure differential valve, metering valve, and proportioning valve. If an unequal hydraulic pressure occurs between the front and rear brakes, the pressure-differential valve senses the condition, activates a brake warning lamp switch, and turns on a warning lamp located on the instrument panel. The metering valve regulates the hydraulic pressure to the front disc brakes, and the proportioning valve controls the pressure to the rear brakes.

As noted above, the pressure-differential valve, Figure 19-8, knows when an unbalanced, hydraulic pressure condition exists between the front and rear brake system. When the brakes are applied and there is a pressure loss in either system, the valve moves off its normal center position and

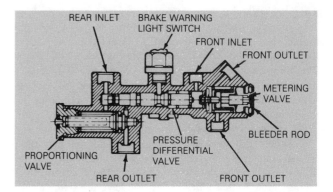

Fig. 19-8. Three-way control-valve assembly—disc/drum brakes. *Courtesy of Ford Motor Company.*

this causes the brake warning light to come on. The lamp will shut off when the brake system is properly serviced and bled and the brakes are applied to recenter the piston.

The brake warning-lamp switch is mounted on top of the control-valve body extrusion. Under normal conditions, the piston of the differential-pressure valve is centrally located, and the spring-loaded, warning-switch plunger fits into the piston's tapered groove. This leaves the contacts of the warning switch open.

The metering valve limits the hydraulic pressure to the front brakes until a predetermined pressure is reached and the rear brakes are activated. The metering valve is located in the forward end of the central bore of the control valve between the front brake inlet port and the two outlet ports. This location provides easy access to the valve's bleeder rod for purging the front brake system after performing brake service.

The proportioning valve regulates the hydraulic pressure in the rear brake section. As shown in Figure 19-10, the valve is located between the inlet and outlet valves of the rear brake system. When the brake pedal is pressed, the full rear-brake fluid pressure passes through the proportioning valve to the rear-brake system until the split-point of the valve is reached. Above this point the proportioning valve begins to reduce the hydraulic pressure to the rear brakes, creating a balanced braking condition between the front and rear wheels to prevent a rear-wheel lock-up.

After the brake system is repaired or bled, the differential-pressure warning light may remain on (valve piston in off-center position). All cars except a few AMC models with four-wheel drum brakes have a self-centering valve. When the repair or bleeding is completed, it is only necessary to apply light pressure on the brake pedal to recenter the valve and turn off the warning light.

To center the valve piston on the AMC models having drum brakes only, proceed as follows:

1. Before repairing or bleeding the brakes, disconnect the switch terminal wire and remove the switch terminal,

contact plunger spring, and plunger (with contact). If any fluid leaks from the center terminal opening while you are removing the terminal, replace the valve assembly. Also, if the switch is faulty, it must be replaced.

2. If the warning light is on, spring pressure may be holding the plunger down. Apply light pressure to the brake pedal to release plunger. The location of any leak is indicated by the position of the plunger in its bore. The top of the plunger leans to the side (front or rear) that has low pressure. Make the repair and bleed the brakes.

3. Install the plunger in the valve with the switch contact facing down.

4. Replace the nylon terminal and reconnect the warning-light wire.

Tandem Master Cylinders

The tandem (dual) master cylinder has been installed on all American-made automobiles since 1967. The two separate hydraulic systems provide some assurance that the loss of pressure in one system (front or back) will not result in the loss of pressure in the other system.

The tandem master cylinder operates on the same basic principles as the single master cylinder described earlier and accomplishes the same purpose.

As noted earlier, the tandem master cylinder contains two reservoirs: a rear (primary) reservoir for the front brakes and a front (secondary) reservoir for the rear brakes. A disassembled view of the cylinder is shown in Figure 19-9. There are two ports leading from each reservoir into the cylinder; the inlet port and the compensating port. There are also two outlet ports for brake-line attachment. To avoid the possibility of connecting the rear brakes to the primary (front brakes) reservoir, the brake lines are usually different in size.

The brake pedal push rod may be part of a power-brake unit. Alternatively, it is attached to the primary piston in the master cylinder. In the latter arrangement, the push rod must be removed from the brake pedal to permit removal of the master cylinder.

At each outlet port, a tube or fitting is pressed into the outlet bore. On master cylinders used with drum brakes only, there is a residual valve under each tube seat. This valve is not present for the front disc brakes in disc/drum braking systems. This valve is shaped like a duck's bill and is used to maintain a residual pressure of about 15 psi in the wheel cylinders. When the brakes are applied, the residual valve opens and lets fluid flow out of the master cylinder.

When the brakes are released, fluid is pushed out of the wheel cylinders and back to the master cylinder. The residual valve then unseats and allows this return flow. A

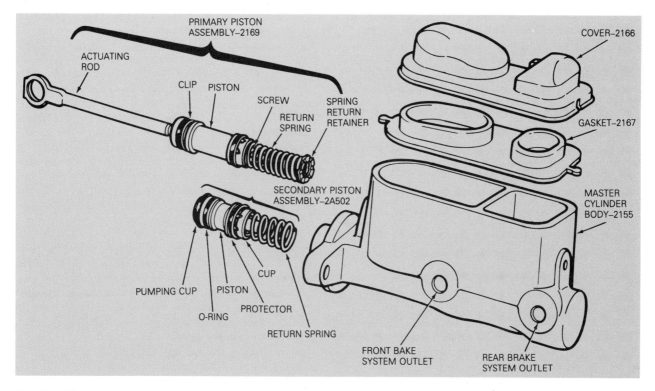

Fig. 19-9. Tandem master cylinder—disassembled. *Courtesy of Ford Motor Company.*

spring in the residual valve overcomes the pressure of the returning fluid at about 15 psi and stops its flow. Thus a constant pressure of approximately 15 psi is maintained on all drum-brake wheel cylinders and holds the seals tight against the wall of the wheel cylinders, thereby sealing in fluid and keeping out air.

When the brakes are applied, the primary piston spring, which is stiffer than the secondary piston spring, pushes the secondary piston forward and both compensating ports are covered up. As long as there are no leaks in the system and the seals are of equal diameter, equal pressure then builds up in both master cylinders.

When the brakes are released, the piston-return springs move the piston assemblies back. Although the residual valve restricts the flow of fluid from the drum-brake wheel cylinders, the return flow continues until pressure drops to about 15 psi. As the piston assemblies move back, a low-pressure area is created in the vacated spaces and atmospheric pressure, acting on the fluid in the reservoirs, pushes fluid through the intake port into the low-pressure areas.

When the piston assemblies have returned to their stops, pressure from the front-wheel cylinders (or calipers on disc brakes) forces any extra brake fluid back through the compensating ports and into the reservoirs.

If pressure is lost in the front brakes (leaky wheel cylinder, ruptured brake line, or faulty seal in master cylinder), there is no hydraulic resistance to the movement of the primary piston assembly. Therefore, when the brakes are applied, the primary piston moves forward and compresses its return spring until the primary piston bottoms out against the secondary piston. When this occurs, a solid link exists between the brake pedal and the secondary piston, and the secondary piston is then operated mechanically to provide rear-wheel braking.

If pressure is lost in the front brakes, there is no hydraulic resistance to the movement of the secondary piston assembly. When the brakes are applied, the heavier primary spring moves the secondary piston until it bottoms out against the end of the master cylinder. When this occurs, the primary piston builds up hydraulic pressure for front-wheel braking.

NOTE: Never remove self-adjusters from brakes equipped with the tandem master cylinder. To do so cancels the safety feature of the tandem system.

Maintenance of Tandem Master Cylinders

Filling. The master cylinder must be kept properly filled to ensure adequate reserve and to keep air from entering the hydraulic system. Because of expansion due to heat absorbed from the brakes and from the engine, however, the cylinder must not be overfilled.

Thoroughly clean the reservoir cover before removal to avoid getting dirt into the reservoir. Remove the cover and diaphragm. Bring the fluid level to one-quarter inch from the lowest portion of the top of each reservoir. Use the fluid recommended by the car manufacturer.

Do not use shock absorber fluid or any other fluid that contains mineral oil. Also, do not use a container that has been used for mineral oil or that is wet from water. Mineral oil will swell and distort rubber parts in the brake system and water will mix with the brake fluid, thereby lowering the boiling point of the fluid. Keep all fluid containers capped to prevent contamination.

To prevent damage to brake parts, use all of the components included in cylinder repair kit. Lubricate rubber parts with clean, fresh brake fluid. Do not use lubricated shop air on brake parts. The torque values specified by the manufacturer are for dry, unlubricated fasteners.

Removal. Disconnect brake pipes from the master cylinder and tape the ends of the pipes to prevent the entry of dirt. Then remove the master-cylinder retaining nuts and remove the cylinder from the vehicle. Be careful not to drip brake fluid on exterior paint.

Disassembly. Clean the outside of the master cylinder thoroughly and then remove the reservoir cover and diaphragm. Turn the cylinder over and pump the push rod by hand to drain all brake fluid. Always discard used fluid.

Then depress the piston and remove the secondary piston stop bolt from the bottom of the front fluid reservoir. Then place the master cylinder in a vise so that the jaws grip the mounting flange. Remove the lock ring and primary piston assembly. Remove the secondary piston and the secondary piston spring and retainer by blowing air through the outlet port.

Now place the master cylinder in the vise so that the outlet holes are up. Enlarge the hole in the tube-fitting insert using a 13/64-inch drill. Place a heavy washer over the outlet on the master cylinder and thread a 1/4-20 by 3/4-inch screw into the insert. Tighten the screw until the insert is unseated. Remove the insert, screw, and washer.

Finally, use clean brake fluid to clean all metal parts thoroughly. Air dry and place the clean parts on paper or a lint-free clean cloth. Do not use anti-freeze, alcohol, gasoline, kerosene, or any other cleaning fluid that might contain even a trace of mineral oil.

Inspection. Inspect the cylinder bore for scoring or corrosion. It is best to replace a corroded cylinder. Corrosion can be identified as pits or excessive roughness.

Polish any discolored or stained areas with crocus cloth by revolving the cylinder on cloth supported by a finger.

Rinse the cylinder in clean brake fluid. Shake excess rinsing fluid from the cylinder. Do not use a rag to dry the cylinder since lint from a rag cannot be kept off the cylinder bore surfaces.

Make sure the compensating ports are clear. If scratches or corroded spots are too deep to be polished satisfactorily, replace the cylinder.

Assembly. Place the brass tube fitting insert (new parts) in outlet holes so that it is in position to be pressed into the hole. To install the tube-fitting insert, thread a spare brake-line nut into the outlet hole and turn nut down until tube-fitting insert bottoms. Remove the tube nut and check the outlet hole for loose burrs, which might have been turned up when the tube-fitting insert was pressed down.

Put a new secondary (rear) seal in groove in end of secondary piston, as shown in Figure 19-10.

Assemble a new primary (front) seal over the end of the secondary piston, also Figure 19-10, so that the flat side of the seal seats against the flange of the piston.

Assemble a new secondary seal into the groove on the end of the secondary piston.

In order to ensure correct assembly of the primary piston, a complete primary piston assembly should be included in the repair kit.

Coat the bore of the master cylinder with clean brake fluid. Coat the primary and secondary seals on the secondary piston with clean brake fluid. Insert the secondary piston-spring retainer into the secondary piston spring. Place the retainer and spring over the end of the secondary piston so that the retainer locates the inside lip of the primary seal.

Hold the master cylinder with the open end of the bore down and push the secondary piston into the bore so that the spring will seat against the closed end of the bore.

Now place the master cylinder in a vise with the open end of the bore up. Coat the primary and secondary seals on the primary piston with clean brake fluid. Push the primary-piston assembly, spring end first, into the bore of the master cylinder. Hold the piston down and snap the lock ring into position in groove in inside diameter of bore.

Continue to hold the primary piston down and install the stop screw (if so equipped).

Install a new reservoir diaphragm in the reservoir cover and install the cover on the master cylinder. The beaded side of the cover faces the master cylinder casting to ensure positive sealing. Baling wire is then pushed into position to hold the reservoir cover.

Installation. Using the correct fastener, reinstall the master cylinder in place and torque the nuts to specifications. Then connect the brake pipes to the master cylinder, bleed the hydraulic system, and road test the vehicle for proper brake performance.

DISC BRAKES

Introduction

The great advantage of disc brakes over drum brakes is their ability to dissipate heat quickly and thereby minimize brake "fading" resulting from the buildup of excessive heat as in drum brakes.

An exploded view of a single-piston caliper disc brake is shown in Figure 19-11. The major components of the assembly are the disc (also called the rotor), the caliper housing with a single enclosed piston, brake shoe and lining assemblies on each side of the disc, a piston seal, and a dust boot.

The rotor is designed to create its own air flow and to provide a much greater surface area for heat dissipation than on drum brakes.

The caliper derives its name from its shape which resembles the instrument used to measure the outside dimensions of objects.

When the brakes are applied, hydraulic pressure (applied by a tandem master cylinder) pushes the inboard shoe into contact with the disc; the reaction force thus generated is used to pull the outboard shoe into friction contact with the disc. This is made possible by allowing the caliper to move slightly along the axle centerlines.

After each brake application, the rectangular seal provides automatic adjustment of the clearance between the disc and the brake linings. This is necessary because disc-brake design does not permit the use of return springs (as on drum brakes). When the brakes are applied, the seal is distorted by hydraulic pressure; the inside of the seal moves out with the piston while the outside holds in the cylinder groove. When the brakes are released, the seal returns to its released position. As the brake lining wears, the piston travel exceeds the deflection limit of the seal and the piston simply slides farther out on the seal. Thus, there is a built-in self-adjusting mechanism on disc brakes.

High pressure must be exerted on the piston in order to achieve effective braking. Therefore, heavier automobiles are equipped with power-brake units. Disc-brake design also requires more fluid reserve in the master cylinder because the piston is large. Consequently, all master cylinders used on disc/drum brake combinations have a larger reservoir for the front brakes than they do for the rear brakes.

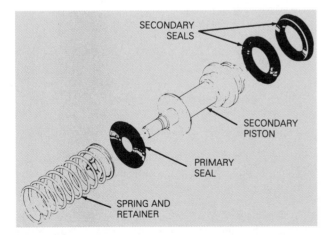

Fig. 19-10. Exploded view of secondary piston assembly. *Courtesy of Chevrolet Division, General Motors Corporation.*

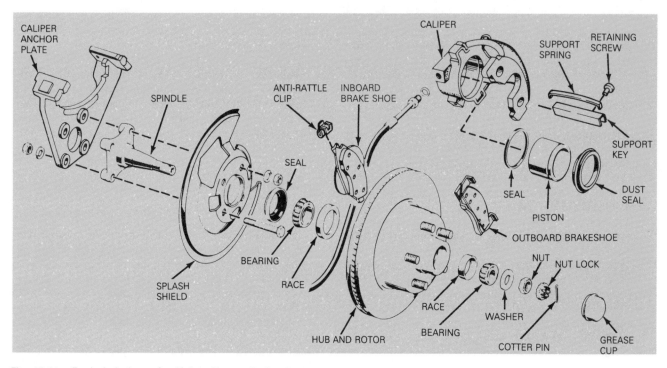

Fig. 19-11. Exploded view of a Kelsey-Hayes single piston caliper disc brake. *Courtesy of American Motors Corporation.*

Some older model disc brakes use a fixed caliper and either two or four pistons (one or two on each side of the caliper). Braking is achieved by hydraulically pushing both brake shoes against the disc sides. No overhaul procedures are given for this type of disc brake.

Servicing Single-Piston Caliper Disc Brakes

General description. On a typical single-piston, sliding-caliper disc brake the cast iron disc is of the ventilated rotor type incorporating non-directional cooling fins, and is integral with the wheel hub. A splash shield bolted to the spindle is used to prevent road contamination from contacting the inboard rotor surface and to direct cool air to the brakes. The wheel provides protection for the outboard surface of the rotor.

Caliper assembly. The caliper assembly consists of a pin-slide caliper housing, inner and outer shoe and lining assemblies, and a single piston. The caliper assembly slides on two locating pins which also act to position the caliper and to attach the outer shoe to the combination anchor plate and spindle.

The piston has a molded rubber dust boot and an outer end that attaches to a cylinder bore groove to prevent cylinder contamination. There is also a rectangular section rubber piston seal located in the cylinder bore, providing sealing between the cylinder and piston. See Figure 19-12.

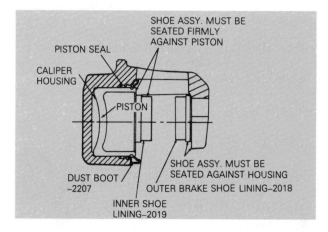

Fig. 19-12. Caliper assembly sectional view (front). *Courtesy of Ford Motor Company.*

The outer brake-shoe and lining assembly is longer than the inner shoe and lining assembly. Both inner and outer shoe lining assemblies are attached to the caliper by spring clips. The outer clip is riveted to the lining assembly. The inner clip attaches to the lining assembly as a separate item. To attach the inner shoe to the caliper, install the spring clip to the inside of the caliper piston. The outer shoe clips directly to the outer housing. A metal wear indicator is attached to the outer shoe and lining assembly. This indicator emits a noise when the lining is worn to a point where replacement is needed. Because of the metal wear indicator, the outer shoes are right and left hand and must not be interchanged. Two rubber insulators with plastic inner sleeves are installed in the caliper attaching holes. The insulators and sleeves prevent metal-to-metal contact between the locating pins and the caliper.

Brake friction materials inherently generate noise and heat in order to dissipate energy. As a result, occasional squeal is possible, and is aggravated by severe environmental conditions such as cold, heat, wetness, snow, salt, mud, etc.

Anchor pin. The anchor plate is an integral part of the spindle. Spindles are right or left hand and are not interchangeable.

Rotor and splash guard. The rotor is cast iron and attaches to the combination spindle/anchor plate. The splash guard is made of glass-filled nylon material. Attachment of the shield to the spindle is accomplished by using three bolts.

Removal and Installation

Removal of caliper assembly. Remove the wheel and tire assembly from the hub. Use care to avoid damage to, or interference with, the bleeder-screw fitting during removal. Disconnect the flexible brake hose from the caliper. To disconnect the hose, loosen the tube fitting that connects the hose to the brake tube at the bracket on the frame. Plug the brake tube. Remove the horseshoe-shaped retaining clip from the hose and bracket, disengage the hose from the bracket, and then remove the hollow bolt that attaches the hose assembly to the caliper. Mark the left and right caliper and hose assemblies with chalk prior to removal from the vehicle so that they can be correctly positioned during the reinstallation procedure. Remove the caliper locating pins. See Figure 19-13. Lift the caliper from the integral spindle and anchor plate and rotor.

Installation of caliper assembly. Install the caliper assembly over the rotor with the outer brake shoe against the rotor's braking surface. This prevents pinching the piston boot between the inner brake shoe and the piston. Make sure the correct caliper is installed on the correct anchor plate according to the way they were marked during disassembly. Connect the locating pins to the integral spindle/anchor plate, the outer shoe and lining, and the caliper insulators. Be sure the locating pins are free of oil, grease, and dirt. The caliper locating pins must be hand-inserted into the outer shoe and hand-started prior to installation with a bolt. Make sure that the large diameter of the pins goes through the outer shoe holes so that possible bonding or bending is prevented. Tighten the caliper locating pins (typically 40-60 foot-pounds). Install the flexible brake hose to the caliper with the hollow bolt and two new sealing washers. Tighten the hose fitting (typically 17-25 foot-pounds). Position the upper end of the flexible brake hose in its bracket and install the retaining clip. Remove the plug from the brake tube. Connect the brake tube to ths hose with the tube-fitting nut and tighten (10-18 foot-pounds). Bleed the brake system and centralize the brake pressure differential valve. Fill the master cylinder to within ¼ of an inch from the top of the reservoir. Install the wheel and tire assembly, and tighten the wheel nuts to specification. To position the brake lining, apply the brake pedal before moving the vehicle. Road test the vehicle.

Removal of brake shoe and lining. Remove the master cylinder cap and check the fluid level in the primary (large) reservoir. Remove brake fluid until the reservoir is half full.

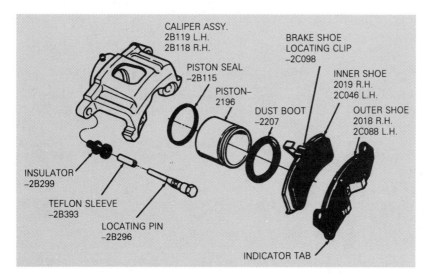

Fig. 19-13. Caliper assembly. *Courtesy of Ford Motor Company.*

Discard removed fluid. Remove the wheel and tire assembly from the hub. Be careful to avoid damage to, or interference with, the caliper splash shield or the bleeder-screw fitting. Remove the caliper locating pins (Figure 19-13). Lift the assembly from the integral spindle/anchor plate and rotor. Remove the outer shoe from the caliper assembly. Remove the inner shoe and lining assembly. Inspect both the rotor and the braking surfaces. Minor scoring or build-up of lining material does not require machining or replacement of the rotor. Suspend the caliper inside the fender housing. Be careful not to damage the caliper or stretch the brake hose. Remove and discard the plastic sleeves that are located inside the caliper locating pin insulators (Figure 19-14). These parts *must not* be reused. Remove and discard the caliper locating insulators (Figure 19-18) and discard.

Installation of brake shoe and lining. Use a 4-inch C-clamp and a block of wood 2¾ inch by 1 inch and approximately ¾ inch thick to seat the caliper hydraulic piston in its bore. This must be done to provide clearance for the caliper assembly to fit over the rotor when it is installed. Remove the C-clamp from the caliper and the caliper piston will remain in its bore. Install new locating pin insulators and plastic sleeves in the caliper housing. Check to see if both insulator flanges straddle the housing holes and the plastic sleeves are bottomed in the insulators as well as slipped under the upper lip. Figure 19-18 shows an installation tool that can help with insulator installation. Install the correct inner shoe and lining assembly in the caliper piston. Care should be taken not to bend the shoe clips in the piston, or distortion and rattles can result. Install the correct outer brake shoe and lining assembly (RH/LH), making sure that the clips are properly seated. The outer shoes are marked LH or RH and must be installed in the correct caliper. Refill master cylinder. Install the caliper in the rotor and connect the locating pins to the integral spindle/anchor plate, the outer brake shoe and lining, and the caliper insulators. Be sure the locating pins are free of oil, grease, and dirt. The locating pins must be hand-inserted into the outer shoe and hand-started prior to tightening. Make sure that the large diameter of the pins is through the outer shoe hole to prevent possible binding or bending. Install the wheel and hub assembly and tighten the wheel nuts to specifications. Pump the brake pedal prior to moving the vehicle in order to position the brake linings. Road test the vehicle.

Removal of hub and rotor. Remove the wheel and tire from the hub, taking care not to damage or cause interfer-

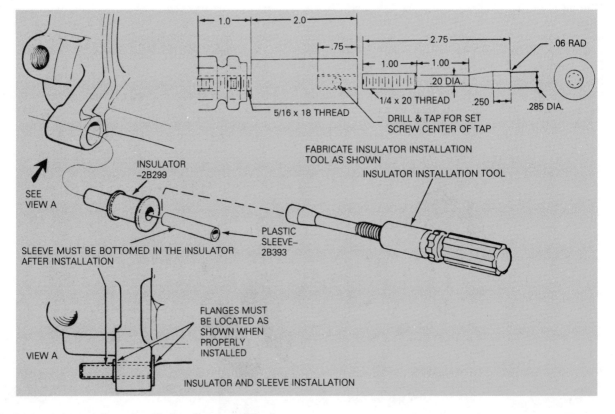

Fig. 19-14. Insulator and sleeve installation. *Courtesy of Ford Motor Company.*

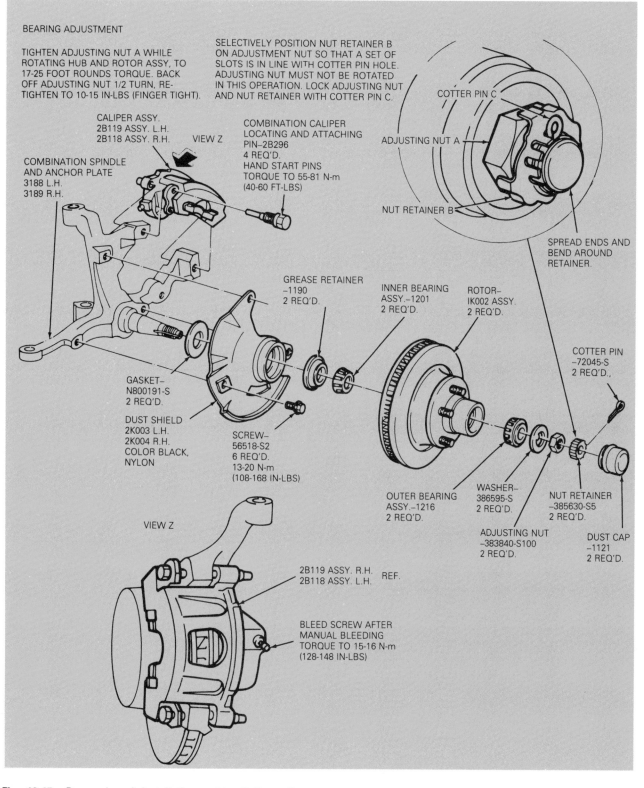

Fig. 19-15. Removal and installation guide. Caliper disc brakes. *Courtesy of Ford Motor Company.*

ence with the bleeder-screw fitting and the caliper splash shield. Remove the caliper assembly from the spindle and the rotor. If the caliper does not require servicing, it is not necessary to disconnect the brake hose or remove the caliper from the vehicle. Position the caliper out of the way, and support it with a wire in order to avoid damaging the caliper or stretching the hose. Insert a clean cardboard spacer between the linings to keep the piston from coming out of the cylinder bore with the caliper removed. Handle the rotor and caliper assemblies carefully to avoid deformation of the rotor and ricking, scratching, or contamination of the brake linings. Remove the grease cap from the hub. (Figure 19-15.) Remove the cotter pin, nut lock, and adjusting nut. Grasp the hub and rotor assembly and pull it outward far enough to lessen the washer and outer wheel bearing. Push the hub and rotor back onto the spindle and remove the washer and outer wheel bearing. Remove the hub and rotor assembly from the spindle.

Installing the hub and rotor.   If the rotor is being replaced, remove the protective coating from the new rotor with carburetor degreaser. Pack a new set of wheel bearings with the specified grease and install the inner bearing cone and roller assembly in the inner cup. Pack grease tightly between the lips of a new grease seal and install the seal. If the original rotor is being installed, make sure the grease in the hub is clean and adequate, the inner bearing and grease seal are lubricated and in good condition, and the rotor braking surfaces are clean. Install the hub and rotor assembly on the spindle. Keep the assembly centered on the spindle to prevent damage to the inner grease retainer or the spindle threads. Install the outer wheel bearing and washer and start the adjusting nut. Adjust the wheel bearing to specification and then install the nut lock, cotter pin, and grease cap. Install the caliper assembly on the spindle. Install the wheel and tire assembly. Tighten wheel stud nuts to specification. Install wheel cover. Apply the brakes several times to properly position the brake shoe and lining assemblies.

Removal and installation of splash shield.   Remove the caliper and the hub and rotor assembly as outlined earlier (it

is not necessary to disconnect hydraulic connections). Remove the three bolts that attach the splash shield to the spindle and remove the shield. Remove and discard the splash shield-to-spindle gasket.

Install a new splash shield-to-splindle gasket. If the shield is bent, replace it with a straight shield. Position the shield on the spindle. Install the attaching nuts and torque to specifications. Install the hub and rotor assembly and the caliper as described earlier.

Overhaul of Disc Brake Caliper

Disassembly.   Remove the caliper assembly as described earlier. Apply air pressure to the fluid port in the caliper with a rubber-tipped nozzle to remove the piston. If the piston is seized and cannot be forced from the caliper, tap lightly around the piston while applying air pressure. Use care because the piston can develop considerable force from pressure buildup. Remove the dust boot from the caliper assembly. Remove the rubber piston seal from the cylinder and discard it.

Cleaning and inspection.   Clean all metal parts with isopropyl alcohol. Then clean out and dry the grooves and passageways with compressed air. Make sure the caliper bore and all component parts are thoroughly clean. Check the cylinder bore and piston for damage or excessive wear. Replace the piston if it is pitted or scored, or if the chrome plating is worn off.

Assembly.   Apply a thin film of clean brake fluid to the new caliper piston seal and install the seal in the cylinder bore. Be sure the seal is not twisted but is firmly seated in the groove. Install a new dust boot by setting the flange squarely in the outer groove of the caliper bore. Coat the piston with brake fluid, and install the piston in the cylinder bore. Spread the dust boot over the piston as it is installed. Seat the dust boot in the piston groove. Install the caliper over the rotor as described earlier.

HYDRAULIC BRAKE (DRUM AND DISC) TROUBLESHOOTING CHART

The following charts were provided by the Ford Motor Company.

Condition	Possible Source	Resolution
■ Brakes do not apply. ■ Service as required.	■ Insufficient brake fluid. ■ Binding or damaged brake pedal linkage. ■ Binding or damaged brake booster linkage.	■ Add fluid, bleed system, check for leaks. ■ Service as required. ■ Service as required.

Condition	Possible Source	Resolution
■ Excessive pedal travel or pedal goes to floor.	■ Air in system.	■ Bleed system.
	■ Loose brake tube end fittings.	■ Tighten to specification.
	■ Malfunctioning master cylinder.	■ See Master Cylinder Diagnosis Guide.
	■ Drum brakes—improperly adjusted.	■ Check adjustment. Inspect brakes. Service as required.
	■ Loose wheel bearings—front.	■ Adjust as required. Check for wear, damage, or bind.
	■ On disc brakes, misaligned anchor plate.	■ Check anchor plate.
	■ Loose/missing pedal bushings/fasteners.	■ Check pedal and illustration for corrections.
	■ Outer shoe torque buttons not properly seated in caliper holes.	■ Check and service.
■ Excessive pedal effort to stop car.	■ Binding or damaged pedal linkage.	■ Inspect. Service as required.
	■ Engine vacuum loss.	■ Check engine vacuum, and vacuum at check valve to booster. Service as required.
	■ Booster inoperative.	■ Perform power-brake function test or see vacuum-booster diagnosis guide.
	■ Malfunctioning master cylinder.	■ See Master Cylinder Diagnosis Guide.
	■ Worn or contaminated linings.	■ Inspect. Replace if necessary.
	■ Brake system.	■ Inspect wheel cylinders or caliper pistons, restricted lines or hoses, contaminated brake fluid, improper operation of proportioning or metering valve. Service as necessary.
■ Spongy pedal.	■ Air in system.	■ Bleed system.
	■ Loose or improper brake pedal, pedal support, booster, master cylinder attachment.	■ Service as required.
	■ Brake system.	■ Inspect for damaged or distorted parts in brake-caliper assemblies, cracked brake drums, mis-machined anchor plates.
■ Brakes drag, slow or incomplete release.	■ Parking-brake cable out of adjustment or binding.	■ Check cables for correct adjustment or bind.
	■ Front-wheel bearings out of adjustment.	■ Check bearings for adjustment, wear, damage, or bind.
	■ Blocked master-cylinder compensator ports.	■ See Master Cylinder Diagnosis Guide.
	■ Brake adjustment (rear).	■ Check and adjust.
	■ Restriction in hydraulic system.	■ Check and service.
	■ Wheel cylinders or caliper piston seizure.	■ Check and service.
	■ On disc brake—excessive rust on front or edge of inboard shoes.	■ Inspect, clean, lubricate. Replace if necessary.
	■ Brake system.	■ Inspect and service.
■ Noise at wheels when brakes are applied—snap or clicks.	■ On drum brakes in 3 places—brake shoes binding at backing plate ledges.	■ Lubricate.*
	■ On drum brakes in 3 places—backing plate ledges worn.	■ Replace backing plate and lubricate ledges.*

Condition	Possible Source	Resolution
	■ Loose or missing disc brake caliper attaching bolts.	■ Replace missing bolts, tighten to proper torque.
	■ On disc brake—excessive rust on front or rear edge of inboard shoes.	■ Inspect. Lubricate, replace if necessary.*
	■ On disc brakes—loose or missing inner shoe anti-rattle clip.	■ Replace.
	■ Loose outer shoe retaining clip.	■ Inspect. Service or replace.
■ Noise at wheels when brakes are applied—scrape or grind.	■ Worn brake linings.	■ Replace. Refinish drums or rotors if heavily scored.
	■ Bent lining-wear indicator.	■ Inspect and adjust if necessary.
	■ Brake-shoe interference with back of drum. Binding at backing-plate guide ledges.	■ Inspect. Replace as necessary. Lubricate.
	■ Caliper to wheel or rotor interference.	■ Replace as required.
	■ Other brake system components: Warped or bent brake backing plate or splash shield, cracked drums or rotors.	■ Inspect and service.
	■ Tires rubbing against chassis or body.	■ Inspect and service.
■ Noise at wheels when brakes are applied—squeaks, squeals, or chatter. NOTE: Brake friction materials inherently generate noise and heat in order to dissipate energy. As a result, occasional squeal is normal, and is aggravated by severe environmental conditions such as cold, heat, wetness, snow, salt, mud, etc. This occasional squeal is not a functional problem and does not indicate any loss of brake effectiveness.	■ Brake drums and linings, rotors and pads worn or scored.	■ Inspect, service or replace.
	■ On disc brakes—missing or damaged brake pad insulators.	■ Replace.
	■ On disc brakes—burred or rusted calipers.	■ Clean or deburr.
	■ Dirty, greased or glazed linings.	■ Clean or replace. Lightly sand rotors.
	■ Improper lining parts.	■ Inspect for correct usage. Replace.
	■ On drum brakes—loose lining rivets, weak, damaged or incorrect shoe retracting springs, loose or damaged shoe retaining pins, springs and clips, and grooved backing plate ledges.	■ Inspect, service or replace.
■ Noise at wheels, brakes not applied—squeak or squeal.	■ Wheel cover attachment.	■ Seat covers with a rubber mallet. Service flanges or replace cover.
	■ Loose wheel-attaching lug nuts.	■ Tighten to correct torque. Replace wheel if stud holes are damaged.
	■ Bent or warped backing plate causing interference with drum or rotor.	■ Service or replace.
	■ Improper machining of drum, causing interference with backing plate or shoe.	■ Replace drum.
	■ Other brake system components: ■ Loose or extra parts in brakes. ■ Drum or brake adjustment too tight, causing lining to glaze. ■ Worn, damaged, or insufficiently lubricated wheel bearings. ■ On drum brakes—weak, damaged, or incorrect shoe retracting springs. ■ On drum brakes—grooved backing-plate ledges.	■ Inspect, service, replace as required.

Condition	Possible Source	Resolution
	■ Improper positioning of shoe in caliper. ■ Outside diameter of rotor rubbing caliper housing. ■ Lack of correct lubricant on disc-brake caliper slides. ■ Improper installation of disc-brake anti-rattle clip.	
■ Noise at wheels, brakes not applied—growling, click or rattle.	■ Outer disc-brake shoe-locating buttons not seated in caliper holes. Usually accompanied by loss of pedal. ■ Stones or foreign material trapped inside wheel covers. ■ Loose grease cap. ■ Loose wheel lug nuts. ■ Disc brake caliper—loose or missing anti-rattle clips and support spring, or crimping on outer shoe. ■ Drum brakes—loose or extra parts. ■ Worn, damaged or dry wheel bearings.	■ Check and replace if necessary. ■ Service or replace. ■ Service or replace. ■ Tighten to correct torque. Replace if stud holes are elongated. ■ Inspect, service or replace. ■ Inspect, remove or service. ■ Inspect, lubricate or replace.

■ Brakes pull to one side.	■ Unequal air pressure in tires.
	■ Grease or fluid on linings. Glazed linings.
	■ Loose or missing disc brake caliper attaching bolts.
	■ Improper size or type lining on one wheel.
	■ Stuck or seized wheel cylinders or calipers.
	■ Restricted brake lines or hoses.
	■ Other brake system components:
	  ■ Improper adjustment of drum or brakes.
	  ■ Improper positioning of disc-brake shoe and lining in the caliper.
	  ■ Improperly adjusted damaged, or worn wheel bearings.
	  ■ Distorted drum brake linings.
	  ■ Missing, broken, or stretched retracting or retaining springs and clips in drum brakes.
		■ Inflate tires to correct pressure.
		■ Replace.
		
		■ Replace missing bolts. Tighten to proper torque.
		■ Replace with correct brake lining in axle sets.
		■ Service or replace.
		
		■ Service or replace.
		
		■ Inspect, service, or replace as required.

■ Brakes grab or lock-up when applied.	■ Tires worn or incorrect pressure. ■ Grease or fluid on linings—damaged linings. ■ Improper size or type of linings. ■ Other brake system components: ■ Bolts for caliper attachment loose or missing.	■ Inflate tires to correct pressure. Replace tires with worn tread. ■ Inspect, service, or replace. ■ Replace with correct brake in axle sets. ■ Inspect, service or replace as required.

Condition	Possible Source	Resolution
	■ Worn, damaged, or dry wheel bearings. ■ Improperly adjusted parking brake.	
■ Brake warning light on.	■ Hydraulic system. ■ Shorted light circuit. ■ Parking brake not returned. ■ Brake warning switch.	■ See Master Cylinder Diagnosis Guide. ■ Correct short in warning circuit. ■ See "Parking brake will not release or fully return" below. ■ Replace.
■ Intermittent loss of pedal.	■ Loose wheel bearing. ■ Stop-light switch (manual brakes only).	■ Adjust as required. ■ Perform Master Cylinder Diagnosis test. ■ Perform steps under "Excessive pedal travel or pedal goes to floor."
■ Rough engine idle or stall, brakes applied—power brakes only.	■ Vacuum leak in neutral switch. ■ Vacuum booster.	■ Check lines for leaks. Service or replace as required. ■ Check vacuum booster for internal leaks. Replace if required.
■ Parking brake control will not latch (manual release).	■ Kinked or binding release cable. ■ Control assembly.	■ Inspect, service, or replace. ■ Inspect, service, or replace.
■ Parking brake control will not latch (automatic release).	■ Vacuum leak. ■ Vacuum switch. ■ Control assembly.	■ Service as required. ■ Test. Replace if necessary. ■ Service or replace.
■ Parking brake will not release or fully return (manual release).	■ Cable disconnected. ■ Control assembly binding. ■ Parking brake linkage binding. ■ Rear brakes.	■ Connect cable or replace. ■ Service or replace. ■ Service or replace. ■ Check rear brakes shoe retracting springs and parking brake levers.
■ Parking brake will not release or fully return (automatic release).	■ Vacuum-line leakage or improper connections. ■ Neutral switch. ■ Control assembly.	■ Inspect and service. ■ Adjust or replace. ■ Service or replace.

POWER BRAKES

Introduction

Several different types of power brake units are used on the various makes of passenger cars, but all have a vacuum cylinder which uses atmospheric pressure to assist in brake application. A discussion of one type of power brake furnishes the basic knowledge needed to make repairs on the other types; however, to give you a broader knowledge, several types in current use are considered and complete servicing data are given for the Bendix Power Unit.

Bendix Power Unit

The Bendix Power Unit, used on many cars, is mounted either on the underside of the toe board or on the engine side of the fire wall. Some manufacturers use a trade name for the Bendix unit mounted on their products, but most operate and are serviced in a similar manner.

See Fig. 19-16. The power unit contains a vacuum power cylinder, hydraulic master cylinder, and control valve. The vacuum power cylinder contains a shell, power piston, and piston-return spring. The hydraulic master cylinder has a piston, compensating valve, residual check

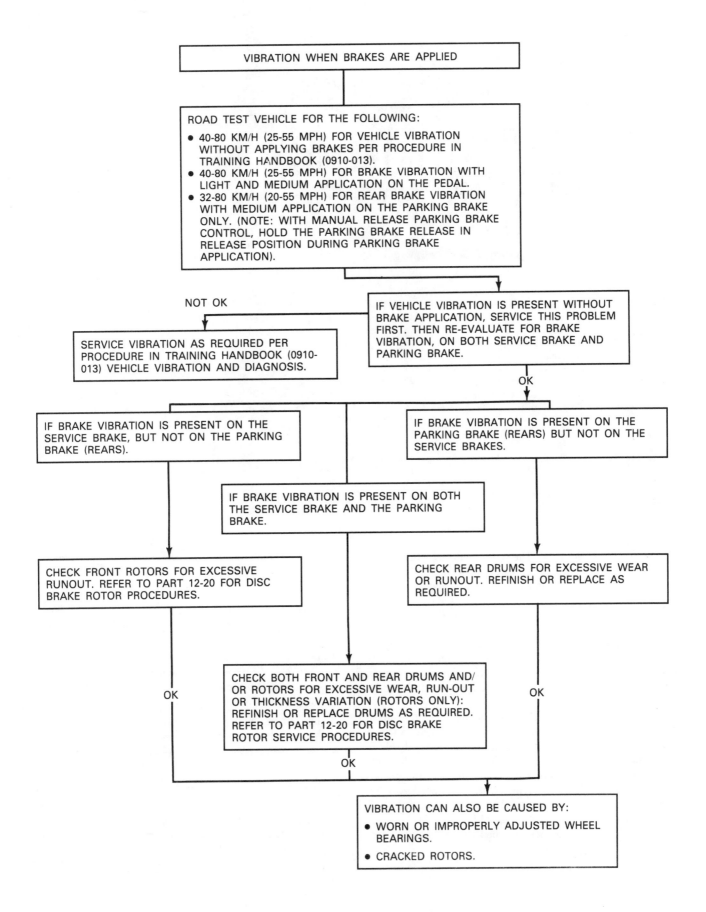

VIBRATION WHEN BRAKES ARE APPLIED

ROAD TEST VEHICLE FOR THE FOLLOWING:
- 40-80 KM/H (25-55 MPH) FOR VEHICLE VIBRATION WITHOUT APPLYING BRAKES PER PROCEDURE IN TRAINING HANDBOOK (0910-013).
- 40-80 KM/H (25-55 MPH) FOR BRAKE VIBRATION WITH LIGHT AND MEDIUM APPLICATION ON THE PEDAL.
- 32-80 KM/H (20-55 MPH) FOR REAR BRAKE VIBRATION WITH MEDIUM APPLICATION ON THE PARKING BRAKE ONLY. (NOTE: WITH MANUAL RELEASE PARKING BRAKE CONTROL, HOLD THE PARKING BRAKE RELEASE IN RELEASE POSITION DURING PARKING BRAKE APPLICATION).

NOT OK

SERVICE VIBRATION AS REQUIRED PER PROCEDURE IN TRAINING HANDBOOK (0910-013) VEHICLE VIBRATION AND DIAGNOSIS.

IF VEHICLE VIBRATION IS PRESENT WITHOUT BRAKE APPLICATION, SERVICE THIS PROBLEM FIRST. THEN RE-EVALUATE FOR BRAKE VIBRATION, ON BOTH SERVICE BRAKE AND PARKING BRAKE.

OK

IF BRAKE VIBRATION IS PRESENT ON THE SERVICE BRAKE, BUT NOT ON THE PARKING BRAKE (REARS).

IF BRAKE VIBRATION IS PRESENT ON THE PARKING BRAKE (REARS) BUT NOT ON THE SERVICE BRAKES.

IF BRAKE VIBRATION IS PRESENT ON BOTH THE SERVICE BRAKE AND THE PARKING BRAKE.

CHECK FRONT ROTORS FOR EXCESSIVE RUNOUT. REFER TO PART 12-20 FOR DISC BRAKE ROTOR PROCEDURES.

CHECK REAR DRUMS FOR EXCESSIVE WEAR OR RUNOUT. REFINISH OR REPLACE AS REQUIRED.

OK

CHECK BOTH FRONT AND REAR DRUMS AND/OR ROTORS FOR EXCESSIVE WEAR, RUN-OUT OR THICKNESS VARIATION (ROTORS ONLY): REFINISH OR REPLACE DRUMS AS REQUIRED. REFER TO PART 12-20 FOR DISC BRAKE ROTOR SERVICE PROCEDURES.

OK

OK

VIBRATION CAN ALSO BE CAUSED BY:
- WORN OR IMPROPERLY ADJUSTED WHEEL BEARINGS.
- CRACKED ROTORS.

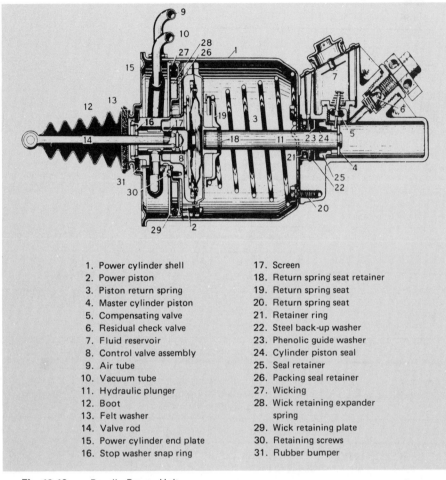

1.	Power cylinder shell	17.	Screen
2.	Power piston	18.	Return spring seat retainer
3.	Piston return spring	19.	Return spring seat
4.	Master cylinder piston	20.	Return spring seat
5.	Compensating valve	21.	Retainer ring
6.	Residual check valve	22.	Steel back-up washer
7.	Fluid reservoir	23.	Phenolic guide washer
8.	Control valve assembly	24.	Cylinder piston seal
9.	Air tube	25.	Seal retainer
10.	Vacuum tube	26.	Packing seal retainer
11.	Hydraulic plunger	27.	Wicking
12.	Boot	28.	Wick retaining expander
13.	Felt washer		spring
14.	Valve rod	29.	Wick retaining plate
15.	Power cylinder end plate	30.	Retaining screws
16.	Stop washer snap ring	31.	Rubber bumper

Fig. 19-16   Bendix Power Unit.

valve, and fluid reservoir. The control valve is actuated mechanically and controls the degree of brake application or release in accordance with foot pressure applied to the brake pedal.

When the brake is in the released position, as it is in Fig. 19-16, atmospheric pressure exists on both sides of the power piston. Usually air is admitted through the air tube, which has an air cleaner fastened to its outer end. Sometimes, however, air is admitted to the cylinder through an atmosphere port and air cleaner mounted on the cylinder shell.

When the brake is applied, vacuum from the intake manifold is admitted to the control valve via the vacuum tube. This reduces the air pressure on the forward side of the piston. Normal atmospheric pressure on the other side then pushes the piston downward and the piston engages a plunger in the hydraulic cylinder. The plunger forces hydraulic fluid through a check valve to the wheel brake cylinders and activates the brakes on all four wheels.

The power brake operates when the car engine is running by creating vacuum on the intake stroke. When the engine is not running, as in the case of a stall, a vacuum reservoir attached to the intake line provides vacuum.

Disassembly.   Removal of the power unit is similar on all vehicles using this type of brake. A typical procedure follows:

1. Disconnect the vacuum-hose line, hydraulic fluid line, and stop-light wiring from the power unit. On some cars you must raise the hydraulic fluid line above the level of the point of disconnection to prevent fluid leakage.

2. Disconnect the brake pedal and pushrod and remove the brake pedal from the pivot bracket.

3. Remove the steering column and clutch-pedal grommets; fold back the carpet.

4. Remove the toe board plate screws and take out the power unit and plate as an assembly.

Before disassembling the vacuum cylinder, clean the outside of the unit thoroughly. Be careful not to let any dirty solvent enter the unit. Remove the hydraulic fluid reservoir filler cap and gasket and empty the reservoir.

To assist in reassembly, scratch alignment marks on all parts before disassembly. Parts that should be marked include the vacuum-cylinder shell, vacuum-cylinder end plate, master-cylinder casting, reservoir cover, hydraulic-cylinder casting, and tube fitting.

To disassemble the hydraulic master cylinder, place the unit in a vise at its normal mounting angle, and remove the six cover screws, cover, and gasket. Next unscrew the compensator port and valve assembly. Remove the rubber seal ring from the compensator port fitting. Unscrew the hydraulic fluid output-fitting bolt, and lift out the fitting and rubber seal. Remove the check-valve assembly and check-valve spring. Finally, remove the unit from the vise and drain any remaining fluid from the reservoir. Do not take out the master-cylinder plunger assembly until the power-cylinder shell is removed from the master-cylinder casting.

Now replace the unit in the vise and remove the boot and felt washer from the valve rod.

Take out the screws holding the power-cylinder end plate, and remove the plate and gasket. Use long, small-nosed pliers to compress the ends of the valve stop washer snap ring and remove the ring, valve rod, and valve assembly. Take the screen away from the vacuum valve. Now remove the vacuum inlet hole and tube assembly. The vacuum piston can then be lifted from the cylinder.

Using care not to move the master-cylinder plunger from its released position, compress the piston-return spring one-half inch and remove the spring-seat retainer, spring seat, and return spring from the cylinder. The master-cylinder casting is fastened to the power-cylinder shell by three cap screws located inside the cylinder shell. Remove these screws. The cylinder shell, gasket, rubber seal ring, and leather seal can now be removed from the hydraulic-cylinder casting.

To disassemble the power piston, remove the piston cup washer-retainer ring. Use special long-nosed pliers for this purpose. Then lift the piston and seal parts as a unit from the hydraulic cylinder. Remove the steel back-up washer, phenolic guide washer, cylinder-piston seal, and seal retainer.

Before disassembling the vacuum piston, scratch alignment marks on the front and rear pistons. With the rear plate facing upward, remove the steel and rubber stop washers and packing plate screws. Remove the retainer plate wick-expander spring, the wick, seal retainer, and seal. Now turn the piston over and remove the piston-plate screws. Separate the front and rear piston plates, diaphragm assembly, counter-reaction spring, gasket, and return spring.

Inspection. With the power unit disassembled, wash all parts in alcohol; wipe them dry with a clean cloth. Blow any dirt or cleaning fluid out of the internal passages. Check the inside of the vacuum-cylinder shell for rust or corrosion. If any is present, clean the surface with a fine emery cloth and finish with crocus cloth. If the cylinder shell is pitted or has any dents, replace it.

Inspect each element of the vacuum piston. Examine the rear piston plate for cracks or damaged threads; examine the bore of the master cylinder for scores, scratches, corrosion, and satisfactory sealing with the rubber hydraulic seal.

Do not attempt to refinish the outside diameter of the vacuum valve or the bore of the piston-plate sleeve. The clearance between the valve and piston-plate sleeve may become too great and serious vacuum leakage will result. Do not attempt to refinish the master-cylinder piston. An undersized piston will cause a serious leakage of hydraulic fluid. Replace any parts that do not come up to inspection standard. To keep dirt out of the power unit, all cleaned and inspected parts should be placed on a clean paper or cloth prior to assembly.

Assembly. Place the rear piston plate on a clean paper with the rear side facing upward. Install the inserts in the recess of the piston plate and place the piston leather packing on the plate. Now, install the piston packing-seal retainer, Fig. 19-17, wicking, wick-retaining expander ring, wick-retaining plate, and retaining screws. Make the screws tight enough to compress the packing seal.

Now, turn the piston plate over and place five dowel pins in the screw holes to help in installing the diaphragm. Place the counter-reaction spring, small end down, on the piston plate. Install the diaphragm and gasket on the dowel pins, with the large diaphragm plate facing toward the rear piston plate. Align the two air-passage cutouts. Install the valve-return spring with its small end into the reaction diaphragm. Place the front piston plate over the dowel pins. Again align the air-passage cutouts. Now, press down on the piston plate to compress the spring, and at the same time replace the dowel pins, one at a time; uniformly tighten the screws. Saturate the wicking and wipe the leather seal with a maximum of two teaspoonfuls of shock-absorber fluid. Fasten the vacuum tube, hose assembly, and gasket to the rear piston plate.

The elements of the master-cylinder piston are assembled in the reverse order of disassembly. Before assembly, dip the hydraulic-cylinder piston and cup in brake fluid. Install the cup retainer on the piston with the smaller diameter facing the washer on the end of the piston. Slide the cup onto the piston and work the lip side of the cup over the cup retainer. Now, with the master-cylinder casting held in the vise, insert the assembly into the cylinder, taking care not to damage the lip of the cup as it enters the bore. Install the phenolic washer and piston cup stop washer on the piston and insert the retaining ring in its groove in the bore of the master-cylinder casting.

Hold the master-cylinder piston assembly in its upward position and install the leather seal with the lip facing the

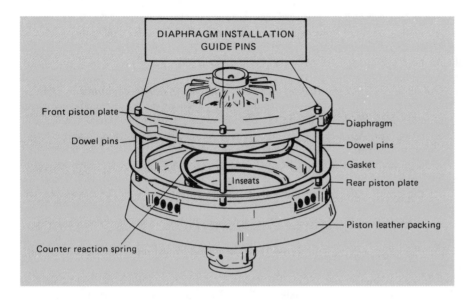

DIAPHRAGM INSTALLATION
GUIDE PINS

Front piston plate
Dowel pins
Inseats
Counter reaction spring

Diaphragm
Dowel pins
Gasket
Rear piston plate
Piston leather packing

Fig. 19-17   Vacuum-piston assembly in Bendix Power Unit.

hydraulic cylinder. Place the rubber seal ring and cylinder gasket on the face of the cylinder casting.

Install the vacuum-cylinder shell by inserting the upper end of the master-cylinder piston in the hole provided in the bottom of the vacuum cylinder. Check the alignment marks on the vacuum cylinder and its casting, and fasten together with mounting bolts and lock washers. Tighten to five foot-pounds of torque. Install the piston-return spring, engaging the hooked end of the spring between one of the mounting bolts and the small hump in the base of the shell. Compress the spring and place the retainer over the end of the master piston. Place the U-shaped retainer washer in the slot in the end of the piston.

Apply a thin coat of shock-absorber fluid to the inside wall of the vacuum cylinder and insert the vacuum-piston assembly into the cylinder. Align the open end of the vacuum hose with the center of the large elongated hole in the cylinder shell. This hole provides an opening for the assembly containing the vacuum and atmospheric-pressure tubes. Push the piston assembly into the cylinder; make sure the bore in the piston front plate fits over the master piston. Rotate the piston 20° to 30° clockwise and then 20° to 30° counterclockwise to assure proper seating. Also, move the piston through its full stroke a number of times to make sure the vacuum hose is aligned with the elongated hole in the cylinder shell after the piston finds its normal working position. Install the tube assembly and gasket into the elongated hole; insert the open end of the vacuum hose over the tube. Again push the piston into the cylinder several times. Let it come back by itself and note if the return spring causes the piston to rotate. If the piston rotates enough to cause the vacuum-hose tube connections to rub against each other, remove the piston from the cylinder and reseat the return spring 120°. Then install the piston and recheck.

Dip the rubber seal ring in fluid and install it on the compensator port fitting. Push the master-cylinder piston inward about one-half inch while installing the compensator-port fitting and valve assembly. Tighten the fitting securely. Dip the rubber cup of the residual check valve in brake fluid and assemble on top of the cup retainer. Place the spring and cup-retainer assembly on the hydraulic-output fitting and screw the fitting into place. Be sure the parts remain in correct alignment. Tighten to 30 to 42 foot-pounds of torque. Place the copper gasket, hydraulic tube fitting, and second copper gasket over the fitting bolt; screw the assembly into the outlet.

Before assembling the vacuum valve, check the movement of the vacuum piston. The movement should be within $3/32$ to $7/32$ inch from its fully released position and should allow the compensator valve to close. If this dimension does not check, examine the unit for faulty assembly.

Place the fluid reservoir cover and gasket over the opening in the master-cylinder casting and fasten the cover screws.

Installation.   The Bendix Power Unit is installed in the reverse procedure of removal. The unit is placed in its proper position. Check the clearance of the valve rod with the hole in the toe board plate before tightening the fastening screws. This clearance should be equal on both the left and right sides. The clearances on the top and bottom should vary, however, with the top clearance being about one-sixteenth inch. When the correct upper clearance is obtained, tighten the toe board plate, install the floor mat and brake pedal. Under the hood of the car, connect the vacuum and atmospheric lines to the cylinder-hose connections. Connect the hydraulic lines and stop-light switch wires.

Table 19-1 Troubleshooting the Bendix Power Brake Unit

Trouble	Cause	Remedy
Hard pedal	Faulty vacuum check valve	Clean if dirty or sticky. Replace if necessary.
	Plugged vacuum fittings	Clean fittings.
	Collapsed vacuum hose (external)	Replace hose.
	Internal vacuum hose loose or collapsed	Tighten connection if loose. Replace hose if collapsed.
	Leaking vacuum-reserve tank	Replace tank.
	Jammed master-cylinder piston	Locate cause of jamming and correct.
	Vacuum leaks caused by loose piston-plate screws	Tighten screws.
	Faulty rubber stop in reaction diaphragm	Replace rubber stop.
	Loose piston wick	The retainer spring is not in place. Reinstall or replace spring.
	Faulty vacuum piston seal	Replace the piston seal.
	Binding pedal pivot	Replace diaphragm.
Grabbing brakes	Reaction diaphragm leakage	Replace diaphragm.
	Broken counter-reaction spring	Replace spring.
	Restricted diaphragm passage	Clean passage.
	Sticking vacuum-valve action	Clean valve with crocus cloth. Do not oil.
Brakes fail to release	Brake pedal pivot binding	Free pedal pivot.
	Restricted air passage	Check air cleaner. If washers have been omitted from behind cleaner, install two.
	Piston sticking	Check piston and see that coiled vacuum line to valve is not sticking in intake ends. Push piston in and out several times. Relocate the piston return spring by rotating 120 degrees.
	Faulty residual check valve	Replace the check valve. Refill reservoir and bleed brakes.
	Vacuum valve sticking	Rough up lightly with crocus cloth. Do not oil.
	Hydraulic plunger sticking	Replace seal on hydraulic piston. Refill reservoir and bleed brakes.
	Compensator valve sticking	Replace valve. Refill reservoir and bleed brakes.
	Broken return spring	Replace spring.
	Compensator port plugged	Clean port. Refill reservoir and bleed brakes.
Pedal goes to floor	Hydraulic fluid leakage	Check system thoroughly and correct leaks.
	Compensating valve leakage	Replace valve assembly.
	Hydraulic piston seal leaking	Recondition master cylinder.
	Output check valve leaking	Bleed lines and refill reservoir.
Brake pedal flutter at light application	Vacuum valve screen dirty or restricted	Clean screen.
	Restriction to air cleaner or hose	Replace air cleaner and/or hose.
	Diaphragm assembly trouble	Check assembly and replace if necessary.

Troubleshooting. Table 19-1 lists the trouble indications, causes, and remedies for the Bendix Power Unit. No adjustments are required on the unit. When it becomes faulty, it should be overhauled by use of a Bendix Power Brake repair kit. During overhaul, discard all old rubber parts. Bleed the brakes in the same way described for hydraulic brakes. Before bleeding the brakes, reduce the vacuum reserve to zero by applying the brake several times when the engine is turned off.

Check the reservoir fluid level every 1,000 miles, and inspect the vacuum hose, tubing, and all connections every 10,000 miles.

Clean the air cleaner twice each year. Use cleaning solvent for the job and let it dry thoroughly before reinstallation of the air cleaner.

Buick Power Brakes

The power cylinder is actuated by means of an extended pushrod. A fluid reservoir is connected to the hydraulic section of the power unit by a tube. A vacuum reserve tank is mounted in the vacuum line near the braking unit to insure quick response.

When the engine is not running, a check valve closes to maintain vacuum in the reserve tank. This reserve vacuum provides two or three normal brake applications with the engine stopped. When the reserve vacuum is used up, the brakes can still be applied manually. Because atmospheric pressure is present on both sides of the power piston in the unapplied stage, this brake is known as an *air-suspended* type.

A cutaway view of the power unit in the released position is shown in Fig. 19-18. A cover closes the end of the cylinder housing to form a chamber in which the power piston and related parts operate. The section on the side cover of the power piston is called the *air chamber*. The section on the opposite side of the power piston is called the *vacuum chamber*.

To seal the vacuum chamber against air leaks, the power piston has a leather cup and a felt lubricating wick on its rim. An attached guide provides a bearing in the cylinder. The piston is connected to the vacuum fitting by a rubber hose. This lets the piston move forward when the brake is applied, as shown in Fig. 19-19. Air leaves the vacuum chamber through passages in the power piston and the vacuum hose when the floating control valve is set for power application by depressing of the foot pedal.

A separate assembly made up of the air valve, floating control valve, hydraulic piston, and reaction mechanism is housed in a pivot plate and cover. The air valve and hydraulic piston move as a unit during power application but move separately during manual application of the brakes.

Two reaction coil springs are used in the vacuum chamber. The heavier spring is used for the power piston and the lighter spring for the air valve and hydraulic piston assembly.

The hydraulic section of the power unit contains a steel piston which extends through a rubber vacuum-cup seal, a rubber secondary cup, and a rubber primary cup. The space between the vacuum-cup seal and the secondary cup is vented to the atmosphere by a small hole. A loose wire is used in the hole to keep dirt from entering the cylinder or blocking the tube.

Application of the brake pedal moves the piston into the hydraulic cylinder. The piston displaces a corresponding amount of fluid, which is forced out through the check valve into the brake lines and wheel cylinders. The counterbored end of the hydraulic piston contains counterbored parts to permit the return of surplus fluid to the reservoir when the brakes are released. Static pressure is maintained in the brake lines and wheel cylinders by the check valve in the hydraulic cylinder.

As the power piston moves, it carries the hydraulic master-cylinder plunger with it until the radial holes in the plunger pass the lip of the primary cup. See Fig. 19-19. Hydraulic pressure then starts to build up in the system. As this buildup takes place, pressure on the end of the plunger causes the reaction plate to move away from its seat and press against the reaction levers. The reaction levers press against the valve-reaction plate and push the plate back against the shoulder on the air valve. In this way, approximately 40 per cent of the load on the hydraulic-cylinder plunger is transferred to the brake pedal to give the operator improved brake control.

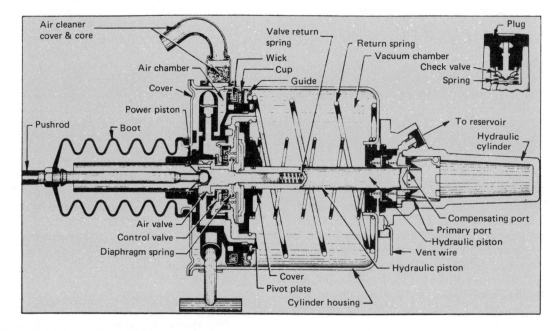

Fig. 19-18 Buick Power Unit with brake released.

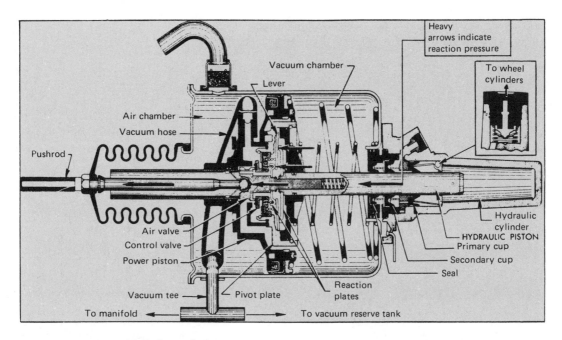

Fig. 19-19   Buick Power Unit with brake applied.

Kelsey-Hayes Power Brake Unit

The Kelsey-Hayes Power Unit is a vacuum-suspended type, having vacuum on both sides of the power piston in the unapplied position. Like most other units, the Kelsey-Hayes consists of three elements: an air-vacuum cylinder, hydraulic cylinder, and control valve. The unit is fastened to the car frame and has a vacuum-reserve reservoir mounted under the hood to assist in stopping the car when the engine is not running. Reserve fluid is also carried in a reserve reservoir mounted under the hood. Both reservoirs are connected to the power unit by tubing. A vacuum check valve is located in the vacuum line to keep vacuum in the reserve tank when the engine is stopped.

With the engine running and the brakes off, vacuum exists on both sides of the power piston. Application of the brake pedal causes the atmospheric port to open and admit air to the cover side of the power piston. The air creates an imbalance in the cylinder and the power piston moves forward to create a thrust on the hydraulic piston. Hydraulic fluid under pressure then increases the line pressure to all four wheels and applies the brake.

See Table 19-2 for troubleshooting procedures.

Power Brake Vacuum Pump

A power brake vacuum pump is used on some cars equipped with the Kelsey-Hayes Power Unit. The pump, with an electric motor driven vacuum-vane with a control relay, is installed between the power brake cylinder and engine intake manifold. Its purpose is to furnish an auxiliary source of vacuum for power-brake application when the engine stops. A check valve, which maintains a reserve vacuum in the cylinder sufficient for two brake applications, is contained in the pump.

The electric motor receives current through the ignition switch and a cutout relay. When the engine is not running, the relay points remain closed. Thus, with the ignition switch on, the electric motor and pump supply vacuum for brake application. When the engine is running, generator voltage energizes the relay coil and separates the points to eliminate pump operation. If the engine stalls, the loss of generator voltage lets the relay points close and the vacuum pump is started.

Bendix Hydrovac Power Unit

The so-called Hydrovac Power Unit is connected between the master cylinder and the brake-line distributor fitting on some cars. It is controlled by hydraulic pressure developed in the master cylinder, but differs from the types described earlier in that it is not actuated directly by a pedal pushrod; instead, it is applied by fluid pressure from the master cylinder. One such unit is shown in Fig. 19-20.

The Hydrovac Power Unit has three elements: a vacuum-power cylinder, hydraulic cylinder, and hydraulically actuated vacuum-control valve. The vacuum-power cylinder contains a vacuum piston and a pushrod which connects the piston to a hydraulic piston in the hydraulic cylinder. The hydraulic cylinder contains a piston with a check valve. The hydraulically actuated vacuum-control valve has a piston, diaphragm, and vacuum poppet. This valve regulates the degree of brake application or release.

A vacuum check valve assembly is located in the vacuum line between the manifold and the power unit. This

Table 19-2   Troubleshooting the Kelsey-Hayes Power Break Unit

Trouble	Cause	Remedy
Hard pedal	Lack of lubrication	Lubricate pedal shaft and push rod clevis.
	Binding or corroded clevis pin	Remove push rod clevis pin and either clean or replace it.
	Misalignment of pedal	Loosen pedal shaft bracket bolts to permit bracket to shift to a free position, then tighten bolts.
	Dry power cylinder piston cup	Remove inspection screw in power cylinder head and inject two or three ounces of power brake cylinder oil. Back off all brake shoes, start engine and pump brake pedal. Readjust shoes.
Brakes fail to release	Push rod adjustment too long	Adjust rod.
	Dry power cylinder piston cup	See hard pedal section.
	Hydraulic cylinder not aligned with piston	Remove power cylinder, loosen hydraulic cylinder flange nuts, depress piston guide to full stroke, and tighten nuts securely.
	Plugged compensation ports	Remove and disassemble power cylinder and clean thoroughly.
	Internal friction	Remove and disassemble power cylinder, look for and replace broken or weak springs, rubber cups, and O-ring seals.
Unit does not boost	Vacuum check valve stuck closed	Remove, open check valve and clean with a dry cloth.
	Vacuum pipe bent, broken, or obstructed	Check vacuum pipe for damage and loose connections. Repair pipe.
	Blocked or restricted vacuum line	Remove restriction or install new vacuum line.
	The ball in the vacuum check valve is stuck	Replace check valve.
	Fluid check valve ball is not seating properly	Remove secondary cylinder from unit, disassemble fluid check valve, and replace any damaged parts. The small end of the spring must always be against the ball.
	Hole in diaphragm or leak in air inlet hose	Replace diaphragm or hose.
	Block air inlet	Check air-breather hose, air-cleaner core, push rod boot. Clean or replace faulty parts.
	Jammed air-valve seat	Remove power piston and clean air-valve seat.
Brakes will not release properly	Improper opening of the fluid check valve	Remove primary cylinder end cap and check for damaged or missing trip rod stop plate or trip rod.
	Screw missing from inspection hole in primary housing	Replace screw.
	Fluid return system seals too tight on the control piston and power piston from returning rapidly	Replace the return system seals. Lubricate seals and shafts with silicon grease.
Loss of brake fluid	Leaky wheel cylinders or loose line connections. Leaky cups and seals in either primary or secondary cylinders	Replace the part or tighten the connection. Remove inspection screw from primary housing. Tip unit to see if any fluid will come out through primary inspection hole or secondary vacuum connection. Replace seals and cups if necessary.

check valve traps vacuum in the power unit so that at least one stop can be made when the engine stalls. The check valve also prevents damage to the power brake in the event of engine backfire.

When the power unit is in its *off* position, Fig. 19-21, the areas on both sides of the vacuum diaphragm and power piston are exposed to manifold vacuum. The ball check in the hydraulic piston is held off its seat and remains so until

it is closed by movement of the vacuum piston. This allows fluid to pass from the master cylinder through the hydraulic piston directly to the wheel cylinders. Thus, the standard brake system operates normally when the engine is not running or when the power system becomes faulty.

As the brake pedal is depressed, Fig. 19-22, hydraulic pressure developed in the master cylinder is transmitted to the hydraulic cylinder and to the control-valve piston. This

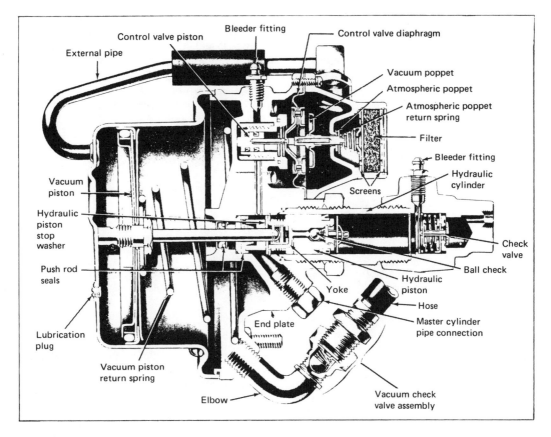

Fig. 19-20   Bendix Hydrovac Power Unit.

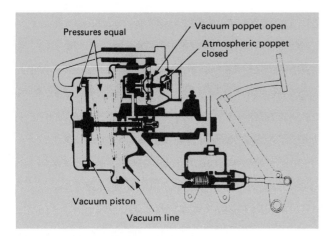

Fig. 19-21   Bendix Hydrovac Power Unit in *off* position.

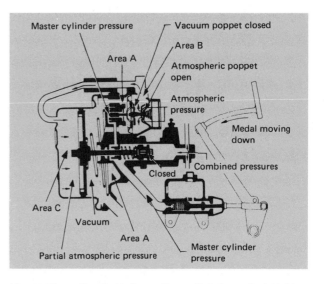

Fig. 19-22   Bendix Hydrovac Power Unit in applied position.

piston actuates the vacuum diaphragm control shaft and forces the diaphragm against the vacuum poppet valve. Area B is then sealed off from manifold vacuum, the atmospheric poppet valve is forced off its seat, and air is admitted to area C from area B. The difference in pressure between areas C and A forces the vacuum piston, pushrod, and hydraulic piston to move to the right. As the hydraulic piston moves to the right, the check valve, no longer held off its seat, closes and traps fluid under pressure ahead of the piston. Hydraulic pressure developed in the hydraulic cylinder is then transmitted to the wheel cylinders.

The degree of power assist is regulated in the vacuum-control valve assembly by controlling the pressure between areas B and A. A hydraulic pressure against the control-valve piston is opposed by air pressure and spring pressure on the area B side of the control-valve diaphragm when the diaphragm is in contact with the vacuum poppet valve. As pressure in area B increases, the forces acting against the vacuum valve and diaphragm also increase, tending to close the atmospheric valve. The degree of power assist is, therefore, proportional to hydraulic pressure.

See Table 19-3 for troubleshooting procedures.

Table 19-3 Troubleshooting the Bedix Hydrovac Power-Brake Unit

Trouble	Cause	Remedy
Hissing noise, engine running, brakes on or off	External vacuum leak on vacuum side of control diaphragm	Correct leak at control valve body to end plate gasket or vacuum cylinder to end plate gasket.
Hissing noise, engine running, brake off	External vacuum leak on atmospheric side of control diaphragm	Correct leak at atmospheric poppet, external tubing, or valve body screws.
Hissing noise, engine running, brake on	Internal vacuum leak	Overhaul unit, check for leak at vacuum poppet, control diaphragm, or vacuum power piston assembly.
Pedal grows harder and kicks back while stopping	Internal hydraulic leak	Overhaul unit, check for small leaks at control valve, valve fitting, or power piston.
	Internal or external vacuum leak	Overhaul unit, check for leak at vacuum poppet, control diaphragm, or vacuum power piston.
Little or no boost from unit accompanied by hissing noise or loss of hydraulic fluid	Internal vacuum leak between atmospheric and vacuum side	Overhaul unit, check for leak at vacuum poppet, control diaphragm, or vacuum power piston.
	Internal hydraulic leak	Check fluid level, overhaul unit, check for brake fluid in inner side of vacuum cylinder or inside of control diaphragm.
	Internal friction	Remove lubricating plug and inject shock-absorber fluid to proper level in vacuum cylinder. If necessary, overhaul unit.
Pedal drops under foot, slow application of power unit	Sticky control valve	Overhaul unit and check for misalignment of control-valve assembly.
	Restriction in atmospheric passage	Clean air filter.
	Internal hydraulic leak	Overhaul unit, check for lead at hydraulic-piston assembly.
	Internal friction	Remove plug and inject shock-absorber fluid to proper level in vacuum cylinder. If necessary, overhaul unit.
Brakes fail to release, or release slowly	Sluggish control valve action	Check for weak or broken vacuum piston-return spring or atmospheric poppet return spring. Correct sticky control valve. Overhaul unit if necessary.
	Internal friction	Remove plug and correct shock-absorber fluid level in vacuum cylinder. If necessary, overhaul unit.
Now power assist on first application after engine is turned off	External or internal vacuum leak	Check for leaks at valve body and power cylinder. Overhaul unit if necessary.

Chrysler Power Brakes

The power brake unit on some Chrysler products is an integral self-contained unit which incorporates an air-vacuum housing, hydraulic cylinder, fluid reservoir, air cleaner, and vacuum check valve. Neither a vacuum reserve tank nor a remote fluid reservoir is needed. The unit is mounted on the engine side of the firewall (see Fig. 19-23).

In a manner similar to other power brake units, the vacuum source tube is connected to the engine intake manifold by a short tube. Additional tubing connects the hydraulic cylinder to the four wheel cylinders.

The unit is applied by a pushrod which is connected to the brake pedal by a pendulum-type linkage. When the brake is applied, the pushrod moves into the unit, closes the vacuum valve, and opens the air valve. The resulting pressure differential causes movement of the diaphragm and power-piston assembly along with the power-piston sleeve. This sleeve, which is actually a hydraulic piston, moves into the hydraulic cylinder, finally forces fluid into the brake lines, and applies the brakes.

Ford Power Brakes

The power unit used on some Ford products is hydraulically operated and is incorporated in the regular brake system between the master cylinder and the wheel cylinders.

The power unit, Fig. 19-24, has a vacuum power chamber, hydraulically actuated vacuum-control valve, and hydraulic slave cylinder. The vacuum check valve is a spring-loaded disk. The power chamber has two pressed-steel bodies divided by a rubber diaphragm and a metal pressure-plate assembly. A pushrod, attached to the metal pressure plate, extends into the slave-cylinder and actuates the slave-cylinder piston when the brakes are applied.

A control-valve assembly consisting of a control-valve disk, diaphragm, disk spring, return spring, and plunger and piston is mounted on the slave-cylinder housing. This control valve is hydraulically operated and controls atmospheric intake when the brake pedal is applied.

The slave cylinder contains a piston assembly, piston cup, check valve, check-valve return spring, and piston return spring.

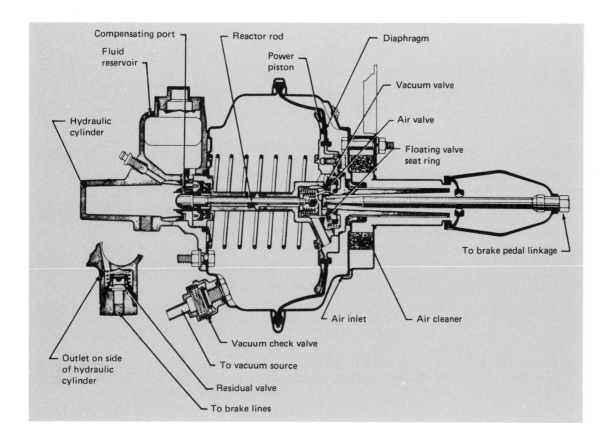

Fig. 19-23　Power unit of Chrysler power brake.

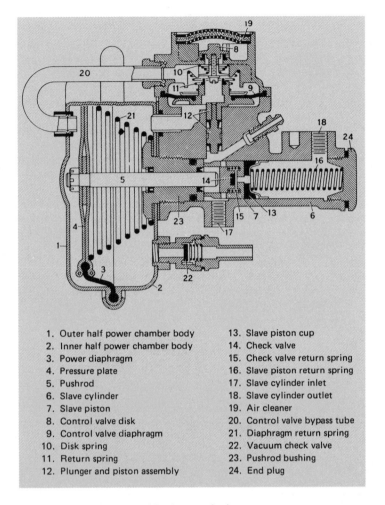

1. Outer half power chamber body
2. Inner half power chamber body
3. Power diaphragm
4. Pressure plate
5. Pushrod
6. Slave cylinder
7. Slave piston
8. Control valve disk
9. Control valve diaphragm
10. Disk spring
11. Return spring
12. Plunger and piston assembly
13. Slave piston cup
14. Check valve
15. Check valve return spring
16. Slave piston return spring
17. Slave cylinder inlet
18. Slave cylinder outlet
19. Air cleaner
20. Control valve bypass tube
21. Diaphragm return spring
22. Vacuum check valve
23. Pushrod bushing
24. End plug

Fig. 19-24   Power unit of Ford power brake.

In the off position, vacuum exists on both sides of the diaphragm and pressure-plate assembly. When the brake pedal is applied, fluid from the master cylinder passes through the slave-cylinder piston openings to the control-valve plunger and piston. The fluid also flows around the slave-cylinder piston check valve and through the piston and cup orifices into the brake system. Fluid pressure against the control-valve piston moves the piston and plunger and seals the vacuum in the rear section of the power chamber. Fluid pressure simultaneously admits air to the front chamber. The unbalanced pressure causes the diaphragm and pressure-plate assembly and the pushrod to move toward the slave cylinder. The pushrod makes the slave piston close the check valve. Movement of the piston into the cylinder builds up hydraulic line pressure to operate the brakes.

If the engine stalls, or the power chamber fails to operate, the brakes are applied directly from the master cylinder. Without the vacuum assist, brake fluid passes through the slave-cylinder piston openings and the piston and cup orifices to the wheel cylinders.

See Table 19-4 for troubleshooting procedures.

Moraine Power Brakes

The Moraine Power Unit is similar in external appearance to the Bendix unit, but can be identified by its cast-iron hydraulic cylinder and filler cap. The Bendix unit has a die-cast hydraulic cylinder and a pressed-steel filler cap. With the exception of the power piston, the construction and operation of the Moraine unit is similar to the Bendix unit.

Table 19-4 Troubleshooting Ford Power Brakes

Trouble	Cause	Remedy
Brake pedal kicks back with engine running	Slave piston cups leaking, hydraulic check valve leaking, or intermittent vacuum leak	Remove and overhaul unit.
Loss of fluid	Leak at end cap, bleeder screw, stop-light switch, or hose connections	Repair leaks by tightening, or, if necessary, replace gasket.
Brakes do not release with engine running	Control valve piston sticking, hydraulic check valve sticking, broken or weak control-valve spring, dented or leaky diaphragm body	Remove and overhaul unit.
Vacuum leak with brakes released, engine idle is normal	Defective O-ring seal or body to slave-cylinder gasket, dirty or worn atmospheric valve seal, or a dirty or defective vacuum check valve	Remove and overhaul unit.
Vacuum leaks with brakes released. Rough engine idle	Leaking power diaphragm, control valve piston or diaphragm, or a leaking control valve vacuum valve seal	Remove and overhaul unit.
Hard pedal, indicating weak or inoperative booster	Clogged air-cleaner element or sticking slave piston	Replace the air-cleaner felt, or, if necessary, remove and overhaul unit.
	Air leak at atmospheric valve seal, control-valve piston, or the power diaphragm	

INDEX

Note: Numbers in italics indicate illustrations.